Chester E. Pryor
2022-L44 Baltimore Road
Rockville, MD 20851

A Guidebook for Teaching
CREATIVE WRITING

A Guidebook for Teaching CREATIVE WRITING

GENE STANFORD

Associate Professor of Education and
Director of Teacher Education Programs,
Utica College of Syracuse University

MARIE SMITH

Teacher of English
Horton Watkins High School
St. Louis, Missouri

Allyn and Bacon, Inc.   Boston • London • Sydney

This book is part of A GUIDEBOOK FOR TEACHING Series

Copyright © 1977 by Allyn and Bacon, Inc.,
470 Atlantic Avenue, Boston, Massachusetts 02210.

All rights reserved. Printed in the United States of America. No part of the material protected by this copyright notice except the Reproduction Pages may be reproduced or utilized in any form or by any means, electronic or mechanical, including photocopying, recording, or by any information storage and retrieval system, without written permission from the copyright owner.

The Reproduction Pages contained within may be reproduced for use with this text, provided such reproductions bear copyright notice, but may not be reproduced in any form for any other purpose without written permission from the copyright owner.

Library of Congress Cataloging in Publication Data

Stanford, Gene.
   A guidebook for teaching creative writing.

   (A Guidebook for teaching series)
   Bibliography: p.
   1. Creative writing (Secondary education)
2. English language—Study and teaching (Secondary)
I. Smith, Marie N., 1920–   joint author.   II. Title.
III. Series.
LB1631.S684   808   77-1453

ISBN 0-205-05873-6

Contents

Preface ix

CHAPTER 1   **PRINCIPLES OF TEACHING CREATING WRITING**   1
Free Students to Express Themselves   1
Allow Students to Explore Who They Are   2
Offer Models of Good Writing   2
Teach Principles and Patterns   3
Provide Students with Appropriate Feedback   4

CHAPTER 2   **STIMULATING STUDENTS TO WRITE**   7
Topic I: *Focusing on Real Issues*   10
     Sample Activity   11
     Suggested Resources   12
Topic II: *Freeing Students to Write What Matters*   13
     Sample Activities   13
     Suggested Resources   14
Topic III: *Reacting to Sensory Stimuli*   14
     Sample Activities   15
     Suggested Resources   17
Topic IV: *Writing for a Reason*   18
     A Sample Approach   19
     Other Sample Activities   20
     Suggested Resources   20
Topic V: *Writing for an Audience*   21
     Ways to Provide Students with an Audience   21
     Suggested Resources   24
Topic VI: *Writing to Understand Oneself and Others*   24
     Sample Activities   24
     Suggested Resources   33

CHAPTER 3   **TEACHING STUDENTS TO CREATE IMAGES**   35
Objectives   35
Learning Experiences   36
     Topic I: Describe—Don't Label   36
     Topic II: Select Details with a Central Purpose in Mind   38
     Topic III: Select Details to Create a Mood   42

Topic IV: Using Sensory Experiences in Writing 46
Topic V: Creating Images in Poetry 47
Assessing Achievement of Objectives 51
Resources for Teaching Creating Images 52
Audio-Visual Materials 52
Books for Students 53
Books for Teachers 53

CHAPTER 4   **TEACHING STUDENTS TO CREATE PEOPLE AND EVENTS**   **55**
Objectives 55
Learning Experiences 56
Topic I: Characterization by Appearance 56
Topic II: Characterization by Dialogue 58
Topic III: Characterization by Actions 63
Topic IV: Putting Characterization Together 65
Topic V: Creating Events for a Purpose 66
Topic VI: Creating Events Rather than Telling about Them 70
Topic VII: Making Events Seem Real 72
Assessing Achievement of Objectives 74
Resources for Teaching Students to Create Characters and Events 75
Audio-Visual Materials 75
Books for Students 76

CHAPTER 5   **TEACHING STUDENTS TO WRITE ABOUT LITERATURE**   **77**
Objectives 78
Learning Experiences 78
Topic I: Writing an Essay about a Novel for Advanced Students 78
Topic II: Writing an Essay about a Novel for Average Students 90
Topic III: Writing an Essay about Poetry 93
Resources for Teaching Students How to Write about Literature 109

APPENDIX A   **ADDRESSES OF PRODUCERS OF RESOURCES**   **111**

APPENDIX B   **REPRODUCTION PAGES**   **115**
RP 1: "The Person Sitting Next to You" 117
RP 2: Example of Labelling 119
RP 3: Good Descriptive Paragraph 121
RP 4: Identifying Labels 123
RP 5: Summarizing Details 125
RP 6: Listing Details 127
RP 7: Excerpts from "Snowbound" by John Greenleaf Whittier 129
RP 8: Revealing Character through Dialogue 131
RP 9: Values in Action Chart 133
RP 10: Describing an Event for a Purpose 135
RP 11: Events and Their Possible Purposes 137

RP 12: "Train Ride in Europe" 139
RP 13: "Cold Turkey" 141
RP 14: "He Should Have Stayed in Bed" 143
RP 15: "Just Dreaming" 145
RP 16: "The Visit" 147
RP 17: "Sensations of My Mind" 149
RP 18: Revising Skeletal Paragraphs 151
RP 19: Creating Rather than Telling about Conversations 153
RP 20: Creating Actual Conversations 155
RP 21: Making an Event Come Alive 157
RP 22: How to Close Read a Novel 159
RP 23: Kinds of Questions to Ask Yourself in Order to Come Up with Answers that Can Provide a Thesis Statement for an Essay of Literary Commentary 161
RP 24: Preparing to Write a Paper about a Novel in Terms of the Author's Purpose 163
RP 25: Steps in Writing a Paper about a Novel 165
RP 26: Sample Essay: The Symbolic Use of the Color Green in Lord of the Flies 167
RP 27: Improving the Style of an Essay about Literature 169
RP 28: Study/Discussion Questions for Alas, Babylon 171
RP 29: Why Study Poetry? 173
RP 30: "The Best Words in the Best Order" 175
RP 31: The Sounds of Poetry 177
RP 32: Metaphorical Language 179
RP 33: Questions for Critical Analysis of a Poem, or What Is in This Poem that I Can Comment on? 181
RP 34: "London" by William Blake 183
RP 35: Chart for Analysis of a Poem 185
RP 36: "On Shakespeare" by John Milton 187
RP 37: "Snow on Easter" by John Stephen Harris 189
RP 38: "Snow on Easter"—An Explication 191
RP 39: Questions for Critical Examination of a Poem 193

APPENDIX C   FEEDBACK FORM   195

Preface

This is not, we hope, just another book about teaching creative writing. From its inception, we have tried to make this a book that will serve a unique purpose: providing the classroom teacher with so many specific ideas and resources for teaching creative writing that he or she could never use them all. There are already too many books that outline in a general way the "best" way to teach creative writing, that urge the teacher to adopt one approach or another. But most of these, although they contain many excellent, thought-provoking ideas, do not go very far beyond describing a general theory of teaching writing and suggesting a few exercises to implement it.

By contrast, we have attempted to produce a comprehensive handbook with an emphasis on practicality. We began by resolving to cover all forms of writing, to dispel the notion that only poetry and fiction can be "creative." But it soon became apparent that if we were going to include the wealth of practical material teachers have been looking for, two volumes would be necessary. And so we have fallen back on that old, admittedly arbitrary distinction between expository and creative writing, principally as a convenience for teachers who emphasize one approach rather than the other and who don't want to have to pay for material they won't use.

This volume, then, deals with the principles of teaching creative writing, stimulating students to write, teaching them to create images and people and events, and analyzing and writing about the creative efforts of others. In the companion volume, *A Guidebook for Teaching Composition,* can be found sections on organizing a composition program, marking student papers, teaching expository paragraphs, essays, and research papers, and teaching skills of revision. Taken together, the two books cover the entire range of high school writing activities. For convenience, the teacher can choose whichever book deals with the kind of writing he or she stresses.

For each type of writing that it deals with, *A Guidebook for Teaching Creative Writing* provides instructional objectives, notes for brief presentations by the teacher to explain new concepts to the class, classroom activities, discussion questions, small group activities, projects, individual assignments, annotated lists of materials, and even sample evaluation items. Perhaps the most valuable feature of the book is the section of Reproduction Pages, which can be used to make masters for spirit duplication or transparencies for the overhead projector—saving the teacher hours of preparation time.

Although the book often suggests a sequence of activities that might be useful in teaching a particular skill, the teacher can choose those materials and strategies that he or she wants to use, without being locked into prescribed lesson plans. In general, for each topic the book provides:

1. An introduction to the concepts that the section or chapter deals with
2. A list of objectives that the methods and materials in the chapter help the student achieve, saving teachers the tedium of writing behavioral objectives for lesson plans
3. Sample evaluation devices, for determining whether the student has achieved the objectives of the unit
4. Annotated lists of materials, including books, films, filmstrips, cassettes, and slide-tape programs.

Rather than promote a single approach to teaching creative writing, our goal has been to suggest activities and materials that teachers with a wide variety of teaching styles and philosophies will find useful. Thus, for example, although we describe numerous activities that put students to work in small groups (since we believe this is an approach that many writing teachers have neglected), we also include explanations of how most of the same activities can be used with students working on their own. The reader is encouraged to understand the rationale for each of the approaches and to choose those which are most consistent with his or her own goals and students' needs.

However, we do have our own set of biases—our own viewpoint, if you will—based on our own philosophy of education developed from a number of years of teaching writing in many different settings. This viewpoint is likely to be evident throughout the book. We believe, for example, that students learn more when they are actively involved in the process than when they are sitting passively. In addition, we believe that learning is enhanced when students are interacting with other persons and that students can learn from one another as well as from the teacher. We believe, also, that developing a skill such as writing is generally most successful when the skill is broken down into small steps or subskills, and approached sequentially rather than randomly. And finally, because writing almost always involves self-disclosure, we are convinced it must take place in a climate that is free from threat.

Most of the activities and approaches included in this book were developed for and used successfully with our own classes. We feel confident, therefore, that many other teachers will find them practical and useful. But we have no way of knowing whether *A Guidebook for Teaching Creative Writing* has been helpful without feedback from those people who use it. We invite you to write us your comments about the book, using the Feedback Form that appears at the end of the book (p. 195). It can be torn out and mailed with a minimum of inconvenience. We promise you a personal reply, and will sincerely appreciate your suggestions. They will help us decide what kinds of changes to make when we revise *A Guidebook for Teaching Creative Writing* and what kinds of activities to include in future books in the *Guidebook for Teaching* Series. (A guide to teaching language and a guide to teaching literature are both presently in development.)

Although most of the material in this book is derived from our own experience, we acknowledge the contributions made by a number of other persons. Raymond J. Rodrigues, Jere I. Hochman, and Robert C. Small, Jr., gave us permission to include teaching materials that they developed. The following students permitted us to include samples of their writing: Ken Cohn, Dennis Weisman, John Stephen Harris, Roger Zehntner, Merilynn Wenzlaff, Ruth Kim, Jim Perkins, Nina Whittier, Sheila Morris, Ben Painter, Jane Clayton, Ron Fredman, Lynn Levin, Ginger Oppenheimer, Nina Palkes, Wendy Davis, Steve Sawolkin, Richard Green, Rochelle Grober, Susan Meyer, Karl Kim, Marian Green, Sally Deitchman, G. P. Georges III, Daphne Rodin, Ellen Wiederholdt, and Barbara Kiem. The National

Council of Teachers of English, and Harcourt Brace Jovanovich made it possible for us to use excerpts from material that they had published previously. And finally, we gratefully acknowledge the assistance of Deborah Perry in preparing the resource lists.

Gene Stanford

Marie Smith

1

Principles of Teaching Creative Writing

There is something about adolescence that seems to cry out for creative expression. Hidden inside those half-child, half-adult bodies painted and disguised by the latest styles that show off the hardness, the secureness, the "coolness" of youth are some of the strongest emotions of a lifetime—fear, love, desire, depression, rage, joy, and hope—all needing some kind of expression. In almost any high school classroom, no matter how deep students' apparent aversion to literature, there is crammed into someone's pocket a tattered declaration of love, filled with all the clichés of last month's Top Forty. In at least one notebook there is likely to be a tear-stained poem of rejection, crossed out and painfully labored over, as a morbid child tested free verse and the sonnet form, not for their sound but for their power to release pain. There are diaries and journals, mostly filled with simple sentences recounting one person's view of what was significant in his or her life. And sometimes there is the work of one whose sensitivity and skill with words may be the early signs of an artist.

Although creative expression seems to be an innate need of high school students, it is not easy to teach. For effective creative writing must combine the natural impulse to express feelings in words, an impulse most students already have, with considerable skill in manipulating words and images. Unfortunately, the teaching techniques that are easiest to use in teaching word skills tend to stifle the impulse to express feelings. Thus, the effective creative writing class is one in which a proper balance is struck between freedom and discipline—the freedom to play with ideas and express deep feelings, and the discipline of literary craftsmanship. In trying to establish this delicate balance, you may find a few principles useful.

FREE STUDENTS TO EXPRESS THEMSELVES

Because most of your students' previous school experiences have probably not encouraged them to express their personal ideas and feelings in a genuine way, you may need to place most of the emphasis at the beginning of the year on helping students feel comfortable expressing their honest feelings. Your goal must be to establish an atmosphere within the classroom and an attitude within yourself that is conducive to creative productivity. Spontaneous creativity flourishes primarily in an atmosphere of trust and acceptance. Since creative writing demands self-disclosure, students need to feel assured that they will not be exposing themselves to ridicule if others learn their inner thoughts. Before most students are willing to trust their classmates and teachers with anything highly personal, they must perceive the others in the classroom as a unified group that behaves responsively, respectfully, and nonjudgmentally. Chapter 2 contains a number of suggestions for building this kind of classroom group.

The role of the teacher is most important in producing the proper climate for growth in creative writing. First, you must convey an attitude of respect and caring for all students and you must insist that class members also display these qualities toward one another. Usually it is helpful if your control and authority over the class become less obtrusive and direct. A strict instructional monitor will restrict and impair the creative flow of ideas. Ideally, the creative writing teacher functions as a sort of senior advisory group member who facilitates creative expression and who views the student as a fairly autonomous creator who must bear the responsibility for his or her own work.

You may further encourage students to express themselves freely by actually doing the same assignments yourself and sharing your own work with the class. This practice has several benefits. First, it convinces students that you believe in what you are teaching; it validates the assignment. Second, it helps to establish a positive model or standard of performance. It also interests and pleases students to discover that teachers are also individuals with personal feelings and opinions.

ALLOW STUDENTS TO EXPLORE WHO THEY ARE

As students begin to feel comfortable expressing their honest feelings, many of them will spontaneously begin to write, often setting down ideas they have been thinking about for a long time. But other students have trouble finding anything to write about. They are likely to feel that their own lives are dull and uneventful, certainly not worth writing something "creative" about. These students can benefit from activities that encourage them to examine and talk about their own pasts, contrasting their experiences with those of other students and seeing the similarities. Group activities, such as those suggested in Chapter 2, which lead students "down memory lane," open up a great reservoir of ideas for creative writing. An exciting by-product of this approach can be that students come to recognize the beauty and significance of the people and things in their everyday lives. They find that memories of childhood, emotion-filled events, people they have known, and humorous incidents all can become meaningful literature.

OFFER MODELS OF GOOD WRITING

Self-expression alone is not creative writing—no matter how genuine it may be. Therefore, in addition to encouraging students to write about things that are meaningful to them, you need to teach the skills and techniques that are the writer's craft. One of the best ways to teach these is through models of good writing.

Virtually anyone who is skilled as a writer is also an enthusiastic reader. Reading serves not only as a stimulus to the writer's thoughts and imagination, but also as an introduction to a variety of styles, to the use of literary devices, and to the approaches a writer can take. Hence, the study of literature is a logical component of the total creative writing program. Identifying the choices made by other writers often motivates students to explore their own skill with various literary forms. In Chapter 5 we have provided detailed suggestions for teaching students to analyze both poetry and fiction, for enhancing their skills in writing either of these forms, as well as for preparing them to write *about* these forms.

Another valuable use of literary models is having students directly imitate them. A poem, a personal essay, or a short piece of fiction can be studied with the class, and then students might be assigned to write a similar composition on a different theme or topic, following as closely as possible the style and form of the original. While an imitation is rarely a creative work itself, practice in using the patterns and techniques of others does develop facility and skill in writing that simply examining a model can never provide.

TEACH PRINCIPLES AND PATTERNS

Giving students direct instruction in the techniques and patterns of writing is an important, but often neglected, approach to teaching creative writing. In their eagerness to give students freedom to express themselves or to avoid stifling the creative impulses of students, some teachers are reluctant to give students any advance instruction in *how* to write. Of course, creative writing follows fewer rules than expository writing, but there are a number of common patterns and basic principles associated with all forms of creative writing that the good writer knows, even if he or she violates them. Rhythm and rhyme patterns in poetry, common plot patterns for the short story, techniques of description and means of character development are all an important part of the writer's repertoire of skills.

Principles and patterns are probably best taught inductively from literature rather than from a list of rules. For one thing, many of the "rules" listed in textbooks on creative writing do not realistically reflect practices that are currently used by good writers. Some of them have little to do with any literary works that ever existed. Before teaching any "rule," therefore, it is often wise to look through three or four contemporary books or magazines that you regard as examples of good writing and evaluate random selections by your "rule." If the good writers you've chosen as models don't seem to adhere to that rule, it's not likely to be useful to your students.

The most effective way to teach a principle or pattern is to start with a work of literature that students themselves respond to, perhaps even the best of their own writing. Lead them to identify the device or pattern. Then give them the proper label for it. For example, students may feel the suspense in a good mystery story, but may need your guidance in identifying the foreshadowing, the descriptive words, and the events that created that response. Once students have perceived a device or pattern and have learned the name for it, encourage them to continue to be alert for this device or pattern in other works they read and to try it out themselves in their own writing. Additional approaches to giving students direct instruction in selected techniques and patterns of creative writing can be found in Chapters 3 and 4.

PROVIDE STUDENTS WITH APPROPRIATE FEEDBACK

Giving students feedback (that is, accurate information about their performance) is one of the most difficult parts of teaching creative writing. Since creative writing is often so much more personal than many other forms of writing, criticism can hurt more. Excessive criticism can quickly stifle creativity, and hence it is difficult to know how much criticism to offer.

All efforts at creative expression deserve at least some praise, unless they are clearly sloppy work done only for a grade. Students need to recognize that a poem does not have to be publishable to be worth writing, and does not even have to be good to give pleasure to the writer and others. Some teachers convey to students the idea that poetry is something produced only by the immortals and that anyone who writes a flawed poem has committed a sacrilege. Far more successful in teaching students to write is the teacher who can enjoy everyday poems—a sentimental valentine poem, an ode to the school band, a new football cheer, or an exuberant paean to the first snow—without either glorifying them as more than a brief enjoyment or degrading them by pointing out their distance from the standards of greatness.

Although it is always important to respond positively to any of your students' creative efforts, if your goal is to help them improve their writing skills, you may wish to provide them with accurate feedback as well as encouragement. Good feedback is focused, specific, and constructive. That is, it is limited to a few important aspects of the piece of writing that the student may be able to improve with continued practice, and it identifies the writer's strengths as well as the weaknesses. In Chapter 1 of *A Guidebook for Teaching Composition,* the companion volume to this book, we have given detailed suggestions for responding to student writing with feedback that is focused, specific, and constructive. You may wish to consult those suggestions in deciding how best to mark students' papers.

Sometimes it may be most helpful to offer students the choice between your simply enjoying their writing or giving them feedback. You might suggest that they produce a number of papers that will not all be marked, selecting only one or two for you to respond to in detail. Giving students this choice allows them to "protect" some of their work if they do not feel comfortable having you assess its quality.

A valuable source of feedback on students' writing is the reactions of other members of the class. You may wish to seat students in a circle and encourage them to share their work by reading it aloud. Encourage them to provide appropriate feedback for one another. One approach is to have students discuss the work, telling what it communicates to them. Then ask the author to explain what he or she meant to communicate. If the author's intention is different from what the other students perceive, the class may wish to discuss what could be done to improve the communication of the author's purpose. Before having students respond to one another's writing, you may wish to present the following guidelines for giving feedback to another person:

1. Urge the author to describe his or her own perceptions of the strengths and weaknesses of the piece of writing before you explain your views.
2. Describe as accurately as possible your own reactions to the composition—both emotional and intellectual.
3. Point out as specifically as you can the aspects of the composition that could be improved. Avoid general or degrading terms (e.g., "Your characterization is

lousy"); instead, find specific examples (e.g., "In the first part of the story Tom seems confident, but later on he seems insecure, but there's no reason given for the change").
4. Ask questions whenever possible, rather than criticizing (e.g., "Did you deliberately portray Tom as changing from confident to insecure, or did that just creep in unintentionally?").

A number of other suggestions for utilizing students as the audience for one another's writing can be found in the chapter that follows.

2

Stimulating Students to Write

Most writing is undertaken "cold" if merely done in response to composition assignments made by a teacher. Students hear the teacher say what they are to write about or read an assignment on a ditto handout, wrack their brains a bit for everything they know on the subject, and then sit down to write. Sometimes the teacher allows students to choose their own topics, but still the process is the same: the student pulls out some pieces of paper and begins to write, usually with little thinking or planning going before.

By contrast, anyone doing "real" writing—that is, writing other than that assigned by a teacher—spends considerable time getting ready. Long before putting pen to paper, the writer mulls over the subject, warms up to it, and gets up courage finally to tackle it. The author may have read extensively in preparation for writing, and may have conversed on the subject for many hours with friends and colleagues. Journal entries made over a period of months or years may now be worth developing in detail. The writer may organize his or her thoughts by jotting down an outline, or may discover that a plan is taking formation in his or her mind without a formal outline. In short, the person engaged in "real" writing almost never selects a topic from a list (or has it assigned by someone else) and certainly never begins to write without much "priming of the pump." Instead, the "real" writer engages in what we sometimes call "pre-writing" to prepare for the actual act of writing.

In addition, "real" writing is virtually always concerned with topics and issues that are of immediate concern to the writer. The writer has a genuine purpose other than to fulfill an assignment or satisfy a teacher. And the "real" writer writes for a real audience, striving to say something of importance to a particular person or group of people, whereas most composition students are asked to devote themselves to communicating in a general, non-personal way with the teacher, who is probably the last person on earth those students have a desire to communicate with.

A successful composition program must engage students, as nearly as possible, in the process of "real" writing. The school situation is artificial enough without asking students to devote themselves to writing without any preparation on topics that don't matter to them, expecting no one except the teacher to read what they produce. Hence, writing topics should emerge naturally from other classroom activities—discussions, literature, role playing, debates, interviews, etc. They should deal as directly as possible with the needs and interests of the student (not those of the teacher). They should be preceded by appropriate motivational activities to start students thinking about the topic. Discussions are frequently ideal for this purpose. Finally, as much as possible, compositions should be written for a particular audience: the other members of the class, a small group of students with whom one is working, the principal of the school, readers of the school literary magazine, etc.

If students are expected to write about things that matter to them, and to share this writing with others in the class, it is imperative that a classroom climate prevail in which they feel comfortable doing these things. None of us wants to reveal our most significant thoughts in a situation where we may be ridiculed, embarrassed, or treated with indifference. We want to be listened to with interest and respect, even though others may not agree with us. And above all, we do not want to be laughed at or belittled.

Therefore, at the very beginning of the term, the teacher is well advised to help students get acquainted with one another through structured activities for name learning and trust building. Even though many students may have known each other for years, or at least have been in previous classes together, it is likely that a large number of students aren't well acquainted with everyone else. Until the level of trust is fairly high, students will be guarded about participating in discussions and sharing their writing with the class.

Don't mistakenly believe that all students in your classes know one another already. (If you think they do, ask them to reveal—via secret ballot—how many members of the class they do not know by their first and last names.) The following activities can be used at any time during the term as a means of assuring that students are acquainted with one another. (Hypothetical statements by the teacher appear in quotation marks; suggestions to the teacher are in parentheses.)

1. "During the first few weeks of this semester, we are going to be spending some time learning how to be better participants in class discussions. I will be asking you to join in a number of exercises and activities which will help you develop better ways of working together.

"The first thing that we should do is start getting to know one another. Look around the room and try to count how many people there are whose names you don't know. How many of you think there are about ten or more people you don't know? Raise your hands. How many of you know the names of all but four or five people? Raise your hands. How many of you know the names of everyone here? . . . So you can see that we ought to begin by learning names and getting acquainted.

"What I'd like you to do is to come up to the chalkboard one at a time, write your name on it, tell us your name and who are are. You can tell us anything about yourself that you wish, anything that would help us get to know you better. I'd also like you to take out a sheet of paper and write down each person's name as he says it and jot down anything next to his name that will help you remember who he is. Okay, does everyone understand? I'll go first to let you see what I want you to do and sort of break the ice. Does everyone have pencil and paper ready? *(Walk to chalkboard and write your name—first and surname—then turn to the group).* I'm Robert Finklemeyer. I've been an English teacher for two years; before that I worked for a publishing company. My hobbies are skiing and tennis. Okay, let's start on this side of the room and take turns until we've all introduced ourselves. Make sure you write down every person's name." *(Call on first student to begin and proceed in order down the rows or around the circle—this is easier on the students than asking for volunteers. If they have trouble knowing what to say about themselves, ask them about hobbies, interests, brothers and sisters, how they like to spend after-school time, etc. Discourage other students from asking questions that might put the person on the spot— each person should be allowed to decide what he or she wants to reveal.)*

2. *(The group is seated in a circle, with the teacher sitting as part of the group.)* "Before we start today's lesson we ought to take a moment to refresh our memories about each other's names. Here's the procedure I'd like you to follow: When it's your turn, say your name clearly and tell the group **one thing you enjoy doing**." *(Start with yourself and then call on the person to your right and proceed in order around the circle. After all students have responded, repeat the procedure.)* "Now let's go around the circle again; tell the group your name and this time tell us **one word that describes you**." *(Start with yourself again—"I'm Robert Finklemeyer and a word that describes me is 'energetic'." Then call on the person to your right to go next. This procedure can continue as many times around as time permits, with students sharing a different aspect of themselves each time.)*

3. *(The group is seated in a circle, with the teacher sitting as part of the group.)* "We've spent a couple of days telling each other our names. Now let's see how well you've been listening. Here's a procedure that will let us test ourselves: I'll start by telling my name. Then the person on my left here will say my name and then his or her own. Then the person on his or her left will give my name, then the second person's name, and then his or her own. We'll continue that way all around the circle—with the list of names getting longer each time!" *(Begin by stating your name—"Robert Finklemeyer"—and nod at the student on your left. If a student gets confused, coach him or her: "Tell my name and then yours." When the student responds, nod at the second person to your left, and so on. When a student forgets a name, say to ask the person whose name he or she has forgotten, rather than telling it yourself.)*

4. *(Group is seated in a circle, with the teacher sitting as part of the group. Instruct students to take out a pencil and sheet of paper—you do the same.)* "At the top of your paper please print the words *I Am* and underneath number from 1 to 5 leaving plenty of room to write. Now I'd like you—working alone, please—to take a few moments to complete that statement, by writing after each number a word or phrase that indicates something that you are. For example, you might wish to say 'the oldest of the children in my family' or 'the owner of a prize-winning registered cocker spaniel' or anything else that will tell us something about you." *(After you and the students have finished your lists, proceed in order around the circle—starting with yourself—having each person read what he or she has written for #3 on the list. If time permits, continue with other numbers in the list until all responses have been read.)*

5. *(Ask students to push back their desks to create empty space in the middle of the room. Have them number off by ones and twos to divide the class into two groups.)* "I'd like all the ones to stand in a circle and the twos to form a circle outside the ones' circle, by standing opposite a one, facing him or her. Do you know your partner's name? If not, ask. Now, tell your partner what you would buy if you had $50 to spend." *(After both partners have responded, continue with the instructions:)* "Now I want the people in the inner circle to move around to the right so that they are facing a new partner." *(After both partners have responded, continue with the same instructions, using the following questions: 1) If you had to change your name, what would the new one be? 2) Who is your hero and why?*

3) What subject in school are you best at? 4) If you could spend an hour talking to some famous person, who would it be? 5) What is one thing that makes you happy? 6) What is one thing that makes you mad?

After the class has become fairly well acquainted, begin to call attention to the process of developing trust, to help them become conscious of the factors that cause students to trust (or distrust) them. Point out how lack of trust keeps persons from participating actively in a discussion.

6. *(Group is seated in a circle, with the teacher as part of the group.)* "I want you to think of your deepest, darkest, inner-most secret—the last thing that you would *ever* tell to the people here. I will *not* ask you to tell that secret or in any way reveal it, so don't be worried. I only want you to imagine that secret in your own mind—remember it. Has everyone thought of a secret which you wouldn't tell this group? Now I want you to imagine, simply imagine, that you had just told that secret right here, right now. What would the reaction of the people in this class be? *(Do not pause for answers yet).* Would they laugh? Would they be understanding? Would they be sad? Would they dislike you? Would they be horrified and never speak to you again? Just how do you think they would react? Can you imagine the expressions on their faces when you told your secret? What would they say to you?" *(Go around the circle—starting with yourself—asking each person to tell how he or she imagines the group would react to hearing the secret.)*

7. *(Group is seated in a circle, with the teacher as part of the group.)* "I'd like us to discuss the following question: What could the people in this group do to make you feel more free to talk in front of them about things that are important to you?" (If time permits, let each person answer; otherwise, call on volunteers. Try to get students to describe the specific behavior on the part of others that makes them feel comfortable, such as listening carefully, not laughing, smiling when I talk, asking me questions.)[1]

We recommend devoting five to ten class periods to trust-building activities such as these. They can be integrated with writing exercises (as we will explain under Topic VI in this chapter, pp. 24-33), so little time is lost from teaching composition. Other resources that can be helpful in establishing a comfortable classroom climate include:

Human Interaction in Education by Gene Stanford and Albert E. Roark (Allyn and Bacon, 1974),
Learning Discussion Skills Through Games by Gene Stanford and Barbara Dodds Stanford (Citation Press, 1969), and
Developing Effective Classroom Groups by Gene Stanford (Hart Publishing, 1977).

TOPIC I: FOCUSING ON REAL ISSUES

All too often the topics students are given for compositions have nothing to do with *them*—their interests, their beliefs, their concerns, their own lives, their selves. Consequently, the

---

1. Gene Stanford, "Taming Restless Cats: Alternatives to the Whip," *English Journal* 62 (November 1973), 1127-32. Copyright © 1973 by the National Council of Teachers of English. Reprinted by permission of the publisher.

writing they produce is sterile, bland, and unimaginative. It lacks substance because the assignment does not touch on anything that matters to them.

Sample Activity

One way to help pupils prepare to write about personally meaningful ideas and experiences is to have them meet in small groups (three to five students) and share their responses to items such as these:

1. Share with the group your earliest memory.
2. Remember and share "the first time I felt guilty."
3. Share a remembered incident in which you were bad and were punished.
4. Describe your earliest memory of "teacher."
5. Remember and share a time when you were injured in some way.
6. Remember and share an early fear or an occasion on which you were afraid.
7. Can you remember your first awareness of sexuality?
8. Can you remember a favorite garment or costume?
9. Recall and describe an early friend or playmate.
10. Can you remember the occasion when you first realized you were a girl— or a boy?

After students have discussed these items, suggest that they choose one and write about it. Here is how one high school student responded to this assignment:

The Principal
Dennis Weisman
(11th Grade Student)

In everyone's life, at one time or another, he fears someone or something so greatly that death would be a better alternative. When I was in kindergarten, I feared the principal of our school in that manner. In the first place, he was bald headed. I had always feared bald-headed men. (I probably would fear bald-headed women too, but I never saw one.) I always thought that these shiny headed creatures had a grudge against children.

In school the principal would walk into our class and my heart would stop. My pulse started racing, and I broke out in hot and cold perspiration. My hands would shake and my pencil would fly away. I just knew he was looking for me. I started my mind working: was it the block I threw at Susan Kincaid or the snake I put in the teacher's desk? Quickly! I would drop my head to the desk, figuring that if I was sick he wouldn't hit me too hard. Yet always he would go away, and never once did he yell at me in class.

One time, right after I had put one of those long red pencils in the pitcher of orange juice we were to drink, the big bald-headed creature, our principal, came into the room. Immediately, I became the good citizen of the class and emptied the pencil sharpener shavings. "Dennis Weisman," he called out.

I came up to the front of the room. My head reached right above his knees. He took my hand and we proceeded out of the room. I was now quite a celebrity. After all, to go to the principal's office in kindergarten you've got to be something. We passed the first and then the second and then the third grade classrooms. I remember saying to myself how nice it would have been to be a first grader next year.

As we walked into his office, he opened a big door: I knew it; this was it. This was the Spanking Machine. I knew now I was to be the only kindergartener ever to die at the hands of the Spanking Machine.

Bravely, chest out, I walked in as if I were to die, and I truly thought I was going to die. It was not there! The Spanking Machine was not there! He said to sit down. I sat in the big chair which I had to climb up on and fall into. I sat there staring at him. He cleared his throat and grasped his hands.

And then: "Dennis, I am surprised at you. Your brother and sister were so well mannered. And then you stick pencils in the orange juice."

I had thought the whole incident was rather amusing and began to laugh. He suddenly started chuckling along with me and before you knew it the whole office echoed with our laughter.

This was the first of many visits I was to make to the principal's office that year. I was better known as the Al Capone of Spoede School Kindergarten. After leaving his office, I limped down the hall, keeping alive the legend of the Spanking Machine. And to this day, the legends are still told about the boy who almost flunked kindergarten.

SUGGESTED RESOURCES

The following materials can be useful in encouraging students to write about topics that interest or concern them. Addresses of publishers can be found in the alphabetical list on pages 111–113. Prices, where given, are only approximate, since changes occur frequently.

A Thousand Topics for Composition revised by the Illinois Association of Teachers of English. Topics found effective by some 250 teachers, classified in nineteen different areas, including my world, religion, character sketches, fantasy, and philosophy. A fine source of ideas for the teacher. Paperbound. $1.00. National Council of Teachers of English.

300 Creative Writing Activities for Composition Classes by Edwin P. Grobe. Interesting topics to which students can respond with many types of writing. Paperbound. $5.00. J. Weston Walch, Publisher.

Composition Situations by Grace E. Wilson. Presents innumerable composition ideas, including personal experiences, language study, mass media, and literature. An excellent reference for teachers. Paperbound. $2.60. National Council of Teachers of English.

Discovering Motives in Writing by Bernard Folta and Richard Trent. A student text that encourages students to examine the motives behind communication and then practice interpreting, writing, composing, and creating. Designed to teach why, not just how, one should write. Teacher's manual available. Paperbound. Harcourt Brace Jovanovich.

The Write Thing by Raymond E. Lemley. A series of student texts with writing activities based on themes such as "Me, Myself, and I" and "Those Alone." Attractive visuals stimulate students' interest. Fine for students of all abilities. Teacher's manual available. Paperbound. Houghton Mifflin Company.

Write On! by Arthur Daigon. A student text containing numerous readings, pictures, excerpts from short stories, poems, and novels—each accompanied by warm-up, writing, and follow-up activities. Designed to give students practice in every imaginable type of writing: letters, slogans, logs, journals, obituaries, etc. Teacher's manual available. Paperbound. Harcourt Brace Jovanovich.

Writing for a Reason by Richard Uhlich. Offers opportunities for students to write about a variety of interesting topics. Excellent workbook format allows students to respond to activities and exercises right in the book. Especially appropriate for average students. Paperbound. $.50. Xerox.

Journal 3/ Journal 4 by Gene Stanford and Barbara Dodds Stanford. Offers numerous interesting, imaginative topics for students to react to and write about in a variety of ways. Journal 3 focuses on personal issues, including childhood, education, values, generations, maturity. Journal 4 focuses on social issues such as war, oppression, technology, world of the future. Paperbound. $2.85. Harcourt Brace Jovanovich.

Invention by John C. Adler. A student text in which students react to and write about quotations and literary excerpts in the areas of commitment, justice, war, hunger, freedom, nature, cities, beauty, love, fear, survival, youth, and individualism. Paperbound. Harcourt Brace Jovanovich.

TOPIC II: FREEING STUDENTS TO WRITE WHAT MATTERS

Years of writing compositions that satisfy English teachers but lack genuineness, originality, and freshness have made many students experts in producing what Ken Macrorie has dubbed "Engfish." Explains Macrorie: Engfish is ". . . the bloated, pretentious language I saw everywhere around me, in the students' themes, in textbooks on writing, in the professors' and administrators' communications to each other. A feel-nothing, say-nothing language, dead like Latin, devoid of the rhythms of contemporary speech. A dialect in which words are almost never 'attached to things,' as Emerson said they should be." Too many students churn out papers that sound like this example cited by Macrorie:

> It is hard to realize just how much you miss someone until you are away from this person. It seems that the time spent away from this person is wasted. You seem to wait and wait till you can see this person again. Then when the time comes, it passes far too quickly.[2]

The teacher of composition confronted with a class of writers of Engfish has the problem, not of teaching the class to write, but of *re*-teaching them to write. He or she must convince them that it is all right to write the same way they speak, to say what's on their minds, to risk making a few errors in mechanics.

Sample Activities

1. Provide students with frequent, regular opportunities to write as much as they like on whatever topic they wish. This could take the form of a journal, in which they make daily entries dealing with whatever is on their minds at the time. Stress that the important thing is that they say what they really mean, and never mark errors in mechanics or suggest revisions. The purpose of an assignment such as this is to get students used to writing regularly without feeling the constraints usually imposed by composition assignments that will be graded.

2. From time to time have students spend ten to twenty minutes writing nonstop. Instruct them to write continuously, as fast as they can, about something that matters to them. Some possible starting points: "often I feel . . . ," or "I never can . . . ," or "other people think I . . . ." Suggest that if students think they've run out of anything to say, they should just copy the last sentence they wrote until they think of something new. Emphasize that the exercise will not be graded and that they are not to worry about errors in mechanics.

---

2. Ken Macrorie. *Telling Writing* (Rochelle Park, New Jersey: Hayden Book Company, 1970), p. 2.

SUGGESTED RESOURCES

The following materials can be useful in helping students free themselves from the inhibitions caused by too much emphasis on the mechanics of writing and not enough emphasis on content. Addresses of publishers can be found in the alphabetical list on pages 111–113. Prices, where given, are only approximate, since changes occur frequently.

A Vulnerable Teacher by Ken Macrorie. The autobiographical account of a college English professor's experiment with a new way of teaching writing. "For seventeen years I heard my students repeating badly to me what I had said to them and hundreds before them. I read their tired, hurriedly written papers conveying in academic dialect what they thought proper to give Teacher. One day in May in an advanced writing class I finally exploded." In the new approach students were allowed to react subjectively to course content, giving personal reactions to literary works rather than pedantic analysis. Students enjoyed the writing when it became relevant to their needs, experiences, and interests. Macrorie presents samples of student work, along with explanations and comments. An inspiration to the teacher who reads it. Paperbound. Hayden Book Company.

Uptaught by Ken Macrorie. Similar in purpose and content to *A Vulnerable Teacher*, though perhaps a bit more readable. Shows how the author developed "The Third Way" of teaching writing. Filled with anecdotes and samples of student writing. Guaranteed to cause any teacher to re-examine how he or she teaches composition. Paperbound. Hayden Book Company.

Writing to Be Read by Ken Macrorie. Intended primarily for high school students, this text includes many excellent approaches to writing freely and provides instruction in keeping a journal, writing reports and columns, creating form, playing with words, etc. A fine antidote for students who have overdosed on topic sentences, outlines, parallel construction, and correct punctuation. Paperbound. $4.96. Hayden Book Company.

Telling Writing by Ken Macrorie. A text intended primarily for college students, but appropriate for advanced high school students as well. Similar in content to *Writing to Be Read*, which is the better choice for use with high school students. Paperbound. Hayden Book Company.

Writer's Journal: Explorations by Dalton H. McBee. A student text that builds an entire program of writing instruction around keeping a personal journal. Students are presented with a stimulus and are then asked to react to it in their journals. Teacher's manual available. Paperbound. Harcourt Brace Jovanovich.

Let the Children Write by Margaret Langdon. Subtitled "An Explanation of Intensive Writing." A teacher's account of her writing program that includes setting up spontaneous writing exercises designed to capture interest and maximize involvement. Includes examples of student work on a variety of open-ended, imaginative topics. An interesting book for teachers of younger students. Hardcover. National Council of Teachers of English.

Imaginary Worlds: Notes on a New Curriculum by Richard Murphy. In an experimental writing program the author instructs students in spontaneous writing activities—descriptions of imaginary places, undiscovered states, and other dimensions. Restrictions are lifted, imaginations liberated. Paperbound. Teachers and Writers Collaborative.

TOPIC III: REACTING TO SENSORY STIMULI

The world of the student's immediate experience is a rich source of ideas for writing. It is the world, Macrorie would say, that students should write about, rather than some abstract, far-fetched world "out there." Yet many students are not in the habit of attending to the world around them. They don't see and hear and feel as keenly as the good writer must.

Their powers of observation must be developed, so that they are sensitive to the world through which they move each day. Only then can they develop the skills for communicating their experiences to others.

In order to provide students with opportunities to improve their powers of observation and their sensory awareness, many teachers now utilize photographs and other stimuli (visual, tactile, and auditory) in the composition class. Some rely on commercially produced materials such as those reviewed on pages 17–18. Others prepare their own and involve the students themselves in the collection and preparation of such materials.

Sample Activities

1. Have students describe the school in terms of the smells (or the sounds, sights, feelings, and tastes) they notice during a walk down the hall.

2. Have students take a walk, and then write about what they experienced in terms of their senses.

3. Have students prepare and drink a glass of iced coffee, and then describe the experience in terms of the senses.

4. Have students describe a Thanksgiving dinner, or a breakfast tray, or a great pizza, or any other "tasteful" experience.

5. Have students listen to the sounds in their homes at various times of day and compare them.

6. Ask students whether morning sounds differ from evening. Does morning *feel* different from evening? Have them write about the differences they've discussed.

7. Have students take their senses through a tour of the four seasons: does autumn smell different from spring? Does winter feel different from summer? What tastes go with which season?

8. Have students sit in study hall (or somewhere else in the school) and write down what they hear.

9. Have students look out a window and describe what they see, including colors, shapes, sizes, patterns, lights and shadows, textures, etc.

10. Take students on a field trip (i.e., to the zoo, a packing house, a farmers' market, a country store, a neighborhood very different from their own, a hospital). Then have them record their sensory impressions.

11. Suggest students listen to various people's voices. Do they sound alike or different? Have them listen to family, friends, strangers, and describe their voices.

12. Have students describe a pain, being hot, cold, sick, hungry, full, sleepy, or alert.

13. Bring to the class pieces of apple, orange, or onion. Have students eat one and describe the experience.

14. Instruct students to hold their arms outstretched as long as they can and then describe the feeling.

15. Play recordings of sounds and have the class identify them.

16. Provide the class with a multitude of smells to experience. Then have them choose one to describe. Do the same with tastes, touch sensations, visual experiences (light show, strobe light, kaleidoscope, etc.).

17. Have each student bring a "sensory experience" to share with the class or a small group.

18. Have the class list on the board all the "feels" they can think of (dizziness, nausea, warmth, coolness, dampness, itchiness, aches, sharp pains, hunger, etc.).

19. Have each student share with a small group a log of a day's observations of sensory impressions.

20. Have each student share a memory of a significant sensory experience.

Here is a sequence of activities that have been suggested by junior high school teacher Jere I. Hochman:[3]

Day 1. Writing sample. Describe anything in the room.

Day 2. Scribbling. Play a record, any record without words. Let students relax and allow the music to dictate their pencil scribblings on paper. (Finger painting would be better.) Repeat this on the opposite side of the paper. Students this time should write any words that come to mind as they are scribbling.

Day 3. This time pick out a song that you feel represents a certain situation such as playing a pinball machine. Usually a song that begins slowly and builds up works best. Tell the students to think of that situation and while free-flowing across the page their scribbling should illustrate the speed and intensity of the music. Again have them write as many words as come to mind along the lines of the situation: flash, ping, ouch, bright lights, reflections, flippers, ding. They may continue writing short phrases.

Day 4. Repeat the music as in Day 3, only have students pretend that THEY are an object in the situation: "You are a pinball!" They should record in their scribbling all their sensations as they listen: slowly, curious, where am I, rolling, faster, ding, ping, cut it out, buddy, embarrassed. Upon conclusion of the song, they should immediately begin writing a brief paragraph (don't worry about punctuation) from the point of view of the pinball, relating its experience. They should use all of the words on the scribbled side, and more.

Day 5. Students read their paragraphs aloud at the same time. Then ask the class if they felt they were the pinball as they listened, or if it read like a newspaper account of a pinball. Have students rewrite paragraphs so that someone reading it could feel what the writer felt as the pinball.

Day 6. Picture description. Students too often do not realize the importance of description. Present one side of the class with a picture. (Slides are even better.) The other half should close their eyes. Ask the "looking" side to describe what they see. They will describe hair color, and maybe an emotion,

---

3. Jere I. Hochman, "What Does a World Smell Like?" (Unpublished manuscript). Used with permission of the author.

but when the other half looks they won't believe it was the same picture. Switch sides. As attempts continue, descriptions become much more detailed. Show and Tell works well, too.

Day 7. Bring in a sample of good description. I am more partial to sports articles than newspaper "what happened" accounts. Students can see from a model how one can communicate feeling. "His face was suffused in agony, a mask of glowing, glitter-like sweat."

Day 8. By now the students think that you are crazy for having them scribble or describe things, so this may be a good time to introduce them to a few essentials. Here introduce them to our old friends: plot, character, setting, theme, and the step ladder approach to writing a story. Action packed TV shows work well here as they usually introduce the setting and characters early in the show and the plot gets better as it continues. Each between-commercial episode is usually a step up the ladder until the climax is reached. Students also see the difference between plot and theme since most shows have the same theme each week with a different plot.

Day 9. Now that the students are beginning to get the feel of things, they are introduced to their senses: sight, smell, taste, touch, and hearing. These are discussed briefly: how often we use them, could we do without them, etc. If time permits, several experiments could be done pretending the loss of vision or hearing. If students can be made to appreciate their senses, their writings will illustrate this awareness. Begin by having students describe visually what they see. They continue by asking what music sounds like, what sandpaper feels like. These are quite simple, but then ask what water tastes like, or what burning rubber smells like. Descriptions can be done on paper or orally. Continue by exploring one sense in relation to another. For example, what does the color red smell like, or what does smoothness sound like? Students will begin to think abstractly.

SUGGESTED RESOURCES

Below is a selected list of resources useful for teaching writing through sensory awareness. Several types of materials are suggested, including books for the teacher, and audio-visual materials. Addresses of publishers can be found in the alphabetical list on pages 111–113. Prices, where given, are only approximate, since changes occur frequently.

Stop, Look and Write/Pictures for Writing/The Writer's Eye/An Eye for People by Hart Day Leavitt and David A. Sohn. Four separate paperbacks, each containing a multitude of dramatic photographs with related suggestions for writing about them. All of the texts share one premise: to stop, look and concentrate on a picture, painting, or scene, and then to write, using accurate language appropriate to the image. Paperbound. $1.50 each. Bantam.

Dig U.S.A./The Good Life U.S.A./Violence U.S.A. by Arthur Daigon and Ronald T. LaConte. Three independent paperbacks, each containing a collection of photographs, documents, charts, cartoons, and other equally interesting items to spur students to react in discussion or in writing. Paperbound. $1.25–$1.95 each. Bantam.

New Approaches to Writing edited by Philip

Werber. A teacher's guide to using the seven books described above. Outlines the rationale for teaching writing through photographs and other visually stimulating items, and provides specific teaching strategies for using the books. Guidebook for the teacher using any of the above books. $1.25. Bantam.

Eye Openers by David A. Sohn and Don Blegen. A writing program of 21 lessons using color slides and related activities to encourage students to use their many different observations and perceptions as they develop important creative writing skills. Also included are 48 black and white prints for use in individual writing assignments. Set contains 97 slides in a carousel tray, 40-page teacher's guide, and photo package of prints. $74.50. Scholastic Book Services.

Come to Your Senses by David A. Sohn. A filmstrip program similar to *Eye Openers* described above. Teaches creative writing through observation skills and awareness. Set contains four filmstrips, 32 supplementary photographs printed on heavy cardboard, seven posters, and an 80-page teaching guide. $49.50. Scholastic Book Services.

Here and Now by Fred Morgan. A student text that approaches writing through perception. Includes chapters on perceiving objects, the immediate environment, emotional attitudes and thoughts, evaluating, identifying, examining, observing, searching, reliving, and looking. Appropriate only for advanced students or as a teacher resource. Paperbound. Harcourt Brace Jovanovich.

Poster Ideas for Personalized Learning by Betsy Caprio. A teacher's guide to using posters to stimulate discussion or as pre-writing stimuli. Includes excellent ideas for creative writing activities, plus open-ended, "run-on" story writing, stimulus-response items, mind-stretching exercises, imaginative writing assignments, and much more. Paperbound. $1.00. Argus Communications.

A Folio for Writers: Exposition/A Folio for Writers: Advertising by Bruce Vance and Michael Milne. Two unique "packages" of photographs and related questions and activities. Twenty-eight prints are included in the back sleeve of each folder, which also contains a guide to small group and individual projects, discussion questions, and writing suggestions. Clarke, Irwin and Company.

The Creative Word by Stephen N. Judy *et al*. A series of student texts that incorporate visually stimulating material with a wide variety of writing activities. No student will find these books dull. Paperbound. Random House.

12,001 Students and Their English Teachers compiled by the Commission on English of the College Entrance Examination Board. Model teaching units in language, literature, and composition for grades 9-12. Includes two composition units based on visual stimuli. Spiralbound with paper cover. $6.30. National Council of Teachers of English.

TOPIC IV: WRITING FOR A REASON

For many students, writing activities assigned in school have no relationship to the life that they lead outside the school or that they will lead as adults. They will not go to college, and have no need to prepare themselves to write the kinds of paper required there. They will not become writers by vocation or even avocation. But they will need to communicate in writing to survive—to get the jobs they want, to hold on to those jobs, to write letters to friends and family, to write thank you and condolence notes, to fill out forms, to complain about inferior services and manufactured goods, and perhaps even to express an opinion in the letters to the editor column.

The more a teacher can link writing assignments to the real world in which students live—or will probably live as adults—the more likely it is that students will produce good writing. To undertake this approach successfully, the teacher must have a clear idea of their post-graduation plans and what kind of lives they are likely to lead as adults. It's impossible to link writing instruction to the real-world lives of students unless you know what those lives actually are.

A Sample Approach

Since an important focus of the high school years is choosing and preparing for a career, writing related to exploring a career can be particularly appropriate. Writing about the teaching of composition skills through career education, Robert C. Small, Jr., suggests:

> In such a unit, students would begin in the traditional manner by examining factual information about a selected career and summarizing those facts in a brief presentation using the skills of outlining and summarizing. This would not be a research report, so there would be no pretense that the result was anything but a condensation of one or more sources. From this summary, the students would then write lists of the characteristics that they have which suit them for that career. At the same time, they would examine want ads or similar materials appropriate to that field and obtain names and addresses of businesses, agencies, institutions, etc., which employ people from it. Each student would choose one and write a letter requesting information about work possibilities. He or she would also ask for copies of job applications, descriptions of application procedures, etc. When such materials have been obtained, the student would go through the formal application procedures for employment used in that career, including possibly a simulated submission to whatever certification processes or examinations it might require.
>
> Up to this point, the unit would resemble many efforts by English teachers to create simulated situations for the writing of job applications; and it is at this point that most units conclude. Unfortunately, however, such a unit concentrates only on the externals of the career under consideration; and the writing exercises and skills are of a rather low level. If, however, the unit were to continue by asking students to pretend that they, in fact, entered the career under consideration, many additional writing skills, especially those of a higher level than the completion of forms, could be included. Through the reading of biographies and autobiographies, novels, short stories, and essays by and about members of a career, students would attempt to develop a sense of what it is like to be a person in that career. Where appropriate, each student would examine specialized manuals such as journals, materials, and books which would form the reading matter of members of the field.
>
> This second phase of the unit would require the creation of a large number of varying types of writing. Each student would be expected to interview a member of the career and present a written report in the manner of journalistic interviews with well-known people. He or she would also write a narrative presenting the details of the public life of a person in that field. In addition, students would write several short papers from the point of view of a member of that career, such as a letter to the editor of a local newspaper reacting to some issue or event like the adoption of a school budget, a letter to a colleague, and a report to a superior. The particular skills involved in each type of composition would, of course, be studied as a preliminary to the writing. Descriptive writing would focus on the details of the place of work where the career is pursued and would involve efforts to capture the various aspects of the mood of the career and those who pursue it. Character sketches would be written about fellow workers, clients, etc. Again, the particular skills involved in each type of writing would be examined as a part of the writing situation.
>
> Finally, in the role of an established practitioner of the career, students would be asked to prepare a job description to be given to someone considering entering that field. They would also prepare an advertisement for a job opening, using the form appropriate to the career, and develop application materials and procedures. The final step in the unit would consist of students' reviewing their own applications from Phase One, deciding whether or not to hire themselves on that basis, preparing a report to some appropriate authority explaining the decision, and writing a letter to the applicant informing him or her of the decision.
>
> Thus, in such a unit, each student would practice the general skills of composing and also the particular skills involved in the following types of writing:

1) a summary,
2) a list of character elements,
3) a letter asking for information,
4) a job application,
5) a journalistic interview,
6) a narrative,
7) a letter to a newspaper editor,
8) a friendly letter,
9) a report to a superior,
10) a description,
11) an impressionistic piece capturing a mood,
12) several character sketches,
13) a job description,
14) an advertisement,
15) an application form, and
16) a letter to a job applicant.

This composition unit, by moving students from the outside of a proposed career to the inside, would carry them from the uninformed novice to the expert who makes decisions about job applicants. Because of the emphasis on the inside details of the career, the unit would provide students with a simulated situation for the practice of many different composing skills, all of which, even the more "creative," would have a meaningful and practical application. Such a unit, then, would meet the challenge of career education and, at the same time, allow for activities appropriate to the objectives of a writing class.[4]

Other Sample Activities

1. Bring to class actual copies of forms, particularly job applications, and have students fill them in. Then let students meet in small groups and compare the ways they have answered.

2. Have students imagine that the mother of a close friend has died. (Have them actually choose which friend, to make the assignment seem more real.) Assign them to write a brief note to the friend, expressing their sympathy and concern. (For practical, interesting suggestions on writing condolence letters, see Chapter 10 of *Widow* by Lynn Caine, published by Bantam Books, $1.75.)

SUGGESTED RESOURCES

Below is a selected list of resources useful for improving students' skills of practical, everyday writing. Both books for the teacher and books for students are suggested. Addresses of publishers can be found in the alphabetical list on pages 111–113. Prices, where given, are only approximate, since changes occur frequently.

Business Writing by J. Harold Janis and Howard R. Dressner. Provides instruction in writing reports, resumes, orders, letters of inquiry, and replies, plus countless other forms. Probably too advanced for use as a student text at the high school level, but could be a valuable reference for teachers.

---

4. "Composition Skills and Career Education" in *On Righting Writing*, copyright © 1975 by the National Council of Teachers of English. Reprinted by permission of the publisher and Robert C. Small, Jr.

Paperbound. $2.95. Barnes and Noble.

Forms in Your Future by M. Goltry. A work-text for students. Activities include sample forms of all types that the student can practice filling out. Forms range from gasoline company credit card application to union membership application. Teacher's guide provides detailed lesson plans. Paperbound. $2.40. Globe Book Company.

The Bantam Book of Correct Letter Writing by Lillian Eichler Watson. Useful as a student text or reference for the teacher. Explains and illustrates correct form and content for all kinds of business and social letters. Includes hundreds of sample letters. Practical and clear. Paperbound. $1.50. Bantam.

The Written Conversation: A Practical Guide to Letter Writing by Jane Eaton. A little booklet available from a major stationery company, containing practical information about correct form for various kinds of letters. Paperbound. $.35. Eaton Paper Company.

Put It in Writing: A Natural Approach to Writing English by Anthony Howatt. A book for students. A continuous story about a teenager and his friends forms the text, with the characters writing letters, postcards, telegrams, diaries, and articles. Focuses on everyday situations and practical writing skills. But since the characters are British, American students may find the situations somewhat strange. Perhaps most useful as a source of ideas for the teacher. Paperbound. Oxford University Press.

TOPIC V: WRITING FOR AN AUDIENCE

Writing that is not read is like the tree that falls in the forest with no one to hear it; one wonders whether it creates any sound at all. A writing assignment that is undertaken for only the teacher to read is not likely to engage the student in any meaningful way. Such writing is merely an exercise, and most students approach it with the same lack of enthusiasm with which they approach most exercises.

No adult writer would be willing to compose much under these circumstances. We all need the reinforcement that comes when others read and respond to our work, even if that response is less than favorable. Hence, it is imperative that we supply students with more of an audience than just a harried teacher wading through a stack of papers. The audience may be simply another student in the class, or the class as a whole, or it could be the entire school or even the community. Several ways to go about providing an audience are suggested below.

Ways to Provide Students with an Audience

1. Allow each student to choose a partner in the classroom to read his or her compositions and respond to them. The partner is *not* to mark errors but to react to the content.

2. Allow each student to choose a classroom partner with whom to correspond on a regular basis. Do not assign or even suggest content. This procedure should entail little teacher intervention; do not correct or inspect the student writing. Allow sufficient time for students to write, pass, and respond to all notes during class. Treat note passing as a legitimate activity, which provides students with a valuable way to practice writing skills while sharing ideas and feelings that otherwise might never be expressed.

3. Assign students to small groups. Have them read their compositions to the other members of their small groups and ask for reactions. As in #1 above, the small group is not to criticize the writing, but to react to the content.

4. Reproduce students' papers for the class to read. Have students type or write their essays, poems, or stories on a ditto master. Run these off and distribute copies to the class to read and comment on. Be sure to warn students that you plan to make their work public in this fashion.

5. Have a class compile the compositions that they like best and reproduce an anthology of the class's writing to be distributed to other classes in the school.

6. Help students become involved in writing for the school newspaper or yearbook. Or create your own weekly class newspaper or newsletter using a spirit duplicator. Give students experience in writing interesting columns, editorials, letters to the editor, news stories, etc. You could have part of the class write letters to the editor and the other part respond to them.

7. Call your local newspaper concerning the following activities:
    a. Ask it to work with you to establish a contest in which students write poems or other short works and a panel of judges (the teacher plus the newspaper's editor for education) chooses the best one for publication in the newspaper.
    b. Find out if the newspaper will allow one or more of your better students to volunteer their services to the newspaper, writing feature stories under the teacher's supervision.

8. John Hollowell suggests playing "The Publishing Game," a classroom simulation in which students decide what kind of magazines they want to publish, choose roles ranging from editor to staff writer, and write and edit their respective magazines. For specifics, see Hollowell's article in *On Righting Writing*, published by the National Council of Teachers of English.

9. Letter writing is the most practical way to give students an audience. The idea of the pen pal in another school has been developed into an exciting approach by Carole Berlin and Nancy Miller in their article "Help! I'm a Prisoner in a Letter Factory." Their students exchanged letters with students in a very different kind of school in another part of the city and learned about people as well as about writing. Their article, providing the interesting details, appears in *On Righting Writing*, published by the National Council of Teachers of English.

10. Raymond J. Rodrigues suggests several ways to use letter writing in the composition program:[5]

The letter has typically been taught to all students at some stage of their education, but what has usually been taught is form, not content. Students learn a "correct" form for personal letters and for business letters, the emphasis being placed upon mechanics—e.g., whether to use a colon or a comma, how far to indent particular items, and how to fold the letter. That letters are motivated communications, that word choice and style vary according to the person and reason one is writing, and that the writer must constantly predict the effect a letter will have upon its reader, are often ignored.

---

5. "In Search of an Audience: Letter Writing" (Unpublished manuscript). Used with permission of the author.

Letters are written for many purposes: condolence, complaint, congratulations, opinion, information seeking, information giving, holiday greetings, requests for assistance, love letters, death notices, get-well wishes. These are the communications of life and are thus highly motivated efforts, not assignment fillers. By incorporating letter writing throughout the language development process, the teacher can be assured of interesting reading.

Letter writing can be not only meaningful, but also lead to publication. Almost every newspaper contains two outlets for the letter writer: letters to the editor and letters to the personal advice columnist. Students who see their words in print know that someone has paid attention to them though obviously an editor who receives thirty to forty letters in the mail one day from a similar source may perceive that some teacher's class is fulfilling an assignment and probably won't print more than one or two. With that in mind, the teacher can make this type of letter an option to other writing assignments which students may select as often as they choose.

Writing to people in the news sometimes leads to pleasant results. True, if students write to a sports figure just after that person has broken a long-standing record or to a movie star who just won an award, they may not receive a response. But if they write to a lesser-known individual, such as a man who had a freak accident and is now in the hospital or a woman who is working to improve her neighborhood, they will very often find a letter in return.

Discouraging students from writing to celebrities is too negative. Even if they cannot reply themselves, famous individuals often have staff members to answer for them. People constantly before the public need letters to boost their egos or provide feedback on their impact. However, students should be prepared for occasional negative results. A New Mexico student who wrote a prominent state journalist for advice received an insulting response telling him never to enter journalism.

We are constantly bombarded with appeals to write our congressperson about some important issue. "How else can they know what you are thinking or respond to your wishes?" One frequent appeal is that such an activity is an essential ingredient in keeping our democracy alive. Yet, how many adults actually do so? A recent survey in Utah revealed that 87 percent of the state's population had never communicated to a state or federal representative or senator, and that figure may be low for the entire country. Most elected federal officials respond to every letter, even if the response is a preprogrammed one. Students who have written to the President of the United States have been both surprised and pleased to receive an answer, even if signed by a presidential aide. Whether they will continue as adults to write congresspeople cannot be predicted, but for the moment, they do write purposefully.

As a part of the study of literature, students can write to poets, novelists, and editors to comment on what they have read, to suggest ways of improving anthologies, and to ask for biographical data, writing suggestions, or explanations of confusing elements in the literature. Well known authors often never reply. As a fantasy exercise, students might write to characters in the literature, giving advice, criticising, or role-playing other characters.

The "pen pal" approach has enabled students to write to others in different parts of the world, not only providing students with someone who will listen, but also enabling them to learn about cultures different from theirs. Why not have an entire class contact an entire class in another school? Teachers can write teachers as well, thus developing an interchange of ideas.

Some teachers establish post offices in their classrooms. Students walk into those classrooms looking forward to letters in their boxes. And when they receive letters, they share them with other students and their teachers. Some even write the correspondent again. The feeling that teaching truly can be worthwhile increases whenever a student asks, "How can I say this better?" or, "He didn't understand what I was talking about—what should I do now?" As the letter writing events increase in scope, the student demand for training in communication skills will also increase, not because the students want to impress the teacher, but because they develop a need to know.

Inevitably, if the teacher does not set an example, the student may begin to wonder why. So the teacher should also write letters in front of the students while they are writing theirs. If the teacher has not had a chance to write that complaint to the local catalogue store or a note to the superintendent of schools bragging about the success of the letter writing project, the time set aside for the students to write is the time for the teacher to do the same.

Oh yes, don't forget: one of the most important steps in writing letters is to mail them.

SUGGESTED RESOURCE

The School Literary Magazine by B. Jo Kinnick. Discusses literary magazines and the high school writer, purposes and advantages of having a literary magazine, a description of a creative writing program, and tips on how to make the school magazine literary. Interesting discussion of successful high school literary magazines around the country. Paperbound. $1.75. National Council of Teachers of English.

TOPIC VI: WRITING TO UNDERSTAND ONESELF AND OTHERS

The two questions, "Who am I?" and "Where do I fit with others?" are perhaps the most basic issues facing the high school student, if not all human beings. Writing that is real and purposeful almost always attempts to handle these questions either directly or indirectly. As communication, writing can serve to strengthen the bonds between persons or groups, or it can be used destructively to create hurt and suspicion. In conjunction with writing activities, students can develop a greater understanding of themselves and can improve their relations with others, including the various members of the class. The following approaches combine human relations training and instruction in composition, and have worked successfully with high school classes:

Sample Activities*

1. At the beginning of the term, seat the class in one large circle and have students introduce themselves to the group. Test students periodically to see how well they are remembering names.

2. Have students choose a partner, and interview that person, trying to learn as many facts about him or her as possible in 15 minutes. Then have each student introduce the partner to the class.

3. Assign the students to groups of three. Have them determine two things that all three agree on, two things all three disagree on, two things all three hope will take place in the class, and two things all three hope the class won't do.

4. Conduct an open-ended discussion on the value of getting to know one another: Should members of a class get acquainted? Why? What are the benefits? What are the risks? What are the obstacles that make it difficult? How can the class overcome them? How do you get to know someone?

---
*See also the trust-building activities suggested previously in this chapter (pp. 8–10).

5. Suggest the following as writing topics related to the process of getting acquainted with a new group or class:
   a. How do I feel about myself as I begin my membership in this group? Do I feel fearful or hopeful or . . . ? Do I *want* to get to know these people, this teacher? Am I afraid? Of what, whom? Do I feel like being really me, or do I feel a need to pretend to be other than I am? Why?
   b. Who am I? What kind of person? How do I show myself to others?
   c. How do I feel about others in this group? One particular person? The teacher?
   d. What was an occasion when I revealed more about myself than I meant to?
   e. What was an occasion when I presented an appearance of myself that was totally and deliberately false? Why did I do this? How did I feel afterwards? Were there any good or bad consequences?
   f. What was an important lesson I learned from someone else, or from a group?
   g. Have I ever learned anything from a teacher that was of great importance and value to me? From a friend?
   h. What was something that happened in class that I felt strongly about?
   i. Was there something someone (a student or the teacher) said in class this week with which I disagreed strongly?
   j. Was there something I said or did in class that I wish I could call back and redo?
   k. What are some things I hope for this year, or in this class? What are some things I fear or dislike about this year or this class?

6. Assign each student in the class a partner, trying to match people who do not know each other well. Have each student interview his or her partner and write either a biographical sketch or a feature story (depending on which is more appropriate for the course) about that person. It is often necessary to prepare students for this assignment, for many show as little skill and imagination in talking to strangers as they do in writing compositions. Untrained efforts at this assignment usually produce little more than the partner's birthdate and record of schools attended. Showing students samples of good biographies or feature stories is a good way to start. The feature story is particularly useful, even for non-journalism students, because it forces the writer to select a main idea and develop it in detail, thus discouraging the mindless listing of events that so often appears in poorly written biographical pieces. Another way to prepare students is to have the class brainstorm leading questions that may help the interviewer find the most interesting things about the interviewee. It is then helpful to break down into pairs to practice interviewing for a while. After five or ten minutes, reconvene the total class and discuss how to explore an area in depth once you've discovered the most interesting things about your interviewee. For example, now that you have found that Chuck is interested in sports and plays on the hockey team, how do you find out the interesting details that will make your story come alive? Conduct a few sample interviews in front of the class, or let the whole class interview you or an interesting guest you've invited.

7. After students have written biographies about one another, encourage them to share their pieces with the entire class so everyone can find out about everyone else.

8. Another way that interviews can be used as both a stimulus for writing and to improve students' understanding of self and others is to interview persons outside the classroom.
    a. Find an older relative or neighbor to interview about dating and courtship patterns during that person's youth.
    b. Interview students in the special education program in your school to find out what games and television programs they enjoy. (This assignment, of course, should be preceded by discussion, but it is potentially very helpful in fostering interaction between students and a group of children who are often ridiculed.)
    c. Interview a person in a career you are interested in to find out either why the person chose that career or what a typical day in that career is like.
    d. Interview your parents to find out what schools were like when they were students.

9. Have students work together in groups on a single composition to which every student contributes ideas and examples from his or her own experience. One approach is to have each student write a paragraph describing his or her own ideas or experiences on a topic, and then have the group write an essay incorporating all of the ideas. For example, students could each be assigned to write a paragraph describing the most effective form of punishment which their parents used. The group as a whole could pool their ideas and write an essay on the topic, "Kinds of parental punishments that are effective." This assignment teaches students how to formulate a general statement to cover a number of examples, and how to use incidents and examples to develop a general statement. Other useful topics for this assignment are:

    Individual Paragraph Topic
    a. One person who taught me how to love (what courage is, the joy of sharing, etc.)
    b. One time I was successful in handling anger (resolving conflict, making a friend out of an enemy, etc.)
    c. The time I was most afraid (embarrassed, etc.)

    Group Essay Topic
    a. How children learn to love (to be courageous, to share, etc.)
    b. How to handle anger (resolve conflicts, make a friend out of an enemy, etc.)
    c. Fear (embarrassment, etc.) is caused by . . .

10. Have students fill out an opinionnaire dealing with issues on which members of the class are likely to be sharply divided. Have students express their opinions as either for, against, or don't care. Then assign each student a partner with whom he or she disagrees on at least one issue and have the students write compositions to each other trying to convince each other of their own positions. Provide students with time at the beginning of the assignment to talk with each other to find out why the partner holds a particular view.

11. Clip from the newspaper a fairly detailed news story in which a person or persons commit(s) an act or holds a position that students are likely to disagree with. (You may have to bring several clippings to assure that every student can disagree

with at least one.) Then assign students to write an essay explaining the point of view of the person they disagree with. For example, after reading about the highjacking of a plane by a terrorist, ask students to write an essay explaining what could have motivated the highjacker.

12. Bring to class newspaper articles about a confrontation between the United States and another country and have students write one paragraph giving their reaction to it. Then have them write another paragraph in the first person, imagining that they are a teenager in the other country reacting to the same incident.

13. Discuss with the class the importance of a writer having empathy for the persons being written about. Read or paraphrase the following excerpt from *Fabric of Fiction* [6]:

The Talent for Experience

What are the most important talents of a writer? We have already suggested six (a talent for experiencing; language; imagination; taste; a talent for discerning the significance of what we observe; and personal integrity). Though these might be added to, and much written about each, here we shall analyze only one, the one essential prerequisite of every writer—the talent for experience.

This talent enables us, first, to saturate ourselves with the impressions arising in our daily lives; and second, to project ourselves into the characters and situations we create in our stories. That is, in our own living we must absorb all kinds of ideas and feelings; but in our writing we must lose our own identities and assume the role of the characters we write about. Their emotions become our emotions; we laugh when they laugh, and cry when they cry. This is not to say that as we write our stories we should indulge in an emotional debauch. But we must more than understand a situation; we must experience it. When we understand a friend, we know about him; when we experience him, we sympathize with—in the literal sense of the word "suffer with"—him. His ordeal becomes ours. Only when we have once experienced are we able to write truly and with a sensitive understanding.

In our search to understand and to experience the joys and the troubles of other people, we will be helped by closer consideration of this talent for experience.

In the first place, we must recognize a difference between experiencing life and merely being informed about it. We may know innumerable cold facts about a person, down to the minutest detail; yet we may be totally incapable of entering into that person's emotional life. We may even be capable of putting the facts together in our minds, so that we can understand our acquaintance's successes or failures. But still we are not necessarily experiencing these feelings; for experiencing does not involve the mind so much as it does the heart. The talent for experience can project us completely into the feelings of another—whether that person be real, or only the product of our imaginations. If we merely understand a fictitious character, we are likely to create an inanimate dummy; but if we possess the talent of experiencing, we are much more likely to create a living and memorable character.

Mere information, then, and cold facts, are not enough. No one ever created a story simply from information compiled from Who's Who or the Encyclopaedia Britannica. We need to have more than seeing eyes; we must have understanding hearts. With our in-

---

6. Douglas Bement and Ross M. Taylor, *Fabric of Fiction*. Copyright, 1943, by Harcourt, Brace Jovanovich, Inc.; renewed, 1971, by Rita R. Coville and Ross M. Taylor. Reprinted by permission of the publishers.

*tellects we may be able to understand another's troubles, but until we really sympathize—
"suffer with"—him, we have not experienced. We need not experience so deeply that the
people and situations we observe upset our emotional equilibrium; yet we must look at
life about us with eyes that* see *and hearts that* feel.

14. Reproduce and distribute to students (or project by means of an overhead projector, or read to the class) the short essay "The Person Sitting Next to You" by Ross Snyder (Reproduction Page 1). Then discuss the following questions:
    a. What "invisible activities" are occurring within us all (hearing, tasting, listening, remembering, knowing, forgetting, dreading, hoping, planning, fearing, loving, hating, feeling tense, etc.)?
    b. Are we suffering? How do we *all* "suffer" (fail, or feel rejected, left out, embarrassed, out of place, ashamed, guilty, unsure, unloved, etc.)?
    c. Do we believe people are sacred? In what way? How does this influence the way we should treat people? Do we treat them as if they were uniquely valuable?
    d. In *Heart of the Matter* Graham Greene says, "If we knew all there is to know about someone, we would forgive them anything." Do we agree? Is a human being (are we) capable of such understanding, such love? (Some are: the Kennedys asked for Sirhan Sirhan not to be executed. Other examples abound.)

15. The following extended activity is useful in introducing more affluent students to the everyday realities of the poor. Begin by distributing to each student a list of the five groups of food a person should have daily for good nutrition. (See the school nurse or home economics teacher for help if you don't have access to this list.)

    Divide the class into groups of three or four students each. Assign them to make up menus for one week (seven days) of breakfast, lunch, and dinner for a family of five—mother, father, 16-year-old boy, 14-year-old girl, and 8-year-old boy. The goal is to come up with meals that are both nutritious and cheap. After the groups have drawn up their menus, send them (during class or after school) to a nearby market to see how much their menus would actually cost. Have them total the cost of feeding the family for a week and compare to see how well each group did.

    Meanwhile, call your local welfare office and see how much public assistance such a family is eligible for if the father can't find work and is not receiving unemployment insurance payments. (In the state of Missouri, for example, the family is eligible for *none.* If the father is disabled, he can get $70.00 per month and can buy food stamps if he has money left after paying rent, heat, light, etc. If the father leaves, a Missouri family can get $170 per month and food stamps if there is enough money to buy them.)

    After groups have compared menus and found the cheapest plan for feeding the family nutritiously, present them with the information about public assistance and ask them whether the family could eat adequately on this amount of money. When students see there really isn't enough money to feed the family, have them return to their small groups and brainstorm all the possible things the family might do in order to eat. Require that students think creatively, rather than give up at once with an "I don't know." They might suggest: send children to grandparents or other employed relative; let children become wards of the court and go to foster homes; have the father forge the mother's name on an Aid to Dependent Children application—if he's not caught, the family gets $170 and if he's caught, he goes to prison, and the family gets $170 while he is gone; beg at churches; go to the Salvation Army; fish in lakes in city parks; grow what they can in the back yard, if any; beg at supermarkets and restaurants at closing time; shoplift; have the mother turn to prostitution; have kids pick up bottles, etc., to sell; have the older boy and girl find part-time jobs through their school's work-study program.

In conjunction with this activity, or as an alternative, calculate how much a family on public assistance can spend per day for food. Have students plan, prepare, and eat one day's meals that do not exceed that amount in cost.

Find a local social worker or other person who works on a day-to-day basis with persons who cannot afford to buy adequate food. Have that person describe the experience to the class and answer questions about poverty conditions in your community. The class may wish to respond by taking some sort of action, such as collecting money and canned goods to assist the persons they have learned about.

16. Another group of people that students can learn to empathize with are prisoners. Begin by having students discuss the following questions, either in small groups or as a total class:

   a. Who is in prison? Have you ever committed a crime and gotten away with it? What kind? Do you think your parents ever have? (Ask students to share whatever they feel is not too personal, pointing out that they may be surprised to learn that many of us are not as perfect as we try to appear.) Can each of you visualize a crime you feel you might commit, or be capable of committing? (Have the group agree on what would be a suitable punishment or debt to society to be paid for each crime. Have students agree or disagree on their own sentences.)

   b. What do you think prisons should be like? What are prisons generally like now, and what are the consequences? Do you think people should be punished? (This may assume that students believe people commit crimes out of free will, not as a result of circumstances beyond their control. Or it may assume that regardless of why people commit crimes, punishment is the best way to respond.) Do you think people should *not* be punished? If not, what should happen in prisons? And what would prisons be like? What kind of prison do you think would profit you most if you were put in one?

   c. What other kinds of sentences can you recommend for your own crime and for other crimes?

   d. What would you find to be the hardest part of going to prison? What would you miss the most? Some people who have never been to prison believe that a good modern prison is like a country club. Invariably those who have been in prison, even a good one, say that nothing makes up for the loss of freedom. How would the loss of freedom affect you?

   e. What do you think constitutes the cruel and unusual punishment forbidden by the Constitution?

Then arrange for the class to take a field trip to a correctional institution near your community. When they return, after a general discussion of what they saw and heard there, ask students—working individually—to make a list of all the words that could be used to describe the institution. When they have finished that list, ask them to make another list of all the words that describe their own feelings while visiting the institution. Finally, have students list words that they think might describe the feelings of the inmates. When they have finished, compile the individual lists into a long list on the board. Here are the lists that resulted from a discussion in one class:

The Place	My Feelings	Their Feelings	
oppressive	*uncomfortable*	*banished*	*resentful*
dismal	*ill at ease*	*outcast*	*envious*
impersonal	*embarrassed*	*forsaken*	*left out*
degrading	*skeptical*	*rejected*	*scornful*
bare	*miserable*	*exploited*	*without hope*
colorless	*self-conscious*	*misunderstood*	*reduced*
gray	*out of place*	*unjustly treated*	*hopeless*
tan	*heavy*	*frightened*	*desperate*
disinfected	*dull*	*lonely*	*despairing*
smelly	*disoriented*	*fearful*	*suicidal*
cheerless	*un-confident*	*terrified*	*wretched*
ugly	*empty*	*full of hatred*	*half alive*
unhomelike	*uncertain*	*cynical*	*depersonalized*
bleak	*vulnerable*	*untrusting*	*humiliated*
desolate	*naive*	*hopeful*	*ashamed*
unwelcoming	*displaced*	*submissive*	*helpless*
public	*untrusting*	*rebellious*	*blue*
stuffy	*shocked*	*hostile*	*up-tight*
institutional	*disapproving*	*frustrated*	*caged*
anti-human	*hopeful*	*determined*	*crushed*
threatening	*unworldly*	*guilty*	*diminished*
regulated	*fortunate*	*degraded*	*wary*
uniform	*confined*	*dejected*	*bored*
forsaken	*depressed*	*unlucky*	
lifeless	*curious*	*isolated*	
unselective	*headachy*	*forgotten*	
undiscriminating	*nervous*	*angry*	
plain	*guilty*	*worried*	
forlorn	*disgusted*	*despised*	
isolated	*claustrophobic*	*scorned*	
depressing	*unsure*	*picked on*	
gloomy	*sympathetic*	*framed*	
enclosing	*realizing*	*nervous*	
solid	*compassionate*	*unsure*	
imposing	*thankful*	*controlled*	
restrictive	*surprised*	*oppressed*	
efficient	*shocked*	*cut off*	
depersonalizing	*suspicious*	*unsatisfied*	
stifling	*crass*	*ugly*	
hollow	*unsafe*	*no good*	
drab	*conspicuous*	*useless*	
surrealistic	*humble*	*cautious*	
dreary	*paranoid*	*watchful*	
	withdrawn	*on-guard*	

Then have students write a composition—either a single paragraph or a complete essay, depending on the maturity of the group—on one of the three topics suggested by this activity: a description of the institution, their own feelings while visiting the institution, or what it feels like to be an inmate in such an institution. Or students could write a persuasive essay on some topic related to prison reform or approaches to dealing with criminals in our society.

17. The handicapped are still another group whom students may need help in learning to empathize with. Books and films can be used to give the class an inside view of what it's like to be handicapped. They they can experience first hand what it's like to be physically disabled by "handicapping" themselves for a 24-hour period. Blindness can be simulated by a tight-fitting blindfold, muteness by a pledge not to speak, lameness by confinement to a wheelchair or by tying an arm behind one's back. Let students choose handicaps to live with for a day and then report to the class how it felt, how they reacted to being dependent on others, what frustrations they experienced, and how other people reacted. For more information about developing empathy for the disabled, see "Living with Differences: A Mini-course on People with Handicaps" by Gene Stanford and Joanne L. Bird in *Miniguides* (Citation Press, 1975).

18. Similarly, students are not likely to have had much contact, knowingly, with homosexuals, and can likewise benefit from class activities that help them develop an understanding of this group of people. In addition to reading books that depict homosexuals sympathetically (e.g., *Trying Hard to Hear You* by Sandra Scoppettone, a Bantam paperback written especially for young people), the class can view audio-visual materials (such as "The Invisible Minority," an excellent filmstrip program distributed by the Unitarian Universalist Association) and interview guest speakers provided by your local Gay Liberation organization. For a complete listing of materials and activities on this topic, see the chapter on homosexuality in *Roles and Relationships: A Practical Guide to Teaching about Masculinity and Femininity* by Gene Stanford and Barbara Stanford (Bantam Books, 1976) and "Freeing Students from Homophobia through Literature" by Gene Stanford in *Responses to Sexism: Classroom Practices in Teaching English* (National Council of Teachers of English, 1976).

19. Divide the class into pairs. Instruct each pair to tell one another all the *facts* (no feelings or reactions) about an event in their lives that had great emotional impact on them. After students have told their partners about the event, reconvene the group in one large circle and have each person tell the group the story of the event he or she heard as if it had happened to him or her (rather than to the partner), sharing "his" or "her" feelings as if the event had occurred to him or her.

20. Have students choose an event the whole class is aware of and tell the class about it, taking the role of someone in the event other than themselves and telling the story in the first person as though they were that person.

21. Give students the following writing assignments to choose from:
    a. Pretend to be your mother (or father) writing about you (the son or daughter) to your grandparents. Or pretend to be your Mom or Dad talking about you together.

b. Describe what you imagine are the feelings and thoughts of a teacher handling some problem with a student. Make up the circumstances.
c. Write of a quarrel you had with someone from the point of view of the other person.
d. Narrate an incident when one person or group of persons puts down someone else, trying to reveal the feelings of the person being put down.
e. Describe a class you've been in which led to uncomfortable feelings of some kind (other than boredom).
f. Put yourself in the place of an old person (someone who perhaps faces loss of good health, loneliness, or poverty) or someone whose life does not look secure for the future. What thoughts might go through the mind of this person?
g. Can you read a news item in the paper and put yourself in the shoes of the person about whom it is written and express your feelings and thoughts as that person? What is former President Nixon feeling and thinking just now? Or former Vice President Agnew? A couple whose child perished in a fire last night? A woman with five children evicted for nonpayment of rent? An old woman mugged near her home?

22. Present students with the following situations that represent moral dilemmas or value choices. Have them either discuss their answers with the class or write brief answers.
    a. You sell minibikes for a living. A number of children, over the space of a few years, have been in accidents or even killed riding bikes you have sold them. Your own seven-year-old is killed. Would you continue selling minibikes?
    b. You ride a motorcycle. A law is passed requiring riders to wear protective helmets. Do you think the government has a right to invade your privacy in this way? Or do you have a right to kill yourself on a motorcycle if you want?
    c. You know the identity of someone who is selling uppers and downers in school. You know that several students have overdosed on them. You know that the pusher is very active. What would you do?
    d. You see a man drop his wallet out of his pocket accidentally. He walks on, not seeing. No one else is about. What would you do?
    e. You find a wallet with $350 in it. There is an identification card in the wallet. What would you do? What if it had only $25 in it? $5.00?
    f. You find a wallet with $40 in it in front of a house in a residential neighborhood. What would you do? What if it is downtown, on the sidewalk?
    g. You are the richest person in your neighborhood. Other families are managing to get along but don't have much to spare. One family is almost starving to death. Other families all get together and ask you to help the starving family. But to do so would upset your entire investment program and cause you a considerable financial loss. What would you do?
    h. You are president of the world's wealthiest food-producing nation. People in a small country are starving to death. You are asked for one million bushels of grain as an emergency measure while other solutions are worked out. To give it would cause an increase in food prices in your own country. What would you do?

i. You are a student. You have a teacher who is consistently rude and thoughtless and inconsiderate of you. What would you do?
j. You are a teacher. You have a student who is rude and negative and makes it difficult for you to do a good job of structuring learning experiences for the class. What would you do? (Answer first as if you yourself are a rude, negative person. Then answer as if you are a person who tries consciously not to be rude and negative.)

SUGGESTED RESOURCES

Below is a selected list of resources useful for integrating composition instruction with human relations training. Addresses of publishers can be found in the alphabetical list on pages 111–113. Prices, where given, are only approximate, since changes occur frequently.

Composition for Personal Growth by Robert C. Hawley, Sidney B. Simon, and D. D. Britton. A very useful handbook for teachers. According to the authors, "Through guided activities and a wide range of written assignments, the approach attempts to promote the student's awareness of self, his ability to relate positively to others, and his ability to translate his values into meaningful actions." Includes many familiar values clarification strategies, along with ways to use them in conjunction with composition instruction. Contains little or no instruction on *how* to write, but provides countless stimuli for pre-writing activities. Paperbound. Hart Publishing Company.

Becoming: A Course in Human Relations by Chester Cromwell, William Ohs, Albert E. Roark, and Gene Stanford. A multimedia program that contains all materials needed for activity-oriented human relations training in the classroom. A leader's guide details instructions for structuring class activities that help students understand themselves and improve their relations with others. Topics include emotions, communication, values, masculinity, femininity, helping, stereotyping, making decisions in groups, perceptions, etc. A kit contains pre-recorded cassettes, photographs, puzzles, and other materials needed for the class activities. A Personal Log serves as a journal in which each student records his or her reactions to class activities and the changes taking place in him or her. The course is divided into three modules (*Relating, Interaction,* and *Individuality*) which can be used independently or in combination. Leader's Guide for *Relating*: $4.20; Personal Log for *Relating*: $1.50; Kit for *Relating*: $51.00; Leader's Guide for *Interaction*: $4.38; Personal Log for *Interaction*: $1.50; Kit for *Interaction*: $45.00; Leader's Guide for *Individuality*: $4.38; Personal Log for *Individuality*: $1.50; Kit for *Individuality*: $39.00. J. B. Lippincott Co.

3

Teaching Students to Create Images

Both in descriptive prose and in poetry the writer attempts, through words, to cause the reader to imagine what the writer is describing or creating. He or she attempts to build images by appealing to the mind's eye, to the mind's ear, and so on. If a writer uses words which cause the reader to imagine the sound of bells pealing triumphantly, then he or she has successfully created an image which involves the reader in his or her writing. If the words cause the reader to imagine the soft, furry feel of a little animal's fuzzy coat, then the writer has captured the reader's imagination with successful imagery that helps the reader have the experience the writer has prepared for him or her.

In order to create strong images, writers must learn to sharpen their own senses, their own imaginations, and their vocabularies. They must learn to go beyond merely labelling an object or experience with a word like "charming" and to provide, instead, specific details that give the reader a clear image. They must learn how to select those details to include in a description and those to omit because, even though they may be vivid and specific, they do not fit the central purpose of the description. They must be able to use words to create a mood in addition to an image, that is, to evoke feelings in the reader toward the object or experience being described. Finally, students need to consider the special role imagery plays in poetry and the importance of creating strong sensory images when writing poems.

OBJECTIVES

As a result of the learning experiences in this chapter, the student should be able to:

1. Explain what imagery is and why it is important in good writing.
2. Describe an object, person, or experience through words which create images rather than mere labels.

> 3. Choose details which fit the central purpose and eliminate those details which do not.
> 4. Create a mood with words.
> 5. Make use of the senses in writing.
> 6. Use clear imagery in writing poetry.

LEARNING EXPERIENCES

TOPIC I: DESCRIBE—DON'T LABEL

1. *Teacher Presentation.* Explain to students that often when a person intends to describe something, he or she puts labels on it instead. The person might say a book or a story is "interesting" or "boring"—a statement that says more about what the writer finds interesting or boring than it does about the book or story. Or, of a girl, one might write: "She is beautiful." Readers will then know that the girl has an appearance which favorably impresses the writer, but they will actually have little notion of what she looks like or whether they would find the girl attractive. A good writer avoids subjective words, such as "interesting" or "exciting" or "beautiful," words which reflect the writer rather than the image. Instead the good writer uses descriptive details, such as "high cheekbones," "skin smooth as porcelain," or "raven black hair" to create an image of the person or thing being described. Good descriptive details, then, refer to the actual observable characteristics of the thing being described rather than to the subjective reaction of the writer.

2. *Activity.* Using Reproduction Page 2, duplicate and distribute to students paragraph A below, or project it with an opaque or overhead projector. Have students circle all labelling (or subjective) words in the paragraph, that is, those that do not really describe. (Possible answers are indicated by underlining in paragraph A below.) Then give students paragraph B below (on Reproduction Page 3) by either duplicating it or projecting it for them to see. Have them compare paragraph B with paragraph A, noting the descriptive details that have replaced the subjective or labelling words.

    A. *Back-packing in the Colorado Rockies is a truly <u>great</u> experience. There's something really <u>wonderful</u> about hiking along Colorado's <u>beautiful</u> mountain trails with the <u>amazing</u> peaks towering overhead. There are literally countless different <u>species of life</u> on all sides, from majestic trees to colorful little wildflowers by the side of the <u>scenic</u> trails. Occasionally from a lookout point one can see across a <u>lovely</u>, peaceful valley where farms nestle in the serene countryside. And sometimes one follows for a while the <u>exciting</u> rush of an exhilarating mountain stream, fresh from the upper levels, soon to be a leisurely stream on the valley floor.*

    B. *Back-packing in the Colorado Rockies is an experience one will never forget and will long to repeat. Colorado's many miles of hiking trails are in rugged terrain unmatched for its natural, unspoiled beauty. Each trail has its own special character: one might wind through miles of shadowy white pine forests; another will lead through fields of granite boulders and over granite bluffs; and still another is bordered by small blue, yellow and pink star-shaped flowers. Over them all, in cold and silent majesty, tower the snow-covered peaks of America's highest mountains. Occasionally, from a barren, rocky promontory, one can look across a small valley enclosed in the green lower slopes of the mountains. From a great height the farm buildings look like toys, and the fields make miniature patchwork patterns, with here a curving row of tiny trees and there a winding gleam of silver that marks a stream. The flood of water that swept down from the peaks, cutting a channel through granite with its force, flows quietly on the valley floor.*

3. *Activity.* Write the paragraph below on the board or dictate it to the class to write in their notebooks:

   Bob's new car is really terrific. It has these really great wheel covers and a finish that you just wouldn't believe. The interior is fabulous with this amazing upholstery and the most beautiful bucket seats you've ever seen.

   Have students read the paragraph and circle all the labelling (or subjective) words, that is, those that do not really describe. Then have them rewrite the paragraph, using specific descriptive details to replace all the labels. In order to do this, of course, they will have to interpret the labels in terms of their own values, opinions, and experiences. Remind students to be as complete as possible and as descriptive as they can be, even though the new paragraph turns out to be much longer than the one above. You can have students work individually on revising the paragraph, or the entire class can work together, with various students suggesting details to replace the labels.

4. *Activity.* Using Reproduction Page 4, duplicate and distribute to students the list of words below, some of which are subjective words or "labels" while others are descriptive details. Have students identify label words by circling them or printing an "L" beside them. (Answers are indicated on the list below, but not, of course, on the Reproduction Page.) After students have marked their answers, go over the list to see if the class agrees on their answers. Point out that these words that they have identified as labels differ from all the descriptive words in one important regard: they are statements of opinion rather than of observation or fact. The descriptive words, on the contrary, relate to an actuality observable through one's senses.

deafening	*green*	*sexy*
threadbare	*fantastic (L)*	*hateful (L)*
ugly (L)	*malodorous*	*fabulous (L)*
moss-covered	*frayed*	*sturdy*
close-cropped	*bumpy*	*great (L)*
boring (L)	*unlikable (L)*	*wonderful (L)*
awful (L)	*immoral (L)*	*upturned*
slow-moving	*sharp-featured*	*awesome*
curly	*sweaty*	*bug-eyed*
lovely (L)	*foul-mouthed*	*horrible (L)*
splotchy	*adorable (L)*	*ragged*
capable	*timid*	*pugnosed*
blue and white checked	*fetid*	*purple*
	amazing (L)	*right (L)*
cautious	*looming*	*exciting (L)*
respectable (L)	*wild-eyed*	*appealing (L)*

reliable	interesting (L)	obese
pink-eyed	bald	leathery
rascal	swarthy	wrong (L)
ideal (L)	itchy	rancid
fuzzy	dumb	inadequate
oval	decent (L)	prudent
growling	admirable (L)	law-abiding
blinding	sickening	attractive (L)
disgusting (L)	square-jawed	active
memorable (L)	popular	inert
crooked	irregular	gleaming
fitful	gorgeous (L)	graceful
impressive (L)	noteworthy (L)	alarming (L)
heroic	unacceptable (L)	straight
winding	remarkable (L)	

5. *Activity.* Have each student choose three *label* words from the list above (Reproduction Page 4) and apply each one to some object or person. Then ask them to see how many descriptive words they can list under each label as specification of it. Suggest they use the label word in a sentence to provide a context.

   EXAMPLE: He is an <u>ugly</u> person.
   LIST: sharp-featured, sweaty, obese, malodorous.
   OR: It is an <u>interesting</u> book.
   LIST: lots of action, suspenseful, sexy hero, intelligent heroine.

   Then have several students who chose the same label word read their lists so that the class can see how similar or different their definitions of these labels are.

6. *Activity.* Have students choose one of the labels and lists of descriptive details they prepared for Activity #5 above. Ask them to make each into a complete, unified, coherent, orderly paragraph by using the label word in the topic sentence and the descriptive details in the sentences that develop the body of the paragraph. Students should feel free to add any other descriptive words or statements they can think of to "flesh out" their paragraph and make it more effective. The best of these paragraphs could be duplicated and distributed to the class, or projected on a screen with the opaque projector.

TOPIC II: SELECT DETAILS WITH A CENTRAL PURPOSE IN MIND

1. *Teacher Presentation.* Point out to students that it is impossible ever to say all there is to be said about anything, as the list of specific details to describe a person or object is virtually limitless. Therefore, a writer must learn to say what *needs* to be said to create an image in the mind's eye (or ear or whatever) of the reader, and to leave out those details which do not contribute to the image the writer is creating. A list of unrelated details chosen at random will convey no particular impression. It will simply confuse the reader, who will likely find it difficult to remember the unrelated details and who will be unable to "see" what the facts add

up to. What is needed is a series of details selected precisely because they *do* add up to a certain impression. The writer must examine carefully the object or scene he or she wishes to recreate in words, and must decide on the impression that is to be conveyed. Then and only then is the writer ready to select the details that will go into the description. The writer will select those details which contribute to the impression *he or she* receives from the object or scene being described, and will simply leave out those details which do not relate to the impression to be conveyed.

2. *Activity.* Pass out to each student the lists of details below or project the lists one at a time with the opaque or overhead projector. (Reproduce the lists, using Reproduction Page 5.) Ask students to summarize each group of details in one sentence which states the impression they receive from the details. Encourage students to be as imaginative as possible in their summary sentences, helping them to see that their statements can take many forms, depending on the imaginary context into which they place the situation suggested by the given details. Sample summary sentences appear in parentheses below, but do not, of course, appear on Reproduction Page 5.

   A. -crickets rasping
      -bass voice of a bull frog
      -jar flies in trees
      -leaves rustling
      -screech owl in distance
      (The night was filled with sounds. Or: Sounds so quiet and customary I almost didn't hear them lulled me to sleep.)

   B. -a huge, golden turkey
      -a bowl of steaming mashed potatoes
      -sweet potatoes swimming in golden syrup
      -home made noodles
      -stuffing in a bowl
      -a platter of fruit
      -a wooden bowl heaped high with greens
      (Dinner was ready to be eaten. Or: The table showed clearly how much we had to be thankful for.)

   C. -one shoelace dangling
      -skirt hem hanging on one side
      -blouse tail half in, half out
      -wisps of hair escaping the knot on top of her head
      -lipstick smeared on chin
      -one earring missing
      (One got the impression that either she had never really gotten herself together or she was rapidly coming apart.)

   D. -a leaning tower of records on the desk
      -a wastebasket full of books
      -one blue sock draped over the lampshade
      -guitar case sticking out from under the bed
      -bath towel slung over open closet door
      -a hockey stick leaning against the bureau
      (George's room demonstrated a reverse axiom, a place for nothing, and nothing in its place.)

   E. -cold gray eyes
      -a frown-wrinkle between his brows
      -a thin, straight mouth

-sharp, beak-like nose
-iron gray hair cut like a Prussian army officer's
(He was a stern, forbidding man whose very appearance cast fear into the hearts of lazy students.)

F. -shrill high notes
-blatant, unmodulated tone
-a vibrato quite out of control
-uncertain pitch tending to chronic flatness
-limited range
-a tendency to nasality in the middle range
(Her singing voice, to put it mildly, left a great deal to be desired. Or: Few who heard her sing shared her illusion that she could find fame as a singer.)

G. -the Three Stooges committing their usual hijinx
-the "Roadrunner" comically surviving a dozen gruesome fates
-a movie made in 1934
-an early "Lucy" episode
-an early "Flintstone" episode
-the Lone Ranger urging Silver "awa-a-a-ay!"
(Saturday morning TV sounds like a series of echoes from TV's less than glorious past.)

3. *Activity.* Have students take each summary sentence they composed for Activity #2 above and add at least three more details that would further support and specify it. You might lead this as a group activity, writing suggested details on the board. Or have students work individually and share their results with the class.

4. *Activity.* Have students, working individually, write complete, orderly, coherent paragraphs using the summary sentences and lists of relevant details from Activity #3. Tell them they may add as many other details as they wish, as long as these all relate to the summary sentence (which will appear, of course, as the topic sentence of the paragraph).

5. *Activity.* Using Reproduction Page 6, provide students with the list of summary sentences below. Have them list under each as many pertinent details as they can think of, making sure, of course, that all the descriptive details contribute to the overall impression summarized in the summary sentence. When they have finished, let students compare their lists with those of other students. Finally, have them choose one summary sentence and list of details to turn into a paragraph.

   1. Walking through the deserted neighborhood, I felt as though I was the only person alive.
   2. The fertile valley seemed to have been cut off from the passage of time.
   3. The street began to fill with activity, as the city roused itself from sleep.
   4. Their garden was still producing a variety of vegetables well into November.
   5. Angry students crowded the student union to take part in a protest meeting.
   6. The front hall of the high school was as crowded and busy as Grand Central Station.
   7. The woods behind the old house provided a magic place for the children to spend their Saturday afternoons.
   8. The market's produce department looked like a brilliant illustration of October for a calendar.
   9. His bachelor apartment revealed his artistic interests and his tendency toward a monkish life.

10. *The living room was tastefully elegant.*
11. *The long table groaned under enough food to feed a regiment.*
12. *Houseplants of every conceivable nature crowded the porch.*
13. *Gino's Pizzeria offered every conceivable kind of pizza in any combination desired.*

6. *Activity.* Seat the class in a circle or double horseshoe and place in the center, so all students can see it, a distinctive object such as one of the following:

    a frilly, graceful fern in a delicate pot
    a primitive African mask or statuette
    a plump, happy looking Buddha
    an unattractive, poorly made garment or piece of handicraft
    a beat-up cooking utensil
    a picture of some distinctive scene.

    Ask students, working individually, to write their overall impressions of the object in one sentence. Let them share these orally, discussing how similar or dissimilar their impressions are. Next, ask each student to support his or her impression with the details about the object that led to it. If the student cannot provide supportive details, encourage him or her to abandon the statement and come up with a new one which *can* be supported. Finally, have each student write a one-paragraph description of the object, using the summary statement as a topic sentence which determines the details to be included, and supporting this statement with descriptive details which are listed in the previous step. Be sure students understand that they are to include no details except those which support their topic sentences.

7. *Activity.* Have students examine carefully the room in which they sit. Ask them, working individually, to identify the five or six elements of the room and its furnishings which most conspicuously contribute to the overall impression the room conveys to them. Then have them, one by one, share their lists with the class to see if other students can compose a statement of the overall impression which summarizes the list. For example, one student might list the following elements:

    spotless floor
    gleaming desk tops
    unmarked blackboard
    neat stacks of papers
    straight rows of books

    Other students might summarize those details with the following statement of central impression: "The classroom looks as if no student has ever entered it." Or another student might list the following elements:

    colorful painting on one wall
    potted plants along the window sill
    a red and orange felt wall-hanging with the words, "If You Love Somebody, Say So"
    a blue poster with a white bird and the word "Peace"
    a stereo with a stack of records

    The other students might summarize those details with the following statement of central impression: "The room was bright and friendly, looking as if students would enjoy being there."

8. *Activity.* As a variation on Activity #7 above, have students compose their own summarizing sentences and see if their classmates can supply a list of specific elements in the room that contribute to that impression.

9. *Activity.* Using the list of summarizing sentences below, ask students to list details which might provide suitable specification. You might wish to do this exercise orally with the entire group, following it with an assignment to write one or more descriptive paragraphs using these topic sentences and the ideas for supportive details they and their classmates have generated.

> *His clothes looked as if they had been thrown on him in the dark.*
> *Her flower garden revealed the hours of loving care she spent on it daily.*
> *His room was a mother's nightmare.*
> *Her house was so perfectly arranged that one felt ill at ease in it.*
> *His lawn was his pride and joy.*
> *There was no extra that he didn't have on his car.*
> *By prom time the gym had been turned into a beautiful ballroom.*
> *His room was his peaceful sanctuary.*
> *The dinner was superb.*
> *On either side of the road the woods stretched, dark and mysterious.*

TOPIC III: SELECT DETAILS TO CREATE A MOOD

1. *Teacher Presentation.* Explain to students that sometimes a writer wants to achieve two things with a description: create an image in the mind of the reader and also create a certain mood or feeling in the reader. For instance, the writer might describe a house as spotlessly clean. At the same time, it is entirely possible to give an impression either of bright, shiny cheerfulness or of cold, sterile drabness. The secret lies in the details the writer chooses to put in and the words used to express them. A writer can describe a deep wood so that it sounds like a peaceful, shady sanctuary, or if he or she prefers, like a gloomy, fearful thicket where one would dislike to linger. After all, the writer *chooses* what details to put in. And as for words, we all know that some words have a "good" feel—cheerful, affirmative, comfortable—and some are "bad" or negative in connotation—gloomy, fearful, or uncomfortable. The writer can choose whatever kinds of words he or she wants, and thus can determine the mood to be created. The two examples of student writing below illustrate how descriptive details can be carefully chosen to fulfill a purpose in addition to merely recreating a scene. In "Plastic Lunch," the student has used details that not only vividly describe the scene in the cafeteria but also convey the writer's point of view toward what he sees. In "Release," the writer uses details that both create feelings in the reader and create an image.

Release
Jane Clayton
(11th grade student)

fasterfasterfasterfasterfaster
honkwhooshpurrrzooooomrumblescreeeech HONK

"Sure. You can't miss it. Just take the Ventura Freeway for another mile and then get on the San Bernardino Freeway which will take you right to the Golden State Freeway. When that forks take the Bakersfield fork for about a half mile to the San Diego Freeway. Go another 5 miles to the 105th St. exit. Turn right at 105th, turn left at the seventh light, and you're there!"

65 m.p.h. = 1000 words per minute at 100% comprehension = 15 miles to a gallon = 5 columns of metal Driver Ants marching to 9 to 5 at $2.75 an hour + $5.50 for over-time-lunch-coffee break = splitsecond tension + a helluva lotta smog.

fasterfasterfasterfasterfaster

"Change lanes, idiot!"

Like a precious blend of sorcerers' panaceas,
the cool ocean rinses away my fretfulness.
A lone gull
cries out
and I follow his liquid flight over the sea.
The quiet swish of the surf caresses my senses
as I, like an idle marionette, collapse on the warm sand.
Pacific. Pacem. Peace.

Plastic Lunch
Ron Fredman
(11th grade student)

I scan the cafeteria:
fifty tables
six chairs each
three hundred chairs
three hundred people
flesh, blood, hunger.

I pick out sounds:
   "what do you think of . . . "
   ". . . a bitch"
   ". . . ever scare the . . . "
I crack a joke,
my noise scares me silent.
People stare.

Plastic spoons, knives, forks
stuff the plastic garbage bags.
Milk, meat and vegetables
leave me hungry.
Everyone leaves,
unsatisfied.

2. *Activity.* The following pairs of words have pretty much the same meaning (denotation) but have very different "feelings" (connotations) to them:

    damp - dank   curious - nosy
    slick - slimy   freckled - splotched
    speechless - tongue-tied   mixed breed - mongrel
    misty - foggy   dog - cur

marsh - swamp
talkative - garrulous
precocious - smart-alecky
polite - obsequious
proud - arrogant
slender - skinny
pudgy - fat
plain - homely
elaborate - ostentatious
delicate - weak
firm - harsh
determined - stubborn
quick - hasty
stately - haughty
simple - stupid

horse - nag
remind - nag
instruct - dictate
reluctant - begrudging
bachelor girl - old maid
hard worker - drudge
good student - greasy grind
reveal - give away
covert - sneaky
unafraid - rash
cautious - fearful
unknowing - ignorant
small - meager
frugal - miserly

There are a number of ways you might make use of this list. Students might work orally as a class, or individually, or in small groups. Give students either the list of "positive" words or the list of "negative" words, and ask them to supply for each word another one that has the same meaning but an opposite connotation. (The word need not be the same one shown here, of course.) Or give them a list in which the positive and negative words have been mixed and ask them to identify which is which.

3. *Activity.* Read students several statements such as the following, in which the connotation of the word referring to oneself is positive, of the word referring to the person spoken to is slightly negative, and of the word referring to a third person is very negative:

I am pleasantly plump; you are putting on weight; he is obese.

I am righteously indignant; you are angry; he is furious.

I am determined; you are unwilling to reexamine your position; she is stubborn.

I winced; you grimaced; he made a face.

I have self-respect; you are proud; she is arrogant.

I make an effort to be well informed; you like to know what is going on; she isn't happy unless she knows it all.

I am very trusting; you are easily taken in; he is a born sucker.

I am highly verbal; you talk a lot; he's a garrulous bore.

I get around; you're into everything; she's a busybody.

I am self-confident; you're very sure of yourself; he's conceited.

I'm decorous; you're prim; she's prudish.

I'm a feeling person; you're sentimental; he's maudlin.

I'm forgetful; you're confused; he's empty-headed.

I eat well; you eat a lot; he's a glutton.

I'm sensitive; you're easily hurt; he's thin-skinned.

I'm slender; you're thin; she's skinny.

I'm thrifty; you're frugal; she's stingy.

I tell tall tales; you stretch the truth; she tells lies.

Then have students choose several words which might describe a person and write a series of comparisons of this type. Or, instead of reading the list of comparisons to the class, type the list on a spirit master, leaving one or two blanks in each comparison empty, and have students supply the word that they think fits each blank.

4. *Activity.* Have students, working in small groups or individually, describe the classroom (or the entire school) as it might be seen by three different people: a teacher, a happy, successful student, and a student who dislikes school intensely. Instruct each group to come up with the list of details they consider suitable to each way of viewing the room. When students have shared and compared their lists, assign each student the task of writing three different one-paragraph descriptions representing the three viewpoints. Remind students that their choice of words will be an important part of conveying different views. The best paragraphs could be duplicated and shared, or shown to the class using the opaque projector.

5. *Activity.* Bring to class a picture of a cat, preferably a regal, dignified adult cat. Divide the class into those who like cats and those who don't. Have students work individually, describing the cat in the language natural to a cat lover or one who doesn't like cats (depending on which group they classified themselves in). Encourage them to include at least four descriptive details based on their observation of the picture. Read some of the descriptions aloud, allowing the class to guess which group the description came from.

6. *Activity.* On a rainy day, ask students to describe the day, using details and words which will set a mood of gloominess or of refreshing cleanliness or whatever mood a rainy day produces in them. Remind students to use as many detailed statements as possible, all carefully chosen and stated to enhance the mood they are trying to convey. Let students exchange papers or pass them in for you to read or project on the screen, and then try to determine the moods portrayed. Students should be reminded that they are not to write about the mood rain causes in them, but to describe the day itself in words that reveal their mood.

7. *Activity.* During the football season (or basketball, or whatever) ask students to describe a game in two ways—first, as a fan of the winning team, and then as a fan of the losing team. Remind the students to be very conscious of the connotations of the language they use in creating moods of joy and gloom. They should be encouraged to avoid direct statement of such emotions, but to create these moods by means of the details they include and the words they use to express them.

8. *Activity.* Put the following list of details about a big house on the board (all details are phrased in carefully neutral words):

> *two stories*
> *white frame construction*
> *20 rooms*
> *big rooms*
> *large lawn, with trees and shrubs*
> *a small barn behind*
> *a porch around the front*
> *a circular driveway*

Instruct students to describe the house in such a way as to create a certain mood in connection with it—spooky, cheerful, full of memories, rich and elegant, shabby and forlorn, etc. Require students to utilize the details that you supply (that is, they cannot describe a house that does not have these characteristics), but to add whatever other details are needed to create the mood they have chosen. When they have finished, have them read their descriptions aloud or exchange them and identify the mood that other students have created. Here is a sample paragraph:

The brooding gloom of Morley's Manor cast a spell over the visitor even as he entered the great iron gates which opened on the circular drive. Huge oak trees towered on either side of the narrow winding track, and dark, misshapen bushes huddled in random groups among the trees. About a quarter of a mile from the gate, through a break in the line of trees, the visitor caught a glimpse of the mansion's upper story gleaming white against the twilight sky, with windows gaping black and empty. Another hundred feet farther on, the drive looped around a small barn, closed and mysterious, walls covered with vines and doors sagging and shrouded with cobwebs. This road led to the back of the sprawling frame house, where a long veranda opened to a back door and circled around the sides of the house to the front. At the front entrance, the wooden steps and porch floor gave back hollow echoes as the visitor approached the half open front door and peered into the darkness. Neither light nor motion broke the gloom; only a dank and musty vapor hovered in the stagnant air.

TOPIC IV: USING SENSORY EXPERIENCES IN WRITING

1. *Teacher Presentation.* Explain to students that the activities that follow are designed to raise their consciousness of their senses. Perhaps they have not realized that they might "listen" to an entire record and not really *hear* more than a few bars of it. Perhaps they have not been silent long enough to notice how noisy their school is. And perhaps they would be surprised to have called to their attention the number of objects around them that they have never consciously observed. It is said that the literary artist "sees" more keenly than others do, and "feels" more deeply and thus is able to convey these feelings poignantly, in words. It is not enough, then, for the student writer to feel. He or she must also be able to identify feeling in words, a process which requires thought, and he or she must be able to write about a sensory experience in such a way as to evoke a given feeling in the reader. The process goes from feeling to thinking to writing—and, one hopes, will result in feeling in the reader.

2. *Activity.* Arrange the class in a large circle, or divide it into small groups seated in small circles. Give the directions for each part of the activity one at a time, stopping after each part to let the students share and compare what they have written.

    a. Have students name five things in this room they have never consciously observed before.
    b. Have students name three things (or five or ten) they have never noticed about the person sitting opposite them.
    c. Have students sit silently for five minutes and list all the sounds they hear.
    d. Have students go around the circle, speaking in certain ways (gruffly, softly, sharply, breathlessly, haughtily, boldly, uncertainly, nasally, etc.) and have the other students write down a word identifying the way each student spoke.
    e. Go around the circle with each person making some kind of abstract sound. Have students identify each sound by naming it or reproducing it on paper.

3. *Activity.* Play a piece of recorded music for the class. Ask them, as they listen, to write down what they think the music is "saying." For this exercise, be sure to use

music that does definitely portray something or create a definite mood, such as "The Moldau" by Bedrich Smetana, "Death and Transfiguration" by Richard Strauss, "The Afternoon of a Faun" by Claude Debussy, "Finlandia" by Jean Sibelius, or "Pictures at an Exhibition" by Modest Moussorgsky. After the music is over, let them share their impressions. Discuss the ways composers use certain kinds of musical effects to convey certain activities or visual images. See if students can come up with examples. Here are a few to prime the pump:

3/4 time for the waltz, for romance

broad and flowing for a river (like "The Moldau")

clash of cymbals and drums for storm or war ("1812 Overture")

ethereal, high violin for heaven, angels

broad oom-pah-pah for clowns or humor or parade

slow, low tones for gloom, sorrow ("Pathétique" Symphony)

brass, brisk and full, for martial effects

4. *Activity.* Play Dukas's original music (not the dramatized version with Mickey Mouse) of "The Sorcerer's Apprentice" and have students write down the story they think they hear. After sharing their stories, they might like to hear the dramatized version, or you could at least tell them the entire story.

5. *Activity.* Bring to class a statue or figure of an animal of some kind—the more unusual the better. Put it in a bag or under a cloth where it cannot be seen and have each student feel it carefully. Ask students to draw the animal they have felt and, then, describe it in words. After these descriptions have been shared and compared, you might ask the student with the most accurate drawing to put it on the board. Only then, show the class the animal figure. (Other students might wish to show their drawings and chuckle over how much they do not resemble the animal figure.)

6. *Activity.* Bring a jar of dill pickles and some chocolate milk (one of the all-time great taste combinations!). Give each student a piece of pickle and a little chocolate milk. On signal have everyone eat the piece of pickle and follow it with the chocolate milk. Then ask the students to write a paragraph describing the taste experience. When all have finished their paragraphs, collect them and read them aloud anonymously. If the writing is praised, encourage the writers to reveal themselves.

7. *Activity.* Place one large barbecue potato chip before each student. On signal, have everyone crunch his or her chip. Then have them describe the taste experience in words. Share and compare the writings. With these last two exercises, it might be useful to discuss the difficulty of describing taste, the limited number of words available, ways to compare taste to other things, and words that the group can think of.

TOPIC V: CREATING IMAGES IN POETRY

1. *Teacher Presentation.* Explain to students that to create strong images in poetry, they must try to be visual rather than auditory in their writing. Too many students

begin writing a poem by searching through their vocabularies for poetic (musical) sounding words. The skill actually is to enter visually into the thing being described, not into one's own vocabulary. Surprisingly often, if one can identify the concrete visual characteristics of the thing being viewed, the words will take care of themselves. If this is not quite the case, the writer can always consider during revision of the poem such other matters as compression (using as few words as possible), redundancy (a trait to be avoided at all costs), and the aural effect of the language. If you or your students want to deal with aspects of poetry other than imagery (the focus of this Topic), consider the material on poetry that appears in Chapter 5.

2. *Activity.* Have students read the snow imagery from the early part of "Snowbound" by John Greenleaf Whittier, by using Reproduction Page 7 to make a master for the spirit duplicator or a transparency for the overhead projector. (This is an ideal activity to use on the occasion of winter's first real snow!) Discuss with students the differences between Whittier's images and the ones that might occur to them. (His are rural and 19th century, for example.) Then ask your students to write down all the images connected with snow that occur to them. Here are some starters:

the scrape of a snow shovel
everything is rounded and smooth; no angles
a car spinning its wheels
bright colors of caps, jackets, scarves on hills
droning sound of school closings on radio

clouds of steam and smoke over cars
a path of tiny paw prints across the back yard
the car is buried at the curb by the snow plow
the barbecue grill, left out, is a fat snow man

3. *Activity.* Have the class visualize snow doing things (in actuality, if it is in fact snowing outside, or in their mind's eye, if not); and make a list on the board. Begin with single words describing what snow does, such as: falls, drifts, piles, blows, covers, blankets, floats, sticks, melts, hardens, etc. Then have students list phrases or sentences about what snow does. Examples: Snow fills the air—blows into my face—makes familiar things mysterious—deadens sounds—covers ugly things—drifts against the door—piles up at windows—falls silently all night long, etc. Follow the listing with an assignment for students to write a brief poem using the images they have generated. Here is the way two students responded to this assignment:

Snowflake
Merilynn Wenzlaff
(12th grade student)

Winter through a snowflake
is a crystal world
of crackling colors
transparent surfaces
and depthless centers
of pine and sky and snow and sun

frozen for a moment—
until the snowflake's white
branches burst
shattering the crystal colors
into moist spring flowers.

Scrim
Rochelle Grober
(11th grade student)

Enfolding earth and trees in white,
snow draws a scrim across our world,
reveals a private view of life;
the sunlight fades to silver glow,
forerunner to the white and black
of silent snow and quiet night.
The truth unfolds before our eyes:
the universe revealed is cold;
life flickers like a spark
within the heart of time.

If you have examined "Snowbound" with the class as part of this activity, some students may wish to write their poems in the same rhyme and rhythm pattern as "Snowbound," as did this student:

"Snowbound" Revisited
Susan Meyer
(12th grade student)

Tonight I draw my loved ones close
about and thank my God
for hours like this. Before the
hearth the sleepy children nod.

The wordless interchange of smiles
the laughter quick and warm
the sound of old familiar songs
that lift above the storm
bring a sweet and joyous flood
of peace and gratitude
that fills my soul with happiness
and gives my spirit food.

The drift of snow, the lash of wind
on casements weather-tried
beat savagely on winter's drum
but we are safe inside.

The cherished cloak of family ties
enfolds us, sure and tight,
as love pulls up an extra chair
and sits with us tonight.

4. *Activity.* All the seasons of the year are good subjects for creating poetic images. Show students, for instance, "Autumn" by John Keats, and discuss the wealth of imagery he uses to depict the fall of the year. See which images *they* can recognize and relate to and which are unfamiliar to them. Then ask them, working individually, to list the images that *they* visualize as having to do with autumn. They

will undoubtedly be quite different from Keats's images, and rightly so, since students' lives are so different from the English poet's. Their images might have to do with football games, winter clothes coming out of closets, smell of moth balls, pumpkins, trick-or-treat, etc. Perhaps you would prefer to lead the entire class in this exercise, writing their images on the board as they suggest them. Stretch the class's imagination to come up with as long a list as possible, in order to push them beyond the obvious, trite ideas that come first to mind. Then have them take their lists of images and use them in writing a brief poem. Here is how some students responded to this assignment:

October Air
Karl Kim
(12th grade student)

*I step from inside
and deeply inhale
the inflaming air.
The sun in the east,
a glowing ember
momentarily
appears to brighten
as green starts to burn.
The flaming leaves drop.
Perceive the beauty!
My spirits rejoice
until finally
they have all come down.
October essence
departs with the burnt leaves.*

Autumn Dusk
Marian Green
(12th grade student)

*Day closes early:
pungent violet smoke creeps through paling light;
thin wind whistles through naked joints of trees;
the garden yields late bounty;
through the rose haze of sunset
crickets cry their last October chorus.*

Indian Summer
Susan Meyer
(12th grade student)

*Not green and not yellow,
dim haze over all;
the day after summer,
the day before fall.*

5. *Activity.* Again as to one of the four seasons: Have students bring pictures from magazines or calendars showing scenes of a particular season of the year, perhaps one you have not yet worked with. Display the pictures where all can see them, and ask the class, as a group, to describe in words the images the eye identifies. After the group has discussed possible images, have students write a description of the scene—in poetry form, if possible, or in sentences or paragraphs, if they prefer. When all are finished, collect and read them aloud, or perhaps project the best ones for all to read.

6. *Activity.* Collect a large number of pictures of vivid scenes. (*National Geographic* is a good source.) Make these available to all students by spreading them out on a large table. Encourage each student to choose one or more picutres to write about. Ask students to write a three line "poem" in which they try to encompass the overall effect or meaning of the scene, much as in a haiku. They may or may not keep to the haiku pattern of a five syllable line followed by a seven syllable line and ending with another five syllable line. If they wish to impose this discipline on themselves, well and good, but it is not necessary, even in haiku writing. The main effort should be to recreate the scene or capture its essence in three short lines. The images should be as sharp, as brief, and as all-inclusive as possible. (Note that several of the materials in the Additional Resources section deal with haiku.) Here

is how several students responded to this assignment, some with haiku, some with other forms:

*Trees flow down the slopes
like streams, like pinion rivers
in a wash of green.*

*Mullein, unpeeling
to the sun its woolly leaves,
shivers in the breeze.*

*The waning moon dusts
its ashen gleam on mushrooms
rising from the earth.*

*In August dry as
night is dark, asters twinkle
among dun grasses.*

Lynn Levin
(11th grade student)

*Jewels of light
spilled in infinite splendor
dim the crescent moon.*

Sally Deitchman
(12th grade student)

Treasure
Ginger Oppenheimer
(11th grade student)

*At the top of the pass
a lone cabin stands against
unceasing winds and driven snow.
The open door leans, clinging to
its rotted frame by a single hinge.
Within, a cast iron stove
rusts from melted snows,
and a shattered crock remains
from long-forgotten lives.
The mountain keeps vigil behind,
guarding its miniature jewel from the past.*

*Under the rising moon
shells glisten on the beach;
the night breeze is cool.*

G. P. Georges III
(12th grade student)

7. *Activity.* Have students choose some activity that is familiar to them and, as a group, list all the images they visualize as being part of that activity. This can be done as a group or individually, with each student writing the images as vividly as possible, spending ample time actually trying to see in his or her mind's eye the event being described. Some suggestions for activities:

football game	*quarrel*	*automobile accident*
rock concert	*picnic in the park*	*visit to a relative*
church service	*float trip*	*going to the supermarket*
school assembly	*going to a movie*	*auto rally*

Allow students to share their images with the class, perhaps in pairs or small groups. Then they might wish to do some revising, selecting more vivid, stronger words. Some students might wish to turn their descriptions into poems.

ASSESSING ACHIEVEMENT OF OBJECTIVES

On-Going Evaluation

The extent to which students have mastered the skills taught in this unit can be measured by having them submit for grading the final products of almost any of the activities suggested earlier.

Final Evaluation

For an overall evaluation of students' achievements, assign an in-class descriptive paragraph. On the previous day, encourage students to be alert for a scene, a

> person, an object, or an experience that they encounter before coming to class for the evaluation. Suggest they choose something that they can describe in detail. On the day of evaluation, give the following instructions:
>
>> Choose a person, object, scene, or experience and describe it in one complete, unified, coherent, orderly paragraph. Make sure your description is as vivid as possible, and that it conveys a central impression or mood.
>
> Some students will not have brought to class an idea to develop. Suggest that they choose one of the following to describe: the waiting room at their dentist's office, the appearance of their locker at school, their English teacher, their most prized possession. Allow students the entire period to compose and revise their paragraphs. Grade the final drafts according to these criteria:
>
> 1. Has the writer used words that describe rather than label?
> 2. Does the paragraph create a single overall impression or has the writer included details that detract from the central purpose?
> 3. Has the writer conveyed a mood through the words used?
> 4. Does the writer use words that appeal to the reader's senses?

RESOURCES FOR TEACHING CREATING IMAGES

Below is a selected list of resources useful for teaching the skills of description and creating images. The list is divided into audio-visual materials (films, filmstrips, slide-tape programs, cassettes, etc.), books for students, and books for the teacher. Addresses of publishers can be found in the alphabetical list on pages 111–113. Prices, where given, are only approximate, since changes occur frequently.

Audio-Visual Materials

Composition Starters: Description by Bruce Reeves. A collection of four silent film loops from the Walt Disney Nature Series. Students view each loop and then respond to their choice of key questions or statements on assignment cards. Effective for independent study or individualization at all grade and ability levels. Doubleday Multimedia.

Eye Openers by David A. Sohn and Don Blegen. Ninety-seven slides in a carousel tray, a 40-page teacher's guide, and a photo package of 48 award-winning black and white prints. Contains 21 lessons that help students develop their writing and observation skills. Lessons begin with simple exercises and continue through increasingly complex descriptive and narrative assignments. Can be adapted to various grade and ability levels. $74.50. Scholastic Book Services.

Come to Your Senses by David A. Sohn. A smaller program similar to *Eye Openers* (above). Contains four filmstrips, a set of supplementary photographs printed on cardboard, seven classroom posters, and a teacher's guide. Very flexible. $49.50. Scholastic Book Services.

The Do-It-Yourself Poetry Kit. Designed to stimulate student interest in writing poetry. Four sound filmstrips: one concerns haiku, another teaches rhythms and limericks, a third explains "Who Am I" poems, and a fourth introduces cinquains. Each concludes with a series of pictures to provide visual inspiration for classroom writing. Twenty extra slides can be used in a variety of ways. Sound on cassettes. Particularly useful for younger or less capable students. Complete kit: $72.00; each filmstrip: $20.00; slides alone: $19.00. Greystone Films, Inc.

Creative Writing by Morris Schreiber. One LP record presenting a general introduction to various forms of creative writing, including description. Most useful as an enrichment experience, since it doesn't provide much in the way of specific instructions on how to write. Advanced students only. $6.95. Scholastic Book Services.

How to Write an Effective Composition: Narrative and Descriptive Writing by Morris Schreiber. One side of an LP record. Presents a cursory introduction to the topic through examination of a brief literary work. Useful as an enrichment experience for better students only. Folkways Records.

Describing What We See. 12 min. color film. Engages viewers in the process of learning how to observe the scenes and events around them. Includes a baseball player in action as the poem, "The Base Stealer" by Robert Francis, is read describing the same scene. The second half is devoted to two scenes for students to describe after the film is over. Excellent for students of all ages and ability levels. Rental: $12.50. S-L Film Productions.

Books for Students

Writing Incredibly Short Plays, Poems, Stories by Francis Gretton and James Norton. Contains a section on imagery and other aspects of poetry. Good explanations and learning activities. Teacher's guide available. Paperbound. $2.85. Harcourt Brace Jovanovich.

Writer's Journal: Experiments by Dalton H. McBee. Contains a section that encourages students to improve their writing of description and poetry by imitating literary models. Teacher's manual available. Paperbound. $3.00. Harcourt Brace Jovanovich.

How I Write/1 by Judson Phillips, Lawson Carter, and Robert Hayden. Contains a substantial section on writing poetry, including an interview with poet Robert Hayden in which he discusses how and why he writes poetry. Most suitable for advanced students. Teacher's guide available. Paperbound. $2.55. Harcourt Brace Jovanovich.

How I Write/2 by MacKinlay Kantor, Lawrence Osgood, and James Emanuel. Contains a section on writing poetry by James Emanuel, who describes how he goes about creating. Likely to be of interest only to more advanced students. Teacher's guide available. $2.55. Harcourt Brace Jovanovich.

Now Poetry by Charles L. Cutler, Edwin A. Hoey, Sarah L. Holden, and Nancy Malone. A splendid way to get reluctant students writing poetry! Suggests "recipes" for writing simple forms of poetry: grooks, haiku, terse verse, etc. For each form, a number of examples written by students are included, along with attractive illustrations. Considering the low price and potential effect on students, this is a best buy. Paperbound. $.50. Xerox Education Publications.

Writing Creatively by J. N. Hook. A comprehensive text which includes chapters on "Observation and Sensory Words," "Description and Imagery," "How Poetry Expresses You" and "How to Express Poetry," as well as other topics. Hardbound. D.C. Heath.

An Eye for Writing by Susan Thesenga and Mary Bell. One of six books on composition in the "Contemporary English Modules" series. A short, appealing paperback—visually attractive—that contains many interesting activities to help students improve their powers of observation and description. An excellent choice for almost all students at almost any grade level. Teacher's guide available. Paperbound. Silver Burdett Company.

Write Now by Anne Wescott Dodd. A series of interesting exercises, activities, and assignments that will appeal to all types of students. Appropriate for slower and average students. Paperbound. $2.10. Globe Book Company.

Poetry by Stephen Dunning, Andrew Carrigan, and Ruth Clay. An instructional package for grades 7-9, including a student handbook with 34 short exercises that lead students to write poetry. Other components are a teaching guide, set of six posters, a recording of poetry, and several paperback anthologies of poetry. Complete program (materials for 35 students): $119.50. Scholastic Book Services.

Poetry 2 by Stephen Dunning, Malcolm Glass, and M. Joe Eaton. An instructional package for grades 9-11. Basic component is a student log/anthology, which encourages students to write poetry, putting to work the techniques they've explored in their reading. Also included are a teaching guide and several supplementary books. Complete program (materials for 35 students): $99.50. Scholastic Book Services.

Books for Teachers

Poetic Composition through the Grades by Robert A. Wolsch. Contains a wealth of workable ideas for encouraging students to develop their ability to write poetically. Although intended for elementary school teachers, it can easily be adapted to other levels. Paperbound. Teachers College Press.

My Sister Looks Like a Pear: Awakening the Poetry in Young People by Douglas Anderson. Describes the author's work with the "Poets in the Schools" project. Includes many strategies for encouraging students to write poetry. Paperbound. $2.95. Hart Publishing Company.

4

Teaching Students to Create People and Events

In writing narrative essays, biographies, autobiographies, short stories, and plays, a successful writer must create or describe characters in such a way that they come alive for the reader, and he or she must create or recreate events in such a way that the reader feels like an actual participant.

To do so requires that the writer master a number of skills, which can be developed in part by the activities suggested in this chapter. The writer must, for example, become adept at characterization, allowing characters to reveal themselves through their appearance, their words, and their actions, rather than merely telling the reader directly what they are like. Similarly, the writer must learn techniques that make a story "happen" rather than simply telling a sequence of events.

OBJECTIVES

As a result of the learning experiences in this chapter, the student should be able to:

1. Describe how characters reveal themselves in good writing,
2. Write a paragraph (or longer composition) in which a person reveals himself through his appearance,
3. Write a dialogue that gives the reader clues to the kinds of persons the speakers are,
4. Write a paragraph (or longer composition) in which a person is revealed through his or her actions,
5. Explain the importance of one's purpose in creating or recreating an event,

> 6. Create an event rather than simply telling about it, and
> 7. Make a created or recreated event seem real to the reader.

LEARNING EXPERIENCES

TOPIC I: CHARACTERIZATION BY APPEARANCE

1. *Teacher Presentation.* People reveal a great deal about themselves by their appearances, and the writer must learn to describe a character's appearance in such a way not only to help the reader picture the character in his or her mind's eye, but also to be consistent with and to reveal the inner nature of the character. In order to achieve such a double purpose, the writer must study the appearance of the person being described—either in real life or in the imagination—and arrive at a conclusion as to the "essence" of the appearance. Then the writer is ready to describe the person, including only such details as are relevant.

    All too often the student writer simply begins with the detail of appearance that first strikes his or her eye or fancy, and follows this with whatever detail occurs next and so on. This results in a random listing which fails utterly to create any kind of image in the mind's eye of the reader. The secret of avoiding such an ineffective description is for the writer to decide what kind of impression the character makes and then to utilize the details which will create the same impression in the mind of the readers. (This is a point made previously in Chapter 3, Topic II; you might wish to review that section with your students.)

2. *Activity.* Conduct a discussion of the question, "What do we reveal about ourselves by our appearance?" Elicit from students examples of ways it is possible to understand the personal qualities of someone from the way that person looks, as well as examples of ways appearances can be deceptive. Do not attempt to lead the class to any particular conclusion; instead, allow students to voice their opinions freely. Encourage students to give specific examples wherever possible.

3. *Activity.* Have students look around the classroom at other students to find examples of consistency between some aspect of a person's appearance and what they know about the personal qualities of that individual. For example, Sandy might point out that Tina's turned up nose suits her vivacious, energetic personality. (In some classes it might be wise to establish a ground rule that no negative qualities are to be discussed.)

4. *Activity.* Seat the class in one large circle. Tell each student to secretly choose another student and to decide which color, animal, food, type of weather, piece of furniture best symbolizes that person. For example, Sandy secretly chooses Jerry, and jots down that he is like the color yellow (he's cheerful), a chipmunk, blackberry pie, a clear sunny day in October, and a deacon's bench. Call for volunteers to read their list of colors, etc., and have the class guess who is being

described metaphorically. As in Activity #3, you may wish to limit the students to positive comparisons.

5. *Activity.* Have students choose someone—either a member of the class or anyone else they know or have observed—and describe the person in terms of an essential element that dominates his or her appearance. Have them compose a single descriptive sentence, followed by a list of the details that led to the dominant impression. Here are some examples to get students started:

> *"He looked as if he had dressed in a great hurry—in a dark room." (shirt out, buttons crooked, socks unmatched, etc.)*
> *"Everything about him was soft and limp looking." (plump body, sloping shoulders, fat cheeks, soft pink hands)*
> *"At forty-nine there was about her, still, an air of childishness." (bow knot mouth, hair ribbon, round eyes, ruffled apron)*

Other examples of dominant impressions: air of genteel poverty; appearance of robust health; romantic depravity; sharp and angular; carefully put together; terribly, perfectly correct; pruny and prudish.

6. *Activity.* Have students write a description of someone in terms of that person's similarity to an animal or a bird in appearance. Point out that the writer must take care to choose an animal or bird which is analogous in reputation (stereotype) to the character type he or she is trying to create. It wouldn't do, for example, to describe a sophisticated urbanite as looking like a plow horse. Here are some examples to get students started:

> *"He had a hawk's face." (beak of a nose, arching brows, flaring nostrils, keen eyes)*
> *"The wolf and the weasel vied for dominance in his face." (fierce look, weak chin; dark brows over beady, busy eyes; slick greasy hair)*
> *"She looked like the over-fed poodle she held in her lap." (pendulous cheeks, little mouth, button nose, round brown eyes)*

Other examples of characteristics associated with animals:

> *sparrow - tiny, quick, brown, bony*
> *race horse - sleek, shiny, fine boned, smooth, satin haired, alert eyes*
> *bulldog - bulging eyes, multiple chins, pug nose, short, bowed legs*
> *bear - huge, shaggy, brown-haired, lumbering gait, awkward*
> *sea lion - sloping forehead, little hair, receding chin, clammy skin*

Here is how one student responded to this assignment:

> *She is truly a wild mustang masquerading in human form. She is excitingly alive— —constantly kicking up her heels in pursuit of fun or adventure. She always appears to move at a full-speed canter, with her long brown mane flapping in the breeze. When she suddenly stops in her tracks for some unknown reason, it is only a matter of seconds before she is off again and running in another direction.*

Nina Palkes
(12th grade student)

7. *Activity.* If a person to be described is not "all of a piece," suggest that students describe his or her appearance in terms of its contrasts, as in the wolf/weasel example in Activity #6 above. As in the other ways of describing, this contrasts method is usually an attempt to reveal basic character through an analysis of appearance. This is a useful technique as long as the writer does not try to "read too much" into appearance. Have students watch for a person whose appearance includes important contrasts and to write a sentence characterizing that person.

For example;
> "The lower part of his face seemed quite at variance with the upper." (sharp eyes, curving lips; beak nose, soft chin)
> "He had the face of a poet and the body of a stevedore."

8. *Activity.* Seat the class in a circle. Have students choose a classmate and write several sentences describing that person's appearance. Encourage them to focus on the essential element they see in the person's appearance. Then call for volunteers to read their descriptions and have the class guess who is being described. Or you might read the papers aloud yourself, doing some tactful editing as you read.

9. *Activity.* Have students choose some person well known to all persons in the class (for example, some school administrator, teacher, TV personality) and write a description of that person's appearance. As in Activity #8, encourage students to focus on the essential element they see in the person's appearance. Then call for volunteers to read their descriptions and have the class guess who is being described.

10. *Activity.* Have students choose one descriptive statement that they have written for one of the activities above and write a paragraph using this statement as the topic sentence. (Development details for the paragraph would be, of course, the various specific aspects of the person's appearance that led to that conclusion.)

TOPIC II: CHARACTERIZATION BY DIALOGUE

1. *Teacher Presentation.* Explain to students that people reveal themselves when they speak, and the writer must learn to create dialogue that truly represents the person being created. People reveal their age, locale, educational level, cultural background, and personal characteristics by their level of polish and ease with language, by their idioms, and by the details they emphasize when they speak. Elicit from the class as many examples as possible of what clues you can get from the way a person speaks as to the nature of that person as well as to his or her background.

2. *Activity.* Read to the class or duplicate and distribute to students (using Reproduction Page 8) the details of one or more of the episodes provided below. Then assign each student one of the following roles:

> eight year old boy
> Vermont farmer
> garrulous old lady
> English teacher
> businessman
> minister
> filling station attendant
> escaped convict
> college professor

plus any others you may wish to add. Have students consider how the person whose role they've been assigned would describe the event. Then have them role-play that person describing the episode or tape record the description or write it.

   A. *Kindergarten class and teacher have gone to a park for a picnic. Teenage hoodlums taunt and tease them. Children are frightened. So is the teacher. Teacher asks big boys to go away. They laugh rudely. The ruffians tip over the table and spill the food. They take the cake the teacher had brought and run away with it. The teacher and children look for a police officer so they can report what has happened.*

   B. *An eighth grade class has a substitute teacher. He is young and unsure of himself. The students take advantage of the situation and misbehave. They mislead him as to their assigned work. They misrepresent the class rules to him. The principal comes in and sees how uncooperative they are being. She lectures them on their rudeness to the substitute. She assigns them all to an extra study hall after school. She is angry with the students and feels sorry for the young teacher.*

   C. *Once there was a mother who insisted that her children eat every bit of food on their plates. She made them eat a serving of everything. One night for dinner she served stewed tomatoes, mashed turnips, and collard greens. The children did not clean their plates. The mother told them they would have to stay at the table until the plates were clean. She and the father went into the other room. One child threw his carrots out the window. The second child fed her turnips to the dog. The third child hid his greens behind a big jar on the pantry shelf. The mother was pleased to see they had all cleaned their plates.*

3. *Activity.* Assign students to eavesdrop on conversations around school, at home, on the street, on the subway, or at social affairs. Urge them to listen for people showing what they are like in their speech. Perhaps they will overhear quarrels, flattery, selfishness, lack of interest, naivete, arrogance, and many other qualities. Then have students write down what they can recall and share it with the class, explaining the insights into the speaker's character that they gained. Here is a composition that resulted from this assignment:

The Show
Wendy Davis
(11th grade student)

The room was swarming with people. I stood off to one side, a mere speck in the mounds of dust. Conversation was a steady hum which buzzed around my ears. Sometimes the loud cackle of an amused woman would amplify itself above the other people's conversation.

We were all in the lobby of a movie theater, waiting for the doors to open. I was bored, so I decided to watch the different styles of clothing the people wore.

Most of the women were in pants-suits. They were in their twenties and evidently on dates. Many had coats pulled over these outfits, as if to make sure that their dates could not glimpse any naked skin. I concluded that these people were on their first date. I edged closer to one such young woman and her male companion, to eavesdrop on their conversation. When something intrigues me, I have no scruples. I listened without appearing to do so.

"Well, yeah, uh, my dad drinks, uh, you know, but I, uh, never have seen him bombed," mumbled the man.

"Yeah, my dad drinks sometimes, but I've never seen him, uh, . . . drink too much," the girl rejoined delicately.

They had to be on their first date, and a blind one at that. The conversation became more inane.

"Well, uh, I, uh, drink, you know, uh, occasionally," revealed the man.

"Well, yeah, uh, me, too," confessed the woman.

They went on, agreeing in about four different ways, that they sometimes drank. Then the man threw a bomb.

"Well, uh, I think drinking is fun," he said. The woman started to agree, but the man cut in, adding, "Sex is fun, too."

"Well," stated the woman, pulling her coat more tightly around her, "It, cough, is, uh, to a, cough, uh, certain extent." She looked flushed.

Glancing nervously at the woman's face, the man said, "Let's change the subject."

"Good idea," agreed the woman.

My hypothesis had to be correct: they were on their first date.

Next, I saw two who apparently knew each other quite well. The woman had her coat off. She and the man were laughing, totally at ease. These people talked the most, constantly keeping the room lively with their laughter.

Last came those couples who had . . . discovered each other. They said nothing. Conversation was not needed between those who were in heavenly bliss. With their arms locked around each other, they gazed longingly into each other's eyes.

And then, finally, that awaited moment arrived. The gates opened and we cattle were herded into the theater. To some, this meant that the tension of creating conversation was momentarily ended. To others, it meant a comfortable seat where they could companionably watch something together. To another group, it meant the lights would go out and the fun would begin. For whatever reason, an inaudible sigh arose as we tramped into the theater.

4. *Activity.* Have students observe themselves and make a list of speech habits they observe in themselves. Then have them observe and make a list of the speech habits shared by the group of friends they associate with. Have them bring these lists to class and share them in group discussion.

5. *Activity.* Have students utilize the information they collected for Activity #4 above and write a dialogue between themselves and a friend, incorporating the speech habits identified during the observation. Below is a composition that resulted from an assignment similar to this:

Kids
Steve Sawolkin
(12th grade student)

Here is a dialogue that occurred about ten years ago between my best friend and me. The scene: a ping-pong game between the seven year olds with no one else in the house:

"Hey!" Corey said in a quiet, almost guilty voice, "Who's your girl friend?"

"I don't have one!" Steve said adamantly.

"I know, but who is she? I won't tell anyone," Corey pleaded.

"I don't have one, I told you!" Steve screamed. In a subdued voice, he added, "I'll tell you if you tell me."

The game went on in silence for a few minutes.

"O.K., you tell me first," Corey said slyly.

Steve, not liking the look in Corey's eyes, said, "I'll tell you after you tell me."

"I don't trust you, Steve."

"I don't trust you, either."

A few more minutes of silence as the game proceeded.

The light bulb lit over Corey's head and he said, "Let's write down who they are."

"O.K."

Steve got the paper, and they both wrote down something.

"O.K., hand it to me," Steve demanded.

"Uhuh, you hand it to me first," Corey wisely decided.

"Put your paper in my hand and I'll put my paper in your hand. O.K., now, when I count to three. Onetwothree!"

Each boy grabbed the other's paper, unfolded it and read it.

"You didn't write anything, you rat. You tricked me!"

"Oh, yeah, you didn't write anything either. Besides, I don't really have a girlfriend," Steve retorted.

They went back to the ping-pong game in silence for a few minutes. Then Corey said, "Want to try again?"

"No tricks this time!" Steve said bitterly.

The boys wrote again, and observed the same ceremony as before in exchanging papers. This time, however, they each put up collateral (a pen knife and baseball card) to make sure no one cheated.

Looking at the paper, Steve grinned sheepishly and said, "They're the same."

"Yeah," Corey mumbled. "But I don't really like her that much," he added.

"Neither do I; I can't stand her. I just needed something to write," Steve countered. "But I think she likes me more than she likes you," he said feebly.

"I doubt it, but I don't really care."

"Me too," Steve said as he shrugged his shoulders. (Shrugging one's shoulders was the ultimate symbol of indifference at that age.)

The game went on in silence for about ten minutes. Then Corey said, "Hey, who is she really?"

6. *Activity.* Point out that in plays the characters are revealed only by their speech and actions, since the author cannot describe them directly. Choose a play and read aloud in class one act or scene which is primarily dialogue rather than action. Have different students read the various roles. Discuss what various characters reveal about themselves by the manner and substance of their speaking. (An excellent resource for this activity is *Great Scenes from the World Theater*, edited by James L. Steffensen, Jr., published by Avon, 1965.)

7. *Activity.* Have students write a scene in dialogue, with a minimum of three or four characters revealing their natures in what they say and the way they say it.

8. *Activity.* Produce the scenes written for Activity #7 above. Have students read the various roles, with the author coaching them on how to play them. Then let the class analyze the characters revealed by the dialogue.

9. *Activity.* Have each student choose a partner and role-play one (or all) of the situations suggested below. After role-playing the scene, have the students in each pair write down, as best they can remember, the dialogue they have improvised. (A tape recorder might be helpful.)

    1. A husband and wife having an argument over a dent in the fender of the car, which he is sure she is responsible for. The couple could be mature or rational, or there could be a hotheaded husband and a meek wife, a mousy husband and domineering wife, two young people very much in love but pretty insecure, etc.
    2. Two young people on a blind date: a visiting prep school fellow who thinks he's hot stuff with a shy neighbor of his cousin; a quiet, studious

fellow with a quiet, studious girl; or a pretty, popular girl with a good looking, intelligent, likable guy.
3. The security guard for a department store and a young person suspected of shoplifting.

10. *Teacher Presentation.* Teach students the rudiments of written dialogue as it appears in novels and short stories:
    1. Mechanics of punctuation, placement of quotation marks, commas, etc.,
    2. Division into paragraphs by speaker,
    3. Avoidance of overusing "fancy" synonyms for "said" and "asked" (for example: "he uttered," "she conveyed"). Good writers seem comfortable using "said" most of the time.
    4. Substitution of identifying activities for a stated attribution of speech: "George ran to the door, grabbing his hat on the way. 'I'm going to follow . . .' "
    5. Placement of "he said" near beginning of a speech, not after a long speech,
    6. Choice of words and sentence structure which truly "sound like speech," and
    7. Reproduction of dialect or regional or cultural speech mannerisms by restrained use of a minimum number of effects rather than attempting to slavishly reproduce actual speech, which makes reading difficult.

11. *Activity.* Divide the class into small groups of three to five persons each, attempting to put together students who don't know one another well. Let each group choose a situation and each member choose to speak as a character in that situation. After the group has improvised some dialogue, have the students write it down. Then have them—working individually—revise the dialogue into finished form following the suggestions in Teacher Presentation #10 above.

12. *Activity.* Point out to students that characters' values are often revealed by their ways of speaking. This is true in literature as in life, and of course each writer must learn to create an assumed value structure or world view for the characters being presented. The writer must be very sure that each character speaks as a person with those values would speak. Have students discuss the question, "How do you reveal your own personal values when you speak? Can others infer your values from what you say and how you say it?" Then have them consider the other members of the class and ask, "What values do other members of this class seem to hold, as revealed by what they say and how they say it?"

13. *Activity.* Have students write a dialogue between two characters with very different values systems. For example:
    1. Two boys in the locker room talking about a girl they both know. Show through dialogue that the boys have very different kinds of values.
    2. Two men talking about scandals in government, such as Watergate,
    3. Two women talking about girls of today,
    4. Two teachers discussing class discipline, or
    5. Two students discussing a teacher.

TOPIC III: CHARACTERIZATION BY ACTIONS

1. *Teacher Presentation.* Call to students' attention that there are many personal characteristics that we may unconsciously reveal by mannerisms, habitual gestures, or constant behavior patterns which others can easily identify as typical of us. Give the class several examples such as the following:

    Shyness - unwillingness to look into others' eyes directly
    reluctance to speak in a group
    speaking in a soft, breathless voice
    blushing when the center of attention

    Boldness - speaking often and loudly
    interrupting or inserting opinions
    expressing opinions without testing views of others
    correcting teacher without hesitation

    Vulgarity - treating others' and one's own materials roughly
    loud, uncontrolled laughter
    hitting others hard, playfully
    spitting on the floor
    using Ming vase as an ash tray
    chewing loudly, scratching

2. *Activity.* Give students a list of personal characteristics such as that below and have them supply revealing behaviors for each. You could have them work in small groups in class, or make their lists individually as homework and then share them with the class.

dishonesty	*compassion*
courtesy	*piety*
concern for others	*intellectual acuteness*
arrogance	*self-centeredness*
self-consciousness	*brutality*

3. *Activity.* Have each student describe (in one fully developed paragraph) a person behaving in such a way that the reader can gain insight into the person's basic nature. Then, to the group as a whole, read each paragraph aloud and see if pupils can properly evaluate and label the character being described. It will help to have each student write underneath his or her paragraph a summary sentence identifying the purpose; e.g., "He was a thoroughly ill-mannered person." Here is a sample paragraph to get students started:

    She sat quietly in the discussion circle, her gaze intent on the face of each speaker in turn. Occasionally, a smile curved her lips as a speaker became animated with enthusiasm, and once or twice she laughed appreciatively as a group member shared an amusing childhood memory. She did not speak often, but when she did, it was usually to respond to a question or to make a comment on a subject of general interest. She could always be counted on to make a contribution to the group when it was needed, but she never tried to dominate and never lost sight of the feelings of others in the group.
    (She was a thoughtful and responsive group member.)

4. *Activity.* Have each student draw from a receptacle a slip on which you have written a personal characteristic or mood. Then have each student write a de-

scription of a person behaving in such a way as to reveal that characteristic or mood. Encourage students to use imagination in choosing the setting and situation in which their characters reveal themselves. You may wish to read these aloud to the class (anonymously) or reproduce them so all students can judge how well each description presents behavior revealing the characteristic or mood the writer had in mind. The following are characteristics/moods that can be used for this activity; add others that are especially suited to your class:

nervous	*coquettish*
restless	*eager to be liked*
bored	*conscious of good looks*
depressed	*narrow minded*
timid	*energetic*
childish	*thoughtless*

5. *Activity.* Point out to students that people reveal their true values—their codes of belief and behavior—more clearly by what they do than any other way including what they say. To clarify this insight in your students' minds, use Reproduction Page 9 to duplicate or project the following chart, which lists a number of human values in the left-hand column. Have students fill in the right-hand columns with those behaviors which would likely accompany each value and those which would not be consistent with it. The first one has been done as an example.

VALUES IN ACTION CHART

A Person Who Values . . .	Would Probably:	Would Probably Not:
1. *loyalty to friends*	loan money to friend stick around when friend is sick or in trouble go out of his or her way to do a favor for friend include friend in plans even when others think friend would be out of place	avoid friend for own convenience shed friend for a richer or more popular friend turn in friend when he or she had done wrong lie to friend or talk about friend to others
2. *fairness*		
3. *individuality*		
4. *equality of the sexes*		
5. *honesty*		
6. *good sportsmanship*		
7. *popularity*		
8. *physical fitness*		
9. *social justice*		
10. *independence*		

6. *Activity.* Ask each student to choose one belief or value from the list given in Activity #5 above and in two or three paragraphs describe a situation or event in which a person behaved in such a way as to reveal devotion to that value. This can be an imaginary or real occasion, as the student chooses.

7. *Activity.* Call to students' attention the incomparable richness of the English language which makes it possible for us to verbalize an action such as sitting in a chair or moving across the room in many different words, and hence with many different implications about the person doing the action. Working with the class as a whole, have them help you list on the board all the possible ways of saying that a person *sat.* Here are some starters:

> *He sprawled in the chair.*
> *She lounged.*
> *She sat bolt upright.*
> *He stretched out.*
> *He straddled.*
> *She settled, squatted, lay back,*
> *crouched, ensconced herself, etc.*

When the list on the board is fairly long, stop and look at each verb, asking the class, "What does this say about the person who is doing this action?" Repeat the process by listing on the board all the possible ways of saying that a person *moved* across the room. For example:

> *He sauntered across the room.*
> *She strolled, darted,*
> *danced, lounged, boogied,*
> *slid, strode, crept, waltzed, tore,*
> *rolled, staggered, tottered, paced,*
> *marched, sidled, slouched, trudged,*
> *skipped, minced . . . .*

Again, go back over the list and ask the class, "What does this say about the person who is doing the action?"

8. *Activity.* Have each student secretly choose one other member of the class to observe closely during the next three class periods. Suggest that they keep a record of that person's manners, mannerisms, body language, response patterns (i.e., to whom and on what occasions the person responds and participates), etc. Recommend that they pay particular attention to behavior that reveals what kind of person their "partner" is. After students have had several days to collect data through observation, assign a paragraph to be written about the person they have observed, with emphasis on the characteristics the person reveals about himself or herself through actions during class. If the trust level in the class is high, you could then read the paragraphs aloud and let the class guess who was being described. (If you feel this activity would be too threatening or that students are not well enough acquainted or kind enough to carry it out without someone being embarrassed, you could easily have students observe some unnamed person from another class or outside of school, rather than someone in the class.)

TOPIC IV: PUTTING CHARACTERIZATION TOGETHER

1. *Teacher Presentation.* Help students understand that good writers do not confine themselves to only one means of characterizing the people they write about, but

often combine some or all the means. Provide the class with examples of good characterization in biographies or fiction and point out the ways the author has combined characterization by appearance, characterization by dialogue, and characterization by actions.

2. *Activity.* Have students write a complete profile on some individual in the class or someone else in the school community. This should be considered a major assignment, in which students utilize all the means of characterization that they have studied. One approach would be to have the students choose someone they would like to find out more about and invite him or her to be interviewed by the class. (A school administrator is often a good choice.) To assure that the interview is most productive, you may wish to have the class compile in advance a list of the questions they want the person to answer. Assign at least one question to each student, with the requirement that the student is responsible for asking it if no one else does. After the interview, have the class discuss what they have learned about the person they interviewed. Then assign the writing of a personality profile of several paragraphs about the person. When they have finished, students may wish to compare their profiles and discuss the different approaches taken by different students.

3. *Activity.* Have students write a complete characterization of themselves. Encourage students to avoid writing an autobiography, a chronology of the events of their lives, but to attempt to tell the reader what kind of person they are.

4. *Activity.* Have each student write a profile of an imaginary person who represents an ideal to him or her, perhaps the person the student would (now or someday) like to be. For best results, before making the assignment conduct an open-ended discussion of what members of the class consider to be an ideal or admirable human being.

TOPIC V: CREATING EVENTS FOR A PURPOSE

1. *Teacher Presentation.* Explain to students that just as they must have a purpose in mind when they write a paragraph or an essay, so must they know exactly what it is they plan to accomplish when they create or recreate an event or series of events. Narrative writing, whether it be fiction or nonfiction, has a purpose. This is particularly true since in any kind of writing it is impossible ever to tell *everything* about any place, person, or event. The writer must choose which details should go into the account and which should be left out. A purpose provides the guiding principle for making these choices.

2. *Activity.* Using Reproduction Page 10, duplicate or project the random and unselected list of details below which are all parts of an event (a family vacation by automobile). Working with the total class as a group, suggest several purposes one might have in mind when writing about this event (examples are provided) and challenge students to name which details would be used to fulfill each purpose.

RANDOM LIST OF DETAILS RELATED TO FAMILY VACATION BY AUTOMOBILE

children were always hungry
had to stop every ten miles
scenery was beautiful
roads were excellent
we took along games, puzzles
we learned to read maps
car was skillfully loaded
motels were expensive
wife drove from back seat
we saw "Old Faithful" geyser
we kept getting lost
it was hot and boring in Kansas and Nebraska

new insights into U.S. history
became good at "20 Questions" game
restaurants were usually awful
stopped often to rest
got ptomaine at a Cheyenne drive-in
became skillful at outdoor eating
saw Grand Canyon
saw storm over the prairies
talked to a wide variety of people
mountains were awe-inspiring
got great mileage in the car
thrilled by the Pacific Ocean

1st purpose: to recreate our view of the beauty of America
2nd purpose: to tell about trip in such a way as to reveal how much we learned about taking a successful trip
3rd purpose: to describe our trip in such a way as to show what a nightmare it was
4th purpose: to describe our trip in such a way as to amuse the reader

3. *Activity.* Using Reproduction Page 11, provide students with the list of events (given below) by duplicating it or projecting it with the overhead or opaque. Have them—working individually or in small groups—list as many really useful purposes as they can that might determine their approach to each event. After they have finished, have them share their results and discuss them. Two events that can be used as examples when making the assignment:

1. EVENT: party where everything went wrong
   POSSIBLE PURPOSES: to recreate the event so accurately one might feel one is there
   to recreate it in such a way that one identifies with the hostess's embarrassment and anguish
   to recreate it in such a way as to amuse the reader
   to recreate it for the purpose of showing what not to do when giving a party

2. EVENT: automobile accident
   POSSIBLE PURPOSES: to recreate mood of horror
   to scare people into safer driving
   to accurately recreate the scene
   to show limits of auto's capacity
   to pay tribute to police
   to sell driving lessons

3. EVENT: an evening of watching television
4. EVENT: the senior class picnic in the park

5. *EVENT:* a family reunion
6. *EVENT:* graduation exercises
7. *EVENT:* lunch in the school cafeteria
8. *EVENT:* a family weekend at the farm
9. *EVENT:* an evening at traffic court
10. *EVENT:* a birthday party
11. *EVENT:* tryouts for a school team
12. *EVENT:* a rock concert

4. *Activity.* Have each student choose one event from the list in Activity #3 above and write about it at least twice, with a different purpose in mind each time. More capable students could be encouraged to write about the event with as many different purposes as possible.

5. *Activity.* Provide students with a list of possible purposes that a writer could have in mind in creating or recreating an event. (The beginning of such a list is given below.) Lead the class in a discussion of the purposes, asking them to determine what *events* the writer might use to serve these purposes:
    1. To demonstrate the untrustworthiness of a character,
    2. To show what a hollow mockery much patriotic verbalization is,
    3. To reveal the insincerity of many people, even with their good friends,
    4. To demonstrate the generation gap,
    5. To reveal the tragedy of old age,
    6. To illustrate the point that students are often treated unfairly by teachers
    7. To show the lengths some people will go to have friends, and
    8. To show change in a character.

    (Other purposes: illustration, characterization, creation of an effect (to shock, amuse, or horrify), to dissuade, to persuade, to teach, etc.)

6. *Activity.* Have students choose one of the purposes suggested in Activity #5 above and create an event or a series of events which successfully fulfills that purpose. When these have been completed, it might be useful to share them with the whole class and let students discuss and evaluate the events and the purposes they were meant to fulfill.

7. *Activity.* Provide the class with a number of examples from literature and from student writing (see list below) of the purposeful creation of events. Read them in class and have students try to identify the purpose(s) an event or an entire plot sequence fulfills in the given work. Then ask them to try to think of events in their own lives which could serve the same purpose(s) if recreated. Following is a list of works that might be useful for this activity, along with possible statements of their purposes:
    1. "Gift of the Magi" by O. Henry - to show how love can "overcome" poverty,
    2. "The Verger" by Maugham - to reveal the shallowness of the view that one must be formally educated to succeed,

3. "The Killers" by Ernest Hemingway - to create a story almost entirely by dialogue, including plot, mood, characterization,
4. "The Sound of Thunder" by Ray Bradbury - to develop the idea that even the most trivial action can have significant consequences,
5. "The Other Foot" by Ray Bradbury - to develop the idea that the identities of the oppressor and the oppressed might well be a matter of circumstances rather than a difference in nature,
6. "Train Ride in Europe" by Sheila Morris (12th grade student) - to juxtapose elements in a scene in order to convey an implication about the ongoing tragedy of war's human cost (see Reproduction Page 12),
7. "Cold Turkey" by Nina Whittier (12th grade student) - to relate a tall tale in such realistic detail and matter of fact style that readers will be tempted to believe in spite of themselves (see Reproduction Page 13),
8. "He Should Have Stayed in Bed" by Jim Perkins (12th grade student) - to amuse the reader with a tall tale about an event told in the manner of oral joke-telling (see Reproduction Page 14),
9. "Just Dreaming" by Ben Painter (11th grade student) - to emphasize a value judgment about our society by recounting an event in two possible versions (see Reproduction Page 15),
10. "The Visit" by Ruth Kim (11th grade student) - to create an event revealing the benefits of old age as perceived from two very different viewpoints (see Reproduction Page 16), and
11. "Sensations of My Mind" by Merilynn Wenzlaff (12th grade student) - to create a fantasy event which seems as if it might really have happened and which reveals strong feelings and emotions (see Reproduction Page 17).

8. *Activity.* As students learned in the preceding section on "Characterization through Actions," people reveal their true nature most surely in their actions, so a valuable exercise would be to have students create an event or a whole plot sequence aimed at revealing the true nature of a character who at the outset is thought to be or to present him or herself as a different kind of person. Begin by having students think about experiences in their own lives in which they discovered that a person was not the kind of person they first thought he or she was or gave the impression of being. Invite several students to tell the class about their experiences. Some students may need some help in thinking of suitable experiences, and you will want to give them suggestions. Following is a list of possible character changes. Have students discuss with one another the kinds of events which might have brought about these revelations of character before they make their own selections and begin to write.
    1. A seemingly self-confident person turns out to have the same fears and self-doubts as you;
    2. The big braggart folds when the chips are down;
    3. A reputed Romeo turns out to be a very nice fellow;
    4. A "perfect gentleman" turns out to be all surface and no substance;
    5. A plain girl turns out to be a beautiful person;
    6. A tough teacher becomes a friend at a time you badly need one;

7. A so-called friend turns out not to be a friend;
8. Your mean, stubborn parent turns out to be right after all; and
9. A fellow you thought was a sissy turns out to be a real man.

TOPIC VI: CREATING EVENTS RATHER THAN TELLING ABOUT THEM

1. *Teacher Presentation.* Tell students that the key to successful narrative writing is to *create* an event rather than to simply *tell* about it. The secret, of course, is in using details rather than making general statements.

2. *Activity.* Tell students to imagine that they had to have an emergency appendectomy and missed a social event that they badly wished to attend. A friend, they are to imagine, wrote the following account of the event:

    The parent-student banquet was wonderful. Everyone was there, X dressed in party clothes. X The cafeteria was beautifully decorated, X and the tables were lovely. X The entertainment pleased everyone X and so did the excellent food which tasted X as good as it looked. X

    Point out that this account really doesn't recreate the banquet for the reader, but simply tells about it using general statements when specific statements would have made the event "come alive." Challenge the class to list—perhaps on the board—the specific details which could then be added at each X-mark to *recreate* the event that here is merely *mentioned*.

3. *Activity.* Have students expand the following skeletal paragraphs that merely tell about an event into paragraphs that recreate the events. (Use Reproduction Page 18.)

    A. *When I went to the park, the weather was just as I like it. We went swimming in a pool that was all right but that needed a few improvements. Then we did a lot of really fun things. Afterwards we all talked around a bonfire and decided to do it again sometime.*

    (Written on purpose by high school student Daphne Rodin)

    B. *The seventh grade trip to Chicago started off in utter chaos on a bad February day. All the seventh graders were dropped off by 6:30 a.m. and began causing all kinds of trouble. Teachers and parents ran around trying to restore order. Finally everyone was aboard the buses and they left.*

    (Written on purpose by high school student Ellen Wiederholdt)

    C. *The synagogue was crowded and noisy, but the service was pleasant and progressed smoothly. Afterwards everyone went to the Kiddush and ate refreshments. People talked to one another about the sermon and about the events of the past week and their plans for the next. Then they left the building to take care of their tasks for the day.*

    (Written on purpose by high school student Barbara Kiem)

4. *Teacher Presentation.* Explain to students that a frequent weakness of narrative writing is *telling about* conversations rather than *creating* them. Using Reproduction Page 19, duplicate and distribute to students the two accounts of the same conversation given below, and help students understand the differences between them. (Both versions were written by 12th grade student Richard Green.)

TEACHING STUDENTS TO CREATE PEOPLE AND EVENTS 71

A. *David told Louie a story to distract him while he got his hair cut. He made up a tale about where the moon goes during the day. Even the barber got interested, and Louie was full of questions. Jane, however, was her usual practical-minded self, interrupting and disagreeing with David's flights of fancy.*

B. *"You know where the moon goes during the day, Louie?"*

"Where?" Louie's eyes grew wide, and he seemed not even to notice the stroking of the barber's trimmer through his hair.

"Well," David began, not entirely sure where he would end up, "they lift up the edge of the sky . . ."

"They do not!" That was crabby Jane, their older sister.

"Don't be a pill, Jane." Louie laughed at David's imitation of their mother's tone of voice. David continued with his story: "Then they let it have the day off."

The barber smiled absently and winked at Jane.

"Anyway, it's a big balloon with craters and canyons and scratchmarks. And it has to be driven by a hundred short midgets. Anyway, these short midgets run around on wire tracks that go roundy-round . . ."

"Like Jake?!" Jake was Louie's mechanical mouse.

"Yes. And they go to a fair."

"A fair?"

"And they fly around and the clouds are green and yellow . . ."

5. *Activity.* Have students choose one of the following accounts of conversations and arguments and turn it into *actual* talking and arguing. Use Reproduction Page 20 for duplicating the accounts.

   1. *My folks and I really got into it over whether I could go to the dance.*

   2. *I told him I really loved him, and he acted so dumb I felt like a fool. Then he apologized.*

   3. *I told her if that was the way she was going to act, I didn't need her for a friend, and she told me off and hung up on me.*

   4. *Janie chattered happily as they walked to the car. Jim answered shortly, if at all, and gradually Janie ran out of things to say. She tried to get Jim to tell her what was the matter, but he turned her questions away with non-answers. At last, she fell silent.*

   5. *Mrs. Garber spent a full five minutes telling her third period pupils how displeased she was with their behavior. Several students tried to speak up in their own defense, but Mrs. Garber easily overrode them in both volume and intensity, and eventually the pupils sat silently, accepting their verbal punishment.*

   6. *This weekend one of my best friends revealed a side I had never seen before. He told me how unsure of himself he is and how uncertain he sometimes feels of his own worth. He told me that his father drinks too much and never seems to have time for him. His mother ignores him most of the time, he told me, because she's so upset about the father's behavior. My friend told me that once he felt so desperate he even considered killing himself but now that he has me for a friend he feels life is more worthwhile. I told him I hoped we'd always be friends.*

   7. *Judy called me on the phone last night but was so upset she could hardly make clear to me what she was trying to say. I finally talked her into settling down a little and she managed to tell me her mother and father had just had an awful fight and were planning to get a divorce.*

6. *Teacher Presentation.* Explain to students the difference between creating an event or simply reporting that an event happened. If writing about actions is to come alive, the actions must happen on the page, with the writer engaging the imagination of the reader. Readers must be able to see with their minds' eye, hear with their minds' ear, etc., whatever is happening on the page. They certainly

cannot respond in that way to a general statement such as the one below, which is duplicated on Reproduction Page 21.

He tried desperately to build a fire with his last matches, but his frozen hands were too stiff. He could not control his body's shivering, and thus scattered his small fire instead of building it. Each twig burned out and he knew he was doomed.

Contrast this passage (above) with Jack London's tense account of such a happening in his famous short story "To Build a Fire." See the excerpt that appears on Reproduction Page 21. Duplicate it and distribute it to students to compare with the first account, or read it to the class and discuss the differences.

7. *Activity.* Have students choose one of the passages below and, working individually or in small groups, turn it into a lively, dramatic, active happening. Urge them to combine dialogue and action with description of a setting, in order to prepare a complete event for the reader.
   1. *We were swept overboard at the same time and managed to stay together in the shark-infested waters most of the night. Rescue came shortly after dawn, too late for him.*
   2. *We made the mistake of pitching camp on a sandbar, barely above the level of the river, and when the storm came up in the night we were flooded out and washed away with next to no warning.*
   3. *When I first picked up the hitchhiker I thought he was very courteous and friendly, but he soon showed me a different side. I was lucky to escape a horrible death.*
   4. *I invited only six friends to come to the party I was going to have when my folks were away. However, I made the mistake of telling each friend she could invite other people. Before that awful night was over our house was a shambles and I had to call the police to help me get some of the people to leave. There must have been a hundred people there. My mother and father were furious and, actually, I can't blame them.*
   5. *The other day in the smoking lounge at school there was a fight that got several students in trouble. It started as an argument between a football player and the boyfriend of one of the cheerleaders and developed quickly into a near riot involving half the football squad and ten band members. Several cheerleaders got into the excitement, and one of them got carried away and threw a book just as the assistant principal walked into the lounge to investigate the noise. Needless to say, he was not pleased.*

8. *Activity.* Bring to class plenty of back issues of *Reader's Digest* and have students look at the "First Person" articles that are a regular feature. Have them find good examples of how writers of these accounts utilize techniques suggested in the preceding activities and teacher presentations for recreating rather than telling about an event. You might even have students attempt deliberately to write a general telling-about account of one of the events that was dramatically recreated by the author of the *Reader's Digest* article.

TOPIC VII: MAKING EVENTS SEEM REAL

1. *Teacher Presentation.* Remind students that they probably read many stories that seemed completely believable, even though they dealt with unreal or farfetched circumstances, as in science fiction. (Perhaps students can cite several examples.) Read one or more of the following passages from well-known works of fiction and help students identify which details lend to the reality—the

credibility—of what the author is creating. (This might be a good time to teach students the meaning of the term, "verisimilitude.")

  a. In the last three paragraphs of Poe's *The Black Cat*, Poe describes his own (the narrator's) feelings in such horrifying detail it is impossible to disbelieve.
  b. In the passage in Camus's *The Stranger* in which Mersault is taken to the Visitor's Room, the exactitude of his description makes the scene very real.
  c. The first four paragraphs of Kafka's *Metamorphosis* boast matter of fact description and total calm acceptance of the bizarre.
  d. Shirley Jackson's *The Lottery* mixes everyday, well known details of life with the unbelievable in such a way that it all seems real and believable.

2. *Activity.* Assign the task of writing about some strange, unusual, or unreal event in such detail as to make it seem real, vivid and believable to the reader. Suggested subjects: sighting of a flying saucer, being arrested and held in jail in a case of mistaken identity, being bitten by a rattlesnake while alone in the woods, discovering that you are a werewolf, etc.

3. *Teacher Presentation.* Point out a phenomenon students may not have noticed: that when they read about actions and events in a piece of skillful writing, they do not *think* they are there amid the action, but it is quite possible for them to *feel* as if they are there. So it is the *feelings* of the reader that the writer must learn to engage. Read the class an excerpt from Sartre's "The Wall" or distribute copies for them to read themselves. Point out that this story creates fear for the reader to experience. Help students identify the *feelings* that seem to make up *fear* in this piece of writing; then have them also identify feelings *they* have had when experiencing fear.

4. *Activity.* Assign students to write about a situation or an event in which the writer experienced great fear. The challenge of this assignment is to describe vividly the feelings that were experienced, and not simply to tell that they were afraid.

5. *Activity.* Read to the class or have students read an excerpt from Katherine Mansfield's "Bliss" or some similar story. Discuss the author's description of the feelings which add up to intense happiness. Have students also identify other feelings they have experienced when *they* were very happy.

6. *Activity.* Have students write at least one paragraph about an occasion when they felt extreme joy. Challenge them to write about their feelings in such a way as to engage the feelings of the reader.

7. *Activity.* Have students read together a description of grief in a work of fiction. Have them discuss the feelings the author associates with sorrow and a sense of loss. Ask them to describe other feelings they, themselves, have experienced related to sorrow.

8. *Activity.* Have students write at least a paragraph about an occasion when they felt intense sorrow, urging each writer to describe this feeling in such a way as to arouse a reader's emotions.

9. *Activity.* Following the procedures utilized in the activities above, focus on other feelings such as anger, frustration, hatred, guilt, affection, loneliness, etc. If students are pleased with the results of these assignments, they might wish to reproduce their writings about emotions in a booklet entitled something like "To Live Is to Feel" and make it available to other students.

10. *Activity.* Have students read the science fiction story "The Long Walk" or some similar work. Or you might want to read it to them. Discuss the vivid description of the character's feelings as he tries desperately to reach his space ship: the fear, the difficult vision, the pain behind his knee as a broken spring gouges into his flesh, etc. Help them see that it is these details about the walker which make it possible for the reader to identify with him and which build the story's suspense. The reader cares about the character in the story and cares what happens to him because the reader identifies with him and his feelings and experiences.

11. *Activity.* Have students bring to class brief book, magazine, or newspaper selections which relate in vivid detail a personal, suspenseful experience with which they identify. Place students in groups of three or four and have them share their selections with one another. Emphasize to them that it is the realism of the descriptive detail which makes us identify with the experience being written about. (As insurance against forgetfulness on the part of some students, you might wish to have several such readings available for students to take to their groups.)

12. *Activity.* Assign students to write about a personal experience which involved strong feelings, an element of risk, endurance and/or great effort, and some degree of suspense. Let students' abilities determine the assignment's length. Challenge them to include as many realistic personal details as possible. If a student insists that no such event has ever occurred in his or her life, instruct the student to write of an event which *might* have occurred or one which he or she *wishes* had occurred. Remind students always to remember *why* they are creating a particular event—in this case, to recreate an experience so vividly and so personally that the reader will identify with the narrator.

ASSESSING ACHIEVEMENT OF OBJECTIVES

On-Going Evaluation

The extent to which students have mastered the skills taught in this unit can be measured by having them submit for grading the final products of almost any of the activities suggested earlier.

Final Evaluation

For an overall evaluation of students' ability to create people and events, assign an in-class character sketch or short piece of fiction or narrative prose. Suggest that students remember an incident that took place in their lives within the past 24 hours and recreate it in writing. Allow students the entire period to plan, write, and revise their compositions. Grade the final drafts according to these criteria:

1. Has the writer utilized the appearance of the character(s) to tell the reader what kinds of persons they are?
2. Has the writer used dialogue to reveal the nature of the character(s)?
3. Has the writer used the characters' actions to reveal the kinds of people they are?
4. Has the writer created or recreated an event rather than just telling about it?
5. Has the writer made the event seem real to the reader?

RESOURCES FOR TEACHING STUDENTS TO CREATE CHARACTERS AND EVENTS

Below is a selected list of resources useful for teaching the skills needed for creating believable characters and events. It is divided into audio-visual materials (films, filmstrips, records, photo sets, slide-tape programs, etc.) and books for students. Addresses of publishers can be found in the alphabetical list on pages 111–113. Prices, where given, are only approximate, since changes occur frequently.

Audio-Visual Materials

A Folio for Writers: Narration by Bruce Vance and Michael Milne. Contains guide and 28 5" x 8" black and white photo reprints, which may be used to stimulate open-ended, spontaneous writing exercises. Guide includes questions for small group discussion and individual study. Fine for all students. Clarke, Irwin and Co., Ltd.

How to Write an Effective Composition: Narrative and Descriptive Writing from "Anatomy of Language" by Morris Schreiber. Contains one LP record, thorough discussion guide, and readings of excerpts from the works of Charles Dickens, along with a group of specific questions related to style, character development, and creative literary devices. Appropriate only for advanced students. $6.98. Folkways Records.

Creative Writing by Morris Schreiber. Contains one LP record along with guide. Topics include self-expression, sources of ideas, writing format, and the art of writing. Readings of creative passages accompanied by specific questions related to style, method, characterization, and expressive quality. Appropriate for advanced students. Scholastic Records.

Creative Writing. LP record plus text. Examination of self-expression through writing, sources of ideas, diverse literary genres, and writing techniques. Numerous literary models. Appropriate for advanced students. $7.50. Applause Productions, Inc.

Developing Creative Ability by Dorothy J. Skeel. Sound series—two cassettes. Designed to provide a conducive atmosphere to creative writing—encourages oral interpretation and recorded readings, and promotes the practical application of creative writing skills. Suitable for all students. Encyclopaedia Britannica.

How to Write a Short Story. Four filmstrips, two cassettes. Designed to help students compose short, creative, fictional works. Instruction in how to create effective characters, settings, and plots. Guide for each filmstrip follows the end frame. Suitable for average and advanced students. $42.65. Eye-Gate.

Writing: From Imagination to Expression. Contains four filmstrips, four LP records/cassettes, and a discussion guide. Recorded excerpts from the works of great writers, followed by skill-building assignments. $77.50. Guidance Associates.

And Then What Happens?: A First Experience in Creative Writing by Jean Fiedler. Contains five color sound filmstrips, program guide, and LP records or cassettes. Students are encouraged to define and develop characters, create new endings to existing stories, and exercise the imagination. The comprehensive program guide provides important teaching tips and classroom activities. Appropriate for all students. $1.00 with records, $1.15 with cassettes. Prentice-Hall.

Creative Writing. Includes twenty-four transparencies, three overlays, and a teacher's guide. An open-ended, overhead transparency set designed to stimulate creative composition. Challenging and interesting for all students. $37.50. Scott Education Division.

Books for Students

Creative Writing by John Freeman. Examination of conflict, description, characterization, and dialogue. Valuable writer's checklist, reading list, and assignments which reinforce the text. Appropriate for average and advanced students. Paperbound. Frederick Muller Limited.

Picture Your Writing/2 by Geraldine Murphy. A brief, informative guide—workbook format. Provides instruction and practice in three-dimensional characterization, stylistic subtlety and nuance, plausible dialogue, and creation of rich scenes. Excellent, clear, and direct. Appropriate for all students. Paperbound. $.50. Xerox Corp.

Composing Humor: Twain, Thurber, and You by Jean Sisk and Jean Saunders. A comprehensive look at literary humor, including definitions of comedy, satire, parody, and wit. Examination of comic perspectives with excerpts from Twain and Thurber serving as excellent models. Suitable for advanced students. Teacher's manual available. Paperbound. $3.45. Harcourt Brace Jovanovich.

You Can Write: A New Approach to Expository and Creative Writing by The Editors of READ Magazine. Provides nine prepared, open-ended story set-ups, casts of characters, and settings. Given this foundation and framework students will, undoubtedly, be able to bypass that difficult first step in creative writing. Valuable experience for all students. Paperbound. $.50. Xerox Corp.

Writing Creatively by J. N. Hook. Substantial sections on writing fiction—characterization, setting, plot, short story, play, and poetry—and techniques on how to bring compositions to life. Also includes general writing principles—sensory words, descriptive writing and imagery. Excellent style index for quick reference. Appropriate for average and advanced students. Hardcover. D.C. Heath and Co.

Character, Plot, and Setting by Susan Thesenga and Mary Bell. One of six titles in the Contemporary English Modules Series. Contains sections on the imagination at work, characters, setting, and the sources of creative writing. Visually attractive, easy-to-follow structure. Exercises and project suggestions. Appropriate for average and advanced students. Paperbound. Silver Burdett

Writing Incredibly Short Plays, Poems, Stories by James H. Norton and Francis Gretton Interesting sections on characterization, precepts of creative writing, structure of a well-made play, the short story—character sketch, autobiographical account, point-of-view, tone, and mood. A valuable handbook. Teacher's guide available. Paperbound. Harcourt Brace Jovanovich.

Writing from the Inside: Alternatives—An Introduction to Creative Writing by James D. Houston. Discussion of characterization, examples of professional writing, interesting model character sketches. Examination of writing in several genres: short story, fable, tale, and fantasy. Valuable writer's checklist included. Fine for average and advanced students. Paperbound. Addison-Wesley Publishing Co.

An Eye for People: A Writer's Guide to Character by Hart Day Leavitt. A new title in the *Stop, Look, and Write* series. Teaches the art of creative thinking, observing, and writing along with the intricacies of character sketch and study. Examples from works of the literary masters. Over 150 illustrations. Appropriate for all students. Teacher's guide available. Paperbound. $1.25. Bantam Books.

The Writers' Eye by Hart Day Leavitt. Another title in the *Stop, Look, and Write* series. Designed to help develop creative compositional skills through the visual medium. Over 160 concrete images extend the student's powers of artistic observation and stimulate and encourage creative writing. Suitable for all students. Teacher's guide available. Paperbound. $1.50. Bantam Books.

Open-Ended Stories. Twenty exciting stories without endings give students the opportunity to compose endings, further develop characters, and make creative, dramatic decisions. Question material appears in a special section at the end of the book. Fine for all students. Teaching guide available. Paperbound. $2.40. Globe Book Co.

Write Now! Insights into Creative Writing by Anne Wescott Dodd. Provides a thorough, developmental writing program—from descriptive phrases through the complete story, poem, and one-act play. Inspirational examples, explanations, and a teacher-student "contract" which facilitates grading of the creative products. Directions for journal keeping and term project are included. Paperbound. $2.10. Globe Book Co.

Inside Story by Stephen Dunning, Henry Maloney, and Laura Diskin. Includes two possibilities—one in which students are the main characters in the open stories, and/or a conventional assignment toward understanding basic literary techniques. Student log included. Fine for average and advanced students. Paperbound. $1.65. Scholastic.

5

Teaching Students to Write About Literature

Many English teachers consider writing about literary works to be a central feature of any writing program. Perhaps because most of us enjoy reading and talking about literature, it seems natural to choose literature as the focus of students' writing. After discussing a work in class, many teachers almost reflexively assign a paper on it, and if they don't require a complete, out-of-class essay, they at least include some essay questions on any tests over a work studied by the class.

As we pointed out in Chapters 1 and 2, we feel that students learn to write better when they are allowed to write about things that are of vital concern to them, and for most students explication of a literary work does not fall into this category. Nevertheless, since many students will ultimately have to demonstrate skill in writing a paper of literary analysis—if not in high school, then most certainly in college—the composition teacher needs to equip the student with the ability to write about literature.

Although many teachers assign essays to be written about literary works, all too rarely do they give students explicit instructions about *how* to write such a paper. Perhaps they are remiss in this way because writing about literature comes very naturally to most English teachers, and thus they have difficulty imagining that someone else simply doesn't know where to begin. But there is a serious difference between merely making an assignment and teaching students the skills they need to carry it out proficiently. The purpose of this chapter is to suggest how you might give students guidance in writing about a literary work, so that they become conscious of the process and know what to do when given a writing assignment related to literature.

The process of *writing* about literature cannot be separated from the process of analyzing and understanding a work of literature. For this reason it will be necessary for us to give attention to the process of literary analysis in this chapter—even though we may be accused of digression from the real purpose of the chapter. Yet we know of no way to help students learn to write about a work unless they are skilled in the close reading of literature.

This chapter is based on the supposition that art, including literary art, is purposive, that every work of art represents a working out of the artist's purpose(s). Art is to be seen as an act of will, not as a result of random behavior. Without such a supposition, the study of literature would be as subjective as the search for meaning in ink blots or the reading of tea leaves in a cup. It is the assumption of purpose on the part of the artist that makes the study of art worthwhile.

The language arts student who accepts this tenet will, it is hoped, be spared the futility of commenting on writings as if they were purposeless productions which mean whatever the student chooses to decide they mean. Such a response to literature is both lazy and arrogant, depriving the student of the rigorous and rewarding task of exploring a work to discover fully and exactly what the author has achieved.

The student should be encouraged to approach each literary work armed with two questions: *what* and *why.* The first question, *what,* demands close, attentive reading and careful identification of the elements which are actually observable in the text. The second question, *why,* assumes that what is in the text has been put there by the author on purpose and, hence, is susceptible to analysis and interpretation. *Why* is the question which directs the student's study and leads to his or her own comment about a literary work.

OBJECTIVES

As a result of the learning experiences in this chapter, the student will be able to:

1. Trace a repetitive element throughout a work of literature to discover the author's purposes for that element.
2. State in the form of a thesis a conclusion as to the author's purpose.
3. Write an expository composition which supports the thesis with textual evidence and interpretation.
4. Demonstrate an understanding of literary art as purposive.

LEARNING EXPERIENCES

TOPIC I: WRITING AN ESSAY ABOUT A NOVEL FOR ADVANCED STUDENTS

Lord of the Flies, by William Golding, is an ideal novel to use in teaching capable students how to study a literary work in terms of the author's purpose. Golding has written a chilling story of boys fighting one another for control of an island on which their plane has crashed during evacuation from the battle zone of some future war.

The story provides enough excitement and suspense to guarantee that secondary school students will read it without complaint. This major asset is, however, only the beginning.

Students tend to read the book in such haste—to find out what happens—that they fail entirely to recognize another level of meaning that the author is conveying through the story of these little boys. Yet this second level of meaning is undeniably present and is worked out in complete detail, with the involvement of practically every element in the book.

Once your students have read and enjoyed the story, then, a splendid opportunity exists to lead them in a search for more serious purposes the author might have had in writing the book. While many students resent and resist being *told* that something exists in a book which they have failed to see, if allowed the pleasure of discovery for themselves, they will relish the new learning and consider it their own. It is very important, therefore, that your students' next entry into the book be truly a search and not a lecture which many students will regard as an effort by the teacher to demonstrate his or her superiority. (What teacher has not experienced the pulling back, the negativism, the downright hostility that goes with, "You're reading things into it!")

Fortunately, in *Lord of the Flies* there exist any number of characters and other elements which serve a symbolic purpose beyond the simple plot level. And, very fortunately, many of these are so completely and so obviously worked out in the course of the book, with various clues to dual purpose repeated over and over throughout, that the most recalcitrant student will be successfully led to satisfying discoveries. It is for this reason that we have chosen *Lord of the Flies* to serve as our example in this sample unit on writing about a novel. But, of course, our suggestions can be applied to any novel the class is studying.

The sequence of activities in the sample unit is designed to guarantee that each student 1) arrives at agreement on the symbolic purpose of one character, as a result of a search by the whole class led by the teacher; 2) learns the technique of tracing one element through a book to see the author's complete purpose for that element; 3) gains practice in such inductive study while working with a small group; and 4) successfully makes such a search on an independent basis and writes an expository paper about his or her discovery.

1. *Activity.* After students have read *Lord of the Flies* at least once, work with the total class in tracing the character of Simon through the book, examining everything he says, does, thinks, and feels, and any other mention that is made of him. Keep a list on the board or on paper of every detail from the book that relates to Simon. Your list is likely to look something like this:

   DEVELOPMENT OF SIMON

   1. *He faints, and the boys laugh. (He is different.)*
   2. *He smiles pallidly at Ralph and says his name is Simon.*
   3. *Ralph chooses him to go explore the island. The boys around Simon giggle.*
   4. *Simon walks between Jack and Ralph—they look at each other over his head.*
   5. *Simon strokes Ralph's arm, shyly.*
   6. *Simon suggests they make a map on bark.*
   7. *Simon looks at Ralph and Jack and nods.*
   8. *Simon sees buds of a bush and says, "Like candles. Candle buds." Ralph says, "You couldn't light them." Jack says, "We can't eat them." (The spiritual Simon, practical Ralph, hunter-killer Jack)*
   9. *Simon says, "Blue flowers." (Ralph says, "Food and drink"; Jack says, "Rocks.")*
   10. *Simon stands up for Piggy: "We used his specs . . . He helped that way."*
   11. *Simon is the only one who helps Ralph build shelters. (Carpenter)*
   12. *He supports Ralph: "You're chief. You tell 'em off."*
   13. *Simon speaks freely about the snake, the beastie. He says, ". . . as if it were real." "Simon intent . . ." as Jack and Ralph discuss the beast.*
   14. *Ralph and Jack agree about Simon, "He's queer. He's funny."*
   15. *Simon is described in detail as he goes into the forest "with an air of purpose."*

16. *Simon pauses to feed the children in a scene described in terms of beauty and brightness.* ("Suffer the little children to come unto me . . .") *This is an insight that might not come until* after *the many parallels to Christ have brought students to a realization of Simon's purpose in the book.)*

17. *He goes into the jungle to a little enclosed place* on a rock, *described in terms connoting a religious place: the candle buds, the canopy, the white petals, the scent.* "Holding his breath he cocked a critical ear at the sounds of the island."

18. *When the boys see a ship, Simon "stood, looking from Ralph to the horizon."*

19. *". . . but Simon cried out as though he had hurt himself, 'Ralph! Ralph!' "*

20. *"Simon put out his hand, timidly, to touch Ralph. . . ."*

21. *"Ralph cried out, 'Oh God, oh God!' and Simon caught his breath." (Almost as if he were the one being called on.)*

22. *On the mountain top, when Jack and his hunters arrive, Simon looks from Ralph to Jack, "as he had looked from Ralph to the horizon." He seems to see the "black" and "white" confrontation coming up (hunting and killing as opposed to building the fire—the link to rescue, civilization). "Piggy sniveled and Simon shushed him quickly as though he had spoken too loudly* in church."

23. *Simon watches the confrontation between Jack and Ralph but says nothing. Jack knocks off Piggy's glasses and Simon "found them for him. Passions beat about Simon on the mountaintop with awful wings" as if the angels of good and evil were contending while Simon does not interfere with free will. "Awful" wings would surely refer to some fearsome being.*

24. *Simon gives his meat to Piggy and "lowered his face in shame," almost, it would seem, as if he were ashamed to participate in this obscene parody of a sacrament, performed with blood and the pig's flesh. Jack flings meat at Simon's feet and says, "Eat! . . . Take it!"*

25. *At the meeting following the scene on the mountain, Simon acknowledges going into the jungle alone, at night, to his special place. The laughter at him is now derisive, condemning.*

26. *Simon says, "Maybe there is a beast . . . Maybe it's only us." He sees that the beast is the evil in themselves, and he alone does not fear it because he alone knows no evil. ". . . laughter beat him cruelly. . . ." He is rejected.*

27. *"However Simon thought of the beast, there rose before his sight the picture of a human at once heroic and sick."*

28. *Simon "bashed into a tree." A sign of his illness?*

29. *Simon seems to read Ralph's mind, his fear. He speaks as if Ralph had spoken: "You'll get back to where you come from." Ralph seems to feel better about this assurance which he accepts on faith, and much later, when the savages have pinned him down, the words go through his mind. With no explanation, Golding inserts these words, "You'll get back," in the middle of that scene of Ralph's deepest defeat and despair. (Simon does not say, "We'll get back," but "You'll get back.")*

30. *When the boys come down from the mountain, thinking they have seen a beast and not knowing what to do, Simon says, "I think we ought to climb the mountain." He is jeered at, derided. Piggy asks, "What's the good of that?" Simon says, "What else is there to do?" In short, one must seek to know the truth, no matter what. Simon moves apart from the others when he is rejected.*

31. *Simon leaves the others and goes to his little place in the forest. He is there when the hunters put the pig's head on a stick wedged into the rock. He has a seizure (epilepsy?—the disease of the gods?) during which he is tempted as if by the Lord of the Flies to forget about the truth on the mountain top and go back to the others. He is tempted* not *to sacrifice himself. (Parallel to Gethsemane.)*

32. *Simon wakens, says, "What else is there to do?" and walks up the mountain. He sees*

that the beast is merely the corpse of a parachuted flier, a picture of death. He knows the truth, that the beast is "harmless and horrible" and he hurries to take the good news down to the others. ("How beautiful upon the mountain are the feet of him who bringeth good tidings.")

33. *Simon staggers onto the beach with the news "about a dead man on a hill" (Golgotha?). The boys are in an orgiastic state, dancing a ritual killing of the beast, and as Simon staggers into their circle with his good news, they see him as a beast and kill him. The heavens open and the storm breaks (as at the crucifixion). The wind rises, fills the parachute on the hill, and the figure of death is blown over the beach and off the island out to sea. (The burden of death is removed.)*

34. *Beautifully descriptive language describes the body of Simon as attended by "strange moonbeam-bodied creatures with fiery eyes." The creatures made a patch of light and "dressed Simon's coarse hair with brightness" (a halo). Silver, marble, pearls, all beautify his body. The earth turns, the tide lifts his "silver shape" toward the "steadfast constellations" (an ascension into Heaven).*

Then condense the list of minute details into a shorter list by combining related details into one idea. The resulting list may look like this:

1) *He is different; he is laughed at, derided, rejected.*
2) *Simon is a Hebrew name. Parallel to Simon Peter—Greek "Petros" for rock. Simon's little chapel was a rock—he gave Ralph faith he would be saved, standing on a rock. (Simon pure, Simon sorcerer, magician).*
3) *He supports Ralph, not Jack. He helps, he builds.*
4) *He is not afraid. Knows the beast is unreal. He has no evil in him, hence does not fear "the beast."*
5) *He stands between Ralph and Jack—good and evil. He does not interfere—free will.*
6) *When Ralph says, "Oh God, Oh God," Simon answers. He later answers thoughts in Ralph's mind. "You'll get back." Ralph accepts on faith, later repeats the words when in extremis.*
7) *He feeds the little children in a scene like Paradise.*
8) *He is tempted, as by the devil in the voice of an anti-Semitic schoolmaster, to forget the truth and join the others.*
9) *He climbs the mountain to get the truth, sees death, and frees the parachute.*
10) *He goes down and is killed by the boys who do not hear his words of reassurance.*
11) *Death is freed and leaves the island.*
12) *Simon ascends into Heaven.*

At some point in the process of tracing all the details about Simon through the book, some student will doubtless recognize the similarities between Simon and Christ. (And at that point you will doubtless want to teach the literary term, "Christ figure.") If you're fortunate, by the time you have collected all the details about Simon and organized them, virtually all students in the class will be convinced that Simon is indeed a "Christ figure." You may then wish to discuss biblical parallels, cautioning students that the parallels found in *this* book are not customary as part of the development of a Christ figure. Conclude the discussion by helping students see how a complete understanding of Simon helps in understanding the whole book: This is a religious book, basically, a parable about how lust for power dominates humanity's spiritual and rational capacities.

2. *Teacher Presentation.* Use the material below as the basis for an oral presentation to the class, or duplicate it (using Reproduction Page 22) and distribute it to

students to read and refer to in the future. If you reproduce the material, go through the sheet with students, answering questions, clarifying, and explaining. Help students understand how the material on this sheet summarizes the process they experienced in Activity #1 above.

How to Close Read a Novel

1. Watch for repetitive elements or words. Circle or underline each and keep, on the inside back page of the book, a record of page numbers for all repetitions. Such a record is a real time-saver when you get ready to choose a subject and write a paper or when you wish to participate in a discussion of the book or story. This technique is particularly helpful when a book includes a number of elements with symbolic meaning or when a character changes over the course of the work, as in *Macbeth*.

2. Watch for statements which, from a strictly literal point of view, do not make sense. When we read quickly, we tend to go right past such statements without noticing them. We are too eager to find out what happens. For instance, early in *Lord of the Flies* by William Golding, there is a statement which literally makes no sense but is very important in terms of the book's symbolic purposes: "Passions beat about Simon on the mountain-top with awful wings." Few students notice this sentence on a first reading. It is fruitful to watch for such revealing passages and to ask about them and to question why the author includes them.

3. Sometimes, in a novel or story, the author makes a comment that seems purely expository, an explanation, perhaps, or a descriptive phrase that seems aimed directly at the reader's understanding. The author is speaking in his or her own voice rather than in that of one of the characters, and it behooves the reader to "listen" well at such times.

    In *Lord of the Flies*, for instance, Golding generally speaks through Ralph or sometimes Simon or Piggy, and engages in an idiom suitable to these young boys. It is noticeable, therefore, when, in the midst of a simply recounted action scene, the author says: "Simon became inarticulate in his effort to express mankind's essential illness." One must suspect that the author is talking to the reader here. Or when Golding says, in describing the weeping of the "littluns": "They were reminded of their personal sorrows; and perhaps felt themselves to share in a sorrow that was universal." Or of Ralph, he says: "He wanted to explain how people were never quite what you thought they were." We must learn to see when the author is addressing us, the readers, and deliberately trying to help us understand his or her deeper purposes.

4. Continually ask the question *Why*, when some element of the book seems to represent a deliberate choice by the author from among a number of possibilities. Why was the fire built on the mountain-top and later moved down to the sand? Why was Jack red-headed? Why did the littluns "buzz" when Jack clouted his knife into a tree? Remember, none of these things really happened; the author made them all up. Assume that he had reasons and try to discover them by asking why.

5. If you wish to make a serious study of any literary work, read it at least twice, once to find out what happens and the second time to find out why it happens and what it all means. The second time through, you should have pen or pencil in hand, marking significant words and passages.

3. *Teacher Presentation.* Use the material below as the basis for an oral presentation to the class, or duplicate it (using Reproduction Page 23) for students to read and keep for future reference. Go through the list with the class, making sure that students understand that these are the *types* of questions that they should ask about *any* book.

**Kinds of Questions to Ask Yourself in Order to Come up with Answers
That Can Provide a Thesis Statement for an Essay of Literary Commentary:**

1. What was the purpose of the _____ incident in this novel?
2. What did the author reveal about the main character by showing him or her as _____?
3. What purpose was served by having _____ treat _____ as he or she did?
4. What was the relationship between _____ and _____? What purpose did the author have in developing this (enmity, friendship, etc.)?
5. Why is it that the author chose to show the mother as a stronger person than the father? (or vice versa?)
6. Why did the author continually emphasize the hero's deep love for _____? What is the author trying to show about the hero?
7. How did the hero react to adults? Are there exceptions? Why? What is revealed by these reactions?
8. Are there religious references? Biblical parallels? Why?
9. Are there constantly repetitive elements? Why? What is the author accomplishing through such emphasis by repetition?
10. Are there symbolic elements? What are they? What larger meanings are suggested by these specific symbols?
11. Is the leading character always sympathetic? Do you identify with the leading character—like the person—always? If so, or if not, why do you suppose the author chose to work it out this way? What is the author showing?
12. Does the author change the kinds of language at various places in the book? Why?
13. Why does the author keep using such and such a word throughout the book, when many other synonyms actually could say the same thing?
14. What purpose is served by the title of the book?
15. Why did the author choose a particular setting?

4. *Activity.* Assign students to small groups of three to five each. Have each group trace one element through the book, attempting to arrive at a conclusion as to the author's symbolic purpose. Let every group choose what element it wishes to trace, using the questions on the worksheet introduced above (Reproduction Page 23) for suggestions. The following could also be used to help small groups select an element to trace: *Why* did William Golding so emphatically and often mention the following in *Lord of the Flies:* butterflies, droppings/dropped, rocks/the big rock, birds, blue flowers, creepers, the scar, the sea, microcosms, the colors red, pink and white, littluns, Percival Wemys Madison? Have the small groups follow these steps in performing the task:

   1. List each appearance of the element in the book.
   2. Attempt to find a logical and consistent interpretation of these repetitions that leads to a conclusion as to the author's purpose.
   3. Choose one member, representing the group, to make an oral presentation of the group's conclusion (*generalization*) and their supporting textual and interpretive detail (*specification*).

After each presentation encourage all class members to ask questions and join in discussion of each group's presentation. Focus particularly on whether they agree with the group's interpretation: is it consistent with their own reading of the book? If students have difficulty drawing generalizations from repetitious elements, reassure them that there is no shame connected with inability to come to a conclusion about some elements. The search is the thing, and pleasure in searching should not be spoiled by uncertainty as to the author's purpose. For instance, we remember a group of students who spent a vigorous and exciting week exploring the meaning of the constant repetition of the words *red* and *pink* in *Lord of the Flies*. They were never satisfied with their own tentative conclusions, but by week's end they were all thoroughly addicted to the pleasures of the search.

5. *Teacher Presentation.* Use the material below as the basis for an oral presentation to the class, or duplicate it (using Reproduction Page 24) and distribute it to students to read and refer to in the future.

Preparing to Write a Paper about a Novel in Terms of the Author's Purpose

One does well to remember that an author setting out to write a novel faces many, many decisions. The author must decide, first and overall, what "statement" he or she wishes to make, what comment about the world and/or the human condition. (This we call the theme.) And then, the author must decide what characters and what events, occurring in what place and under what circumstances, will best reveal or demonstrate the chosen theme. (Or perhaps the author starts with the story and sees in it a theme to be developed by careful selection of details.)

But these gross decisions are merely a beginning. Think how many minute selections the author must make: what color shall the hero's hair be? How tall is he? Where was he born? In what idiom does he speak? What is his disposition? How does he get along with his family, with friends, etc.? And how about the leading character's best friend? And the heroine? Is she sweet and gentle or tomboyish and slangy? What setting will best serve thematic purposes? What scenes—dramatic events—must occur to work out the plot? Who shall tell the story: the leading character, a bystander, an omniscient author, etc.? Which serves the author's purposes most efficiently? All these and literally hundreds of other questions must be answered in the writing of the novel.

How do you suppose the author answers all these questions? Some of them are doubtless answered very easily. Maybe it doesn't matter in the least what color the hero's hair is—unless you're Golding writing *Lord of the Flies,* and you need to portray Jack as one kind of boy and Ralph as another, and so give Jack red hair and Ralph light hair. Maybe it wouldn't really matter what the setting is, unless you are trying to show the difficulties children have in growing up amid racial prejudice and bigotry as in *To Kill a Mocking Bird*. Then it becomes important indeed that the small Southern town be carefully portrayed. In *Heart of Darkness* it is important that Marlowe sits with legs crossed like an "idol"—like some "eastern god." It is important that shoes keep turning up in the jungle, that words denoting or connoting light and dark are constantly used. One wonders how Conrad could keep so many purposes in mind, as well as all the ways to fulfill those purposes.

The study of a novel should, if pursued skillfully, reveal the author's purpose or purposes. Remember to begin with the question: Why? Why is that in the book? Why is this character shown as antagonistic to that character? And so on. Finally, you arrive at an understanding of the overall purpose (theme) of the book. Once you feel that you know this larger purpose, you can check on everything in the book, to see whether it is consistent with this larger purpose. Once you know that Golding in *Lord of the Flies* is showing the evil in people that wrecks all we try to build, you can check through the book to see if or how everything in it supports that purpose. If you find elements in the book that don't make contributions or that actually are not consistent with it, you have grounds on which to make negative criticism of the book.

To prepare to write a paper of literary analysis or criticism, it is wise to ask yourself questions beginning with "why." Why is this in the book? Why did the author have this happen as it did? Then, when you have arrived at the answer, you have the thesis for the paper. Examples: By doing so and so, John Doe accomplishes the dual purpose of showing the hero's inability to cope with his wife as well as the tendency of people to interfere where they are not wanted. 2) In such and such a book, John Doe uses the rain to create an atmosphere of darkness and gloom, as well as to screen the events from reality as if they were occurring behind a curtain. 3) Golding accomplishes a number of important purposes by having the bright faced little boy named Simon.

6. *Teacher Presentation.* Use the material below as the basis for an oral presentation to the class. You may wish to duplicate the material (using Reproduction Page 25) so that students have the list in front of them as you explain it and so they will have the material to refer to again when they write their first paper about a novel. Go through the steps with students, explaining and clarifying each.

Steps in Writing a Paper about a Novel

1. Ask yourself questions about the author's purposes. These questions should all begin with "why," or "what did the author accomplish by . . . ."
2. When you've read the book thoroughly enough to think of a good question, study the book with this question in mind, and use the answer as the thesis for your paper.
3. Introduce that thesis in the first paragraph. Many writers feel that the best place for the thesis statement is at the very end of the introductory paragraph. They believe that one does well to lead up to it by general statements about the book in which mention is made of the name of the book, the name of the author, and the general gist or purpose of the book. This introductory paragraph might be planned as if it were a funnel: it opens with a broad, general statement about the book and narrows down to the specific statement which you intend to develop in your paper.
4. If your thesis statement is a limited one which doesn't have to be divided into various parts, you are ready to develop it, to make it specific instead of general by writing with details. If your thesis needs explanation, explain it, and then make it clear by giving examples from the pages of the book.
5. If your thesis is a complex one and needs dividing into parts, name those parts—they comprise your "outline." Each of these now needs to be explained and made clear with examples from the book. (The pattern for each is: state it, explain it, give examples of it.)
6. Remember that you write by paragraphs, and that you never handle more than one idea in one paragraph. If you have many examples from the text, you usually do well to devote a paragraph to each example.
7. It is seldom sufficient simply to announce an example and let it lie there without any interpretation. It's up to you to show the readers exactly how the example supports your thesis. Don't trust the readers to figure out anything for themselves, because they won't. That's your job.
8. Don't madden your readers by referring to your examples only by page number. Maybe they are reading another edition of the book and the pages are different. Besides, you have no right to ask extra work of your readers. It's your job to explain references by their context.
9. If you're lucky and throughout the book there are many demonstrations (what we're calling examples) of the validity of your thesis, you won't want to bore your readers to death with all of them. Instead, select those which are most significant to the book and will be most convincing to your audience.
10. Plan your paper from beginning to end before writing. Know what points you intend to make, how you intend to make them, and the textual references you intend to

use to prove them. And decide on the order in which you will do these things. Then—and not before—start writing.
11. Use your last paragraph to wind up, summarize, and restate your thesis in different language.
12. Proofread for errors in grammar, spelling, and punctuation.
13. Relax. You did your best.

7. *Activity.* Have each student select one element of the novel and trace that element throughout the book to discover the author's purpose for that element on the symbolic level. See the list below for suggestions of topics in addition to those mentioned in Activity #4. The student should follow these steps:
1. List each appearance of the element in the book.
2. Attempt to find a logical and consistent interpretation of these repetitions that leads to a conclusion as to the author's purpose.
3. State this interpretation as a thesis sentence.
4. Develop the thesis sentence using textual evidence collected in step 1 and interpretation of that evidence.

Remind students that this essay can be approached just like any other essay in terms of organization, etc. See Chapters 2 and 3 in *A Guidebook for Teaching Composition,* the companion volume for this book. To assure that each student has a successful experience writing the paper, you may wish to confer with each student at each stage of preparation: 1) choice of element, 2) listing of details from the book, 3) interpretation of details and formulation of thesis, 4) outline of development of essay.

Suggested Topics

Ralph—the civilization builder, doing his best to establish a just society for all
Jack—the hunter with a lust for power, seeking to control by force
Roger—the sadist—the absolute, irresponsible, totalitarian dictator is possible in him. Had the boys not been rescued, he would have unseated Jack.
Piggy—man's rational capacity, in thrall to self-interest
Simon—man's capacity for good, his spiritual self
Sam 'n' Eric—the conformers, the cannon fodder
The conch—the symbol of parliamentary rule, protection of the weak by law
glasses—the ability to see clearly, to perceive what is best, destroyed by Jack's power
the fire—represents religion, the hope of returning to God, brought down from the mountain, built on the sand
the sun—like the finger of God
the breezes—the author's pointer, like a spotlight, always points to where attention should go
the scar—like a birth scar, or a birth mark or defect—on the island or on the little boy who first feared the "beastie" and who was burned up
the masks—the ritualization of evil, means of hiding self from self, shedding cultural inhibitions
the beast—three meanings: pig's head on a stick, the fantasy tempter in Simon's "dream," and symbol of the evil in the boys (in humanity)
the "flies"—the little boys "buzzed" when Jack brandished his knife; the followers of Beelzebub, the Lord of the Flies, the devil
the title—Lord of the Flies
the names of boys—meanings and derivations
Piggy's asthma and nearsightedness, etc.

8. *Teacher Presentation.* Reproduce and distribute to students the essay below, written by a high school student. Use Reproduction Page 26 to make a master for spirit duplication; or project it using the overhead or opaque projector. Explain to students the ways that Cohn's paper embodies the principles discussed previously and suggest that they use it as a model for their own essays about a novel.

The Symbolic Use of the Color Green in
Lord of the Flies

Ken Cohn
(12th grade student)

<u>Lord of the Flies</u>, by William Golding, is the story of boys evacuated from England during an atomic war at some unspecified future time. The boys land on a tropical island in a passenger tube which drops from a flaming airplane, and in their struggle for survival they encounter conflicts similar to the antagonisms of the society from which they have come. But without the traditional society and the guidance of adults, the natural evil in the boys overwhelms their weak social system, and their civilization itself is threatened. In the plot Golding's major theme becomes apparent as an attempt to display evil as the inborn characteristic of man which gives rise to the defects of a community. In order to present this theme, Golding builds a many layered structure interwoven with numerous motifs with varying degrees of prominence. An inconspicuous but highly significant motif is the word green.

Green has almost innumerable meanings but is often used to express the idea of immaturity or inexperience. The meaning of these two words can be combined into one specific word, innocence, meaning the innocence of the child and the innocence of nature. Nature is green and nature is innocent. But it is the innocence of the wild and the untamed, for the quiet forest cannot conceal the bitter fight for survival among the different species of animals. A child is innocent, and the child is also "green." Hidden behind the mask of innocent youth is an animal instinct and desire. When the natural instinct of man becomes apparent, he has become "green"; he has become like the wild animal. In the novel the retrogression of the boys from civilization to savagery is paralleled with the motif green which first describes the "feathery tops of the palms" but later describes the green which the boys crave.

In the beginning of the story Golding describes the "green feathers" of the palm tree and the "dense green" of "the jungly flat of the island." These phrases introduce the reader to the idea that green is a symbol of the natural state. Similar statements are made throughout the novel in order that the reader will continue to associate green with nature. Further into the book the author attempts to show the reader the different sides of nature. Reference is made to "waxen green" flowers and the "green candle-like buds" which surround Simon's "little cabin." But there is also reference to "a mass of twisted stems, black and green and impenetrable." The former is representative of the peaceful and beautiful side of nature, and the latter is representative of the wild and ugly side of nature. This idea of green as a force of nature must be kept in mind while considering all other repetitions of the color.

After the motif green is established as a symbol of nature's power, the reader notices how frequently the boys have been found in green shadows. At the beginning of the novel when Ralph removes his clothes to go swimming, he "stood there among the skull-like coconuts with green shadows from the palms and the forests sliding over his skin;" when he leaves the water he "decided that the shadows on his body were really green." Shortly after, Ralph blows the conch and watches the boys coming up the beach, "their heads clustered above the trunks in the green shade." Golding narrates: "Some were naked and carrying their clothes, others half naked, or more or less dressed . . ." It is *through these references to green that Golding begins to build a parallel to the retrogression of the boys. The clothing which they have shed is the first link to civilization which they have broken. It is indeed ironic that at the end of the novel, the boys are rescued by a naval officer who also stands in a "green shade."*

At this point Golding presents the reader with an outstanding analogy to his theme. While Piggy and Ralph are speaking of the conch, Piggy tells where he has seen another. Someone he knew "had it on his garden wall . . . . He had some white stones too, an' a bird cage with a green parrot." The conch was suspended on the wall for everyone to admire and respect, but the green parrot was in a cage. To be allowed in society, green must remain caged or hidden. Otherwise, this inborn characteristic of man becomes apparent and leads to the defects of society. In effect, Golding is presenting a summary of his theme in the words of his intellectual character, Piggy.

With the progression of the story, the boys become more dependent on materials associated with green. They procure food from the forest with "the palms that made a green roof." Even by "the place of assembly," one of the boys' major links to civilization, stand trees which form a "green roof." If the boys are to be rescued, they must build a fire which will emit smoke, and for this "green branches" are necessary. And with the retrogression of the island society, these dependencies become ironic. The forest which is necessary for the boys' survival is also believed to be the home of the beast. The pigs which provide the meat the boys cherish leave "olive green" droppings, and the boys believe droppings to be "the dirtiest thing there is." Also, the boys do not have enough organization to keep the fire, a symbol of rescue and hope, burning. The boys are even warned that "green" is responsible for their social decline. They believe the beast to be the threat to their survival, but as Jack, Roger and Ralph lie by the "soft ashes of the fire" and look for the beast, "green lights of nausea appeared for a moment and ate into the darkness." When they thought they saw the beast, "green lights were opening again and growing." Indeed, they were seeing the beast when they saw the green, for the beast was the natural or animalistic part of each boy, and this was exactly what green symbolized.

The boys pass from the stage in which they seek a dependency on green to the phase in which they crave green, to the point at which they actually "become" green. While Jack smears clay on his face before going on a hunt he says to Roger, "If only I'd some green!" But Jack and his followers do at last find green to smear on their faces, and it is then that the animal instinct in each becomes overwhelming. They become like the "black and irridescent green" flies. When they "attack" Ralph's camp for fire, Golding describes them as "Demoniac figures with faces of white and red and green rushing out howling, . . ." Later there are several references to the "black and green mask" that Jack wears, and Ralph attempts "to remember what Jack looked like"; he "cries out hopelessly against the black and green mask." But his cry is indeed hopeless, for Jack and Roger and their followers are now more animal than human. The "green glow" of the horizon is the author's symbolization of the animalistic state which now encompasses the island.

Golding finishes the novel with a highly significant reference to green in a description of the naval officer who, ironically, stands in "the green shade of the peak" of his cap. Although he represents the authority which the boys have needed on the island, he is also representative of the animalistic force which critically weakens the society from which he comes. It is ironic that the boys are rescued from the green which has lowered them to savagery by an adult who also stands in green shade. And it is indeed "the end of innocence" for all the boys on the island. They have seen the power in "the darkness of man's heart" and have witnessed the animal instinct which attempts to destroy every society.

9. *Teacher Presentation.* Discuss with the class the following suggestions for improving the style of an essay about a work of literature. Using Reproduction Page 27, you may wish to duplicate and distribute to students the list of suggestions. In some cases it may be best to let them write their first essay about a short story or novel before introducing this information, to preclude overloading them with requirements and directives on the first round. After the first paper is perhaps the best time to provide these "helpful hints"—either to help them revise the first one or before they write a second one.

   A. Do not use the title of the book or short story as the title of your paper about that novel/story. Instead indicate what you are trying to prove: "A Study of Point of View in Willa Cather's *Paul's Case.*"

   B. Identify the title and author of the work somewhere in the introduction of your paper.

   C. You may need to provide a one or two sentence summary of what the novel/story is about in case the reader is not familiar with it. Do not assume that other people know as much about the story as you; therefore, identify all characters, events, and the like.

   D. A specific detail from the story/novel can be introduced in several ways:
      1) By mentioning it in your own words. This involves no direct quotation from the story. For example:

         At the meeting following the scene on the mountain, Simon acknowledges going into the jungle alone, at night, to his special place. The laughter at him is now derisive and condemning.

      2) By incorporating a key word or phrase used in the novel/story by quoting directly only a word or two within one of your own sentences. For example:

         Simon gives his meat to Piggy and "lowered his face in shame," almost as if he is embarrassed to participate in this obscene parody of a sacrament.

      3) By quoting directly an important sentence or series of sentences:

         The church is foreboding to Jackie: "Within the old church was no stained glass; it was cold and dark and desolate, and in the silence, the trees in the yard knocked hollowly at the tall windows."

   E. Just like any other specific details in a paragraph, the details from the novel/story should not simply be listed after the topic sentence in grocery list form. Instead:
      1) Introduce the detail. But do not use an expression so obvious as "As this quotation shows..." or "The following quotation from the novel reveals..." Try using a colon to connect your generalization (interpretation) and the quotation (as in #3 above).
      2) Interpret the detail. Show how it proves your thesis. Do not expect readers to see the connection for themselves.
      3) Explain the detail.
      4) Provide connecting ideas between specifics, so that you leave no gaps in thought for readers to leap over.

TOPIC II: WRITING AN ESSAY ABOUT A NOVEL FOR AVERAGE STUDENTS

Lord of the Flies is not a book for every student. Reading for inference is undoubtedly the most difficult kind of reading, and, for this reason, students whose reading skills are not well developed might flounder unhappily if asked to study Golding's book. A very effective novel for such students is *Alas, Babylon* by Pat Frank. Frank's novel is not as intricately symbolic as Golding's, but it does have something important to say about our society, and it does, also, spin a tale so engrossing that student interest is easily maintained.

Alas, Babylon qualifies as science fiction, since it occurs in the future—albeit near future—and describes the survival and reorganization of an American community after an atomic war has destroyed the national government and the nationwide communication and transportation systems. It is evident that in the pre-war society people are valued in terms of wealth and status and afterwards they find their place in terms of the contributions they are able to make to the survival and rebuilding of society.

Individuals who before the war were considered to be socially inferior make positions of significance for themselves in the new society. Persons of affluence and status in the community before the bomb are often unable to change their values sufficiently to survive in a post-bomb society no longer motivated by money or social position. Randy Bragg, a middling and poorly motivated lawyer, apparently heading into early alcoholism, is challenged by the new situation to develop his latent strengths and become the natural leader of the post-bomb society. Contrasting the life of each character before and after the atomic disaster provides an effective means of studying the book, and students can find, to their satisfaction, that Frank did everything on purpose—there are no random elements in this book. It is a popular book rather than a highly "literary" one, but it is planned and written with admirable craftsmanship, and provides excellent practice in literary analysis by students who might not profit from working with a more sophisticated novel. For that reason we have chosen to use it as our example in this sample unit on helping average students write about a novel. But, of course, our suggestions can be applied to any novel the class is studying.

1. *Teacher Presentation.* If you think it is appropriate for the ability level of the class, reproduce and distribute to students the worksheet entitled "Preparing to Write a Paper about a Novel in Terms of the Author's Purpose" (Reproduction Page 24). Or use it as the basis for an informal presentation on the process of literary analysis more appropriate for the level of sophistication and ability of your students. Other material that may be useful to present to students can be found on Reproduction Pages 22 and 23.

2. *Activity.* After students have read the book at least once, conduct a total class discussion of the book, using questions such as those below. Or duplicate and distribute to students the list of questions (using Reproduction Page 28) and have them work in small groups to come up with the answers.

Study/Discussion Questions for *Alas, Babylon*

1. The title of the novel comes from the Bible (Revelation 18:9–10: And the kings of the earth, who committed fornication and were wanton

with her, will weep and wail over her when they see the smoke of her burning; they will stand far off, in fear of her torment, and say, "Alas! alas! thou great city, thou mighty city, Babylon! In one hour has thy judgment come.") Can you explain the significance to the book? What useful way of examining and discussing the book is provided by an understanding of the title?

2. Trace the character of Randy Bragg through the book. What changes occur in him, and what is their significance? (In short, why does Frank show him changing in these exact ways?) This question will require much thought and discussion. Perhaps you will need to reread the book, marking appropriate passages. You may want to wait to discuss this question, or you may think it helpful to do this problem early in your discussion. Whatever your decision, do the work carefully and thoroughly.
3. What comment does the author seem to be making through the development of Florence Wechek as the book progresses? Is this also true for Bill McGovern, Dan Gunn, Edgar Quisenberry, etc.?
4. Why does Florence have a cat, two lovebirds, and a tank of goldfish? What other animals are mentioned in the book? Why?
5. What part does religion play in the book? Does it seem to occupy the same position in Frank's post-bomb society as in your own?
6. Does Mr. Frank make any comment about the nature of law in this book?
7. Why do you think Frank included the incident about the "wolf" in the chicken pen?
8. What does the author have to say about race relations? How does he use the Henry family in this connection?
9. Why is Preacher Henry in the book?
10. Why is Lavinia McGovern in the book?
11. Examine the character of Edgar Quisenberry. What does Frank show us through this character? How about Henrietta, his wife?
12. The subject of death appears many times in the book. In what ways do the attitudes toward death in *Alas, Babylon* differ from those observed today?
13. Why do you believe, in the end, no one wanted to be taken out of Fort Repose?
14. Why is Alice Cooksey in the book? How is she characterized by Frank?
15. Examine Graf's role in the book. What purpose does he serve?
16. What is the significance of Porky Logan? In what ways does he relate to the author's theme? Why was he not the natural leader of the community rather than Randy?
17. What kind of person is Dan Gunn? How does he change? What do you think about his plan to marry Helen Bragg? Do you think they are in love? What do you think about her wanting to marry him before she knows for sure that Mark is dead?
18. Examine the purpose in the book of Bubbe and Kitty Offenhaus.
19. How does Frank characterize Helen Bragg? How are she and Lib McGovern different?

20. Through Helen and Lib, as well as other females, what does Frank seem to be saying about women?
21. Examine the relationship between the sexes. What might Frank be showing by contrast to our present society? Do men and women seem to be more different from one another in the novel than is presently true in our world?
22. Do standards of morality seem different in post-bomb society than in our own? Can you locate those portions of plot which reveal Frank's comments on morality? What is the root—the source—of morality?
23. What is the significance of Frank's mention of automobiles in the book?
24. What do you think of Ben Franklin and Peyton as compared to youngsters in our society? Does their outlook on maturing seem about the same as yours?
25. Why are Sam Hazzard and Bill McGovern in the book? How are their lives different from what they would have been without the bomb? Trace the ways they change.
26. Can you identify any minor characters who contribute significant meanings to the book?
27. What were the qualities in Randy Bragg which finally made him the natural leader of Fort Repose?
28. What do you think the chances of survival would be for your own family if you were caught in circumstances like those in *Alas, Babylon*? What kind of person do you think you might turn out to be?
29. What elements in your present world are better than those in the post-bomb world of Ben Franklin Bragg?
30. If you were to be stuck in a small group after a nuclear holocaust, who would you choose to be with and what would you take with you? What would you miss most? What would you gladly give up?
31. In *Lord of the Flies* William Golding seems to say that humanity is basically evil, and that our social structures mirror our inherently evil nature. Do you think Frank agrees with him?
32. Why do you think Frank implies that our society is similar to Babylon? Do you agree with him? Do you think we will come to the hour of judgment? Do you think we deserve to survive or deserve to be wiped out?
33. Do you believe we will eventually suffer nuclear cataclysm in this country? Do you want to be among the survivors, those who must face the "thousand-year night?"
34. Examine all references early in the novel to "life not being worth living." Why were those inserted? How do they contribute to your understanding of the theme of the novel?

3. *Activity.* To demonstrate to students the process of literary analysis, choose one character other than Randy Bragg (e.g., Florence Wechek, Bill McGovern, Dan Gunn, or Edgar Quisenberry) and trace the character through the novel, recording (as suggested for Simon in Activity #1 of the preceding topic) every reference to the character. Students should be able to see the changes that take place in the character as a result of the bomb.

4. *Activity.* As in Activity #4 of the preceding topic, assign each small group to make an exhaustive list of the details from the novel related to one element or theme. The study questions on Reproduction Page 28 suggest a number of possibilities. Perhaps the best focus for this activity is the change in a character; thus, each group could be assigned to trace one character from the novel (other than Randy Bragg and the one you used for Activity #3). See Activity #4 on page 83 for a detailed explanation of how to structure this small group activity.

5. *Activity.* Have students write an essay in which they describe how Randy Bragg is different at the end of the novel from the way he was before the bomb dropped. This is, of course, the same concept dealt with in the second study/discussion question on Reproduction Page 28. Another way to approach it is to indicate how Randy was different from Mark in the beginning and became much like him at the end. Use the instructions given for Activity #7 (page 86) to structure this assignment.

6. *Teacher Presentation.* Coach students on some of the stylistic conventions used in writing about literature. See Activity #9 in the previous topic.

TOPIC III: WRITING AN ESSAY ABOUT POETRY

As in the case of fiction, it is essential that the student setting out to write about a poem know what to look for in poetry, or, in other words, know how to identify *what* is there and know how to ask *why* it's there. The most successful essays written about poetry are the products of systematic, informed literary analysis rather than general opinion or pedantic rhetoric. Thus, although spontaneous emotional reactions to poetry are certainly important, if students are to write about poetry they must first learn to analyze a poem intelligently and critically. The focus of this topic, therefore, must necessarily be the skills of reading poetry as much as the skills of writing about it. Specific goals that must be met if the student is to undertake writing about poetry successfully are:

1) To come to an improved understanding of what poetry is and how it differs from prose
2) To learn to identify and comment on the following characteristics of poetry:
    a) Sound devices such as rhythm, rhyme, alliteration, etc.
    b) Metaphorical language
    c) Imagery
    d) Connotative language
    e) Symbolism and the universalization of specific experiences
    f) Originality and uniqueness, justification for the poem
3) To develop a critical capacity with regard to poetry, in terms of the above possibilities available to the poet; in short, to learn to respond to poetry in an informed and knowledgeable way
4) To develop personal preferences, and thus individual taste, with regard to different poets and kinds of poetry.

1. *Teacher Presentation.* Since many students will have already developed considerable prejudice against poetry long before arriving in your class, the first step you may need to take is to explore with the class the reasons for studying poetry. The material below can be used as the basis for this exploration. You may wish to paraphrase it in an oral presentation or, since it is available on Reproduction Page 29, you may wish to duplicate and distribute it to students to read.

Why Study Poetry?

Hardly any two people will agree as to exactly what poetry is. It appears that there are almost as many definitions of poetry as there are poetry lovers—or poetry haters! Unfortunately, many students number themselves among those who "hate poetry" or think poetry is "stupid," and one comes to believe that there is one definition of poetry which can help explain why this is. Samuel T. Coleridge, the great English poet and critic, said that while prose is words in their best order, poetry consists of "the best words in the best order."

In order to be sure of selecting, out of all those words available, the very best word to suit the purpose, the poet spends a great deal of time and effort in considering all alternatives and in finally choosing just the word that he or she is convinced is "best." In fact, it might surprise you to learn that a poet can devote years to writing one poem. Thomas Gray, for instance, spent nine years working on "Elegy Written in a Country Churchyard." (Undeniably, there are instances in which a poem is almost literally dashed off in final form during the white heat of inspiration— some Bob Dylan works are examples—but evidence indicates that such occasions are not frequent.)

Now, if a poet spends weeks or months—or even years—in writing a poem, how fair—or sensible—is it for a reader to say it is a stupid poem, or to say he or she doesn't like it, after reading it through just once, in the same way one reads prose? To read a poem as if one were seeking information or receiving instruction is to miss all that the poet has worked so diligently to create. In fact, to read a poem in such a way is usually to persuade oneself that poetry makes no sense, for it is hard to get the sense of a poem without reading it with care almost equal to that expended by the poet in writing it. We can hardly be expected, of course, to study a poem for weeks, months, or years, but is is certain that we won't get the advantage of the poet's talent and skill unless we read with a great deal more attention and awareness than we find necessary to expend on prose. Many students—as well as some people no longer in school—have not learned to read in this different way, in this more creative way required by poetry, and this is the reason they fail to get any pleasure out of poetry.

What is it, then, that you are supposed to be looking for, that you are supposed to discover when you read poetry with such care and sensitivity? What is supposed to happen that will make you decide you like poetry after all? These are the important questions. It is clear that if you don't know what you are looking for, if you don't know what poetry is or what the poet was creating for you to experience, it is going to be difficult for you to know how to react to it, and it is unlikely that you will enjoy it. It's hard to like something you don't understand, and, in fact, it's a temptation to say that the reason you don't see anything worthwhile in a poem is because there just isn't anything worthwhile there!

Yet, if you are fair and completely honest with yourself, surely you would not suggest that the countless people throughout the ages who have said that poetry has enriched their lives are liars or hypocrites or not very bright! No, you would certainly admit the likelihood that these people are telling the truth, that they have simply been able to find something in poetry that you have not yet learned to find.

The student's purpose, then, is to find that "something" that so many other people have found in poetry, not just so you will *know* more, or *understand* more, but so you will *enjoy* more.

Surely one of the major purposes of education is to enlarge people's capacity to enjoy life. And that purpose alone justifies the effort to learn to read poetry with understanding.

2. *Teacher Presentation.* Use the material below as the basis for an oral presentation to the class, or duplicate it (using Reproduction Page 30) and distribute it to students to read. If you reproduce the material, read through it with the class, answering questions and clarifying points as you go along. Specifically discuss and give examples of imagery, metaphorical language, symbols, etc.

"The Best Words in the Best Order"

You may already be asking yourself, "best for what?" If someone tells you that a dog, for instance, is *the very best one,* you immediately wonder, "best for what?" Best as a pet, best as a watchdog? As a hunter, as a retriever? And you do well to ask this same question about poetry. If, as Coleridge said, poetry consists of the best words in the best order, what purpose did he have in mind for the words to fill? Best for what? Best to convey precise information? Best to impress the reader with the poet's superior education? Or did he mean best to take up the least space or best not to stir up any unwanted questions?

It is at once apparent that one must identify a poet's purpose before it can be decided whether the poet did indeed choose the "best" words. "What was he or she trying to achieve with that word?" is the first question to be answered.

In a very specific sense, each individual poet has a separate and distinct purpose for each poem he or she writes. But in a more general sense, we can identify one or two overall purposes that poets seem to have in common, and then we can identify some very concrete aims which govern the words they choose.

First, here are two major poetic purposes that will give us some guidelines as to what all poetry aims to do:

I. *The Poet Shows Us to Ourselves.* He or she attempts to write so vividly, with so sharp and clear a focus, that we stand revealed to ourselves in our truest and deepest nature. The poet sees us, our world and our lives, and he uses words to reveal this vision to us.

II. *The Poet Creates an Experience for Us to Have.* The poet does not tell us about an experience or a place. The poet creates it for us, attempting to use words that evoke an experience, a vision, a feeling, or an emotion, so that we ourselves might experience what he or she has experienced and is recreating for us. The poet uses words to make us feel the same emotions, remember the same memories, hear the same sounds as he or she has felt, remembered, or heard.

In pursuit of these poetic aspirations the poet has at least six ways of using language which must be considered in choosing just the word which is best. It is these uses of language which will provide our standards for the word "best."

1. *The use of language to sound a certain way,* either to evoke some emotional response in the reader, to create a literary effect, to create a pattern which arouses the reader's attention on behalf of some emphasis the poet has in mind, to imitate some other sound which the poet wants the reader to think of, or for the simple purpose of decoration. Such use of language for its sound involves rhyme and rhythm as well as the sounds of individual words and combinations of words.

2. *The use of metaphorical language*—that is, saying one thing to mean another. In prose, particularly scientific or instructive prose, we try to say precisely what we mean. The poet, however, often says something other than what he or she means, but which arouses a more emotional response in the reader than precisely informative words would have done. For example, "I have measured out my life with coffee spoons" certainly evokes a sharper personal response than more precisely descriptive wording such as, "I have involved myself with trivial happenings all my life." The use of metaphor is an attempt to engage the reader emotionally, to make personal to the reader the experience being written about.

3. *The creation of images: imagery.* The poet attempts, with words, to cause the reader to imagine what he or she is describing or creating. The poet attempts to create images. These are appeals to the mind's eye, to the mind's ear, and so on. By using words which cause you to imagine the sound of bells pealing triumphantly, the poet successfully creates an image which involves you, the reader, in the poem. If he or she uses words which cause you to imagine the soft, furry feel of a little animal's fuzzy coat, then the poet has captured your imagination with a successful image, and has brought you into the experience created for you. Imagery often helps the reader have the experience the poet has prepared for him or her.

4. *The use of connotative language.* Different words which mean practically the same thing, so far as dictionary definition is concerned, still strike us differently and make us respond in different ways, perhaps as a result of experiences, memories, values, or habits that we associate with certain words. The poet knows this, and tries to figure out how readers will respond to these words and what their emotional reactions will be. The poet chooses specific words with an aim of evoking the emotion which best suits the purpose of the poem.

Certainly "a thrifty dame" calls forth a different response from "an economical woman" or "a penurious female," and "a tiny huddled kitten" strikes you as quite different from "a small, bunched-up young feline." The poet knows how he or she wants you to feel, and tries to choose words which you associate with that very feeling. The poet's sensitivity to connotation helps to capture your emotions.

5. *The use of symbols to make a specific experience or thing take on a more universal meaning.* Human beings seem to be the only animals capable of symbolism, as witnessed by the fact that we are the only animal with language. Words are simply symbols of things, symbols that we humans have chosen for our own use. We go far beyond this in our use of symbols, however. We tend to vest in one thing all the significance of another, as with our country's flag, for instance. We tend to consider the flag sacred because it stands for the country which means so much to us. We say that white stands for purity, black for evil. We say that water represents salvation, that the cross is the central symbol of Christianity and that a certain kind of star is the symbol of Judaism.

Poets often speak of specific things, but they know that our minds will leap to the larger meanings symbolized by those things, and they thus make larger the significance of what they are saying. A small green leaf thrusting up through snow is no longer just a natural phenomenon, but a symbol of hope, of renewal, of rebirth and of humanity's capacity for regeneration. Through symbolism poets make concrete things abstract and specific things general. They widen our vision.

6. *The use of original language.* Poets attempt to create unique expressions. They know they must be able to justify their poetry not only in terms of the significance and validity of its comment about the human condition, but also in terms of its originality and singularity. This standard applies both to the message of the poem and to its form, to the words the poem uses. The poet, therefore, strives to use words in new ways, to say things in ways they have never been said before, to imbue old words and phrases with new meanings in new contexts and to command the reader's attention with the uniqueness of his or her art.

These are some of the purposes a poet might have in mind when choosing a word. These are the standards we shall use in considering whether the poet has chosen the "best" word.

3. *Activity.* Using Reproduction Page 31, duplicate and distribute to students the material below ("The Sounds of Poetry"). Read through it with the class, giving them examples of each term. Then give the class a poem and have them, as a group, identify all poetic devices associated with sound or auditory imagery. Have them discuss why the poet uses a particular sound device—how effective it is, what it communicates, in what way it adds to or detracts from the poem as a total work, etc.

The Sounds of Poetry

Long before the alphabet was invented, there was poetry. Poems were recited and sung, not read. Therefore the sound of the poem was very important. Different sound effects were used for a number of purposes:

1. Rhythmic words and lines were more easily memorized and more easily sung than lines with no rhythmic flow.
2. Alliterative lines also were easily memorized. ("True is the tale I tell of my travels" is surely more memorable than "Accurate is the history I shall relate of my journeys.")
3. The poet-singer could hold an audience's attention more easily if there was interest contained in the word pattern in addition to the story being told. People enjoy patterns, rhymes, repetitive sounds and rhythms. This seems to be inborn, as even small infants respond with a seeming show of pleasure to such sound effects. Have you ever heard a little child crooning to itself, rhyming nonsense syllables: roon, spoon, doon, rote, cote, dote? Youngsters do this as naturally as they smile—it's only later that they need to be reminded of poetry!
4. It became the mark of a poet's craftsmanship—or of his or her art—to be able to make poetry sound like what he or she was telling about: a battle scene should be recounted in rough, bruising, strong language, but a lovely dawn scene should be described in soft, harmonious, flowing sounds. This unity of sound and sense is still a characteristic of the skilled poet.

Definitions

Alliteration - repetition of consonants, especially at the beginning of words, or of stressed syllables. In Old English poetry alliteration was a regular element of each line, but since then it has been used for special effects only.

Assonance - repetition of identical or related vowel sounds, especially in stressed syllables. (The spelling of the word is not pertinent; it is the sound which is assonant.)

Consonance - repetition of a pattern of consonants, with changes in the intervening vowels (a diller, a dollar, a duller scholar.).

Onomatopoeia - use of words whose sounds seem to resemble the sounds they describe (hiss, buzz, rustle, bang).

Cacophony - use of harsh and unmusical sounds, discordancy. (Adj.: cacophonous)

Euphony - a pleasant, melodious effect. (Adj.: euphonious)

4. *Activity.* Using Reproduction Page 32, duplicate and distribute to students the material below ("Metaphorical Language"). Read through it with the class, giving additional examples, answering questions and clarifying points as you go along. Then give the class a poem and have them, as a group, identify all instances of metaphorical language in it.

Metaphorical Language

Simile - a comparison between two essentially different items is expressly indicated by a term such as "like" or "as." (A pretty girl is like a lovely tune.)

Metaphor - a word which in ordinary usage signifies one kind of thing, quality or action is applied to another, without express indication of the relationship between them. (One says one thing to mean another.) (His name is mud. Her kid brother is a pain in the neck. He was a true Galahad. Life is a song.)

Synecdoche - a metaphor in which a part of something is used to signify the whole. Pronounced: sin-eck-doe-key. (She gave her hand in marriage. He bought a new set of wheels.)

Metonymy - a metaphor in which the name of one thing is applied to another thing with which it is closely associated. (The crown is secure. The press is irresponsible. Is there word from the capital?)

Personification - a metaphor in which either an inanimate object or an abstract concept is described as being endowed with human attributes, powers, or feelings. (Justice is blind.)

Hyperbole - extravagant exaggeration of fact used either for serious or comic effect. (He shook when he laughed like a bowlful of jelly.)

Kenning - a metaphorical compound word which names something in terms of function. The Anglo-Saxons often used kennings to describe the sea: whale road. (lipstick, spotlight, pencil-pusher, slave-driver)

Litotes - a deliberate understatement as if to avoid censure for boasting, to emphasize by indirection in order to get credit for modesty. (Not a bad halfback. Not a half bad little town. He is a man of no mean talent. I'd say she can hold her own.)

Paradox - a statement that seems absurd and self-contradictory, but which turns out to have a tenable and coherent meaning. (He who is last among you shall be first. He who would save his life must lose it. Fair is foul and foul is fair. So fair and foul a day I have not seen. (These last two examples are from *Macbeth,* an equivocal play rich with paradoxes.))

Oxymoron - a paradoxical statement combining two terms that in ordinary usage are contraries, such as "pleasing pains," "loving hate." (It was a bitter joy. Missing the plane was a fortuitous misfortune. Had he caught it he would have been killed.)

5. *Activity.* Review with the class the material on "The Best Words in the Best Order" used for Teacher Presentation #2 above (or from Reproduction Page 30). Then distribute a poem to them and have them, either individually or in small groups, identify each of the elements discussed.

6. *Teacher Presentation.* Use the material below to give students further guidance in what to look for in a poem. You may wish to paraphrase it in an oral presentation, or you may wish to use Reproduction Page 33 to duplicate and distribute it to students to read and keep for future reference.

Questions for Analysis of a Poem, or What Is in This Poem that I Can Comment on?

I. *Unity.* Every aspect of a poem should be planned to support the poet's overall purposes. All is unified around one aim.
   A. Tone. Does the poet create a mood of dread? Amuse you throughout with light-hearted humor? Plod along ponderously, seem very serious or pedantic, etc.?

B. Diction. What words can you identify that seem congruent with the poet's major purpose(s) for the poem? Does he or she use language that suits (or sounds like) the subject, as does Keats with the lazy, drowsy sounds in his poem, "Autumn"?

C. Rhyme - Rhythm - Alliteration - Consonance - Assonance. Does the poet use any of these poetic devices? Does he or she use hard, voiced consonants or soft, unvoiced, unstopped sounds? Do the sounds of the poem bear a relationship to the poem's overall subject, purpose, and mood?

II. *Purpose.* The poet's purpose must be revealed—for each poem—*in* the poem. If you cannot decide what a poem means or what kind of experience it was meant to convey, you must determine who is at fault, the poet or the reader. The poet creates a poem so the reader can have—from the words of the poem—the same experiences the poet had in real life; and so the reader can gain from the poem the same insight the poet gained from the real life experience.

A. What kind of experience is being created in this poem?

B. What insight do you seem to be expected to gain from this experience?

III. *Connotation.* What words can you identify that contribute to the emotional experience the poet means you to have? What particular words, in short, can you identify as having connotative value in the poem?

IV. *Metaphorical Language.*

A. What metaphorical (figurative) usages can you identify? Identify metaphors, similes, personifications, etc.—all ways the poet says one thing to mean another.

B. What emotional responses does the poet seem to want to arouse in you by this figurative language?

V. *Imagery.*

A. Can you identify all the images the poet uses—all the words or statements that make us imagine sounds, tastes, smells, sights, feelings?

B. Are there many different images in the poem?

C. Does the poet depend on one of the senses more than the others? (all sight images, perhaps—or mostly sound images)

VI. Do you find examples of original, exciting language?

7. *Activity.* Following is a sample poem and analytical chart which you can use as a demonstration model for the class. Have students read the poem, by projecting it using the opaque or overhead projector. (Use Reproduction Page 34 for making the overhead transparency.) Or make a master for the spirit duplicator from Reproduction Page 34 and distribute a copy to each student. To guide students in analyzing the poem, give each a copy of the blank Chart for Analysis of a Poem found on Reproduction Page 35. The chart has the same headings as the chart below, but does not have the data from the poem filled in. Lead the class as a whole in identifying the various elements in the poem that they can see and comment about. Have students fill in the chart as the discussion proceeds. Their completed charts might look like that below.

London
William Blake (1757-1827)

I wander through each chartered street,
Near where the chartered Thames does flow
And mark in every face I meet
Marks of weakness, marks of woe.

*In every cry of every man,
In every infant's cry of fear,
In every voice, in every ban,
The mind-forged manacles I hear.*

*How the chimney-sweeper's cry
Every blackening church appalls,
And the hapless soldier's sigh
Runs in blood down palace-walls.*

*But most, through midnight streets I hear
How the youthful harlot's curse
Blasts the new-born infant's tear,
And blights with plagues the marriage-hearse.*

CHART FOR ANALYSIS OF A POEM

Sound Devices	*Images*
Rhyme scheme: ABAB in each stanza	Marks of weakness and woe on every face
Rhythm: Iambic tetrameter	Cries of men, infants' cries of fear
	Chimney-sweeper's cry
	The hapless soldier's sigh runs in blood down palace-walls
	Midnight streets
	Youthful harlot's curse
	Sounds over and over of "cry," and of "sigh," "curse"

Metaphors	*Words with Connotative Value*	
mind-forged manacles	chartered	sigh
blackening church	mark	blood
runs in blood down palace-walls	ban	midnight
midnight streets	manacles	blights
the marriage-hearse	blackening	plagues
	appalls	hearse
	hapless	

Allusions	*Symbols*
	blackening church (religion)
	palace-walls (the state)

Original usages	*Other Notable Devices*
chartered streets	Repetition of *chartered*
chartered Thames	Repetition of *mark*
mind-forged manacles	Repetition of *every*
the blackening church	Repetition of *cry*
the marriage-hearse	Personalization - use of *I*

8. *Activity.* Using the completed chart breaking "London" into its components (from Activity #7 above), lead the class in discussing what comments they might

now be able to make about this poem. You might wish to use questions like the following:
1. What can be said of all the images? (They are all sad, all related to human misery.)
2. What is accomplished by the repetition of the word "chartered"? (The emphasis is placed on "planned, man-made environment, not natural.")
3. What is accomplished by the repetition of the word "marks"? (the idea of signs or "scars" imposed on man, not natural to him but the consequence of experiences)
4. Repetition of "every"? (emphasis on the universality of this tragic human experience)
5. What examples are given of mind-forged manacles (shackles to humanity devised by humanity itself)? (Call attention to the colon preceding the stanza naming the "blackening church" and the "palace-walls," symbols of religion and government, human-created institutions which Blake perceived as adding to our misery rather than alleviating it.)
6. In metaphors, the poet says one thing to mean another. In the metaphors we have identified, what does Blake say and what does he mean?
7. What associations, memories, or feelings are brought to mind by the connotative words we have identified? Do the words in our list have anything in common?
8. What does Blake achieve by writing in first person, as of a personal experience?
9. In your imagination, can you hear the cry of the chimney sweeper (perhaps a small child lowered into the chimney as was the custom)?
10. Remembering the words "chartered" and "mind-forged manacles," can you state in a sentence or two the insight Blake gained on his wanderings through London? Do you think we can gain the same insight by studying his poem? (Human beings have, themselves, created much of the misery that blights their lives.)
11. What are the *sounds* of this poem? What does the poet hear? What do we readers hear?

9. *Activity.* Divide the class into small groups of three to five students each. Challenge the groups to list the comments they now feel capable of making about Blake's "London." (See previous activities.) Depending on the grade level and talent of your students, these comments might range from a generalization suitable to be a thesis of a long critical essay to a statement that could be a topic sentence for a paragraph. Following are some examples you might wish to use to get students started:

Thesis Statements

William Blake's poem "London" creates a tragic view of 18th century city life.

In his poem "London," William Blake uses the repetition of certain significant words to emphasize his view that we are victimized by the civilization we have created.

The imagery in William Blake's poem "London" is powerfully appealing to both eye and ear.

Two of the most powerful metaphors in English literature are found in William Blake's "London," where he characterizes both church and state as ignoring and exploiting those they should serve.

The language of William Blake's poem "London" is rich in connotation.

Topic Sentences

The phrase "midnight streets" calls to mind many images.

The oxymoron "marriage-hearse" includes two opposing human experiences.

I can imagine the sound of the little chimney sweeper's cry.

Sometimes we are indeed as shackled by ideas as by actual manacles.

If I walked through any major city, I would see and hear the same marks and cries William Blake saw and heard.

10. *Activity.* When students have finished Activity #9 above, compile a list of all the possible comments the various groups feel they could now make about Blake's poem. Lead a discussion by the entire class of these comments, with emphasis on details in the poem which support the comments. It might be helpful to duplicate the entire list and give each student a copy.

11. *Activity.* Ask each student to choose a comment he or she feels able to make about Blake's poem and to develop it into either a paragraph or an essay, depending on your assessment of the students' needs and capacities.

12. *Activity.* Using Reproduction Page 36, duplicate and distribute to students a copy of Milton's "On Shakespeare." Have them read the poem and then—either in the total class, led by you, or in small groups—analyze the poem as suggested in Activity #7 above. You might wish to give each student a copy of the "Chart for Analysis of a Poem" (Reproduction Page 35). A list of the important elements in the poem is provided following the poem below, along with some general questions for discussion. After the class has analyzed the poem, have them formulate comments about the poem as in Activity #10 above. Then have each student choose a comment and develop it into a paragraph or essay (see Activity #11 above).

On Shakespeare

John Milton

What needs my Shakespeare for his honored bones
The labor of an age in piled stones?
Or that his hallowed relics should be hid
Under a star-ypointing[1] pyramid?
Dear son of memory, great heir of fame,
What need'st thou such weak witness of thy name?
Thou in our wonder and astonishment
Hast built thyself a livelong monument.
For whilst, to the shame of slow-endeavoring art[2]
Thy easy numbers flow, and that each heart
Hath from the leaves of thy unvalued[3] book

---

[1] (meaning pointing toward the stars)
[2] (most of us have to work hard at it)
[3] (it is so great it is beyond value)

Those Delphic lines with deep impression took,
Then thou, our fancy of itself bereaving[4]
Dost make us marble[5] *with too much conceiving.*
And so sepulchred[6] *in such pomp dost lie*
That kings for such a tomb would wish to die.

Metaphors
the labor of an age in piled stones
dear son of memory
great heir of fame
weak witness of thy name
in our wonder and astonishment,
    thou has built a monument
thy easy numbers flow
each bearer hath taken those lines
our fancy of itself bereaving
dost make us marble

Images
labor of an age in piled stones
star-ypointing pyramid
dost make us marble

Sound Devices

labor - age	hallowed - hid
pointing - pyramid	weak - witness
thou - our	wonder - astonishment
built - livelong	heart - hath
leaves - unvalued	Delphic - deep
Then - thou - our	make - marble - much
so sepulchred - such	would - wish

Words About Which One Would Ask, "Why?" (Here one finds connotation, symbolism, originality, implication, etc.)

"my" Shakespeare	*hallowed* relics - hid	easy numbers
honored bones	star-ypointing pyramid	unvalued book
piled stones	weak witness	Delphic lines
dear son of memory	wonder - astonishment	deep impression
great heir of fame	slow-endeavoring art	conceiving pomp

What is the poet's purpose in this poem? Does he fulfill it? Is it worthwhile?
Does he choose words throughout that are consistent with his purpose?
Is his writing creative rather than expository?
Is the language more connotative than denotative?
Does he use language figuratively with success? Does he successfully create images
    or does he rely on other poetic devices?
Does he use "the best words in the best order"?

13. *Activity.* Give students still another poem to analyze in the same way they analyzed "London" and "On Shakespeare." Have them work either individually or in small groups. An excellent poem for this purpose is "Field of Autumn" by Laurie Lee.

14. *Activity.* Advanced students may profit from being challenged to derive from their own individual analysis of a poem a comment which they can then turn into a thesis statement for an essay about the poem.

15. *Activity.* Have students choose a poem and give an oral explication of it before the class, basing their presentation on their own analysis chart.

---

[4] (taking us out of ourselves)
[5] (as still as marble in our thoughtful attention)
[6] (sepulchred = entombed)

16. *Activity.* Using Reproduction Page 37, duplicate and distribute to students the poem "Snow on Easter" below. Have them, working in small groups, analyze the poem considering all the elements introduced in the teacher presentations above. After the groups have finished, conduct a total class examination of the poem, making sure that students have perceived all the elements listed after the poem below (but not on Reproduction Page 37).

Snow on Easter

John Stephen Harris

The cast of mind that put a Hamlet through his paces
kept me working at his whether or not to be
as if the back and forth, each intellective strut,
could build me closer to the other lip of the abyss.
All the walking in my mind began to leave traces
before my eyes, and sunrise found me nearly
blind, eyes almost swollen shut
on the amazing Easter morning I was converted to my senses.
None of the natural shocks before or since
has, like snow on the pale blooming blood of the quince,
the burden of the bright and bent forsythia, so moved
my heavy wits, like a weightless cave-stone, or proved,
like my first breath of the honeysuckle cold,
how better bright the air is once they're rolled.

Sound Devices
distant rhymes in first eight lines: a b c d, a b c d
couplets in sestet: e e, f f, g g
thin, short, unevocative words in octave
long, full, slow, alliterative, assonant sounds in sestet
m: amazing, morning
b: blooming, blood, burden, bright, bent

Images
eyes swollen shut
snow on pale blooming
    blood of quince
bright and bent forsythia
breath of honeysuckle cold
moved my heavy wits
bright the air is
(rich images all in sestet)

Metaphors
Hamlet - representing the intellectual
intellective strut building me closer to the other lip of the abyss (bridging the void of
    meaninglessness by intellectual effort?)
walking in my mind (back and forth)
blood of the quince
heavy wits moved like a weightless cave-stone (once they're rolled)
honeysuckle cold
Easter - signifying rebirth
Resurrection, escape from the tomb - representing a conversion to the senses, to
    beauty, to emotion

"Snow on Easter" by John Stephen Harris. Used with permission of the author.

Allusions

Hamlet - "To be or not to be"
Shakespeare - "Cast of thought"
Biblical passages concerning the resurrection
Easter - Christianity

Symbols

Hamlet (the intellectual)
Easter (conversion, resurrection)

Connotative Words (Words About Which to Ask Why)

Hamlet	sunrise	converted	burden	heavy	cold
paces	blind	natural	bright	weightless	bright
strut	swollen	snow	bent	cave-stone	air
abyss	amazing	blooming	forsythia	breath	
traces	Easter	blood	moved	honeysuckle	

17. *Activity.* Working with the total class, examine the explication of "Snow on Easter" by Roger Zehntner below (available on Reproduction Page 38). Have students compare their own analyses of the poem (Activity #16 above) with Zehntner's.

"Snow on Easter" — An Explication

Roger Zehntner

John Stephen Harris' "Snow on Easter" opens with an explicit reference to Hamlet's famous existential soliloquy. "Cast of mind" is but Shakespeare's "cast of thought" and by alluding to it the poet cues the reader to an understanding of the poem's meaning. The "other lip of the abyss" is the goal for which the poet strives. It is the "abyss" of meaninglessness, and its "other" edge signifies existential completeness. The poet, like Hamlet, seeks to achieve a wholeness of being; but like Hamlet's, his struggles are ineffectual and unsatisfactory. Prince Hamlet, of course, was the eternal intellectualizer, philosophical and cerebral, but, alas, unable to will a sense of resolute meaning upon his life. The poet, in the initial lines of his sonnet, faces a similar dilemma and, like the melancholy Dane, approaches his existential plight in a similar, ultimately unsatisfactory manner. He hopes, by "intellective strut," to "build" himself, calculating like a careful mason, nearer to a sense of being, when life has purpose and yawning nothingness has been traversed. The poet, however, in the initial lines, fails to achieve his aim. His wholly cerebral labors leave his "eyes almost swollen shut," cut off from life's experience, and in the throes of a Hamlet-like meaninglessness. It is then that what Shakespeare termed the "native hue of resolution," the feeling of human potency, is at its lowest ebb. Thus, the poet, now sightless from his futile intellectual strivings, ruminates in the darkness of the night, symbolically in the darkness of existential despair.

The "sunrise," a near perfect pun foreshadowing the Christian imagery to follow, signifies the rejuvenation of the poet's spirit, his conversion to the value of living, to an exalted sense that one's existence is whole, purposeful, and satisfying. Appropriately, the poet now selects the Easter myth as the source of his imagery. It is, indeed, Christ healing the blind, restoring the "native hue of resolution" to the once despairing. This conversion or reconfirmation is eloquently and alliteratively contained in the last three couplets of

---

" 'Snow on Easter'—An Explication" by Roger Zehntner. Used with permission of the author.

the sonnet. The "natural shocks," again a Shakespearian borrowing, are all striking sensations — "pale blooming blood of the quince," "bright and bent forsythia" and "honeysuckle cold." These final lines are in marked contrast to the first two quatrains of the sonnet which are relatively imageless, comparatively blunt and composed in distant rhymes. Consequently, the poetic devices of the sonnet reflect its own theme. The narrative conversion from the barren intellectuality of the initial quatrains is dramatically marked by a profusion of images, metaphors and explosive rhymes in the ending couplets. The sonnet, therefore, exemplifying its own doctrine, and corresponding to the poet's revelation, has its own poetic "conversion."

Moreover, Easter allusions are particularly befitting to the poet's transformation when his intellectual preoccupation is abandoned. For the Christian, Easter is theoretically the most triumphant moment of his religious life, when the worshipper celebrates the ultimate value of his experience. He has achieved, hopefully, at least for one eternal moment, a glimpse of his salvation, when his life, with all its sinful weaknesses and mundane confusion, ultimately has meaning. For the poet, a nearly identical psycho-emotional experience transpires, although with wider pantheistic aspects. Easter here is used as the Christian metaphor for spring, the rebirth of nature. The Christian imagery emphasizes the Easter-like experience of the poet, the intensity of his renewed awareness, and signals his conversion to his senses. Thus, his "heavy wits," once dulled, have been "rolled," remarkably, like Christ's "cavestone," by the sensations of the new season. It is then that life is most sensible and most sensuous, whole and integrated, like a well-wrought sonnet, a breathing microcosm unto itself.

Finally, there is the significance of the poem's title. Snow, of course, symbolizes the barrenness of the winter experience, the season when the cosmos has "died" to be symbolically reborn in spring. Easter, as noted, signifies that rebirth. Thus, as initially hinted in the title and then developed in the body of the poem, there is, by the poet, a successful juxtaposition of metaphors — Hamlet's struggle for existential meaning representing the sterility of the intellect, the Easter narrative symbolizing the rebirth of the senses, and the dramatic change of the spring cycle - to express, symbolically, the evolution of being through sensual experience in the face of, and, perhaps, partly as a consequence of, our futile attempts to make rational sense of an essentially irrational world. Neatly imposed on these is the sonnet's poetic "conversion," reflecting through the richness of the images of the ending couplets, and the unifying tightness of its accompanying rhyme scheme, the thematic transformation. Indeed, "Snow on Easter" is a nice example of what Robert Frost calls "moving easy in harness."

18. *Activity.* Ask students to choose a poem or assign one to the entire class and have them write an analytical essay about the poem, following all the suggestions given in previous teacher presentations and activities.

19. *Activity.* The preceding activities focus primarily on analysis of a poem, and writing such an analysis, rather than on *critical* examination of a poem. However, under certain circumstances it may be valuable to help students develop guidelines for critical evaluation. For example, those students involved in evaluating the work of other students in determining what material to include in the school literary magazine will certainly need this skill. Also, students who are interested in writing their own poetry need a set of guidelines for assessing their own work. The following questions (which can be duplicated using Reproduction Page 39) are useful for both purposes.

Questions for Critical Examination of a Poem

1. *Is There Unity?* Every aspect of the poem should be consciously planned to support the poet's overall purpose. *All* is unified into one aim.
   A. *Tone.* Is there consistency in whatever tone is chosen, as opposed to slipping in or out of mood and feeling to no discernible purpose?
   B. *Diction.* Does the poet select words that consistently are congruent with the purpose? Or can you see instances when a different word would have been more suitable to the purpose? Are harsh sounding words used when writing of a butterfly? Are offensive functional words used when trying to arouse compassion or sympathy? Etc.
   C. Does the poet shift purposes anywhere in the poem—so that he or she seems in the beginning to be expressing one meaning, pursuing one purpose, and later in the poem seems to be writing on behalf of another?
   D. *Rhyme - Rhythm - Alliteration - Consonance - Assonance* — does the poet use incongruous mixtures of these literary devices? For instance, do the lines stagger along with broken and halting rhythms when describing the swift gliding of a sleigh over snow? This would be out of place and unsuitable in terms of unity. Does the poet use a sibilant hiss of s's when describing the piling up of granite blocks? This, too, would seem to violate principles of unity.

2. Is the poet's *purpose* recognizable?

   Is the poet's purpose revealed by what is written? *It must be.* If you cannot decide what the poem means—or if it means anything that you can express in words—or what kind of experience it was meant to convey, then you must determine who is at fault, the poet or the reader. If many readers fail to grasp the poet's purpose, the poet would do well to recognize a failure to communicate successfully with the chosen readers.

3. Is the poet's *purpose* fulfilled?

   Does the poet achieve what you believe (from reading the poem) to be the goal of writing it? Is the poem not only unified, but also whole and complete? Is it developed in detail, or does it remain on a broad, general, unimmediate level that evokes little personal response from you?

4. Does the *purpose* seem significant and valuable?

   Is the comment being made, or the experience being prepared, fresh and original—or moving—or stimulating—or insightful? Or is it trite—shallow—insignificant? Has the thought been conveyed often before—perhaps better? Is it a truism, self-evident and well known to most readers?

These questions are not meant to suggest that all poetry must be solemn and weighted with universal meanings. Of course, there is no such necessity. Humor, for instance, is entirely at home in poetry. But some purpose must be served, even if it is only to make us see something funny or ludicrous in what we have previously considered grave and forbidding.

5. Is the writing *creative* rather than *expository*?

   A poet is expected to create an emotional experience for the reader to have. A poet does not tell the reader—as in expository writing—in denotative, informative, symbolic writing, that he or she feels a certain way or has certain insights. Rather, the poet creates an arrangement of words that hopefully will evoke in the reader the same feeling or the same insight. The poet is, in short, performing the artist's half of the creative experience, and it is up to the reader to read creatively in order to respond "suitably," that is, by having the feelings and achieving the insight the poet intended. It is in the measure of the reader's success that the poet's success or failure is seen.

6. Is the poet's language successfully *connotative* as well as denotative?

    Poets are expected to create emotional experiences for their readers. To do their share, poets use words connotatively rather than denotatively. They choose words for their associations—for the memories or attitudes they evoke in the reader—and they rely on their knowledge both of words and of the life experiences of the people for whom they write. They would know, for instance, that in America the word "mother" awakens feelings of warmth and unconscious echoes of such associated words as home and love, whereas the word "mom" evokes negative reactions expressed in such words as bossy, possessive, and domineering. (Or at least this would be true of those who have read any of the several essays on momism in America.) When wishing to designate a female parent, therefore, the poet would make conscious choices of words in terms of the emotions he or she wishes to evoke in the reader.

7. Does the poet use language *figuratively*, in order to make meaning come alive to the reader?

    The poet uses words figuratively (metaphorically) rather than symbolically. The purposes of science are best served when each designative word used denotes exactly and precisely what it symbolizes. This is pure symbolic language, in which the words "test-tube" symbolize only the glass cylinder into which chemicals are put for testing. In poetry, however, the symbol may be used far less precisely or designatively. One might refer to a situation or an occasion as a test-tube, meaning not that it is a glass cylinder, etc., but that it permits or occasions testing of people. Thus the poet *says one thing to mean another.* This is called figurative, or metaphorical language.

8. Does the poet create *images* that appeal to the senses, arousing response in the imagination?

    Does the poet evoke sensory—imaginary—impressions by the use of words? Does he or she make us imagine sounds, tastes, smells, sights, or feelings and bring these sensory reactions into our imaginations? Do the images evoked suit the poet's purpose? Are they sharp? Is your imagination stirred?

9. Can every word in the poem be justified?

    A good exercise for any poet is to ask himself or herself, "Why did I use that word?" If it can be explained in terms of meaning, connotation, imagery, rhythm, rhyme, assonance, consonance or alliteration, or in a reasonable combination of any of these—or if it can be shown that there is no "better" word available (that is, better in the sense of what poetry is and what it demands in the use of words), then the word is justified. Get in the habit of asking why. Why is a comma there? Why break the line there? Why a yellow flower? The poet must be able to answer all the why's or stand convicted of random, purposeless behavior. A poet who answers, "Because I felt like it," is not in any way justifying his or her work but only justifying his or her feeling.

20. *Activity.* Divide the class into small groups (three to five students to a group). Give students a poem and have them analyze and criticize it using the questions above. You may wish to have them record their group's answer to each question.

21. *Activity.* Have students, working individually, locate five poems which they especially like and five which they strongly dislike. Have them write a brief explanation of why they like or dislike each poem. This should be written on a personal level and can be quite subjective. Then require that they list all the

positive and negative literary or poetic elements in each poem. Suggest that they use the list of "Questions for Critical Examination of a Poem" (above) as a basis. Then have each student compare his or her personal statements and the more objective critical evaluations—did personal preference influence his or her critical judgments, was he or she able to find positive elements in a poem he or she disliked? In general, what were the characteristics (revealed in the critical evaluation) of the poems that he or she liked or disliked?

RESOURCES FOR TEACHING STUDENTS HOW TO WRITE ABOUT LITERATURE

Below is a selected list of resources useful for teaching the skills of writing about literature. Addresses of publishers can be found in the alphabetical list on pages 111–113 in the Appendix. Prices, where given, are only approximate, since changes occur frequently.

Working with Poetry by John Shaw and Prudence Dyer. Deals with the explication of poetic devices directly related to critical analysis. Helpful discussion of symbolism, simile, metaphor, irony, sensory images, and a variety of rhetorical devices. Provides students with an understanding of the basic concepts needed for lucid, succinct analysis. Paperbound. Educators Publishing Service, Inc.

Writing Themes about Literature by Edgar V. Roberts. Detailed explanation of planning, organizing, and writing a theme. Examination of the general critique of a literary work (model critiques provided), analysis of a theme on a close reading of a passage. Discussion of many diverse types of essays about literature—metaphysical, comparison-contrast, historical, and character-oriented. Also discusses analysis of structure, style, and prosodic analysis of poetry. Provides examples and models throughout. Useful only for advanced students, and, better yet, as a guide for the teacher. Paperbound. Prentice-Hall, Inc.

Writing about Writing by Norman L. Haider. One of six titles in the Contemporary English Modules Series. Contains chapters on literary analysis of short stories, novels, plays, and poetry. Contains excerpts from several works, with accompanying exercises and assignments. Probably the only book on writing about literature for the average student or junior high school level. Paperbound. Silver Burdett.

Writing about Literature by Bernard Cohen. Almost as difficult as the above Roberts book, but much more comprehensive. Begins by teaching the student what to look for in a literary work, then discusses how to organize the essay about literature and explains stylistic and mechanical aspects. Too advanced for most students; excellent guide for the teacher. Paperbound. Scott, Foresman and Co.

A Preface to Composition: Problems in Structure by Jean McColley and Thomas Hemmens. Focuses on "The Portable Phonograph" as an example, and discusses how to choose a problem, gather evidence, organize details, etc. Paperbound. Prentice-Hall, Inc.

A Short Guide to Writing a Critical Review by Eliot D. Allen and Ethel B. Colbrunn. Detailed explanations of the critical review, outlining, analysis of the novel, short story, biography, non-fiction prose, poetry, plays and movies. Excellent sample reviews of literary works of all genres. Helpful diagrams and models throughout. Fine for all students. Paperbound. $1.50. Everett/Edwards, Inc.

Practical English Handbook by Floyd C. Watkins, William B. Dillingham, and Edwin T. Marin. An excellent handbook covering every aspect of writing including writing about literature—choice of topic, development, analysis as opposed to summary, substantiation of general contentions, originality, organization and structure of critiques. Model of an analytical paper provided. For advanced students or as a teacher resource. Paperbound. Houghton Mifflin.

APPENDIX A

Addresses of Producers of Resources

Addison Wesley Publishing Company
Reading, Massachusetts 01867

Allyn and Bacon, Inc.
470 Atlantic Avenue
Boston, Massachusetts 02210

Amsco School Publications
315 Hudson Street
New York, New York 10013

Applause Productions
85 Longview Road
Port Washington, New York 11050

Arco Publishing Company
219 Park Avenue South
New York, New York 10003

Argus Communications
7440 Natchez Avenue
Niles, Illinois 60648

Bantam Books
666 Fifth Avenue
New York, New York 10019

Barnes and Noble
Division of Harper and Row, Publishers
10 East 53rd Street
New York, New York 10022

Barron's Education Series
113 Crossways Park Drive
Woodbury, New York 11797

Channing L. Bete Company
45 Federal Street
Greenfield, Massachusetts 01301

Cambridge Book Company
488 Madison Avenue
New York, New York 10022

CEBCO/Standard Publishing
104 Fifth Avenue
New York, New York 10011

Center for the Humanities
Two Holland Avenue
White Plains, New York 10603

Citation Press
906 Sylvan Avenue
Englewood Cliffs, New Jersey 07632

Clarke, Irwin and Company, Ltd.
791 St. Claire Avenue, W.
Toronto, Ontario M6C 1B8 Canada

College Entrance Publications
104 Fifth Avenue
New York, New York 10011

Dodd, Mead and Company
79 Madison Avenue
New York, New York 10016

Doubleday Multimedia
1371 Reynolds Avenue
P. O. Box 11607
Santa Ana, California 92702

Eaton Paper Company
Pittsfield, Massachusetts 01201

Educational Research Associates
Box 767
Amherst, Massachusetts 01002

Educators Publishing Service
75 Moulton Street
Cambridge, Massachusetts 02138

Encyclopaedia Britannica Educational Corp.
425 N. Michigan Avenue
Chicago, Illinois 60611

Everett/Edwards, Inc.
Post Office Box 1060
Deland, Florida 32720

Eye-Gate
146-01 Archer Avenue
Jamaica, New York 11435

Filmstrip House
6633 West Howard Street
Niles, Illinois 60648

Folkways Records
701 Seventh Avenue
New York, New York 10036

Follett Publishing Co.
1010 W. Washington Blvd.
Chicago, Illinois 60607

Frederick Muller Ltd.
Victoria Works,
Edgware Road
London NW 2, 6 LE, England

Glencoe Press
8701 Wilshire Blvd.
Beverly Hills, California 90211

Globe Book Company
175 Fifth Avenue
New York, New York 10010

Greystone Films Inc.
Box 303, Kingsbridge Station
Riverdale, New York 10463

Guidance Associates
757 Third Avenue
New York, New York 10017

Harcourt Brace Jovanovich
757 Third Avenue
New York, New York 10017

Hart Publishing Company
15 West Fourth Street
New York, New York 10012

Hayden Book Co., Inc.
50 Essex Street
Rochelle Park, New Jersey 07662

D.C. Heath and Company
125 Spring Street
Lexington, Massachusetts 02173

Holt, Rinehart & Winston
383 Madison Avenue
New York, New York 10017

Houghton Mifflin Co.
2 Park Street
Boston, Massachusetts 02107

Independent School Press
51 River Street
Wellesley Hills, Massachusetts 02181

Interact
P.O. Box 262
Lakeside, California 92040

Thomas Klise Company
P.O. Box 3418
Peoria, Illinois 61614

Laidlaw Brothers
Thatcher & Madison
River Forest, Illinois 60305

J. B. Lippincott Company
East Washington Square
Philadelphia, Pennsylvania 19105

Littlefield, Adams, & Co.
81 Adams Drive
Totowa, New Jersey 07512

London Association for the Teaching of English
Blackie & Son, Ltd.
5 Fitzhardinge Street
London, W.I., England

Loyola University Press
3441 North Ashland Avenue
Chicago, Illinois 60657

Macmillan Publishing Co., Inc.
866 Third Avenue
New York, New York 10022

McDougal, Littell & Co.
P. O. Box 1667
Evanston, Illinois 60204

Mentor Book Company
1301 Avenue of the Americas
New York, New York 10019

National Council of Teachers of English
1111 Kenyon Road
Urbana, Illinois 61801

New York State English Council
Alan Nelson, Executive Secretary
Union College Humanities Center
Schenectady, New York 12308

Oxford University Press
200 Madison Avenue
New York, New York 10016

Pendulum Press, Inc.
The Academic Building
Saw Mill Road
West Haven, Connecticut 06516

Prentice-Hall, Inc.
Educational Book Division
Englewood Cliffs, New Jersey 07632

Prentice-Hall Media
150 White Plains Road, Box 186
Tarrytown, New York 10591

Random House, Inc.
201 E. 50th Street
New York, New York 10022

The Reading Lab, Inc.
55 Day Street
South Norwalk, Connecticut 06854

RMI Educational Films, Inc.
701 Westport Road
Kansas City, Missouri 64111

S-L Film Productions
P. O. Box 41108
Los Angeles, California 90041

Scholastic Book Services
904 Sylvan Avenue
Englewood Cliffs, New Jersey 07632

Scholastic Records
906 Sylvan Avenue
Englewood Cliffs, New Jersey 07632

Scott Education Division
104 Lower Westfield Road
Holyoke, Massachusetts 01040

Silver Burdett Company
Morristown, New Jersey 07960

Teachers College Press
1234 Amsterdam Avenue
New York, New York 10027

Teachers & Writers Collaborative
490 Hudson Street
New York, New York 10014

The University of Chicago Press
5801 Ellis Avenue
Chicago, Illinois 60637

J. Weston Walch, Publisher
Portland, Maine 04104

Westwood Educational Production
701 Westport Road
Kansas City, Missouri 64111

John Wiley & Sons, Inc.
605 3rd Avenue
New York, New York 10016

H. W. Wilson Co.
950 University Avenue
Bronx, New York 10452

Xerox Educational Publications
Education Center
1250 Fairwood Avenue
Columbus, Ohio 43216

APPENDIX B

Reproduction Pages

The pages that follow have been provided to facilitate the reproducing of exercises, sample compositions, and materials needed for activities suggested in the preceding pages. Each page is perforated to make removal from this book easier. Once removed, a page can be used in several ways:

1. *For projection with an opaque projector.* No further preparation is necessary if the page is to be used with an opaque projector. Simply insert it in the projector and the page can be viewed by the entire class.

2. *For projection with an overhead projector.* The Reproduction Page must be converted to a transparency for use on an overhead projector. Overlay the Reproduction Page with a blank transparency and run both of them through a copying machine.

3. *For duplication with a spirit duplicator.* A master can be made from the Reproduction Page by overlaying it with a special heat sensitive spirit master and running both through a copying machine. The spirit master can then be used to reproduce 50 to 100 copies on paper.

NAME _____ SECTION _____

The Person Sitting Next to You

Ross Snyder

Who is the person sitting next to you? You might say a name, and describe how tall he is, and the color eyes and hair. But none of these things are what the person is. A person is invisible activities.

Who then is the person sitting next to you? The person sitting next to you is suffering. He is working away at problems. He has fears. He wonders how he is doing. Often he doesn't feel too good about how he is doing; and he finds that he can't respect or be a good friend of himself. When he feels that way about himself, he has a hard time loving others. When he doesn't feel good about himself and finds it hard to love others, he suffers . . .

The person sitting next to you has a right to be a person; that is, he has a right to choose and decide, to have a private life of his own. He also has a right to be understood. And unless he can be understood by other people, he is thwarted from being a person.

The person sitting next to you is an inexhaustible store of possibilities. Within him are energies that have been only partially awakened. Nine-tenths of his potential has not been yet touched off. There are all kinds of good struggling to be born from way within that person. There are also worries, fears and hates that are struggling to get themselves expressed. Sometimes if only these could be expressed, he would be free to love other people.

Thus, the person sitting next to you is a cluster of memories of the past and expectations of the future. He is really a whole colony of persons, of people met all during a life. Something of these people has entered into this person forever. So that the person sitting next to you is really a city—a community. In that community live the father and mother of this person, the boys and girls who have played with him most, the people with whom he went to school; all the live things of this world that came and interacted with this person. They are still deep within . . .

The person sitting next to you is the greatest miracle and the greatest mystery that you will ever meet. The person sitting next to you is sacred.

Copyright © 1977 by Allyn and Bacon, Inc. Reproduction of this material is restricted to use with <u>A Guidebook for Teaching Creative Writing</u>, by Gene Stanford and Marie N. Smith.

REPRODUCTION PAGE 2

NAME_____ SECTION_____

Example of Labelling

INSTRUCTIONS: In the paragraph below circle all labelling (or subjective) words, that is, those that do not report the observable characteristics of the thing being described, but instead refer to the subjective reaction of the writer.

A.   Back-packing in the Colorado Rockies is a truly great experience. There's something really wonderful about hiking along Colorado's beautiful mountain trails with the amazing peaks towering overhead. There are literally countless different species of life on all sides, from majestic trees to colorful little wildflowers by the side of the scenic trails. Occasionally from a lookout point one can see across a lovely, peaceful valley where farms nestle in the serene countryside. And sometimes one follows for a while the exciting rush of an exhilarating mountain stream, fresh from the upper levels, soon to be a leisurely stream on the valley floor.

Copyright © 1977 by Allyn and Bacon, Inc. Reproduction of this material is restricted to use with A Guidebook for Teaching Creative Writing, by Gene Stanford and Marie N. Smith.

NAME_____ SECTION_____

Good Descriptive Paragraph

B.   Back-packing in the Colorado Rockies is an experience one will never forget and will long to repeat. Colorado's many miles of hiking trails are in rugged terrain unmatched for its natural, unspoiled beauty. Each trail has its own special character: one might wind through miles of shadowy white pine forests; another will lead through fields of granite boulders and over granite bluffs; and still another is bordered by small blue, yellow and pink star-shaped flowers. Over them all, in cold and silent majesty, tower the snow-covered peaks of America's highest mountains. Occasionally, from a barren, rocky promontory, one can look across a small valley, enclosed in the green lower slopes of the mountains. From a great height the farm buildings look like toys, and the fields make miniature patchwork patterns, with here a curving row of tiny trees and there a winding gleam of silver that marks a stream. The flood of water that swept down from the peaks, cutting a channel through granite with its force, flows quietly on the valley floor.

Copyright © 1977 by Allyn and Bacon, Inc. Reproduction of this material is restricted to use with A Guidebook for Teaching Creative Writing, by Gene Stanford and Marie N. Smith.

REPRODUCTION PAGE 4

NAME _____ SECTION _____

Identifying Labels

INSTRUCTIONS: Find every label word in the list below and indicate it by printing "L" beside it.

deafening	green	sexy
threadbare	fantastic	hateful
ugly	malodorous	fabulous
moss-covered	frayed	sturdy
close-cropped	bumpy	great
boring	unlikable	wonderful
awful	immoral	upturned
slow-moving	sharp-featured	awesome
curly	sweaty	bug-eyed
lovely	foul-mouthed	horrible
splotchy	adorable	ragged
capable	timid	purple
blue and white checked	fetid	right
pug-nosed	amazing	exciting
cautious	looming	obese
respectable	wild-eyed	leathery
appealing	interesting	wrong
reliable	bald	rancid
pink-eyed	swarthy	inadequate
rascal	itchy	prudent
ideal	dumb	law-abiding
fuzzy	decent	attractive
oval	admirable	active
growling	sickening	inert
blinding	square-jawed	gleaming
disgusting	popular	graceful
memorable	irregular	alarming
crooked	gorgeous	straight
fitful	noteworthy	
impressive	unacceptable	
heroic	remarkable	
winding		

Copyright © 1977 by Allyn and Bacon, Inc. Reproduction of this material is restricted to use with <u>A Guidebook for Teaching Creative Writing</u>, by Gene Stanford and Marie N. Smith.

REPRODUCTION PAGE 5

NAME _____ SECTION _____

Summarizing Details

INSTRUCTIONS: For each list of descriptive details below, compose a sentence that states the impression you receive from the details or that summarizes all the details. Be as imaginative as you wish. Your statements can take many forms, depending on the imaginary context into which you place the situation suggested by the given details.

A. crickets rasping
   bass voice of a bull frog
   jar flies in trees
   leaves rustling
   screech owl in distance
   SUMMARY SENTENCE: _____
   _____
   _____

B. a huge, golden turkey
   a bowl of steaming mashed potatoes
   sweet potatoes swimming in golden syrup
   home made noodles
   stuffing in a bowl
   a platter of fruit
   a wooden bowl heaped high with greens
   SUMMARY SENTENCE: _____
   _____
   _____

C. one shoelace dangling
   skirt hem hanging on one side
   blouse tail half in, half out
   wisps of hair escaping the knot on top of her head
   lipstick smeared on chin
   one earring missing
   SUMMARY SENTENCE: _____
   _____
   _____

D. a leaning tower of records on the desk
   a wastebasket full of books
   one blue sock draped over the lampshade
   guitar case sticking out from under the bed
   bath towel slung over open closet door
   hockey stick leaning against the bureau

Copyright © 1977 by Allyn and Bacon, Inc. Reproduction of this material is restricted to use with <u>A Guidebook for Teaching Creative Writing,</u> by Gene Stanford and Marie N. Smith.

REPRODUCTION PAGE 5   **SUMMARIZING DETAILS**

SUMMARY SENTENCE: _____
_____
_____

E. cold gray eyes
    a frown-wrinkle between his brows
    a thin, straight mouth
    sharp, beak-like nose
    iron gray hair cut like a Prussian army officer's
    SUMMARY SENTENCE: _____
    _____
    _____

F. shrill high notes
    blatant, unmodulated tone
    a vibrato quite out of control
    uncertain pitch tending to chronic flatness
    limited range
    a tendency to nasality in the middle range
    SUMMARY SENTENCE: _____
    _____
    _____

G. the Three Stooges committing their usual hijinx
    the "Roadrunner" comically surviving a dozen gruesome fates
    a movie made in 1934
    an early "Lucy" episode
    an early "Flintstone" episode
    the Lone Ranger urging Silver "awa-a-a-ay!"
    SUMMARY SENTENCE: _____
    _____
    _____

Copyright © 1977 by Allyn and Bacon, Inc. Reproduction of this material is restricted to use with <u>A Guidebook for Teaching Creative Writing</u>, by Gene Stanford and Marie N. Smith.

REPRODUCTION PAGE 6

NAME_____ SECTION_____

Listing Details

INSTRUCTIONS: For each of the summary sentences below make a list of as many pertinent descriptive details as you can think of, making sure that all descriptive details contribute to the overall impression summarized in the summary sentence.

1. Walking through the deserted neighborhood, I felt as though I was the only person alive.

2. The fertile valley seemed to have been cut off from the passage of time.

3. The street began to fill with activity, as the city roused itself from sleep.

4. Their garden was still producing a variety of vegetables well into November.

5. Angry students crowded the student union to take part in a protest meeting.

6. The front hall of the high school was as crowded and busy as Grand Central Station.

7. The woods behind the old house provided a magic place for the children to spend their Saturday afternoons.

8. The market's produce department looked like a brilliant illustration of October for a calendar.

9. His bachelor apartment revealed his artistic interests and his tendency toward a monkish life.

10. The living room was tastefully elegant.

11. The long table groaned under enough food to feed a regiment.

12. Houseplants of every conceivable nature crowded the porch.

13. Gino's Pizzeria offered every conceivable kind of pizza in any combination desired.

Copyright © 1977 by Allyn and Bacon, Inc. Reproduction of this material is restricted to use with <u>A Guidebook for Teaching Creative Writing</u>, by Gene Stanford and Marie N. Smith.

NAME _____ SECTION _____

Excerpts from "Snowbound"

John Greenleaf Whittier

The sun that brief December day
Rose cheerless over hills of gray,
And, darkly circled, gave at noon
A sadder light than waning moon.

Slow tracing down the thickening sky
Its mute and ominous prophecy;
A portent seeming less than threat,
It sank from sight before it set.
A chill no coat, however stout,
Of homespun stuff could quite shut out,
A hard, dull bitterness of cold,
    That checked, mid-vein the circling race
    Of life-blood in the sharpened face,
The coming of the snowstorm told.
The wind blew east; we heard the roar
Of Ocean on his wintry shore,
And felt the strong pulse throbbing there
Beat with low rhythm our inland air.

. . .

Unwarmed by any sunset light
The gray day darkened into night,
A night made hoary with the swarm
And whirl-dance of the blinding storm,
As zigzag wavering to and fro
Crossed and recrossed the winged snow:
And ere the early bedtime came
The white drift piled the window-frame,
And through the glass the clothes-line posts
Looked in like tall and sheeted ghosts.

So all night long the storm roared on:
The morning broke without a sun;
In tiny spherule traced with lines
Of Nature's geometric signs,
In starry flake and pellicle
All day the hoary meteor fell;
And, when the second morning shone,
We looked upon a world unknown,
On nothing we could call our own.
Around the glistening wonder bent
The blue walls of the firmament,
No cloud above, no earth below, —
A universe of sky and snow!

. . .

All day the gusty north-wind bore
The loosening drift its breath before;
Low circling round its southern zone,
The sun through dazzling snow-mist shone.
The shrieking of the mindless wind,
The moaning tree-boughs swaying blind,
And on the glass the unmeaning beat
Of ghostly finger-tips of sleet.
Beyond the circle of our hearth
No welcome sound of toil or mirth
Unbound the spell and testified
Of human life and thought outside.
We minded that the sharpest ear
The buried brooklet could not hear,
The music of whose liquid lip
Had been to us companionship,
And, in our lonely life, had grown
To have an almost human tone.

As night drew on, and, from the crest
Of wooded knolls that ridged the west,
The sun, a snow-blown traveler, sank
From sight beneath the smothering bank.

. . .

The moon above the eastern wood
Shown at its full; the hill-range stood
Transfigured in the silver flood,
Its blown snows flashing cold and keen,
Dead white, save where some sharp ravine
Took shadow, or the somber green
Of hemlocks turned to pitchy black
Against the whiteness at their back.
For such a world and such a night
Most fitting that unwarming light,
Which only seemed where'er it fell
To make the coldness visible.

Copyright © 1977 by Allyn and Bacon, Inc. Reproduction of this material is restricted to use with <u>A Guidebook for Teaching Creative Writing</u>, by Gene Stanford and Marie N. Smith.

REPRODUCTION PAGE 8

NAME_____ SECTION_____

Revealing Character Through Dialogue

INSTRUCTIONS: Your teacher will assign you a role to play. You are to pretend that you are that person. You are to describe each episode below from the point of view of that person. Be sure to use the same kind of words, spoken in the same way, that you think that person would use to describe the episode.

A. Kindergarten class and teacher have gone to a park for a picnic. Teenage hoodlums taunt and tease them. Children are frightened. So is the teacher. Teacher asks big boys to go away. They laugh rudely. The ruffians tip over the table and spill the food. They take the cake the teacher has brought and run away with it. The teacher and children look for a police officer so they can report what has happened.

B. An eighth grade class has a substitute teacher. He is young and unsure of himself. The students take advantage of the situation and misbehave. They mislead him as to their assigned work. They misrepresent the class rules to him. The principal comes in and sees how uncooperative they are being. She lectures them on their rudeness to the substitute. She assigns them all to an extra study hall after school. She is angry with the students and feels sorry for the young teacher.

C. Once there was a mother who insisted that her children eat every bite of food on their plates. She made them eat a serving of everything. One night for dinner she served stewed tomatoes, mashed turnips, and collard greens. The children did not clean their plates. The mother told them they would have to stay at the table until the plates were clean. She and the father went into the other room. One child threw his carrots out the window. The second child fed her turnips to the dog. The third child hid his greens behind a big jar on the pantry shelf. The mother was pleased to see they had all cleaned their plates.

Copyright © 1977 by Allyn and Bacon, Inc. Reproduction of this material is restricted to use with A Guidebook for Teaching Creative Writing, by Gene Stanford and Marie N. Smith.

NAME_____ SECTION_____

Values in Action Chart

INSTRUCTIONS: Fill in the two right-hand columns with those behaviors which would be likely with each value in the left-hand column and those which would not be consistent with it. The first has been done as an example.

A Person Who Values...	Would Probably:	Would Probably Not:
1. loyalty to friends	loan money to friend stick around when friend is sick or in trouble go out of his or her way to do a favor for friend include friend in plans even when others think friend would be out of place	avoid friend for own convenience shed friend for a richer or more popular friend turn in friend when he or she had done wrong lie to friend or talk about friend to others
2. fairness		
3. individuality		
4. equality of the sexes		
5. honesty		
6. good sportsmanship		
7. popularity		
8. physical fitness		
9. social justice		
10. independence		

Copyright © 1977 by Allyn and Bacon, Inc. Reproduction of this material is restricted to use with A Guidebook for Teaching Creative Writing, by Gene Stanford and Marie N. Smith.

REPRODUCTION PAGE 10

NAME_____ SECTION_____

Describing an Event for a Purpose

INSTRUCTIONS: Examine the list of random details below, all of which are related to a family vacation by automobile. List as many purposes as you can think of that one might have in mind when writing about this event and indicate which details would be used to fulfill each purpose.

children were always hungry
had to stop every ten miles
scenery was beautiful
roads were excellent
we took along games, puzzles
we learned to read maps
car was skillfully loaded
motels were expensive
wife drove from back seat
we saw "Old Faithful" geyser
we kept getting lost
it was hot and boring in Kansas and Nebraska

new insights into U.S. history
became good at "20 Questions" game
restaurants were usually awful
stopped often to rest
got ptomaine at a Cheyenne drive-in
became skillful at outdoor eating
saw Grand Canyon
saw storm over the prairies
talked to wide variety of people
mountains were awe-inspiring
got great mileage in the car
thrilled by the Pacific Ocean

Copyright © 1977 by Allyn and Bacon, Inc. Reproduction of this material is restricted to use with A Guidebook for Teaching Creative Writing, by Gene Stanford and Marie N. Smith.

NAME _____   SECTION _____

Events and Their Possible Purposes

INSTRUCTIONS: Using the list of events given below, list as many useful purposes as you can that might determine your approach to each event.

EXAMPLE:

1. *Event:* party where everything went wrong
   Possible purposes: to recreate the event so accurately one might feel one is there
   to recreate it in such a way that one identifies with the hostess's embarrassment and anguish
   to recreate it in such a way as to amuse the reader
   to recreate it for the purpose of showing what not to do when giving a party

2. *Event:* Automobile accident
   Possible purposes: _____

3. *Event:* an evening of watching television
   Possible purposes: _____

4. *Event:* the senior class picnic in the park
   Possible purposes: _____

5. *Event:* a family reunion
   Possible purposes: _____

6. *Event:* graduation exercises
   Possible purposes: _____

Copyright © 1977 by Allyn and Bacon, Inc. Reproduction of this material is restricted to use with A Guidebook for Teaching Creative Writing, by Gene Stanford and Marie N. Smith.

REPRODUCTION PAGE 11 EVENTS AND THEIR POSSIBLE PURPOSES

7. *Event:* lunch in the school cafeteria
   Possible purposes: _____
   _____
   _____
   _____

8. *Event:* a family weekend at the farm
   Possible purposes: _____
   _____
   _____
   _____

9. *Event:* an evening at traffic court
   Possible purposes: _____
   _____
   _____
   _____

10. *Event:* a birthday party
    Possible purposes: _____
    _____
    _____
    _____

11. *Event:* tryouts for a school team
    Possible purposes: _____
    _____
    _____
    _____

12. *Event:* a rock concert
    Possible purposes: _____
    _____
    _____
    _____

Copyright © 1977 by Allyn and Bacon, Inc. Reproduction of this material is restricted to use with A Guidebook for Teaching Creative Writing, by Gene Stanford and Marie N. Smith.

REPRODUCTION PAGE 12

NAME_____ SECTION_____

"Train Ride in Europe"

Sheila Morris
(12th grade student)

On a train, eastward bound, I sat in a shiny red seat. The scenery was beautiful: golden mountains cut by silvery water in the setting sun, green trees, barren rocks; they all rushed past my eyes in an instant.

But growing tired of the scenes outside my window, I realized that inside the train was beautiful scenery too: the passengers. Tiny children running down the aisles, laughing, big mothers grabbing and shouting at their tiny children; old men with cigars, young girls returning home. They all made up the scenery inside my window.

A soldier sitting directly across from me interested me most. What struck me was the sweet baby innocence written on his face. He had upturned, laughing eyes, a small button nose, and a smiling baby mouth. His hair was soft and blond, cut short to his head, leaving his pink ears showing. His skin was soft looking, blushing and freckled. He had the look of a two year old.

We exchanged a few words, and I learned that he was twenty-one and had just that day been released from the army. It seemed ironic to me that this boy with his baby look had fought, perhaps killed, in war.

What occurred later that same day's journey affected me greatly and is the reason I am writing of this soldier. I had returned to gazing out the window at mountains, now dark, and, inside, at the children now asleep in their mothers' arms. The young soldier himself had dozed off and seemed peaceful and relaxed. But suddenly a violent tremor shook his body. Every muscle stiffened; even his soft baby face twitched spasmodically. Then his body relaxed again and he seemed to sink into peaceful rest.

I watched him in amazement as this happened again and again. Every few minutes, his muscles would tighten and the spasms would shake his peacefulness. Then he would relax once more.

I wondered what terrible thoughts ran through his mind that would not let him rest. In a peaceful moment I looked at this face of a child who in a moment would twitch in some unknown pain or fear. I looked at the tiny children, asleep in their mothers' arms, then again at the soldier just a few years older. I have not been able to forget his face.

Copyright © 1977 by Allyn and Bacon, Inc. Reproduction of this material is restricted to use with A Guidebook for Teaching Creative Writing, by Gene Stanford and Marie N. Smith.

NAME _____ SECTION _____

"Cold Turkey"
Nina Whittier (12th grade student)

Our family has never had a turkey dinner and the reason for this finally came out last Thanksgiving. We children learned of my parents' first holiday, when my mother tried to cook a turkey.

It seems my father had persuaded my mother to buy a live turkey and had also left her in charge of killing it. She thought she knew how, from watching her mother so many holidays during her childhood.

Yet it wasn't from lack of knowledge that she hesitated, when the time came. Rather, she hesitated because she had grown attached to the bird. He was very pretty, with his soft, ashen feathers and the cunning way he gobbled when someone spoke to him.

Yes, my mother even talked to the turkey; named him, too. Tom Turkey, she called him. Not very original, but all turkeys were Tom to her.

In her mind she realized that all it would take to kill Tom would be a quick, strong twist of the neck and he would be dead, having felt little pain. She told herself that his would be a humane death.

She thought of taking him back to the poultry dealer and buying a turkey already killed and dressed to cook. But no. She had agreed to do the job and she must kill him.

My mother, though, could not kill the turkey with the very hand that he ate from, and so, she decided on a different solution. She would put him in the oven and turn on the gas. This way she would never have to look into his frightened, pleading eyes as he died.

Having made this decision, she walked quickly out to the pen where Tom was being kept. Unable to call Tom to his death, she chased him about the cage until she was able to grab his two strong legs. Tomorrow they would be drumsticks. Hugging the gobbling creature in her arms, my mom hurried into the kitchen, opened the oven and stuffed him in. Turning on the gas, she ran from the kitchen, tears blurring her sight.

Fifteen minutes later she returned, sure that the turkey by now must be peacefully dead. Peeping through the oven window, she could see the hulking body of the motionless bird. Opening the oven door, she grabbed the turkey and let him hang limply upside down. Now Mother found that she could make herself handle the dead bird, so she let him drop to the table. Then she settled into the task of plucking.

After a long time, there lay a skinny, naked turkey and a large pile of beautiful feather duster material. Thinking she had finished with the bird until the next day, she stuffed him into the refrigerator to keep.

Not long afterwards, she began to prepare dinner. As she opened the refrigerator for milk, a bombardment of jars crashed to the floor, and she saw, on the refrigerator shelf, an enraged, shivering turkey.

Gobbling indignantly, he tried to fly from the shelf, but his wings flapped uselessly as he fell to the floor. Gawking in bewilderment at the fallen bird, my mother stood rooted to the ground, unsure of her next step.

Tom quickly recovered his feet and strutted over to her, gobbling in a friendly manner. He did not seem to realize that my mother was the cause of his problem, but saw her as his rescuer from his freezing ordeal. Knowing full well that she couldn't kill the grateful Tom—not a second time—she quickly mixed a hot turkey mash and fixed a small pan by a heater. Then, gathering up her knitting needles and a nice rusty brown yarn, my mother started to knit a small fuzzy sweater.

Copyright © 1977 by Allyn and Bacon, Inc. Reproduction of this material is restricted to use with <u>A Guidebook for Teaching Creative Writing</u>, by Gene Stanford and Marie N. Smith.

NAME _____ SECTION _____

"He Should Have Stayed in Bed"

Jim Perkins
(12th grade student)

It happened the night before, during a big wind storm: this man's chimney blew off.

The next day he plans on fixing it. So he rigs up a beam on his roof and puts a pulley on the beam and puts a rope through the pulley and ties it to a fifty-five gallon drum.

So he gets up on the roof and loads all the old bricks into the fifty-five gallon drum. Then he gets the drum over to the edge of the roof and climbs down the ladder and goes to the rope.

He tugs on the rope to get the drum over the edge. He gets it over the edge and the drum just happens to be heavier than he is, so the drum comes crashing down and he goes flying up. On the way down, the barrel hits him on the shoulder. So now he's in great pain as he keeps on going up, and he hits his head on the beam while at the same time the drum hits the ground and the bottom breaks out so that now he is heavier than the drum and he comes down and the barrel flies up.

On the way up the barrel cracks him on the shin. Now this man is in extreme pain. So he hits the ground and is dazed for a minute and lets go of the rope and the barrel comes back down and hits him on the head.

This poor fellow is now in the hospital. In my own opinion, he should have stayed in bed.

Copyright © 1977 by Allyn and Bacon, Inc. Reproduction of this material is restricted to use with <u>A Guidebook for Teaching Creative Writing</u>, by Gene Stanford and Marie N. Smith.

REPRODUCTION PAGE 15

NAME_____ SECTION_____

"Just Dreaming"
Ben Painter   (11th grade student)

Jonathon Baker quietly said goodnight to his father and walked up to his bedroom. His feet felt like two blocks of concrete as he mounted the stairs. His mind was totally occupied with one item: the death of his mother that day. As he changed, in the very detached manner of a robot, his head spun with the events of the killing. It was so horribly vivid . . . .

Jonathon had gone along with his mother on a shopping trip. They made four stops in town, and stopped at the bank on the way home, in order to make a deposit.

After completing this chore, they walked across the empty parking lot towards the car. They both saw the Cadillac careen around the corner of the bank and head directly for them. Jonathon had reacted quickly, running away from the car's path. But his mother did not have her son's quickness. The car struck his mother on the hip with incredible impact, throwing her head-first to the pavement twenty feet away. Jonathon got up and rushed toward his mother. It was obvious to him when he reached her that she was very badly hurt. Her head had a huge cut, and blood was pouring out of the laceration.

Although he had had first-aid training, Jonathon panicked and left his mother to get help. He ran headlong to the front of the bank. To his horror, he realized that the bank had just closed. The guard was turning away from the door with keys in his hand. Jonathon ran to the glass doors and banged at them with all his might. The guard turned, looked at Jonathon with an annoyed look, and turned around again. Jonathon continued his hysterical drummings. The guard turned once more, shrugged his shoulders, and walked off.

Jonathon, now with tears in his eyes, turned and ran to the edge of the street and waved his arms madly. But, amazingly, none of the cars helped. Moments later, Jonathon ran into the middle of the street, still frantically signalling the uncaring machines. After what seemed like hours, Jonathon collapsed, hysterical and more frustrated than he had ever imagined he could be.

The police told him the rest: they had found him a few minutes later, and suspecting something, had found his mother. They had brought her to the hospital, where she died two hours later.

Jonathon got into bed and closed his eyes. He fell asleep moments later, dreaming. . . .

Jonathon ran to the front of the bank and banged at the locked door with his fists. The guard, who had been walking away, turned around and unlocked the door.

"What's the matter? Can I help?" asked the guard.

"My mother . . . out in back . . . badly hurt," Jonathon gasped haltingly.

The guard ran to one of the phones and called for an ambulance.

A passing motorist, who had noticed Jonathon's frantic banging, had stopped and he now asked, "Is there anything I can do?"

Jonathon, who had now regained some of his composure, said, "My mother is hurt out back."

The man sprinted out of sight toward Jonathon's mother.

The ambulance arrived within three minutes. His mother was carefully loaded into the ambulance, and it hurried off. Jonathon turned to thank the guard and motorist, but both had vanished.

"Jonathon? Jonathon? What's wrong?"

His father's voice brought him back to consciousness.

"Just dreaming, Dad. Just dreaming," Jonathon replied bitterly.

Copyright © 1977 by Allyn and Bacon, Inc. Reproduction of this material is restricted to use with <u>A Guidebook for Teaching Creative Writing</u>, by Gene Stanford and Marie N. Smith.

REPRODUCTION PAGE 16

NAME_____ SECTION_____

"The Visit"

Ruth Kim
(11th grade student)

"What is it like to be old?" asked the curious little boy.

"Well," the old woman said, "I don't have to go to school, and I don't work."

"Really? You must have fun all the time!"

"Oh yes, I don't have to be responsible for little children who go poking their funny little heads into everything. There just isn't much that I have to do."

"I wish I could be old too," the little boy said wistfully.

"You will . . . someday."

"When I get old, will I ever get to live in a nice place like this? You are friends with all these people, aren't you?"

"You are a smart little man. Yes, we are all friends. Maybe someday, after your children are all married, they will send you to a place like this."

"Did your children put you in this nice place? I would like to live with my friends. That would be fun, wouldn't it?"

"Yes, it is fun," the old woman said, her voice quiet and emotionless. "Maybe a long time from now you will be just like me . . . perhaps even doing the same things."

"Oh, boy! I can't wait 'til I'm old. You really have it great, Grandma."

The old woman breathed a sigh, and waited for him to continue. The little boy glanced past his grandmother, out the window. A car was pulling up at the curb.

"I'm sorry I can't stay longer, Grandma, but it's time for me to go now. Maybe I can see you again next year, if Mommy and Daddy decide to visit."

The little boy stretched up and put his arms around the old woman's neck. He gently kissed her on the cheek. She hugged him tightly and whispered her good-bye. Then he ran out the door.

She went to her window and in a moment saw him running out to the car. He did not see his grandmother standing at the window, hand upraised in a last wave. He was too busy telling his mother and father how great old age would be.

Copyright © 1977 by Allyn and Bacon, Inc. Reproduction of this material is restricted to use with A Guidebook for Teaching Creative Writing, by Gene Stanford and Marie N. Smith.

REPRODUCTION PAGE 17

NAME_____ SECTION_____

"Sensations of My Mind"

Merilynn Wenzlaff
(12th grade student)

    I was at the edge of a wood on a summer day, sunlight dappling the brown path and small blue wild flowers gleaming at my feet. I walked around a bend, and there a buck, in full antlerage, stood, tensely poised, big ears straight, eyes bright. He looked at me, alert eyes showing no fear, and I understood him. I climbed aboard his chestnut back, and together we turned to flee the hunter.

    As we jumped over a crooked wooden fence and through young trees and underbrush, we were one, truly one: I, the mind and rationality the deer lacked, and he, the fleetness and grace I would never have. I could feel each muscle flex beneath me, the steady graceful gallop, his heart beating quickly between my knees. As one we had no fear, only a sense of urgency. We burst out of the woods onto a field of knee-high grass and clover; it was a downhill slope, and so our pace quickened—his stride must have covered twenty feet. I could hear only the wind whistling past me, chilling my face; but I sensed more urgency in the warm vitality beneath me which could hear the sounds of the hunters.

    We reached the bottom of the valley, the small plateau before the climb upward. His bounds steadied, his cloven black feet cutting into the deep turf and springing out again. The red fur was deep in my hands as I held his neck. Here in the plateau we were at our most vulnerable, yet we felt no fear.

    There was a road just ahead before the uphill climb began. It was a wide road with huge rain ditches cutting deeply along each side—a seemingly impossible leap. Yet we had no doubt; the gallop did not falter except to collect itself, then a spring of strong hind legs. We flew. He gathered his hocks beneath him, fragile forelegs stretched out, and I leaned forward with his neck, feeling the tense back muscles, the wind, the joy in the incredible power and freedom of the leap. It seemed to last an eternity, a sensation never before realized and never to be forgotten. The hind legs swept farther forward as we angled downward; the small hooves dug into the turf of the hill, and with a surge of his hind legs we continued our steady flight up towards the safe woods on the other side of the valley.

Copyright © 1977 by Allyn and Bacon, Inc. Reproduction of this material is restricted to use with <u>A Guidebook for Teaching Creative Writing</u>, by Gene Stanford and Marie N. Smith.

REPRODUCTION PAGE 18

NAME_____ SECTION_____

Revising Skeletal Paragraphs

INSTRUCTIONS: The paragraphs below were written on purpose by high school students as examples of poorly recreated events. They can be thought of as "skeletal" paragraphs, because the writers have merely outlined the stories rather than providing the details which would actually recreate the events. Revise the paragraphs by expanding them into recreated events.

A. When I went to the park, the weather was just as I like it. We went swimming in a pool that was all right but that needed a few improvements. Then we did a lot of really fun things. Afterwards we all talked around a bonfire and decided to do it again sometime.

written on purpose by
high school student Daphne Rodin

B. The seventh grade trip to Chicago started off in utter chaos on a bad February day. All the seventh graders were dropped off by 6:30 a.m. and began causing all kinds of trouble. Teachers and parents ran around trying to restore order. Finally everyone was aboard the busses and they left.

written on purpose by
high school student Ellen Wiederholdt

C. The synagogue was crowded and noisy, but the service was pleasant and progressed smoothly. Afterwards everyone went to the Kiddush and ate refreshments. People talked to one another about the sermon and about the events of the past week and their plans for the next. Then they left the building to take care of their tasks for the day.

written on purpose by
high school student Barbara Kiem

Copyright © 1977 by Allyn and Bacon, Inc. Reproduction of this material is restricted to use with A Guidebook for Teaching Creative Writing, by Gene Stanford and Marie N. Smith.

REPRODUCTION PAGE 19

NAME_____ SECTION_____

Creating Rather than Telling about Conversations

A.   David told Louie a story to distract him while he got his hair cut. He made up a tale about where the moon goes during the day. Even the barber got interested, and Louie was full of questions. Jane, however, was her usual practical minded self, interrupting and disagreeing with David's flights of fancy.

B.   "You know where the moon goes during the day, Louie?"
   "Where?" Louie's eyes grew wide, and he seemed not even to notice the stroking of the barber's trimmer through his hair.
   "Well," David began, not entirely sure where he would end up, "they lift up the edge of the sky..."
   "They do *not!*" That was crabby Jane, their older sister.
   "Don't be a *pill,* Jane." Louie laughed at David's imitation of their mother's tone of voice. David continued with his story: "Then they let it have the day off."
   The barber smiled absently and winked at Jane.
   "Anyway, it's a big balloon with craters and canyons and scratchmarks. And it has to be driven by a hundred short midgets. Anyway, these short midgets run around on wire tracks that go roundy-round..."
   "Like Jake?!" Jake was Louie's mechanical mouse.
   "Yes. And they go to a fair."
   "A fair?"
   "And they fly around and the clouds are green and yellow..."

_____
Written by Richard Green (12th grade student). Used with permission.

Copyright © 1977 by Allyn and Bacon, Inc. Reproduction of this material is restricted to use with A Guidebook for Teaching Creative Writing, by Gene Stanford and Marie N. Smith.

REPRODUCTION PAGE 20

NAME_____ SECTION_____

Creating Actual Conversations

INSTRUCTIONS: Choose one or more of the following accounts of conversations and arguments and turn it into <u>actual</u> talking and arguing.

1. My folks and I really got into it over whether I could go to the dance.

2. I told him I really loved him, and he acted so dumb I felt like a fool. Then he apologized.

3. I told her if that was the way she was going to act, I didn't need her for a friend, and she told me off and hung up on me.

4. Janie chattered happily as they walked to the car. Jim answered shortly, if at all, and gradually Janie ran out of things to say. She tried to get Jim to tell her what was the matter, but he turned her questions away with non-answers. At last, she fell silent.

5. Mrs. Garber spent a full five minutes telling her third period pupils how displeased she was with their behavior. Several students tried to speak up in their own defense, but Mrs. Garber easily overrode them in both volume and intensity, and eventually the pupils sat silently, accepting their verbal punishment.

6. This weekend one of my best friends revealed a side I had never seen before. He told me how unsure of himself he is and how uncertain he sometimes feels of his own worth. He told me that his father drinks too much and never seems to have time for him. His mother ignores him most of the time, he told me, because she's so upset about the father's behavior. My friend told me that once he felt so desperate he even considered killing himself but now that he has me for a friend he feels life is more worthwhile. I told him I hoped we'd always be friends.

7. Judy called me on the phone last night but was so upset she could hardly make clear to me what she was trying to say. I finally talked her into settling down a little and she managed to tell me her mother and father had just had an awful fight and were planning to get a divorce.

Copyright © 1977 by Allyn and Bacon, Inc. Reproduction of this material is restricted to use with <u>A Guidebook for Teaching Creative Writing</u>, by Gene Stanford and Marie N. Smith.

NAME_____ SECTION_____

Making an Event Come Alive

INSTRUCTIONS: Compare the short paragraph below, which reports that an event happened, with the excerpt from Jack London's "To Build a Fire," which vividly recreates that event.

He tried desperately to build a fire with his last matches, but his frozen hands were too stiff. He could not control his body's shivering, and thus scattered his small fire instead of building it. Each twig burned out and he knew he was doomed.

FROM "TO BUILD A FIRE" BY JACK LONDON

... Well, it was up to him to build the fire over again, and this second time there must be no failure. Even if he succeeded, he would most likely lose some toes. His feet must be badly frozen by now, and there would be some time before the second fire was ready.

Such were his thoughts, but he did not sit and think them. He was busy all the time they were passing through his mind. He made a new foundation for a fire, this time in the open, where no treacherous tree could blot it out. Next, he gathered dry grasses and tiny twigs from the high-water flotsam. He could not bring his fingers together to pull them out, but he was able to gather them by the handful. In this way he got many rotten twigs and bits of green moss that were undesirable, but it was the best he could do. He worked methodically, even collecting an armful of the larger branches to be used later when the fire gathered strength. And all the while the dog sat and watched him, a certain yearning wistfulness in its eyes, for it looked upon him as the fire-provider, and the fire was slow in coming.

When all was ready, the man reached in his pocket for a second piece of birch-bark. He knew the bark was there, and, though he could not feel it with his fingers, he could hear its crisp rustling as he fumbled for it. Try as he would, he could not clutch hold of it. And all the time, in his consciousness, was the knowledge that each instant his feet were freezing. This thought tended to put him in a panic, but he fought against it and kept calm. He pulled on his mittens with his teeth, and threshed his arms back and forth, beating his hands with all his might against his sides. He did this sitting down, and he stood up to do it; and all the while the dog sat in the snow, its wolf-brush of a tail curled around warmly over its forefeet, its sharp wolf-ears pricked forward intently as it watched the man. And the man, as he beat and threshed with his arms and hands, felt a great surge of envy as he regarded the creature that was warm and secure in its natural covering.

After a time he was aware of the first faraway signals of sensation in his beaten fingers. The faint tingling grew stronger till it evolved into a stinging ache that was excruciating, but which the man hailed with satisfaction. He stripped the mitten from his right hand and fetched forth the birch-bark. The exposed fingers were quickly going numb again. Next he brought out his bunch of sulphur matches. But the tremendous cold had already driven the life out of his fingers. In his effort to separate one match from the others, the whole bunch fell in the snow. He tried to pick it out of the snow, but failed. The dead fingers could

Copyright © 1977 by Allyn and Bacon, Inc. Reproduction of this material is restricted to use with A Guidebook for Teaching Creative Writing, by Gene Stanford and Marie N. Smith.

REPRODUCTION PAGE 21   **MAKING AN EVENT COME ALIVE**

neither touch nor clutch. He was very careful. He drove the thought of his freezing feet, and nose, and cheeks, out of his mind, devoting his whole soul to the matches. He watched, using the sense of vision in place of that of touch, and when he saw his fingers on each side of the bunch, he closed them—that is, he willed to close them, for the wires were down, and the fingers did not obey. He pulled the mitten on the right hand, and beat it fiercely against his knee. Then, with both mittened hands, he scooped the bunch of matches, along with much snow, into his lap. Yet he was no better off.

After some manipulation he managed to get the bunch between the heels of his mittened hands. In this fashion he carried it to his mouth. The ice crackled and snapped when by a violent effort he opened his mouth. He drew the lower jaw in, curled the upper lip out of the way, and scraped the bunch with his upper teeth in order to separate a match. He succeeded in getting one, which he dropped on his lap. He was no better off. He could not pick it up. Then he devised a way. He picked it up in his teeth and scratched it on his leg. Twenty times he scratched before he succeeded in lighting it. As it flamed he held it with his teeth to the birch-bark. But the burning brimstone went up his nostrils and into his lungs, causing him to cough spasmodically. The match fell into the snow and went out.

The old-timer on Sulphur Creek was right, he thought in the moment of controlled despair that ensued; after fifty below, a man should travel with a partner. He beat his hands, but failed in exciting any sensation. Suddenly he bared both hands, removing the mittens with his teeth. He caught the whole bunch between the heels of his hands. His arm-muscles not being frozen enabled him to press the hand-heels tightly against the matches. Then he scratched the bunch along his leg. It flared into flame, seventy sulphur matches at once! There was no wind to blow them out. He kept his head to one side to escape the strangling fumes, and held the blazing bunch to the birch-bark. As he so held it, he became aware of sensation in his hand. His flesh was burning. He could smell it. Deep down below the surface he could feel it. The sensation developed into pain that grew acute. And still he endured it, holding the flame of the matches clumsily to the bark that would not light readily because his own burning hands were in the way, absorbing most of the flame.

At last, when he could endure no more, he jerked his hands apart. The blazing matches fell sizzling into the snow, but the birch-bark was alight. He began laying dry grasses and the tiniest twigs on the flame. He could not pick and choose, for he had to lift the fuel between the heels of his hands. Small pieces of rotten wood and green moss clung to the twigs, and he bit them off as well as he could with his teeth. He cherished the flame carefully and awkwardly. It meant life, and it must not perish. The withdrawal of blood from the surface of his body now made him begin to shiver, and he grew more awkward. A large piece of green moss fell squarely on the little fire. He tried to poke it out with his fingers, but his shivering frame made him poke too far, and he disrupted the nucleus of the little fire, the burning grasses and tiny twigs separating and scattering. He tried to poke them together again, but in spite of the tenseness of the effort, his shivering got away with him, and the twigs were hopelessly scattered. Each twig gushed a puff of smoke and went out. The fire-provider had failed. . . .

Copyright © 1977 by Allyn and Bacon, Inc. Reproduction of this material is restricted to use with <u>A Guidebook for Teaching Creative Writing</u>, by Gene Stanford and Marie N. Smith.

REPRODUCTION PAGE 22

NAME_____ SECTION_____

How to Close Read a Novel

1. Watch for repetitive elements or words. Circle or underline each and keep, on the inside back page of the book, a record of page numbers for all repetitions. Such a record is a real time-saver when you get ready to choose a subject and write a paper or when you wish to participate in a discussion of the book or story. This technique is particularly helpful when a book includes a number of elements with symbolic meaning or when a character changes over the course of the work, as in *Macbeth*.

2. Watch for statements which, from a strictly literal point of view, do not make sense. When we read quickly, we tend to go right past such statements without noticing them. We are too eager to find out what happens. For instance, early in *Lord of the Flies* by William Golding, there is a statement which literally makes no sense but is very important in terms of the book's symbolic purposes: "Passions beat about Simon on the mountain-top with awful wings." Few students notice this sentence on a first reading. It is fruitful to watch for such revealing passages, to ask about them and to question why the author includes them.

3. Sometimes, in a novel or story, the author makes a comment that seems purely expository, an explanation, perhaps, or a descriptive phrase that seems aimed directly at the reader's understanding. The author is speaking in his or her own voice rather than in that of one of the characters, and it behooves the reader to "listen" well at such times.

    In *Lord of the Flies,* for instance, Golding generally speaks through Ralph or sometimes Simon or Piggy, and engages in an idiom suitable to these young boys. It is noticeable, therefore, when, in the midst of a simply recounted action scene, the author says: "Simon became inarticulate in his effort to express mankind's essential illness." One must suspect that the author is talking to the reader here. Or when Golding says, in describing the weeping of the "littluns": "They were reminded of their personal sorrows; and perhaps felt themselves to share in a sorrow that was universal." Or of Ralph, he says: "He wanted to explain how people were never quite what you thought they were." We must learn to see when the author is addressing us, the readers, and deliberately trying to help us understand his or her deeper purposes.

4. Continually ask the question *Why,* when some element of the book seems to represent a deliberate choice by the author from among a number of possibilities. Why was the fire built on the mountaintop and later moved down to the sand? Why was Jack redheaded? Why did the littluns "buzz" when Jack clouted his knife into a tree? Remember, none of these things really happened; the author made them all up. Assume that he had reasons and try to discover them by asking why.

5. If you wish to make a serious study of any literary work, read it at least twice, once to find out what happens and the second time to find out why it happens and what it all means. The second time through, you should have pen or pencil in hand, marking significant words and passages.

Copyright © 1977 by Allyn and Bacon, Inc. Reproduction of this material is restricted to use with A Guidebook for Teaching Creative Writing, by Gene Stanford and Marie N. Smith.

REPRODUCTION PAGE 23

NAME_____ SECTION_____

Kinds of Questions to Ask Yourself in Order to Come up with Answers that Can Provide a Thesis Statement for an Essay of Literary Commentary:

1. What was the purpose of the _____ incident in this novel?
2. What did the author reveal about the main character by showing him or her as _____?
3. What purpose was served by having _____ treat _____ as he or she did?
4. What was the relationship between _____ and _____? What purpose did the author have in developing this (enmity, friendship, etc.)?
5. Why is it that the author chose to show the mother as a stronger person than the father (or vice versa)?
6. Why did the author continually emphasize the hero's deep love for _____? What is the author trying to show about the hero?
7. How did the hero react to adults? Are there exceptions? Why? What is revealed by these reactions?
8. Are there religious references? Biblical parallels? Why?
9. Are there constantly repetitive elements? What is the author accomplishing through such emphasis by repetition?
10. Are there symbolic elements? What are they? What larger meanings are suggested by these specific symbols?
11. Is the leading character always sympathetic? Do you identify with the leading character —like the person—always? If so, or if not, why do you suppose the author chose to work it out this way? What is the author showing?
12. Does the author change the kinds of language at various places in the book? Why?
13. Why does the author keep using such and such a word throughout the book, when many other synonyms actually could say the same thing?
14. What purpose is served by the title of the book?
15. Why did the author choose a particular setting?

Copyright © 1977 by Allyn and Bacon, Inc. Reproduction of this material is restricted to use with A Guidebook for Teaching Creative Writing, by Gene Stanford and Marie N. Smith.

NAME_____ SECTION_____

Preparing to Write a Paper about a Novel in Terms of the Author's Purpose

One does well to remember that an author setting out to write a novel faces many, many decisions. The author must decide, first and overall, what "statement" he or she wishes to make, what comment about the world and/or the human condition. (This we call the theme.) And then, the author must decide what characters, what events, occurring in what place and under what circumstances, will best reveal or demonstrate the chosen theme. (Or perhaps the author starts with the story and sees in it a theme to be developed by careful selection of details.)

But these gross decisions are merely a beginning. Think how many minute selections the author must make: what color shall the hero's hair be? How tall is he? Where was he born? In what idiom does he speak? What is his disposition? How does he get along with his family, with friends, etc.? And how about the leading character's best friend? And the heroine? Is she sweet and gentle or tomboyish and slangy? What setting will best serve thematic purposes? What scenes—dramatic events—must occur to work out the plot? Who shall tell the story: the leading character, a bystander, an omniscient author, etc.? Which serves the author's purposes most efficiently? All these and literally hundreds of other questions must be answered in the writing of the novel.

How do you suppose the author answers all these questions? Some of them are doubtless answered very easily. Maybe it doesn't matter in the least what color the hero's hair is—unless you're Golding writing *Lord of the Flies,* and you need to portray Jack as one kind of boy and Ralph as another, and so give Jack red hair and Ralph light hair. Maybe it wouldn't really matter what the setting is, unless you are trying to show the difficulties children have in growing up amid racial prejudice and bigotry as in *To Kill a Mocking Bird.* Then it becomes important indeed that the small Southern town be carefully portrayed. In *Heart of Darkness* it is important that Marlowe sits with legs crossed like an "idol"—like some "eastern god." It is important that shoes keep turning up in the jungle, that words denoting or connoting light and dark are constantly used. One wonders how Conrad could keep so many purposes in mind, as well as all the ways to fulfill those purposes.

The study of a novel should, if pursued skillfully, reveal the author's purpose or purposes. Remember to begin with the question: Why? Why is that in this book? Why is this character shown as antagonistic to that character? And so on. Finally, you arrive at an understanding of the overall purposes (theme) of the book. Once you feel that you know this larger purpose, you can check on everything in the book, to see whether it is consistent with this larger purpose. Once you know that Golding in *Lord of the Flies* is showing the evil in people that wrecks all we try to build, you can check through the book to see if or how everything in it supports that purpose. If you find elements in the book that don't make contributions, or that actually are not consistent with it, you have grounds on which to make negative criticism of the book.

To prepare to write a paper of literary analysis or criticism, it is wise to ask yourself questions beginning with "why." Why is this in the book? Why did the author have this happen as it did? Then, when you have arrived at the answer, you have the thesis for the paper. Examples: By doing so and so, John Doe accomplishes the dual purpose of showing the hero's inability to cope with his wife as well as the tendency of people to interfere where they are not wanted. 2) In such and such a book, John Doe uses the rain to create an atmosphere of darkness and gloom, as well as to screen the events from reality as if they were occurring behind a curtain. 3) Golding accomplishes a number of important purposes by having the bright faced little boy named Simon.

Copyright © 1977 by Allyn and Bacon, Inc. Reproduction of this material is restricted to use with <u>A Guidebook for Teaching Creative Writing,</u> by Gene Stanford and Marie N. Smith.

REPRODUCTION PAGE 25

NAME_____ SECTION_____

Steps in Writing a Paper about a Novel

1. Ask yourself questions about the author's purposes. These questions should all begin with "why," or "what did the author accomplish by..."

2. When you've read the book thoroughly enough to think of a good question, study the book with this question in mind, and use the answer as the thesis for your paper.

3. Introduce that thesis in the first paragraph. Many writers feel that the best place for the thesis statement is at the very end of the introductory paragraph. They believe that one does well to lead up to it by general statements about the book in which mention is made of the name of the book, the name of the author, and the general gist or purpose of the book. This introductory paragraph might be planned as if it were a funnel: it opens with a broad, general statement about the book and narrows down to the specific statement which you intend to develop in your paper.

4. If your thesis statement is a limited one which doesn't have to be divided into various parts, you are ready to develop it, to make it specific instead of general by writing with details. If your thesis needs explanation, explain it, and then make it clear by giving examples from the pages of the book.

5. If your thesis is a complex one and needs dividing into parts, name those parts—they comprise your "outline." Each of these now needs to be explained and made clear with examples from the book. (The pattern for each is: state it, explain it, give examples of it.)

6. Remember that you write by paragraphs, and that you never handle more than one idea in one paragraph. If you have many examples from the text, you usually do well to devote a paragraph to each example.

7. It is seldom sufficient simply to announce an example and let it lie there without any interpretation. It's up to you to show the readers exactly how the example supports your thesis. Don't trust the readers to figure out anything for themselves, because they won't. That's your job.

8. Don't madden your readers by referring to your examples only by page number. Maybe they are reading another edition of the book and the pages are different. Besides, you have no right to ask extra work of your readers. It's your job to explain references by their content.

9. If you're lucky and throughout the book there are many demonstrations (what we're calling examples) of the validity of your thesis, you won't want to bore your readers to death with all of them. Instead, select those which are most significant to the book and will be most convincing to your audience.

10. Plan your paper from beginning to end before writing. Know what points you intend to make, how you intend to make them, and the textual references you intend to use to prove them. And decide on the order in which you will do these things. Then—and not before—start writing.

Copyright © 1977 by Allyn and Bacon, Inc. Reproduction of this material is restricted to use with A Guidebook for Teaching Creative Writing, by Gene Stanford and Marie N. Smith.

REPRODUCTION PAGE 25   STEPS IN WRITING A PAPER ABOUT A NOVEL

11. Use your last paragraph to wind up, summarize, and restate your thesis in different language.

12. Proofread for errors in grammar, spelling, and punctuation.

13. Relax. You did your best.

Copyright © 1977 by Allyn and Bacon, Inc. Reproduction of this material is restricted to use with A Guidebook for Teaching Creative Writing, by Gene Stanford and Marie N. Smith.

NAME _____   SECTION _____

Sample Essay
The Symbolic Use of the Color Green in *Lord of the Flies*
Ken Cohn   (12th grade student)

Lord of the Flies, by William Golding, is the story of boys evacuated from England during an atomic war at some unspecified future time. The boys land on a tropical island in a passenger tube which drops from a flaming airplane, and in their struggle for survival they encounter conflicts similar to the antagonisms of the society from which they have come. But without the traditional society and the guidance of adults, the natural evil in the boys overwhelms their weak social system, and their civilization itself is threatened. In the plot Golding's major theme becomes apparent as an attempt to display evil as the inborn characteristic of man which gives rise to the defects of a community. In order to present this theme, Golding builds a many layered structure interwoven with numerous motifs with varying degrees of prominence. An inconspicuous but highly significant motif is the word green.

Green has almost innumerable meanings but is often used to express the idea of immaturity or inexperience. The meaning of these two words can be combined into one specific word, innocence, meaning the innocence of the child and the innocence of nature. Nature is green and nature is innocent. But it is the innocence of the wild and the untamed, for the quiet forest cannot conceal the bitter fight for survival among the different species of animals. A child is innocent, and the child is also "green." Hidden behind the mask of innocent youth is an animal instinct and desire. When the natural instinct of man becomes apparent, he has become "green"; he has become like the wild animal. In the novel the retrogression of the boys from civilization to savagery is paralleled with the motif green which first describes the "feathery tops of the palms" but later describes the green which the boys crave.

In the beginning of the story Golding describes the "green feathers" of the palm tree and the "dense green" of "the jungly flat of the island." These phrases introduce the reader to the idea that green is a symbol of the natural state. Similar statements are made throughout the novel in order that the reader will continue to associate green with nature. Further into the book the author attempts to show the reader the different sides of nature. Reference is made to "waxen green" flowers and the "green candle-like buds" which surround Simon's "little cabin." But there is also reference to "a mass of twisted stems, black and green and impenetrable." The former is representative of the peaceful and beautiful side of nature, and the latter is representative of the wild and ugly side of nature. This idea of green as a force of nature must be kept in mind while considering all other repetitions of the color.

After the motif green is established as a symbol of nature's power, the reader notices how frequently the boys have been found in green shadows. At the beginning of the novel when Ralph removes his clothes to go swimming, he "stood there among the skull-like coconuts with green shadows from the palms and the forests sliding over his skin;" when he leaves the water he "decided that the shadows on his body were really green." Shortly after, Ralph blows the conch and watches the boys coming up the beach, "their heads clustered above the trunks in the green shade." Golding narrates: "Some were naked and carrying their clothes, others half naked, or more or less dressed . . ." It is through these references to green that Golding begins to build a parallel to the retrogression of the boys. The clothing which they had shed is the first link to civilization which they have broken. It is indeed

Copyright © 1977 by Allyn and Bacon, Inc. Reproduction of this material is restricted to use with <u>A Guidebook for Teaching Creative Writing</u>, by Gene Stanford and Marie N. Smith.

REPRODUCTION PAGE 26 **SAMPLE ESSAY**

ironic that at the end of the novel, the boys are rescued by a naval officer who also stands in a "green shade."

At this point Golding presents the reader with an outstanding analogy to his theme. While Piggy and Ralph are speaking of the conch, Piggy tells where he has seen another. Someone he knew "had it on his garden wall . . . . He had some white stones too, an' a bird cage with a green parrot." The conch was suspended on the wall for everyone to admire and respect, but the green parrot was in a cage. To be allowed in society, green must remain caged or hidden. Otherwise, this inborn characteristic of man becomes apparent and leads to the defects of society. In effect, Golding is presenting a summary of his theme in the words of his intellectual character, Piggy.

With the progression of the story, the boys become more dependent on materials associated with green. They procure food from the forest with "the palms that made a green roof." Even by "the place of assembly," one of the boys' major links to civilization, stand trees which form a "green roof." If the boys are to be rescued, they must build a fire which will emit smoke, and for this "green branches" are necessary. And with the retrogression of the island society, these dependencies become ironic. The forest which is necessary for the boys' survival is also believed to be the home of the beast. The pigs which provide the meat the boys cherish leave "olive green" droppings, and the boys believe droppings to be "the dirtiest thing there is." Also, the boys do not have enough organization to keep the fire, a symbol of rescue and hope, burning. The boys are even warned that "green" is responsible for their social decline. They believe the beast to be the threat to their survival, but as Jack, Roger and Ralph lie by the "soft ashes of the fire" and look for the beast, "green lights of nausea appeared for a moment and ate into the darkness." When they thought they saw the beast, "green lights were opening again and growing." Indeed, they were seeing the beast when they saw the green, for the beast was the natural or animalistic part of each boy, and this was exactly what green symbolized.

The boys pass from the stage in which they seek a dependency on green to the phase in which they crave green, to the point at which they actually "become" green. While Jack smears clay on his face before going on a hunt he says to Roger, "If only I'd some green!" But Jack and his followers do at last find green to smear on their faces, and it is then that the animal instinct in each becomes overwhelming. They become like the "black and irridescent green" flies. When they "attack" Ralph's camp for fire, Golding describes them as "Demoniac figures with faces of white and red and green rushing out howling, . . ." Later there are several references to the "black and green mask" that Jack wears, and Ralph attempts "to remember what Jack looked like"; he "cries out hopelessly against the black and green mask." But his cry is indeed hopeless, for Jack and Roger and their followers are now more animal than human. The "green glow" of the horizon is the author's symbolization of the animalistic state which now encompasses the island.

Golding finishes the novel with a highly significant reference to green in a description of the naval officer who, ironically, stands in "the green shade of the peak" of his cap. Although he represents the authority which the boys have needed on the island, he is also representative of the animalistic force which critically weakens the society from which he comes. It is ironic that the boys are rescued from the green which has lowered them to savagery by an adult who also stands in green shade. And it is indeed "the end of innocence" for all the boys on the island. They have seen the power in "the darkness of man's heart" and have witnessed the animal instinct which attempts to destroy every society.

Copyright © 1977 by Allyn and Bacon, Inc. Reproduction of this material is restricted to use with A Guidebook for Teaching Creative Writing, by Gene Stanford and Marie N. Smith.

REPRODUCTION PAGE 27

NAME_____ SECTION_____

Improving the Style of an Essay about Literature

A. Do not use the title of the book or short story as the title of your paper about that novel/story. Instead, indicate what you are trying to prove: "A Study of Point of View in Willa Cather's *Paul's Case.*"

B. Identify the title and author of the work somewhere in the introduction of your paper.

C. You may need to provide a one or two sentence summary of what the novel/story is about in case the reader is not familiar with it. Do not assume that other people know as much about the story as you; therefore, identify all characters, events, and the like.

D. A specific detail from the story/novel can be introduced in several ways:
  1) By mentioning it in your own words. This involves no direct quotation from the story. For example:
     At the meeting following the scene on the mountain, Simon acknowledges going into the jungle alone, at night, to his special place. The laughter at him is now derisive and condemning.
  2) By incorporating a key word or phrase used in the novel/story by quoting directly only a word or two within one of your own sentences. For example:
     Simon gives his meat to Piggy and "lowered his face in shame," almost as if he is embarrassed to participate in this obscene parody of a sacrament.
  3) By quoting directly an important sentence or series of sentences:
     The church is foreboding to Jackie: "Within the old church was no stained glass; it was cold and dark and desolate, and in the silence, the trees in the yard knocked hollowly at the tall windows."

E. Just like any other specific details in a paragraph, the details from the novel/story should not simply be listed after the topic sentence in grocery list form. Instead:
  1) Introduce the detail. But do not use an expression so obvious as "As this quotation shows..." or "The following quotation from the novel reveals..." Try using a colon to connect your generalization (interpretation) and the quotation (as in #3 above).
  2) Interpret the detail. Show how it proves your thesis. Do not expect readers to see the connection for themselves.
  3) Explain the detail.
  4) Provide connecting ideas between specifics, so that you leave no gaps in thought for readers to leap over.

Copyright © 1977 by Allyn and Bacon, Inc. Reproduction of this material is restricted to use with <u>A Guidebook for Teaching Creative Writing</u>, by Gene Stanford and Marie N. Smith.

REPRODUCTION PAGE 28

NAME _____ SECTION _____

Study/Discussion Questions for *Alas, Babylon*

1. The title of the novel comes from the Bible, Revelation 18:9–10:

    And the kings of the earth, who committed fornication and were wanton with her, will weep and wail over her when they see the smoke of her burning; they will stand far off, in fear of her torment, and say, "Alas! alas! thou great city, thou mighty city, Babylon! In one hour has thy judgment come."

    Can you explain its significance to the book? What useful way of examining and discussing the book is provided by an understanding of the title?

2. Trace the character of Randy Bragg through the book. What changes occur in him, and what is their significance? (In short, why does Frank show him changing in these exact ways?) This question will require much thought and discussion. Perhaps you will need to reread the book, marking appropriate passages. You may want to wait to discuss this question, or you may think it helpful to do this problem early in your discussion. Whatever your decision, do the work carefully and thoroughly.

3. What comment does the author seem to be making through the development of Florence Wechek as the book progresses? Is this also true for Bill McGovern, Dan Gunn, Edgar Quisenberry, etc.?

4. Why does Florence have a cat, two lovebirds, and a tank of goldfish? What other animals are mentioned in the book? Why?

5. What part does religion play in the book? Does it seem to occupy the same position in Frank's post-bomb society as in your own?

6. Does Mr. Frank make any comment about the nature of law in this book?

7. Why do you think Frank included the incident about the "wolf" in the chicken pen?

8. What does the author have to say about race relations? How does he use the Henry family in this connection?

9. Why is Preacher Henry in the book?

10. Why is Lavinia McGovern in the book?

11. Examine the character of Edgar Quisenberry. What does Frank show us through this character? How about Henrietta, his wife?

12. The subject of death appears many times in the book. In what ways do the attitudes toward death in *Alas, Babylon* differ from those observed today?

13. Why do you believe, in the end, no one wanted to be taken out of Fort Repose?

14. Why is Alice Cooksey in the book? How is she characterized by Frank?

15. Examine Graf's role in the book. What purpose does he serve?

16. What is the significance of Porky Logan? In what ways does he relate to the author's theme? Why was he not the natural leader of the community rather than Randy?

Copyright © 1977 by Allyn and Bacon, Inc. Reproduction of this material is restricted to use with <u>A Guidebook for Teaching Creative Writing</u>, by Gene Stanford and Marie N. Smith.

REPRODUCTION PAGE 28   STUDY/DISCUSSION QUESTIONS FOR *ALAS, BABYLON*

17. What kind of person is Dan Gunn? How does he change? What do you think about his plan to marry Helen Bragg? Do you think they are in love? What do you think about her wanting to marry him before she knows for sure that Mark is dead?

18. Examine the purpose in the book of Bubbe and Kitty Offenhaus.

19. How does Frank characterize Helen Bragg? How are she and Lib McGovern different?

20. Through Helen and Lib, as well as other females, what does Frank seem to be saying about women?

21. Examine the relationship between the sexes. What might Frank be showing by contrast to our present society? Do men and women seem to be more different from one another in the novel than is presently true in our world?

22. Do standards of morality seem different in post-bomb society than in our own? Can you locate those portions of plot which reveal Frank's comments on morality? What is the root—the source—of morality?

23. What is the significance of Frank's mention of automobiles in the book?

24. What do you think of Ben Franklin and Peyton as compared to youngsters in our society? Does their outlook on maturing seem about the same as yours?

25. Why are Sam Hazzard and Bill McGovern in the book? How were their lives different from what they would have been without the bomb? Trace the ways they change.

26. Can you identify any minor characters who contribute significant meanings to the book?

27. What were the qualities in Randy Bragg which finally made him the natural leader of Fort Repose?

28. What do you think the chances of survival would be for your family if you were caught in circumstances like those in *Alas, Babylon*? What kind of person do you think you might turn out to be?

29. What elements in your present world are better than those in the post-bomb world of Ben Franklin Bragg?

30. If you were to be stuck in a small group after a nuclear holocaust, whom would you choose to be with and what would you take with you? What would you miss most? What would you gladly give up?

31. In *Lord of the Flies*, William Golding seemed to say that humankind is basically evil, and that our social structures mirror our inherently evil nature. Do you think Frank agrees with him?

32. Why do you think Frank implies that our society is similar to Babylon? Do you agree with him? Do you think we will come to the hour of judgment? Do you think we deserve to survive or deserve to be wiped out?

33. Do you believe we will eventually suffer nuclear cataclysm in this country? Do you want to be among the survivors, those who must face the "thousand-year night?"

34. Examine all references early in the novel to "life not being worth living." Why were those inserted? How do they contribute to your understanding of the theme of the novel?

Copyright © 1977 by Allyn and Bacon, Inc. Reproduction of this material is restricted to use with A Guidebook for Teaching Creative Writing, by Gene Stanford and Marie N. Smith.

REPRODUCTION PAGE 29

NAME_____ SECTION_____

Why Study Poetry?

Hardly any two people will agree as to exactly what poetry is. It appears that there are almost as many definitions of poetry as there are poetry lovers—or poetry haters! Unfortunately, many students number themselves among those who "hate poetry" or think poetry is "stupid," and one comes to believe that there is one definition of poetry which can help explain why this is. Samuel T. Coleridge, the great English poet and critic, said that while prose is words in their best order, poetry consists of "the best words in the best order."

In order to be sure of selecting, out of all those words available, the very best word to suit the purpose, the poet spends a great deal of time and effort in considering all alternatives and in finally choosing just the word that he or she is convinced is "best." In fact, it might surprise you to learn that a poet can devote years to writing one poem. Thomas Gray, for instance, spent nine years working on "Elegy Written in a Country Churchyard." (Undeniably, there are instances in which a poem is almost literally dashed off in final form during the white heat of inspiration—some Bob Dylan works are examples—but evidence indicates that such occasions are not frequent.)

Now, if a poet spends weeks or months—or even years—in writing a poem, how fair—or how sensible—is it for a reader to say it is a stupid poem, or to say he or she doesn't like it, after reading it through just once, in the same way one reads prose? To read a poem as if one were seeking information or receiving instruction is to miss all that the poet has worked so diligently to create. In fact, to read a poem in such a way is usually to persuade oneself that poetry makes no sense, for it is hard to get the sense of a poem without reading it with care almost equal to that expended by the poet in writing it. We can hardly be expected, of course, to study a poem for weeks, months, or years, but it is certain that we won't get the advantage of the poet's talent and skill unless we read with a great deal more attention and awareness than we find necessary to expend on prose. Many students—as well as some people no longer in school—have not learned to read in this different way, in this more creative way required by poetry, and this is the reason they fail to get any pleasure out of poetry.

What is it, then, that you are supposed to be looking for, that you are supposed to discover when you read poetry with such care and sensitivity? What is supposed to happen that will make you decide you like poetry after all? These are the important questions. It is clear that if you don't know what you are looking for, if you don't know, that is, what poetry is or what the poet was creating for you to experience, it's going to be difficult for you to know how to react to it, and it is unlikely that you will enjoy it. It's hard to like something you don't understand, and, in fact, it's a temptation to say that the reason you don't see anything worthwhile in a poem is because there just isn't anything worthwhile there!

Yet, it you are fair and completely honest with yourself, surely you would not suggest that the countless people throughout the ages who have said that poetry has enriched their lives are liars or hypocrites or not very bright! No, you would certainly admit the likelihood that these people are telling the truth, that they have simply been able to find something in poetry that you have not yet learned to find.

The student's purpose, then, is to find that "something" that so many other people have found in poetry, not just so you will *know* more, or *understand* more, but so you will *enjoy* more.

Surely one of the major purposes of education is to enlarge people's capacity to enjoy life. And that purpose alone justifies the effort to learn to read poetry with understanding.

Copyright © 1977 by Allyn and Bacon, Inc. Reproduction of this material is restricted to use with A Guidebook for Teaching Creative Writing, by Gene Stanford and Marie N. Smith.

NAME_____   SECTION_____

"The Best Words in the Best Order"

You may already be asking yourself, "best for what?" If someone tells you that a dog, for instance, is *the very best* one, you immediately wonder, "best for what?" Best as a pet, best as a watchdog? As a hunter, as a retriever? And you do well to ask this same question about poetry. If, as Coleridge said, poetry consists of the best words in the best order, what purpose did he have in mind for the words to fill? Best for what? Best to convey precise information? Best to impress the reader with the poet's superior education? Or did he mean to take up the least space or best not to stir up any unwanted questions?

It is at once apparent that one must identify a poet's purpose before it can be decided whether the poet did indeed choose the "best" words. "What was he or she trying to achieve with that word?" is the first question to be answered.

In a very specific sense, each individual poet has a separate and distinct purpose for each poem he or she writes. But in a more general sense, we can identify one or two overall purposes which poets seem to have in common, and then we can identify some very concrete aims which govern the words they choose.

First, here are two major poetic purposes which will give us some guidelines as to what all poetry aims to do:

I. *The Poet Shows Us to Ourselves.* He or she attempts to write so vividly, with so sharp and clear a focus, that we stand revealed to ourselves in our truest and deepest nature. The poet sees us and our world and our lives and uses words to reveal this vision to us.

II. *The Poet Creates an Experience for Us to Have.* The poet does not tell us about an experience, or a place. The poet creates it for us, attempting to use words that evoke an experience, a vision, a feeling, or an emotion, so that we ourselves might experience what he or she has experienced and is recreating for us. The poet uses words to make us feel the same emotions, remember the same memories, hear the same sounds as he or she felt, remembered, or heard.

In pursuit of these poetic aspirations the poet has at least six ways of using language which must be considered in choosing just the word which is best. It is these uses of language which will provide our standards for the word "best."

1. *The use of language to sound a certain way,* either to evoke some emotional response in the reader, to create a literary effect, to create a pattern which arouses the reader's attention on behalf of some emphasis the poet has in mind, to imitate some other sound which the poet wants the reader to think of, or for the simple purpose of decoration. Such use of language for its sound involves rhyme and rhythm as well as the sounds of individual words and combinations of words.

2. *The use of metaphorical language*—that is, saying one thing to mean another. In prose, particularly scientific or instructive prose, we try to say precisely what we mean. The poet, however, often says something other than what he or she means, but which arouses a more emotional response in the reader than precisely informative words would have done. For example, "I have measured out my life with coffee spoons" certainly evokes a sharper personal response than more precisely descriptive wording such as, "I have involved myself

Copyright © 1977 by Allyn and Bacon, Inc. Reproduction of this material is restricted to use with A Guidebook for Teaching Creative Writing, by Gene Stanford and Marie N. Smith.

with trivial happenings all my life." The use of metaphor is an attempt to engage the reader emotionally, to make personal to the reader the experience being written about.

3. *The creation of images: imagery.* The poet attempts, with words, to cause the reader to imagine what he or she is describing or creating. The poet attempts to create images. These are appeals to the mind's eye, to the mind's ear, and so on. By using words which cause you to imagine the sound of bells pealing triumphantly, the poet successfully creates an image which involves you, the reader, in the poem. If he or she uses words which cause you to imagine the soft, furry feel of a little animal's fuzzy coat, then the poet has captured your imagination with a successful image, and has brought you into the experience created for you. Imagery often helps the reader have the experience the poet has prepared for him or her

4. *The use of connotative language.* Different words which mean practically the same thing, so far as dictionary definition is concerned, still strike us differently and make us respond in different ways, perhaps as a result of experiences, memories, values, or habits that we associate with certain words. The poet knows this, and tries to figure out how readers will respond to these words and what their emotional reactions will be. The poet chooses specific words with an aim of evoking the emotion which suits best the purpose of the poem.

Certainly "a thrifty dame" calls forth a different response from "an economical woman" or "a penurious female," and "a tiny huddled kitten" strikes you as quite a different thing from "a small, bunched-up young feline." The poet knows how he or she wants you to feel, and tries to choose words which you associate with that very feeling. The poet's sensitivity to connotation helps to capture your emotions.

5. *The use of symbols to make a specific experience or thing take on a more universal meaning.* Human beings seem to be the only animals capable of symbolism, as witnessed by the fact that we are the only animal with language. Words are simply symbols of things, symbols that we humans have chosen for our own use. We go far beyond this in our use of symbols, however. We tend to vest in one thing all the significance of another, as with our country's flag, for instance. We tend to consider the flag sacred because it stands for the country which means so much to us. We say that white stands for purity, black for evil. We say that water represents salvation, that the cross is the central symbol of Christianity and that a certain kind of star is the symbol of Judaism.

Poets often speak of specific things, but they know that our minds will leap to the larger meanings symbolized by those things, and they thus make larger the significance of what they are saying. A small green leaf thrusting up through snow is no longer just a natural phenomenon, but a symbol of hope, of renewal, of rebirth and of humanity's capacity for regeneration. Through symbolism poets make concrete things abstract and specific things general. They widen our vision.

6. *The use of original language.* Poets attempt to create unique expressions. They must be able to justify their poetry not only in terms of the significance and validity of its comment about the human condition, but also in terms of its originality and singularity. This standard applies both to the message of the poem and to its form, to the words the poem uses. The poet, therefore, strives to use words in new ways, to say things in ways they have never been said before, to imbue old words and phrases with new meanings in new contexts and to command the reader's attention with the uniqueness of his or her art.

These are some of the purposes a poet might have in mind when choosing a word. These are the standards we shall use in considering whether the poet has chosen the "best" word.

Copyright © 1977 by Allyn and Bacon, Inc. Reproduction of this material is restricted to use with A Guidebook for Teaching Creative Writing, by Gene Stanford and Marie N. Smith.

NAME_____ SECTION_____

The Sounds of Poetry

Long before the alphabet was invented, there was poetry. Poems were recited and sung, not read. Therefore the sound of the poem was very important. Different sound effects were used for a number of purposes:

1. Rhythmic words and lines were more easily memorized and more easily sung than lines with no rhythmic flow.

2. Alliterative lines also were easily memorized. ("True is the tale I tell of my travels" is surely more memorable than "Accurate is the history I shall relate of my journeys.")

3. The poet-singer could hold an audience's attention more easily if there was interest contained in the word pattern in addition to the story being told. People enjoy patterns, rhymes, repetitive sounds and rhythms. This seems to be inborn, as even small infants respond with a seeming show of pleasure to such sound effects. Have you ever heard a little child crooning to itself, rhyming nonsense syllables: roon, spoon, doon, rote, cote, dote? Youngsters do this as naturally as they smile—it's only later that they need to be reminded of poetry!

4. It became the mark of a poet's craftsmanship—or of his or her art—to be able to make poetry sound like what he or she was telling about: a battle scene should be recounted in rough, bruising, strong language, but a lovely dawn scene should be described in soft, harmonious, flowing sounds. This unity of sound and sense is still characteristic of the skilled poet.

Definitions

Alliteration—repetition of consonants, especially at the beginning of words, or of stressed syllables. In Old English poetry alliteration was a regular element of each line, but since then it has been used for special effects only.

Assonance—repetition of identical or related vowel sounds, especially in stressed syllables. (The spelling of the word is not pertinent; it is the sound which is assonant.)

Consonance—repetition of a pattern of consonants, with changes in the intervening vowels (a diller, a dollar, a duller scholar).

Onomatopoeia—use of words whose sounds seem to resemble the sounds they describe (hiss, buzz, rustle, bang)

Cacophony—use of harsh and unmusical sounds, discordancy. (Adj.: cacophonous).

Euphony—a pleasant, melodious effect. (Adj.: euphonious)

Copyright © 1977 by Allyn and Bacon, Inc. Reproduction of this material is restricted to use with A Guidebook for Teaching Creative Writing, by Gene Stanford and Marie N. Smith.

REPRODUCTION PAGE 32

NAME_____ SECTION_____

Metaphorical Language

Simile—a comparison between two essentially different items is expressly indicated by a term such as "like" or "as." (A pretty girl is like a lovely tune.)

Metaphor—a word which in ordinary usage signifies one kind of thing, quality or action is applied to another, without express indication of the relationship between them. (One says one thing to mean another.) (His name is mud. Her kid brother is a pain in the neck. He was a true Galahad. Life is a song.)

Synecdoche—a metaphor in which a part of something is used to signify the whole. Pronounced: sin-eck-doe-key. (She gave her hand in marriage. He bought a new set of wheels.)

Metonymy—a metaphor in which the name of one thing is applied to another thing with which it is closely associated. (The crown is secure. The press is irresponsible. Is there word from the capital?)

Personification—a metaphor in which either an inanimate object or an abstract concept is described as being endowed with human attributes, powers, or feelings. (Justice is blind.)

Hyperbole—extravagant exaggeration of fact used either for serious or comic effect. (He shook when he laughed like a bowlful of jelly.)

Kenning—a metaphorical compound word which names something in terms of function. The Anglo-Saxons often used kennings to describe the sea: whale road. (lipstick, spotlight, pencil-pusher, slave-driver.)

Litotes—a deliberate understatement as if to avoid censure for boasting, to emphasize by indirection in order to get credit for modesty. (Not a bad halfback. Not a half bad little town. He is a man of no mean talent. I'd say she can hold her own.)

Paradox—a statement that seems absurd and self-contradictory, but which turns out to have a tenable and coherent meaning. (He who is last among you shall be first. He who would save his life must lose it. Fair is foul and foul is fair. So fair and foul a day I have not seen. (These last two examples are from *Macbeth,* a very equivocal play, rich with paradoxes.))

Oxymoron—a paradoxical statement combining two terms that in ordinary usage are contraries, such as "pleasing pains," "loving hate." (It was a bitter joy. Missing the plane was a fortuitous misfortune. Had he caught it he would have been killed.)

Copyright © 1977 by Allyn and Bacon, Inc. Reproduction of this material is restricted to use with <u>A Guidebook for Teaching Creative Writing</u>, by Gene Stanford and Marie N. Smith.

REPRODUCTION PAGE 33

NAME _____ SECTION _____

Questions for Critical Analysis of a Poem, or What Is in This Poem that I Can Comment on?

I. *Unity.* Every aspect of a poem should be planned to support the poet's overall purposes. All is unified around one aim.
   A. Tone. Does the poet create a mood of dread? Amuse you throughout with lighthearted humor? Plod along ponderously, seem very serious or pedantic, etc.?
   B. Diction. What words can you identify that seem congruent with the poet's major purpose(s) for the poem? Does he or she use language that suits (or sounds like) the subject, as does Keats with the lazy, drowsy sounds in his poem, "Autumn"?
   C. Rhyme – Rhythm – Alliteration – Consonance – Assonance. Does the poet use any of these poetic devices? Does he or she use hard, voiced consonants or soft, unvoiced, unstopped sounds? Do the sounds of the poem bear a relationship to the poem's overall subject, purpose, and mood?

II. *Purpose.* The poet's purpose must be revealed—for each poem—*in* the poem. If you cannot decide what a poem means or what kind of experience it was meant to convey, you must determine who is at fault, the poet or the reader. The poet creates a poem so the reader can have—from the words of the poem—the same experiences the poet had in real life; and so the reader can gain from the poem the same insight the poet gained from the real life experience.
   A. What kind of experience is being created in this poem?
   B. What insight do you seem to be expected to gain from this experience?

III. *Connotation.* What words can you identify that contribute to the emotional experience the poet means you to have? What particular words, in short, can you identify as having connotative value in the poem?

IV. *Metaphorical Language.*
   A. What metaphorical (figurative) usages can you identify? Identify metaphors, similes, personifications, etc.—all ways the poet says one thing to mean another.
   B. What emotional responses does the poet seem to want to arouse in you by this figurative language?

V. *Imagery.*
   A. Can you identify all the images the poet uses—all the words or statements that make us imagine sounds, tastes, smells, sights, feelings?
   B. Are there many different images in the poem?
   C. Does the poet depend on one of the senses more than the others? (all sight images, perhaps—or mostly sound images)

VI. Do you find examples of original, exciting language?

Copyright © 1977 by Allyn and Bacon, Inc. Reproduction of this material is restricted to use with <u>A Guidebook for Teaching Creative Writing</u>, by Gene Stanford and Marie N. Smith.

NAME _____ SECTION _____

"London"
William Blake (1757–1827)

I wander through each chartered street,
Near where the chartered Thames does flow
And mark in every face I meet
Marks of weakness, marks of woe.

In every cry of every man,
In every infant's cry of fear,
In every voice, in every ban,
The mind-forged manacles I hear.

How the chimney-sweeper's cry
Every blackening church appalls,
And the hapless soldier's sigh
Runs in blood down palace-walls.

But most, through midnight streets I hear
How the youthful harlot's curse
Blasts the new-born infant's tear,
And blights with plagues the marriage-hearse.

Copyright © 1977 by Allyn and Bacon, Inc. Reproduction of this material is restricted to use with <u>A Guidebook for Teaching Creative Writing</u>, by Gene Stanford and Marie N. Smith.

REPRODUCTION PAGE 35

NAME _____ SECTION _____

Chart for Analysis of a Poem

Sound Devices									Images

Metaphors									Words with Connotative Value

Allusions									Symbols

Original Usages									Other Notable Devices

Copyright © 1977 by Allyn and Bacon, Inc. Reproduction of this material is restricted to use with <u>A Guidebook for Teaching Creative Writing</u>, by Gene Stanford and Marie N. Smith.

NAME_____ SECTION_____

"On Shakespeare"
John Milton

What needs my Shakespeare for his honored bones
The labor of an age in piled stones?
Or that his hallowed relics should be hid
Under a star-ypointing pyramid?
Dear son of memory, great heir of fame,
What need'st thou such weak witness of thy name?
Thou in our wonder and astonishment
Hast built thyself a livelong monument.
For whilst, to the shame of slow-endeavoring art
Thy easy numbers flow, and that each heart
Hath from the leaves of thy unvalued book
Those Delphic lines with deep impression took,
Then thou, our fancy of itself bereaving
Dost make us marble with too much conceiving.
And so sepulchred in such pomp dost lie
That kings for such a tomb would wish to die.

REPRODUCTION PAGE 37

NAME_____ SECTION_____

"Snow on Easter"
John Stephen Harris

The cast of mind that put a Hamlet through his paces
kept me working at his whether or not to be
as if the back and forth, each intellective strut,
could build me closer to the other lip of the abyss.
All the walking in my mind began to leave traces
before my eyes, and sunrise found me nearly
blind, eyes almost swollen shut
on the amazing Easter morning I was converted to my senses.
None of the natural shocks before or since
has, like snow on the pale blooming blood of the quince,
the burden of the bright and bent forsythia, so moved
my heavy wits, like a weightless cave-stone, or proved,
like my first breath of the honeysuckle cold,
how better bright the air is once they're rolled.

"Snow on Easter" by John Stephen Harris. Used with permission of the author.

Copyright © 1977 by Allyn and Bacon, Inc. Reproduction of this material is restricted to use with <u>A Guidebook for Teaching Creative Writing</u>, by Gene Stanford and Marie N. Smith.

REPRODUCTION PAGE 38

NAME _____   SECTION _____

"Snow on Easter" – An Explication
Roger Zehntner

    Steve Harris' "Snow on Easter" opens with an explicit reference to Hamlet's existential soliloquy. "Cast of mind" is but Shakespeare's "cast of thought" and by alluding to it the poet cues the reader to an understanding of the poem's meaning. The "other lip of the abyss" is the goal for which the poet strives. It is the "abyss" of meaninglessness, and its "other" edge signifies existential completeness. The poet, like Hamlet, seeks to achieve a wholeness of being; but like Hamlet's, his struggles are ineffectual and unsatisfactory. Prince Hamlet, of course, was the eternal intellectualizer, philosophical and cerebral, but, alas, unable to will a sense of resolute meaning upon his life. The poet, in the initial lines of his sonnet, faces a similar dilemma and, like the melancholy Dane, approaches his existential plight in a similar, ultimately unsatisfactory manner. He hopes, by "intellective strut," to "build" himself, calculating like a careful mason, nearer to a sense of being, when life has purpose and yawning nothingness has been traversed. The poet, however, in the initial lines, fails to achieve his aim. His wholly cerebral labors leave his "eyes almost swollen shut," cut off from life's experience, and in the throes of a Hamlet-like meaninglessness. It is then that what Shakespeare termed the "native hue of resolution," the feeling of human potency, is at its lowest ebb. Thus, the poet, now sightless from his futile intellectual strivings, ruminates in the darkness of the night, symbolically in the darkness of existential despair.

    The "sunrise," a near perfect pun foreshadowing the Christian imagery to follow, signifies the rejuvenation of the poet's spirit, his conversion to the value of living, to an exalted sense that one's existence is whole, purposeful, and satisfying. Appropriately, the poet now selects the Easter myth as the source of his imagery. It is, indeed, Christ healing the blind, restoring the "native hue of resolution" to the once despairing. This conversion or reconfirmation is eloquently and alliteratively contained in the last three couplets of the sonnet. The "natural shocks," again a Shakespearian borrowing, are all striking sensations—"pale blooming blood of the quince," "bright and bent forsythia" and "honeysuckle cold." These final lines are in marked contrast to the first two quatrains of the sonnet which are relatively imageless, comparatively blunt and composed in distant rhymes. Consequently, the poetic devices of the sonnet reflect its own theme. The narrative conversion from the barren intellectuality of the initial quatrains is dramatically marked by a profusion of images, metaphors and explosive rhymes in the ending couplets. The sonnet, therefore, exemplifying its own doctrine, and corresponding to the poet's revelation, has its own poetic "conversion."

    Moreover, Easter allusions are particularly befitting to the poet's transformation when his intellectual preoccupation is abandoned. For the Christian, Easter is theoretically the most triumphant moment of his religious life, when the worshipper celebrates the ultimate value of his experience. He has achieved, hopefully, at least for one eternal moment, a glimpse of his salvation, when his life, with all its sinful weaknesses and mundane confusion, ultimately has meaning. For the poet, a nearly identical psycho-emotional experience transpires, although with wider pantheistic aspects. Easter here is used as the Christian metaphor for spring, the rebirth of nature. The Christian imagery emphasizes the Easter-like experience

---

" 'Snow on Easter' – An Explication" by Roger Zehntner · Used with permission of the author.

Copyright © 1977 by Allyn and Bacon, Inc. Reproduction of this material is restricted to use with <u>A Guidebook for Teaching Creative Writing</u>, by Gene Stanford and Marie N. Smith.

of the poet, the intensity of his renewed awareness, and signals his conversion to his senses. Thus, his "heavy wits," once dulled, have been "rolled," remarkably, like Christ's "cavestone" by the sensations of the new season. It is then that life is most sensible and most sensuous, whole and integrated, like a well-wrought sonnet, a breathing microcosm unto itself.

Finally, there is the significance of the poem's title. Snow, of course, symbolizes the barrenness of the winter experience, the season when the cosmos has "died" to be symbolically reborn in spring. Easter, as noted, signifies that rebirth. Thus, as initially hinted in the title and then developed in the body of the poem, there is, by the poet, a successful juxtaposition of metaphors—Hamlet's struggle for existential meaning representing the sterility of the intellect, the Easter narrative symbolizing the rebirth of the senses, and the dramatic change of the spring cycle—to express, symbolically, the evolution of being through sensual experience in the face of, and, perhaps, partly as the consequence of our futile attempts to make rational sense of an essentially irrational world. Neatly imposed on these is the sonnet's poetic "conversion," reflecting through the richness of the images of the ending couplets, and the unifying tightness of its accompanying rhyme scheme, the thematic transformation. Indeed, "Snow on Easter" is a nice example of what Robert Frost calls "moving easy in harness."

REPRODUCTION PAGE 39

NAME_____ SECTION_____

Questions for Critical Examination of a Poem

1. *Is There Unity?* Every aspect of the poem should be consciously planned to support the poet's overall purpose. *All* is unified into one aim.

   A. *Tone.* Is there consistency in whatever tone is chosen, as opposed to slipping in or out of mood and feeling to no discernible purpose?

   B. *Diction.* Does the poet select words that consistently are congruent with the purpose? Or can you see instances when a different word would have been more suitable to the purpose? Are harsh sounding words used when writing of a butterfly? Are offensive functional words used when trying to arouse compassion or sympathy? Etc.

   C. Does the poet shift purposes anywhere in the poem—so that he or she seems in the beginning to be expressing one meaning, pursuing one purpose, and later in the poem seems to be writing on behalf of another?

   D. *Rhyme - Rhythm - Alliteration - Consonance - Assonance*—does the poet use incongruous mixtures of these literary devices? For instance, do the lines stagger along with broken and halting rhythms when describing the swift gliding of a sleigh over snow? This would be out of place and unsuitable in terms of unity. Does the poet use a sibilant hiss of s's when describing the piling up of granite blocks? This, too, would seem to violate principles of unity.

2. Is the poet's *purpose* recognizable?

   Is the poet's purpose revealed by what is written? *It must be.* If you cannot decide what the poem means—or if it means anything that you can express in words—or what kind of experience it was meant to convey, then you must determine who is at fault, the poet or the reader. If many readers fail to grasp the poet's purpose, the poet would do well to recognize a failure to communicate successfully with the chosen readers.

3. Is the poet's *purpose* fulfilled?

   Does the poet achieve what you believe (from reading the poem) to be the goal of writing it? Is the poem not only unified, but whole and complete? Is it developed in detail, or does it remain on a broad, general, unimmediate level that evokes little personal response from you?

4. Does the *purpose* seem significant and valuable?

   Is the comment being made, or the experience being prepared, fresh and original—or moving—or stimulating—or insightful? Or is it trite—shallow—insignificant? Has the thought been conveyed often before—perhaps better? Is it a truism, self-evident and well known to most readers?

These questions are not meant to suggest that all poetry must be solemn and weighted with universal meanings. Of course, there is no such necessity. Humor, for instance, is entirely at home in poetry. But some purpose must be served, even if it is only to make us see something funny or ludicrous in what we have previously considered as grave and forbidding.

Copyright © 1977 by Allyn and Bacon, Inc. Reproduction of this material is restricted to use with A Guidebook for Teaching Creative Writing, by Gene Stanford and Marie N. Smith.

REPRODUCTION PAGE 39 **QUESTIONS FOR CRITICAL EXAMINATION OF A POEM**

5. Is the writing *creative* rather than *expository*?
   A poet is expected to create an emotional experience for the reader to have. A poet does not tell the reader—as in expository writing—in denotative, informative, symbolic writing, that he or she feels a certain way or has certain insights. Rather, the poet creates an arrangement of words that hopefully will evoke in his reader the same feeling or the same insight. The poet is, in short, performing the artist's half of the creative experience, and it is up to the reader to read creatively in order to respond "suitably," that is, by having the feelings and achieving the insight the poet intended. It is in the measure of the reader's success that the poet's success or failure is seen.

6. Is the poet's language successfully *connotative* as well as denotative?
   Poets are expected to create emotional experiences for their readers. To do their share, the poets use words connotatively rather than denotatively. They choose words for their associations—for the memories or attitudes they evoke in the reader—and they rely on their knowledge both of words and of the life experiences of the people for whom they write. They would know, for instance, that in America the word "mother" awakens feelings of warmth and unconscious echoes of such associated words as home and love, whereas the word "mom" evokes negative reactions expressed in such words as bossy, possessive, and domineering. (Or at least this would be true of those who have read any of the several essays on momism in America.) When wishing to designate a female parent, therefore, the poet would make conscious choices of words in terms of the emotions he or she wishes to evoke in the reader.

7. Does the poet use language *figuratively* in order to make meaning come alive to the reader?
   The poet uses words figuratively (metaphorically) rather than symbolically. The purposes of science are best served when each designative word used denotes exactly and precisely what it symbolizes. This is pure symbolic language, in which the words "test-tube" symbolize only the glass cylinder into which chemicals are put for testing. In poetry, however, the symbol may be used far less precisely or designatively. One might refer to a situation or an occasion as a test-tube, meaning not that it is a glass cylinder, etc., but that it permits or occasions testing of people. Thus the poet *says one thing to mean another.* This is called figurative, or metaphorical language.

8. Does the poet create *images* that appeal to the senses, arousing response in the imagination?
   Does the poet evoke sensory—imaginary—impressions by the use of words? Does he or she make us imagine sounds, tastes, smells, sights, or feelings, and bring these sensory reactions into our imaginations? Do the images evoked suit the poet's purpose? Are they sharp? Is your imagination stirred?

9. Can every word in the poem be justified?
   A good exercise for any poet is to ask himself or herself, "Why did I use that word?" If it can be explained in terms of meaning, connotation, imagery, rhythm, rhyme, assonance, consonance or alliteration, or in reasonable combination of any of these—or if it can be shown that there is no "better" word available (that is, better in the sense of what poetry is and what it demands in the use of words), then the word is justified. Get in the habit of asking why. Why is a comma there? Why break the line there? Why a yellow flower? The poet must be able to answer all the why's or stand convicted of random, purposeless behavior. A poet who answers, "Because I felt like it," is not in any way justifying his or her work but only justifying his or her feeling.

Copyright © 1977 by Allyn and Bacon, Inc. Reproduction of this material is restricted to use with <u>A Guidebook for Teaching Creative Writing</u>, by Gene Stanford and Marie N. Smith.

APPENDIX C

Feedback Form

Your comments about this book will be very helpful to us in planning other books in the *Guidebook for Teaching* Series and in making revisions in *A Guidebook for Teaching Creative Writing*. Please tear out the form that appears on the following page and use it to let us know your reactions to *A Guidebook for Teaching Creative Writing*. The authors promise a personal reply. Mail the form to:

Dr. Gene Stanford and Mrs. Marie Smith
c/o Longwood Division
Allyn and Bacon, Inc.
470 Atlantic Avenue
Boston, Massachusetts 02210

Your school: _____
Address: _____
City and state: _____
Date: _____

Dr. Gene Stanford and
Mrs. Marie Smith
c/o Longwood Division
Allyn and Bacon, Inc.
470 Atlantic Avenue
Boston, Massachusetts 02210

Dear Gene and Marie:

My name is _____ and I wanted to tell you what I thought of your book *A Guidebook for Teaching Creative Writing*. I liked certain things about the book, including:

I do, however, feel that the book could be improved in the following ways:

There were some other things that I wish the book had included, such as:

Here is something that happened in my class when I used an idea from your book:

Sincerely yours,

_____

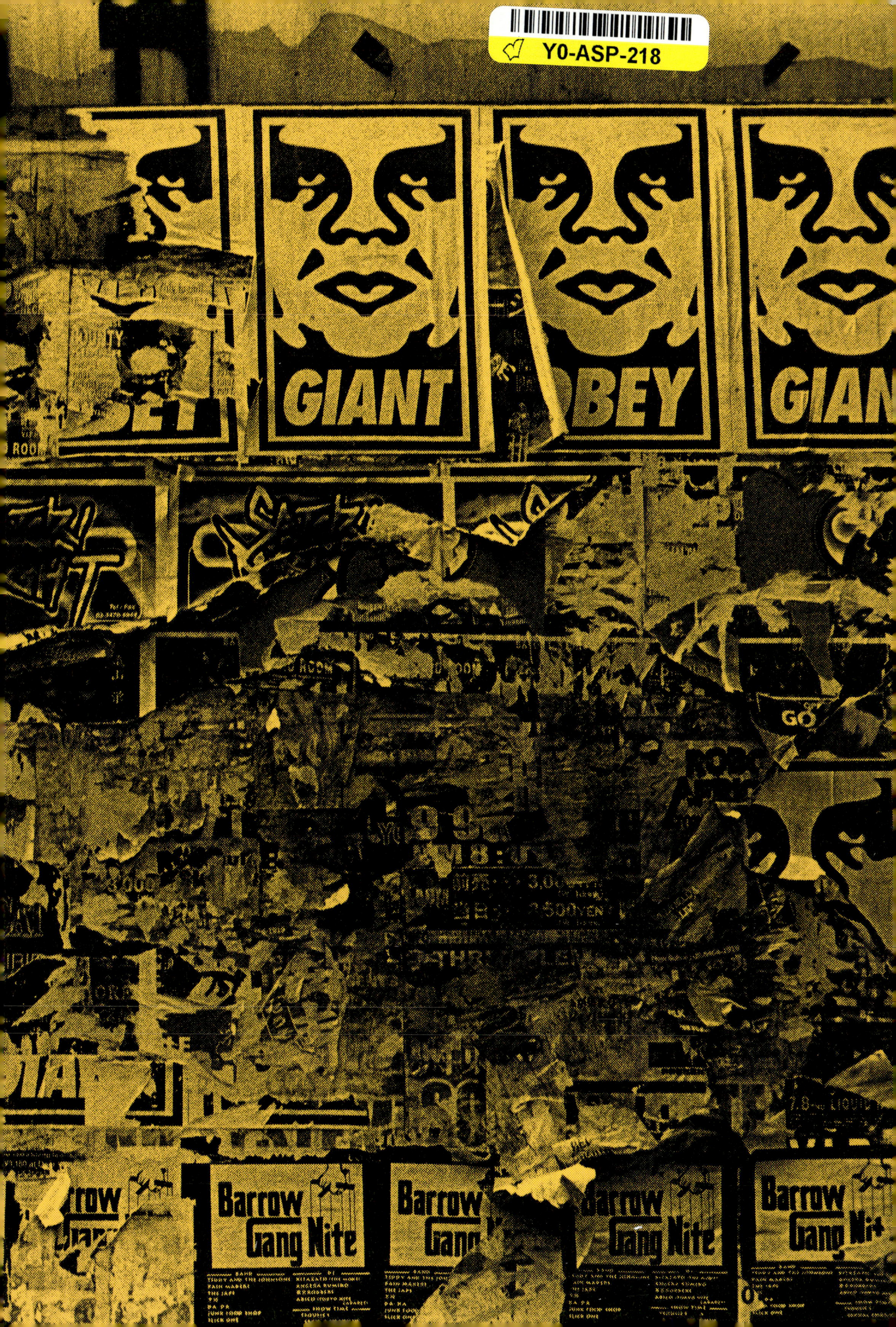

Shunji Ohkura
Tokyo X

KODANSHA INTERNATIONAL
Tokyo • New York • London

In Ohkura's stark vision Tokyo is an inorganic machine where
everyone and everything exists only to serve the ringmaster of commerce.
Activity, however frenetic, is futile. Work, leisure, love,
pleasure, all are just forms of human bondage.
Giles Murray

Photographs by Shunji Ohkura

Cover design by Toru Watanabe.
"Why 'Tokyo X'?" translated by Ralph F. McCarthy. All other parts translated by Shinji Ichiba.

Published by Kodansha International Ltd., 17-14, Otowa 1-chome, Bunkyo-ku, Tokyo 112-8652, and Kodansha America, Inc.
Distributed in the United States by Kodansha America, Inc., 575 Lexington Avenue, New York, New York 10022,
and in the United Kingdom and continental Europe by Kodansha Europe Ltd., 95 Aldwych, London WC2B 4JF.

Copyright © 2000 by Shunji Ohkura and Kodansha International Ltd. All rights reserved.
Printed in Japan. Printed by Fukuin Co., Ltd. (President: Yoshito Namura, Executive: Osamu Muramoto, Staff: Susumu Yoshikawa, Takehiko Ito, Atsushi Ishiguro, Shun'ichi Fujiwara, Atsushi Kuwata, Taketoshi Endo, and Hiroyuki Matsushima.)
First edition, 2000

1 2 3 4 5 6 7 8 9 04 03 02 01 00
ISBN 4-7700-2738-9

1

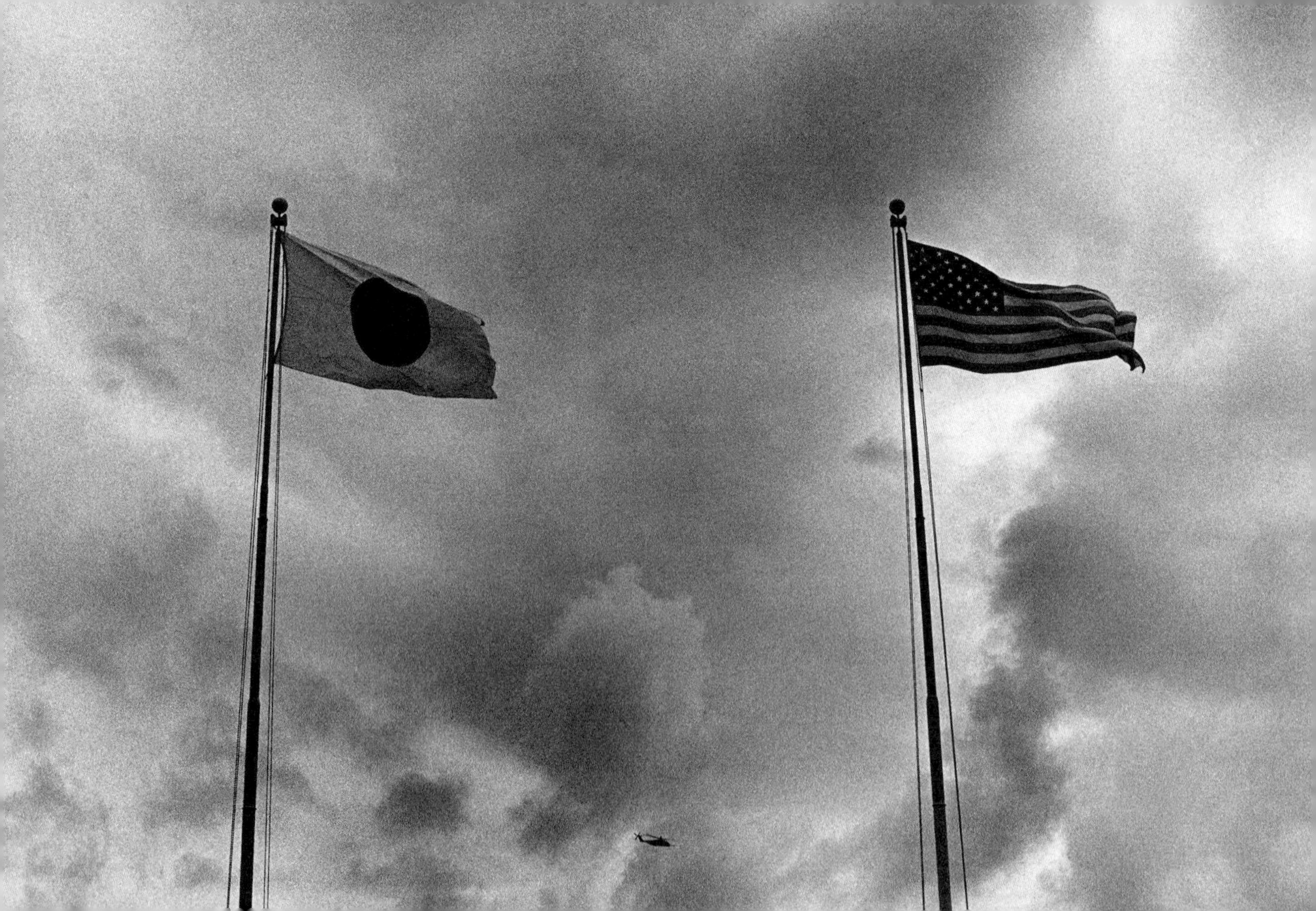

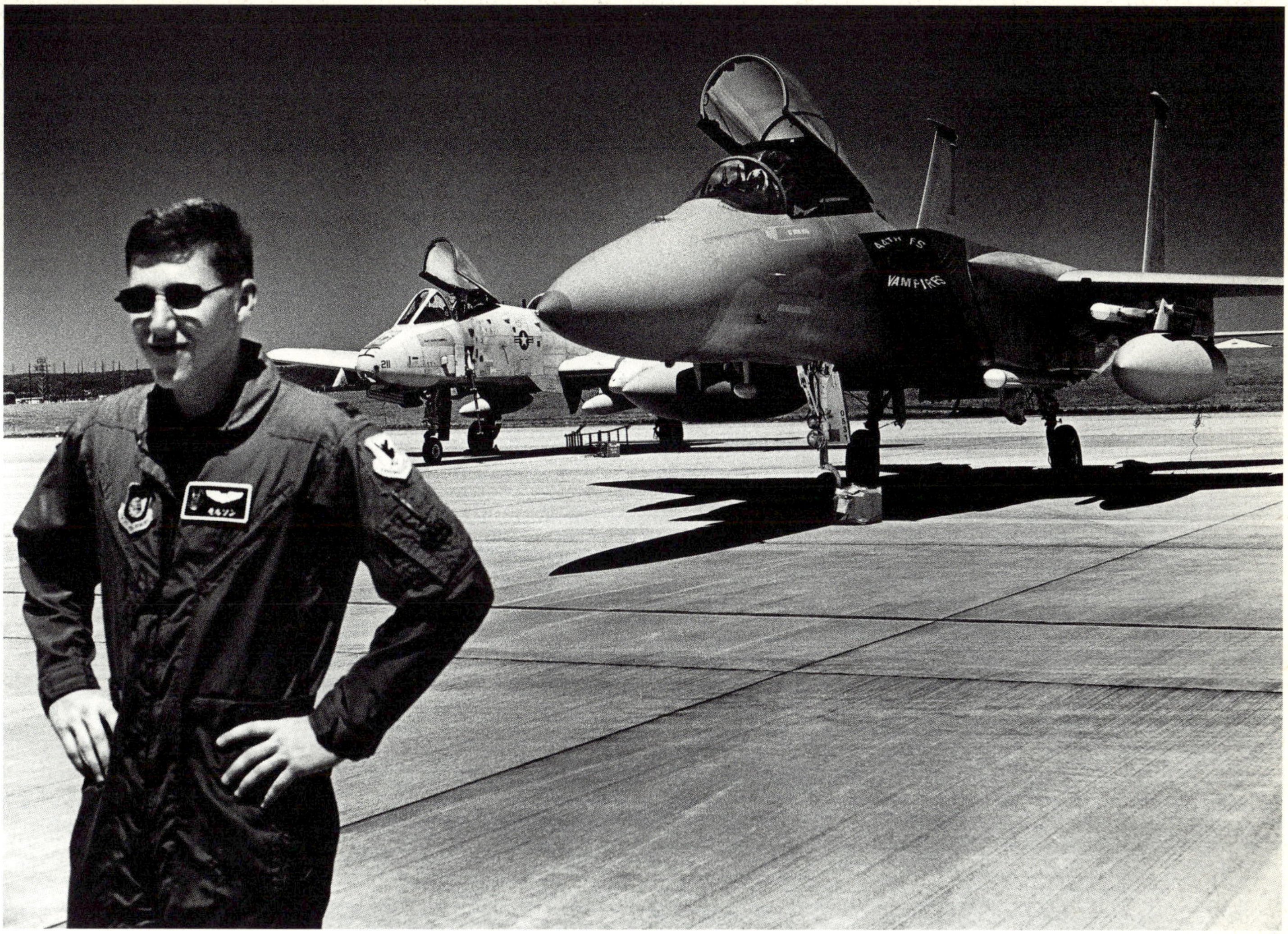

3

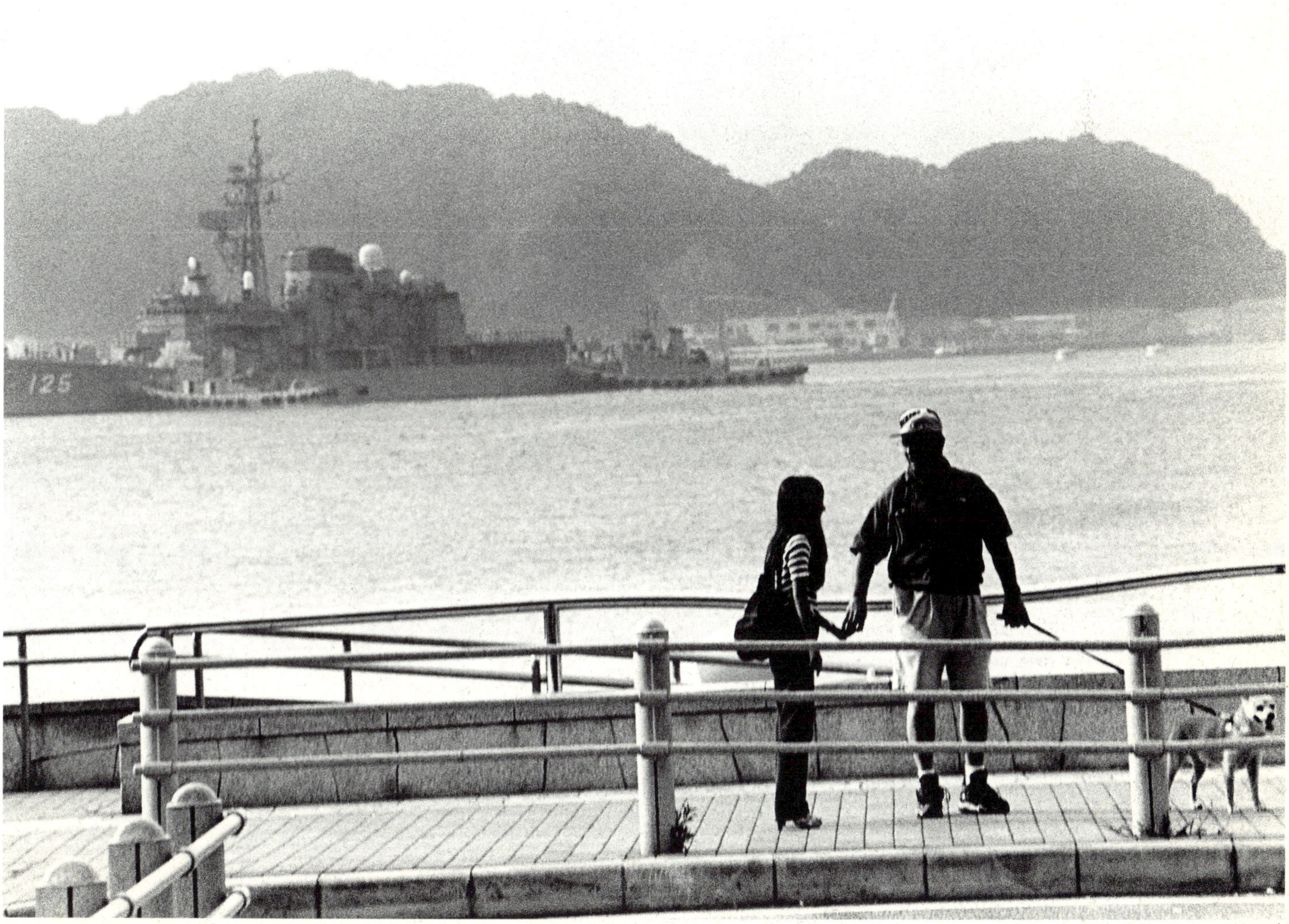

4

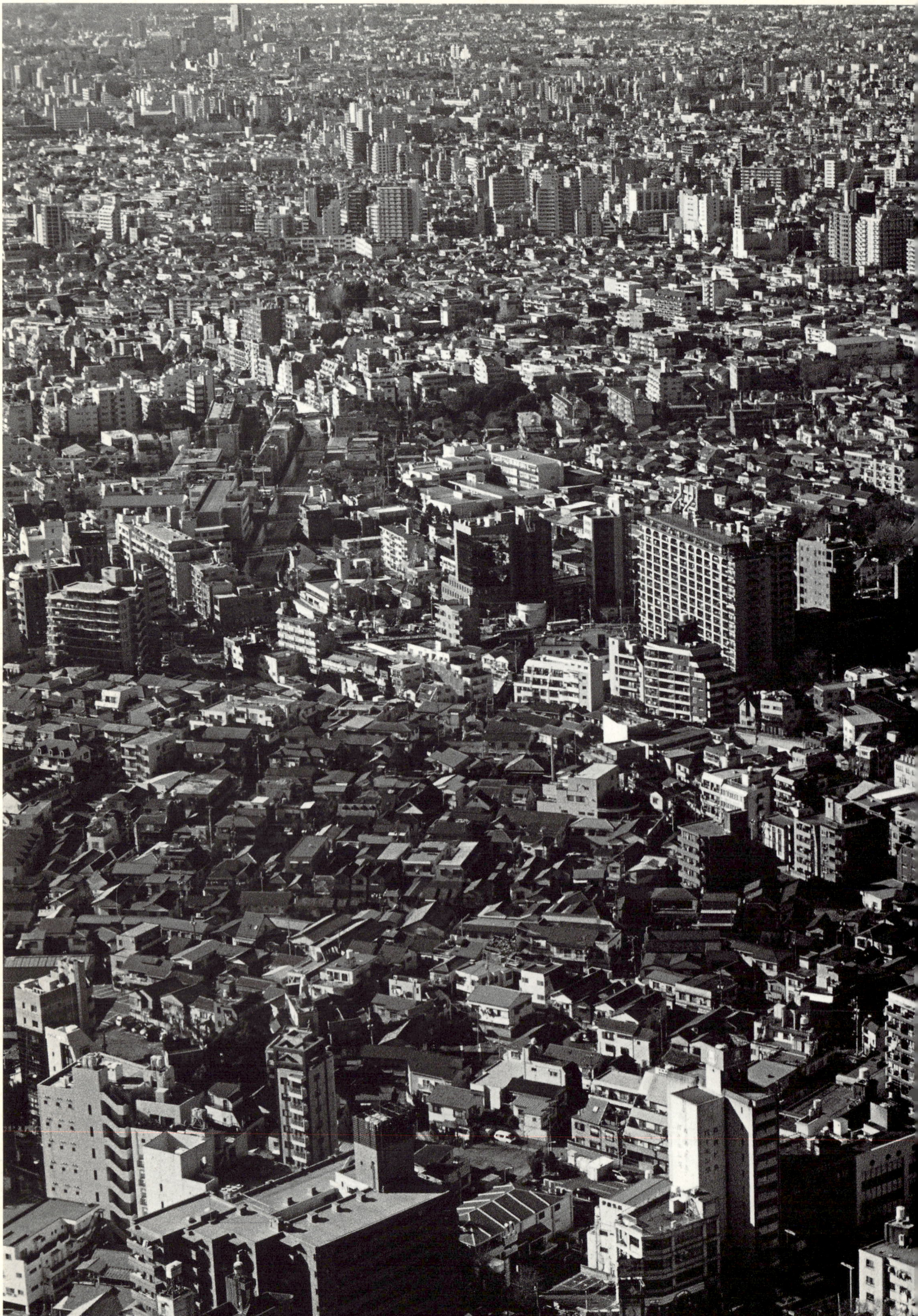

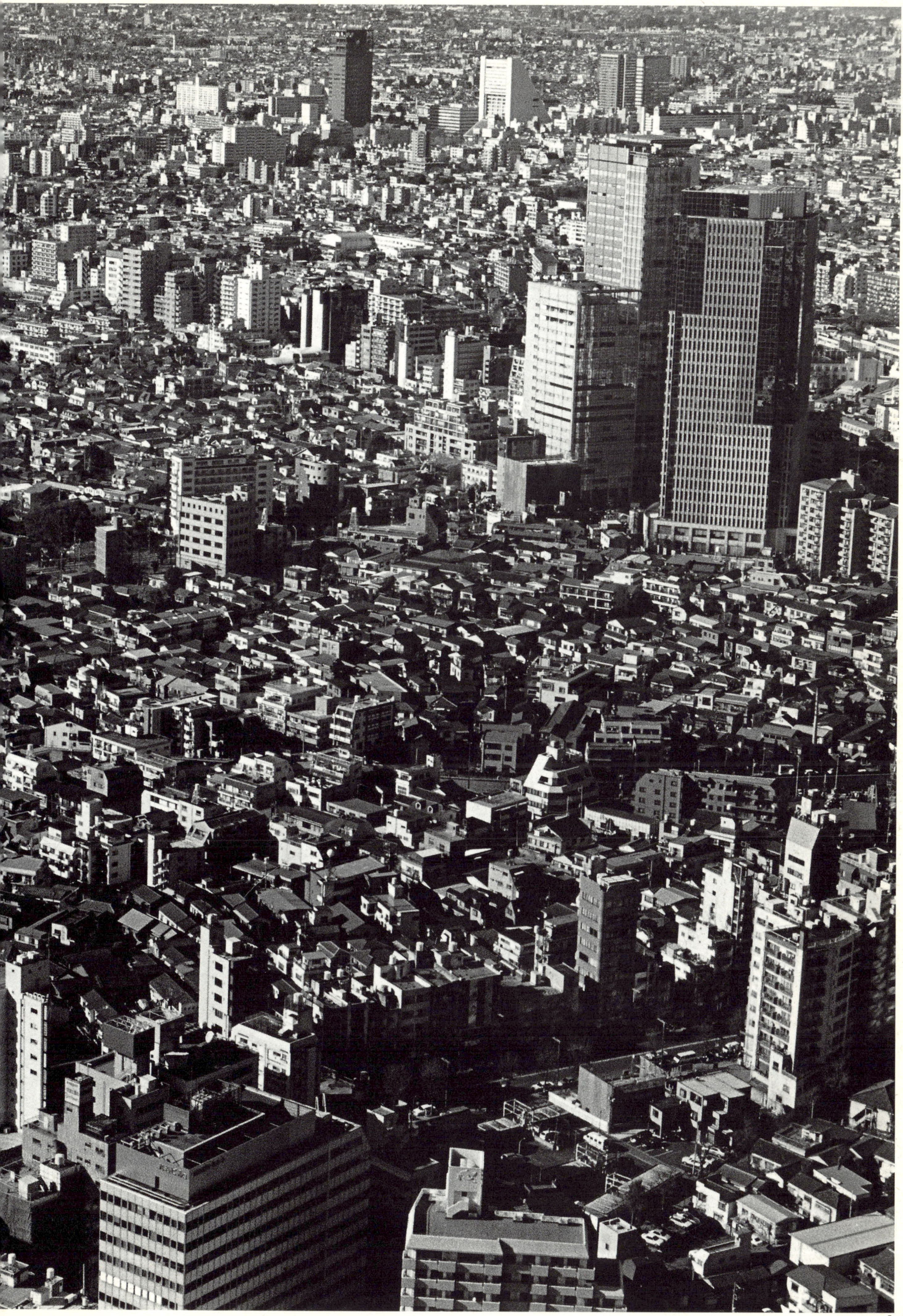

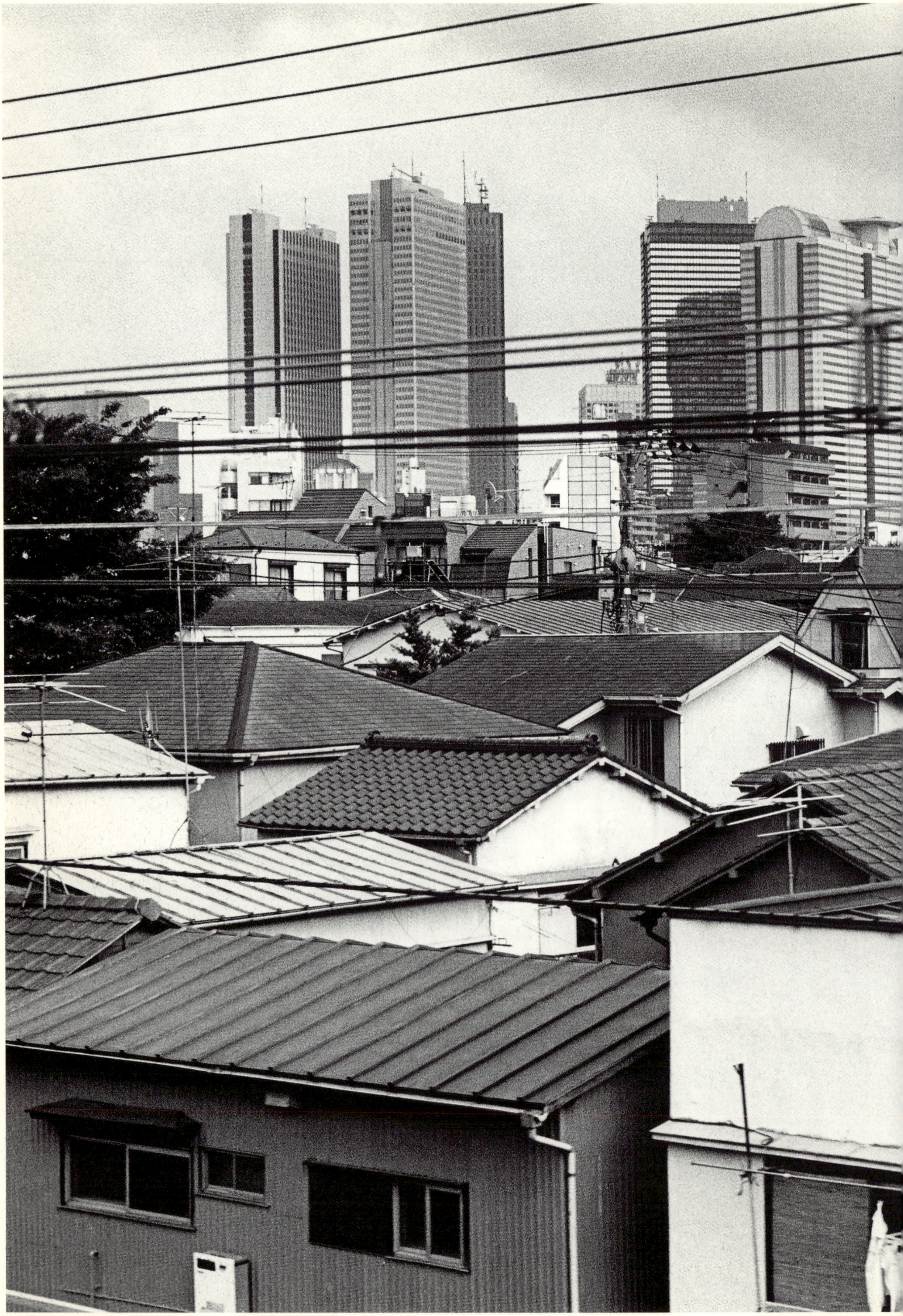

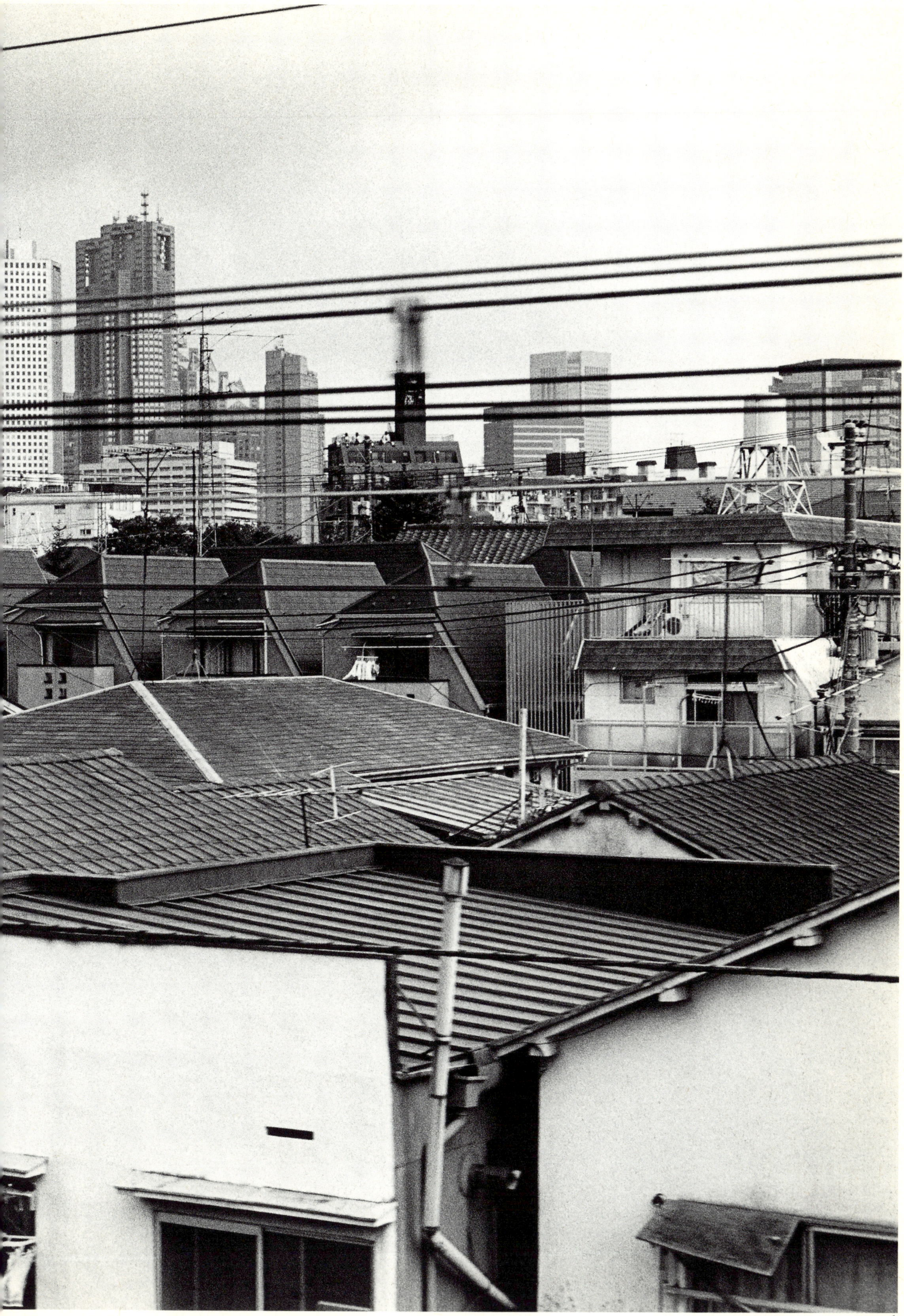

7

8

9

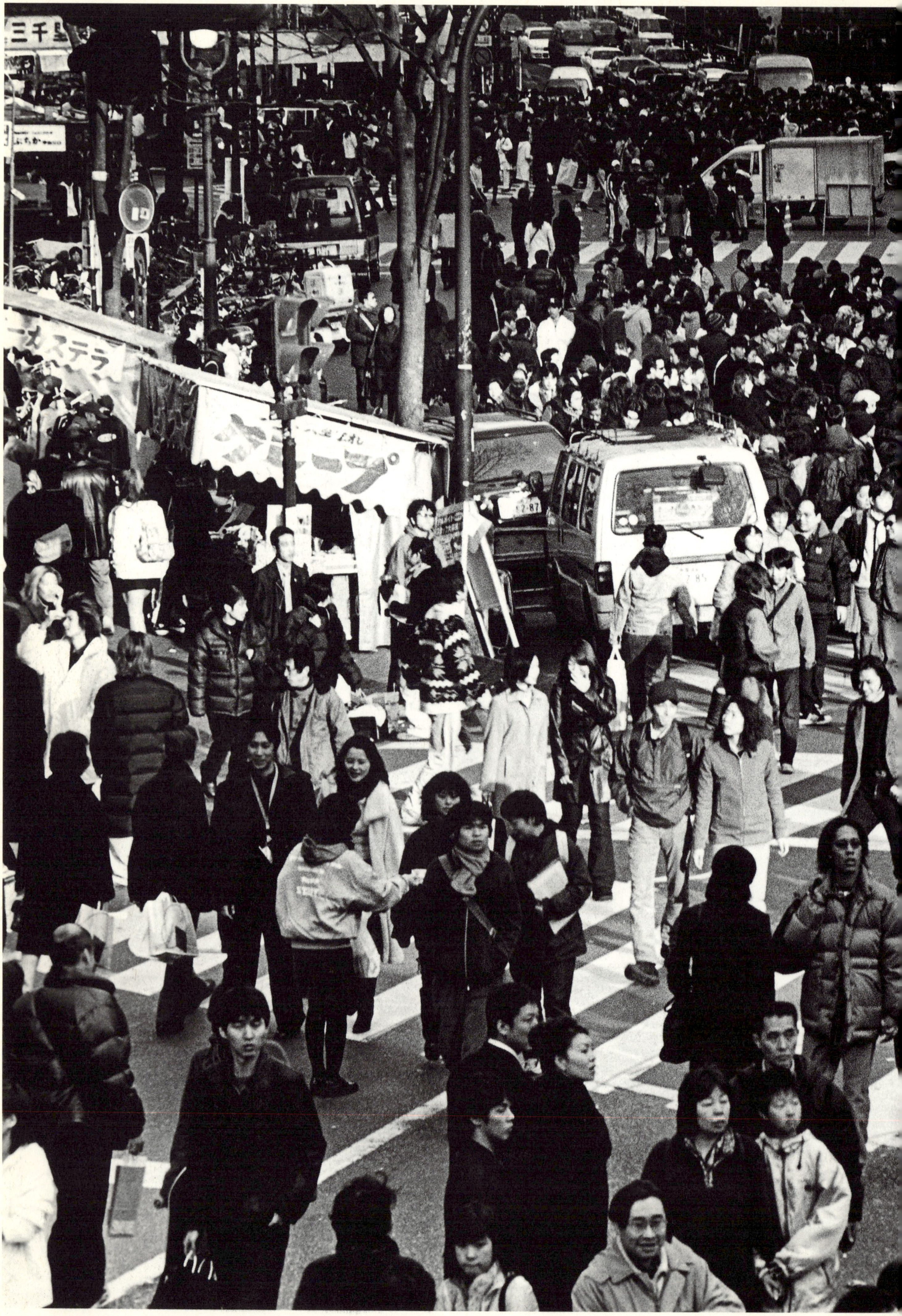

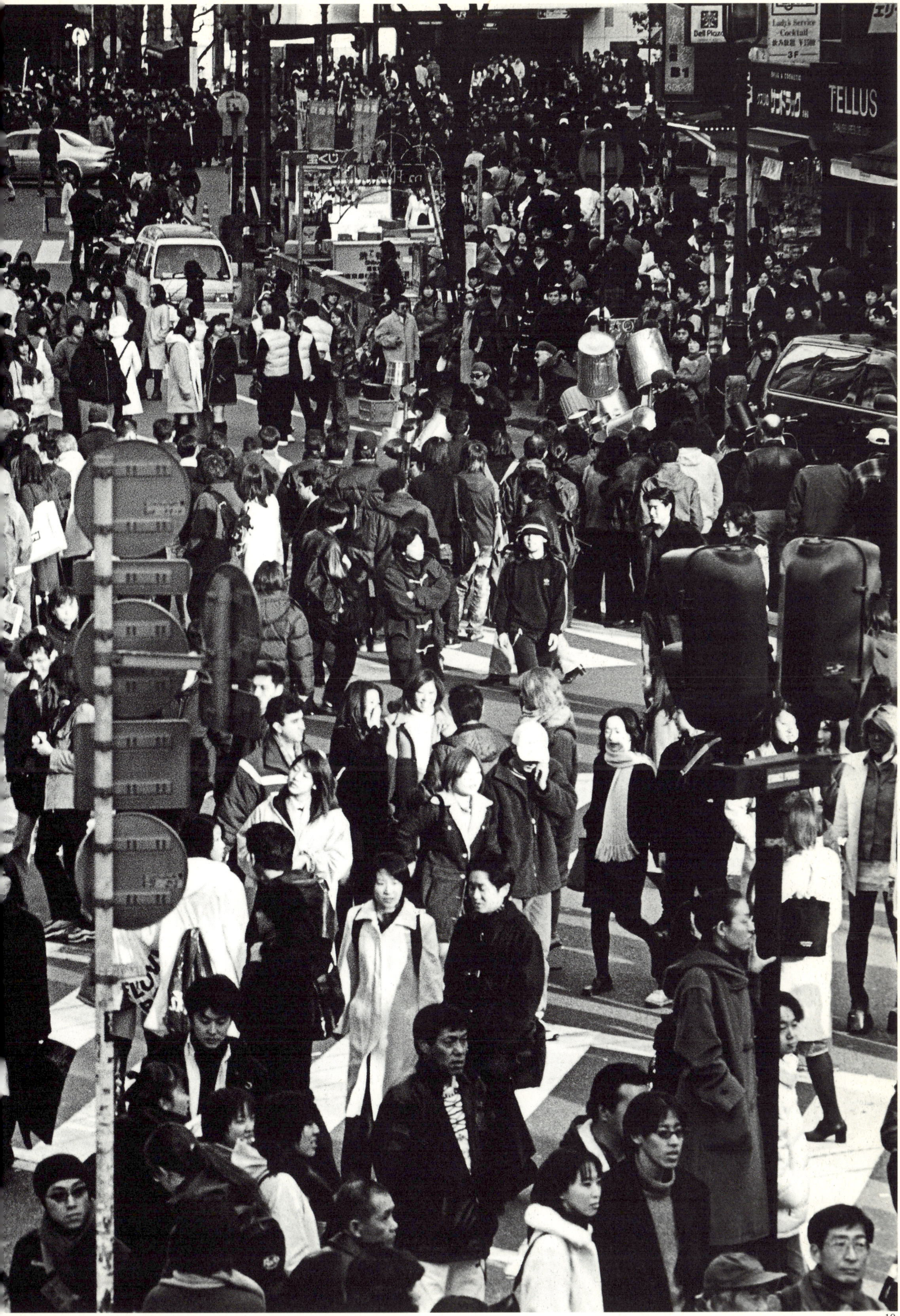
TELLUS

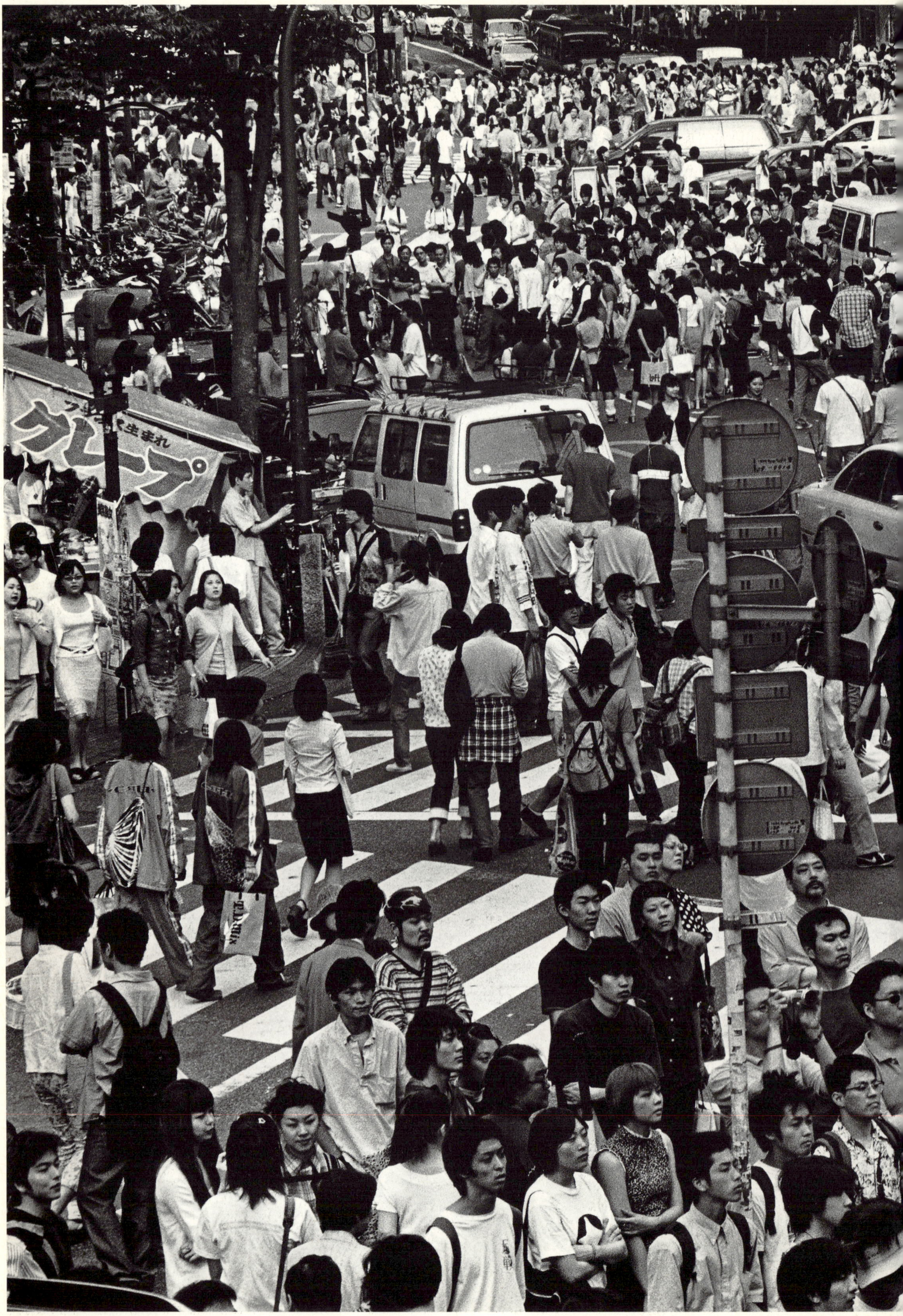
クレープ

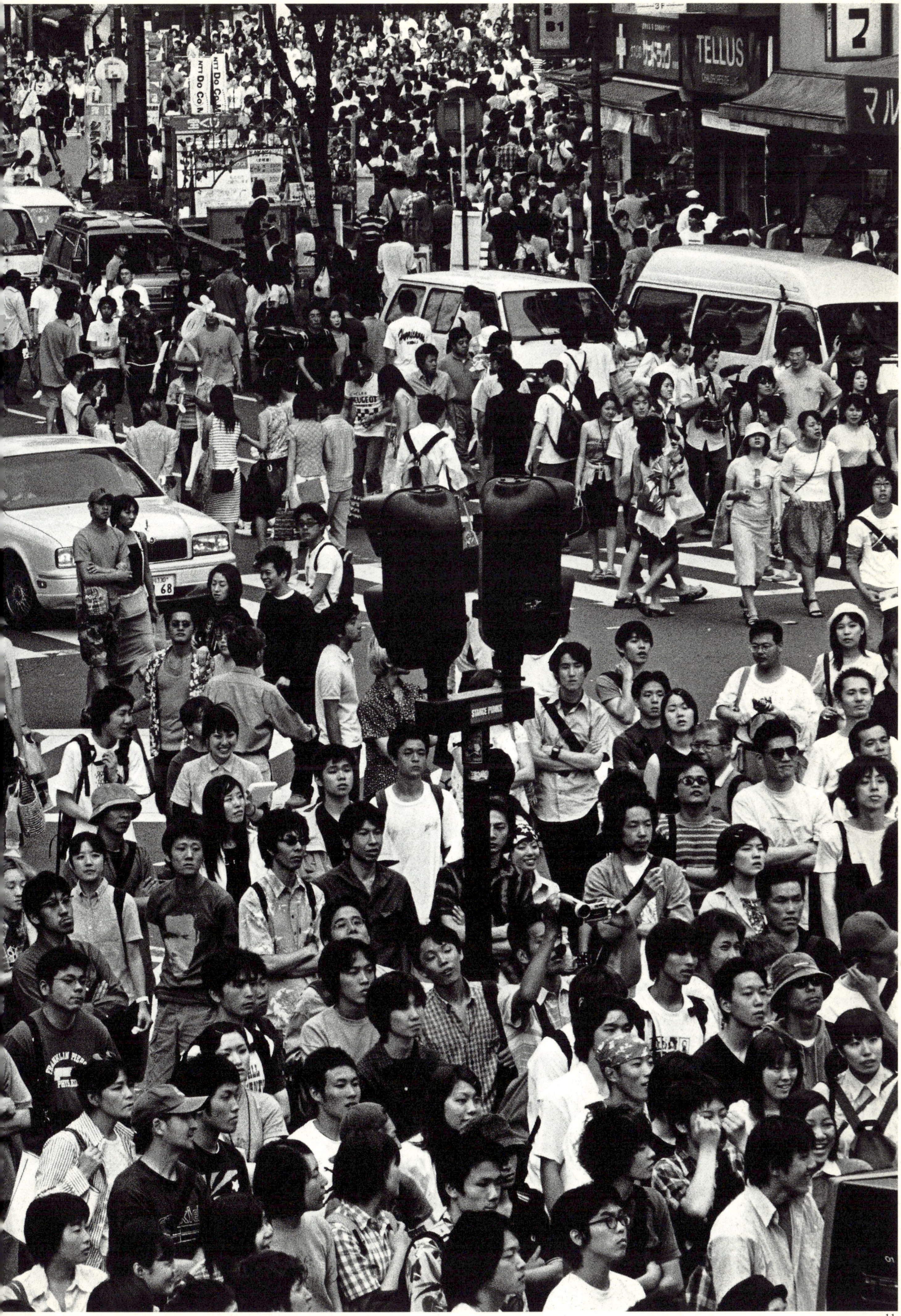

12

13

HOTEL
Prestige
しばらく
お待ち下さい
消火栓

14

SHOPPING CENTER
江古田銀座
低利一括貸金

15

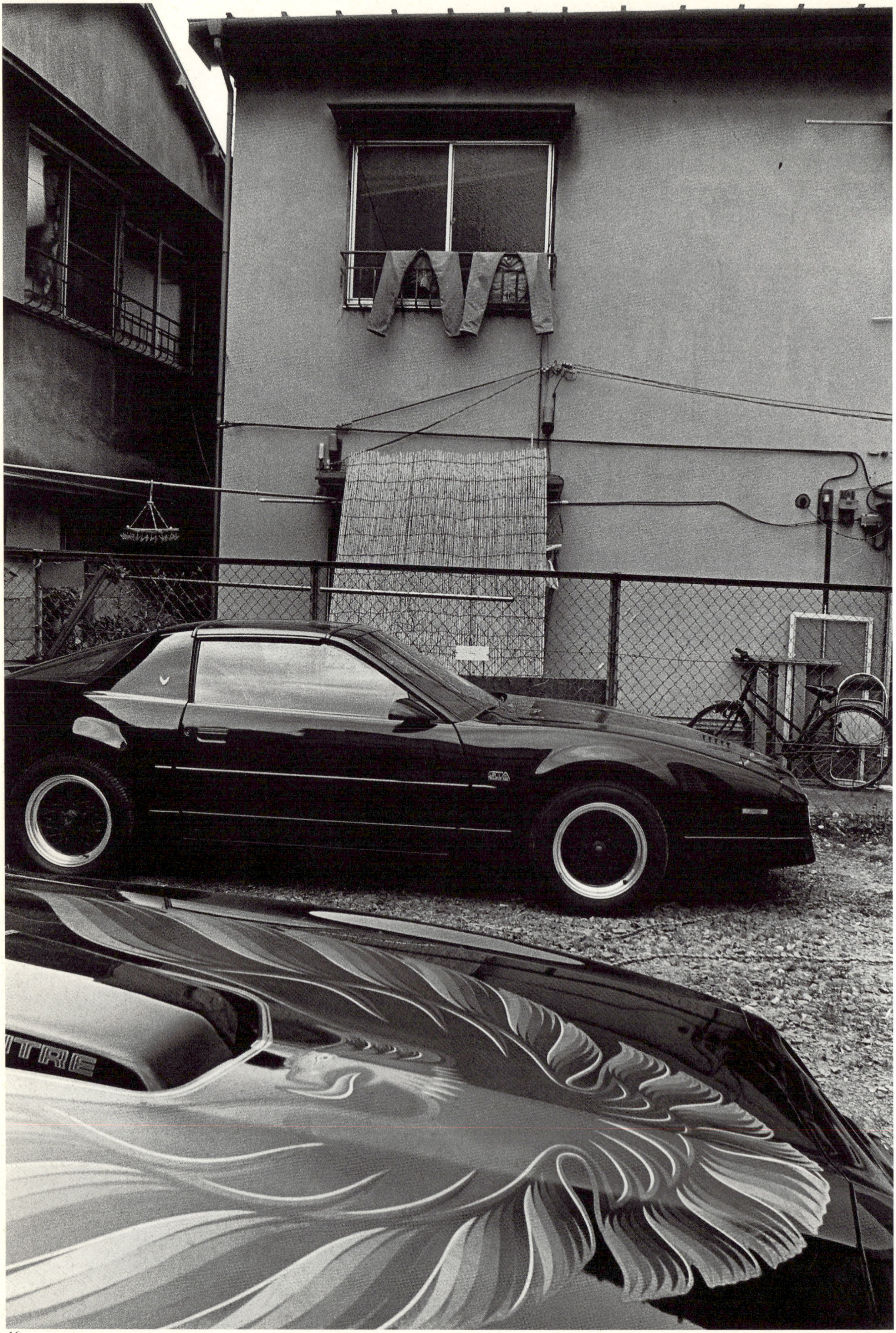

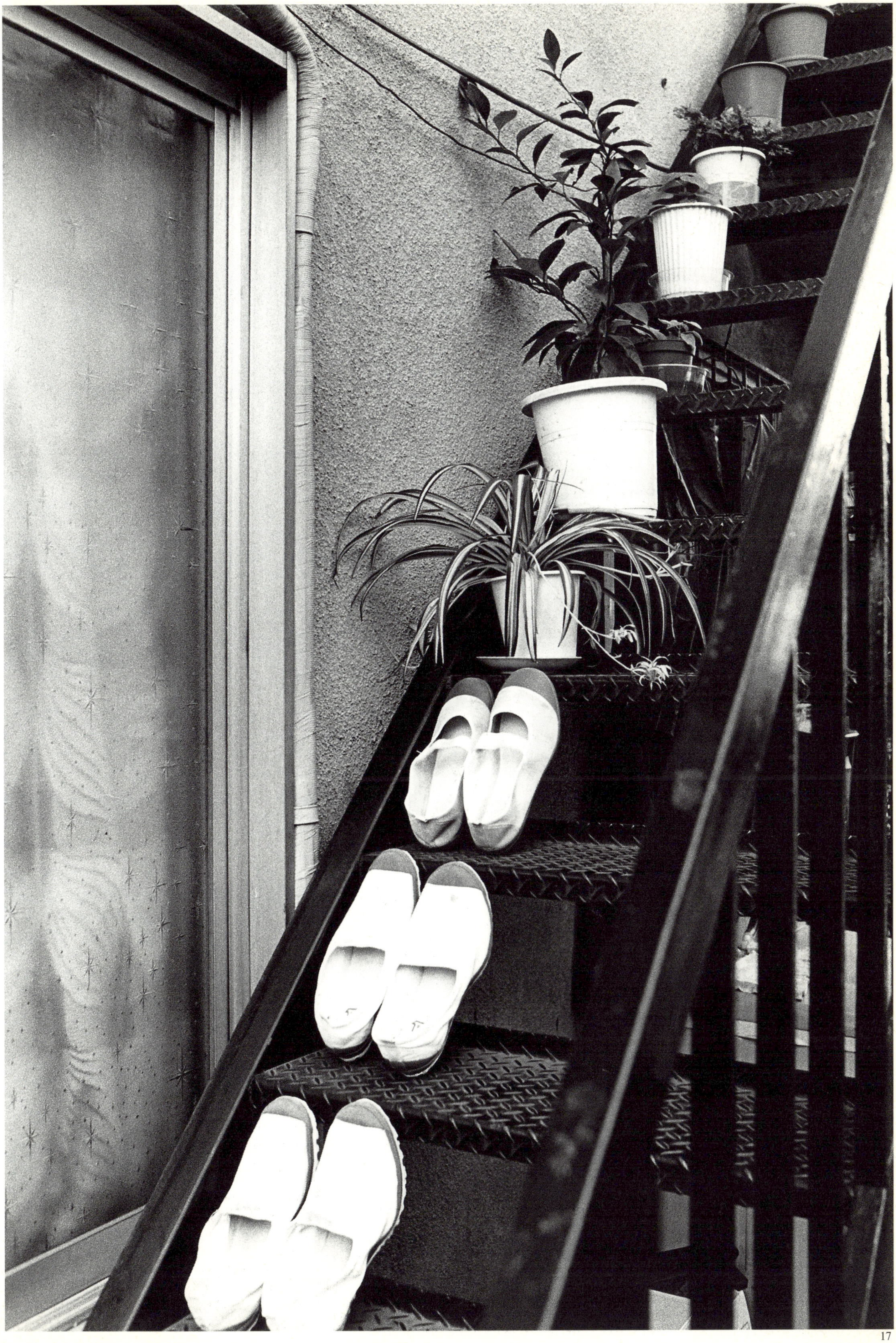

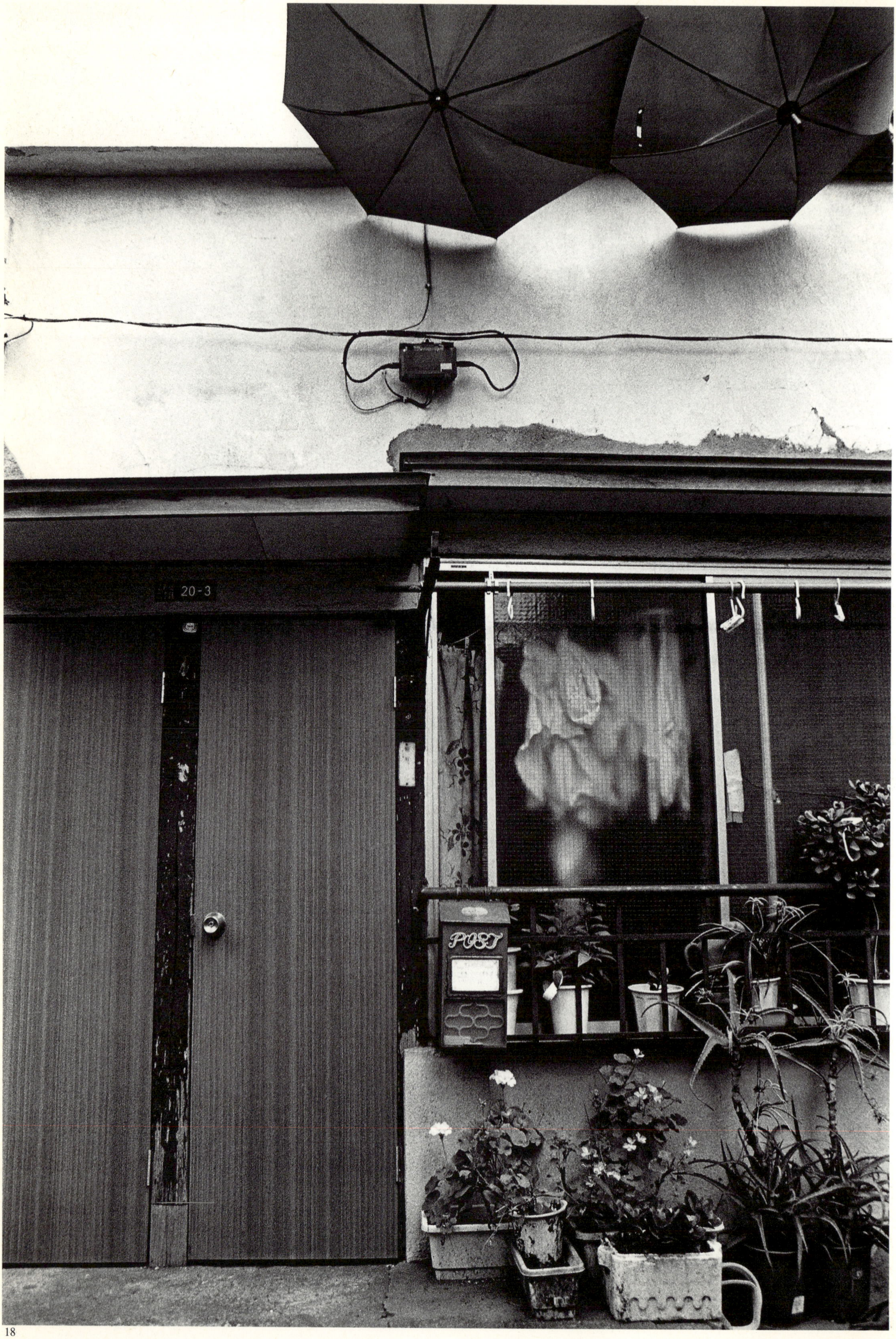
20-3
POST

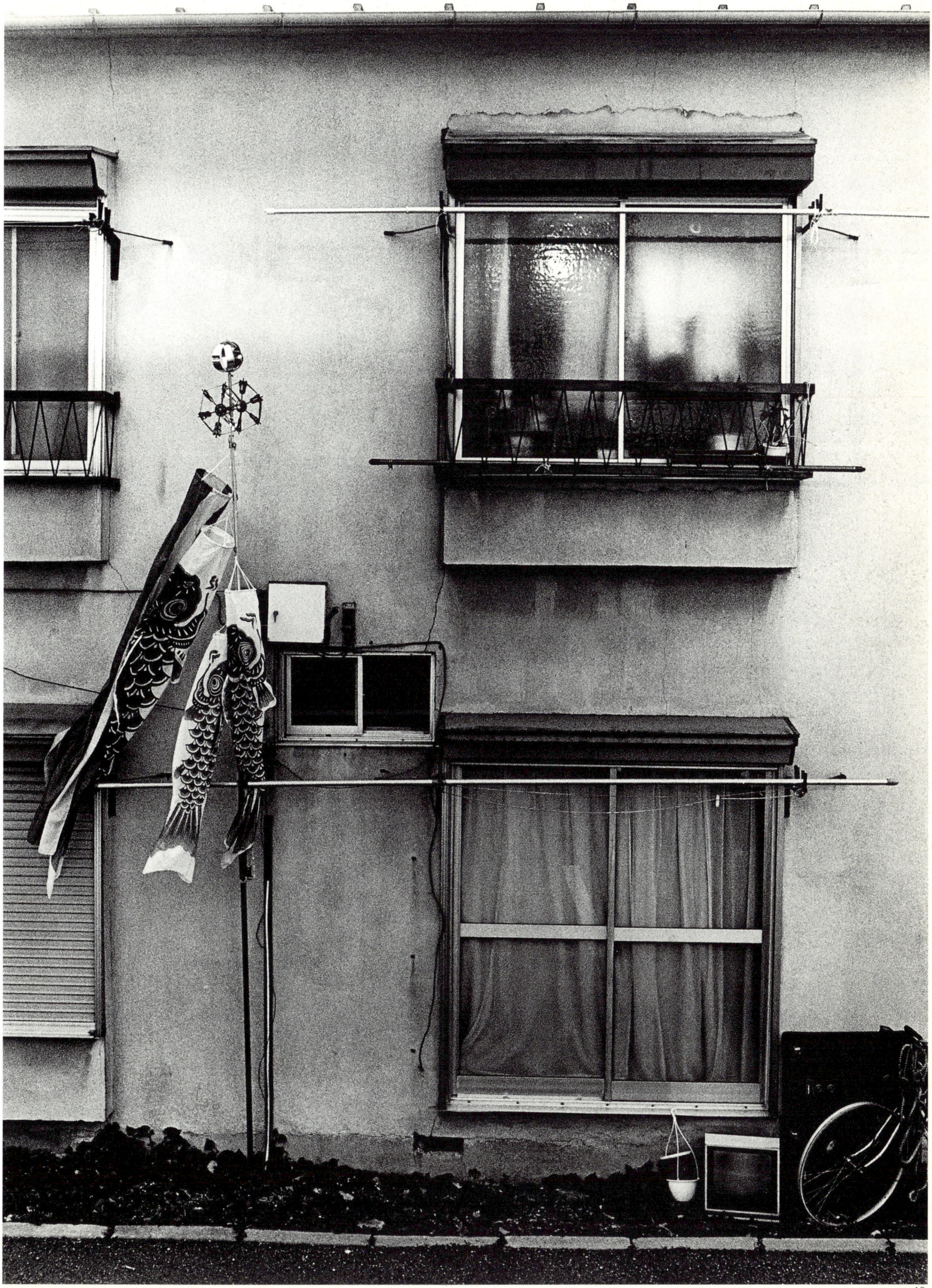

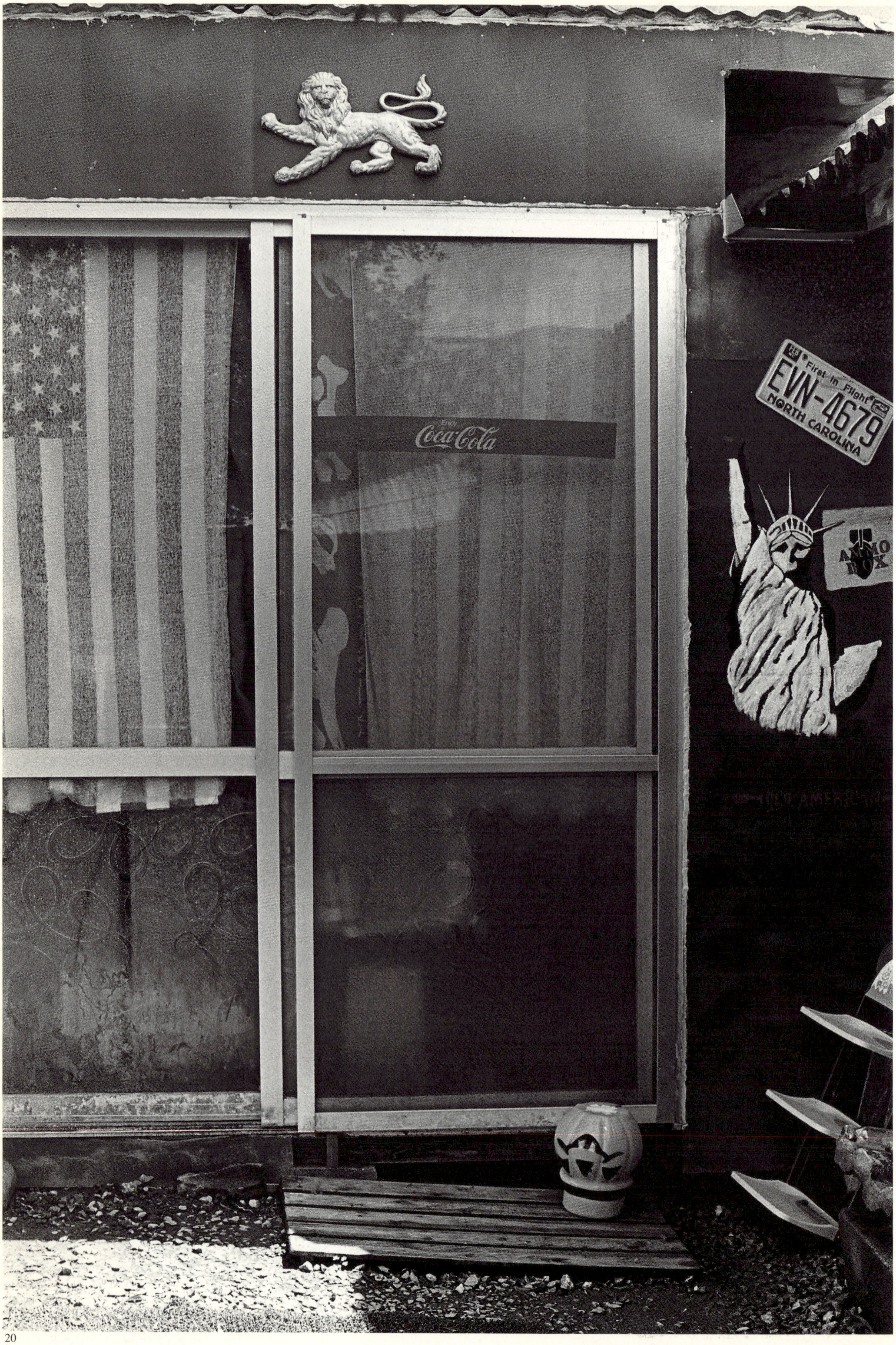
Coca-Cola
EVN-4679
First in Flight
NORTH CAROLINA

一池春水綠於苔水上
花枝間竹開
聰子書

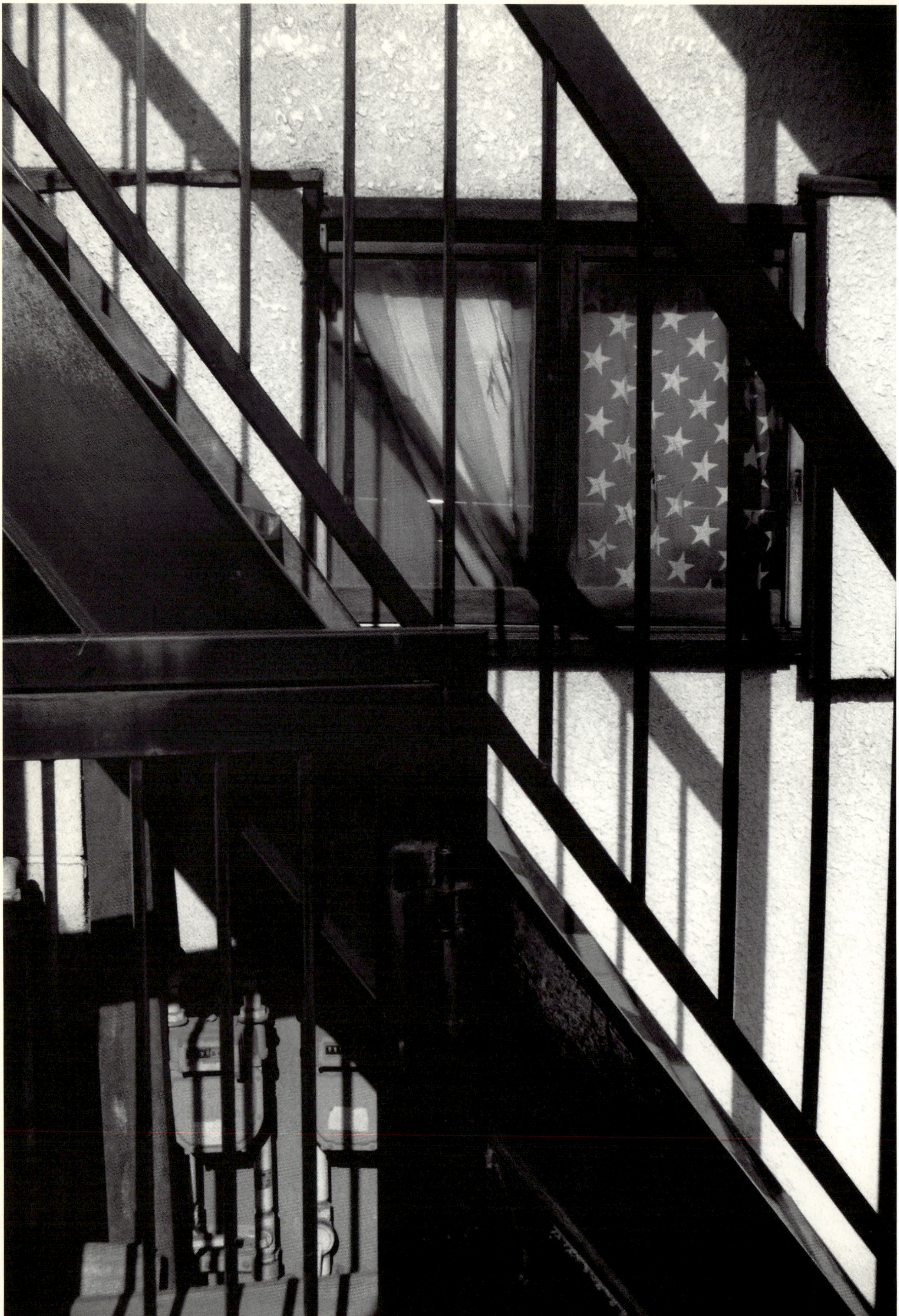

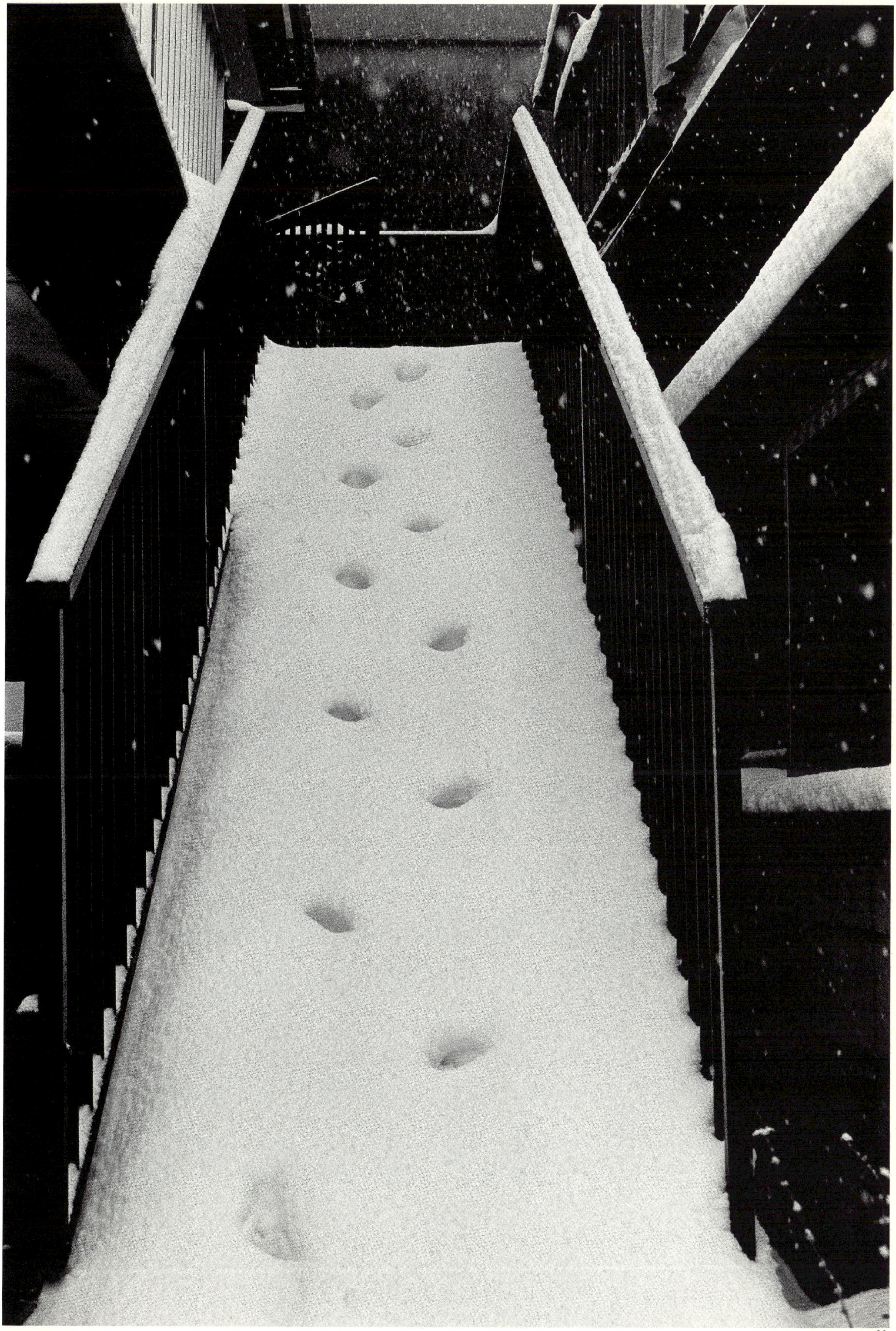

救国の予言者
赤尾敏
生誕100年
愛国党
総本部03-3957-6493
三島由紀夫・森田必勝 両烈士追悼
野分祭
11月24日(火)
シチズンプラザ2階
開場 午後6時
東京都新宿区高田馬場4-29-27
Tel.03-3363-2211
愛国党

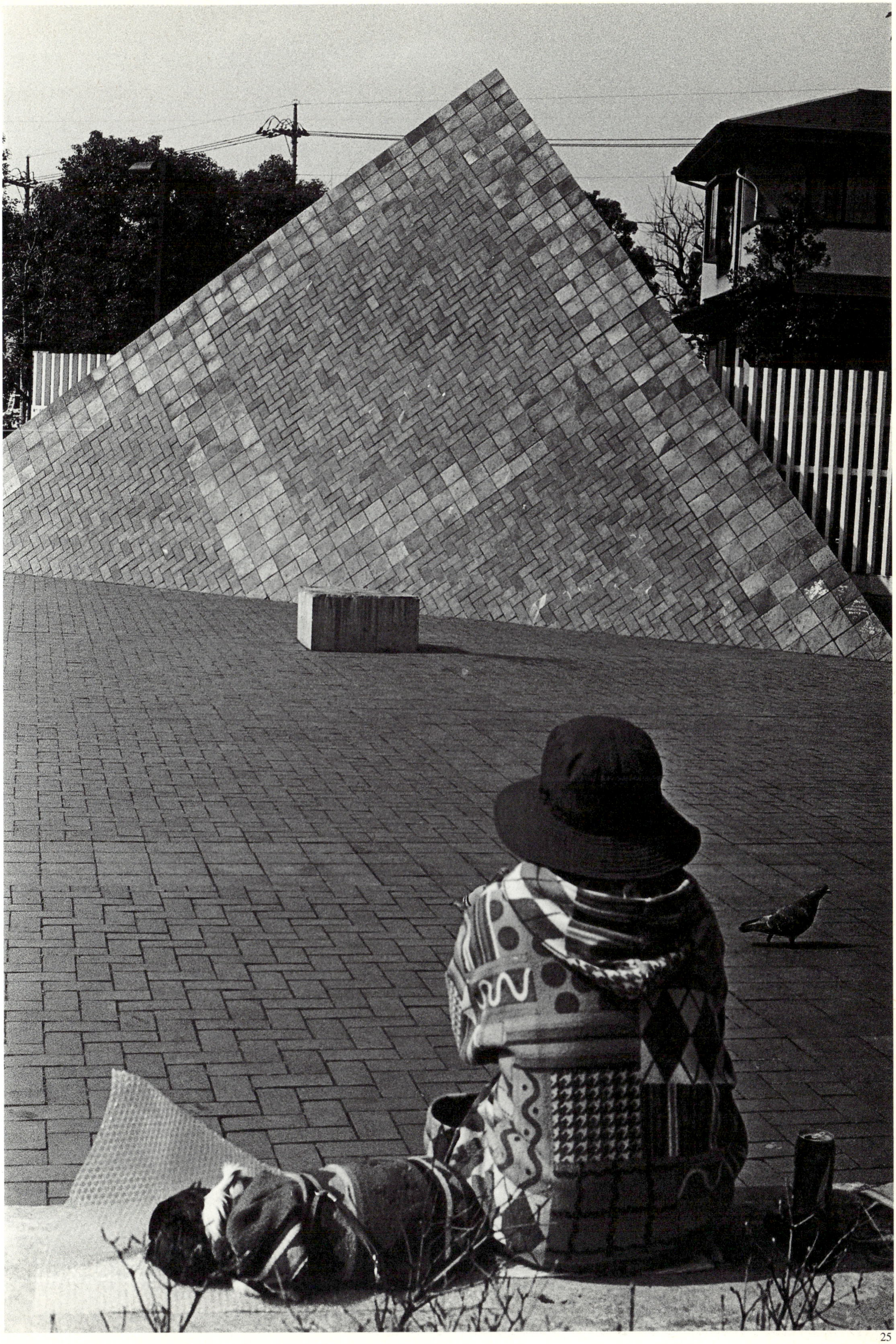

26

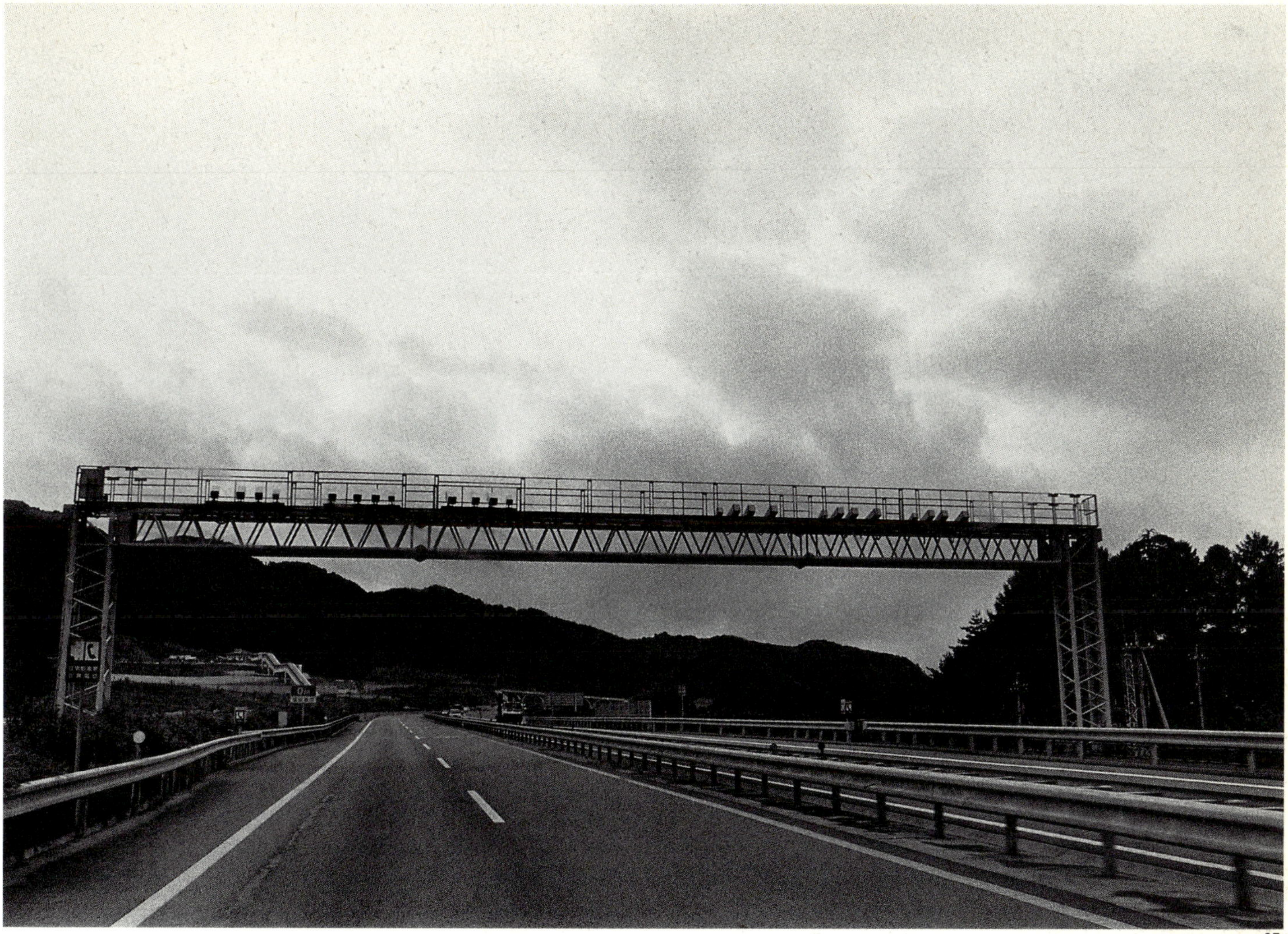

27

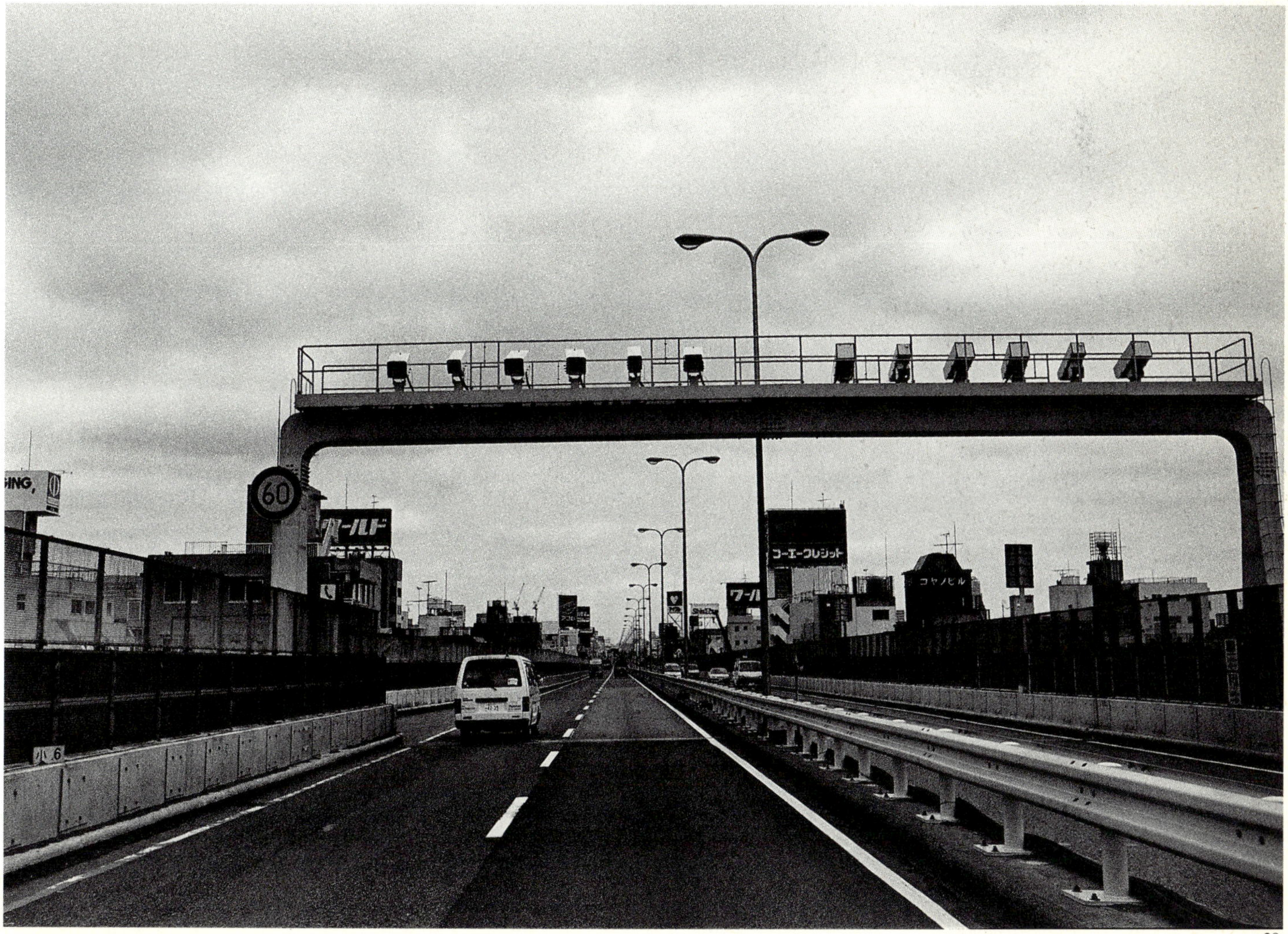

28

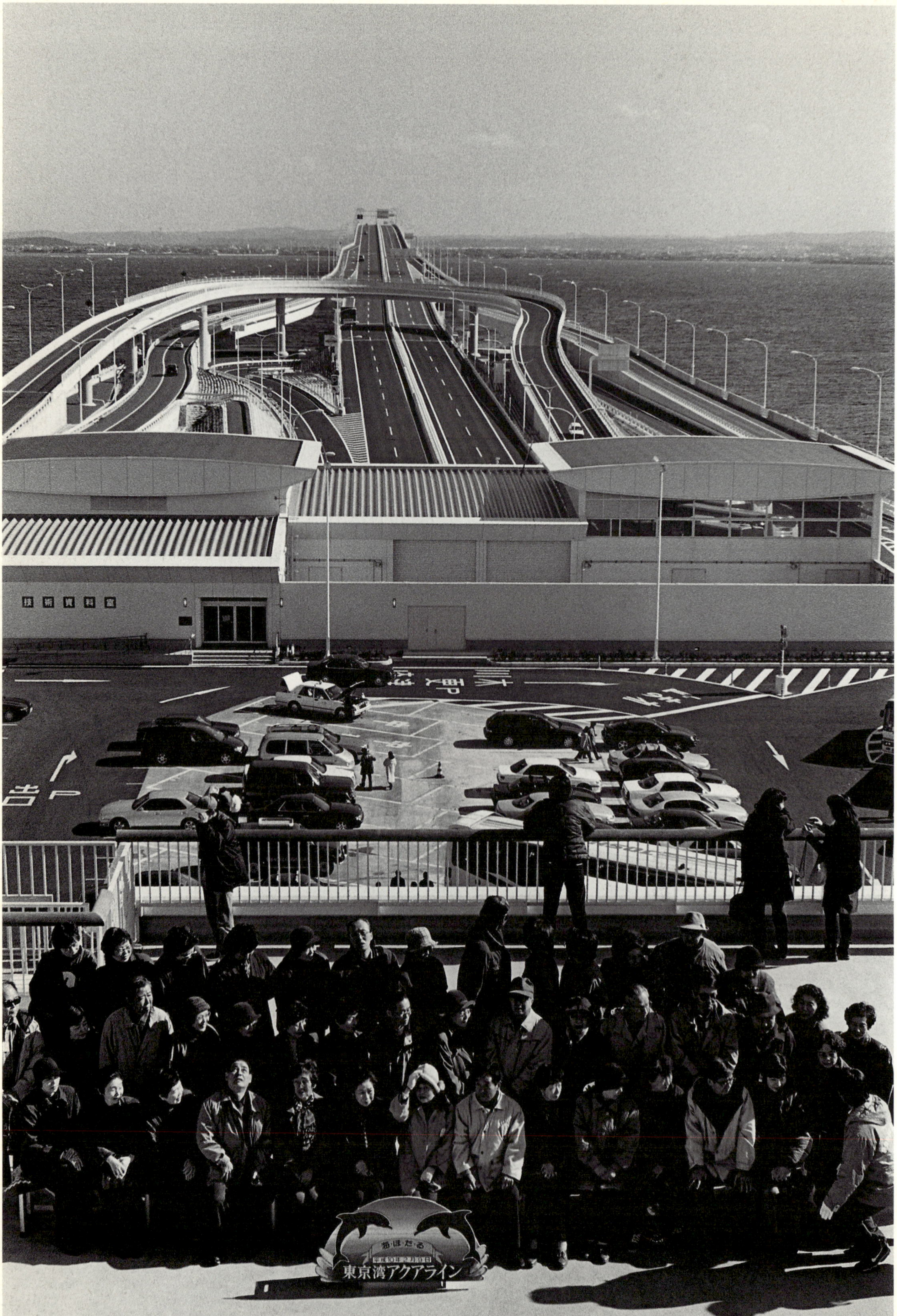
海·ほ·た·る
東京湾アクアライン

30

31

32

33

34

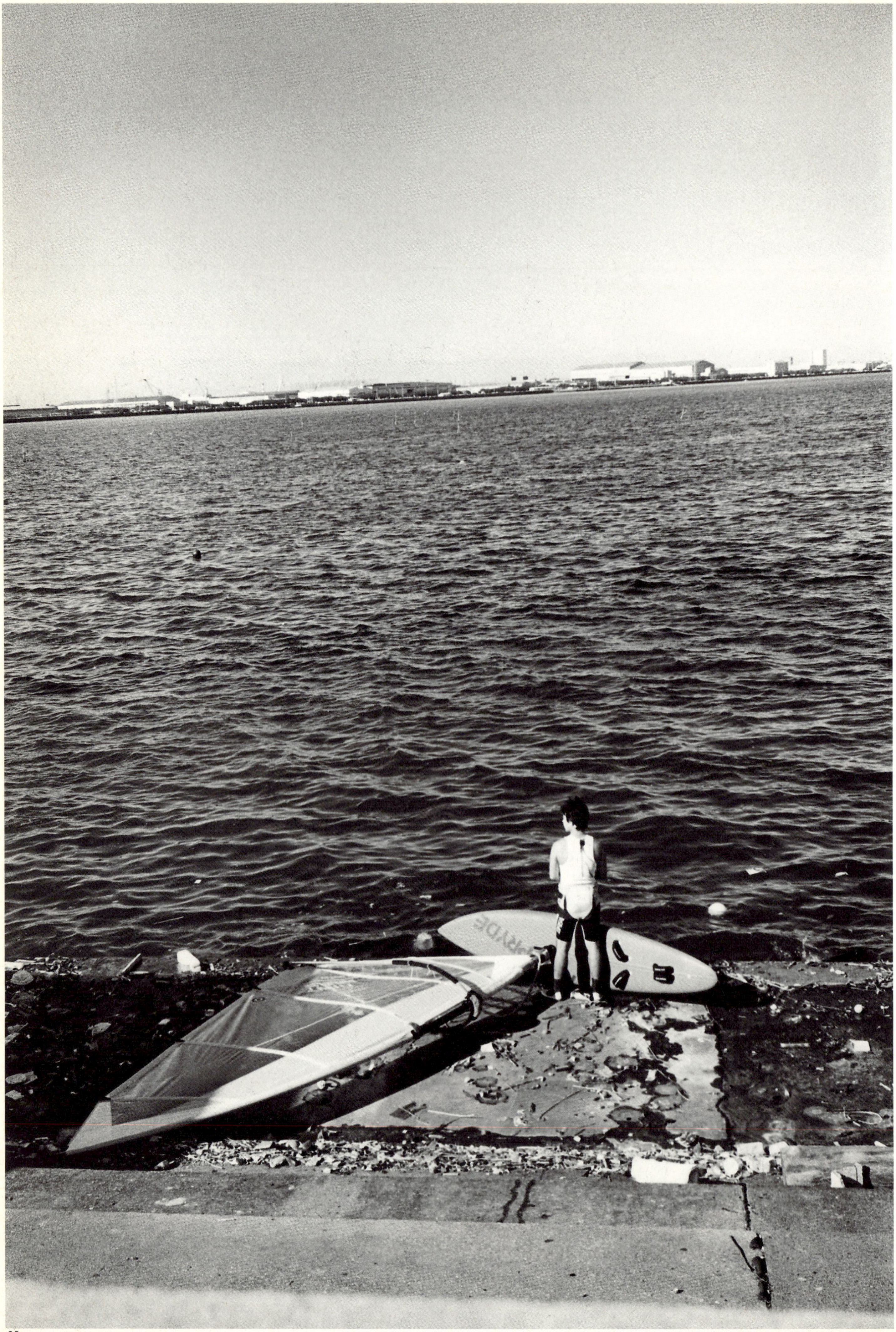

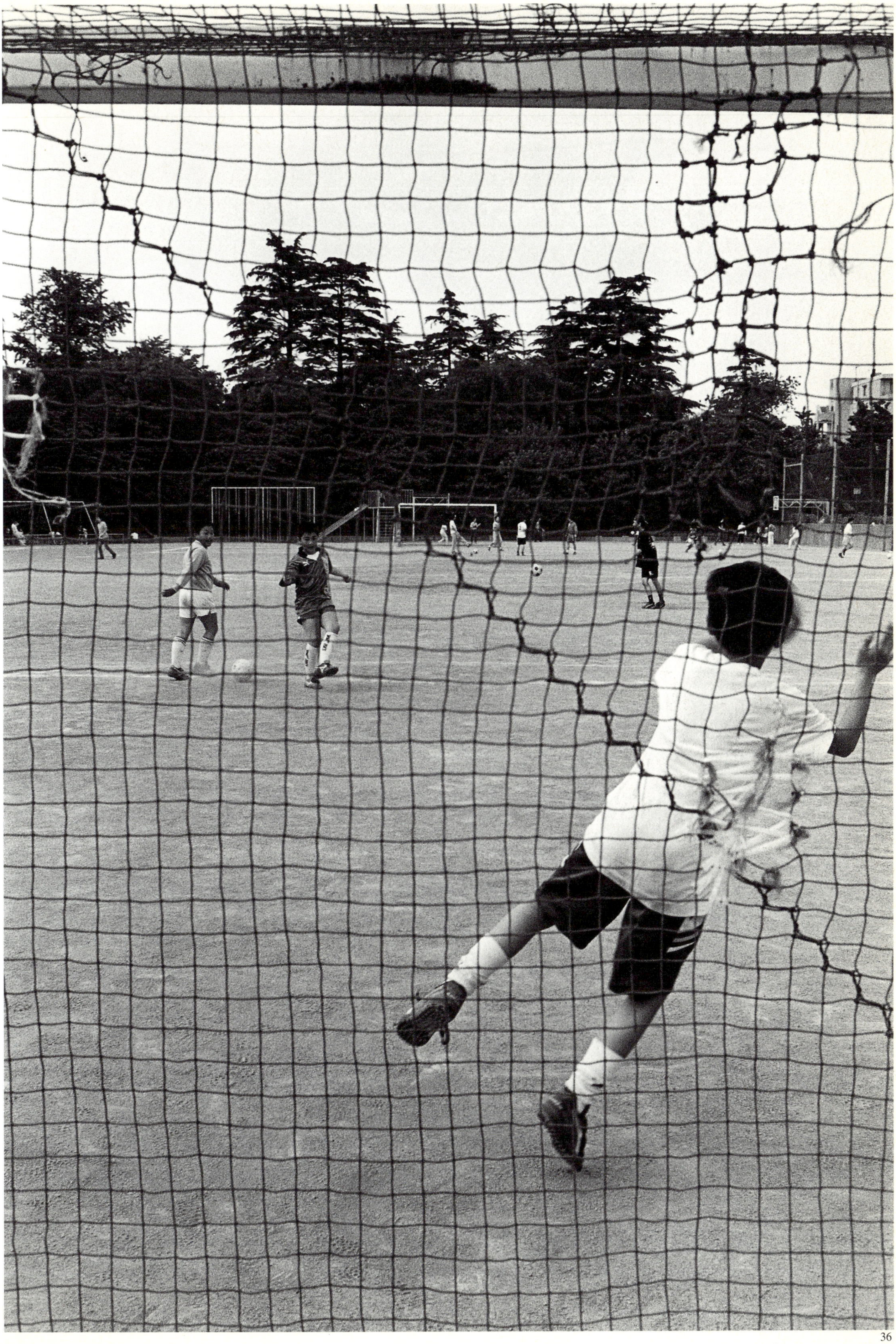

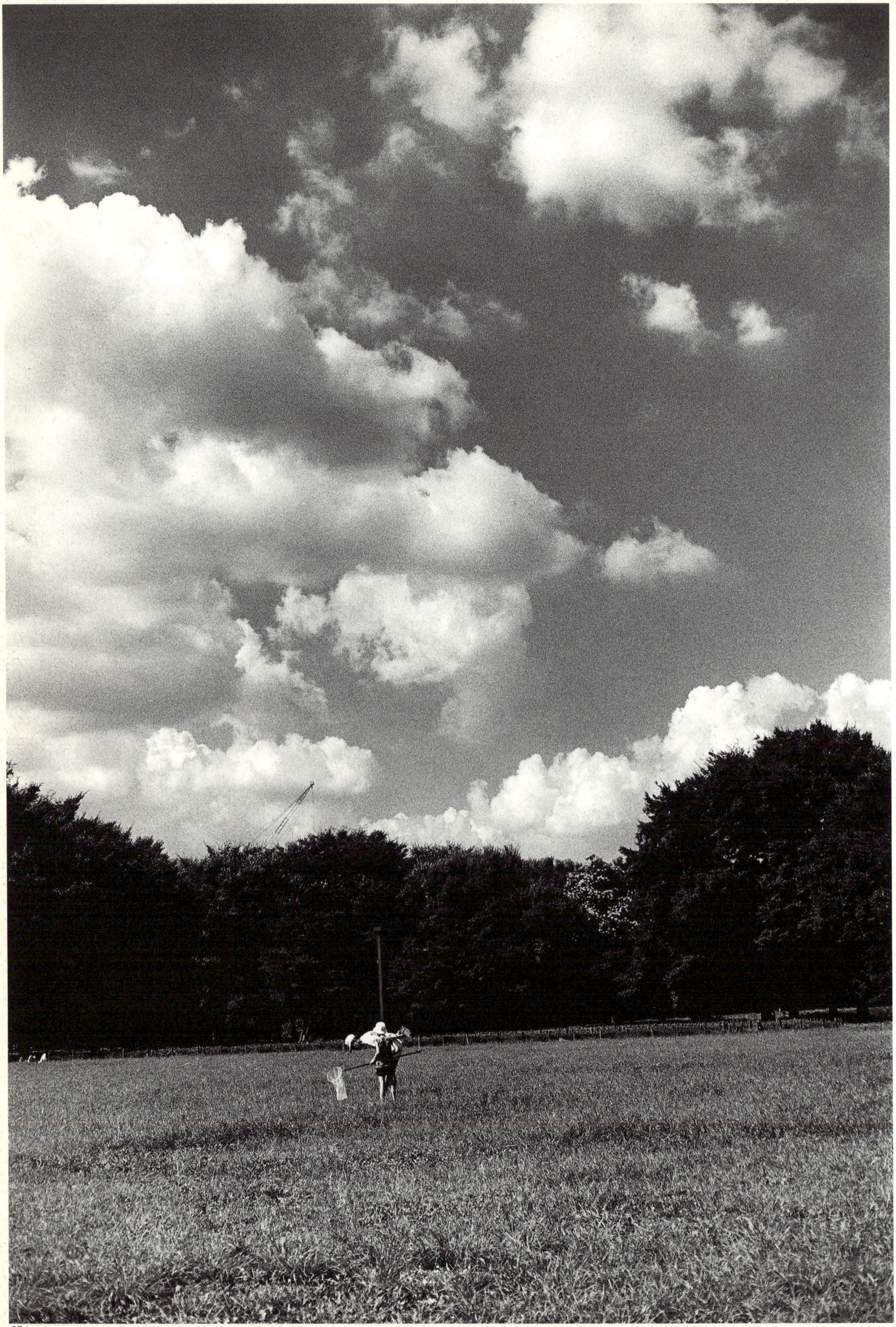

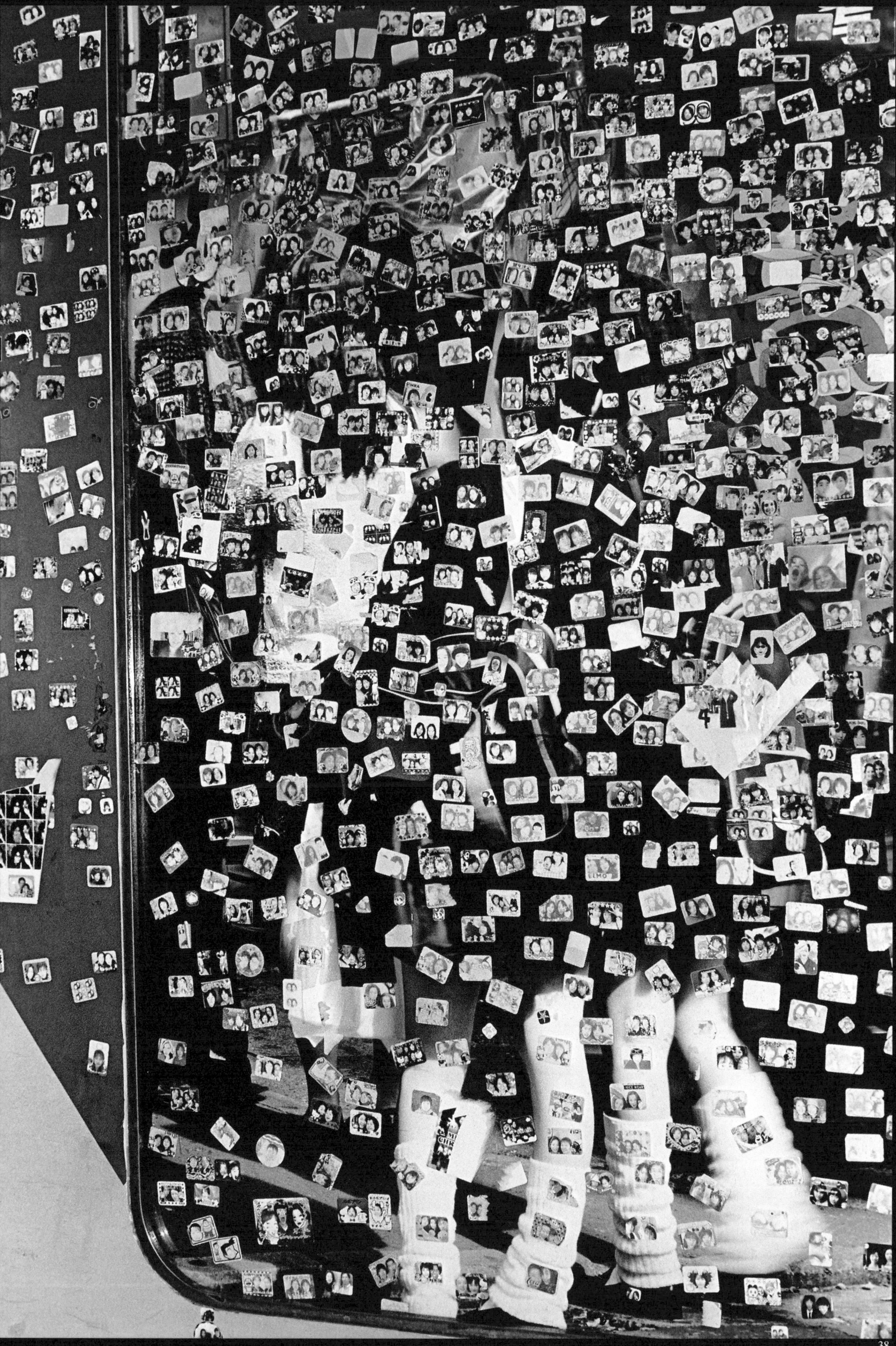

39

40

41

42

43

44

45

46

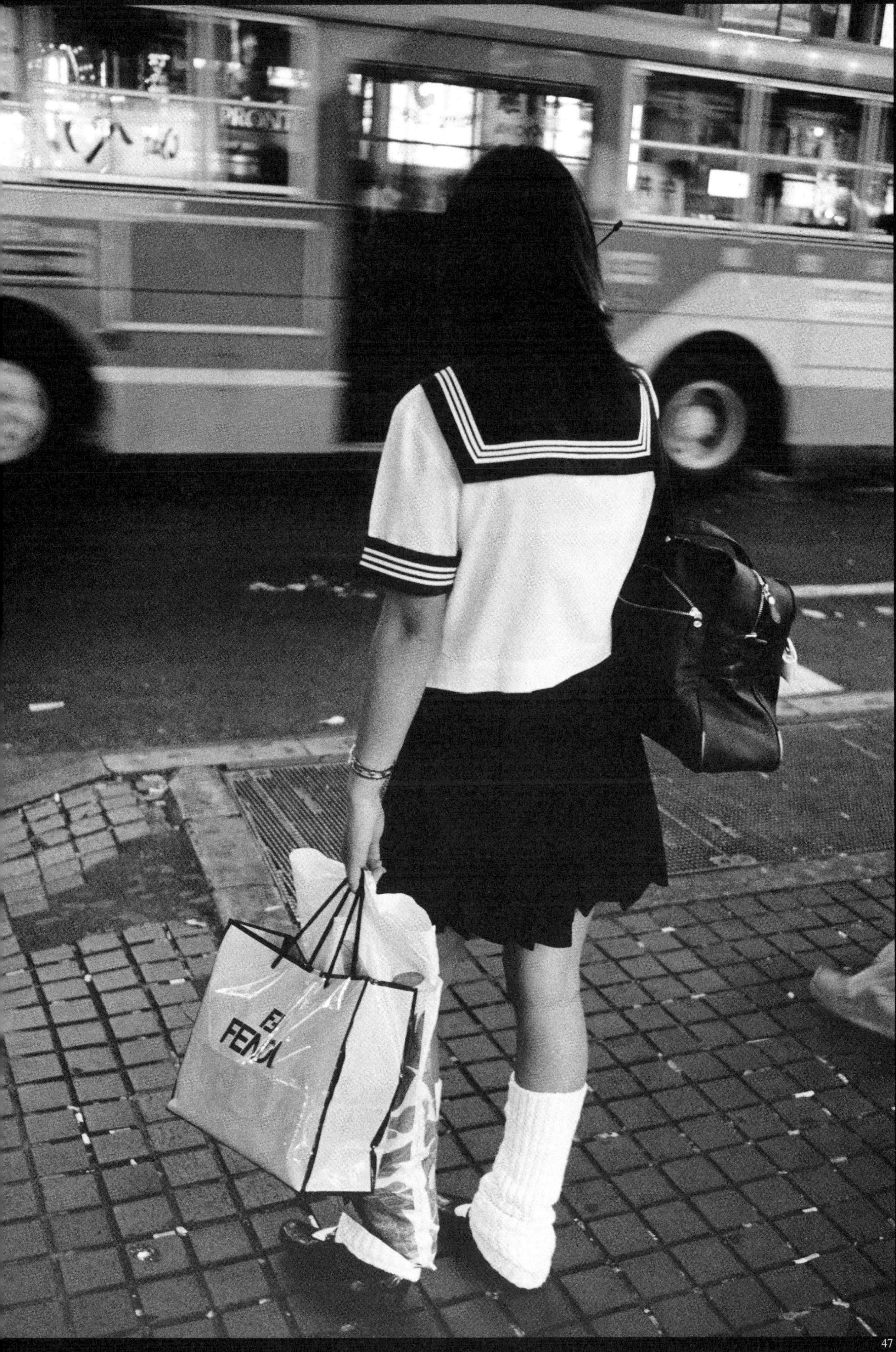
FENDI

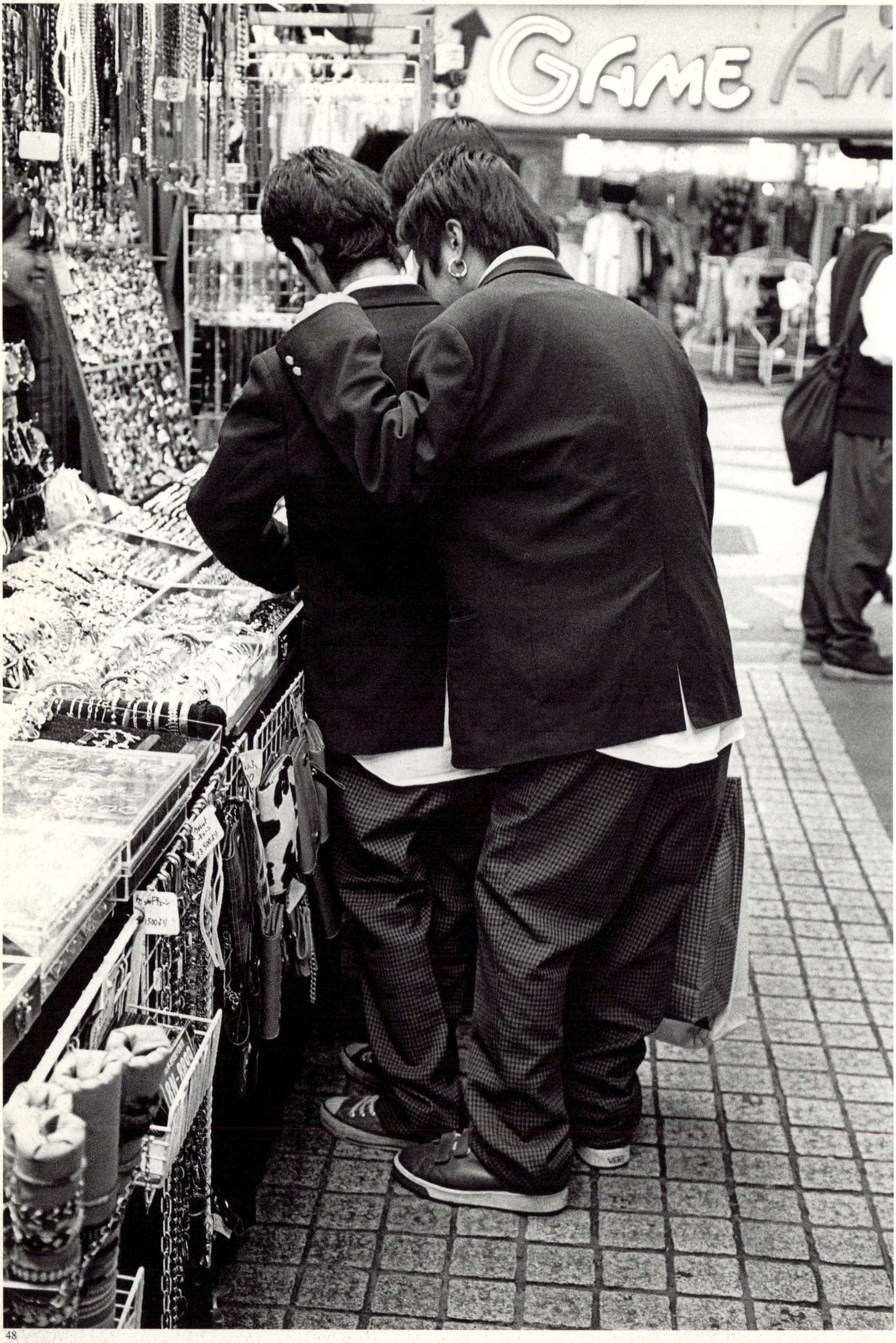
GAME

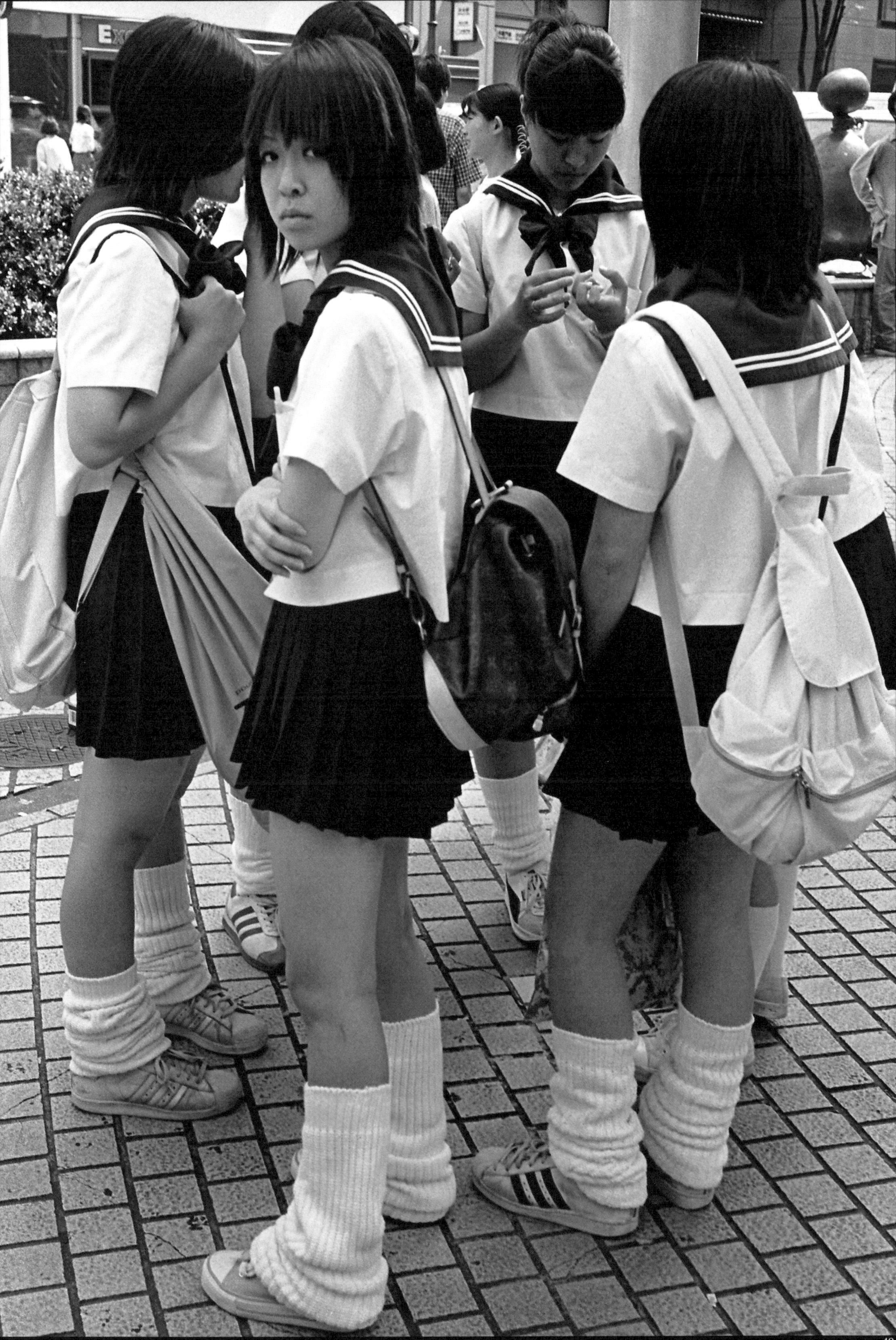

50

51

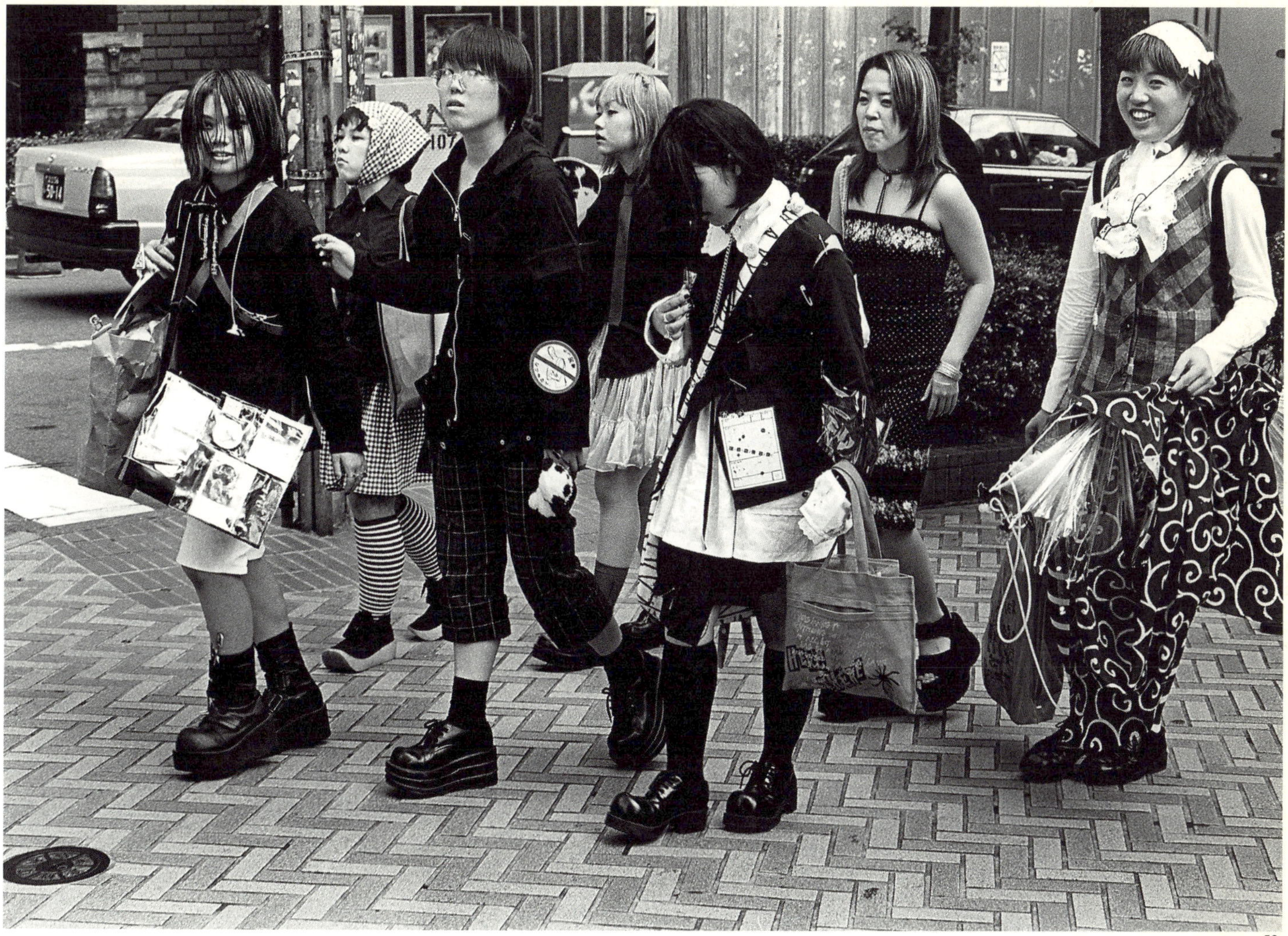

52

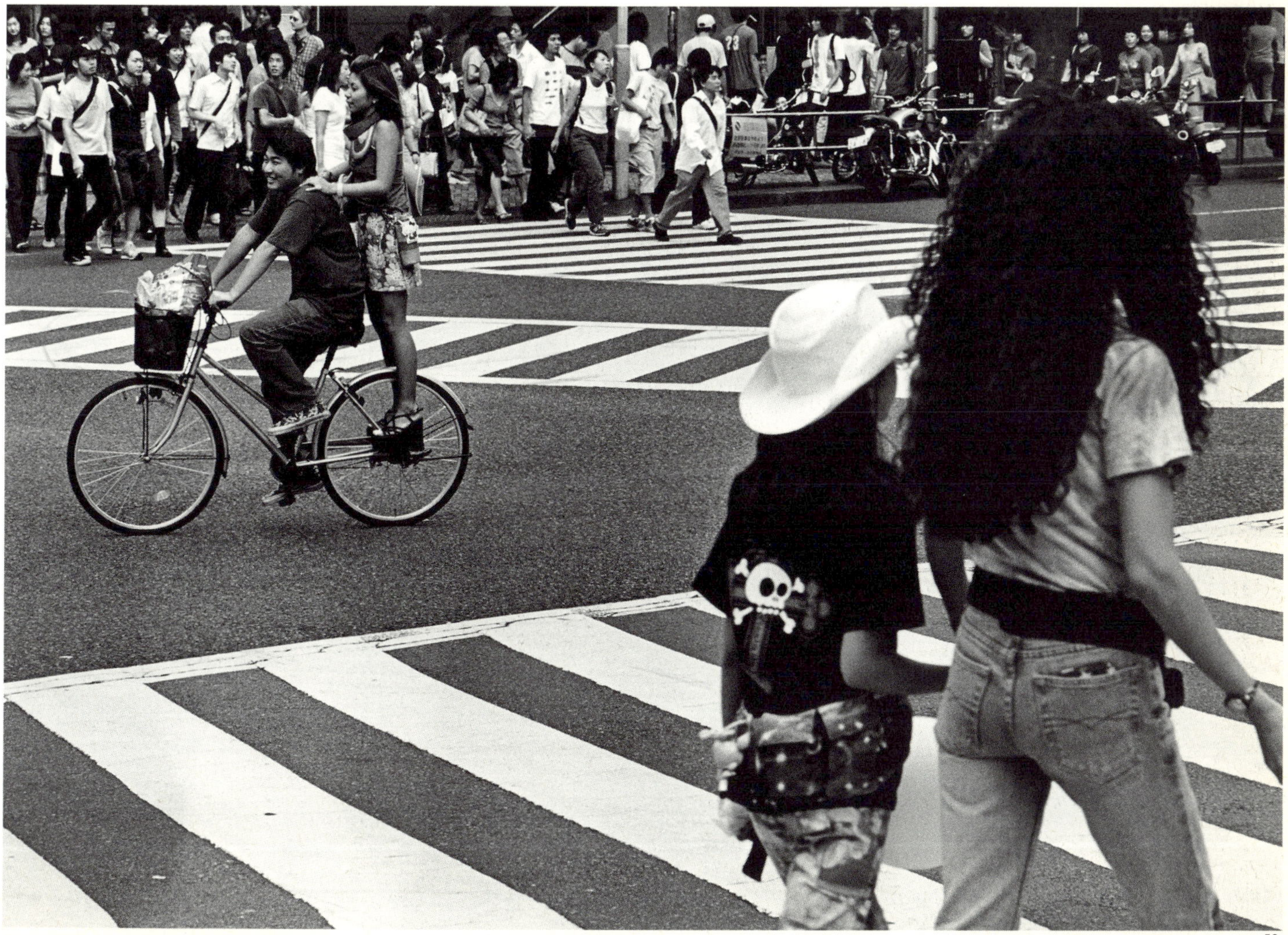

54 55

56

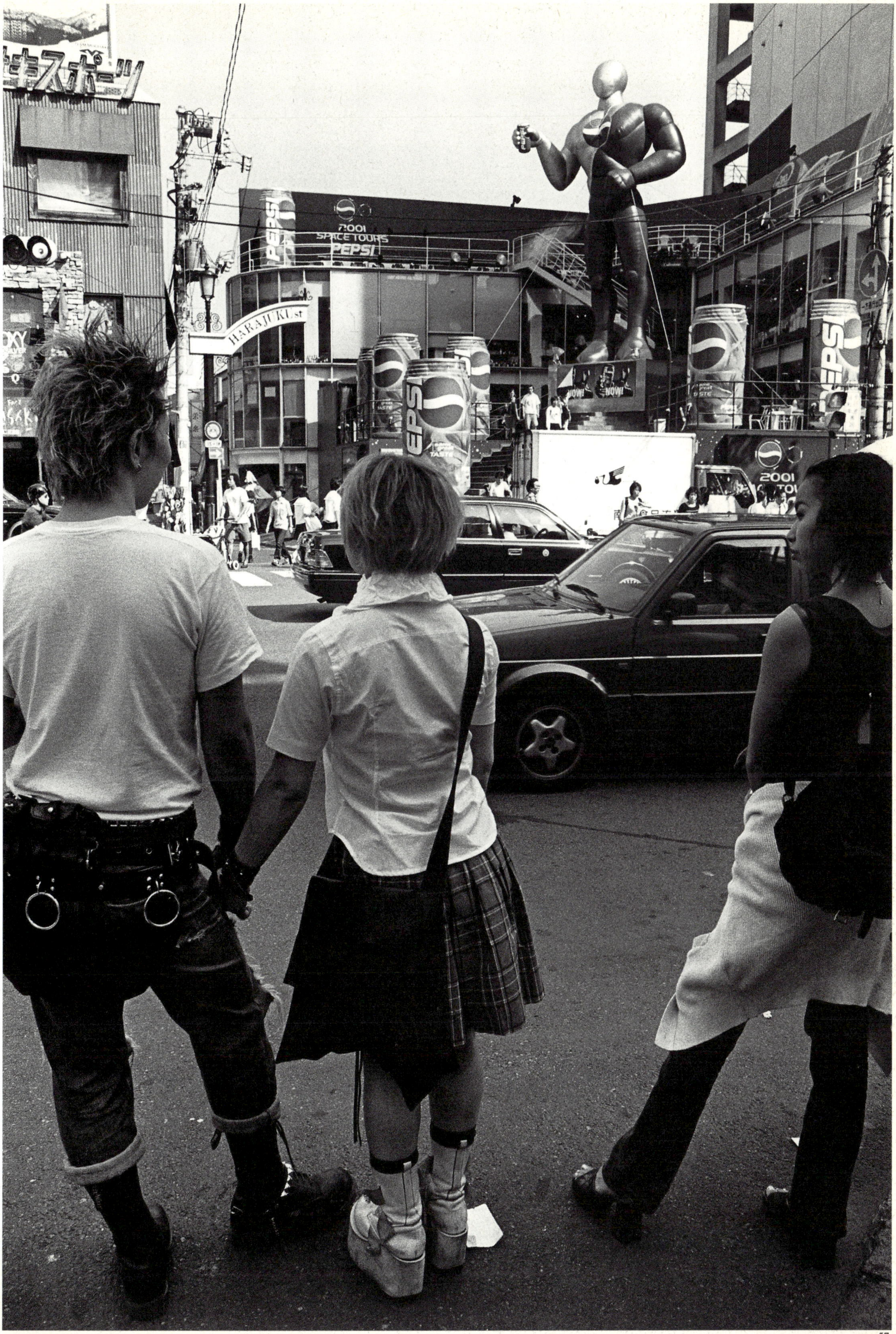
PEPSI
2001
SPACE TOURS
PEPSI
HARAJUKU st

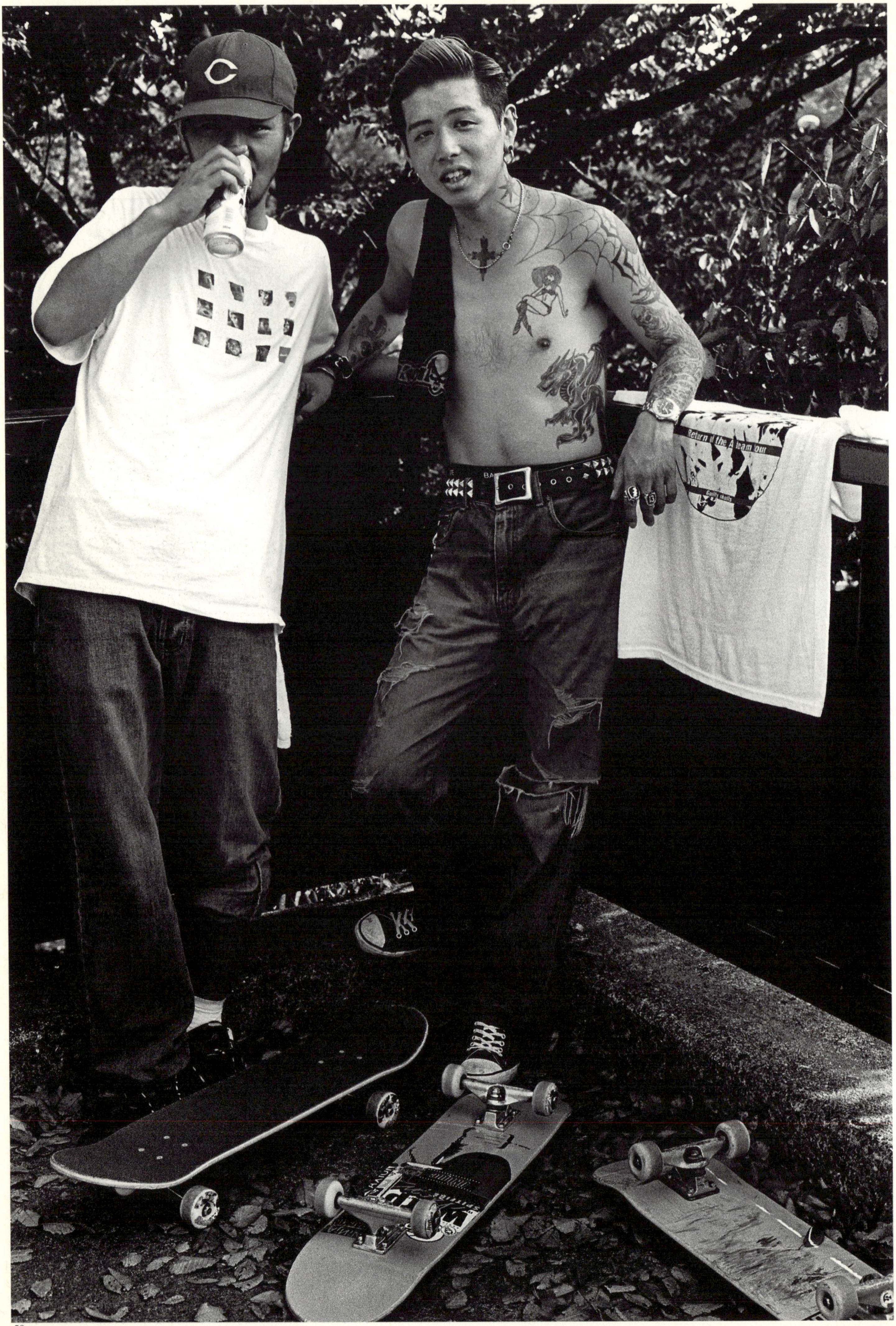

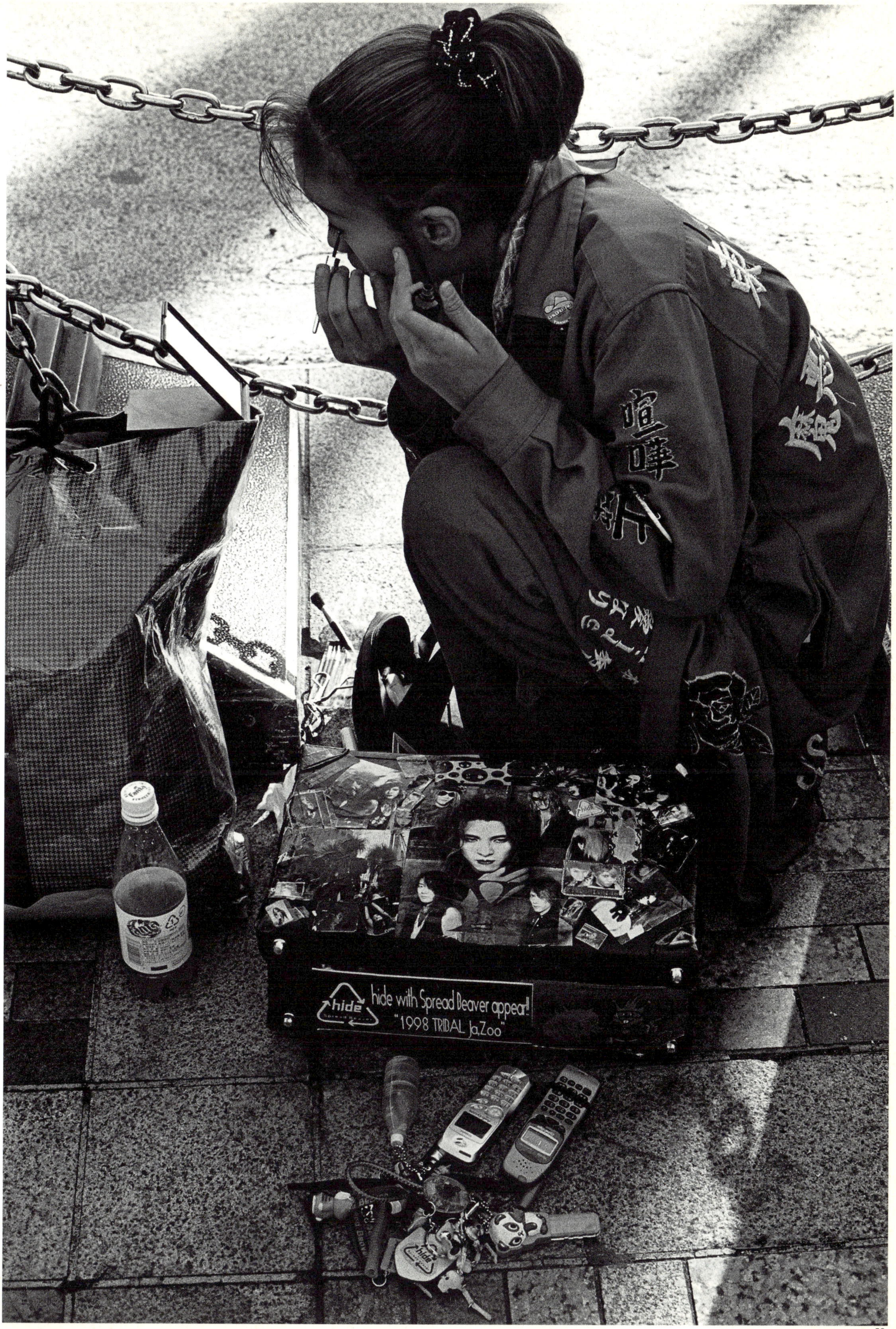
喧嘩
hide with Spread Beaver appear!!
"1998 TRIBAL Ja,Zoo"
hide

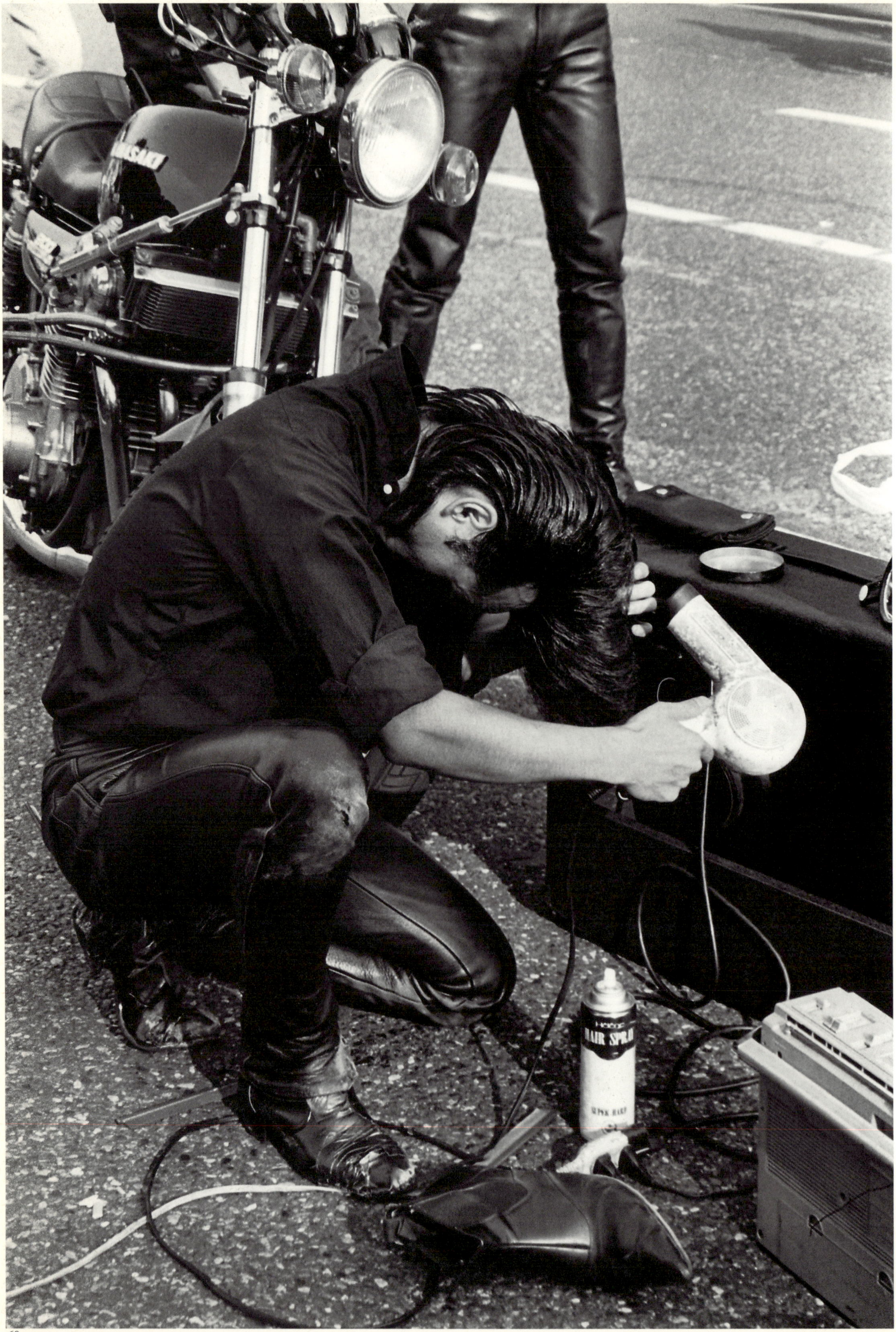

61

62

63

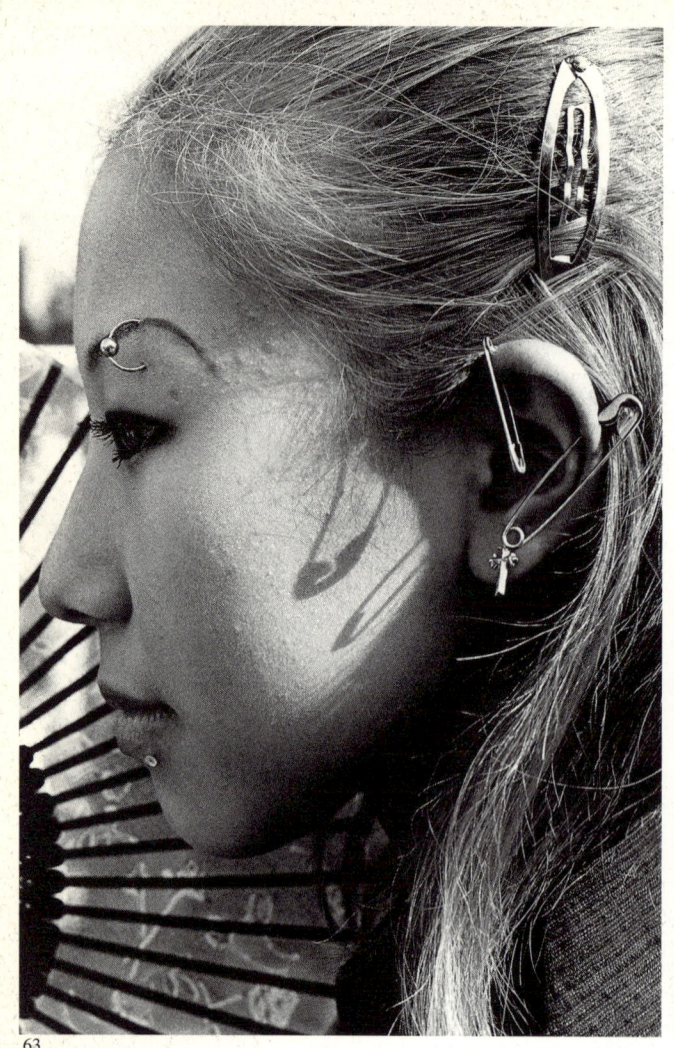

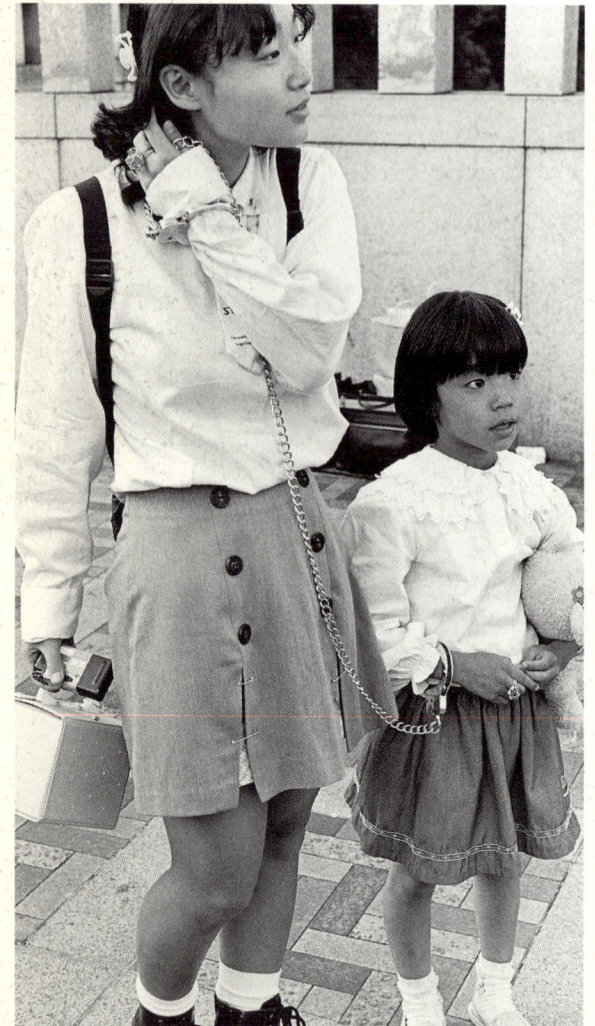

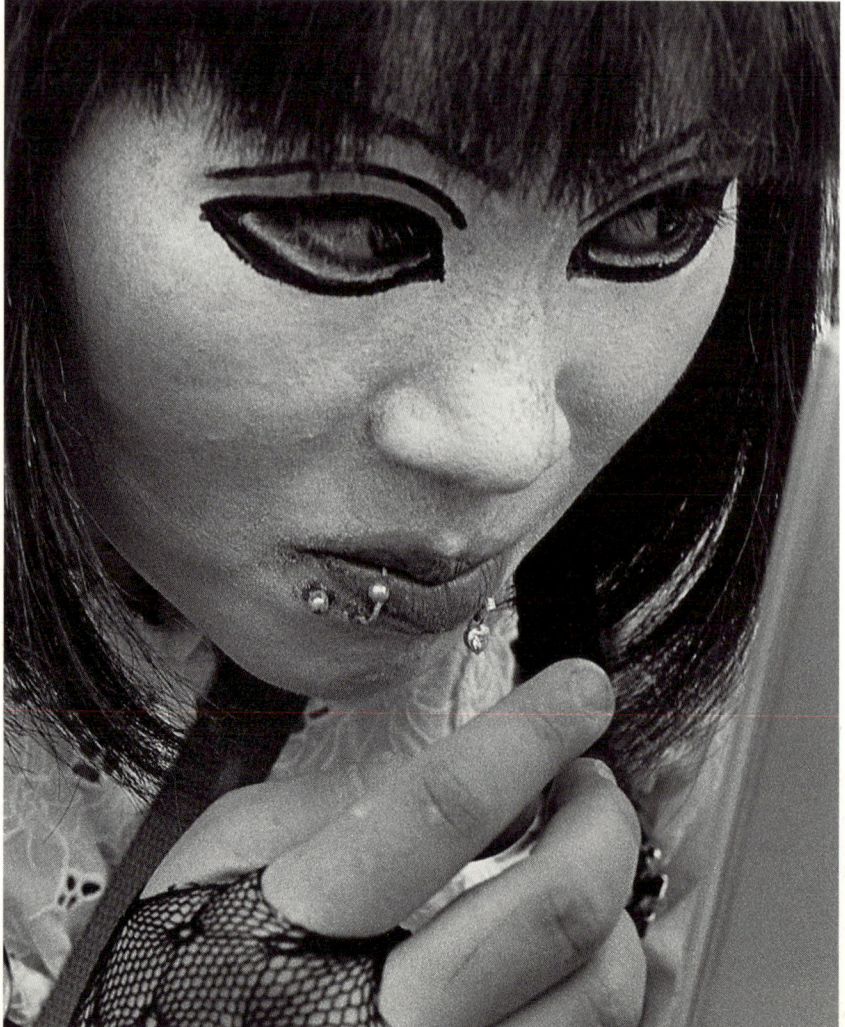

65

64

66

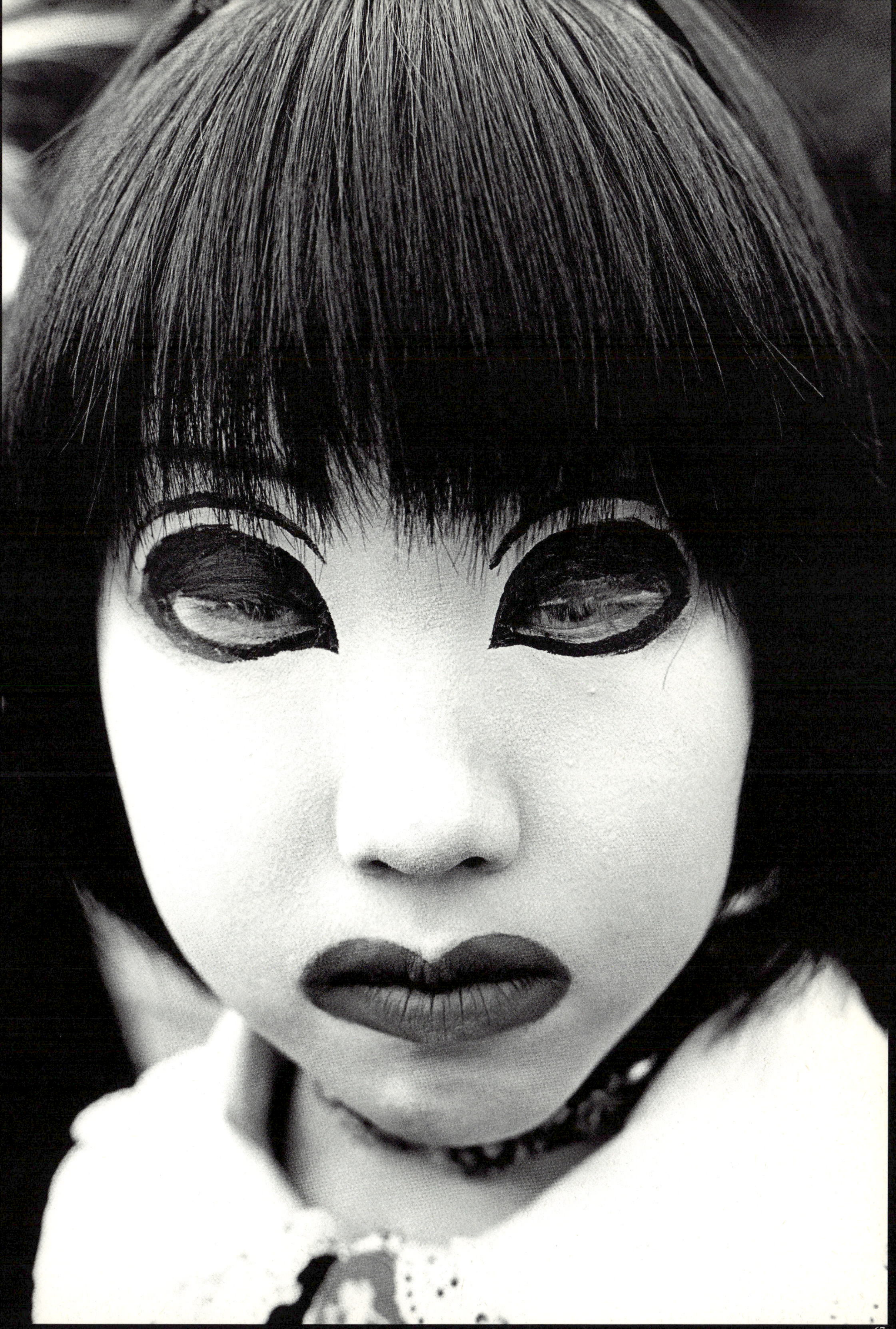

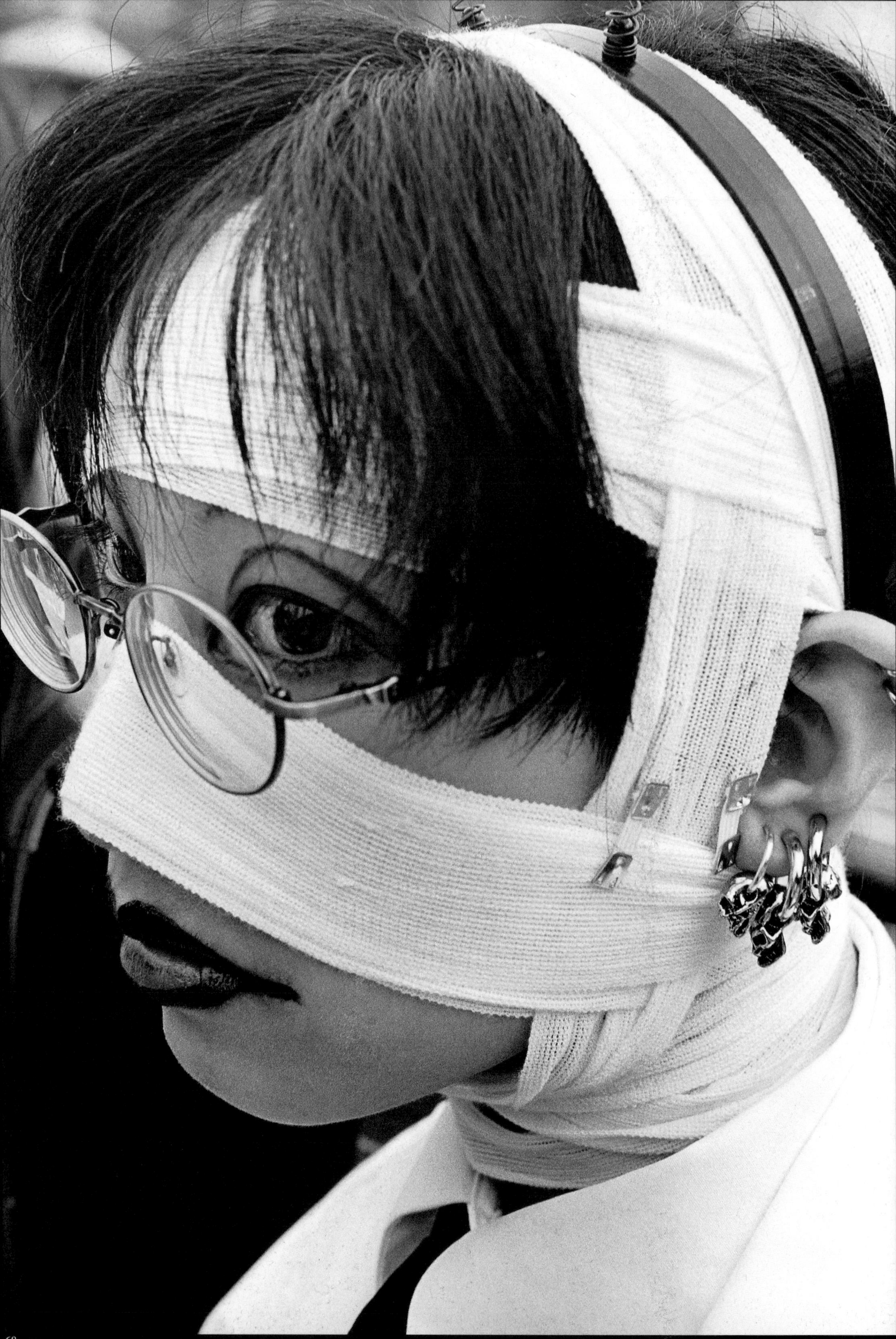

69

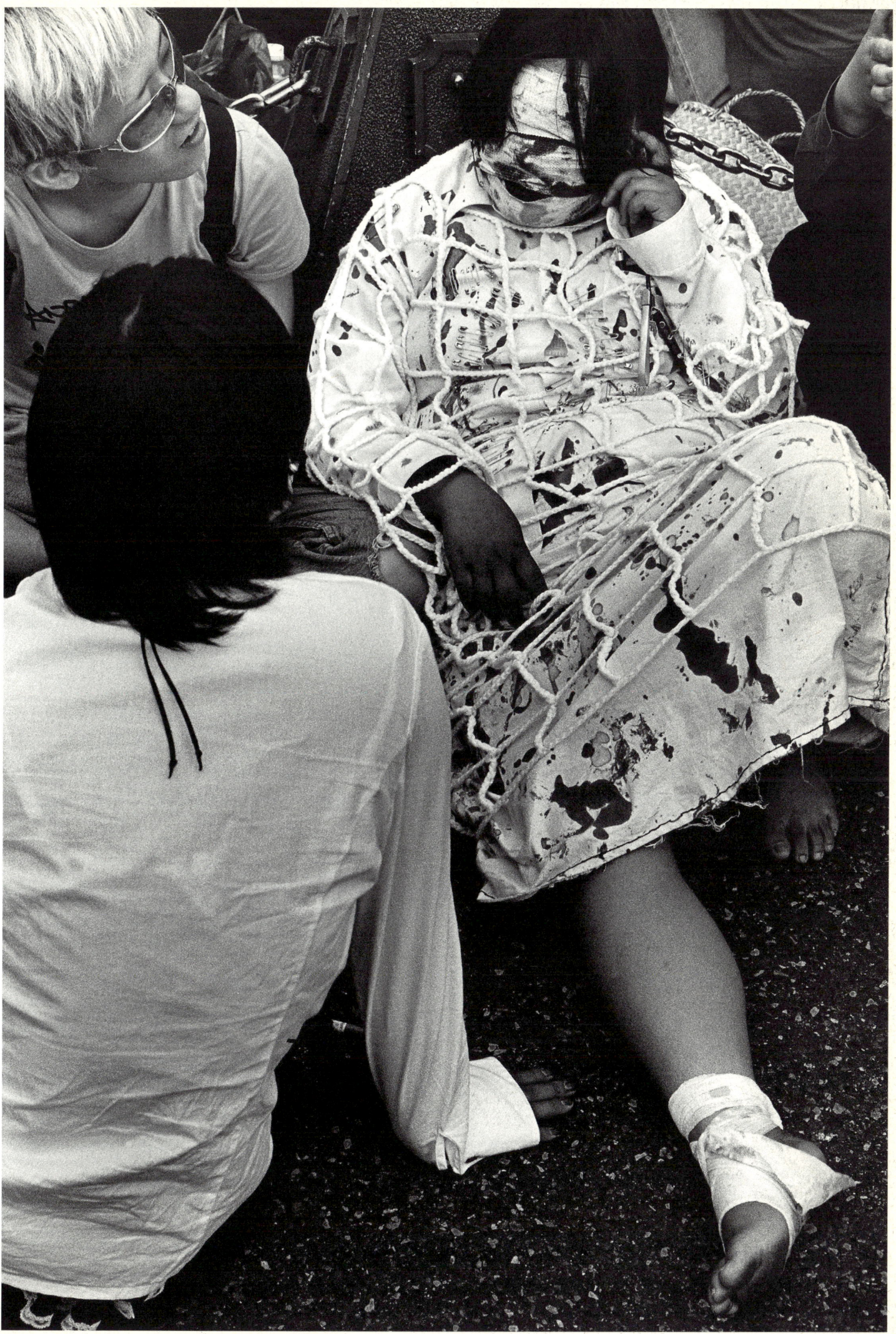

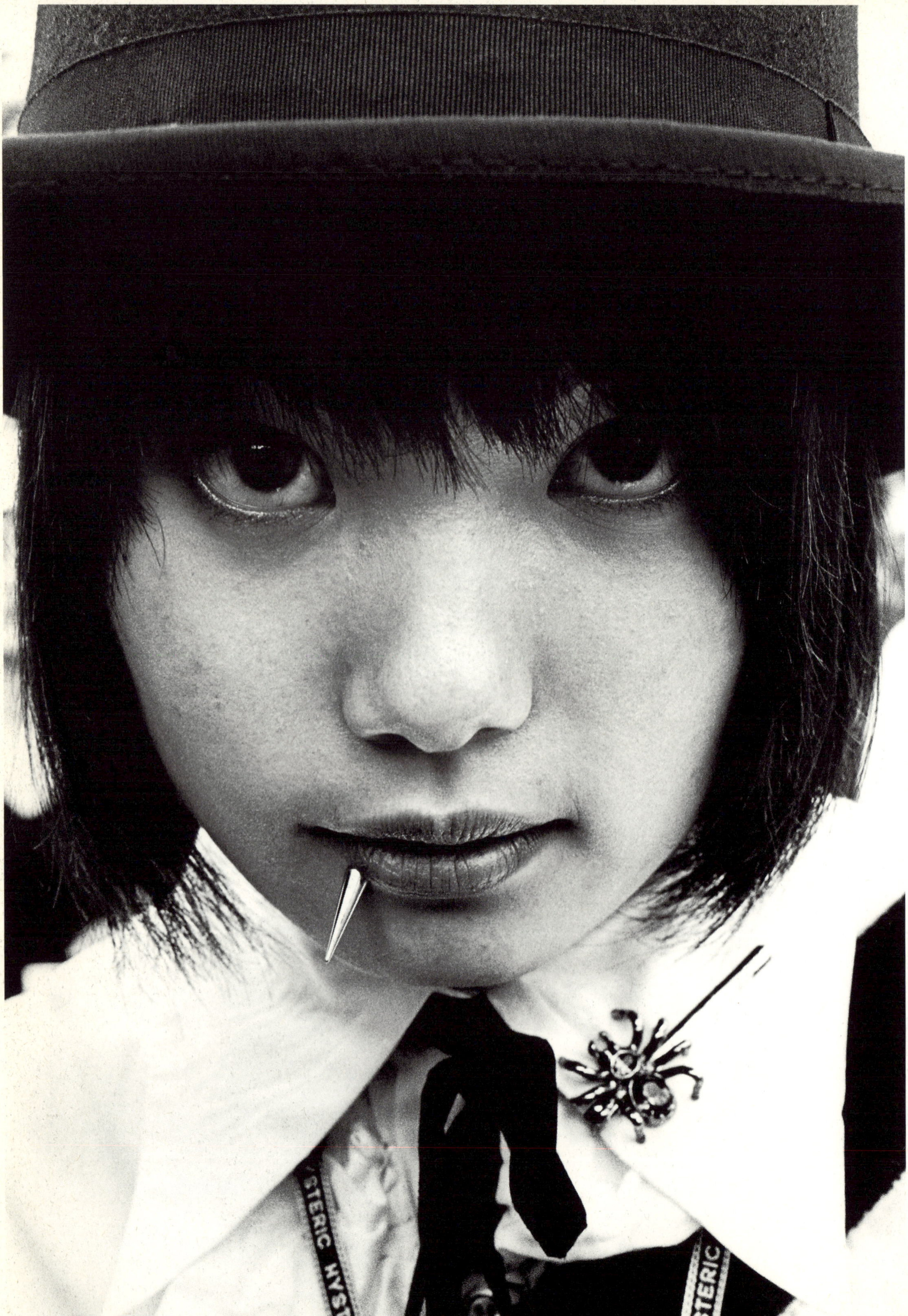
HYSTERIC
HYSTERIC

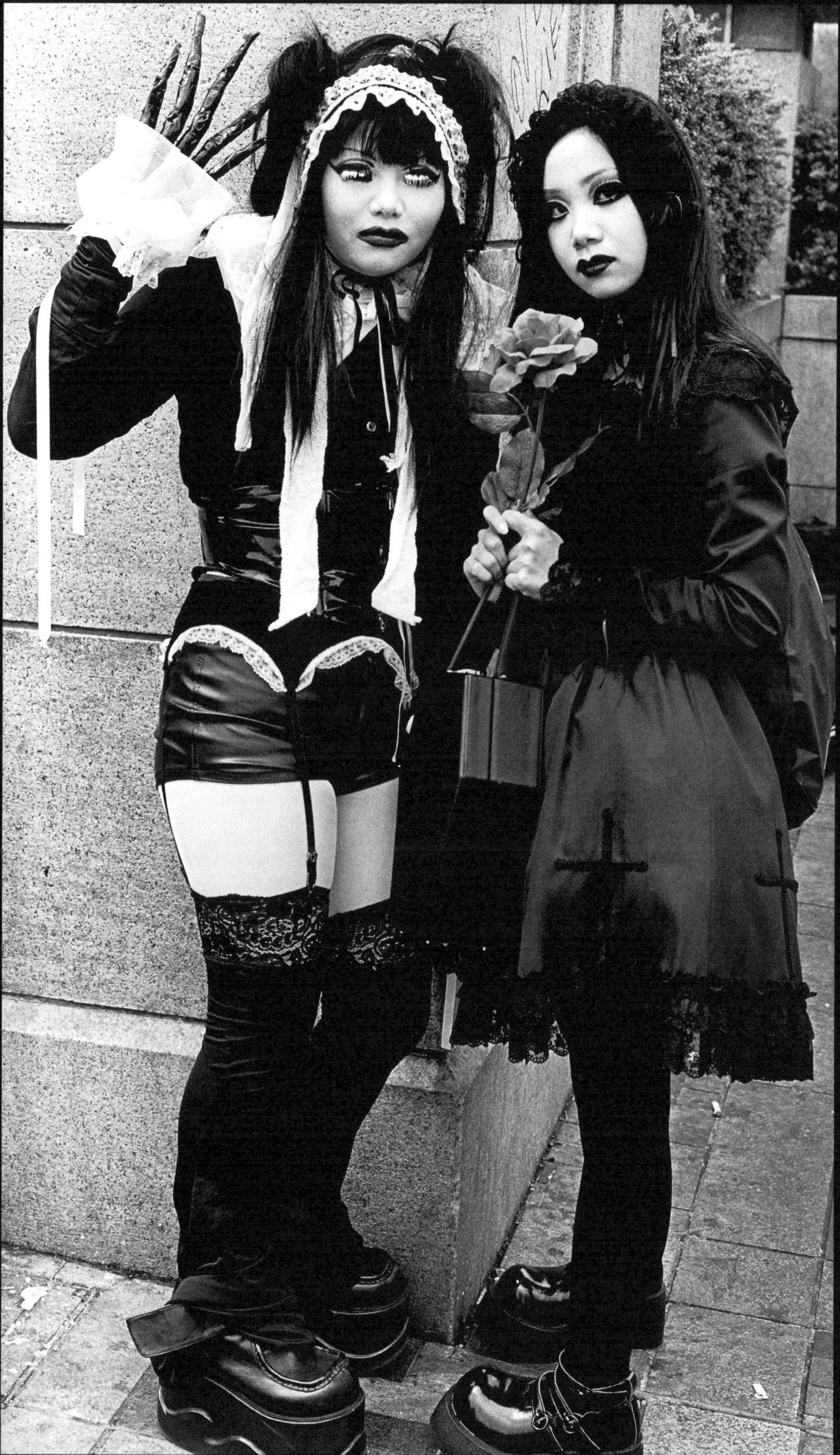

72

73

74

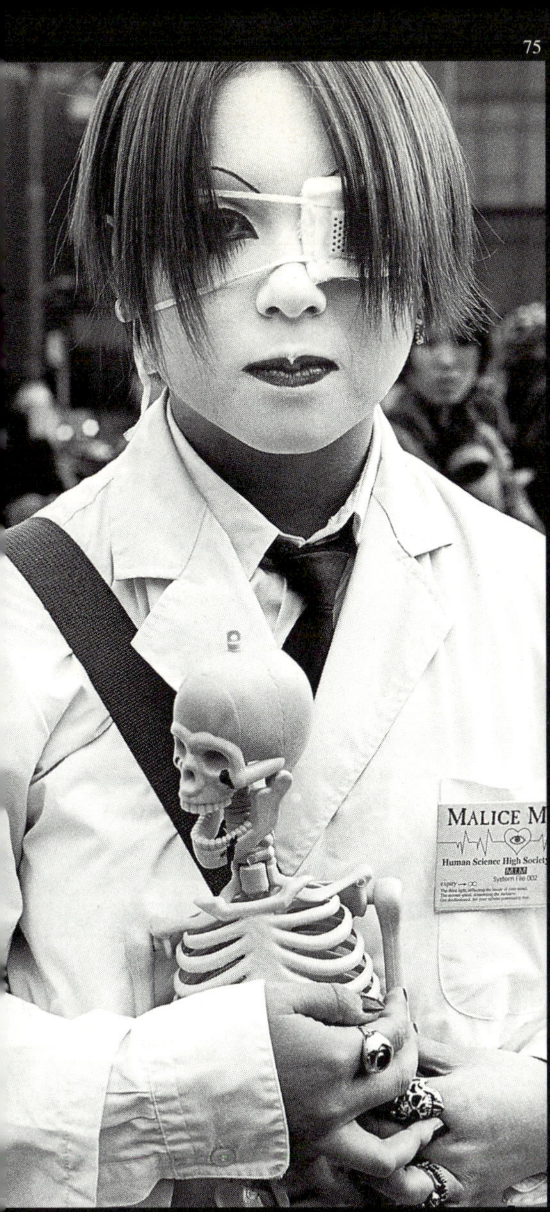

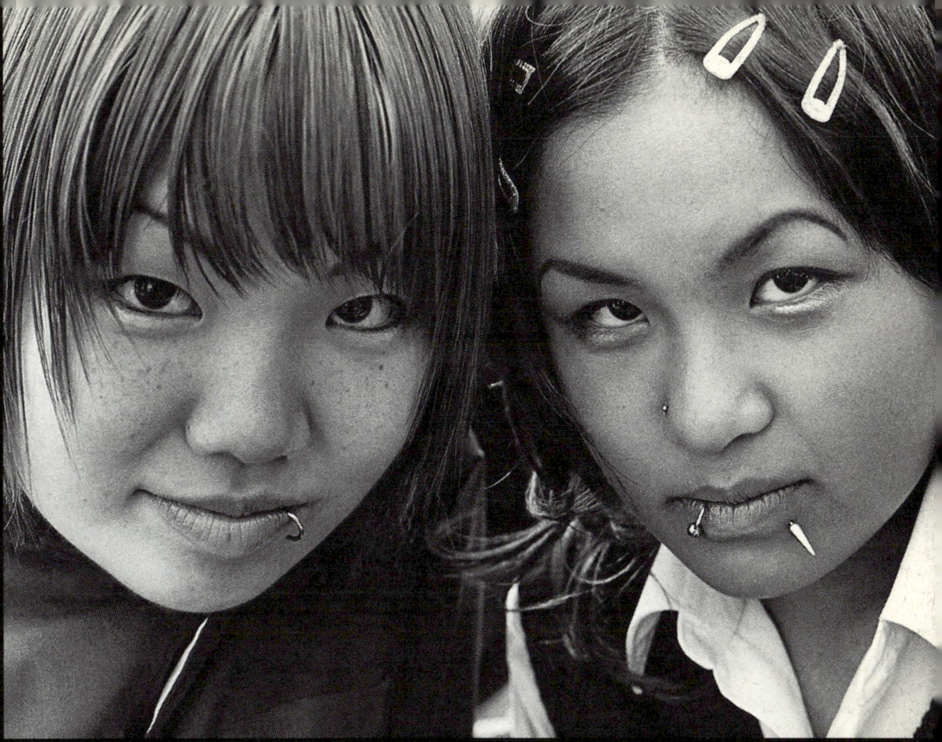

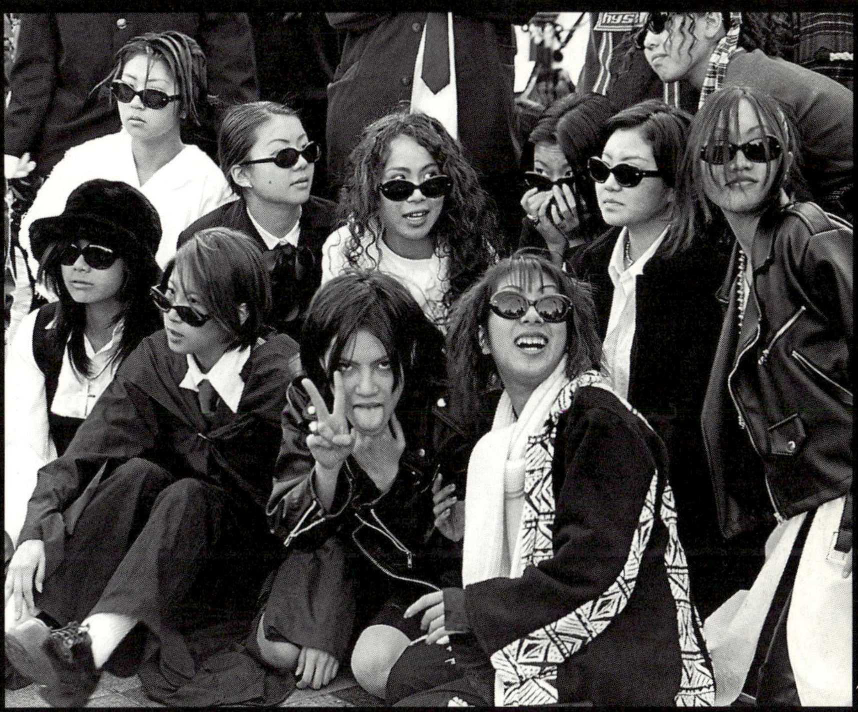

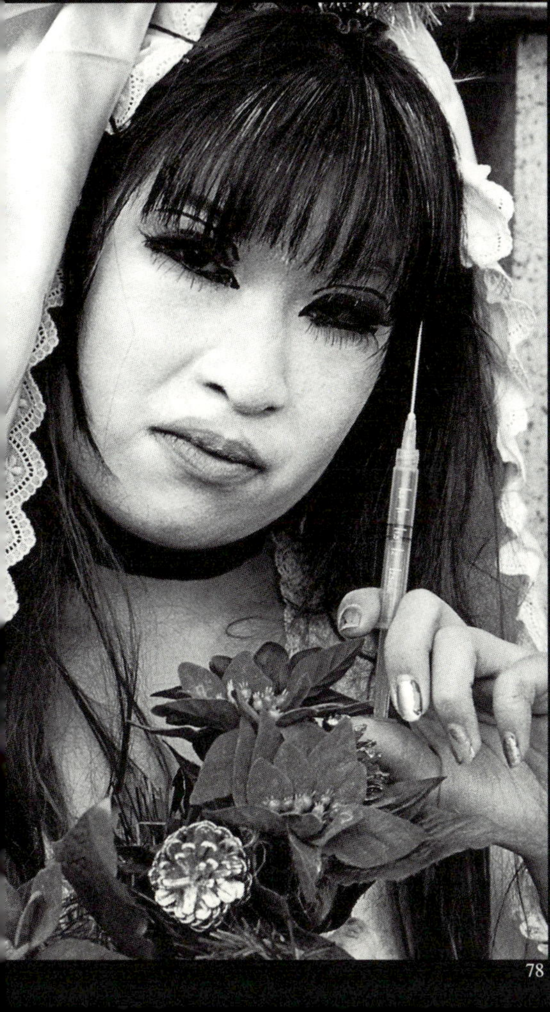

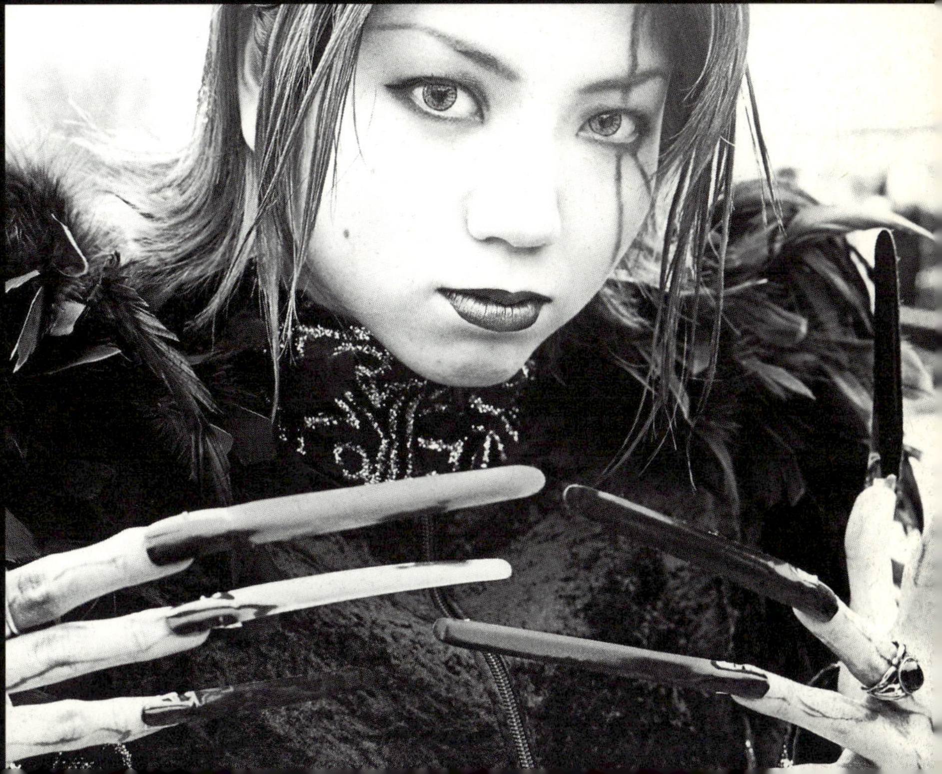

80
81
82
83
84
85

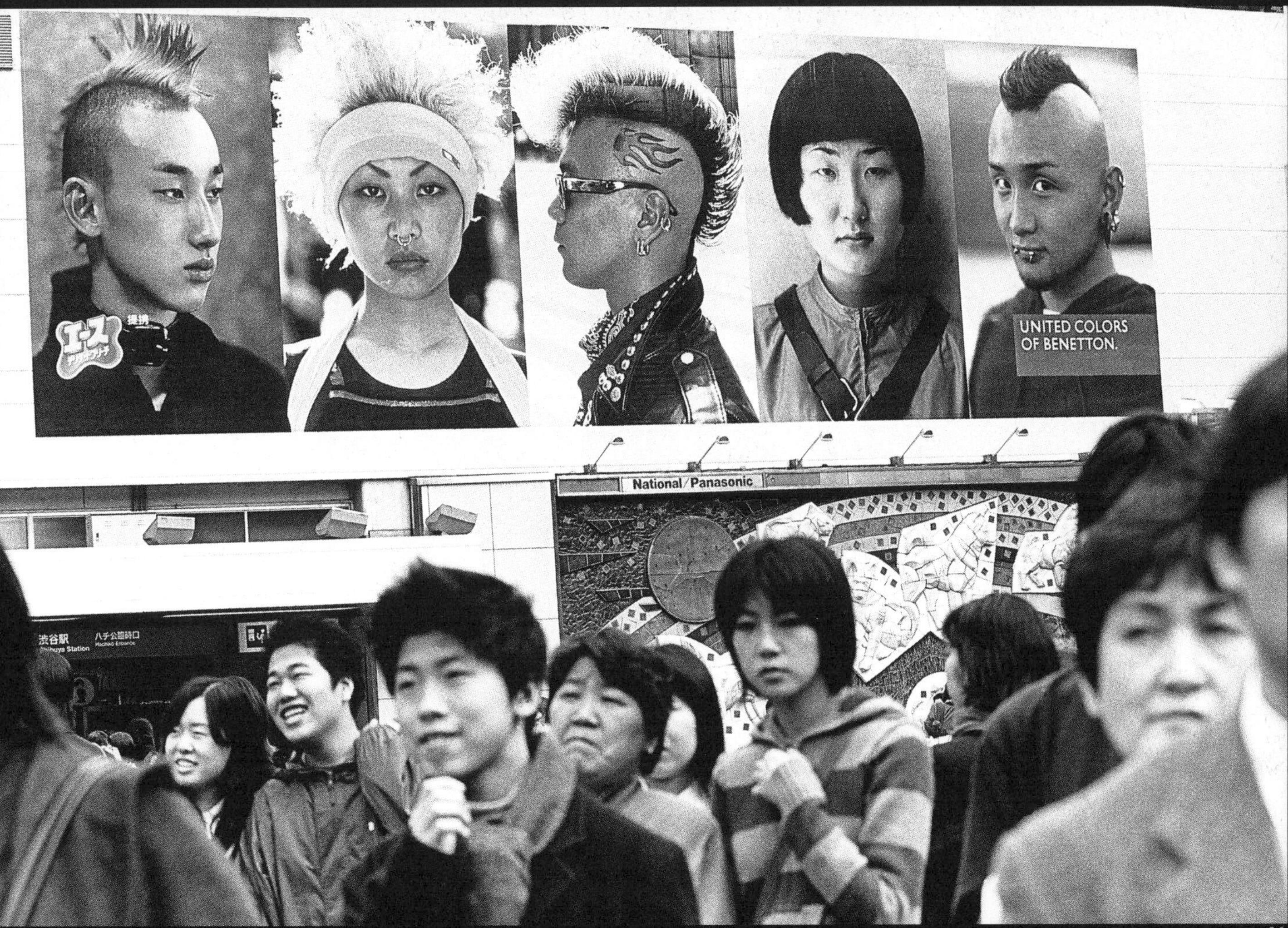

86

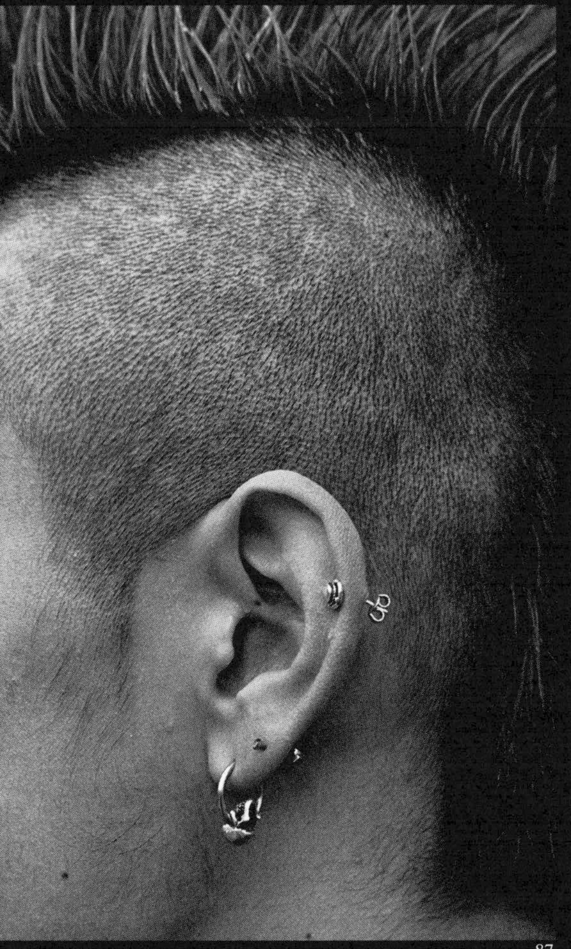

87

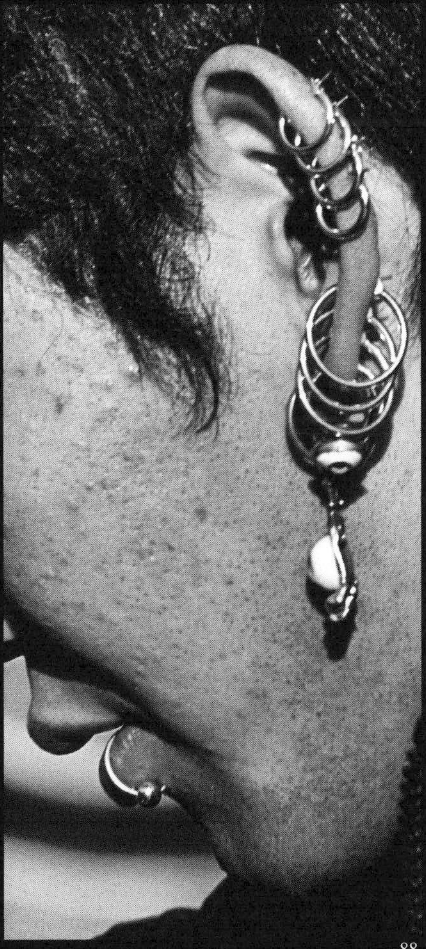

88

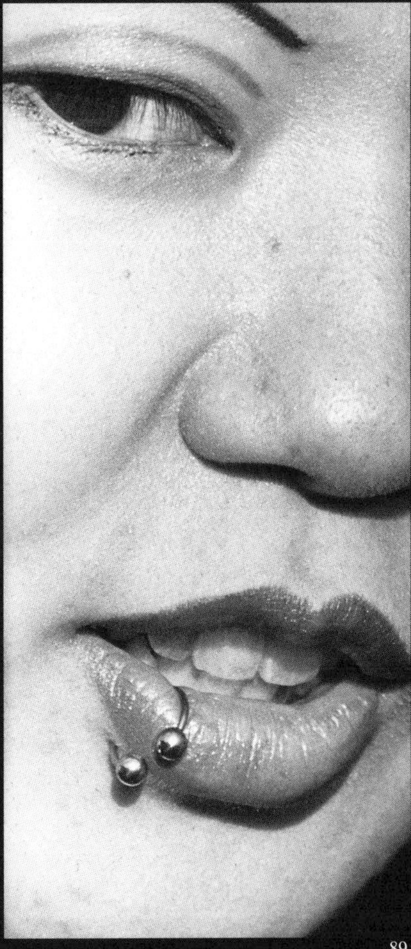

89

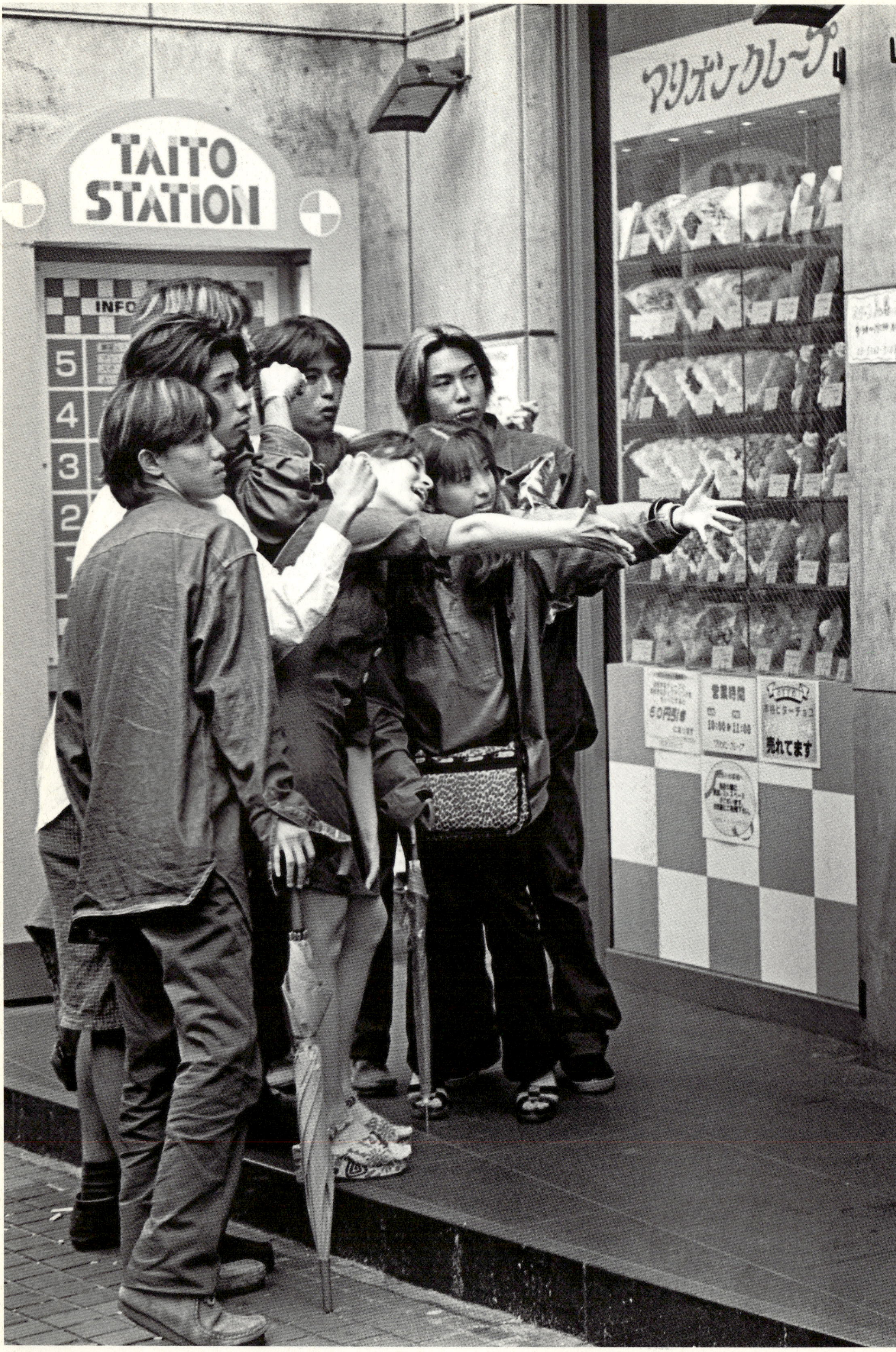
TAITO
STATION
INFO
マリオンクレープ
営業時間
売れてます

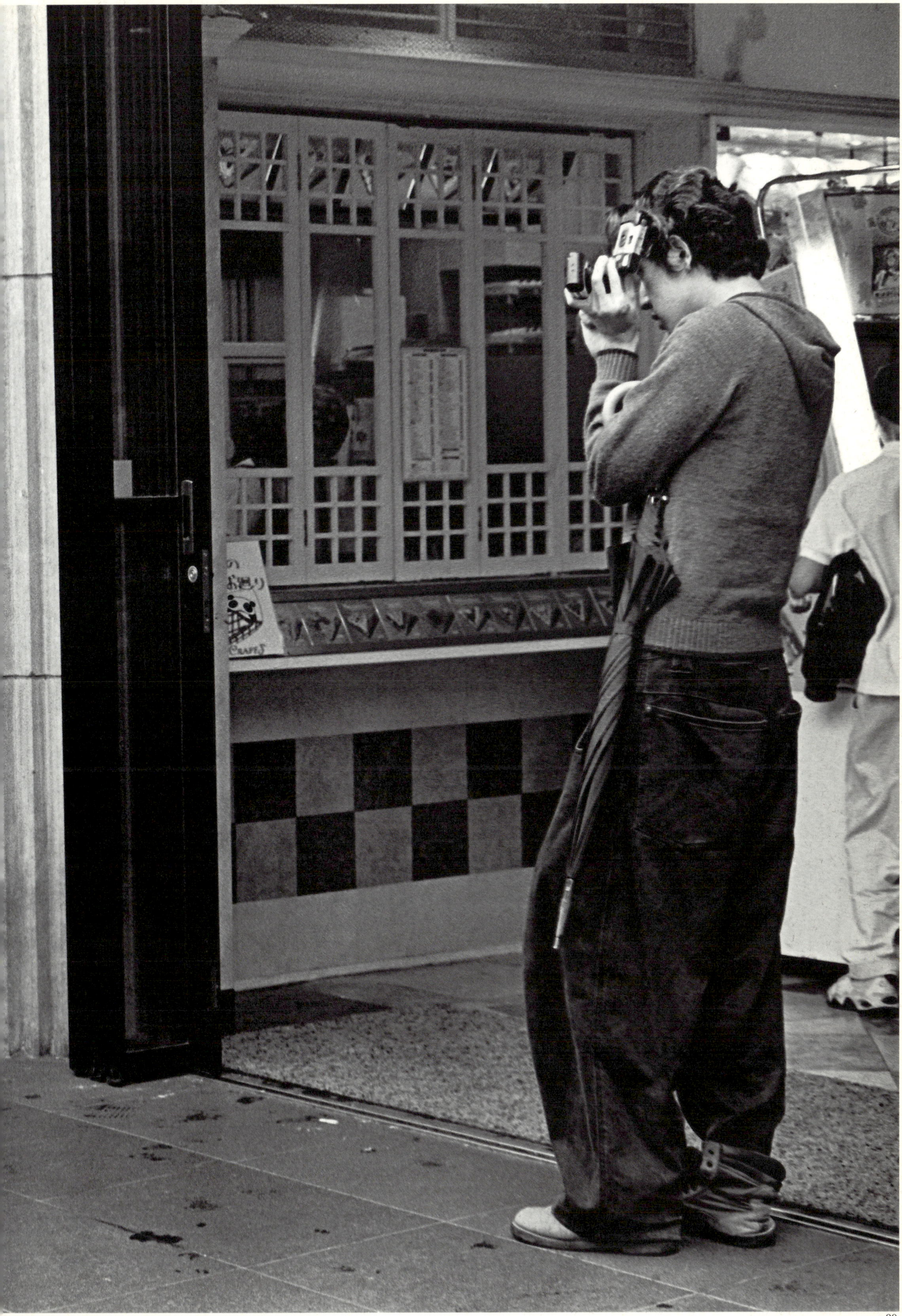

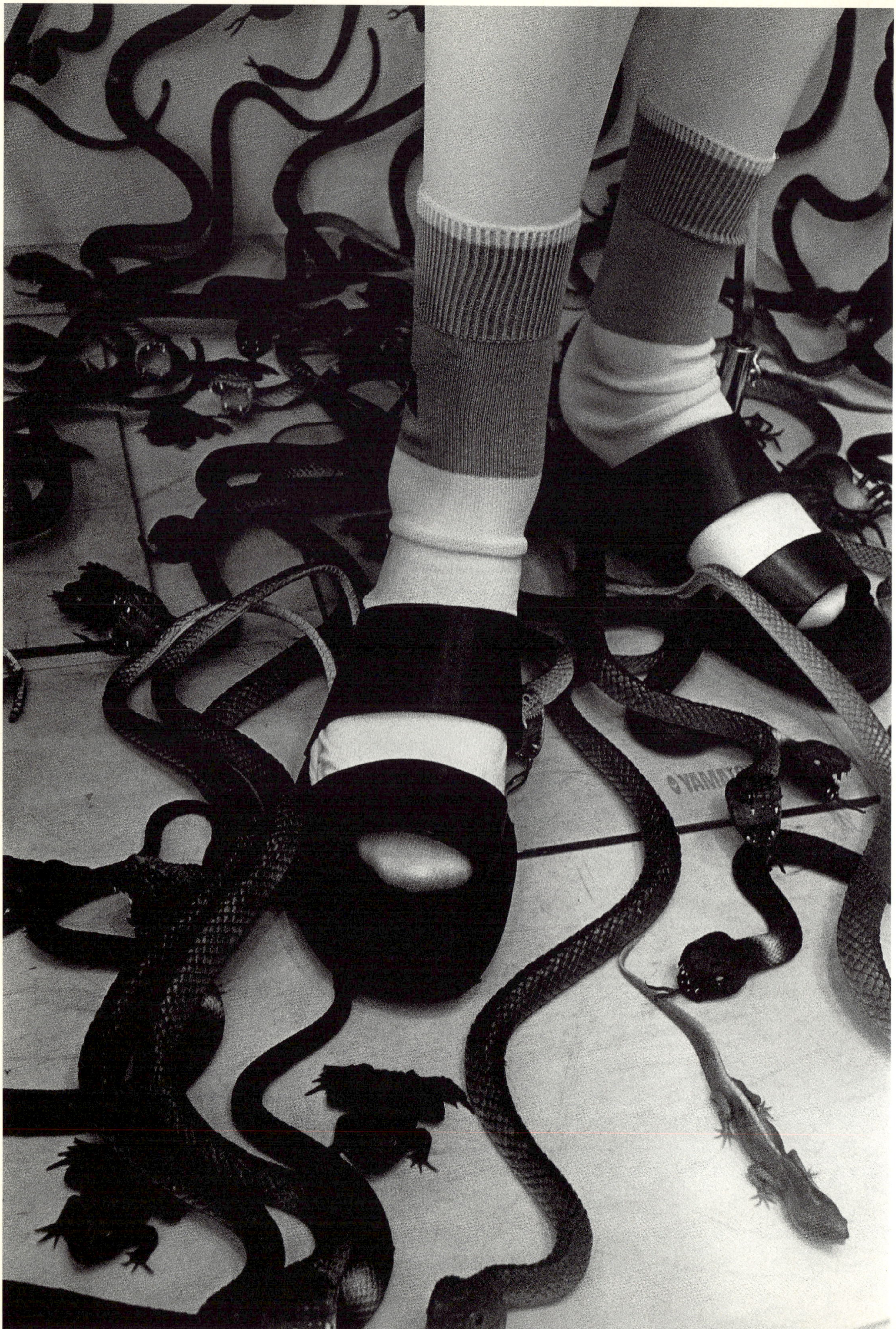

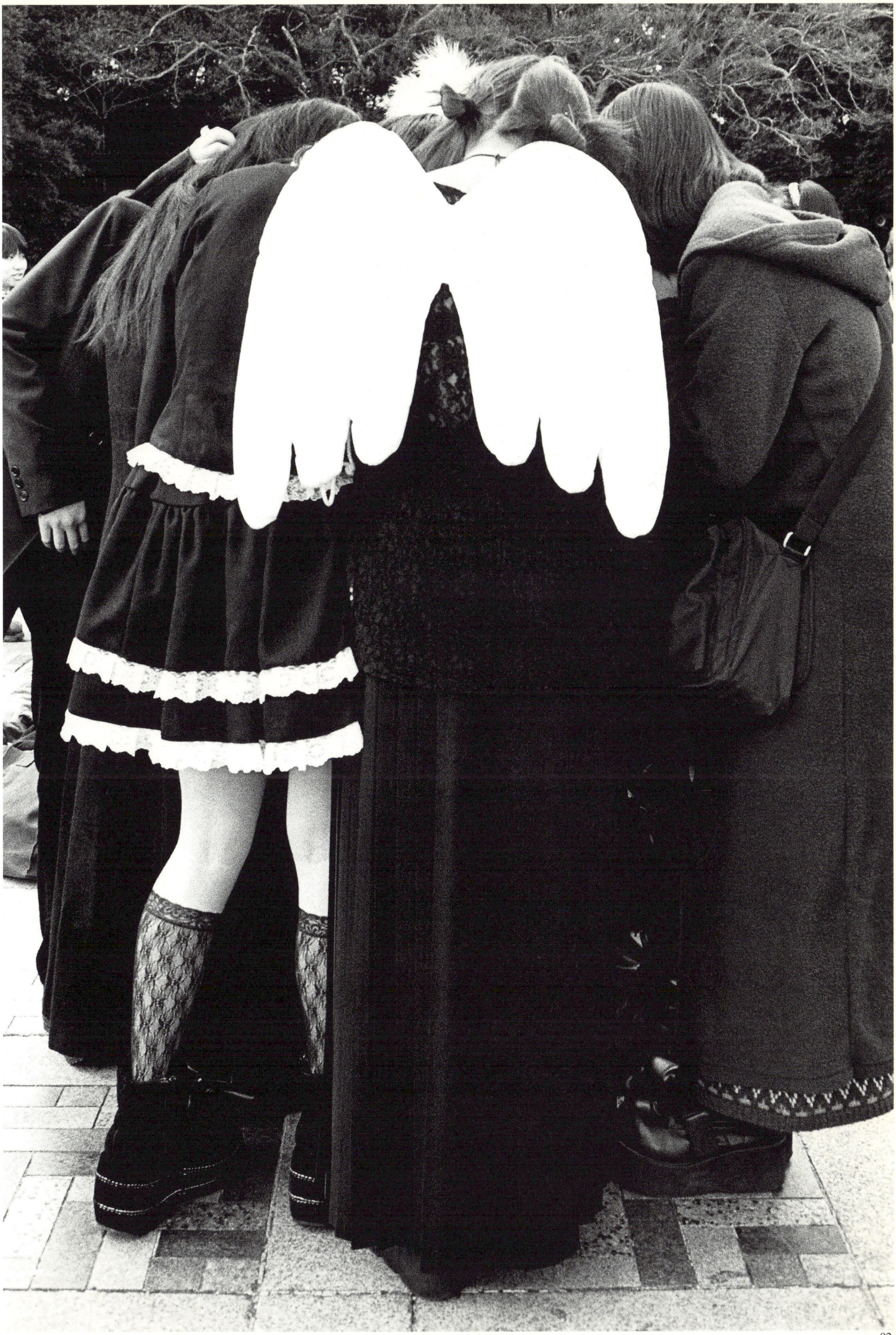

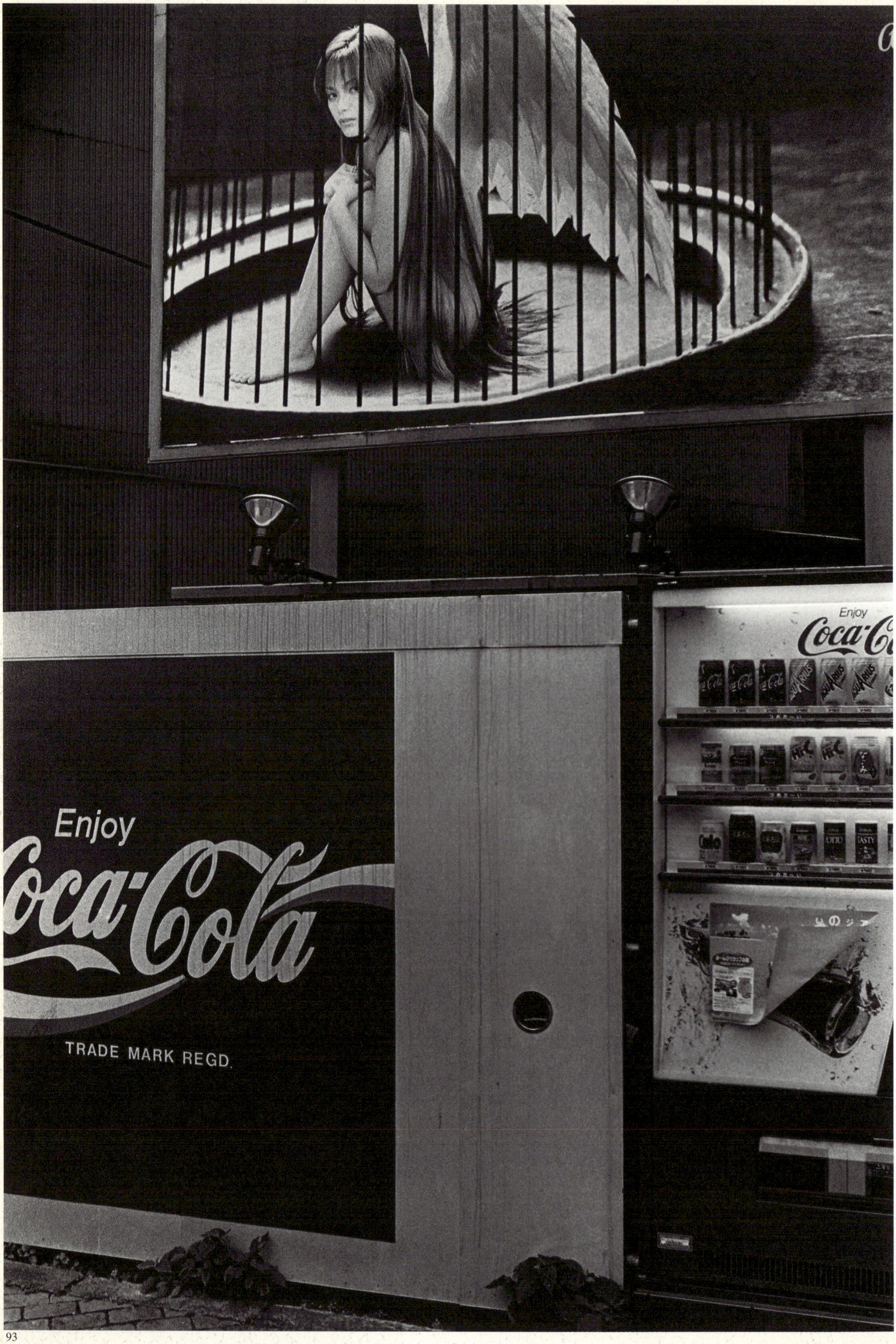
Enjoy
TRADE MARK REGD.
Enjoy

94

THE SYMBOL OF FREEDO
YOUR SOUTHER
PI KETCH CAL INNA DE ACT
TOKYO SKUNX

THE SYMBOL OF FREEDOM FOR YOUR
MI KETCH
GAL INNA
DE ACT
6/23
AC/DC

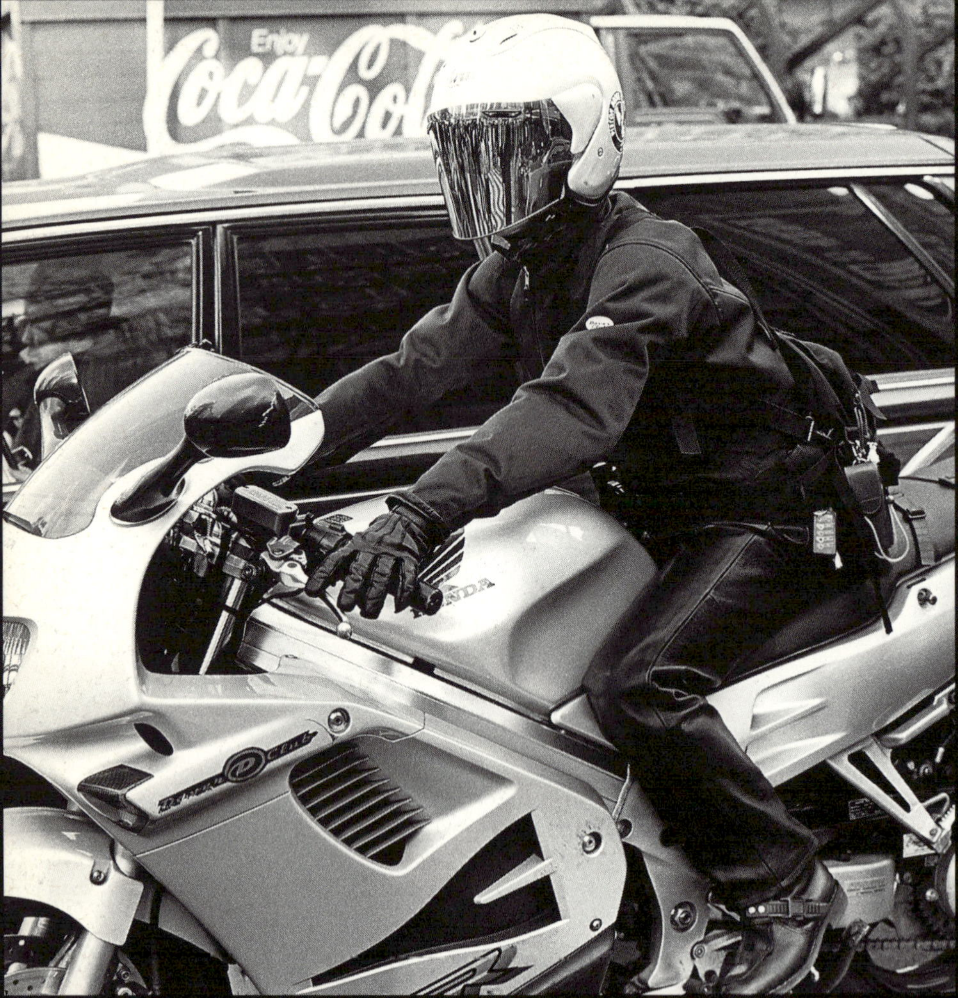

96

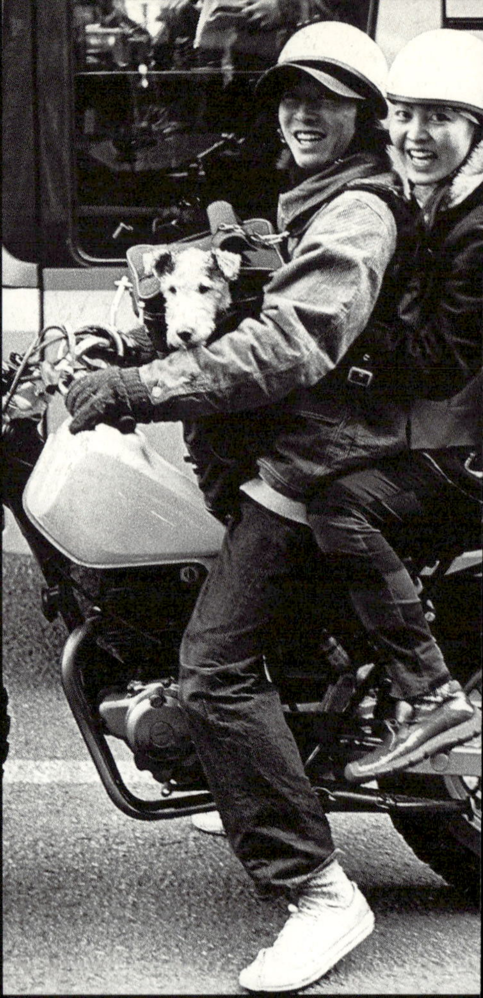

97

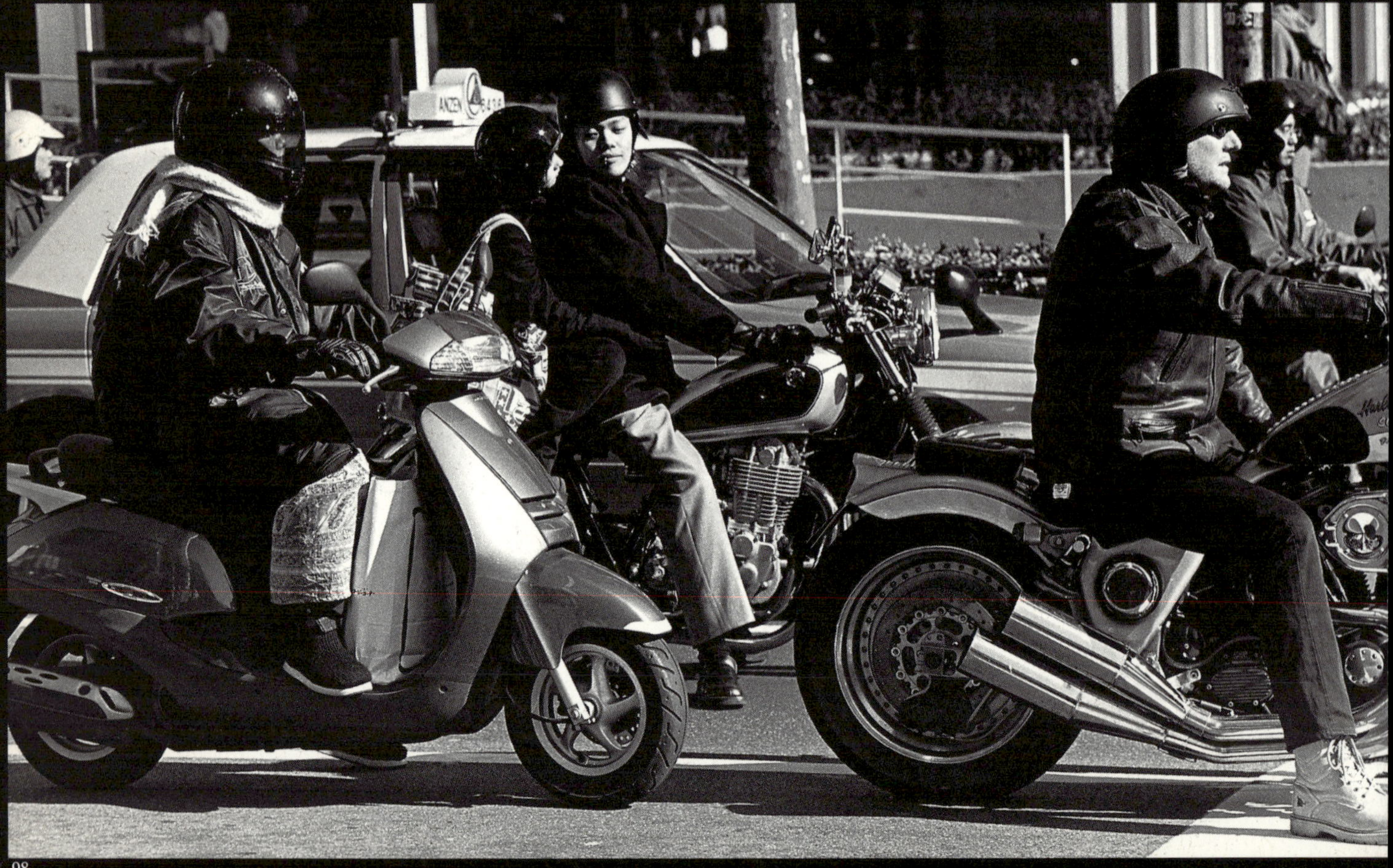

98

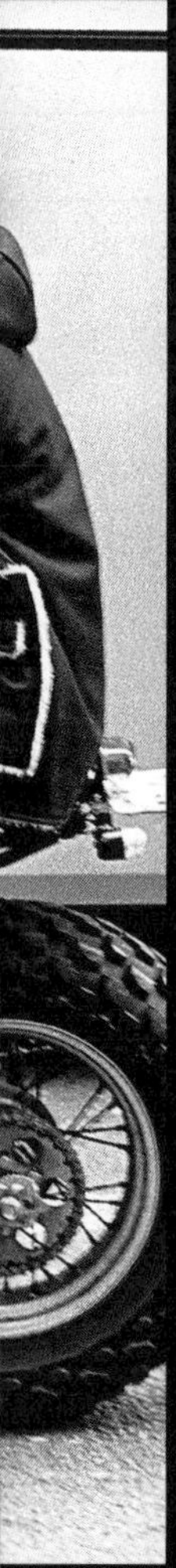

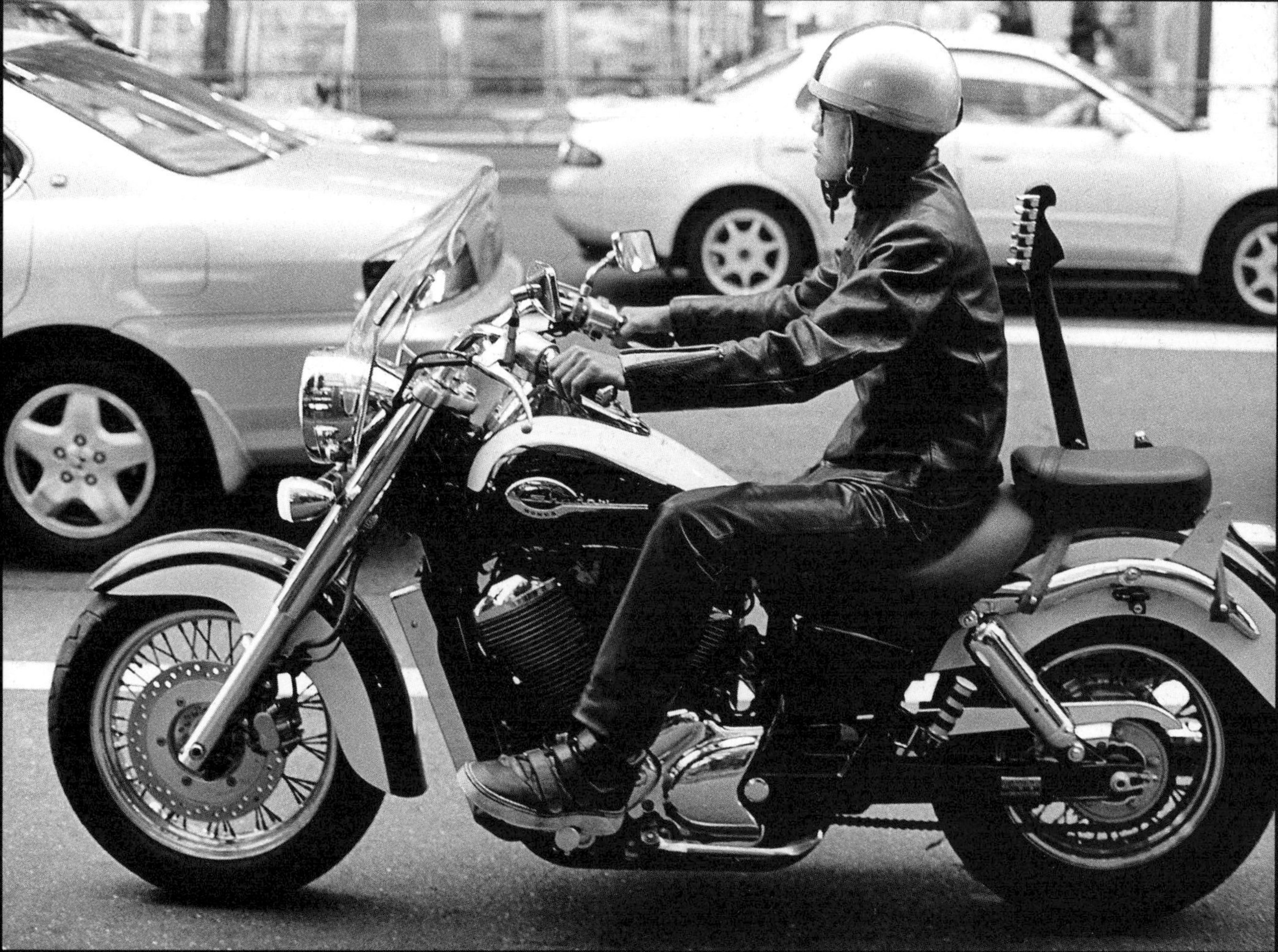

99

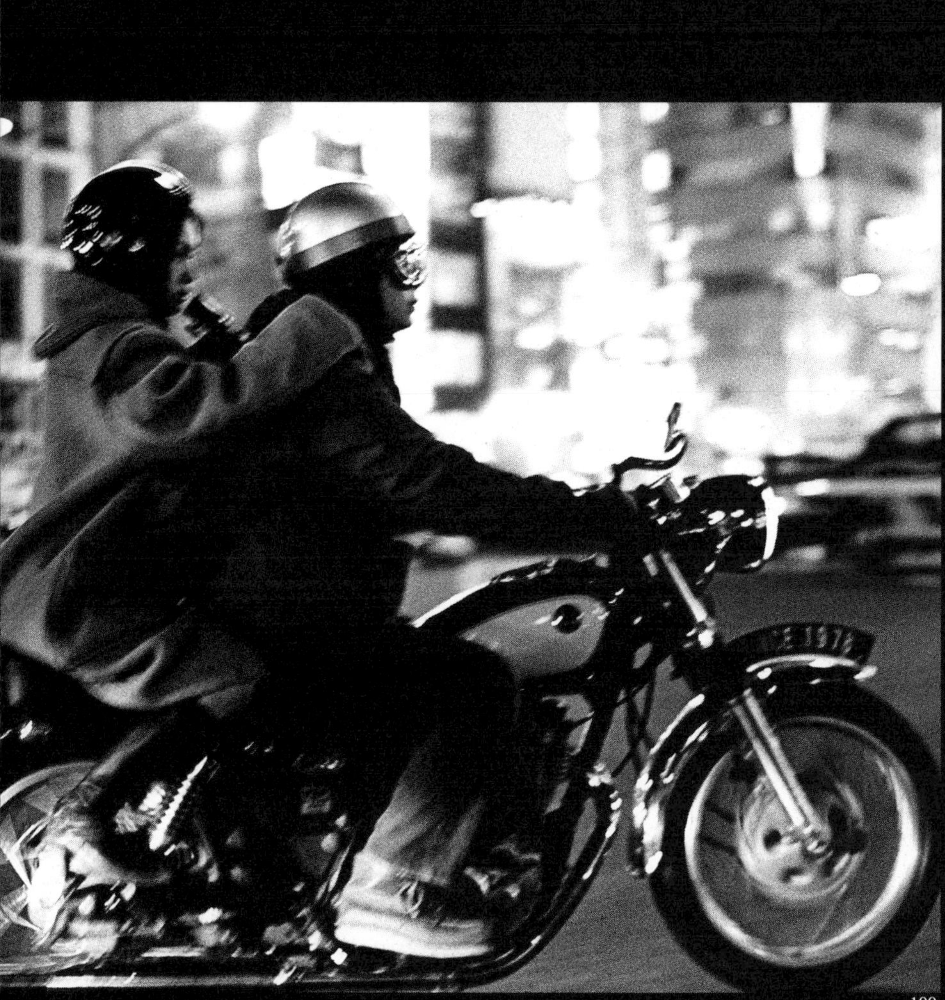

100

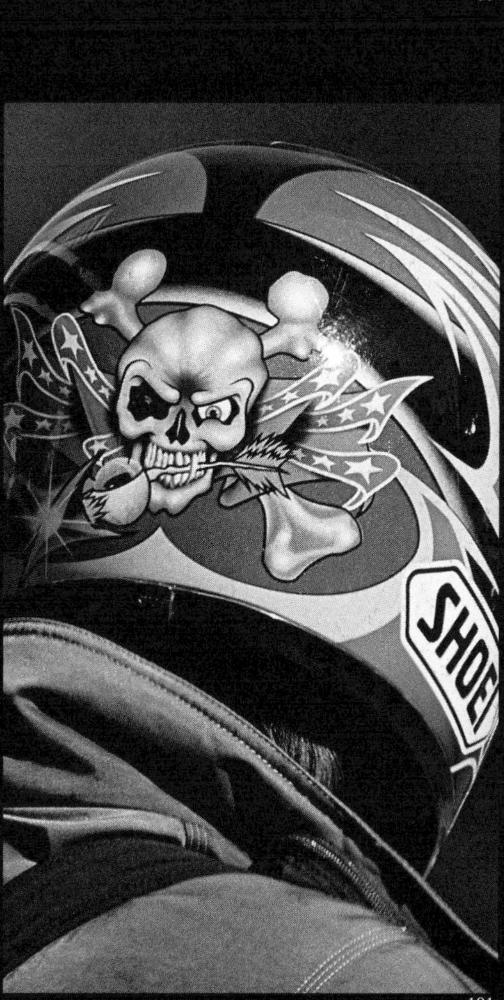

101

I AM A SELFISH,
POSSESIVE TWAT
MAYBE I'LL GROW UP ONE DAY.
title
DOCUME
ATTENTI
KRN
-2203
MORE HIROSHIMAS

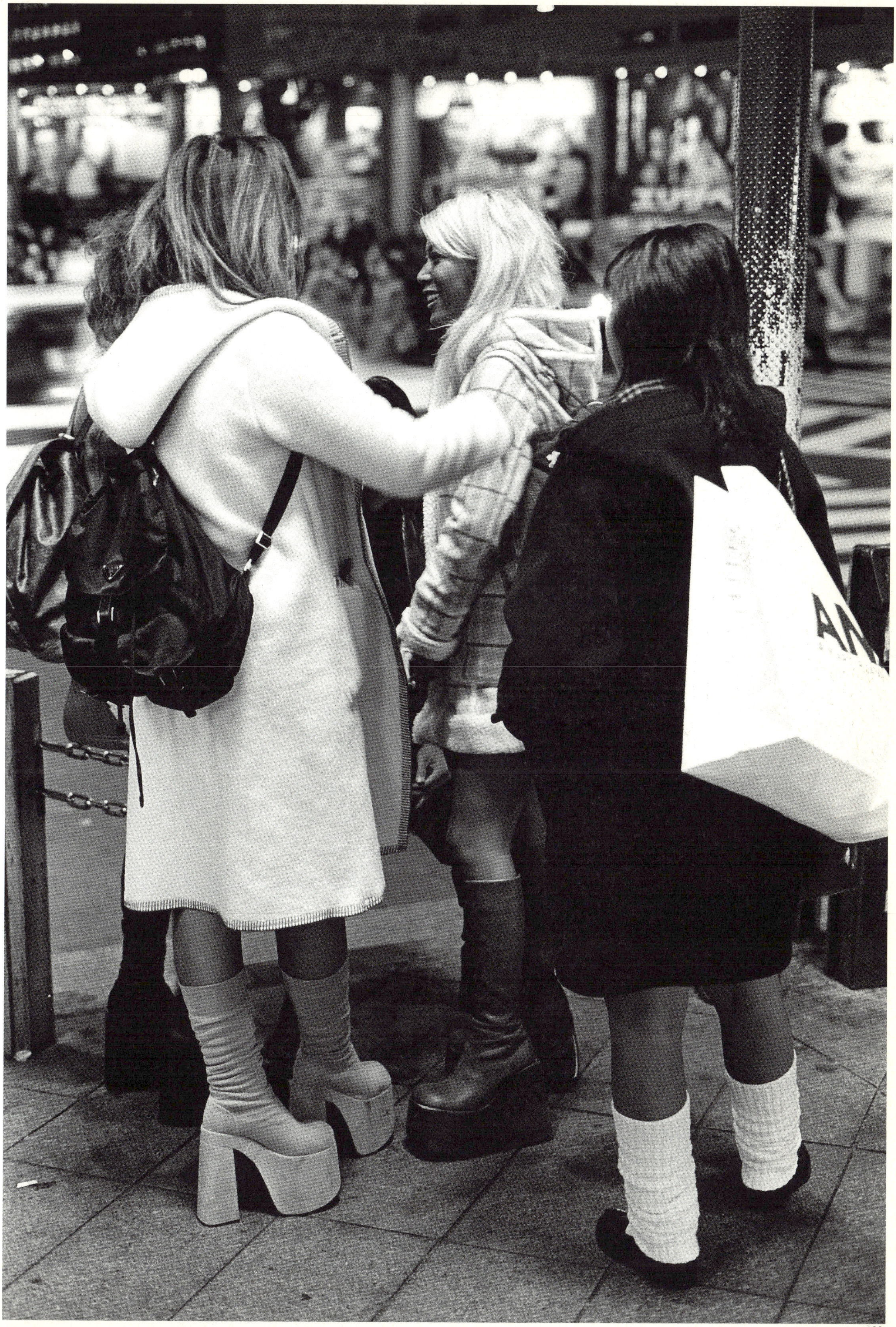

104

105

107

108

106

109

110

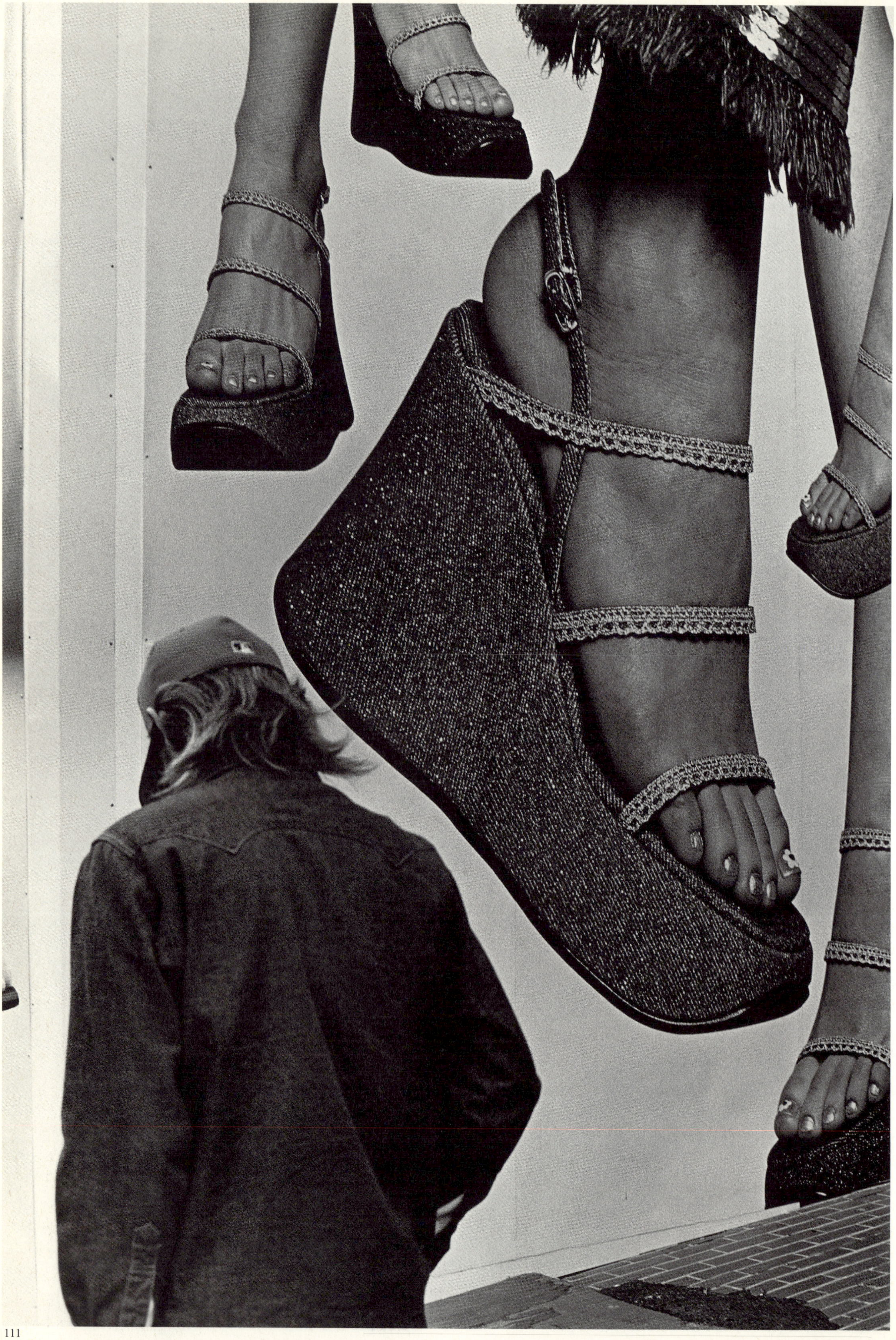

112

113

2F
ROCK'N' ROLL MUSEUM
Elvis
ELVIS AARON PRESLEY
January 8,1935 – August 16,1977

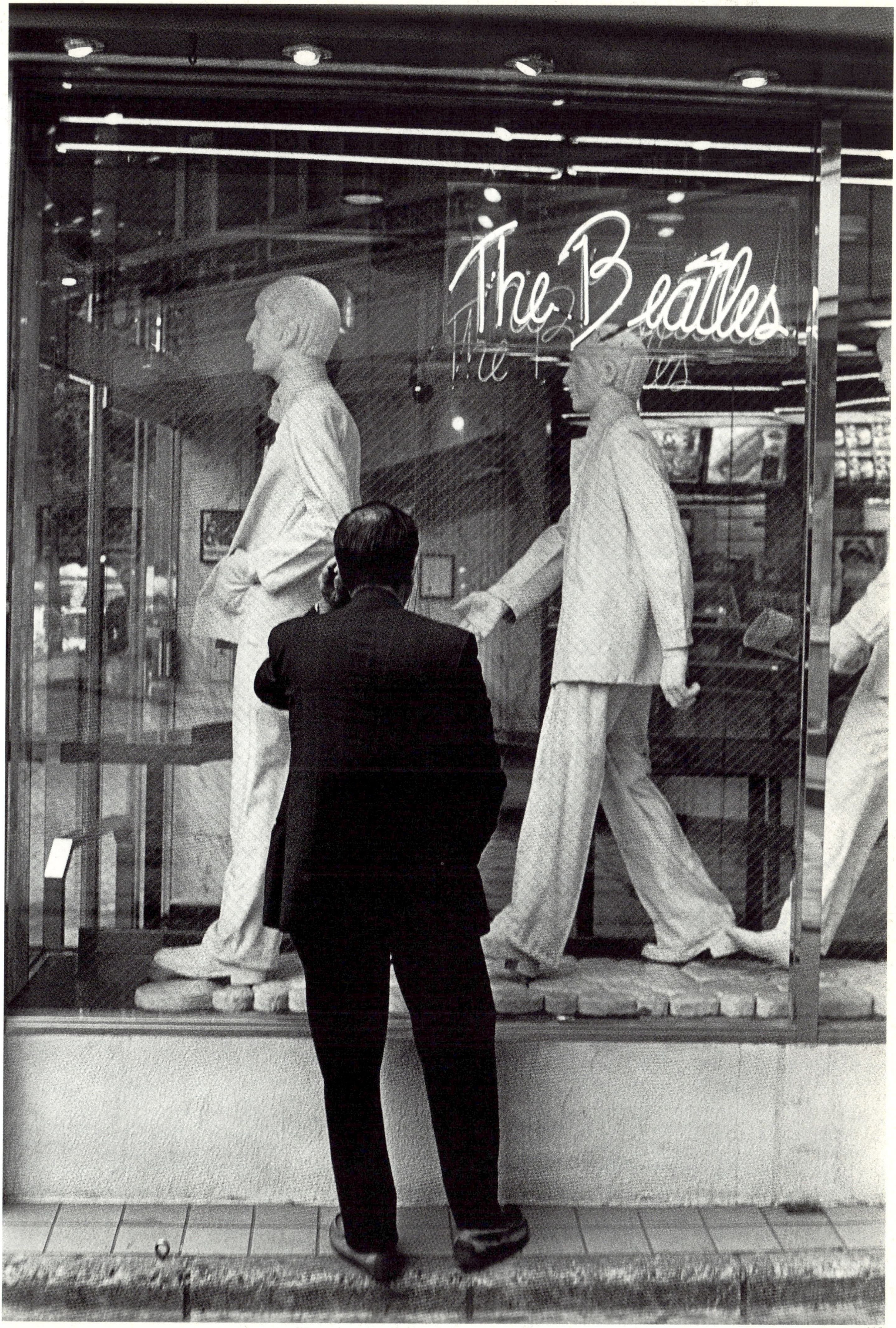
The Beatles

116

117 118

119 120

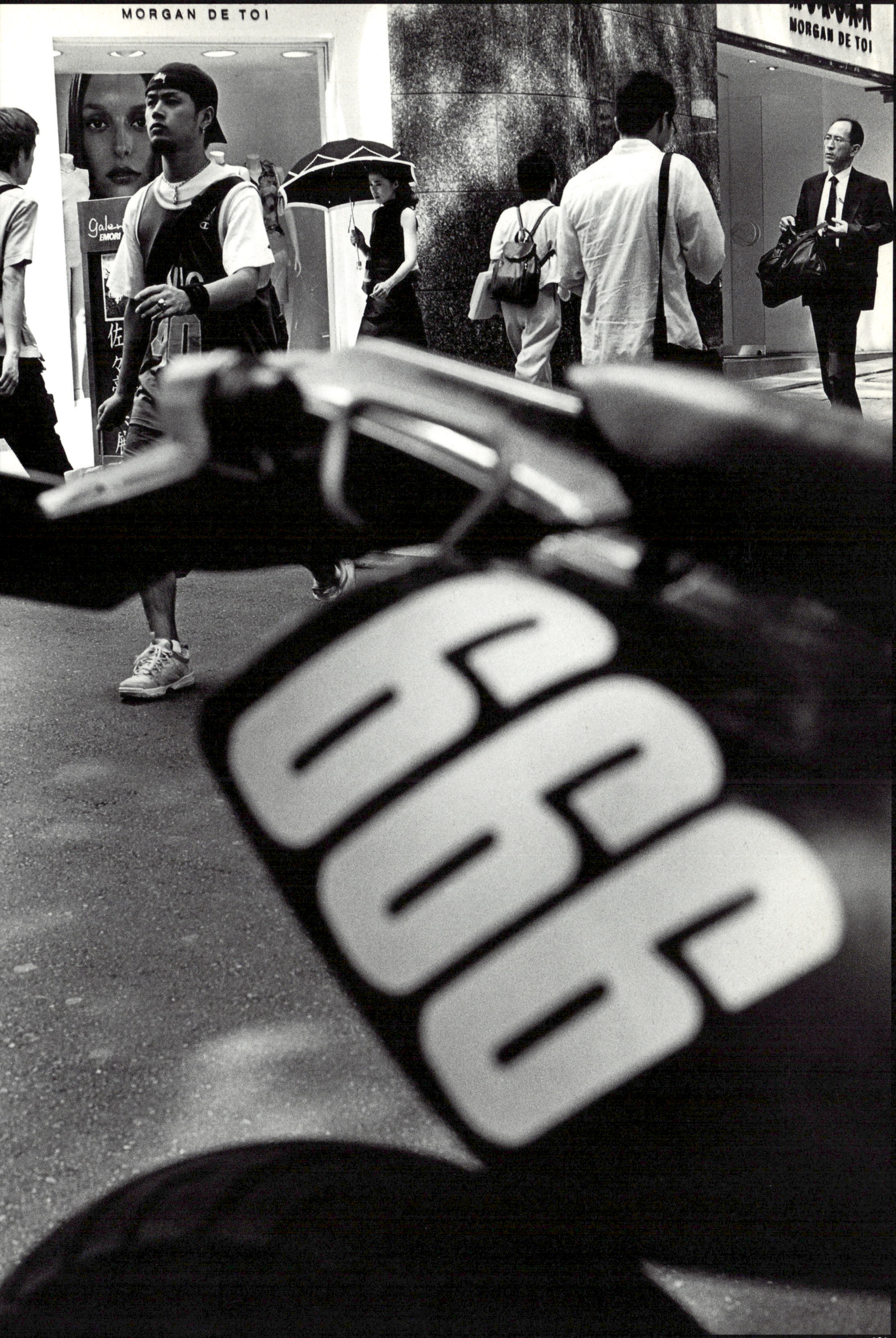
MORGAN DE TOI
MORGAN DE TOI

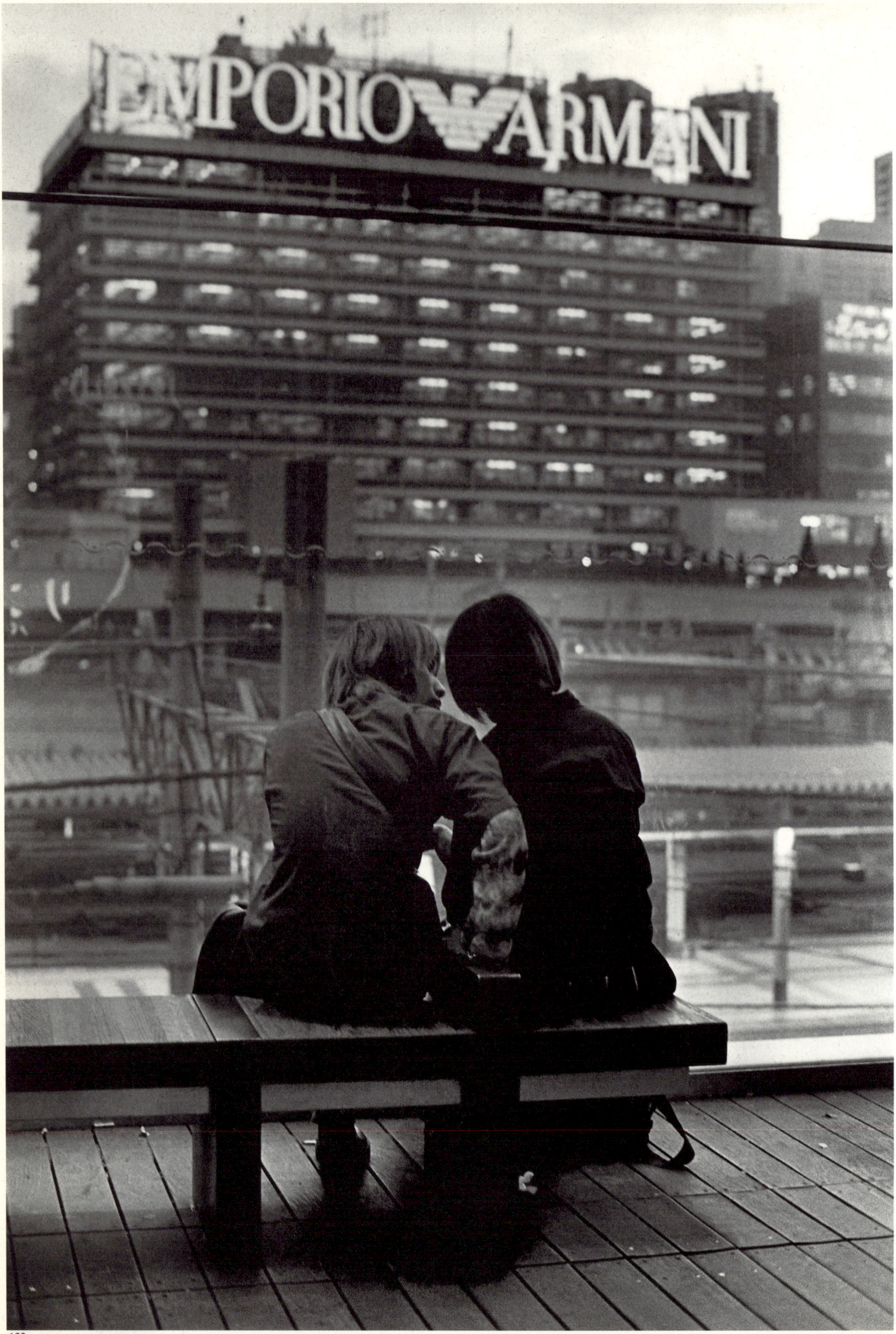
EMPORIO ARMANI

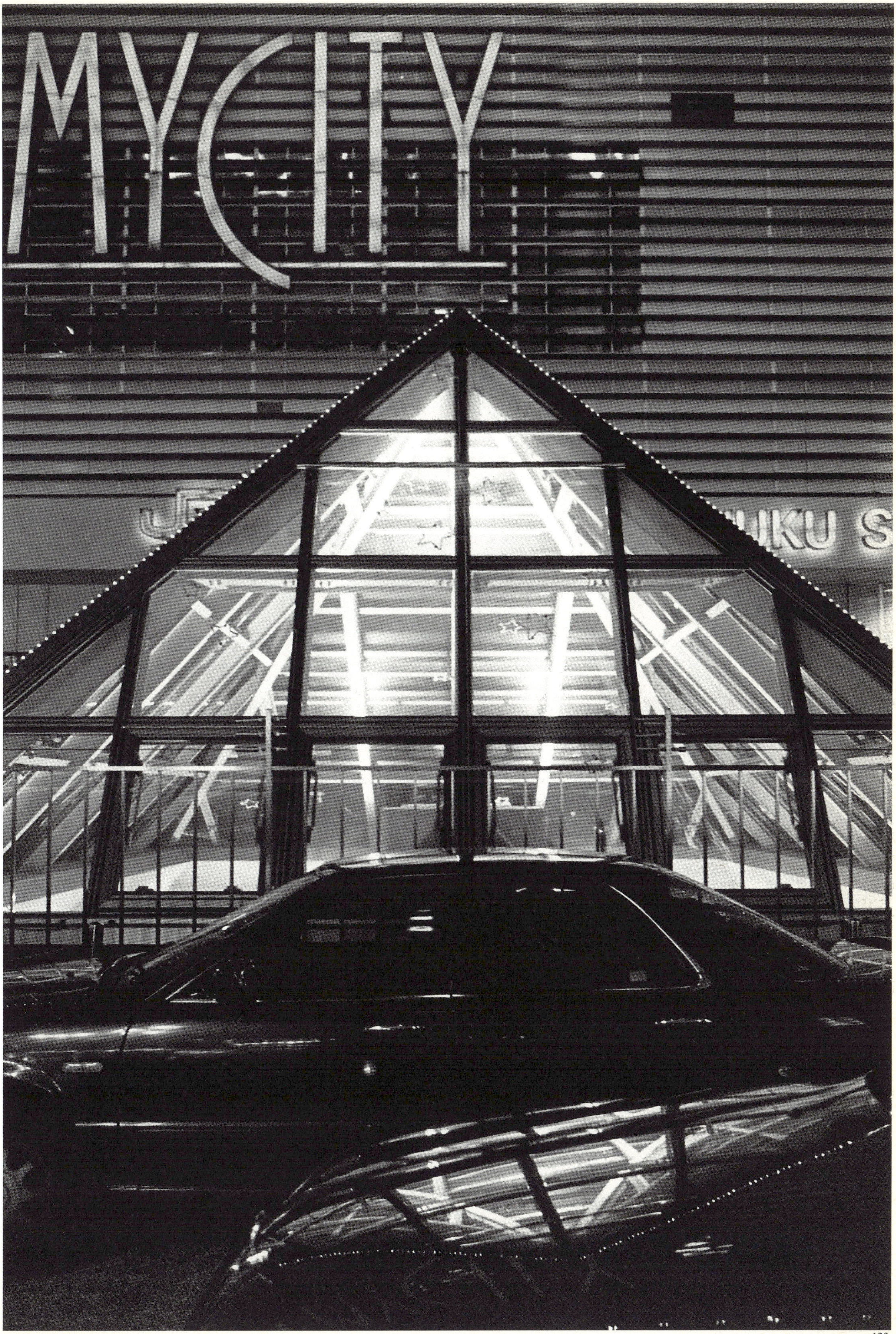
MYCITY
UKU S

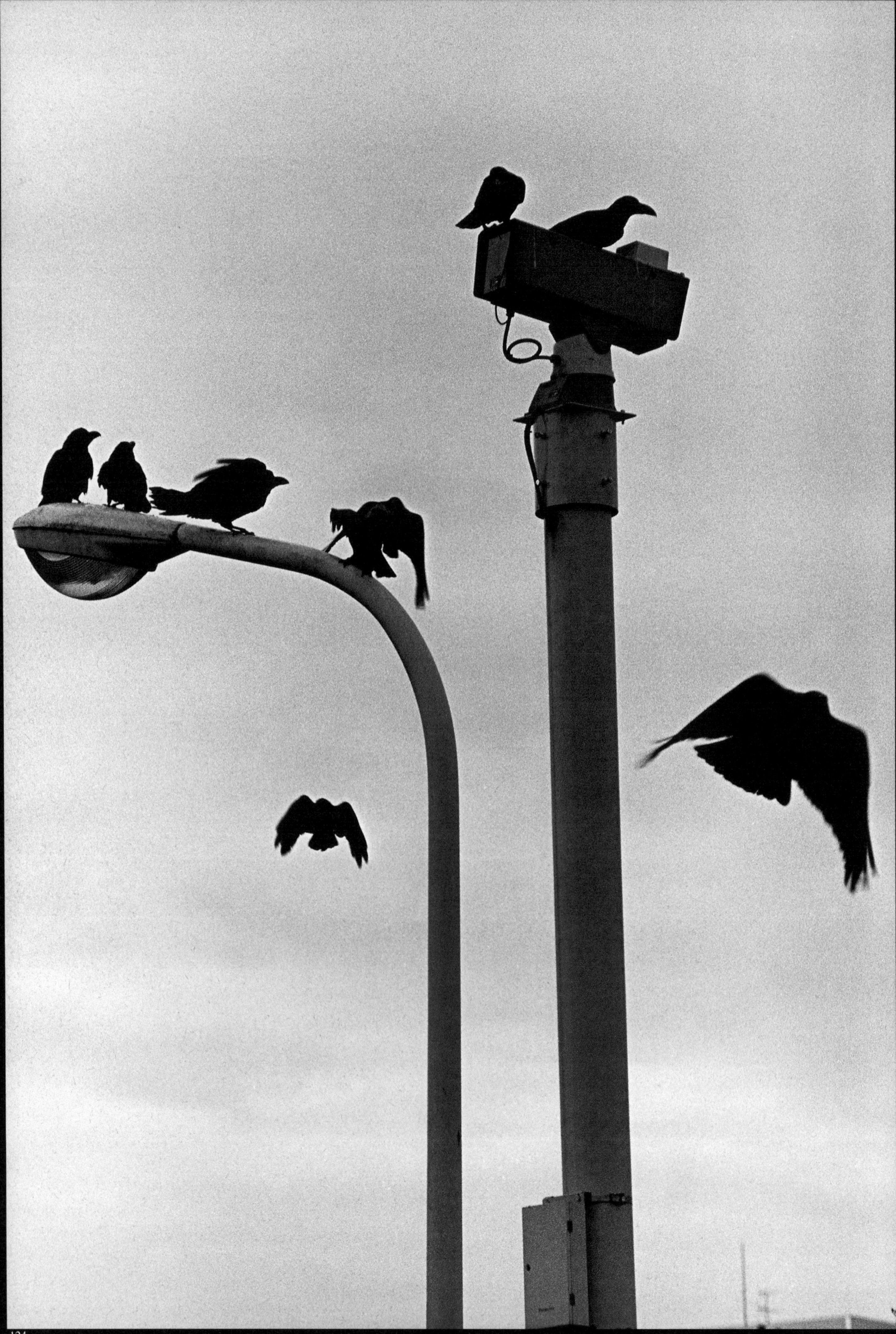

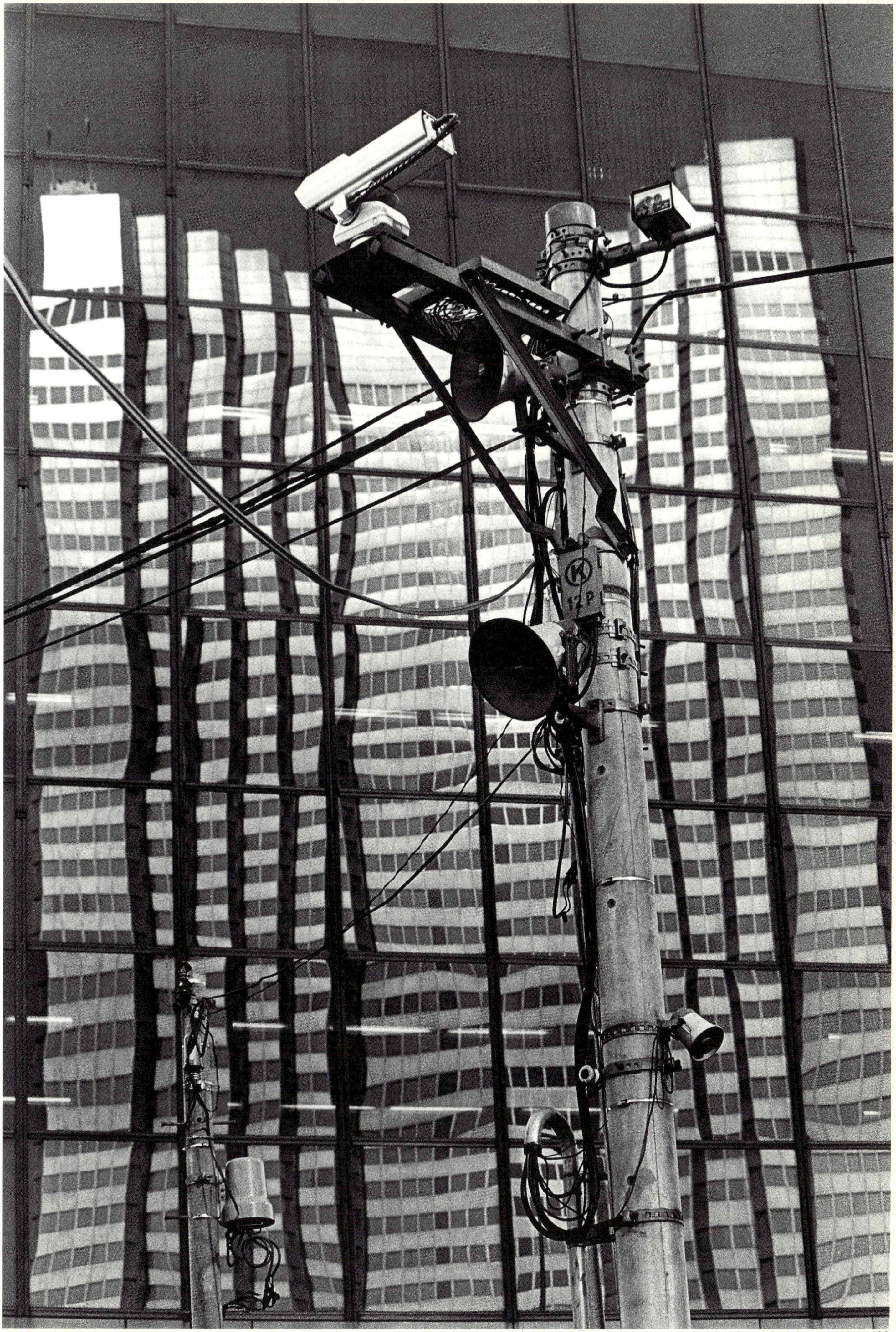
K

126

GUNNER 1
REMAIN TIME
41.134 PTS
GUNNER 1
GUNNER
128

129

Dance Dance Revolution
3rd MIX
6月1日発売予定!
ドリームキャスト用
実況パワフルプロ野球
ドリームキャストエディション
ドリームキャスト用
ロールプレイングゲーム
上映中の
ソフトは
130

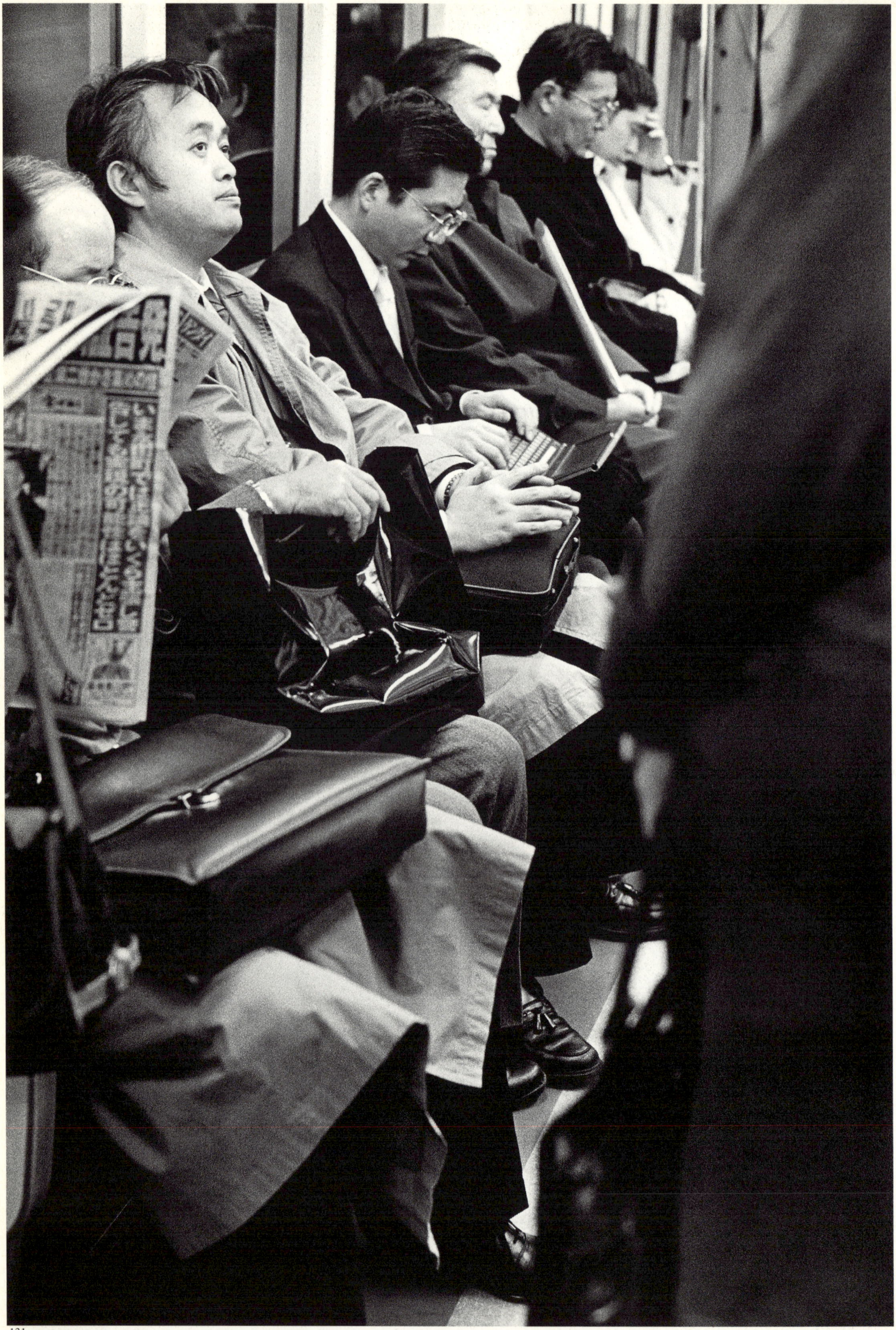

132

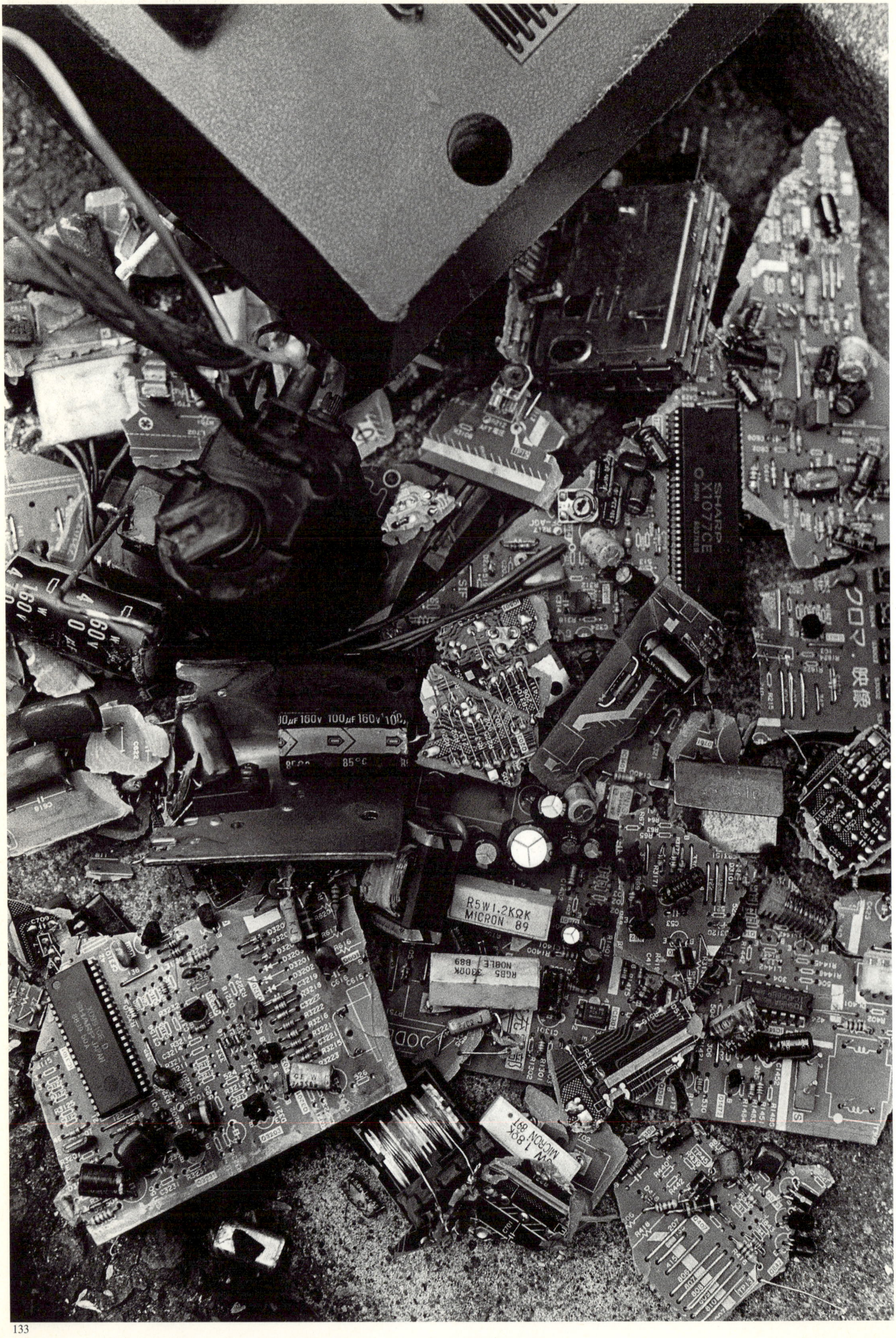

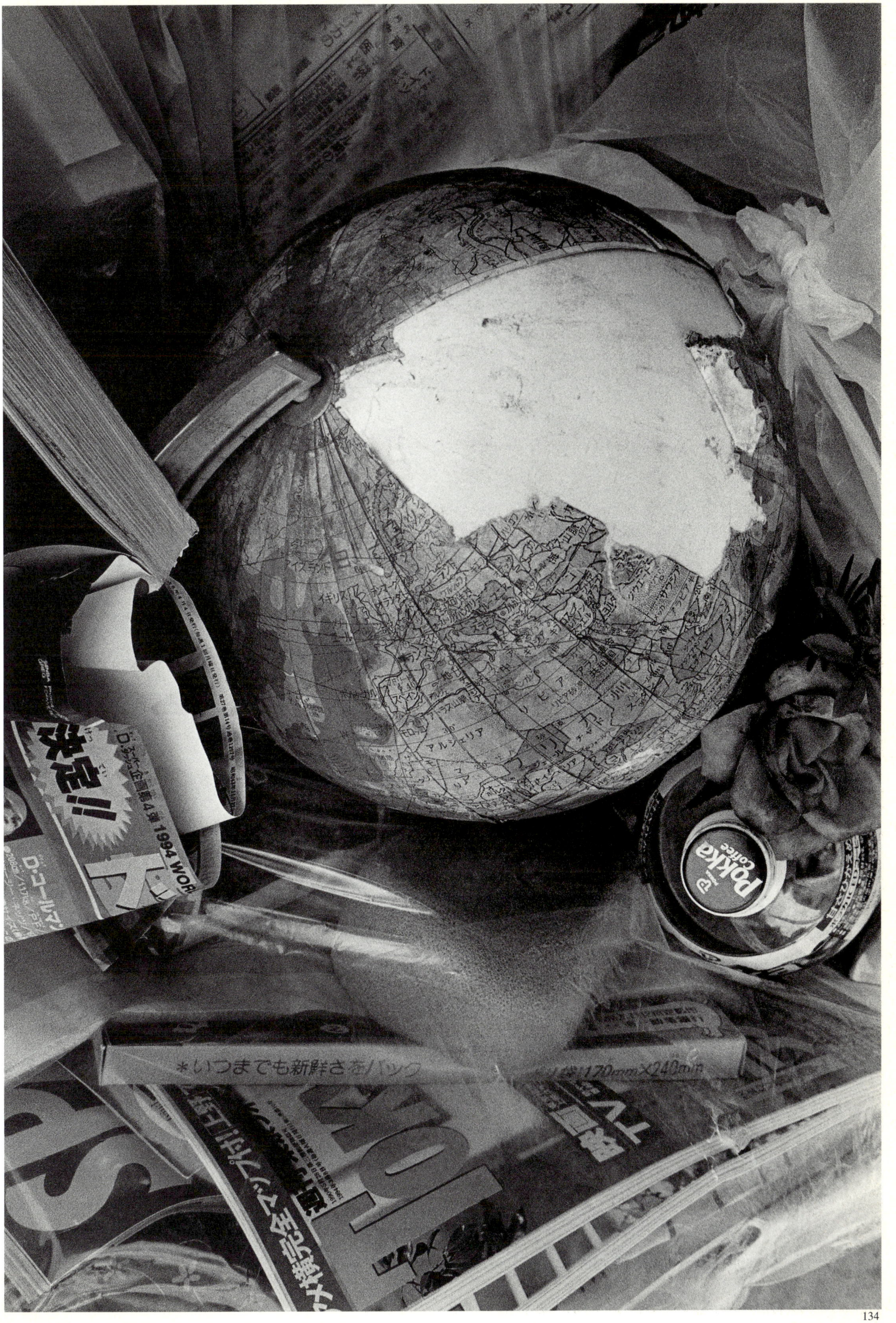
＊いつまでも新鮮さをパック
Pokka
Coffee
決定!!
1994 WOR
アルジェリア

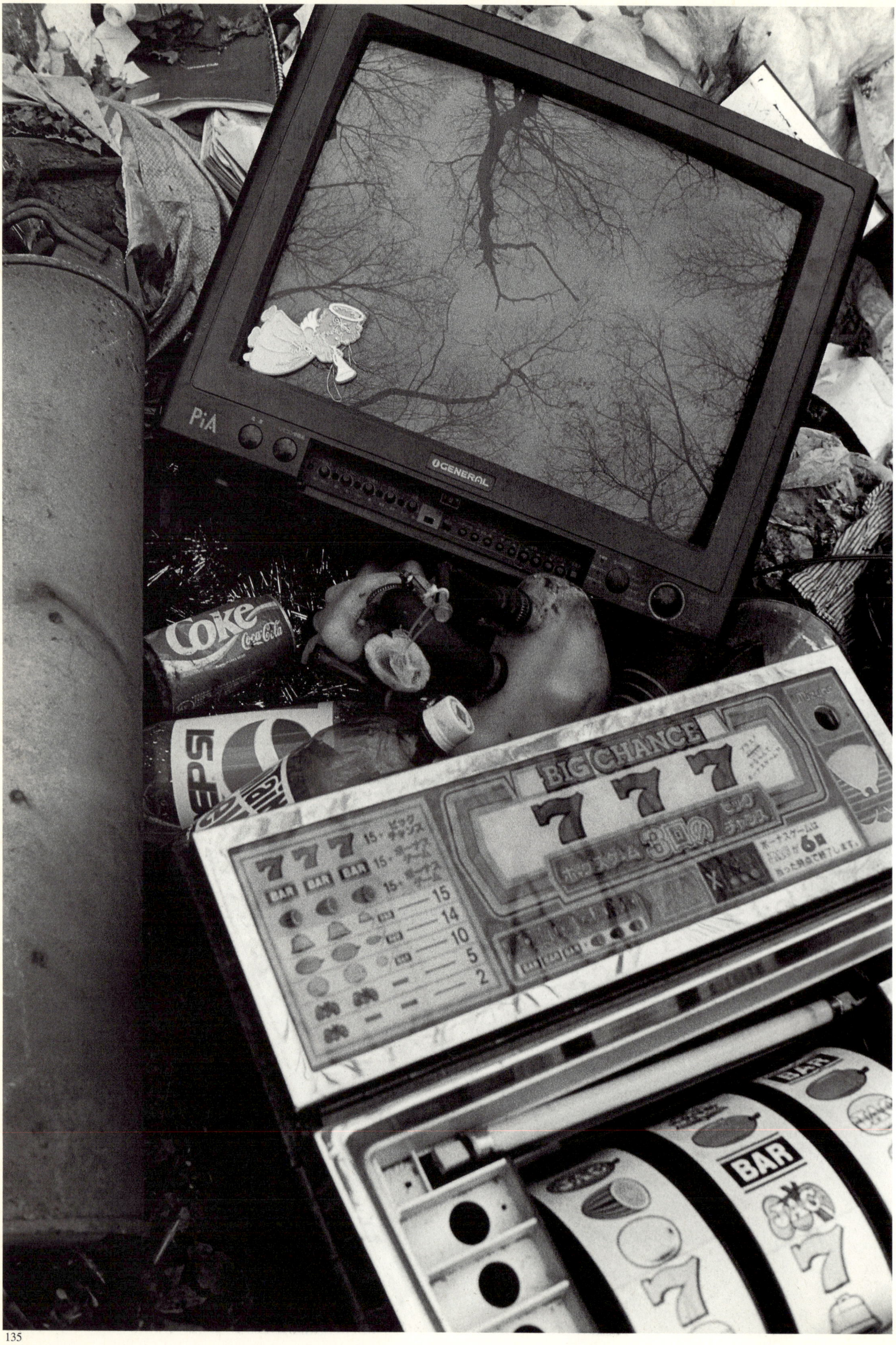
PiA
GENERAL
Coke
Coca-Cola
BIG CHANCE
BAR

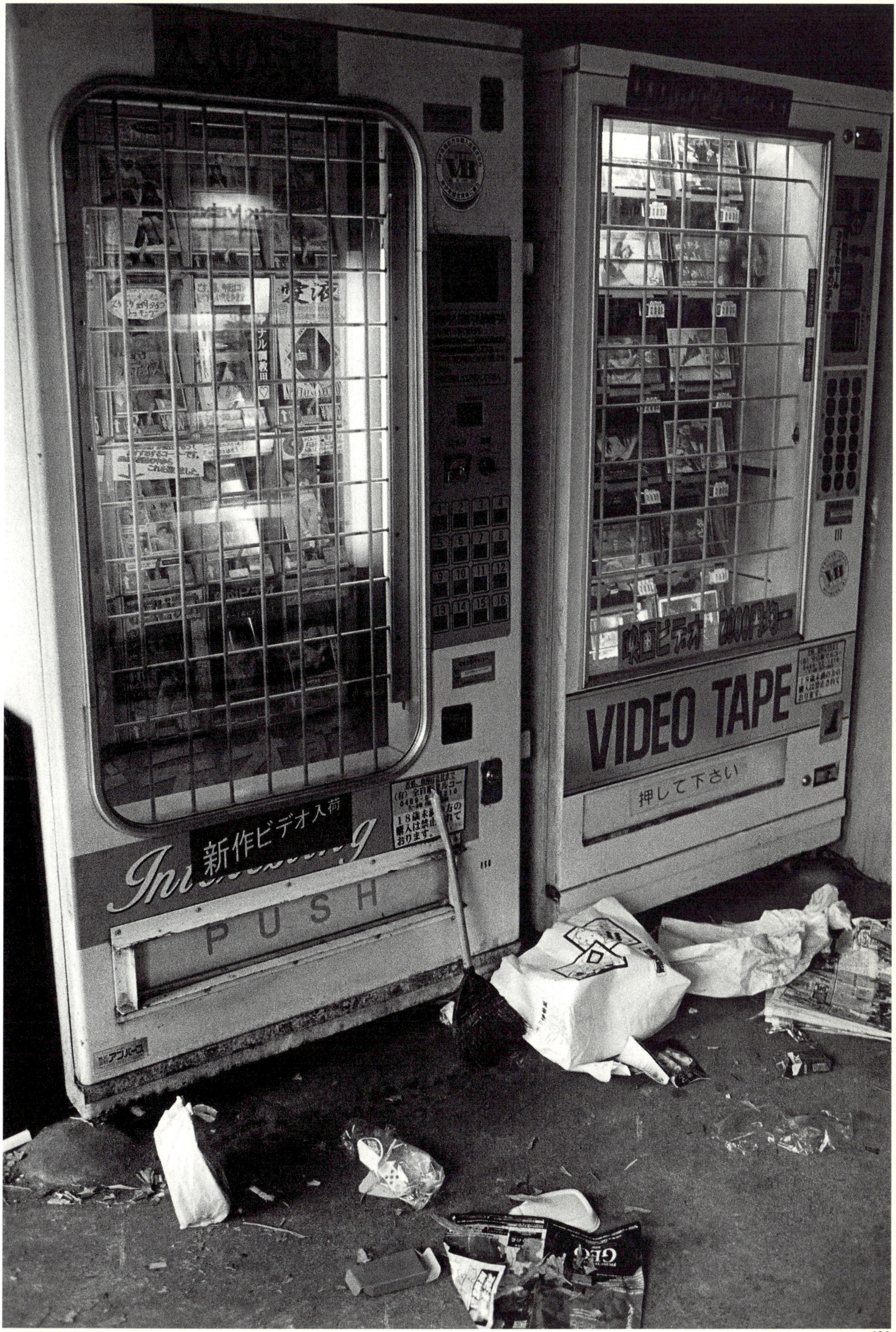
新作ビデオ入荷
PUSH
VIDEO TAPE
押して下さい

パンスト破り無料

〜たくさんのコスチュームから選べて、ナメ放題、サワリ放題〜

セーラー【夏】	セーラー【冬】	ベスト	私立女子校〈A〉
セーラー【青】	セーラー【緑】	セーラー【桃】	セーラー【紫】	セーラー【黄】
紺ブルマ	黒ブルマ	黄ブルマ	赤ブルマ	青ブルマ	桃ブルマ
ナース	ミニスカポリス	バドガール	レースクィーン	チャイナ
OL	Yシャツ	メイド	スチュワーデス	テニス	エプロン

『今、パンスト破りがおもしろい』

破ってよし

かぶってよし

〜ならパンストが無料だ!!

138

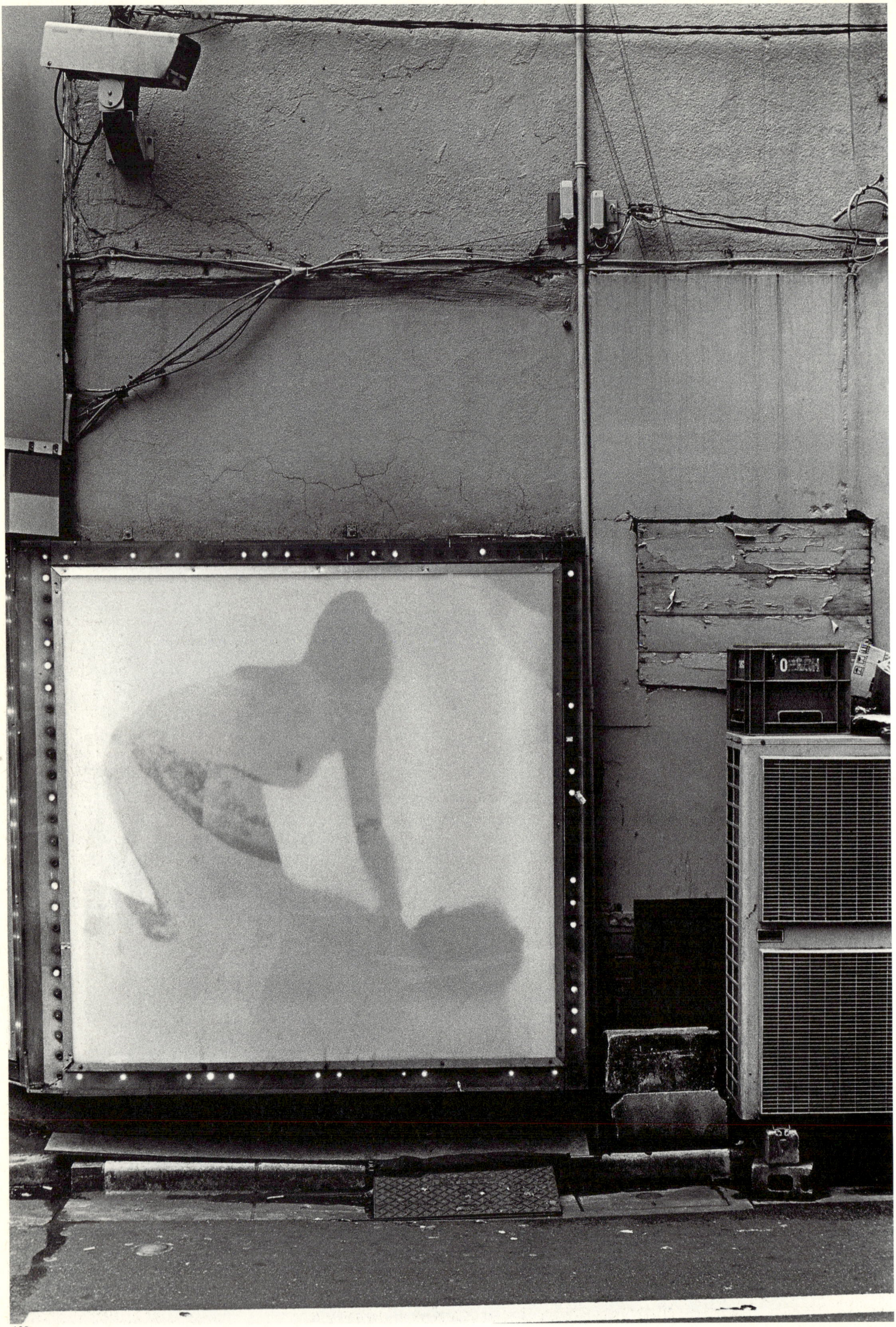

140

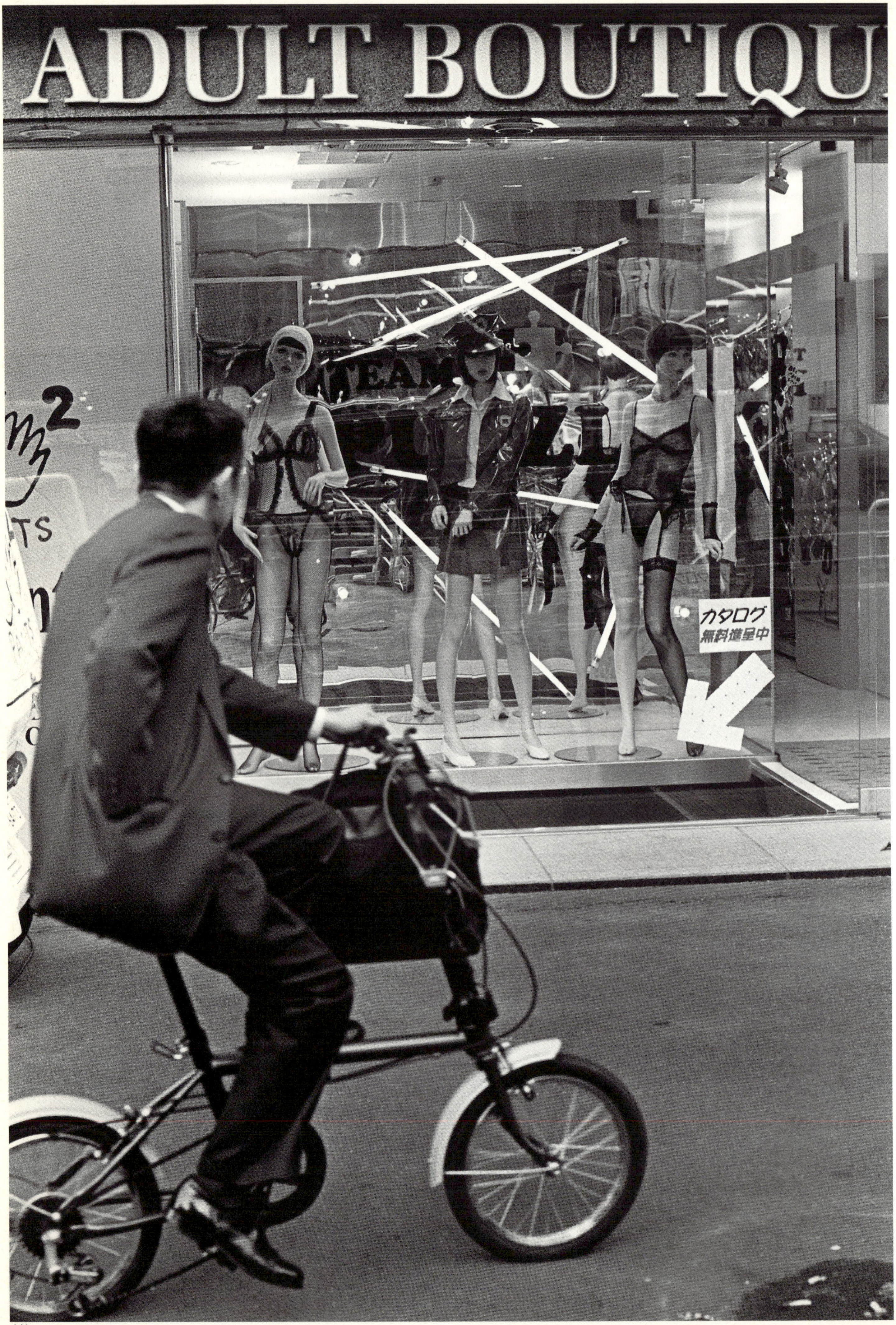
ADULT BOUTIQU
カタログ
無料進呈中

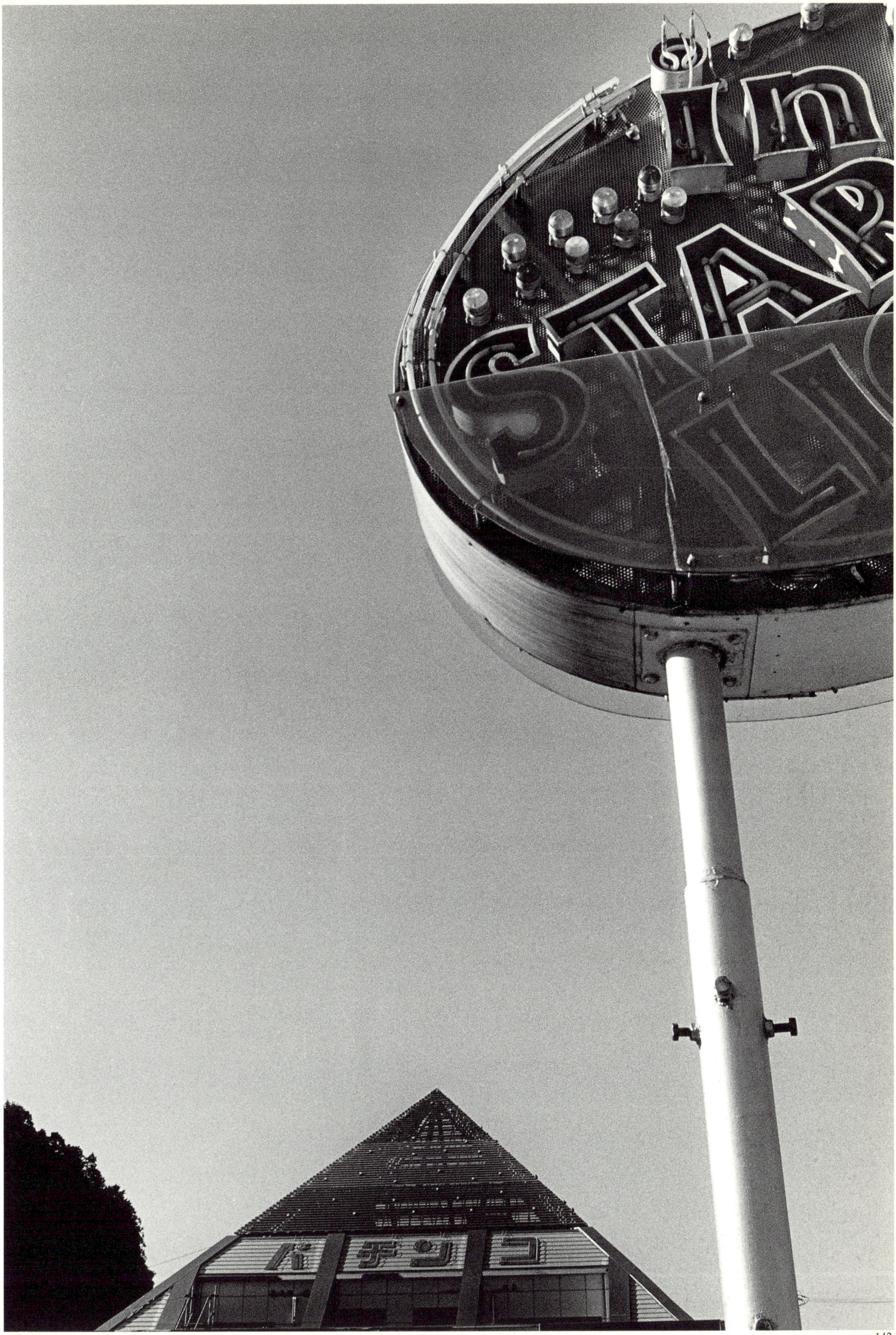
in
パチンコ

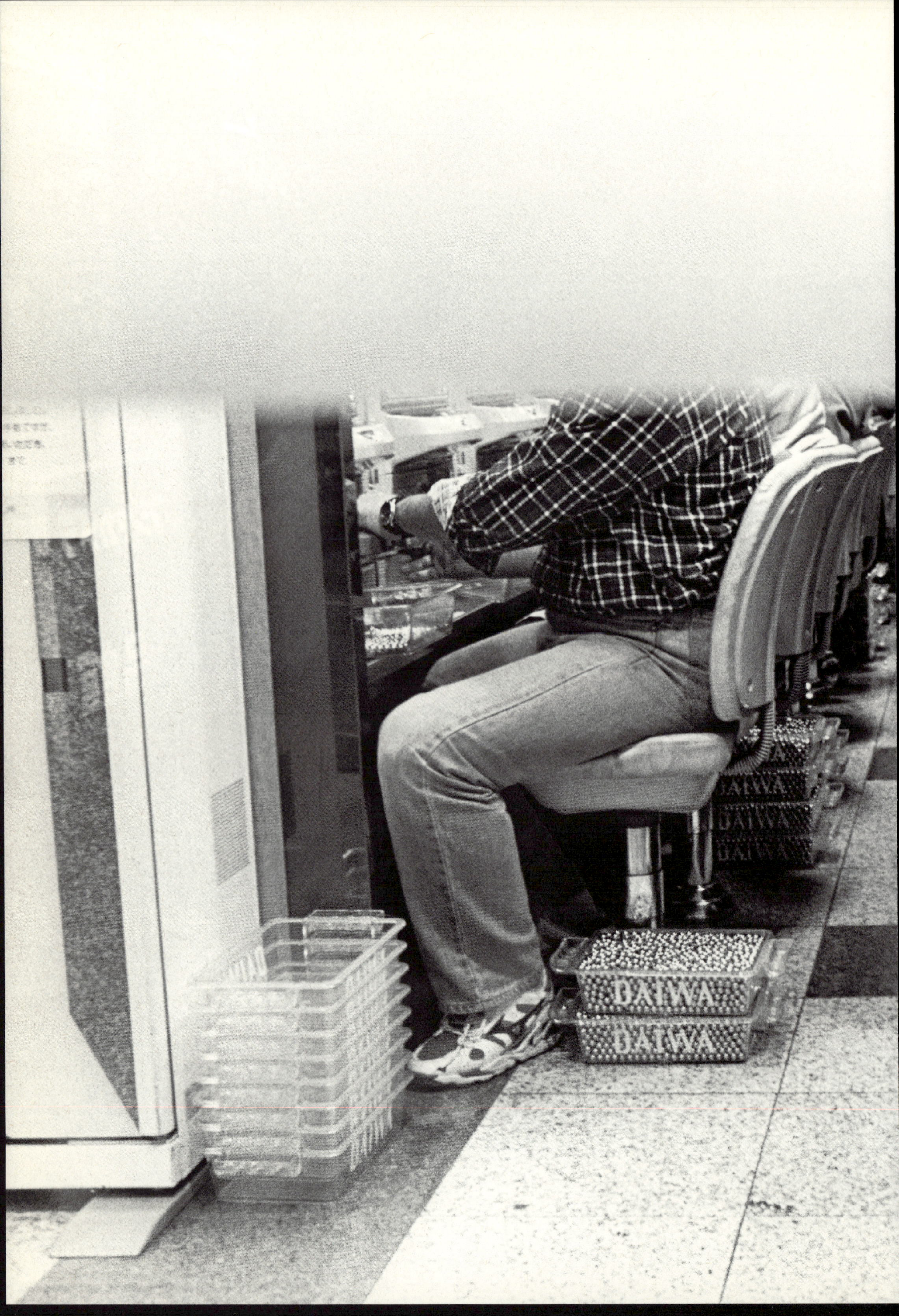
DAIWA
DAIWA

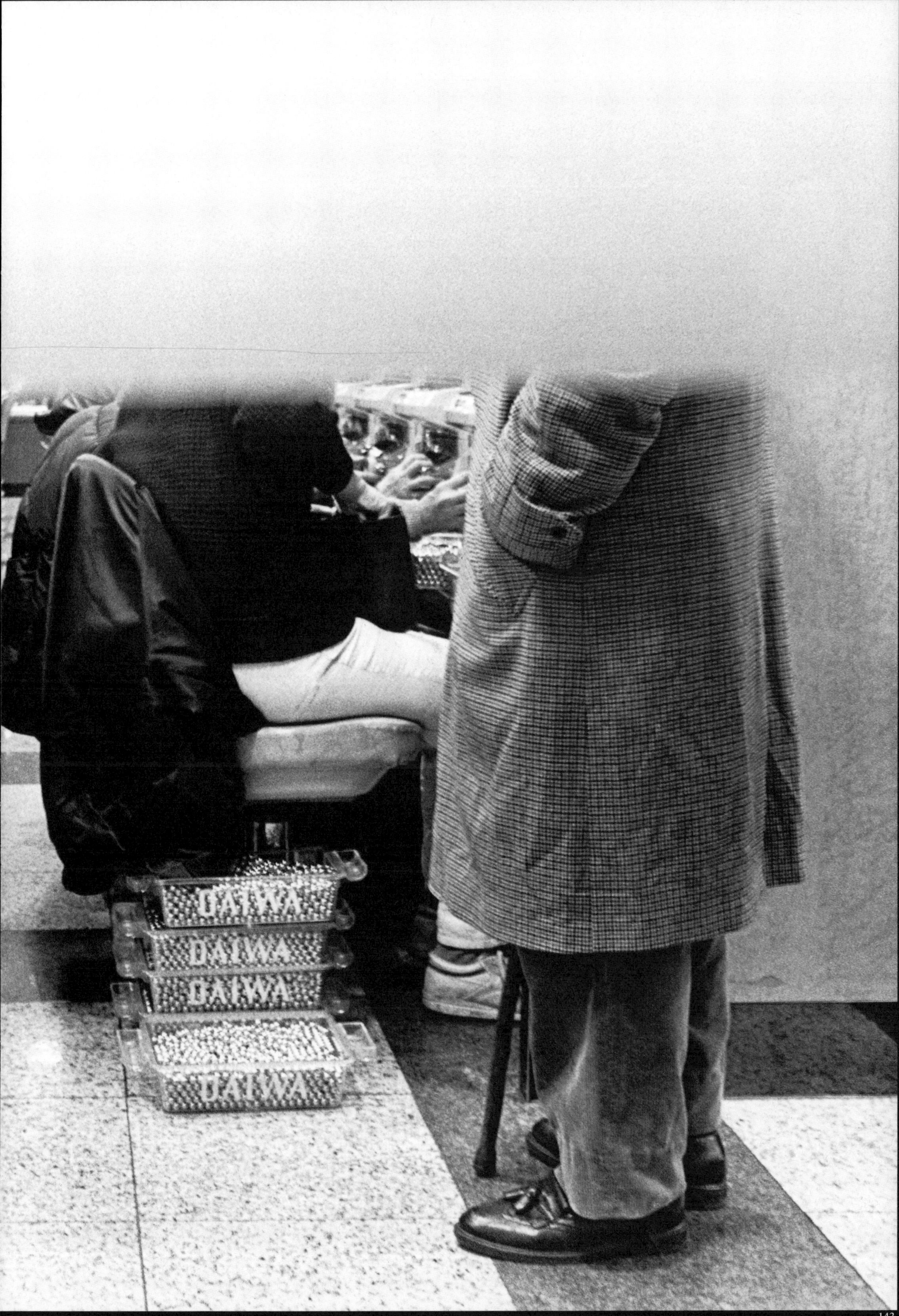
DAIWA
DAIWA
DAIWA
DAIWA

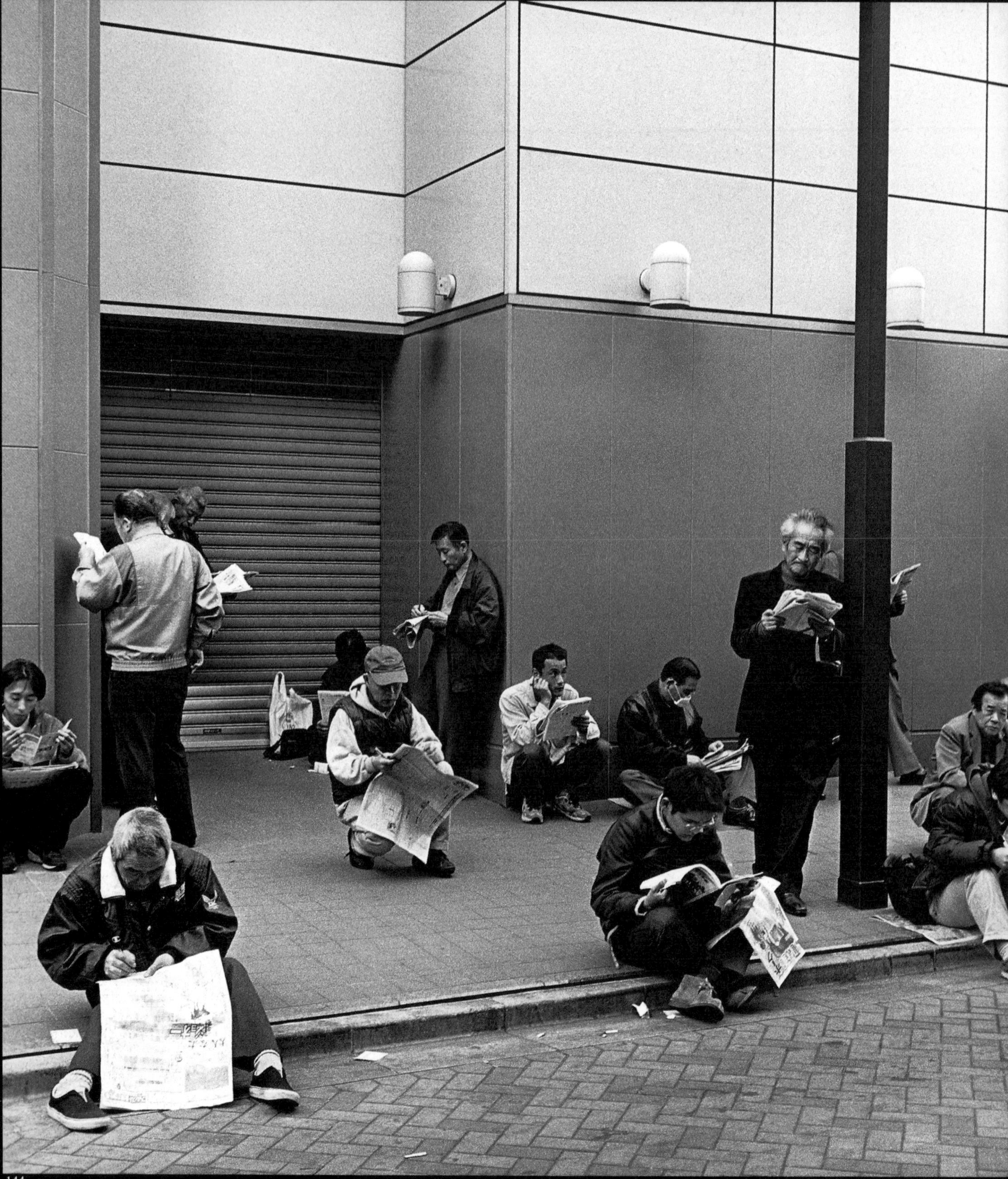

ALTAVISION
Panasonic
2.25.9
TOKYO 10R
イシティ
住銀うえ
アコム
21世紀まで
'98年12月20日
チケット好評発売中!!
0120-489-444
四季劇場
STUDIO ALTA
宝くじ
LOTTERY
ATMコーナー 1F
むじんくんコーナー B1
自動契約受付機
年中無休・24時間
リサイクルフリーマーケット

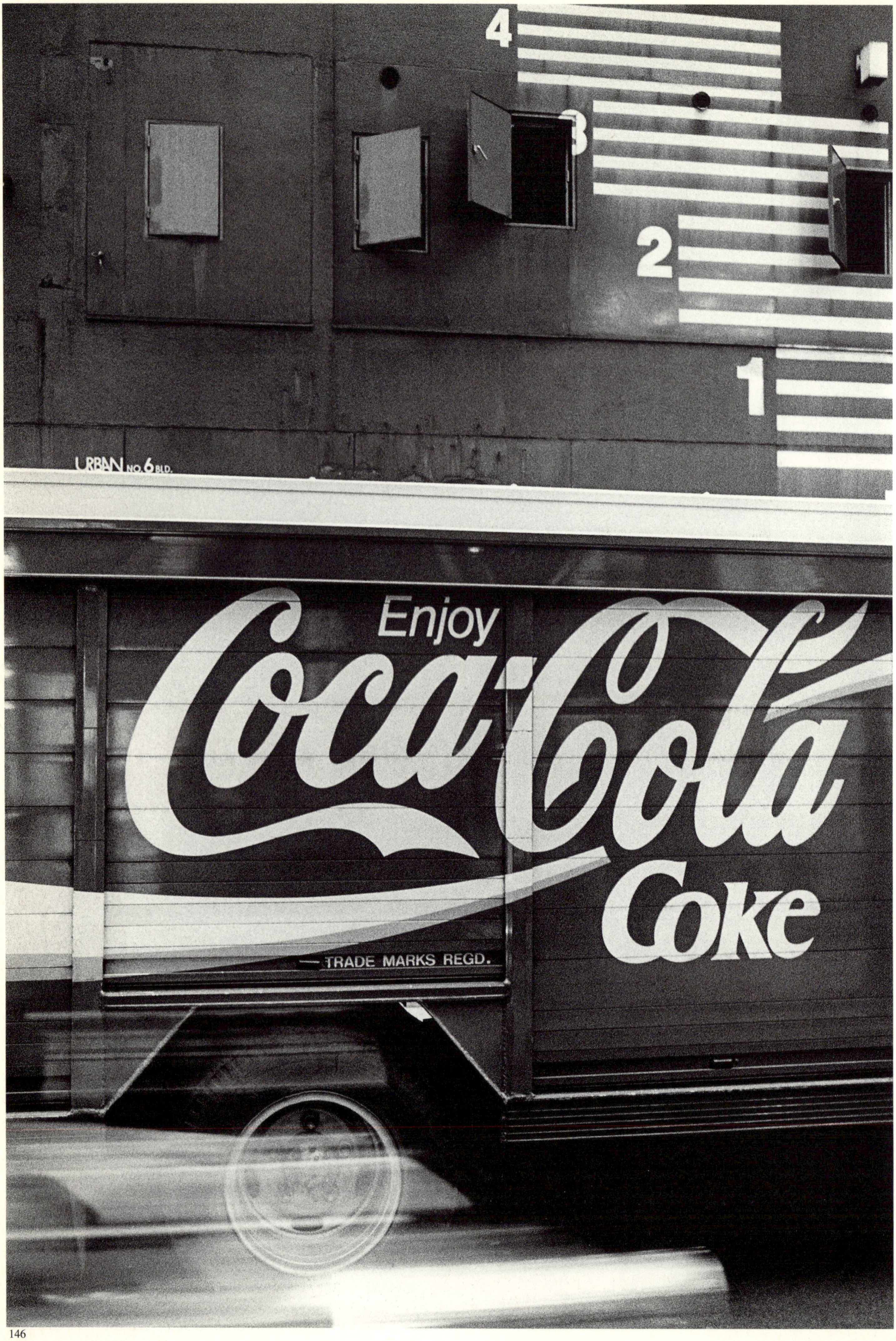
4
3
2
1
URBAN NO. 6 BLD.
Enjoy
Coca-Cola
Coke
TRADE MARKS REGD.

OLIVE des OLIVE on 3F

Rouge vif on 4F

CHILD WOMAN

自社貸付 30万円
3255-9006
すみれ信販
スミトモリース ☎3256-0005
信頼と実績の
協和信販
5~50万迄
03-5295-2728
☎03(5296)0009
50万円まで
アクロシティ
ローンズ大栄 ☎03-3251-2020
ローンズ大栄 ☎03-3251-2020
他店の返済金
貸します!!
三井信販
5256-0055(代)
新規/会員受付中
野村信販
アイドライズ
30万円迄
5283-5553
富士トラスト
☎5256-9666
ピースファイナンス
☎0120-676-001
マネーショップ トライ
☎0120-696-033
新規会員募集!!
自社審査貸付
1万円~30万円迄
ウエスト
☎03-3257-0318
アトムクレジット
コスモ信販
コウセイ
本日即融資
30万円迄
自社貸付
ユタカコーポレーション
3254-5400
3254-5400
30万円迄 スピード融資
5281-0033
ヴェルディ
2000年堂々オープン
BIG
3279-0103
3246-63
神田駅 アシスト
西口 ☎5296-4455
☎5280-0650
スマイル
新規大歓迎!!
50万迄即融資
ローンズ フェニックス
03-5204-8100
03-5204-8100
新規OPEN
1万~50万
03-3258-3933
今すぐ必要だから
融資100%
必ずお役に立ちます。
サンライズ
国民信販
03-3255-3434
新店オープン!!
アスコ
0120-660-499
10~50万迄
3258-4250
貸します!!
丸三信販
アイビー
明光リース 03-5295-0003
借りて安心!!
まで審査なし
100万迄
ヤマキファイナンス
☎3275-190
☎3275-190
5295-0005
1~30万まで
(5256) 8128
サクセス
新規オープン
マルセイ
3526-5858
アサヒ
03-3254-2744
アサヒ
03-3254-2744
ワールドリース
ゴールドリース
5289-7366
オープン
10万迄審査なし
ムサシ信販
5256-0991
すぐ貸します
3255-8889
ユーライフ
ローンズガリバー
3256-0333
NTT
ISDN
5296-34
3251-

明治通り側
エレベーターAをご利用下さい
土・日
祝・6時まで
特別受付中!!
平日/夜8時まで
土・日・祝日/6時まで
ニュー
ラスベガス
AM10:00~PM12:00
無人

お自動さん コーナー 平日朝8時半から営業中!
アイフル
店頭窓口5F
誰にも会わずにカードが
デキル、新 キャッシング
お自動さん
無人契約受付機
コーナー 6F
土・日・祝日
平日夜8時まで
営業中!!
土・日・祝日/AM10:00~PM6:00
商工ローン・不動産担保ローン
好評受付中!!
エレベーター4F
クレジットの
リッチ
まかしと機
アコム
むじんくん
自動契約受付機
むじんくんコーナー 1F
ATMコーナー
店頭窓口 2F
平日夜8時、土・日・祝6時迄
新規受付中

日 水
日コムシス
ハウス食
日本製紙
武田薬
ブリヂストン
日鉱金属
日 立
ミツミ
現在値
前日比
三井山
日本粉
日清食
昭電工
エーザイ
旭硝子
古河電工
東 芝
アルプス電
帝 石
明治菓
J T
住友化
O L C
太平洋セメ
住友電
三菱電
パイオニア
大成建
山崎パン
日清紡
呉羽化
フジテレビ
TOTO
トステム
NEC
松下通
大林組
雪印乳
日東紡
日曹達
富士写
新日鉄
タクマ
富士通
ビクター
清水建
ヤクルト
コニカ
川 鉄
アマダ
鹿 島
日ハム
NKK
森精機
丸大食
日軽金

ヤマハ
イトーヨーカ
三井不
日テレ
現在値
前日比
任天堂
興銀
三菱地所
KDD
コクヨ
第一勧銀
東急
NTT
伊藤忠
富士銀
JR東日本
NTTドコモ
ミズノ
あさひ銀
JR西日本
東電
東エレク
三井信
JR東海
関西電
住友商
野村証
ヤマト運
東ガス
三菱商
新日本証
郵船
NTTデータ
和光証
商船三井
よみランド
東京海上
日航
セコム
三井海
全日空
CSK
日本火
TBS
ソフトバンク

娘GAL
バイブでオナニー
4000円
258-6960
東口一番街
女王様
性感ローション
ソフト
性感
ミキ
クレジット
サービス
ミキ
無人受付
コーナー 7F
大成 クレジット 03-3256-9011
クレジット 6F
自動契約コーナー
クレジットのキャスニ
お自動さんコーナー
アイフル
カードは アース 土・日・祝日営業中
無人契約機 3F
アコム
8-20
銀座
PINK

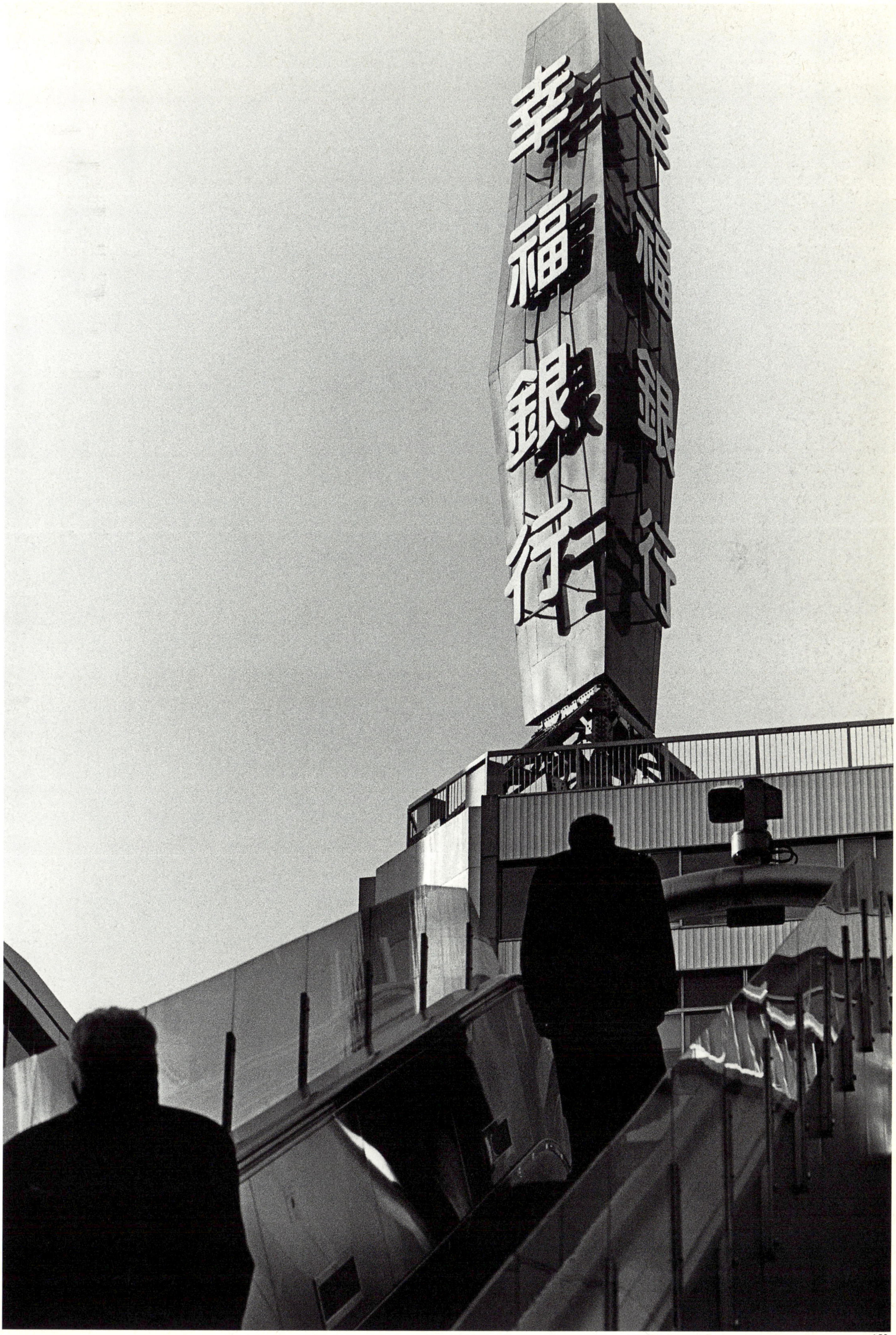
幸福銀行

罪の報いは死
神の賜物は、永遠の

アコム
むじんくん
むじんくんコーナー
武富士
TOWA
東和
むじん 契約機
4F
富士火災
太平洋証券
王朝料理
個室宴会
居酒屋
カラオケ&パーティー
3F 747 5F
新宿将棋センター
東和
むじん契約機
武富士
SHiDAX
富士火災
赤石保険事務所

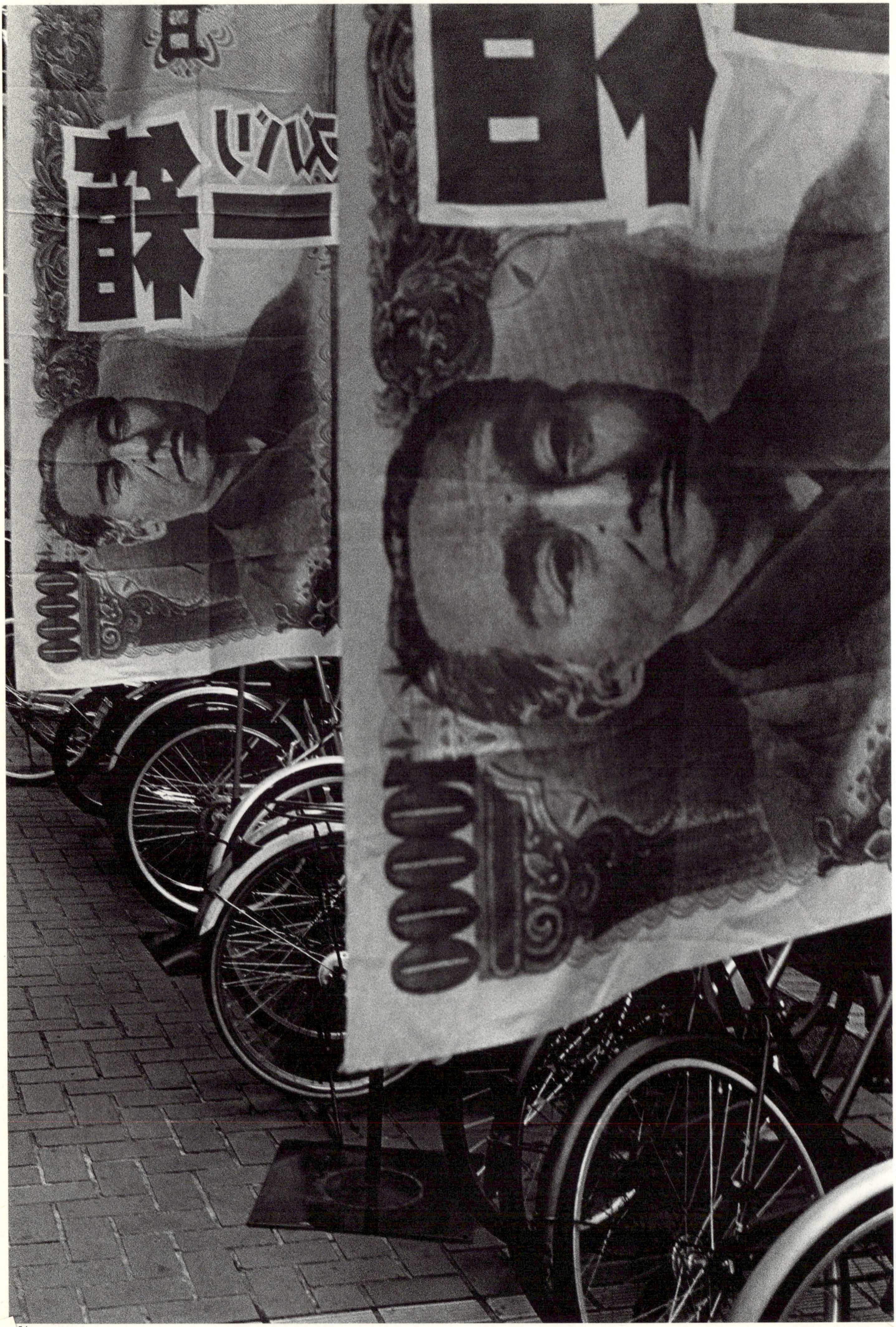
10000

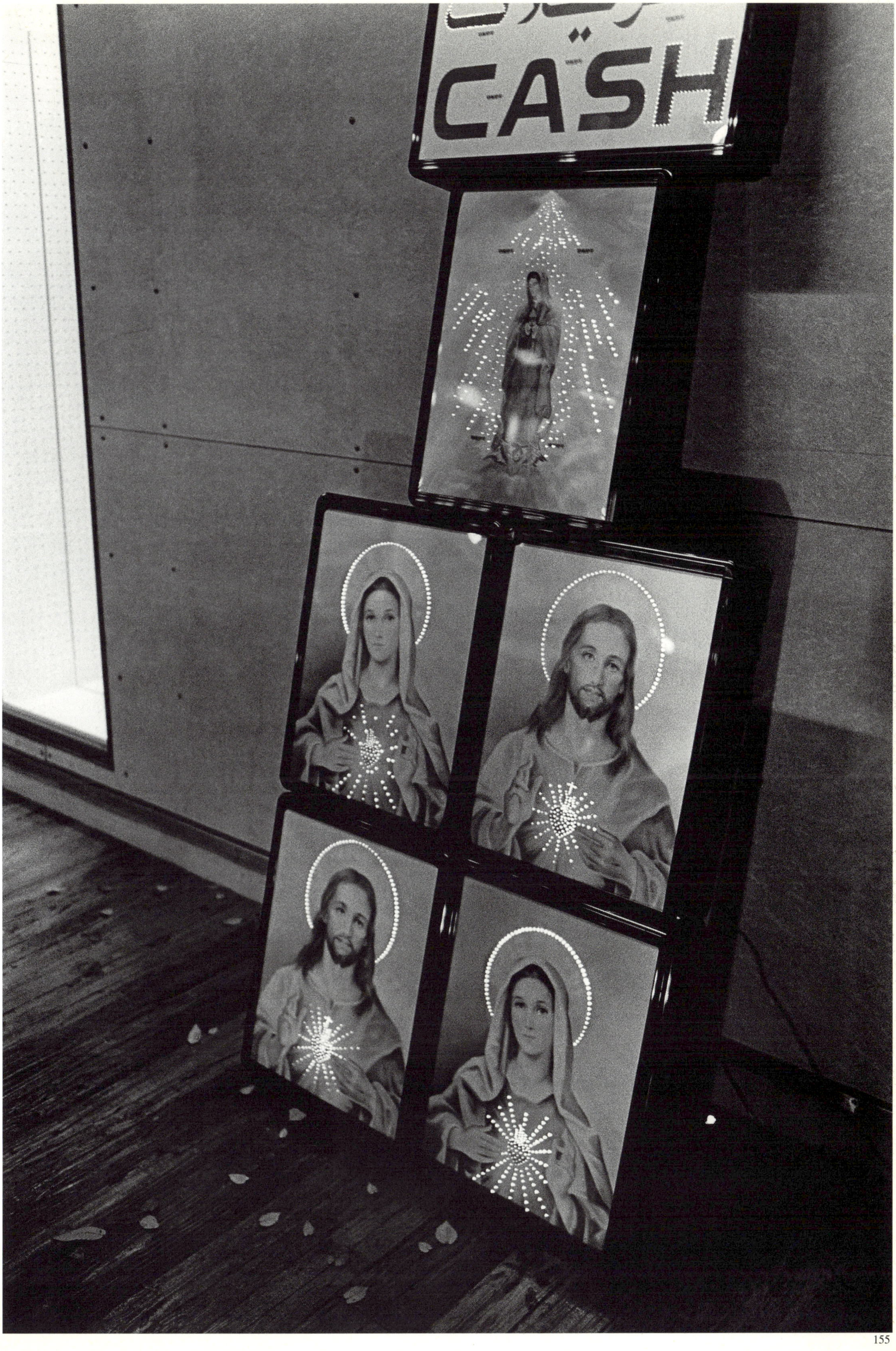
CASH

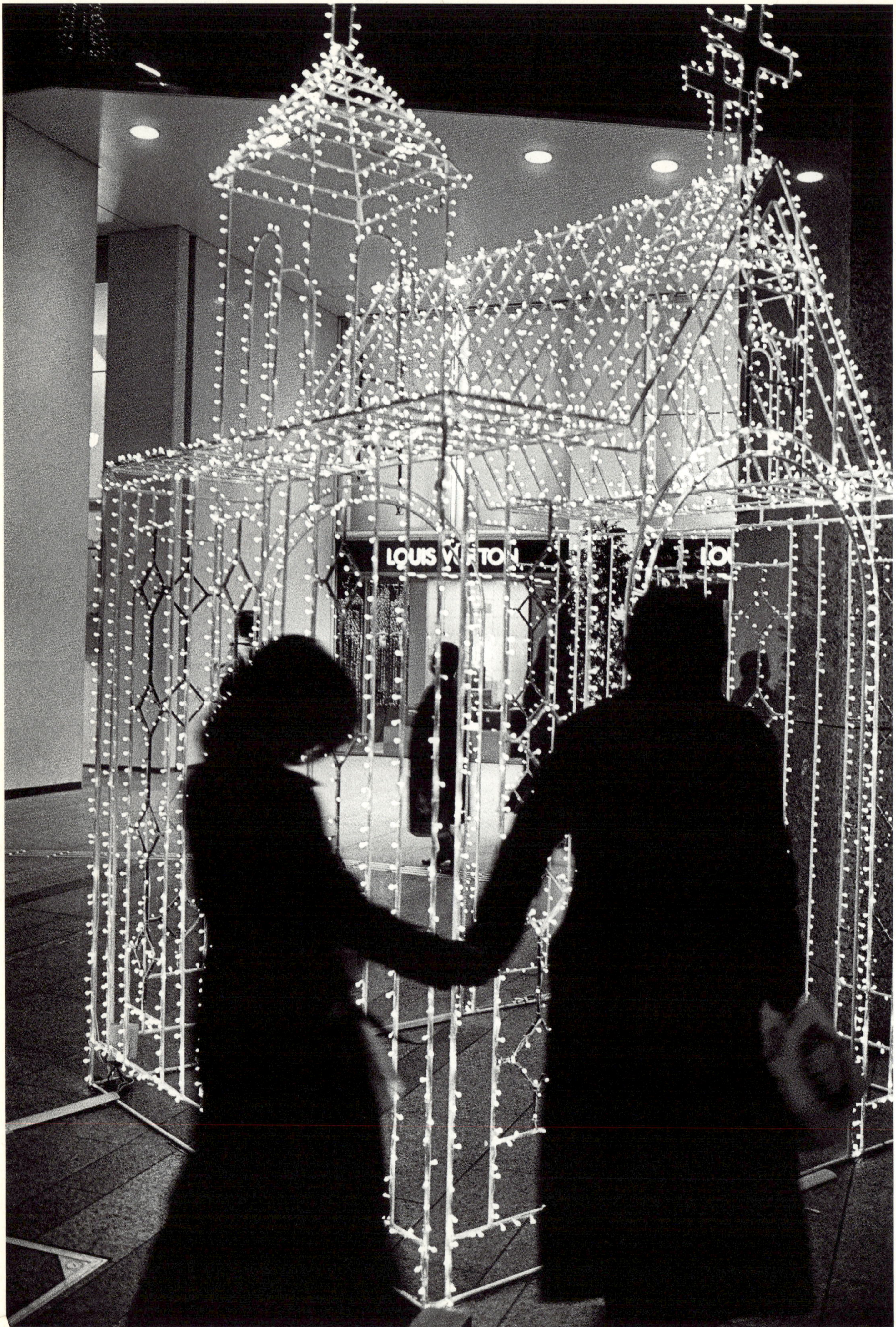
LOUIS

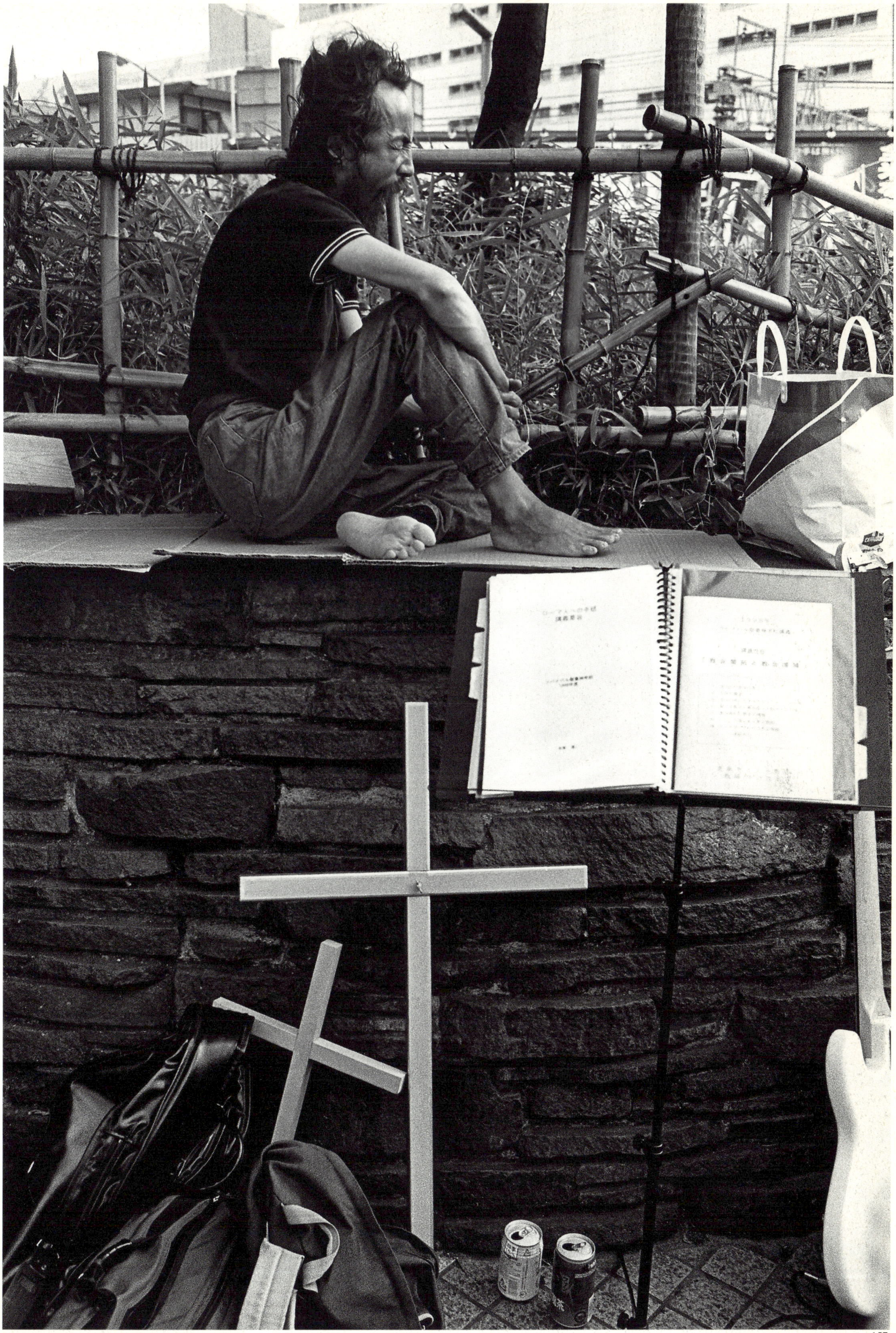

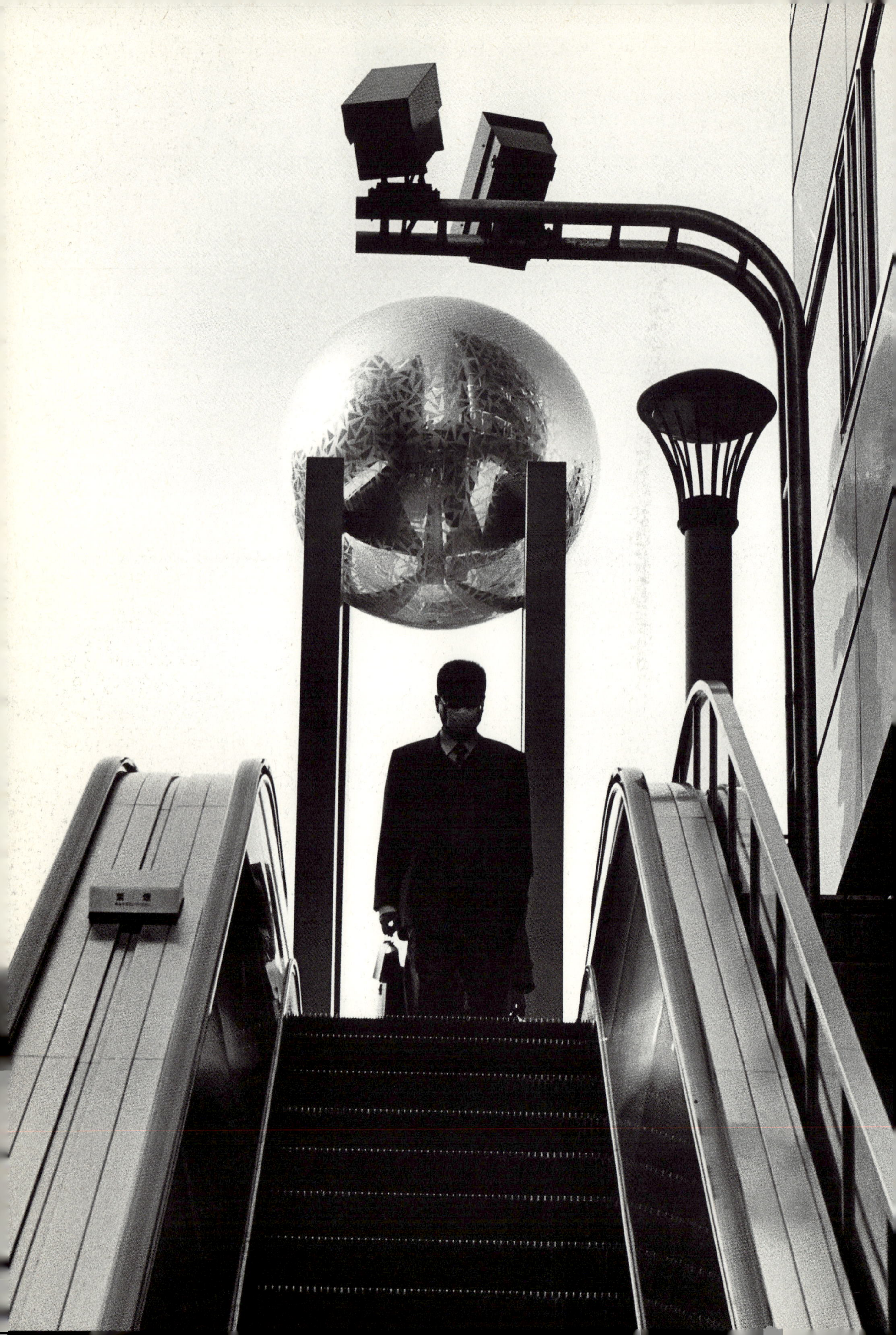

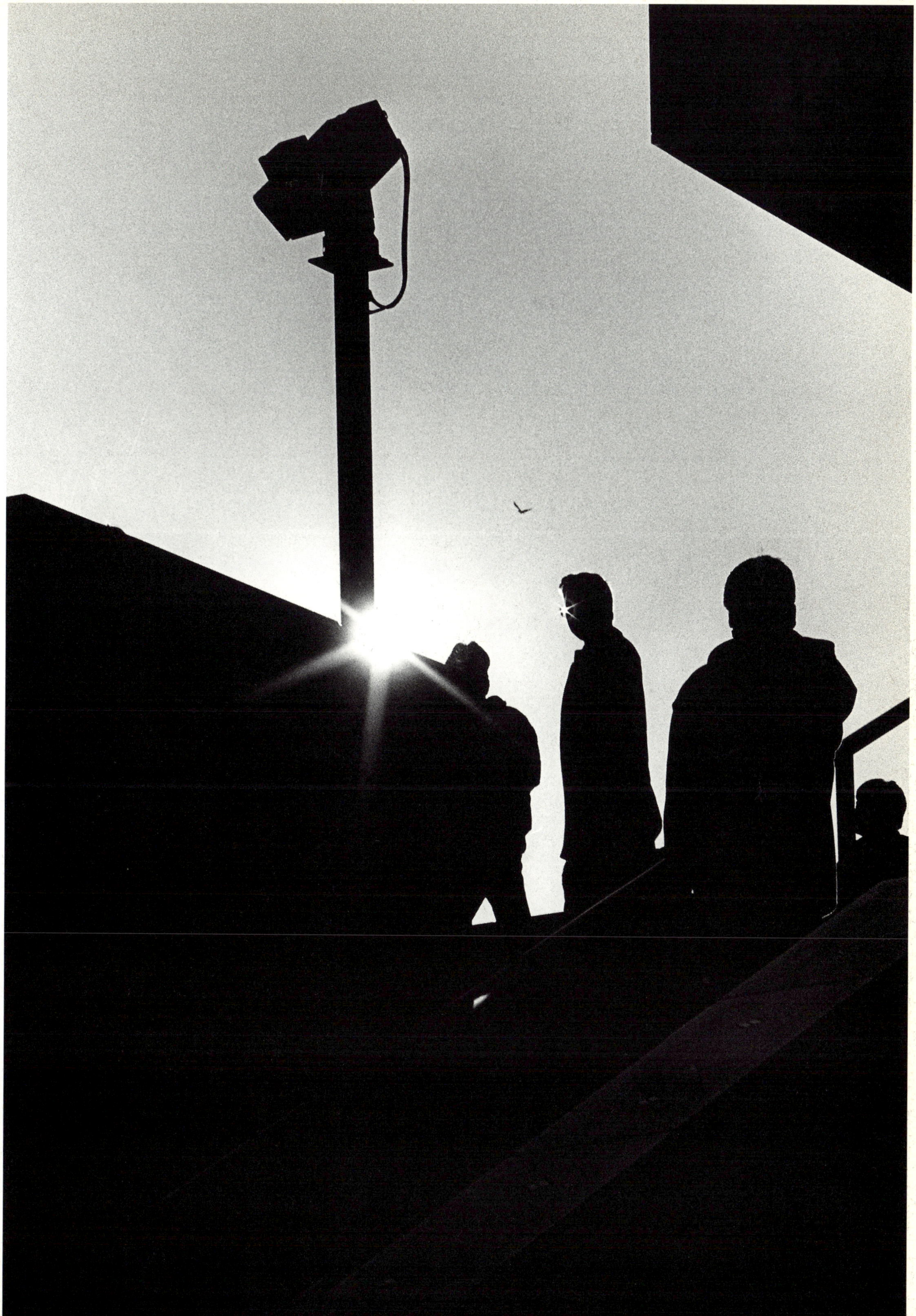

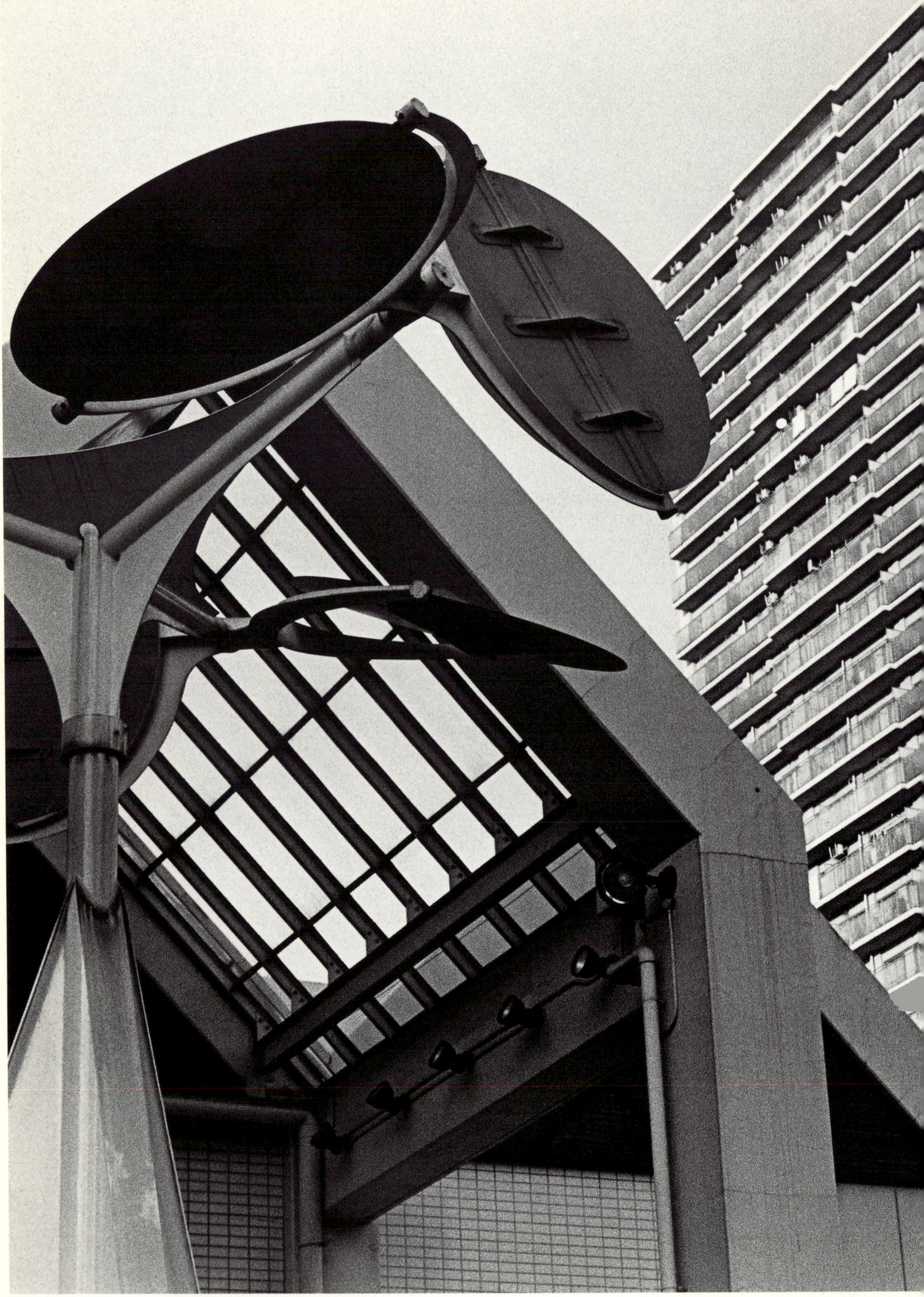

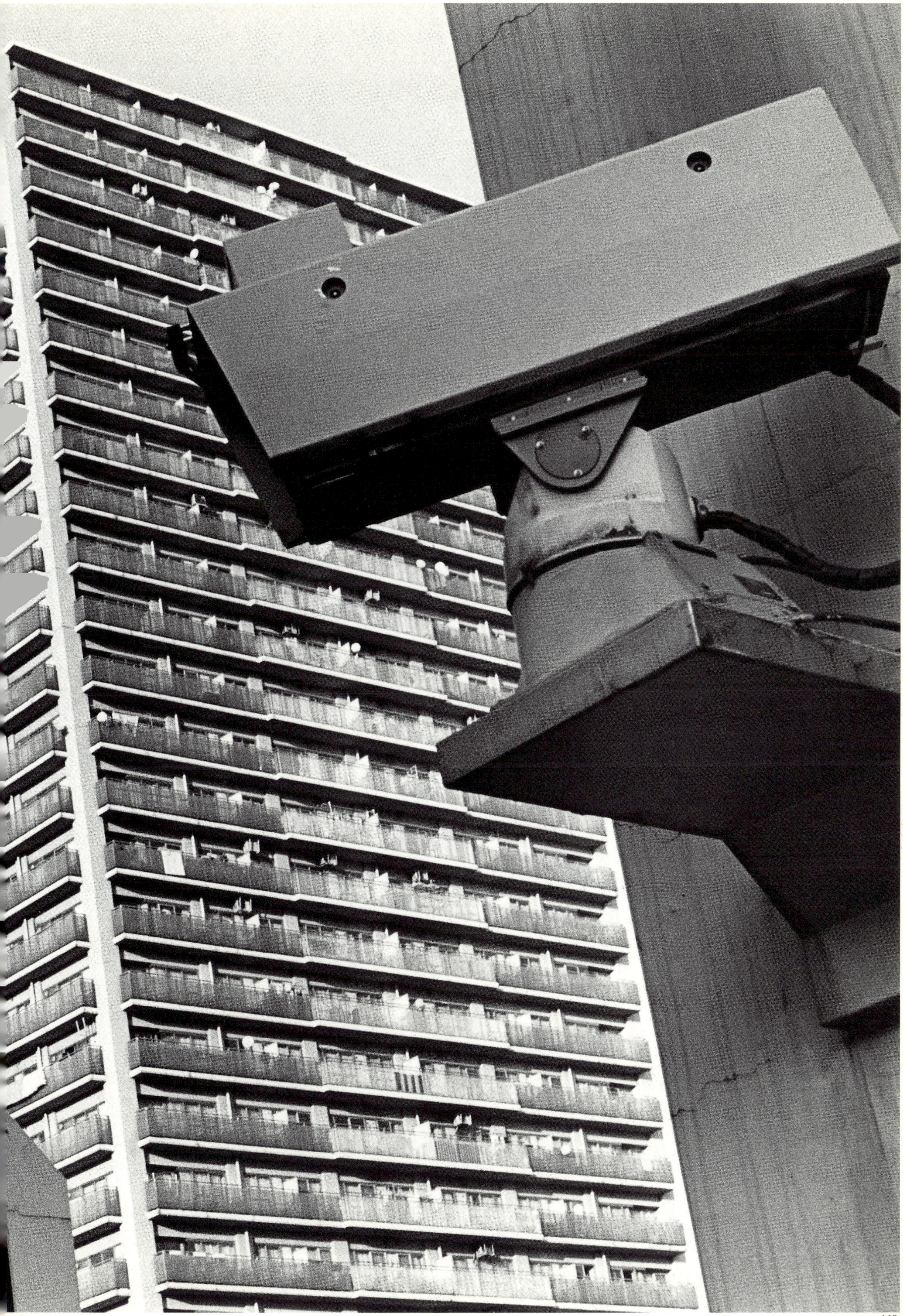

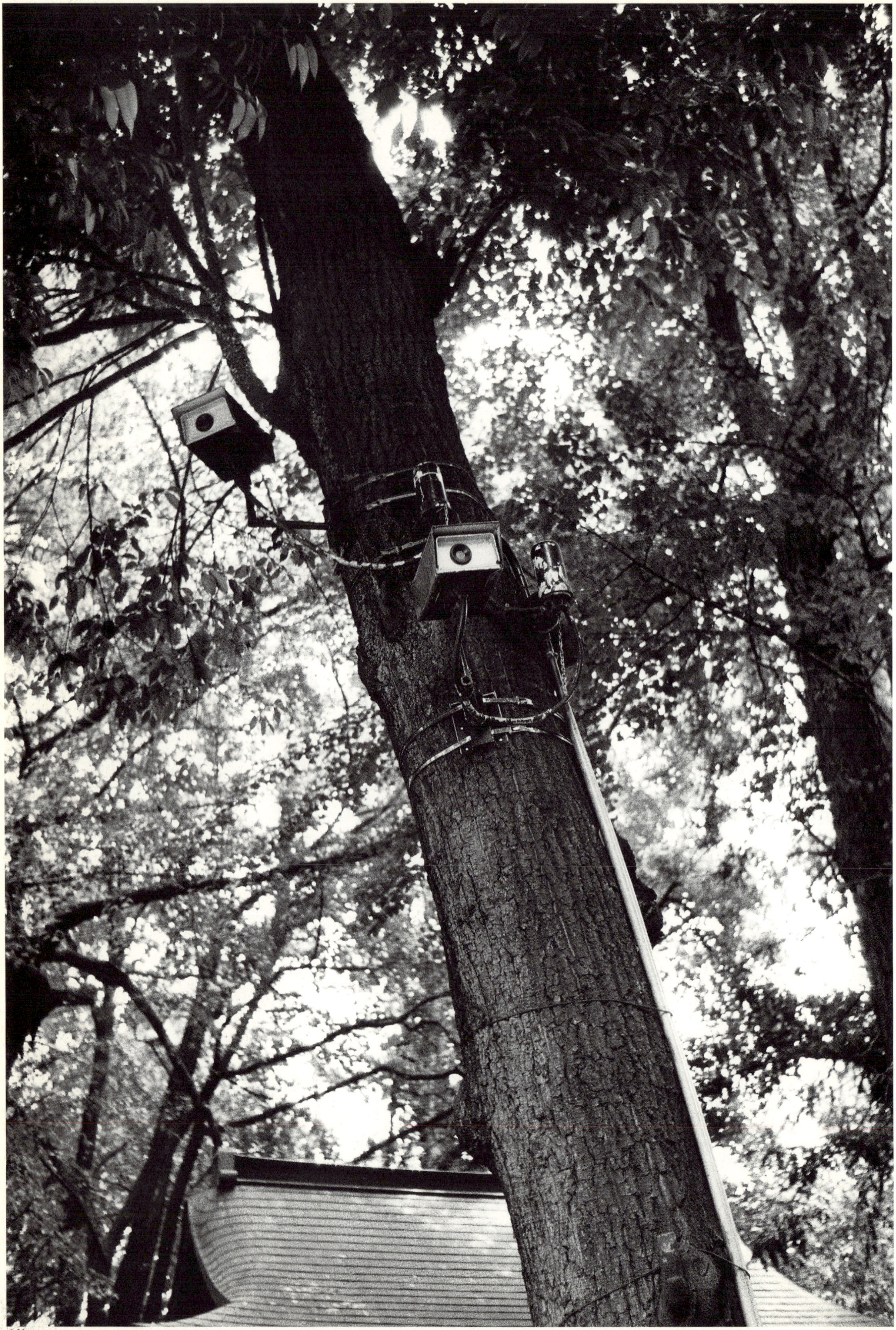

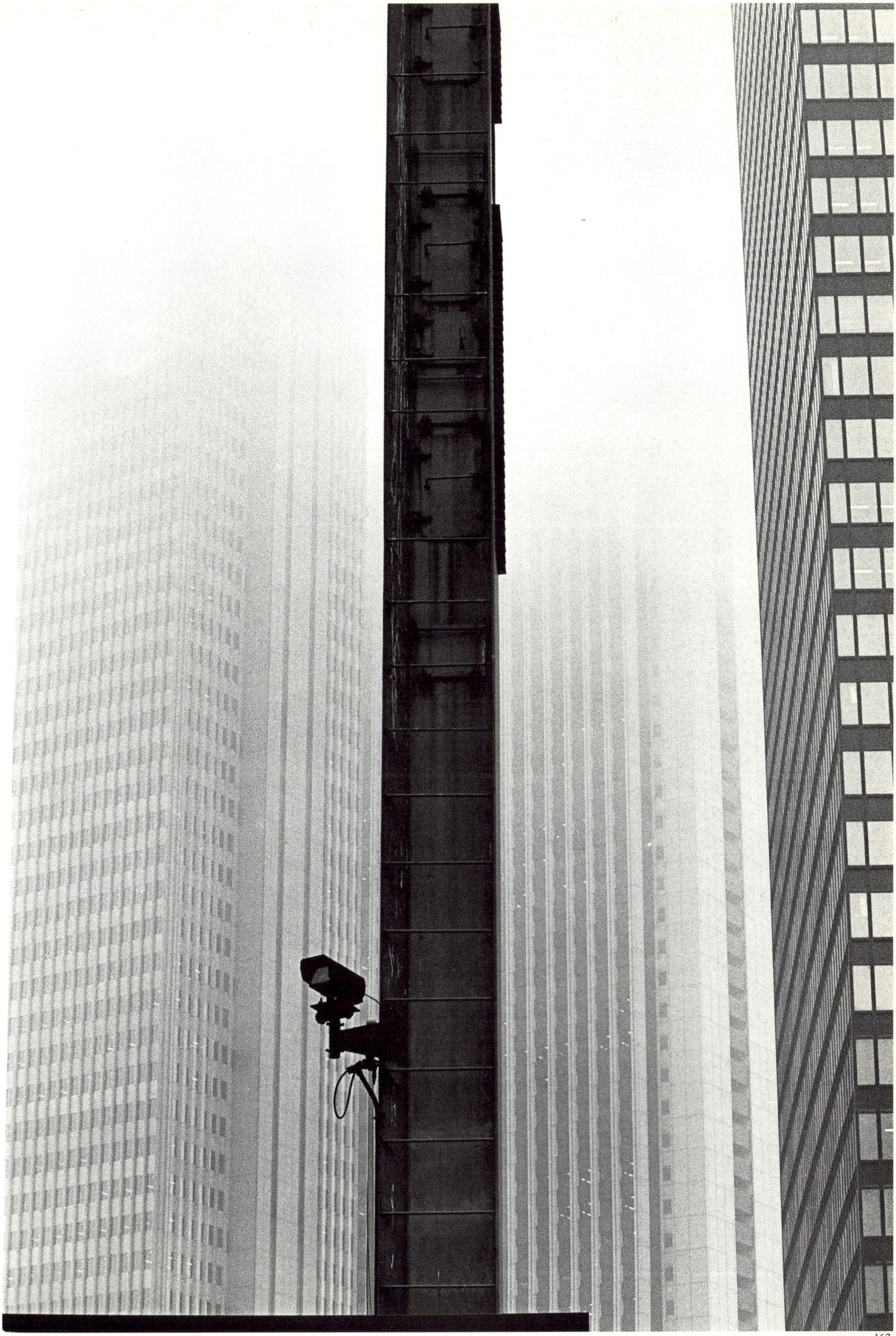

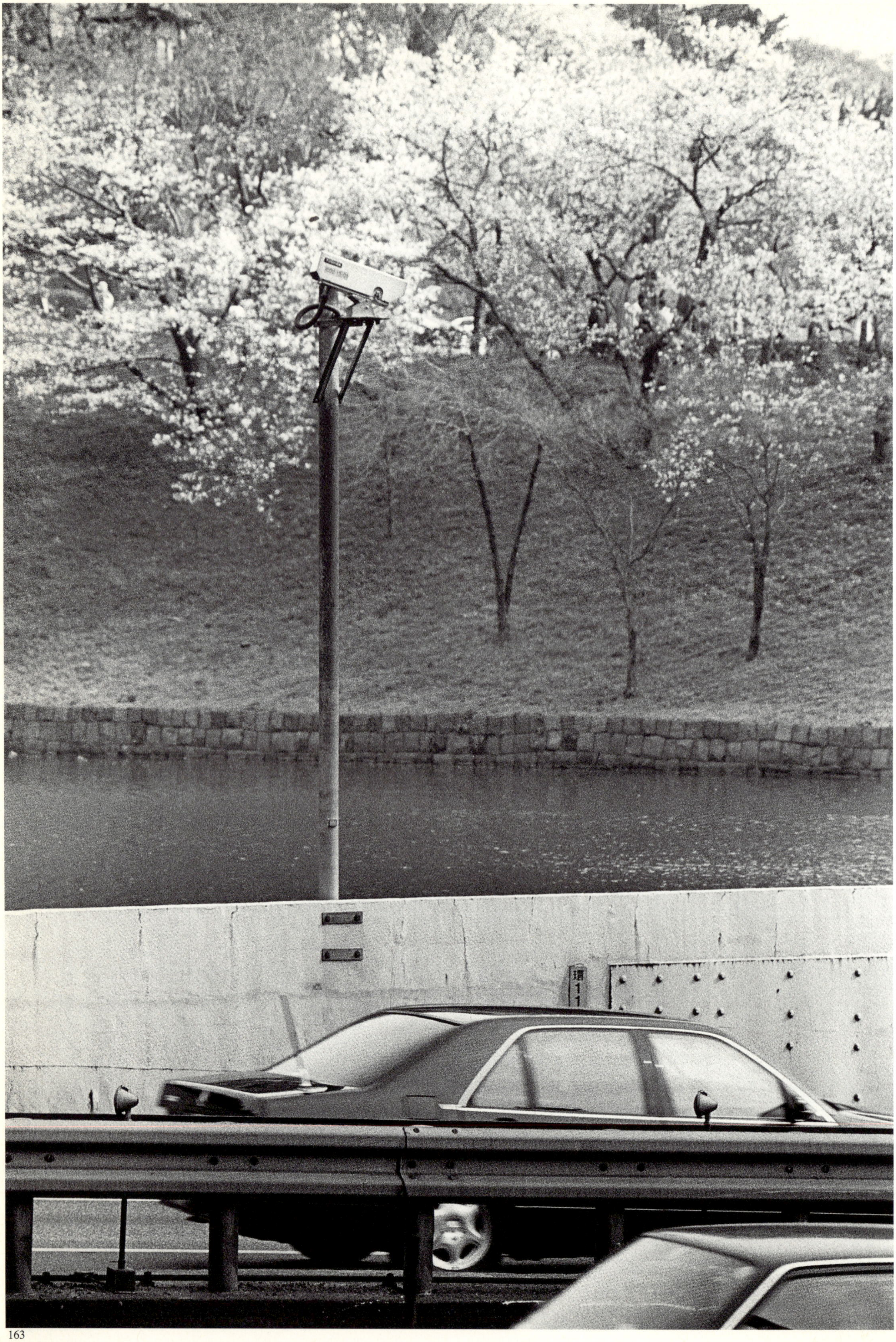

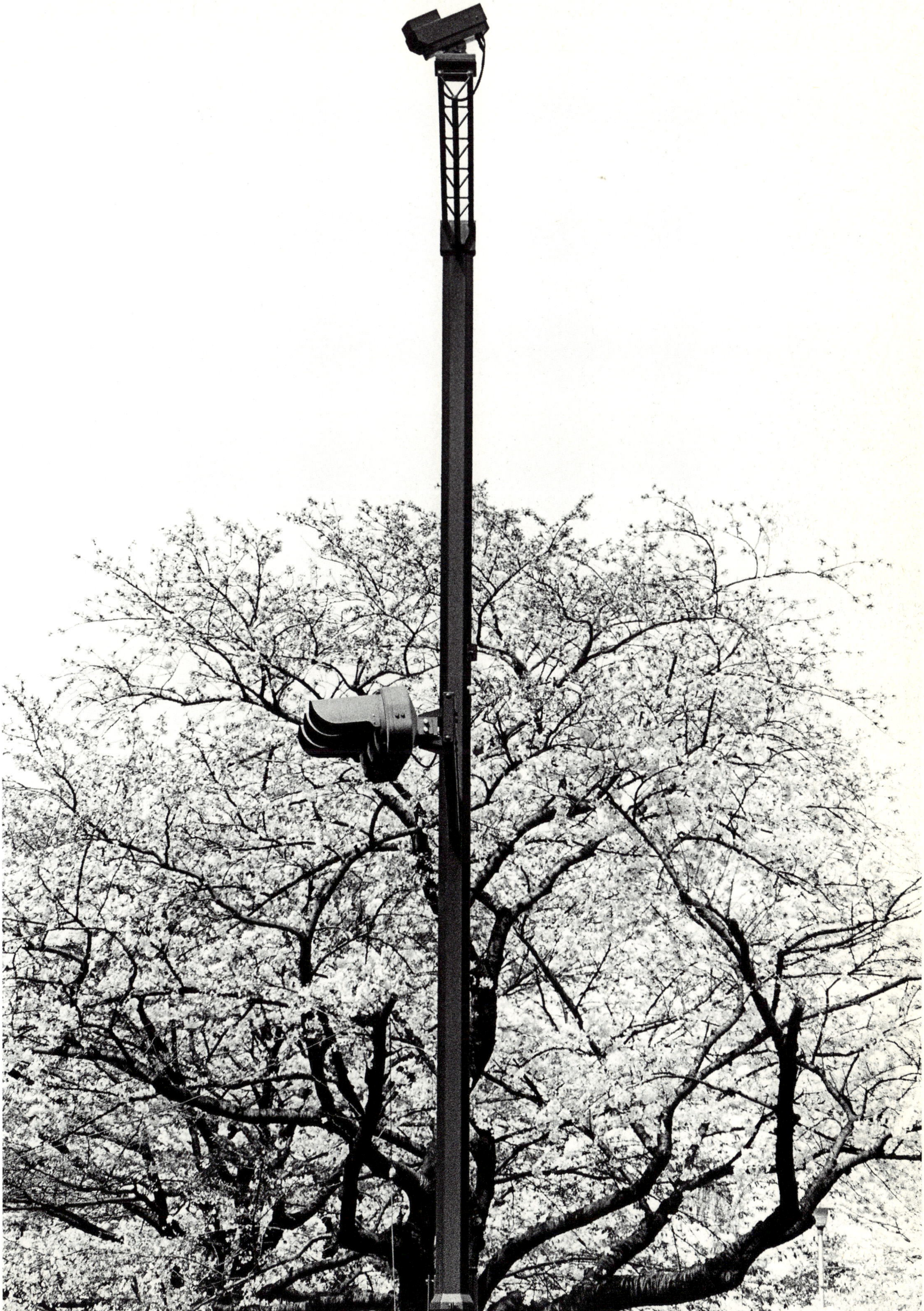

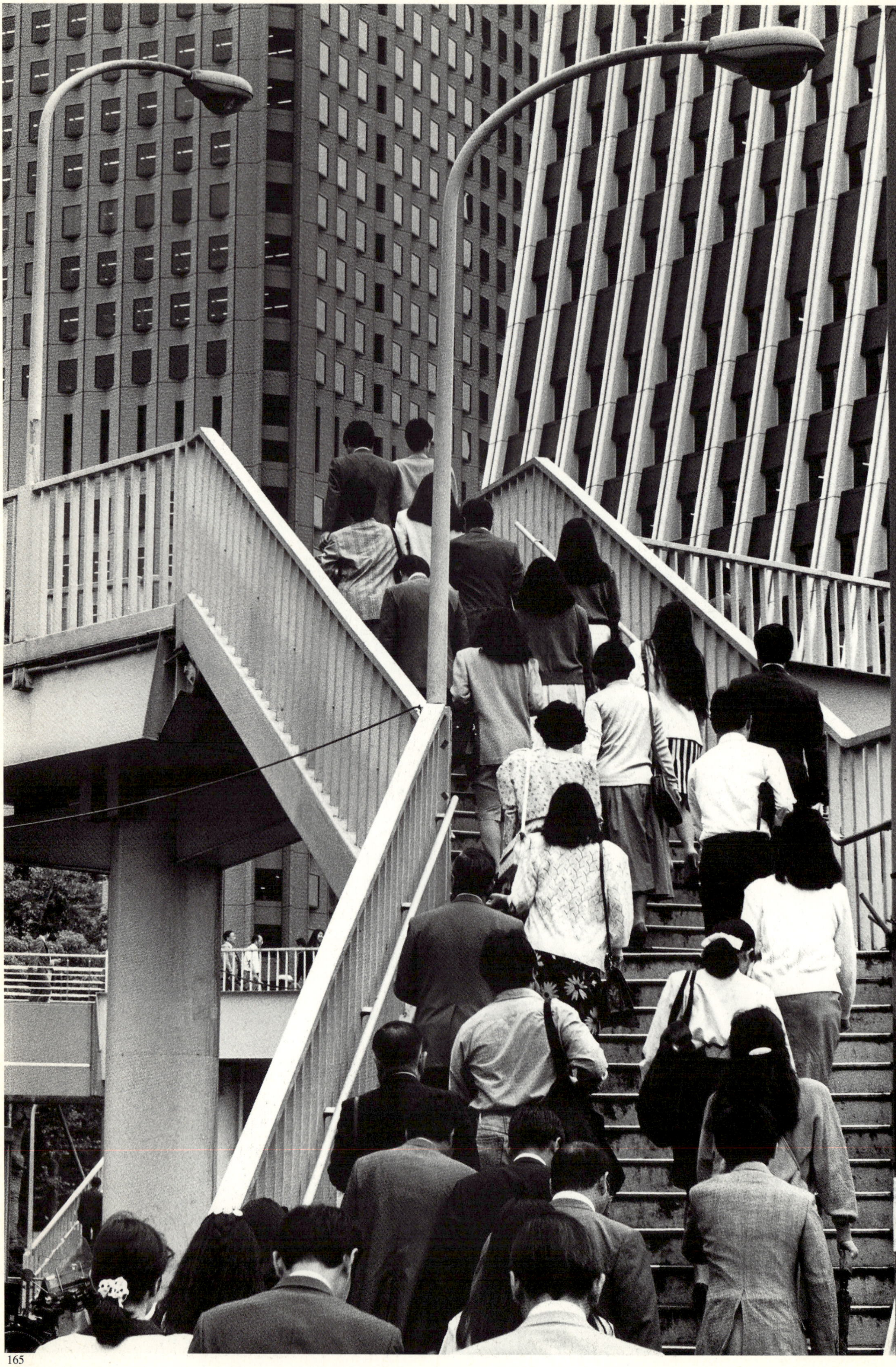

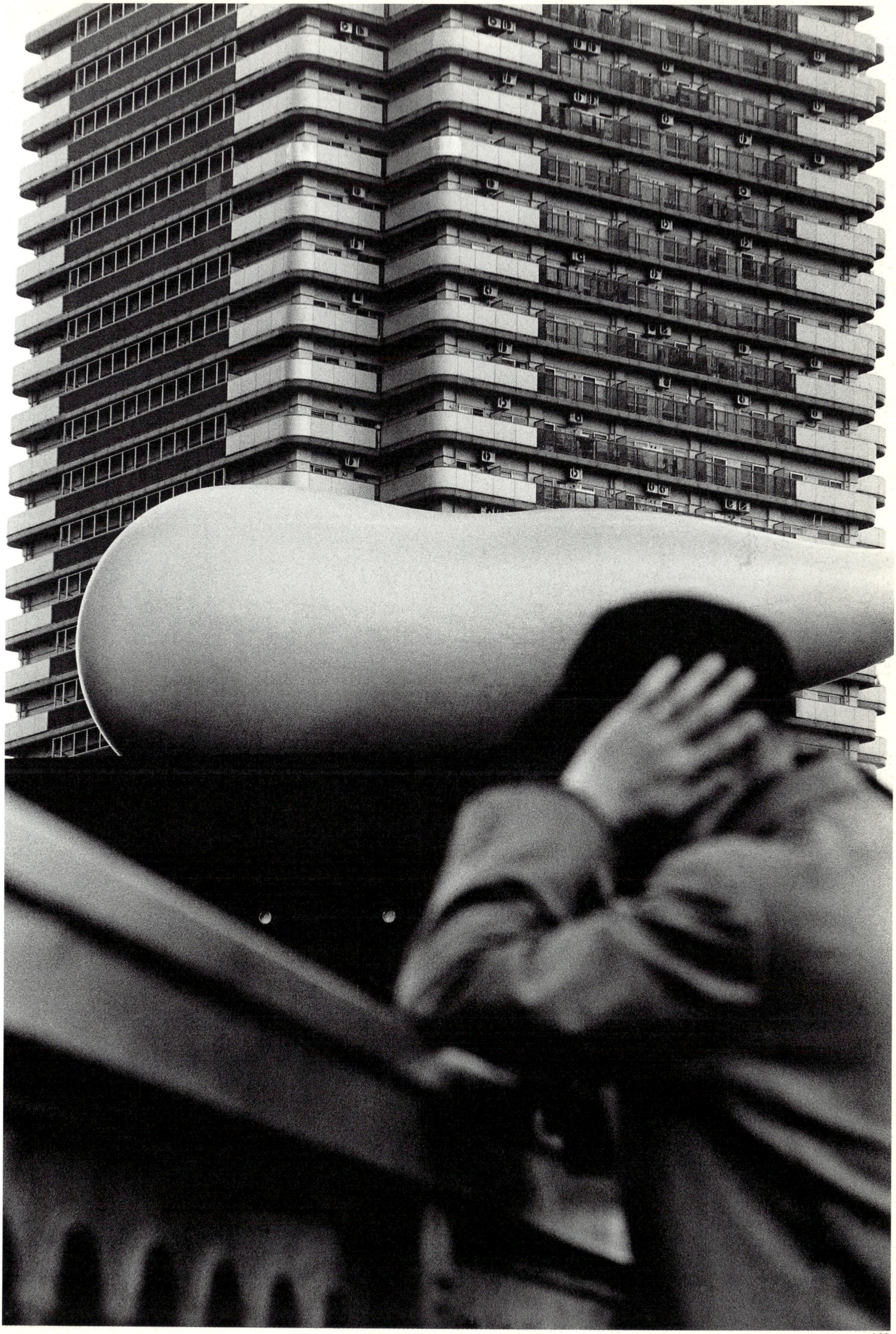

167

168

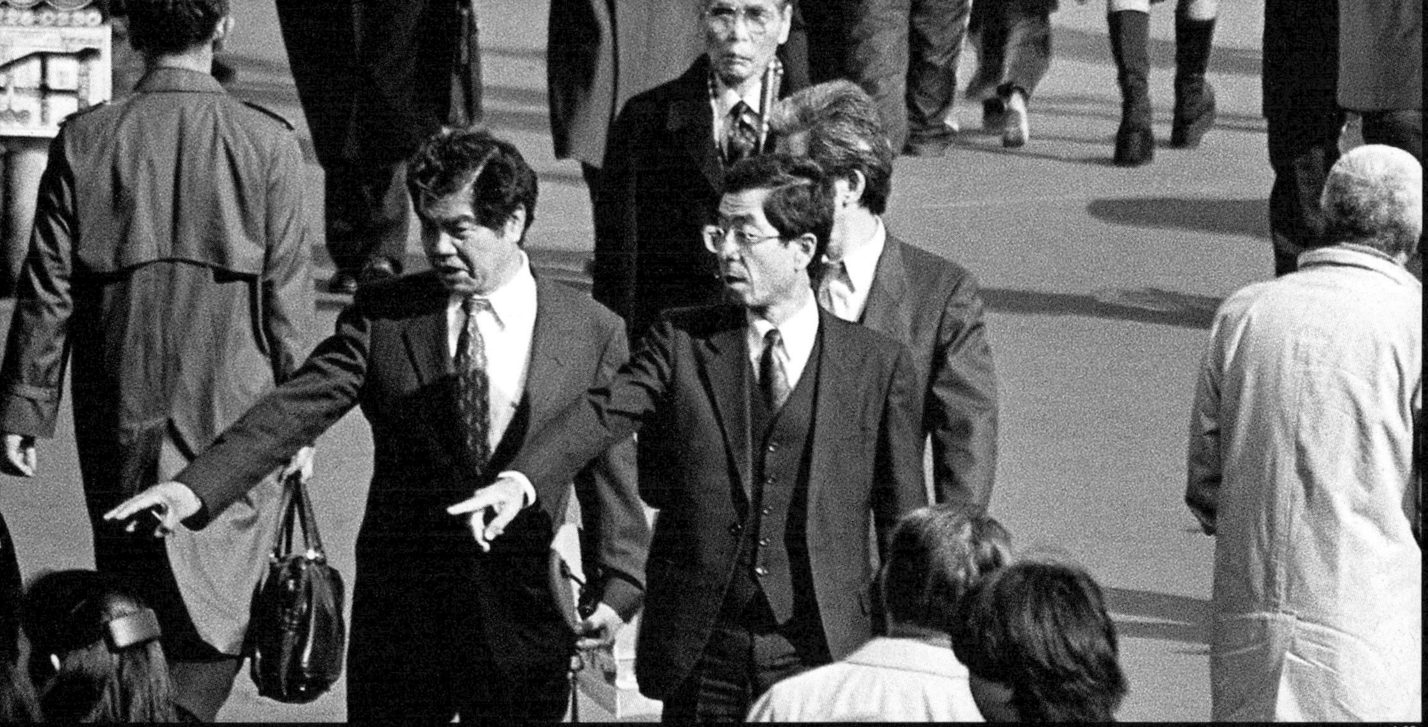

169

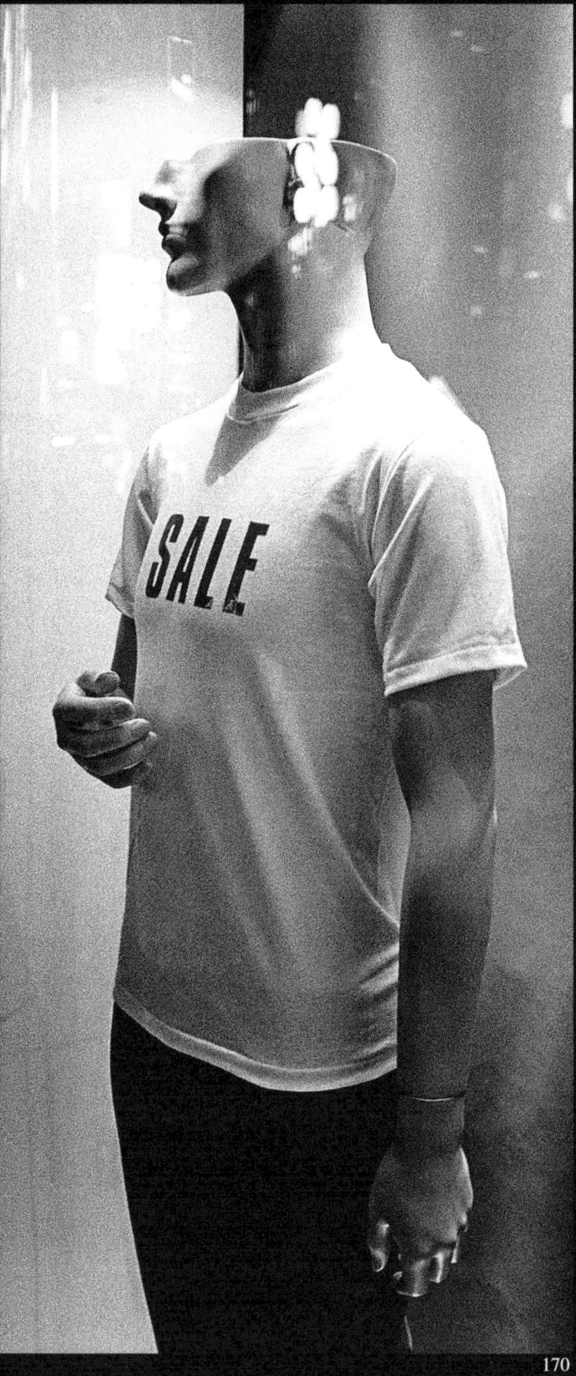

170

171

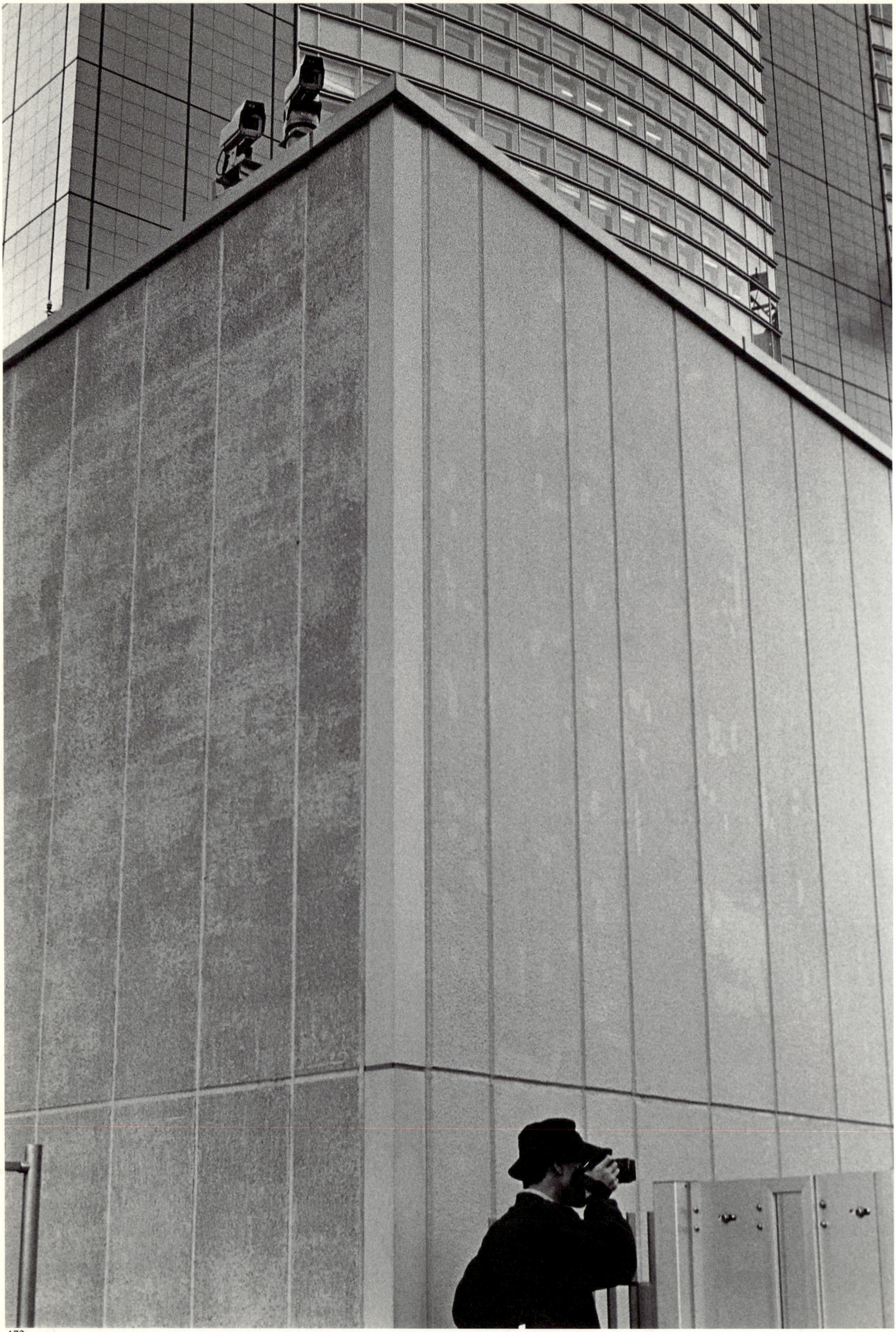

173

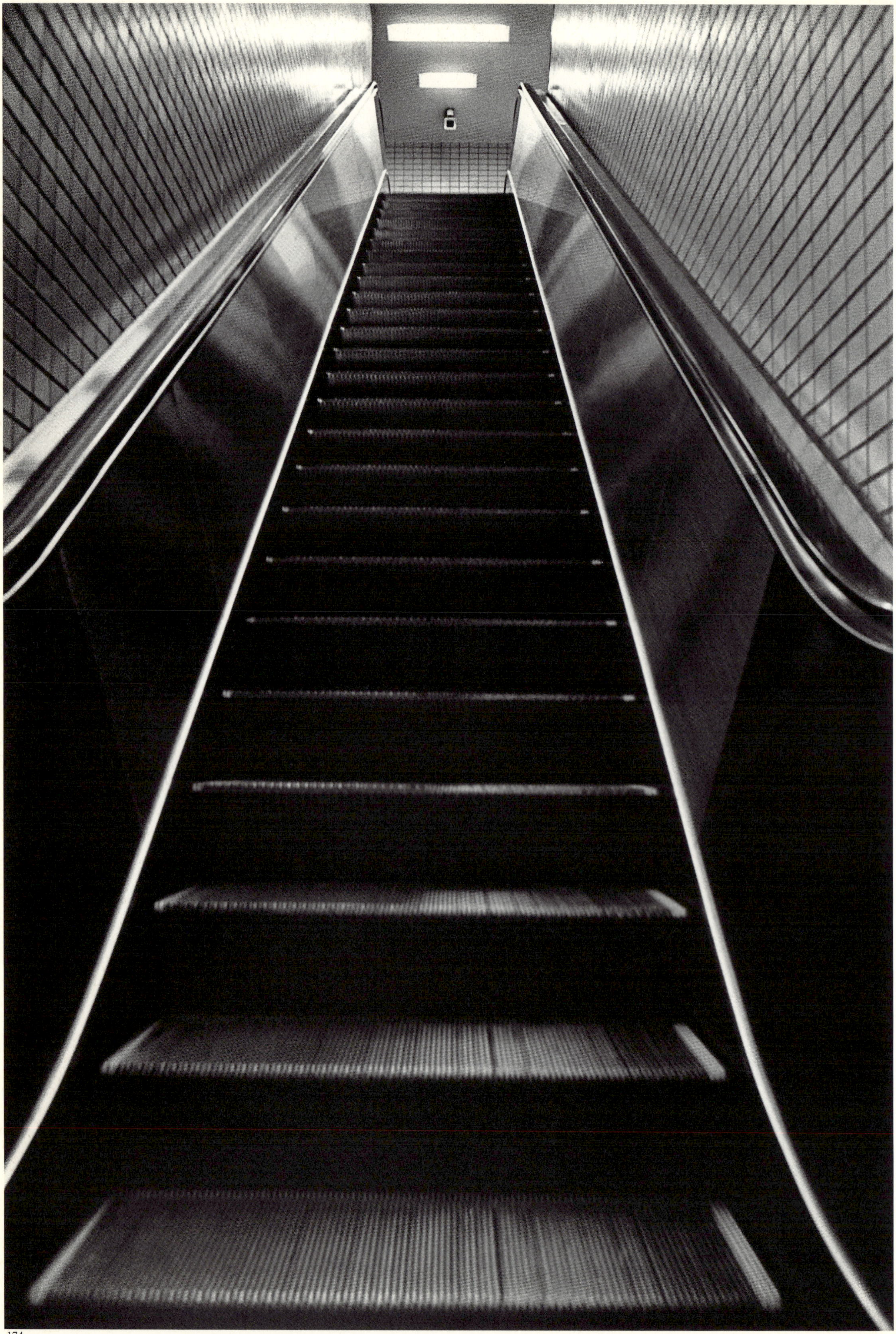

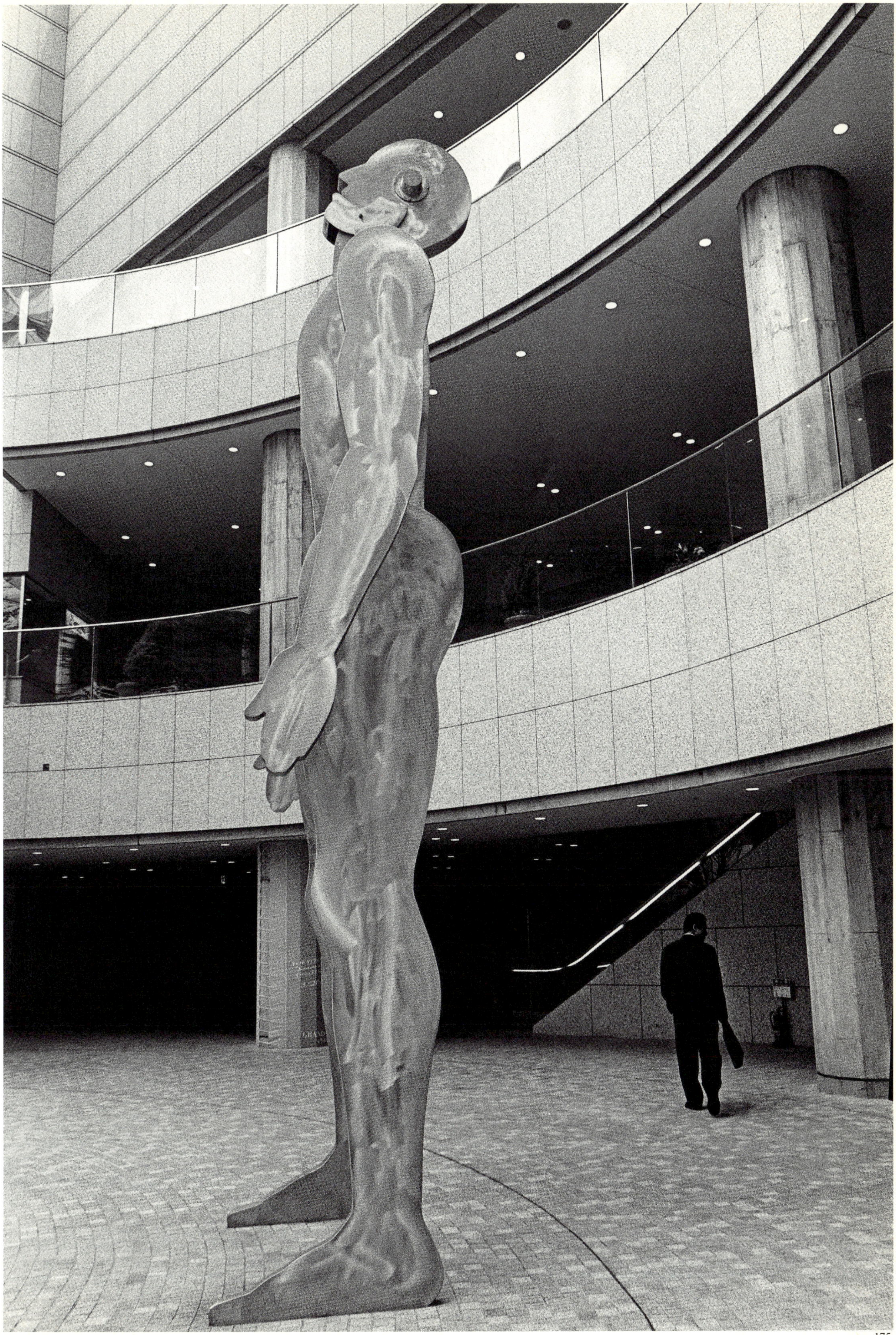

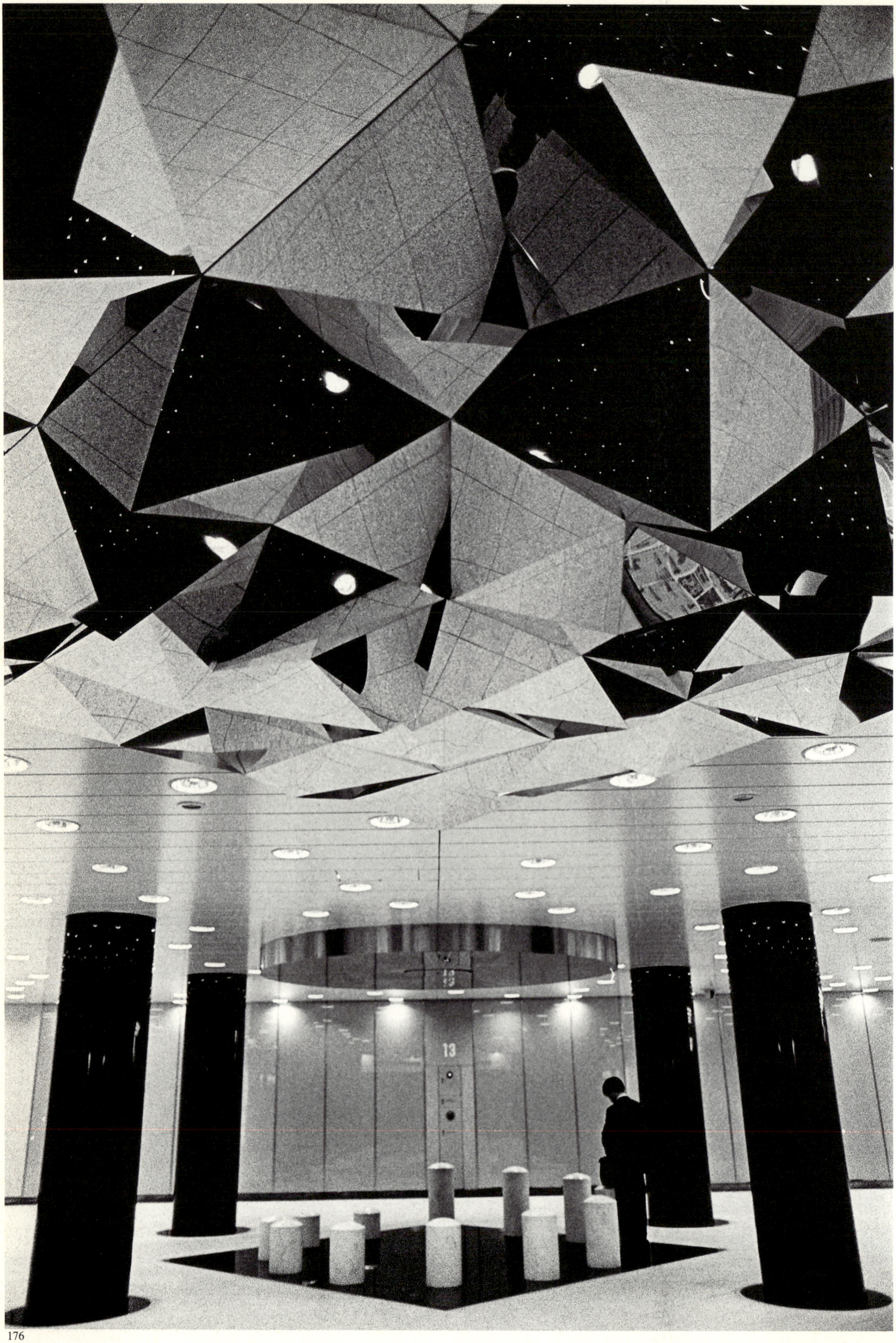
13

177

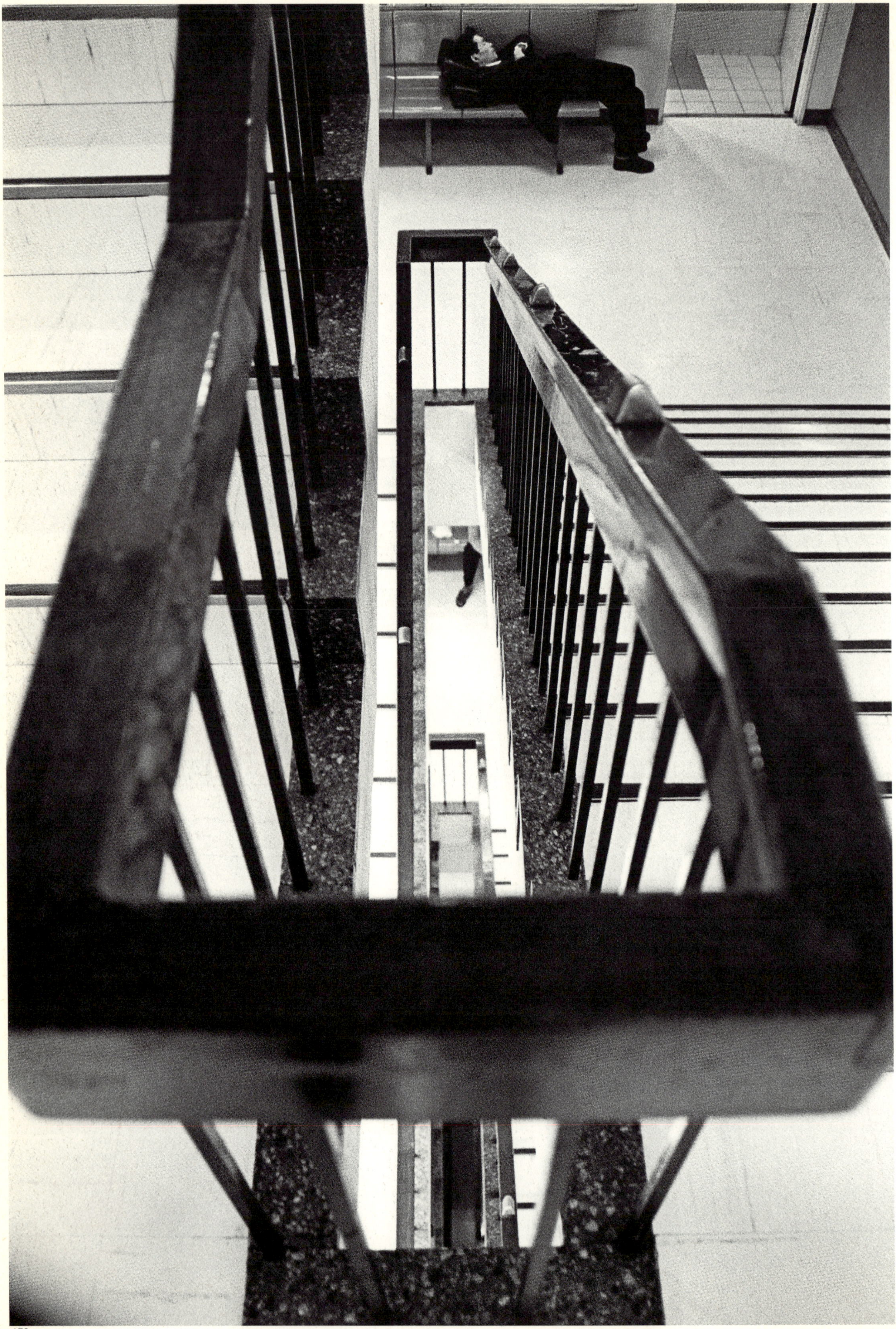

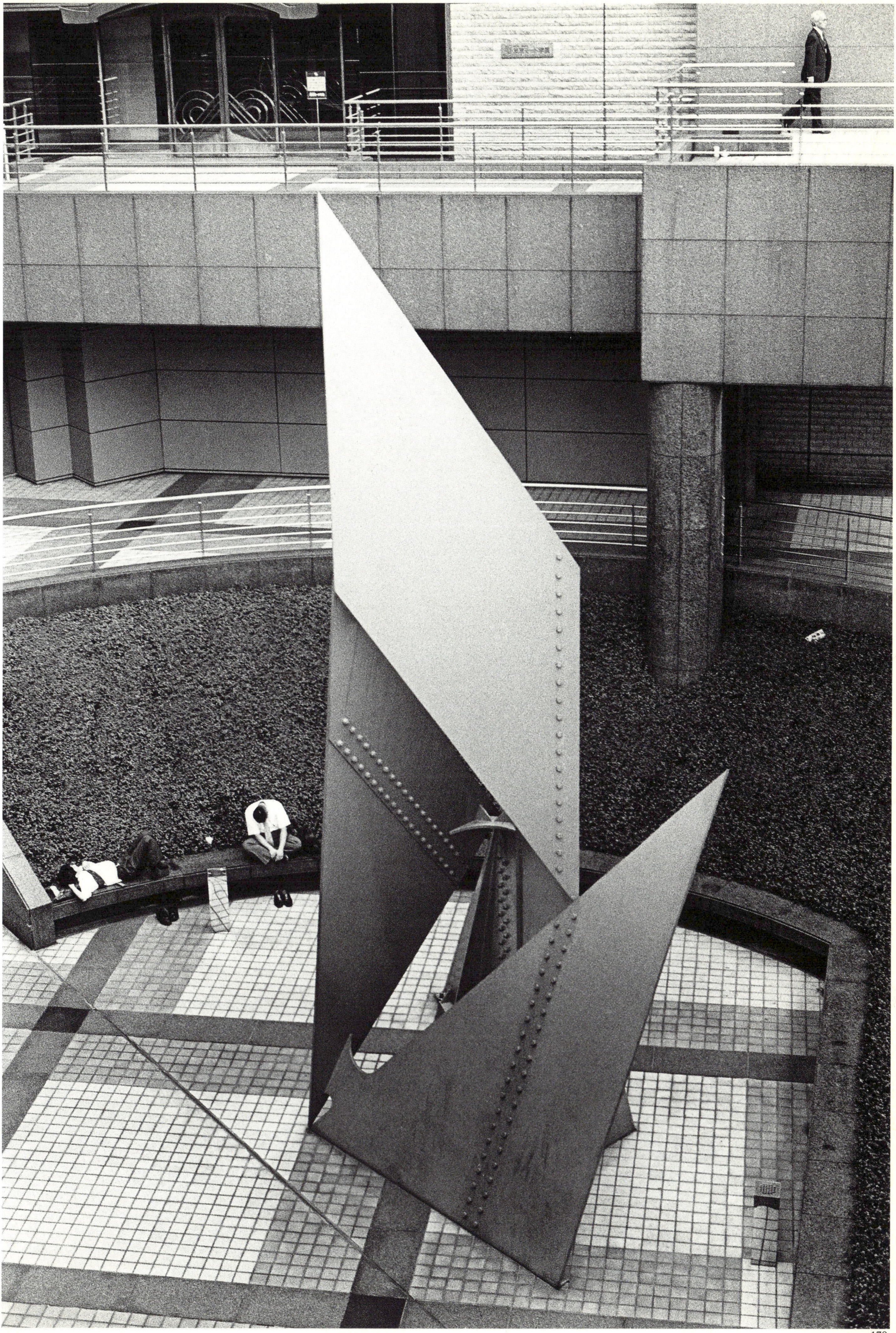

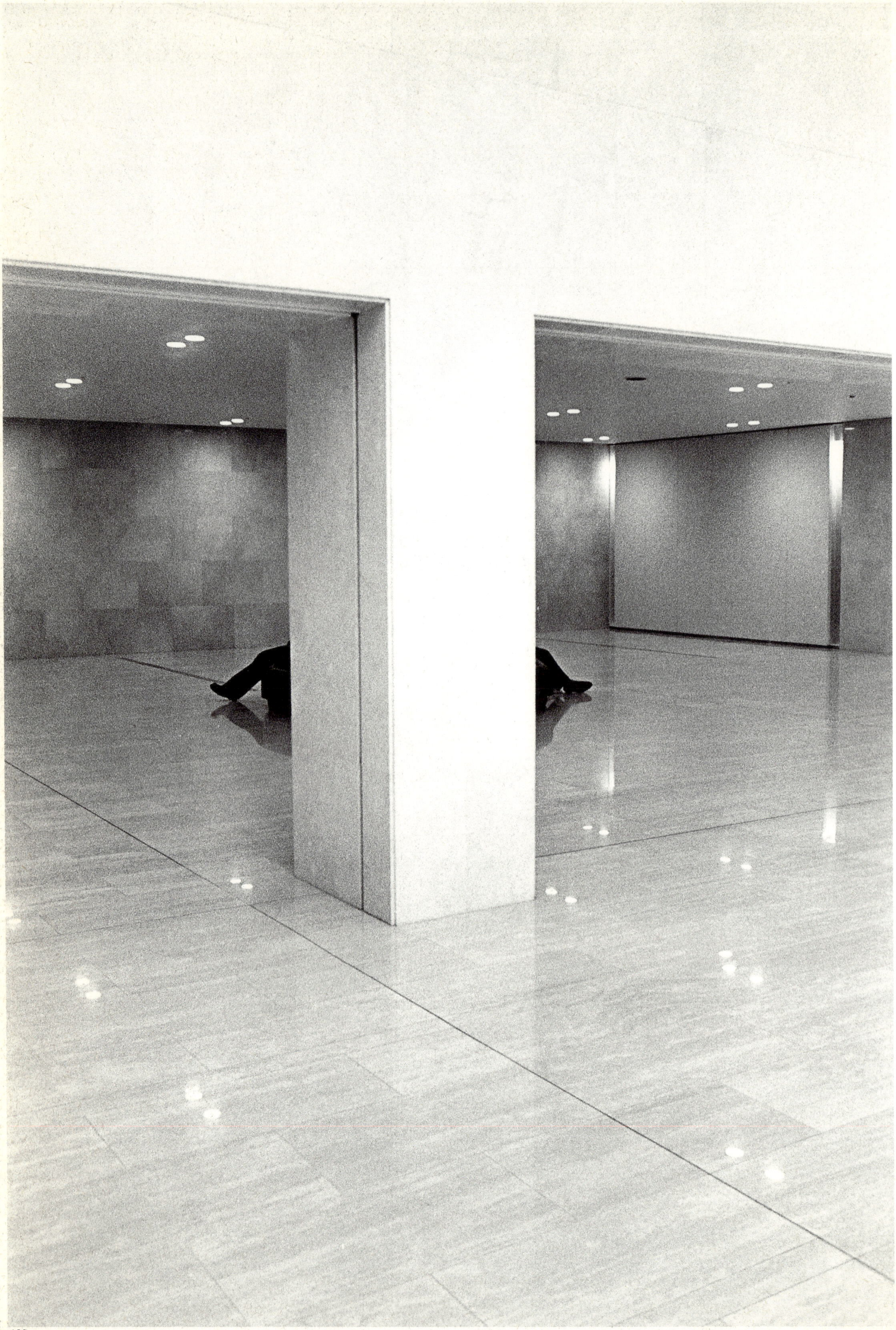

181

182

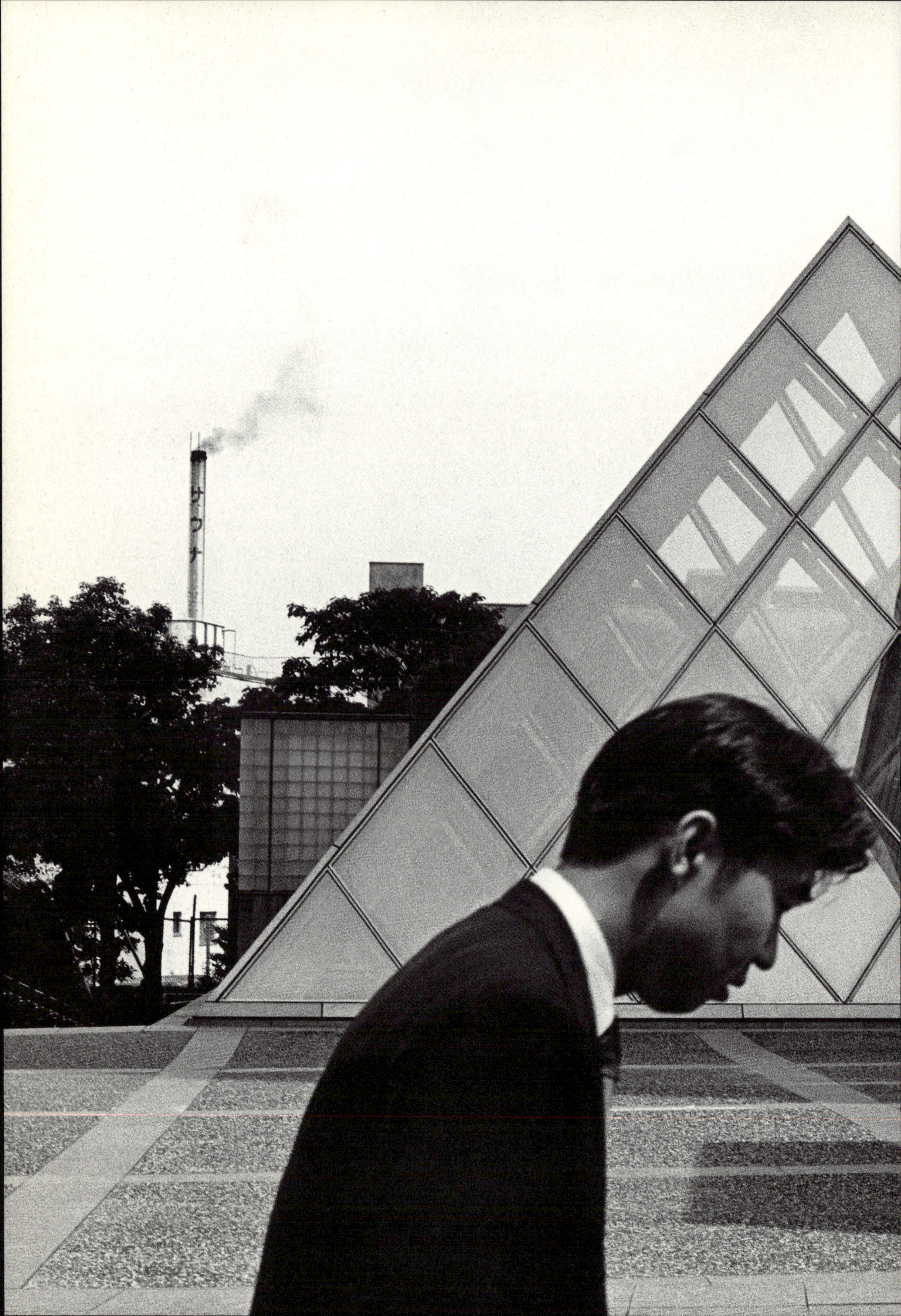
サウナ

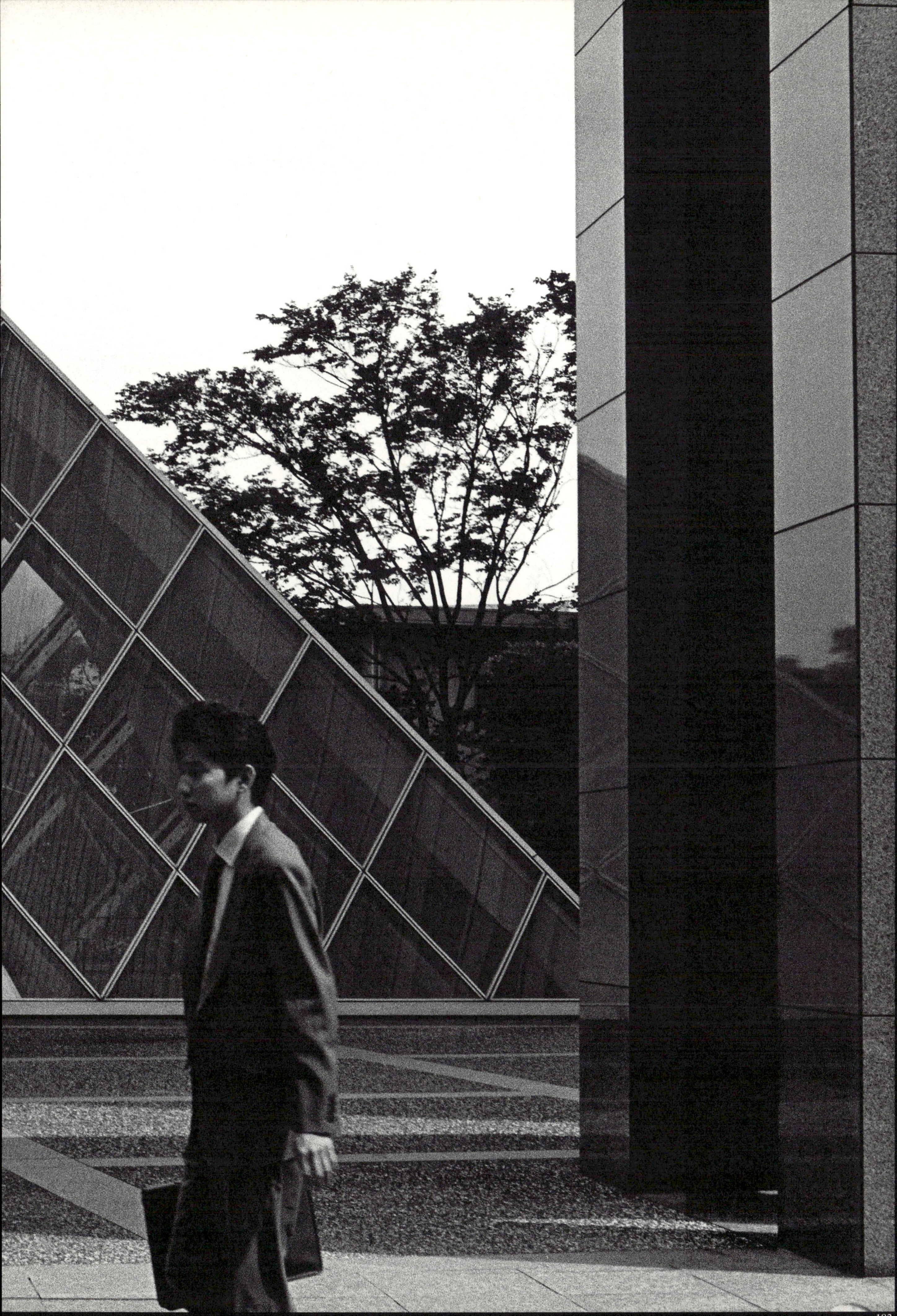

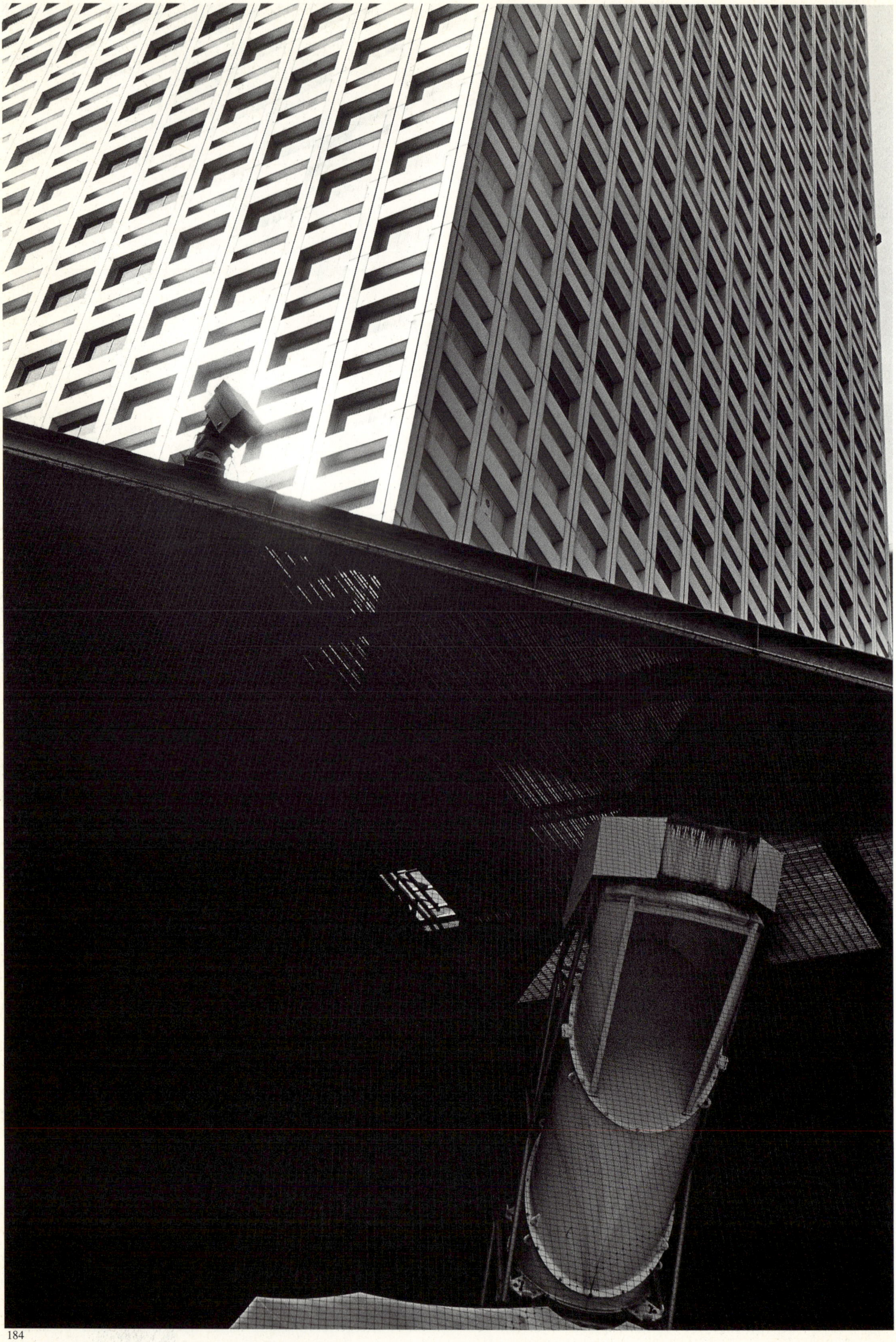

185

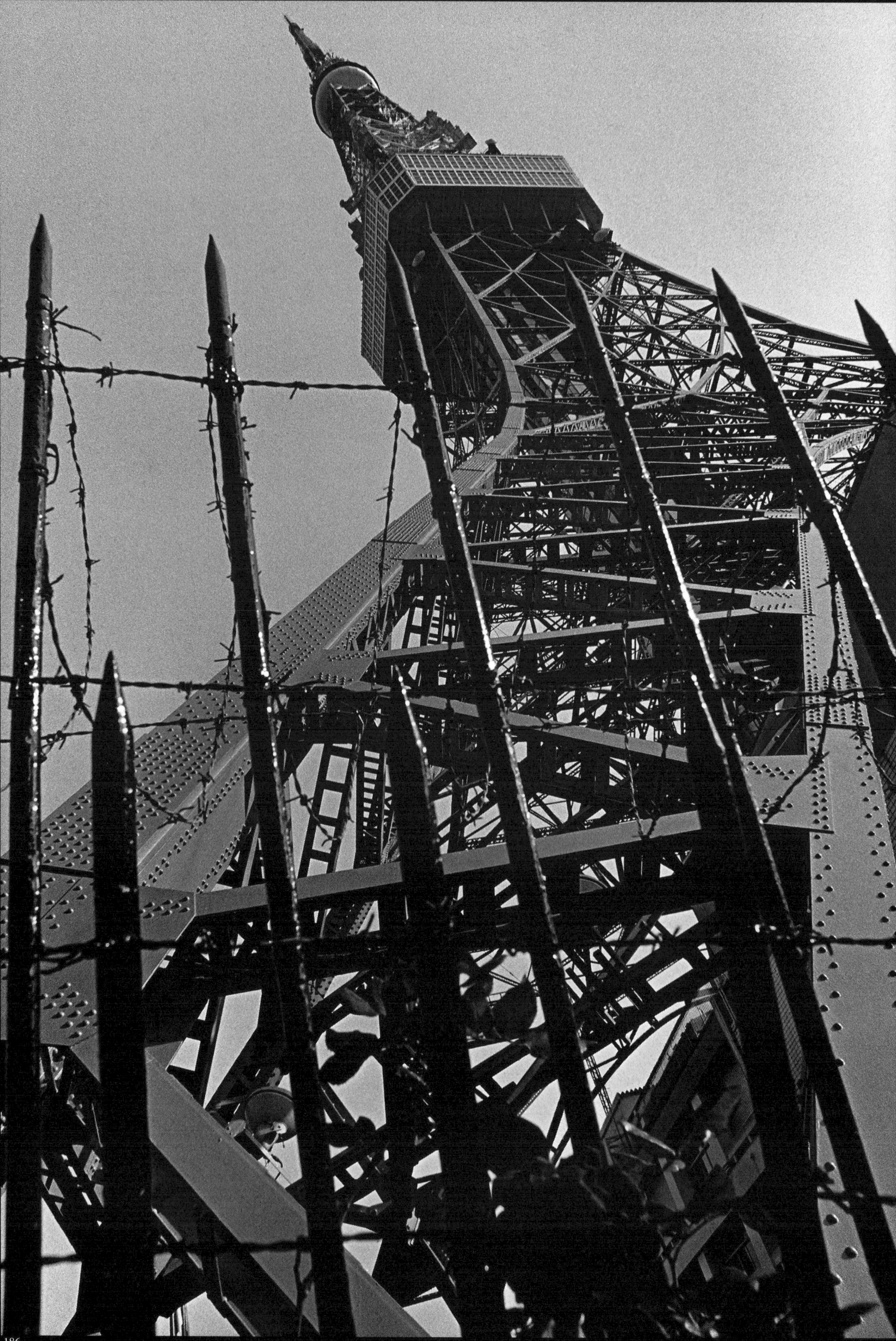

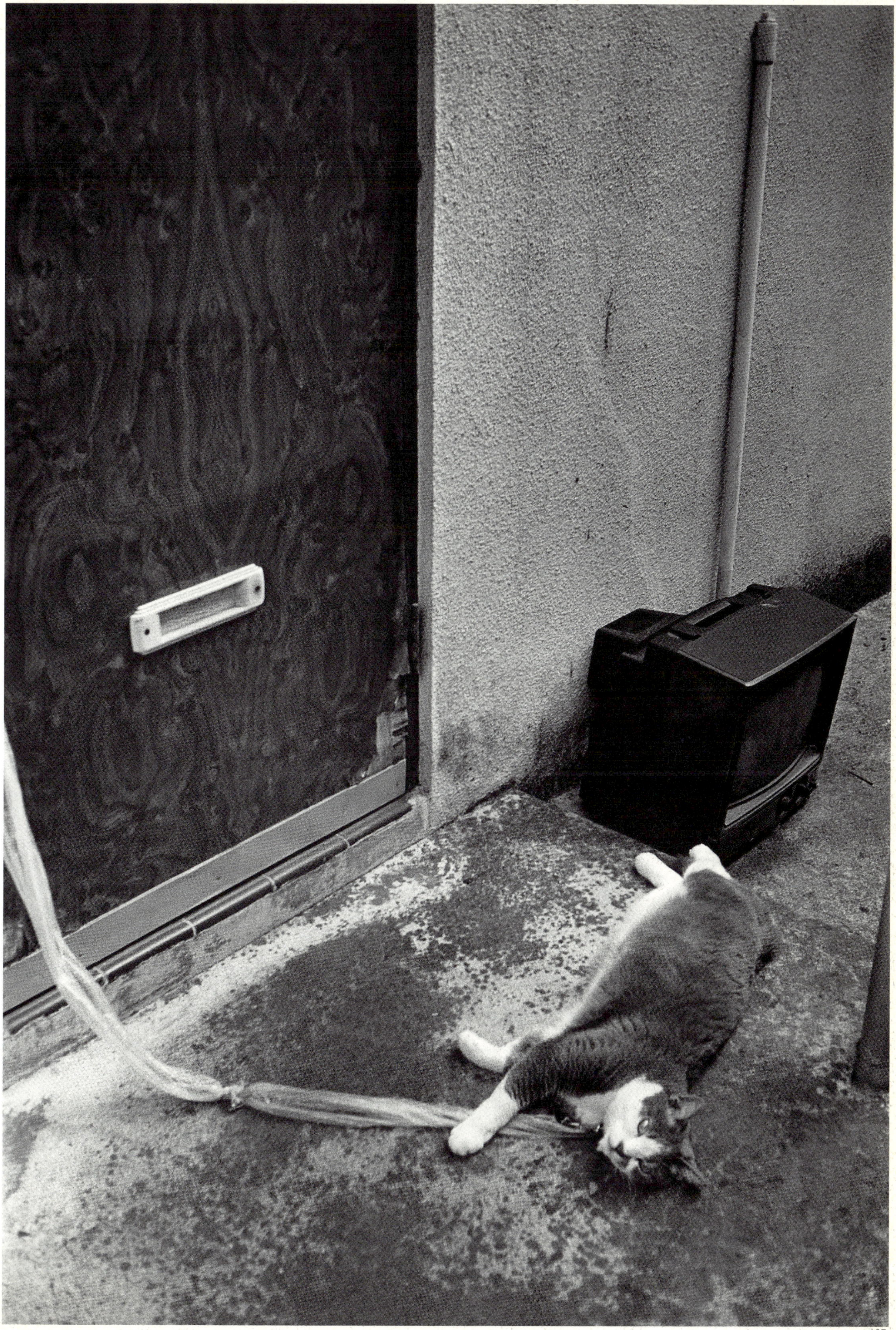

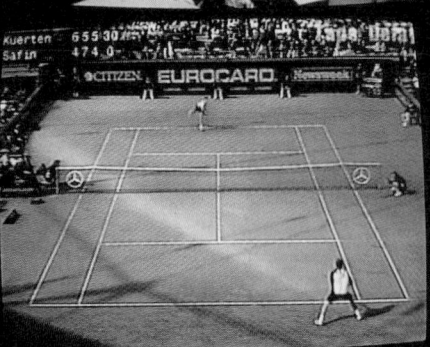

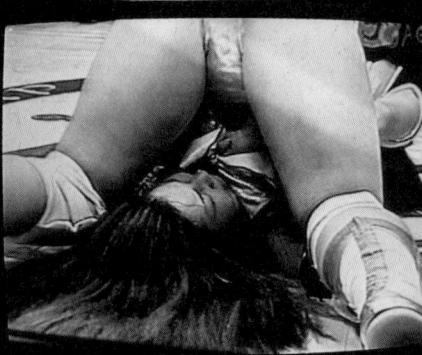

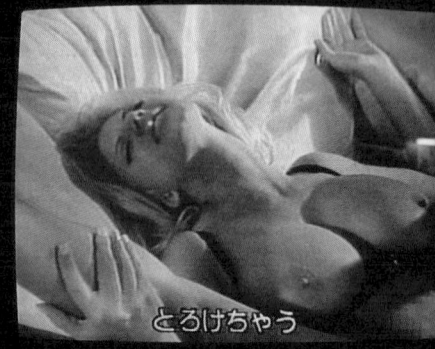

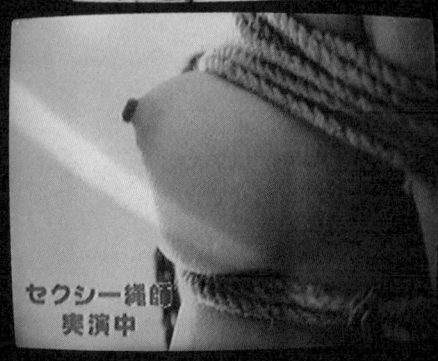

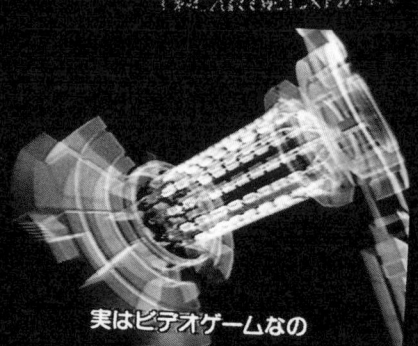

吸いついてる

評議会
現政権は退陣 暫定政権発足

ニューヨーク市場、
ナスダック指数が下落

とろけちゃう

セクシー縄師
実演中

実はビデオゲームなの

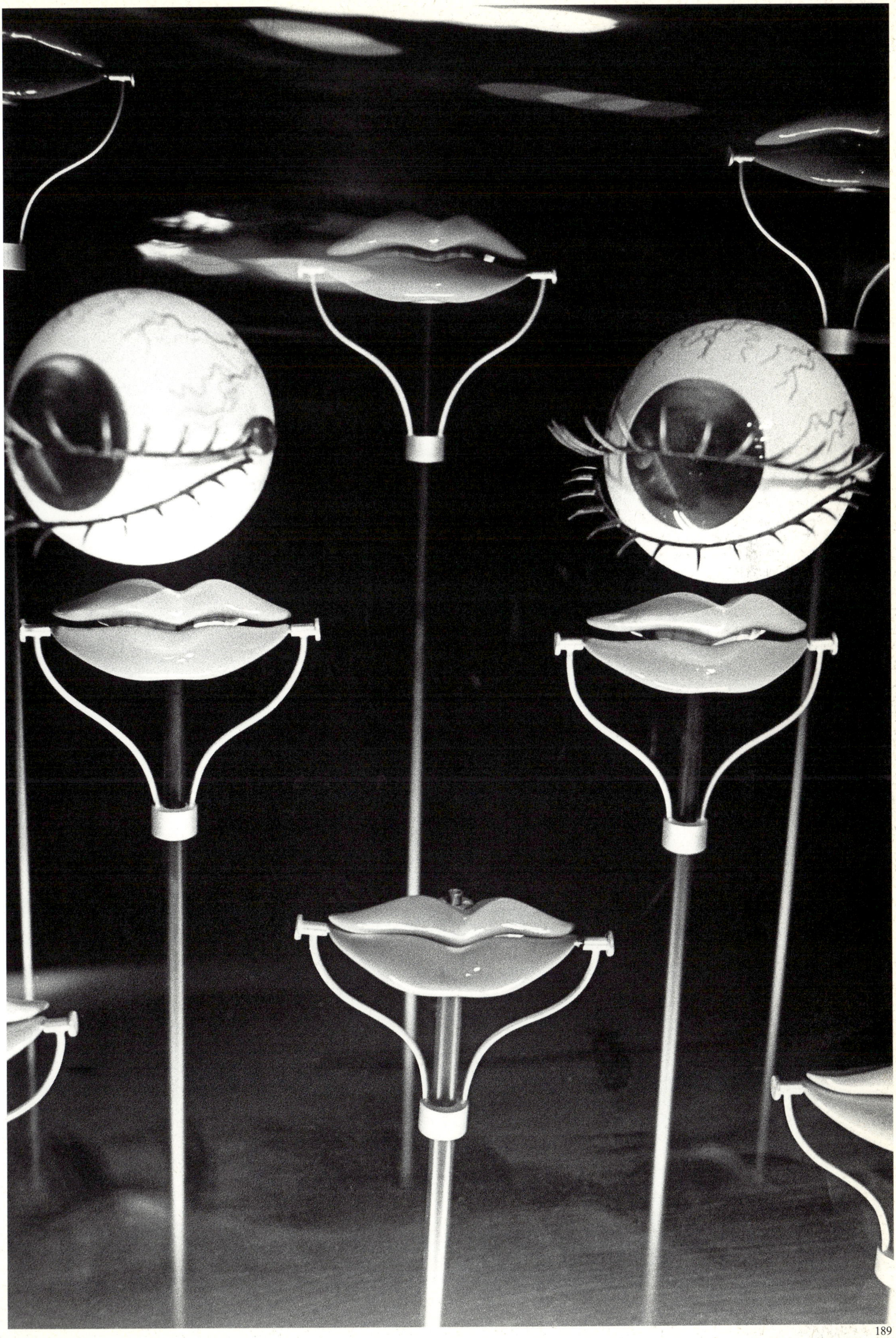

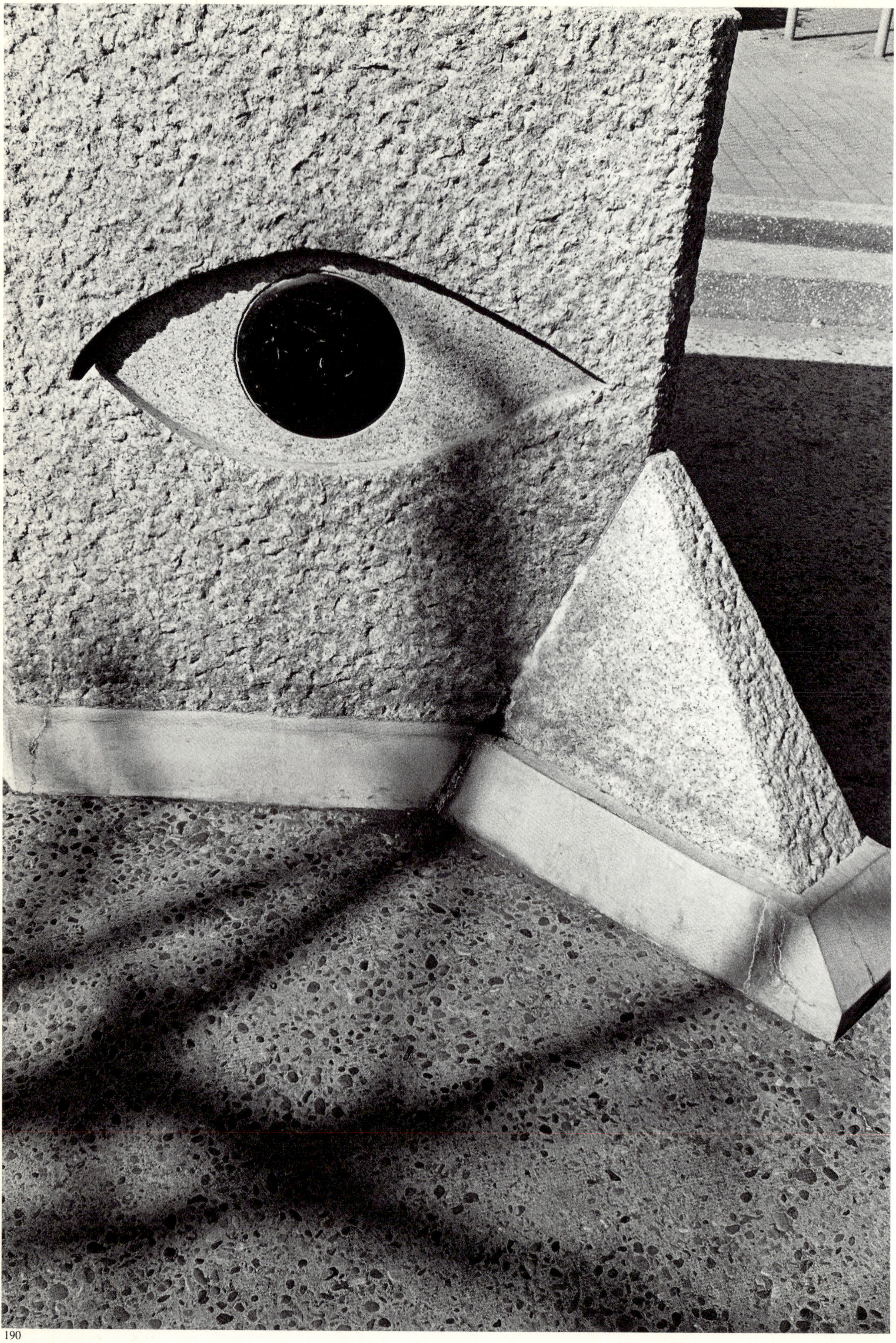

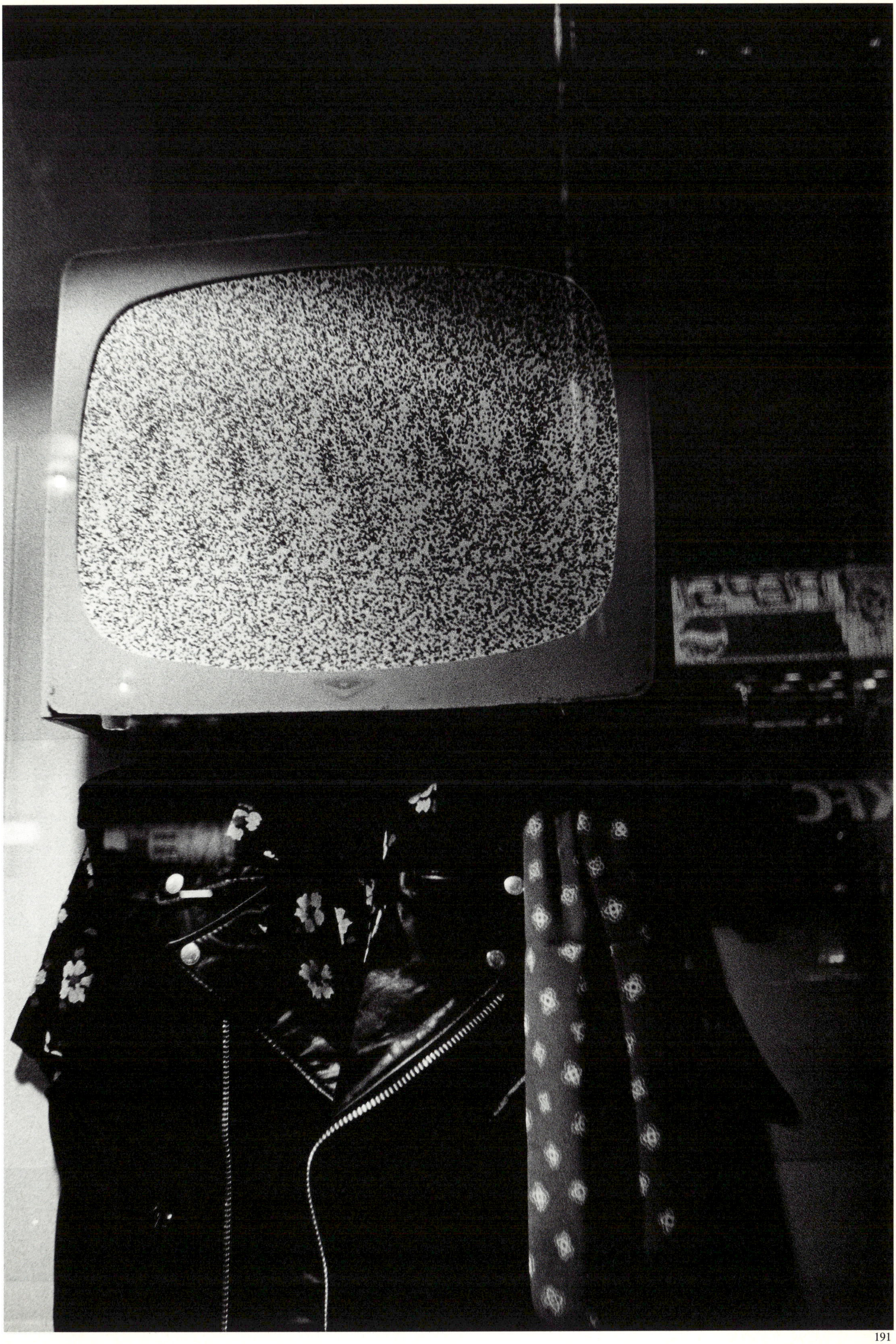

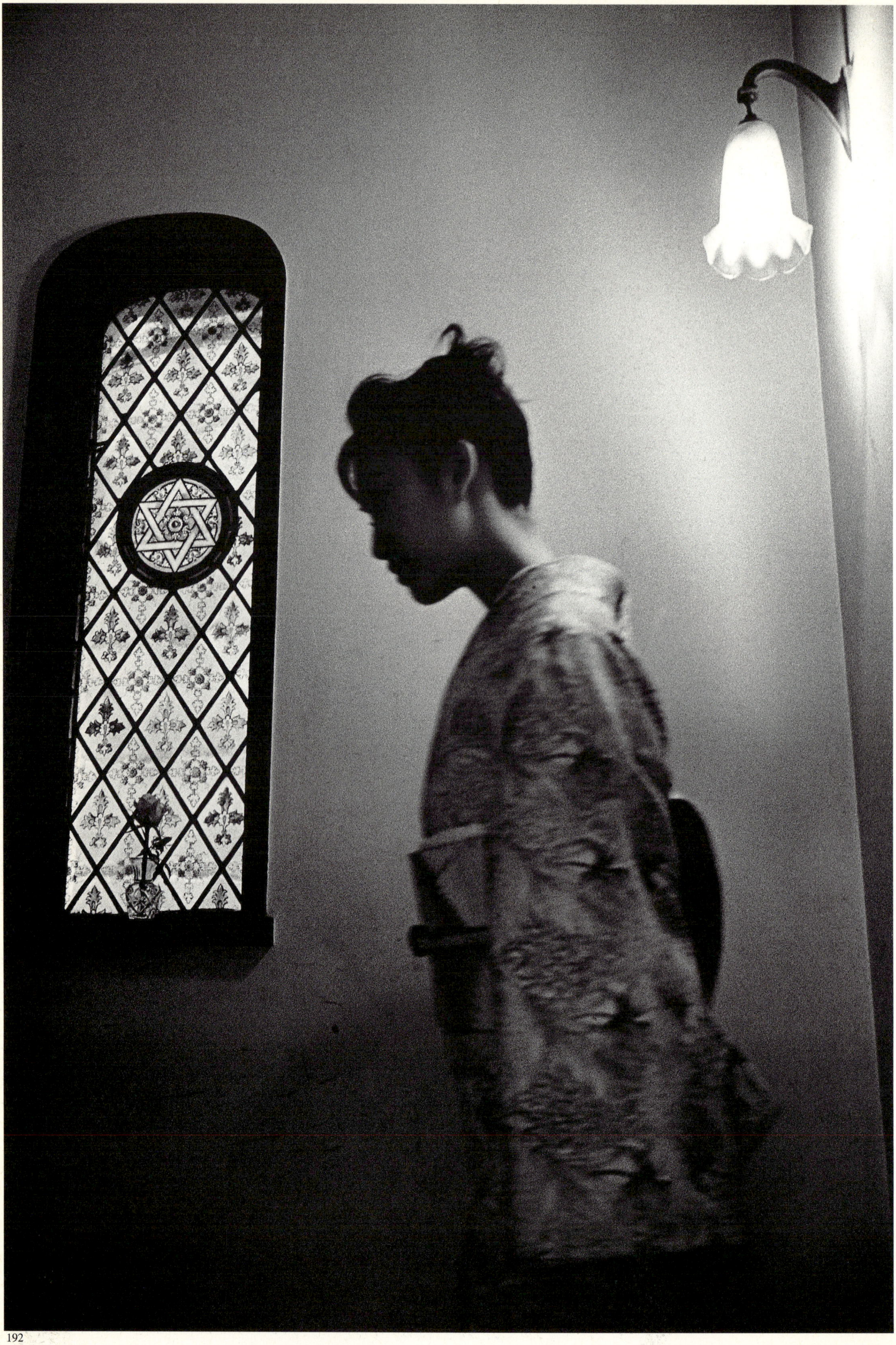

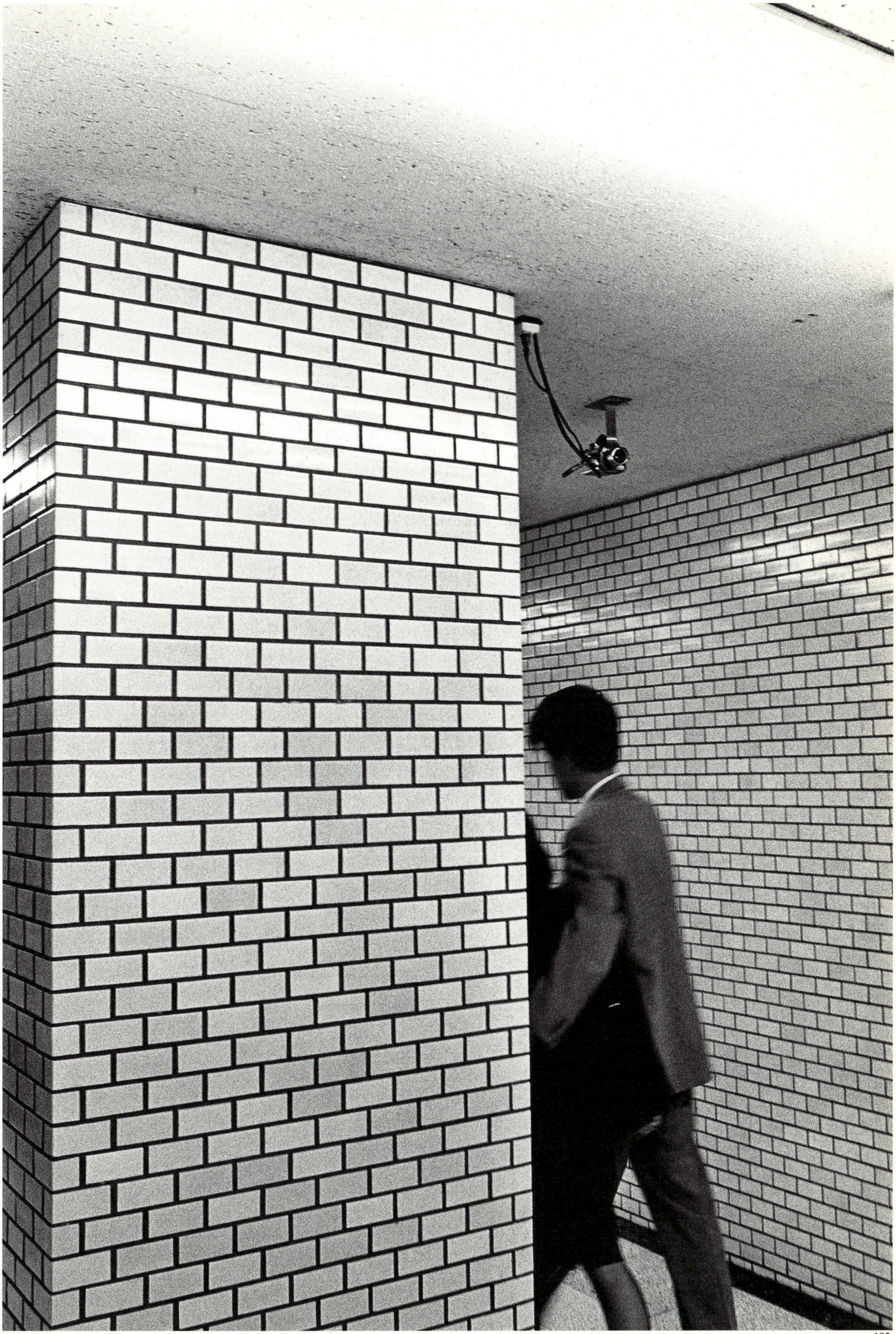

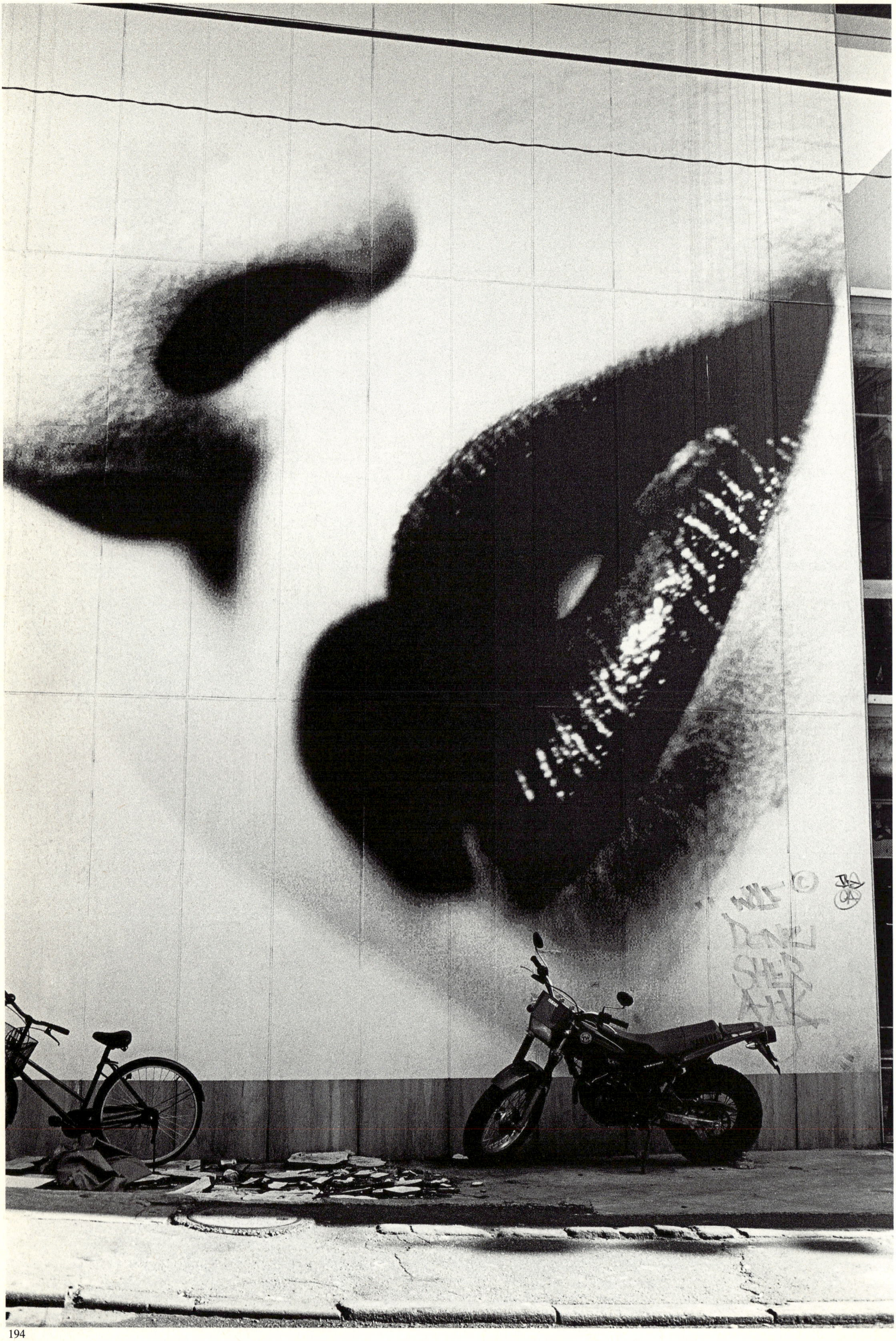

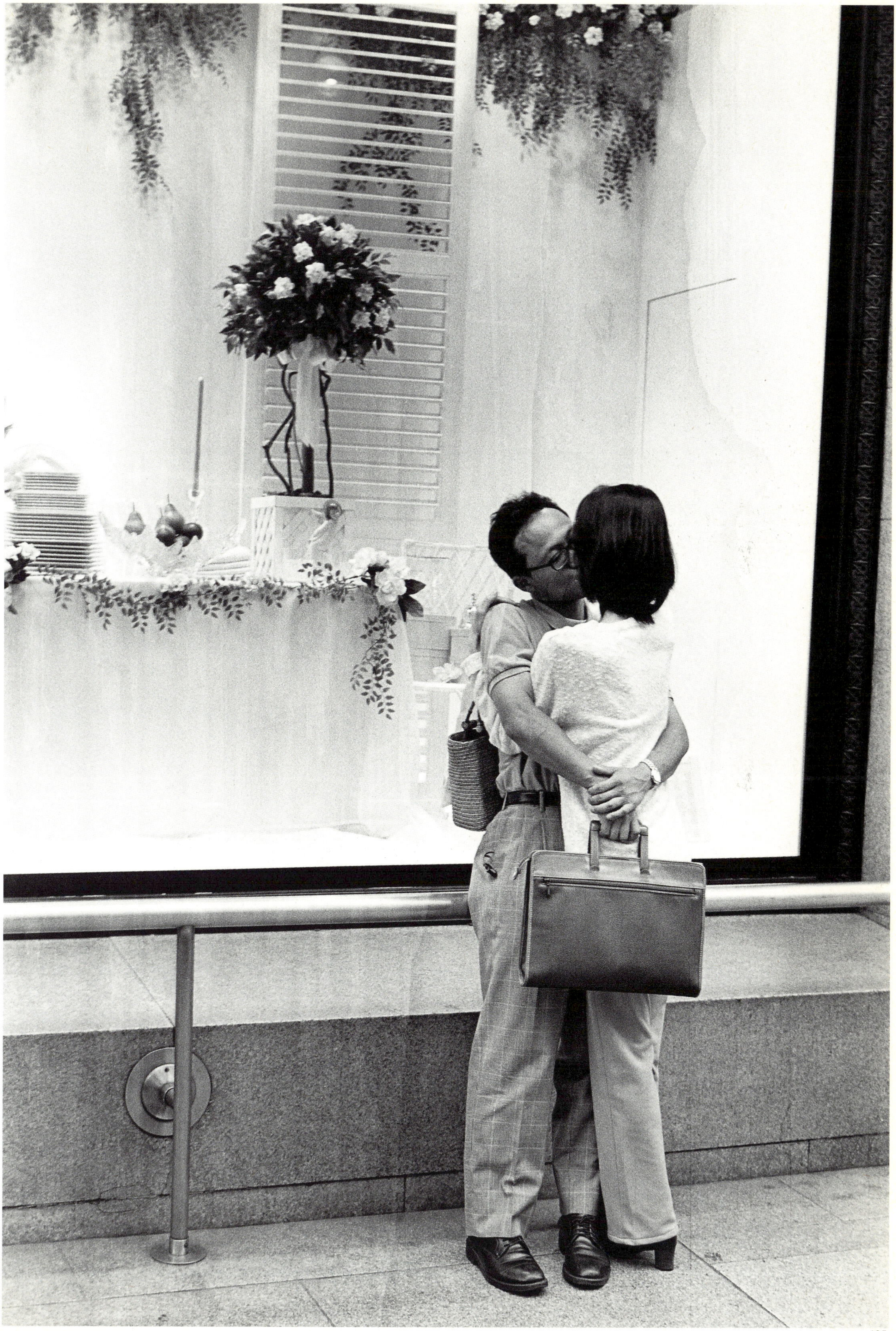

196

197

198

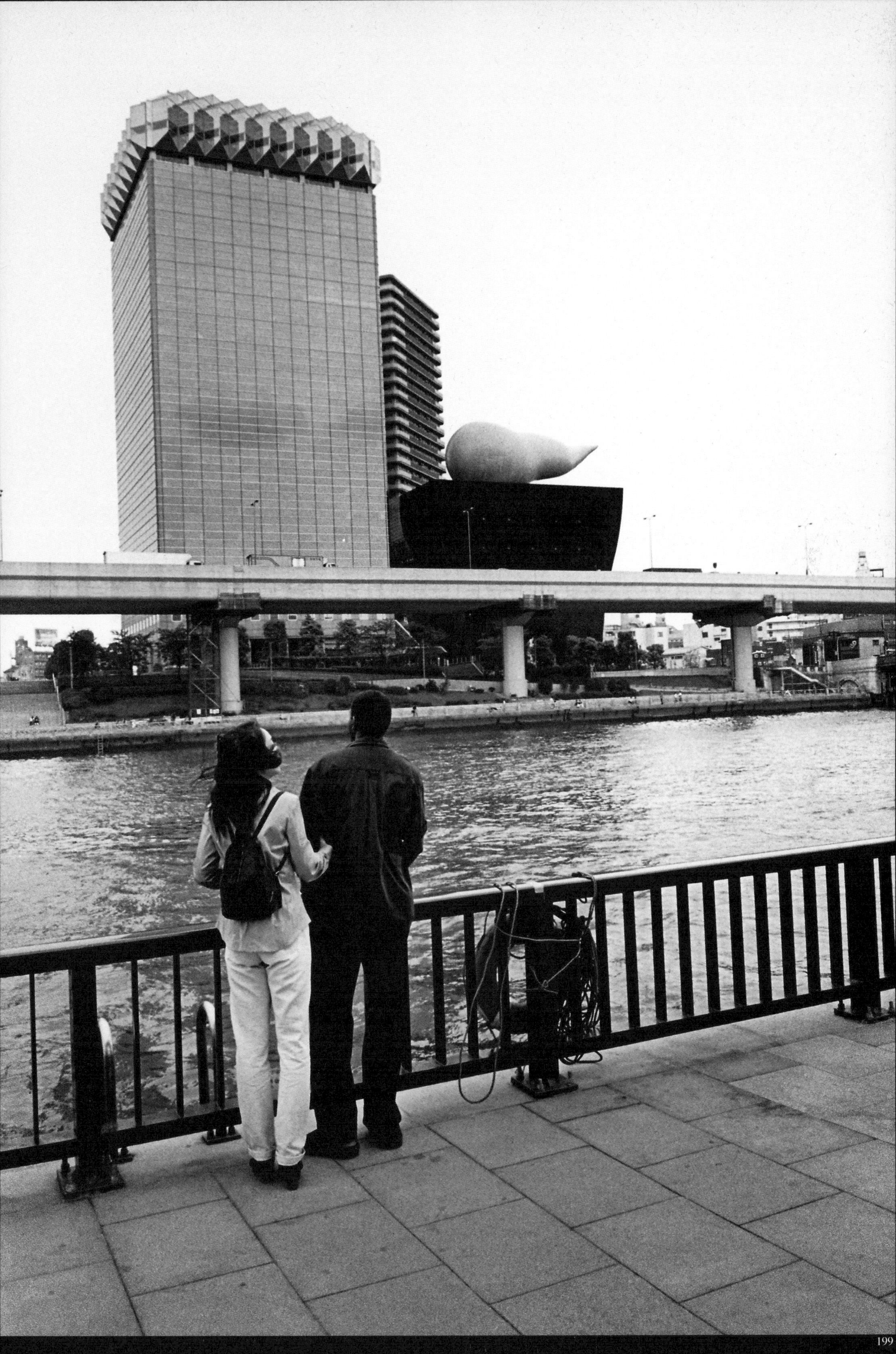

200

201

202

203

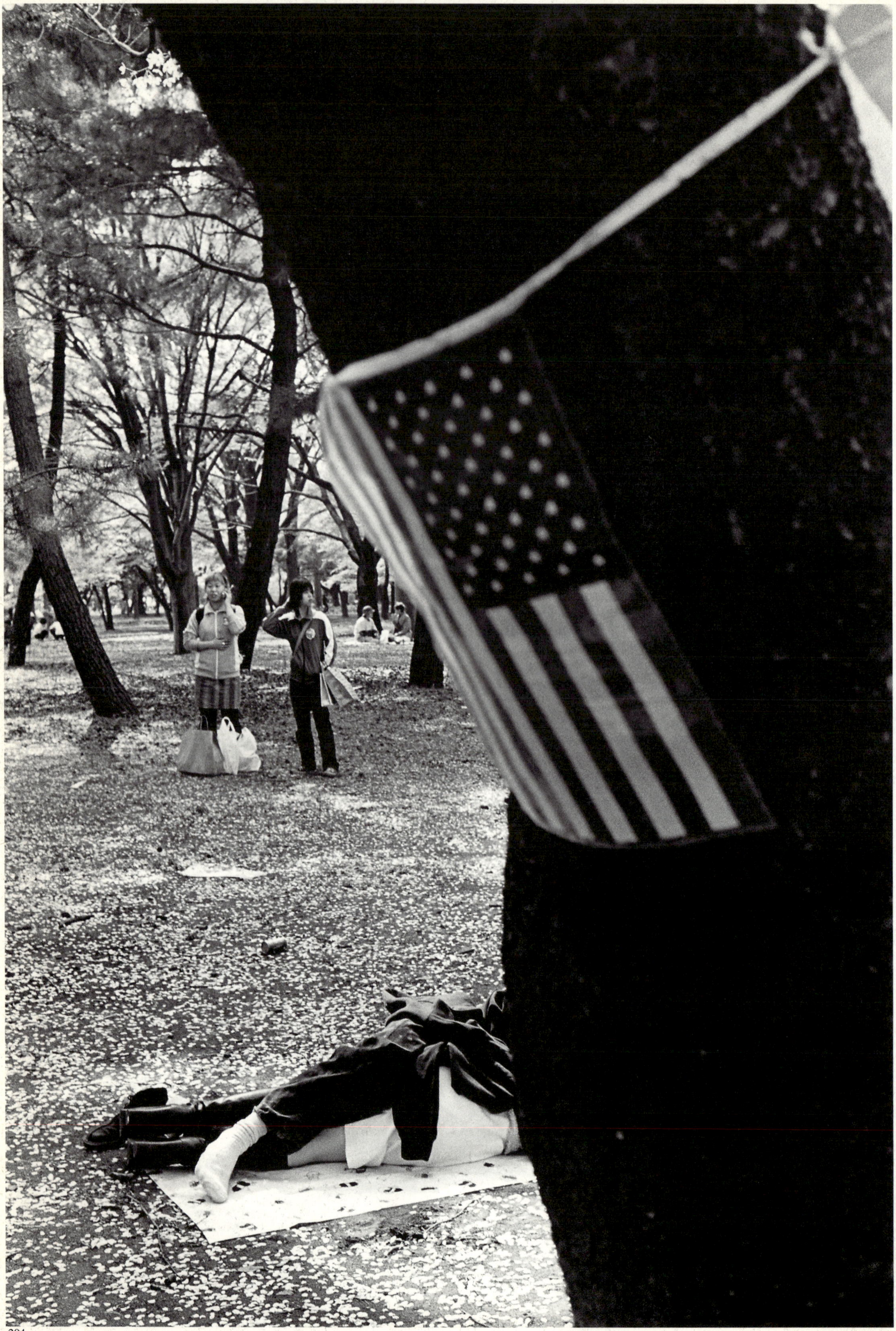

205

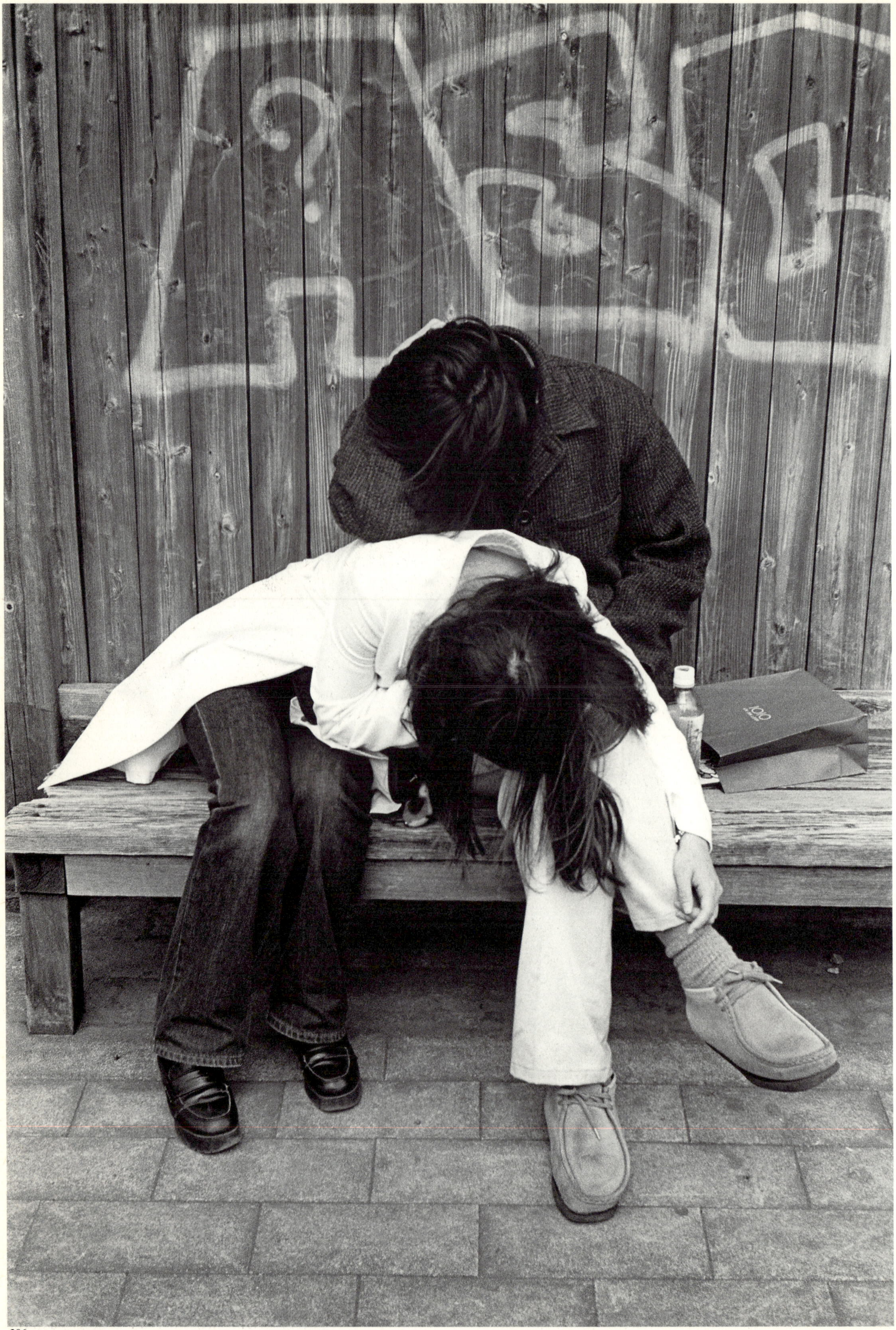

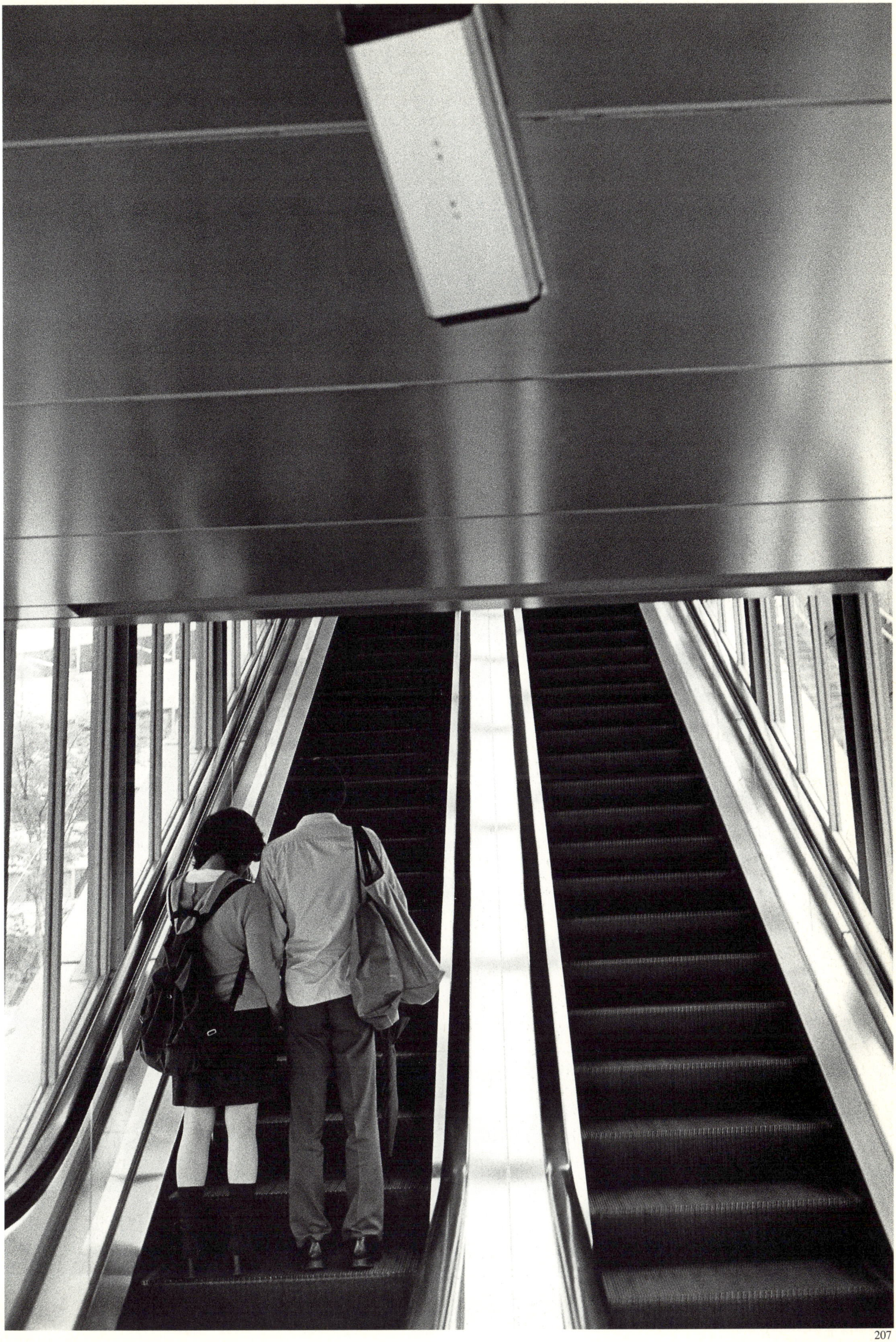

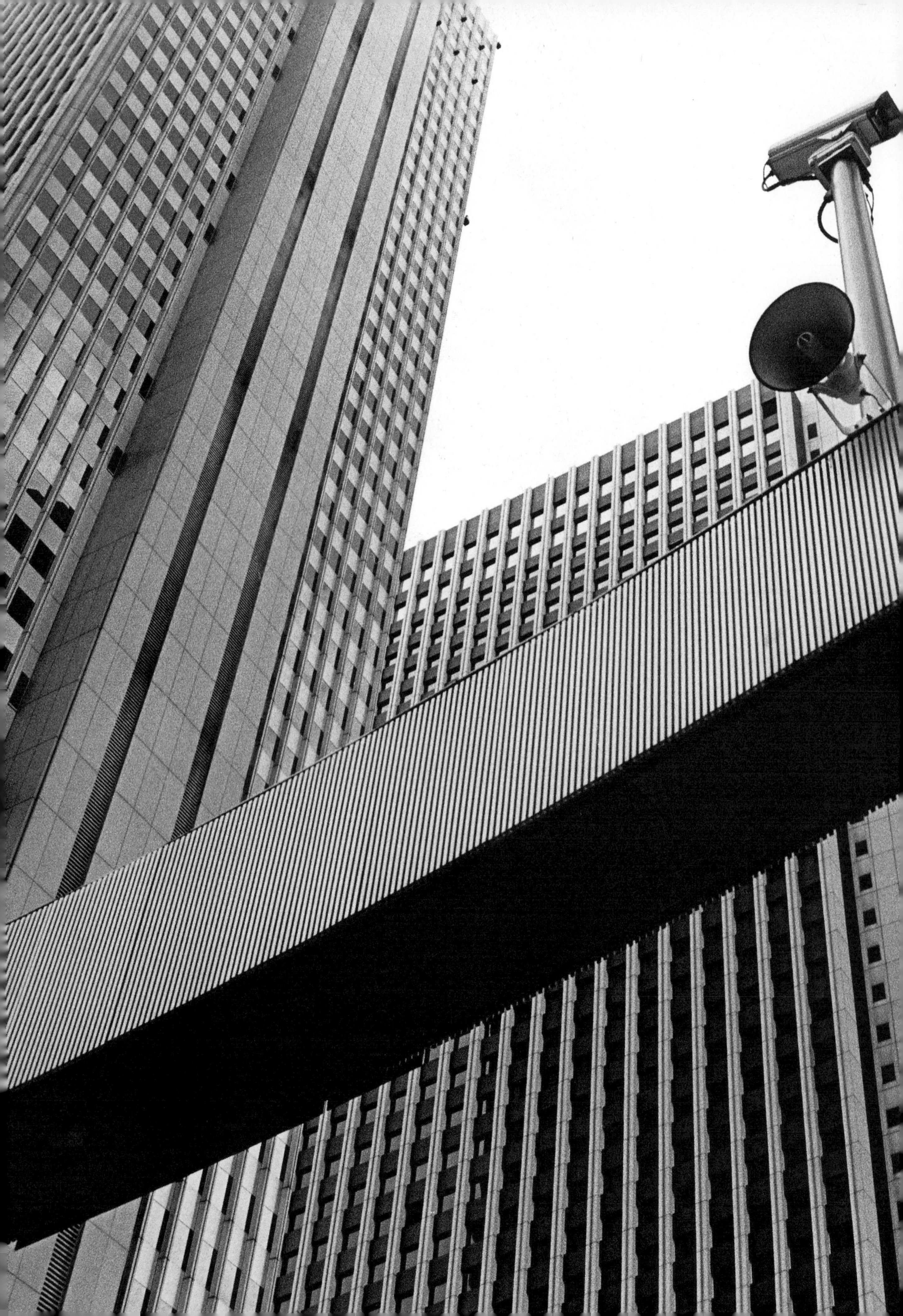

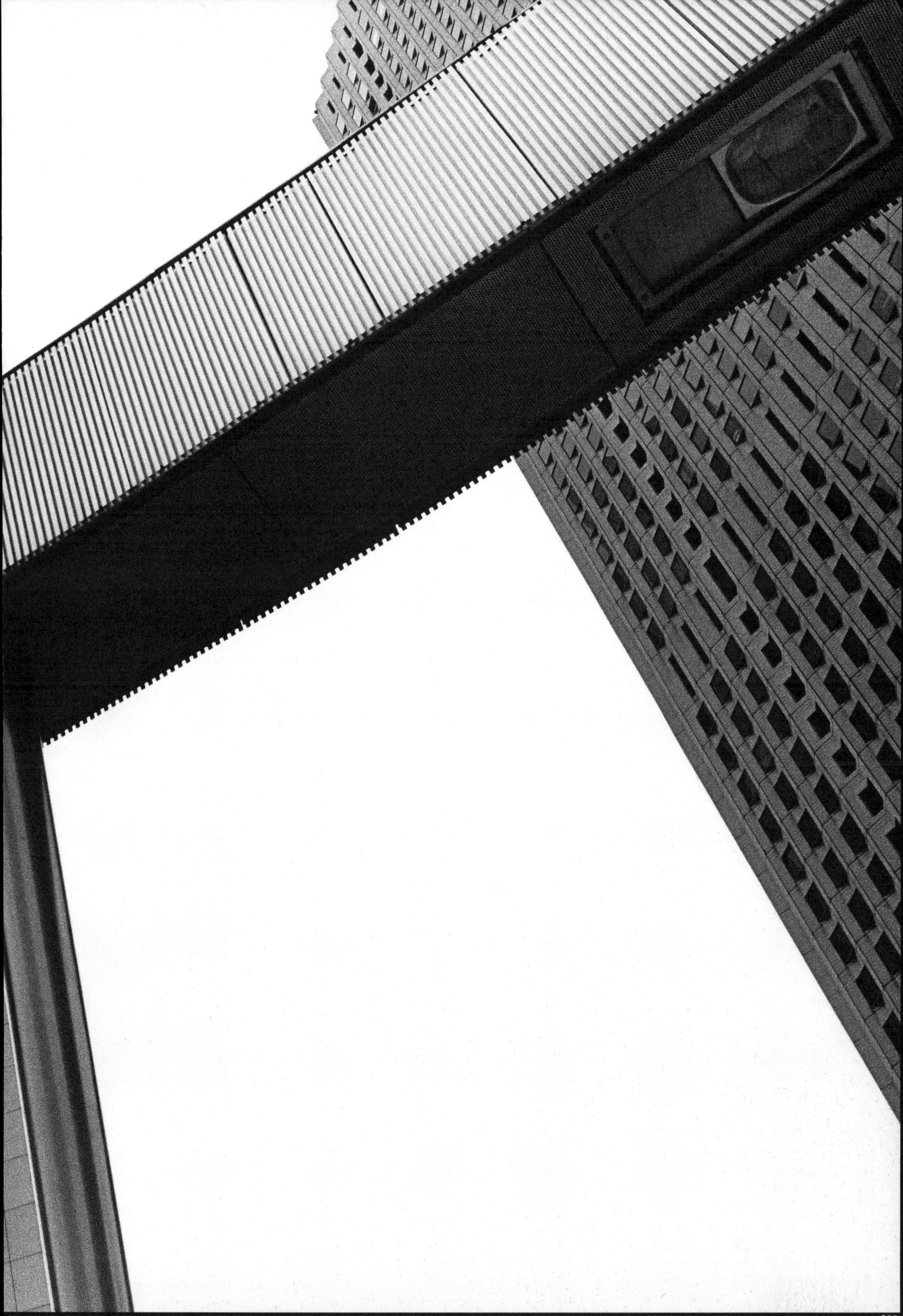

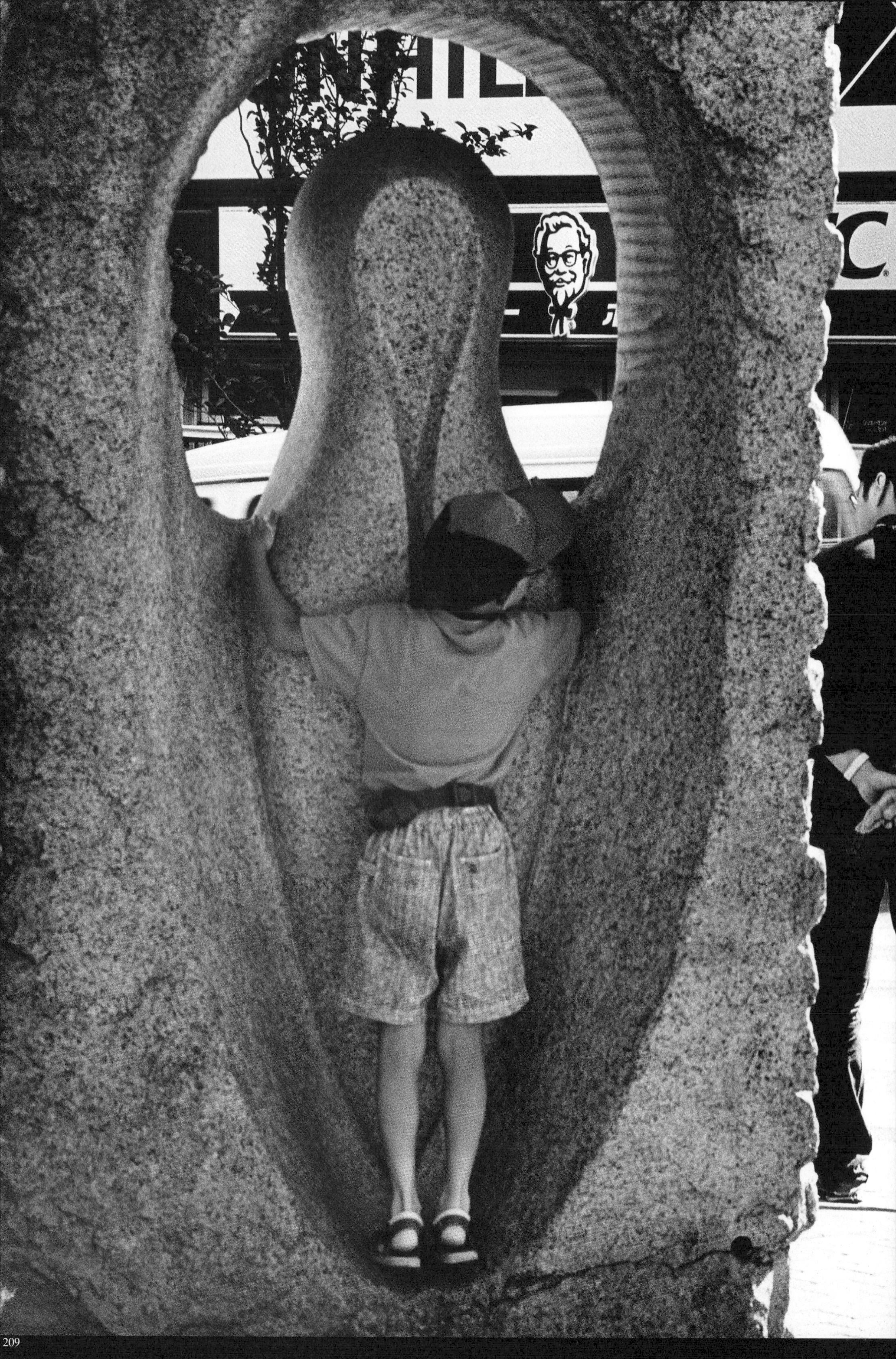

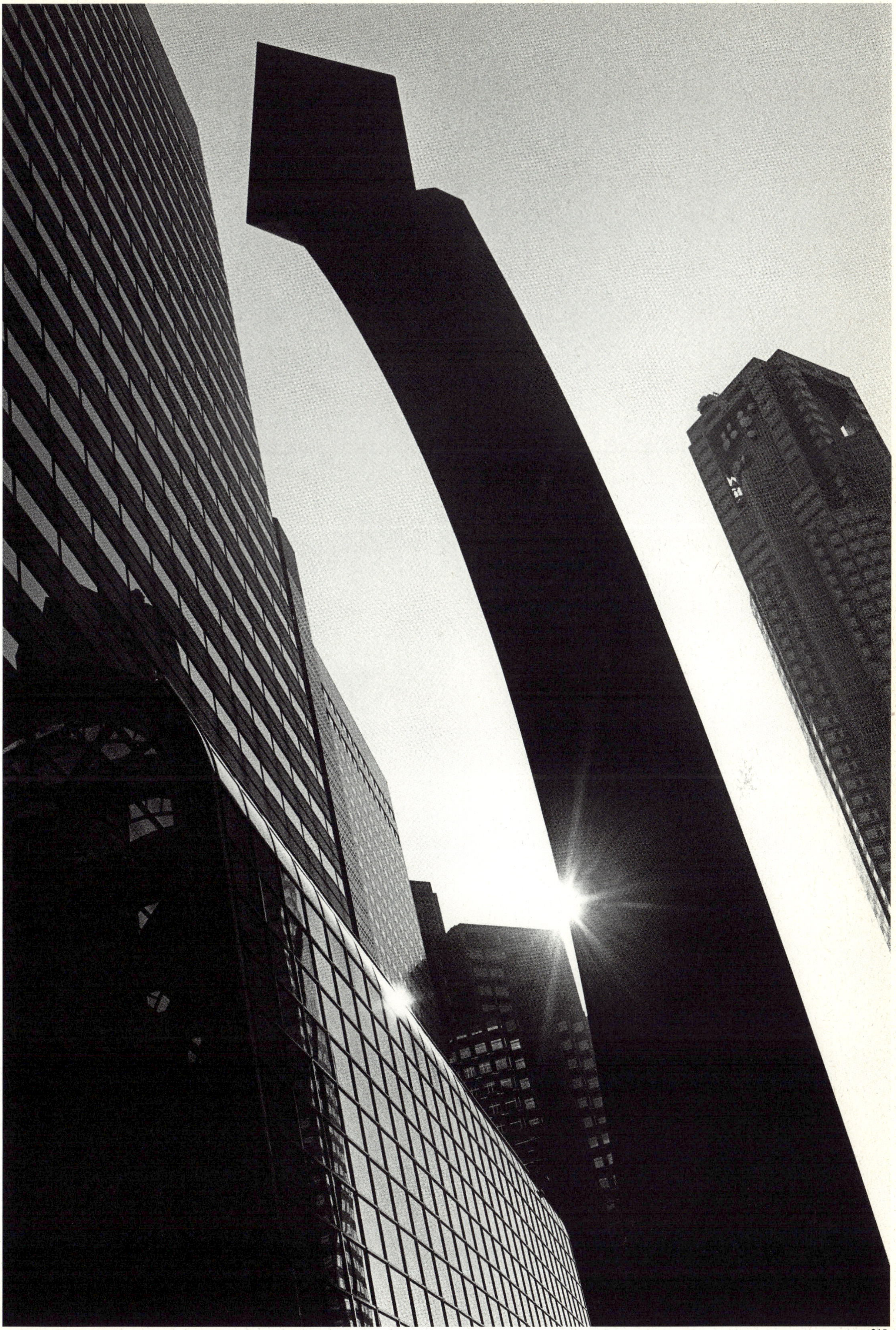

1997 WORLD AIDS DAY

212

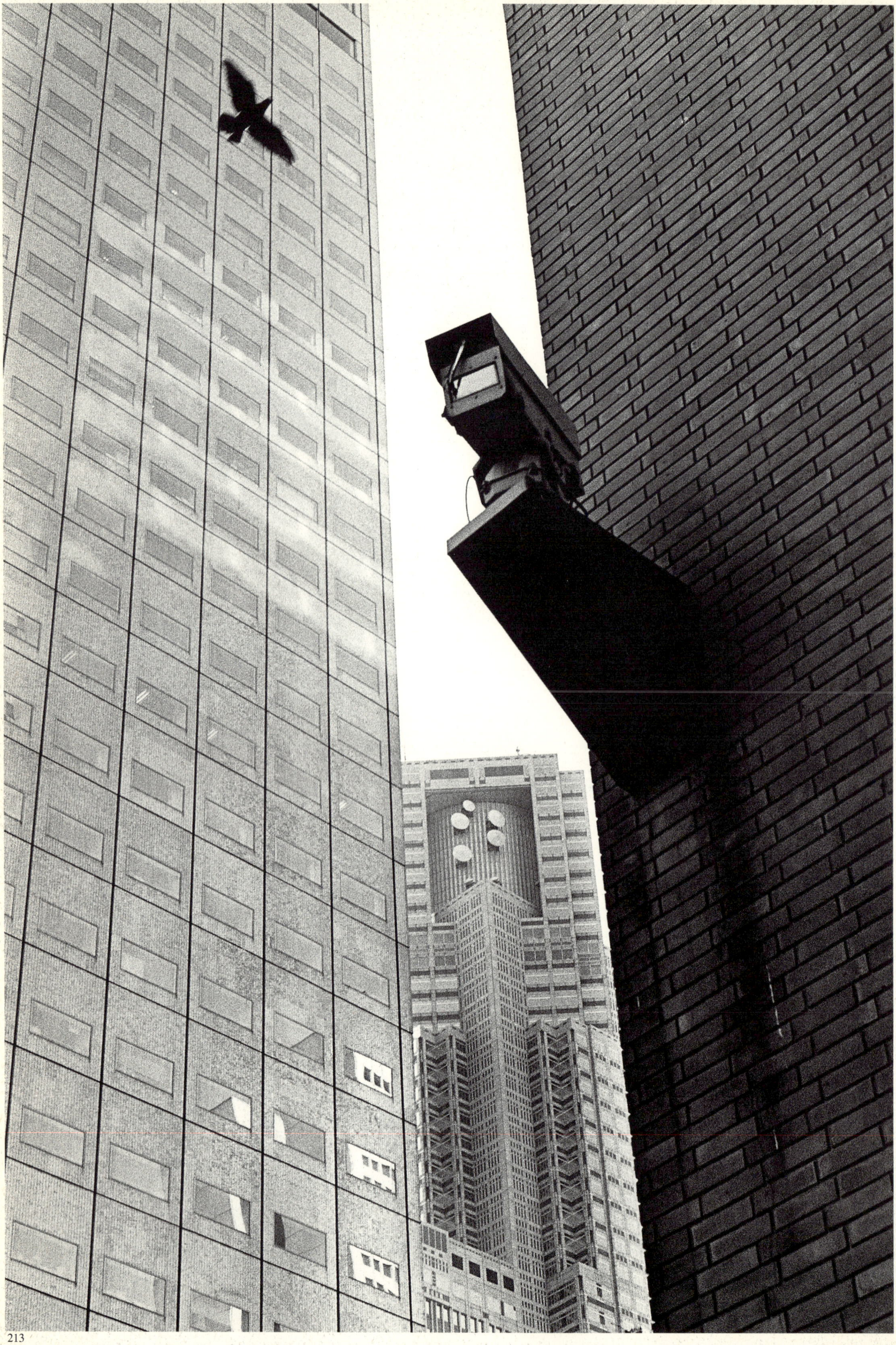

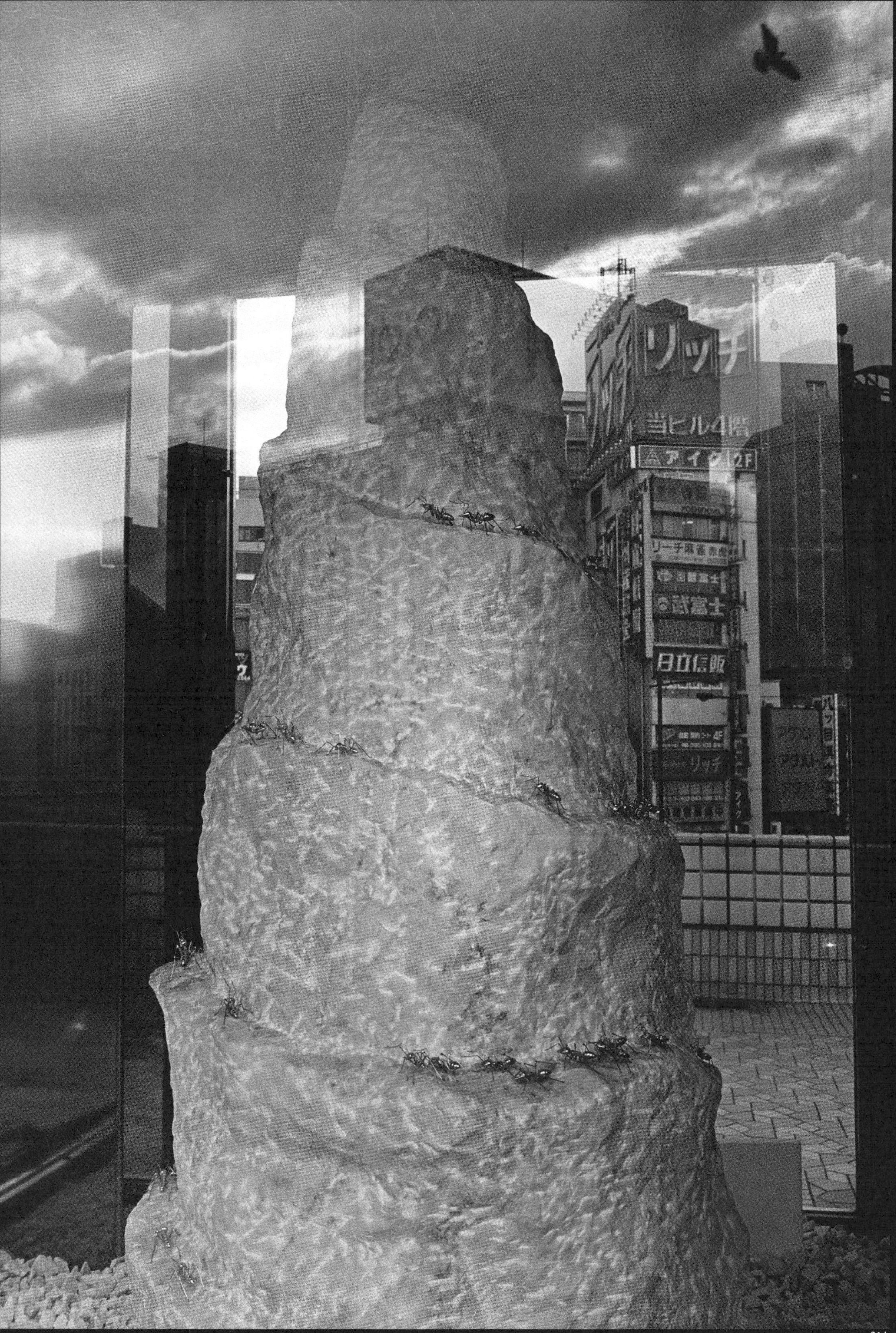
リッチ
当ビル4階
アイク
2F
武富士
日立信販

215

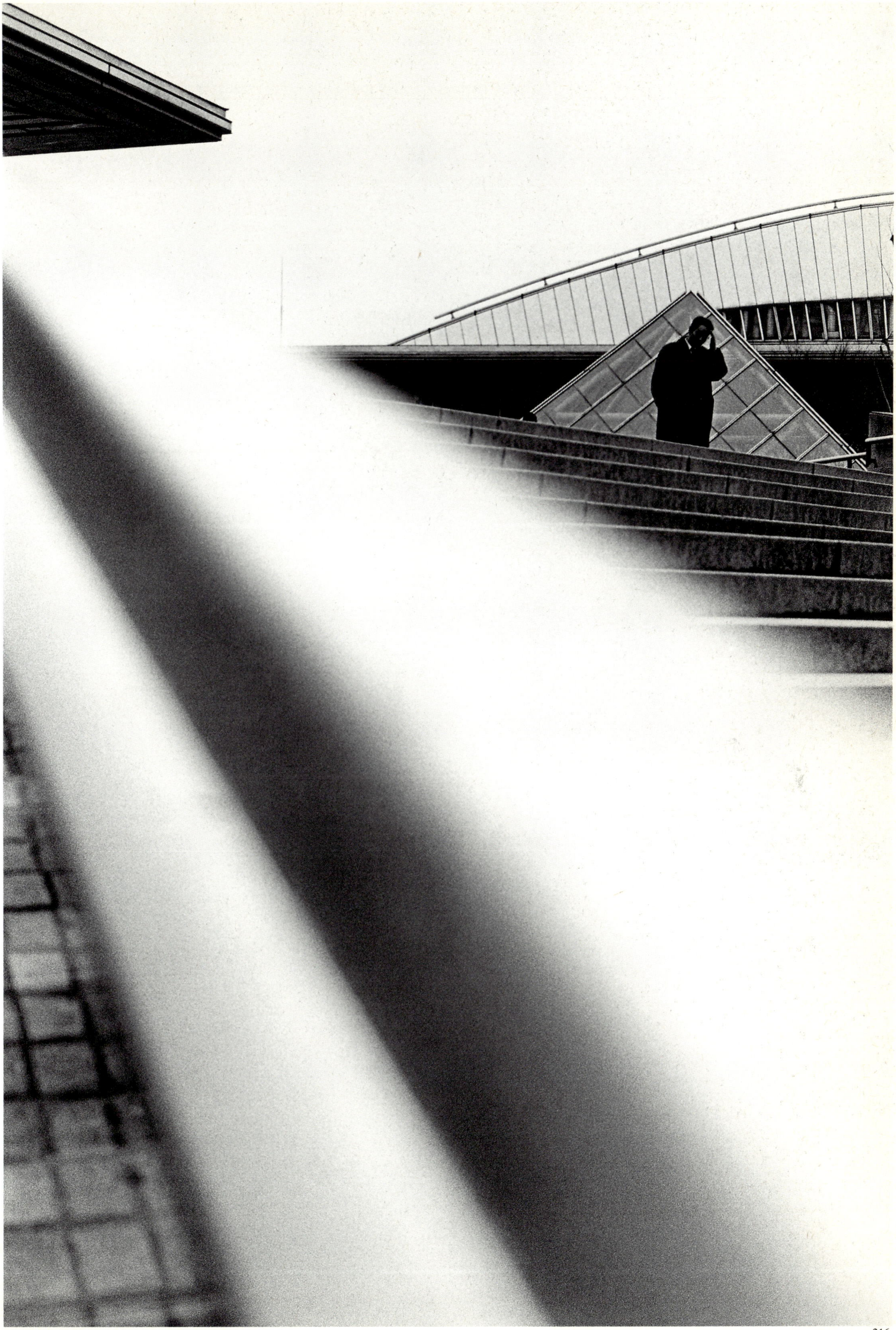

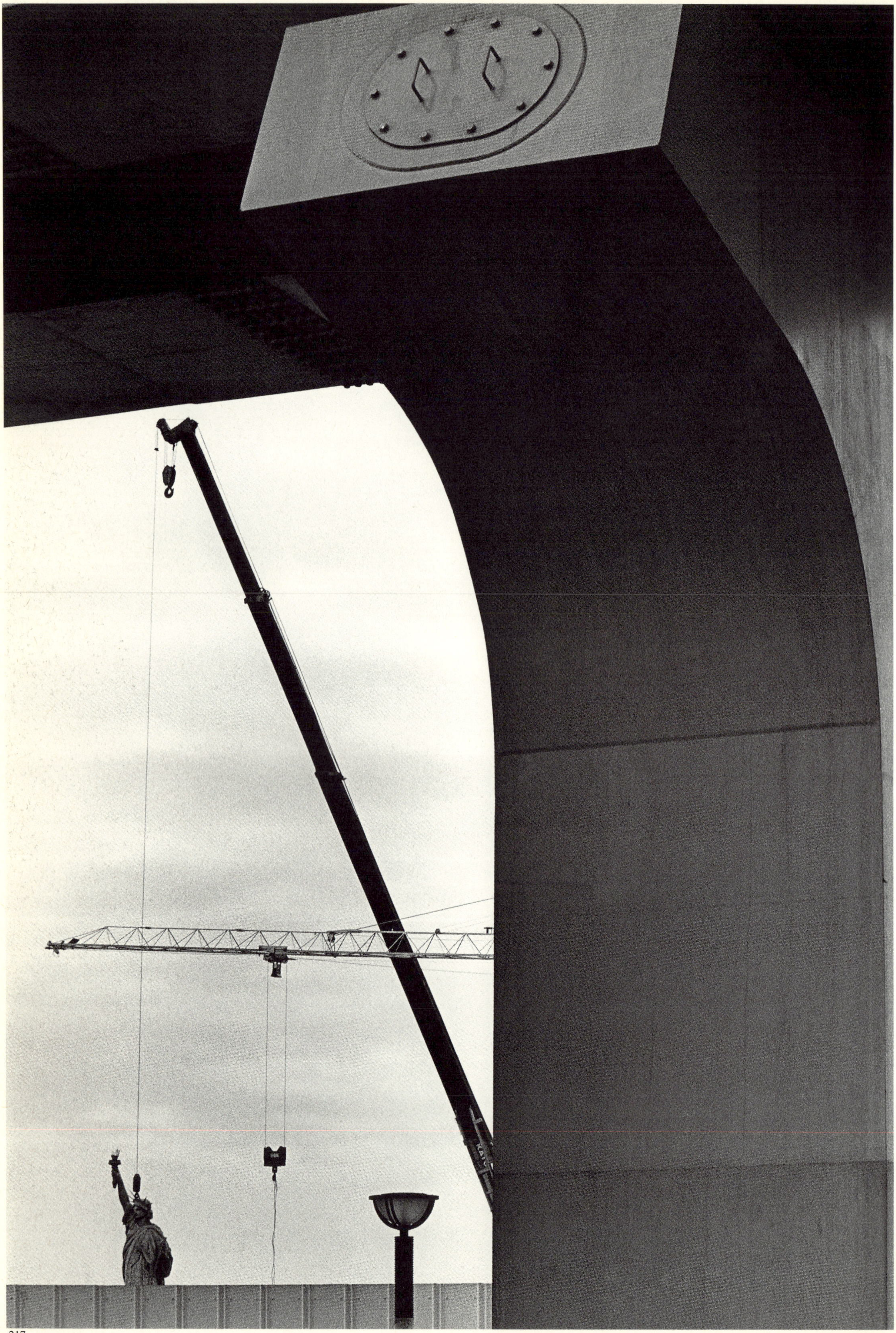

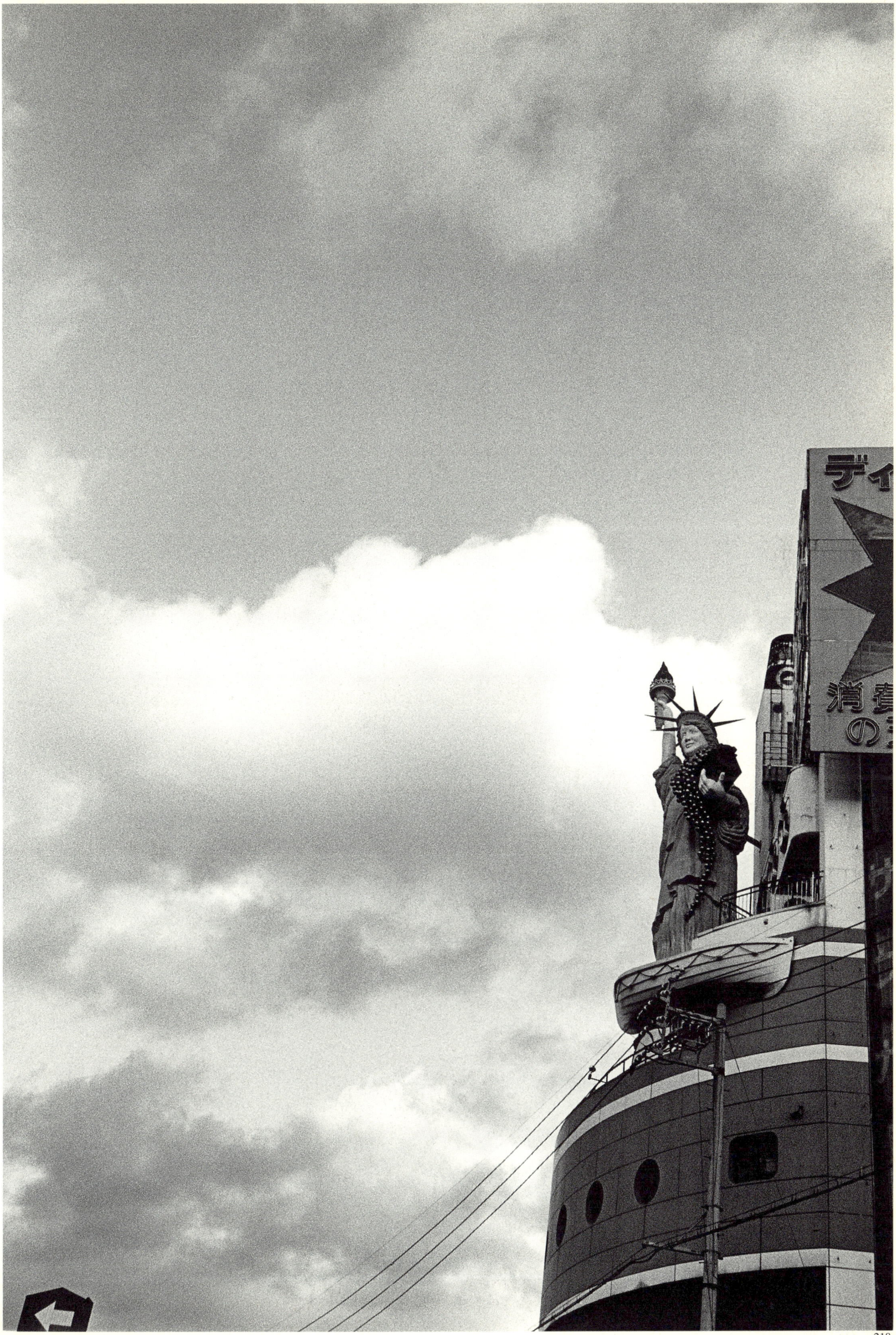

219

220

221

222

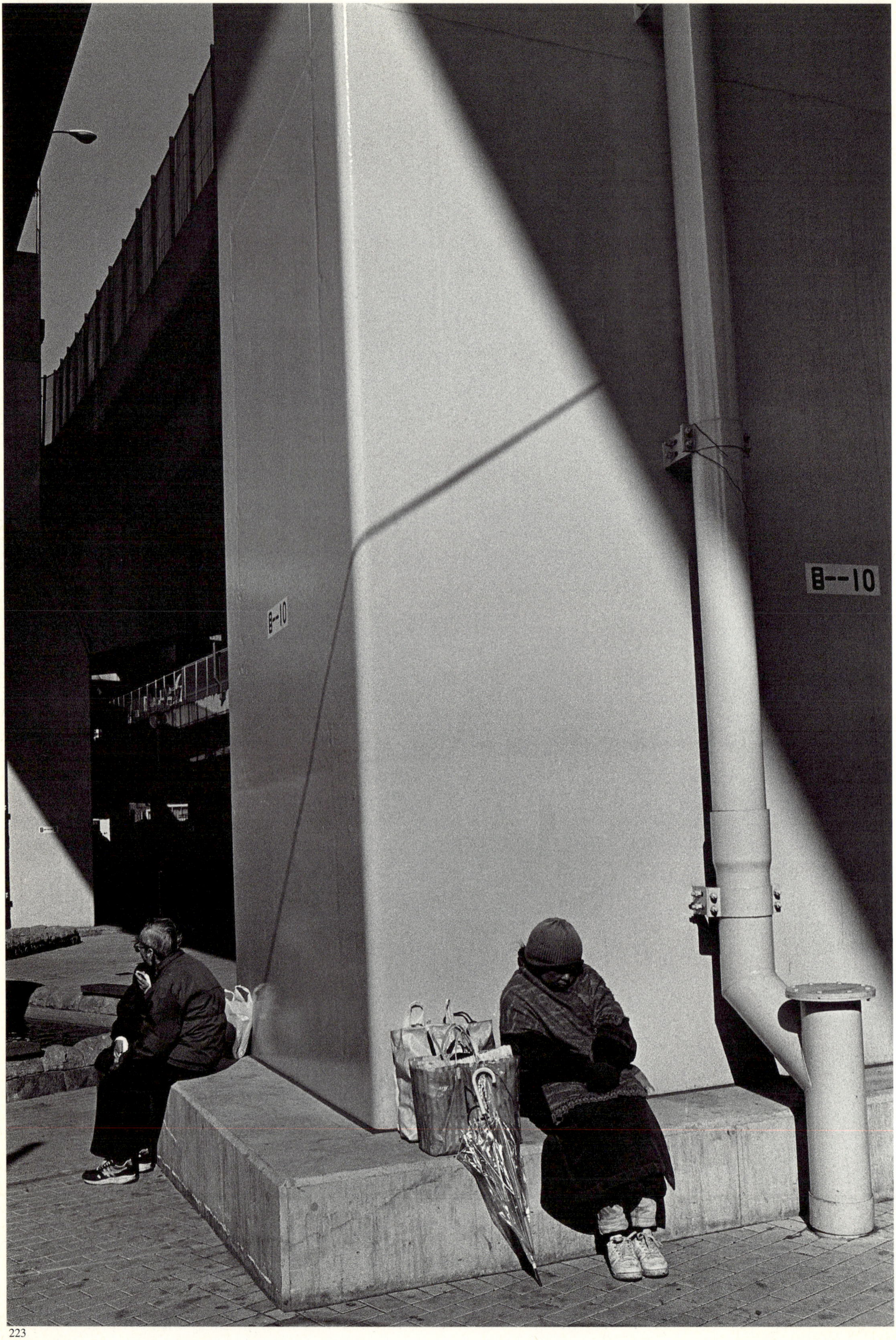
目--10

Half Time
BOMBAY
SAPPHIRE
DRY GIN
Budweiser
SMIRNOFF
Half Time
Heineken

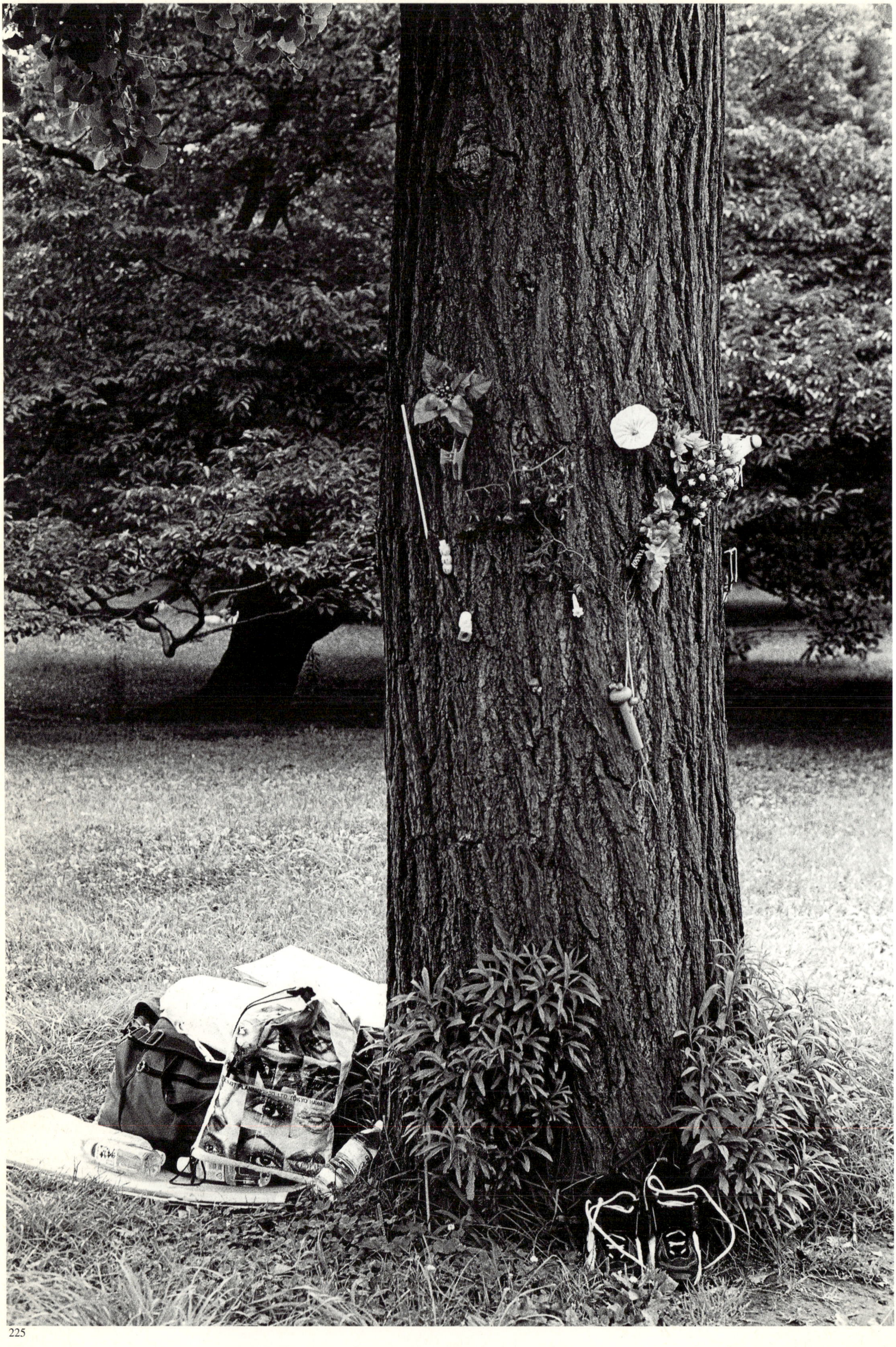

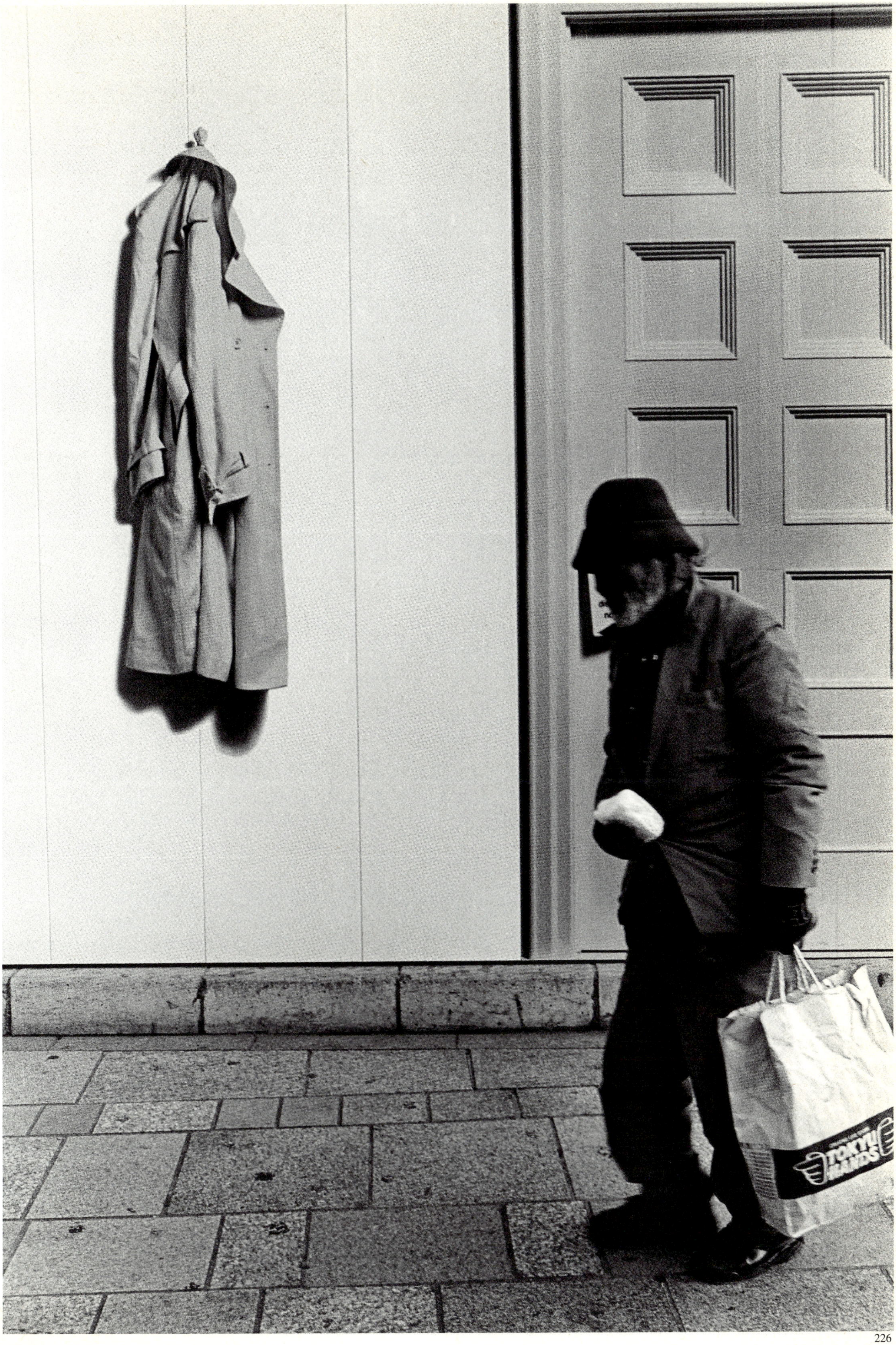
TOKYU
HANDS

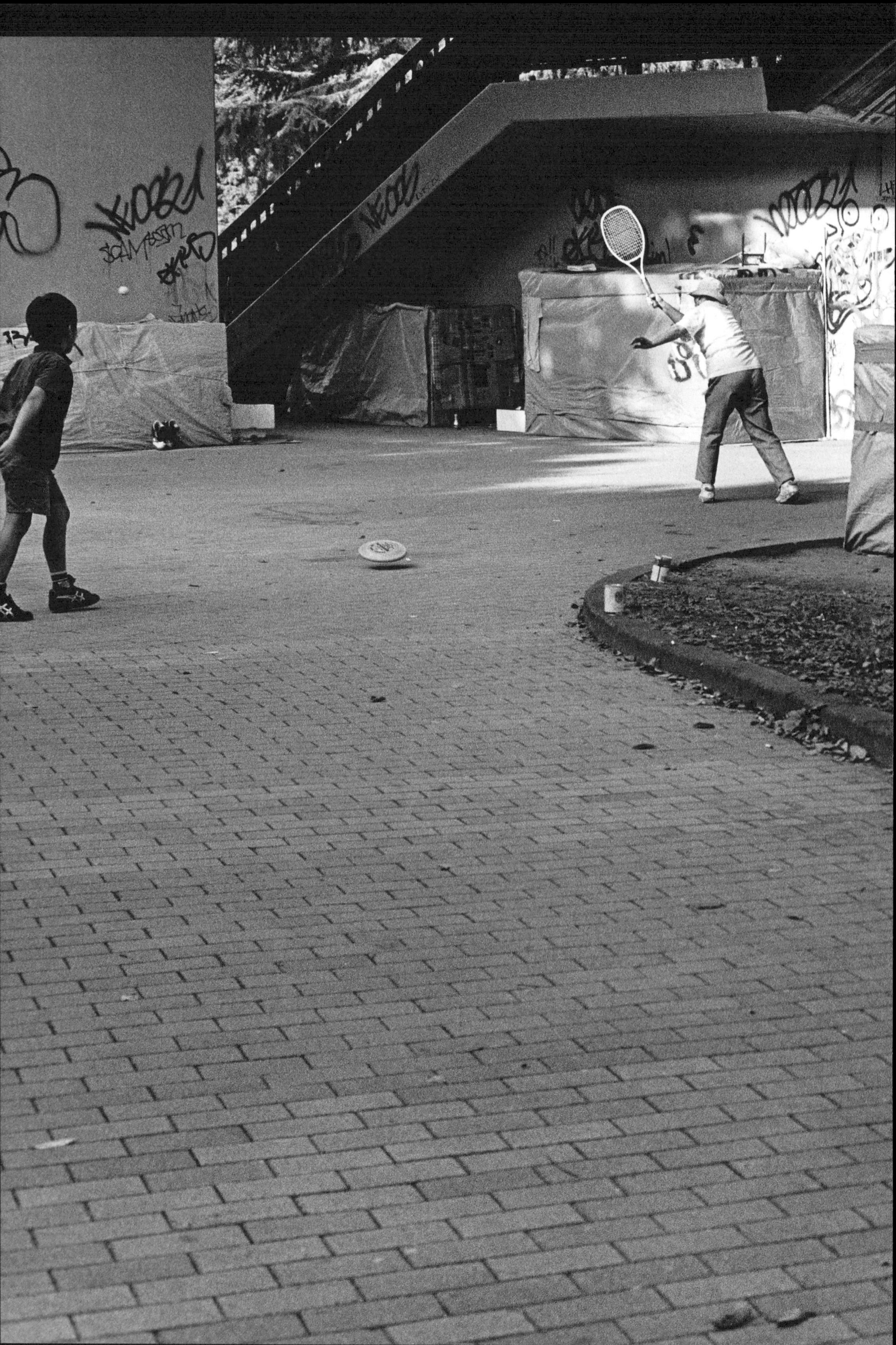

227

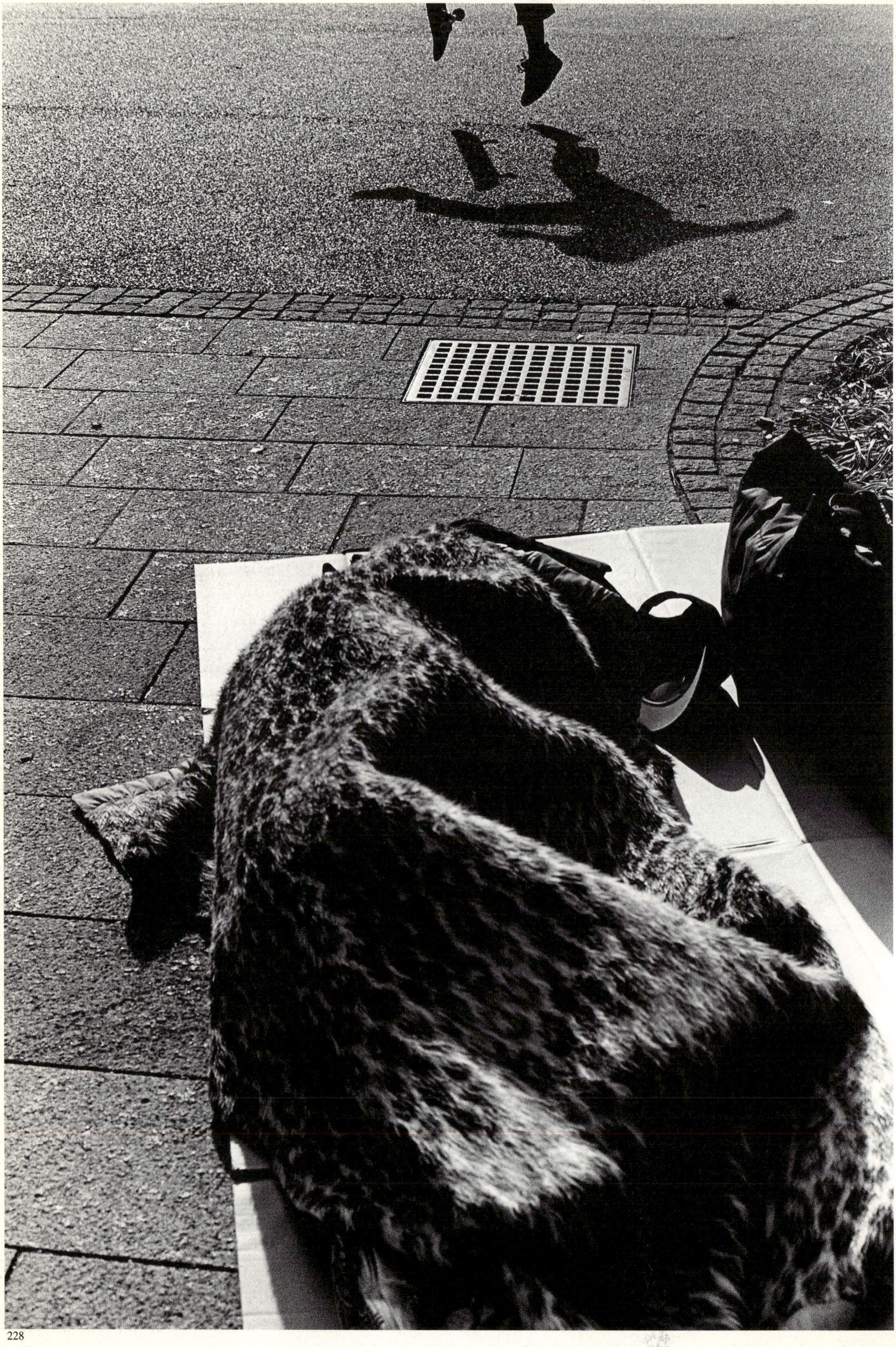

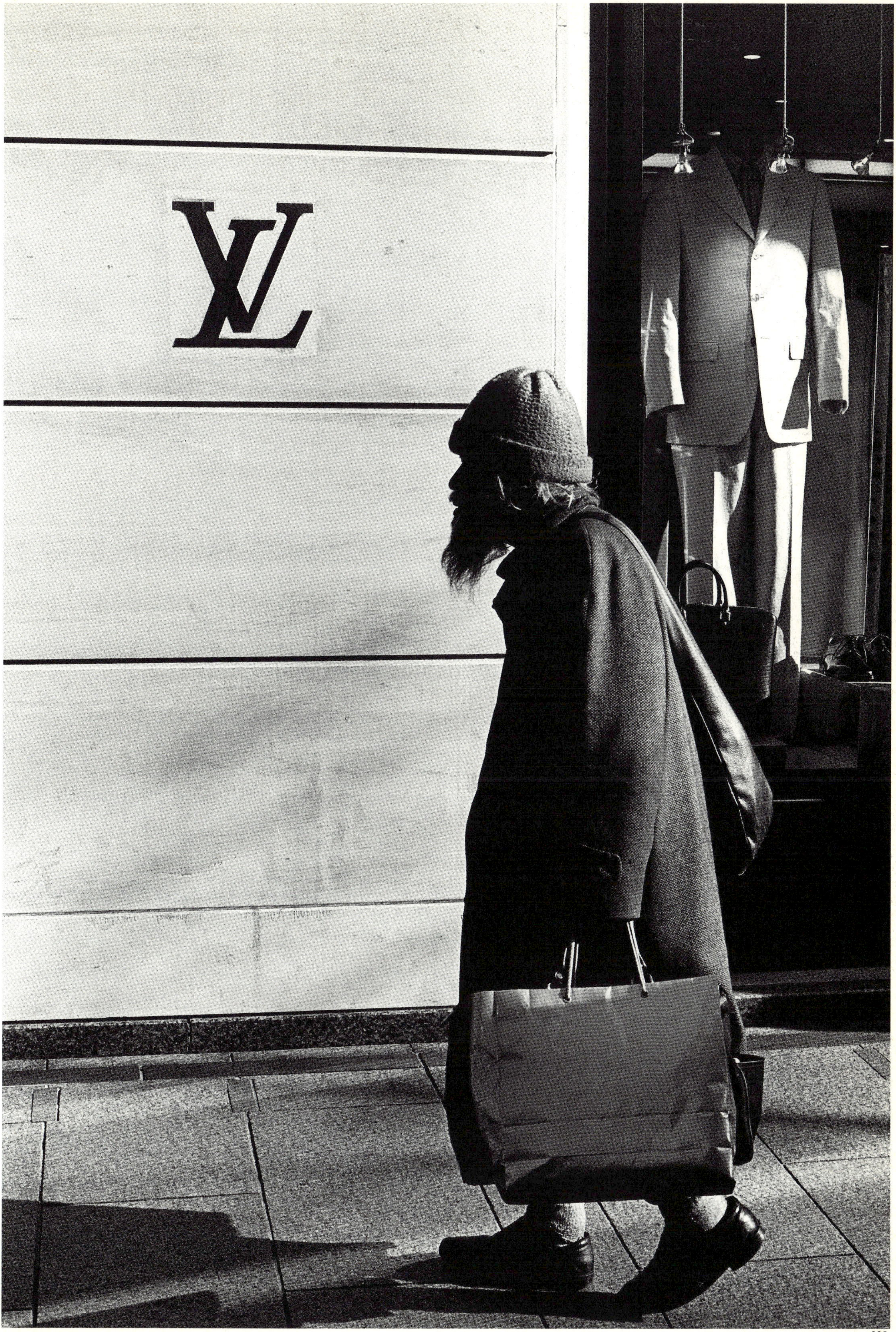

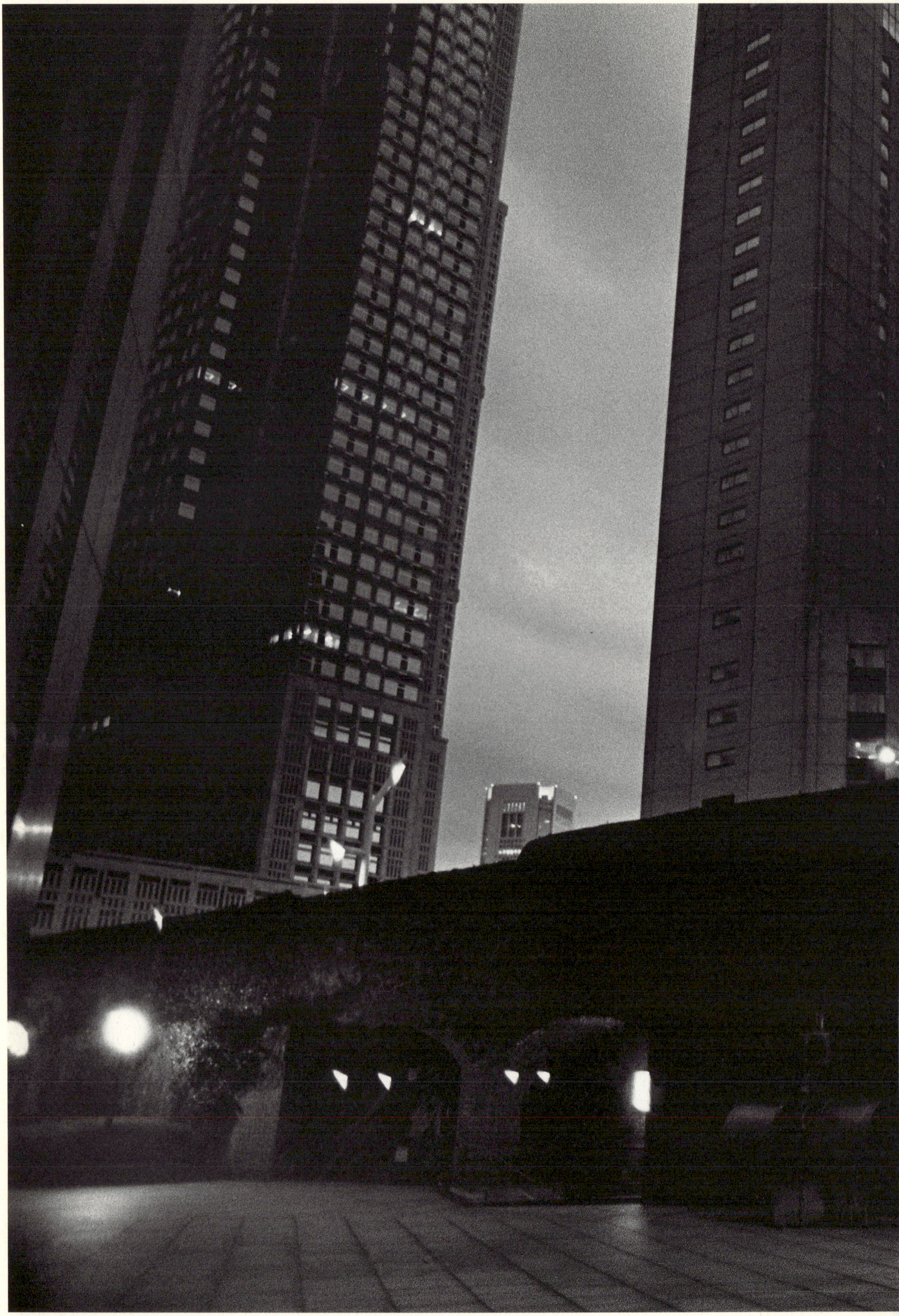

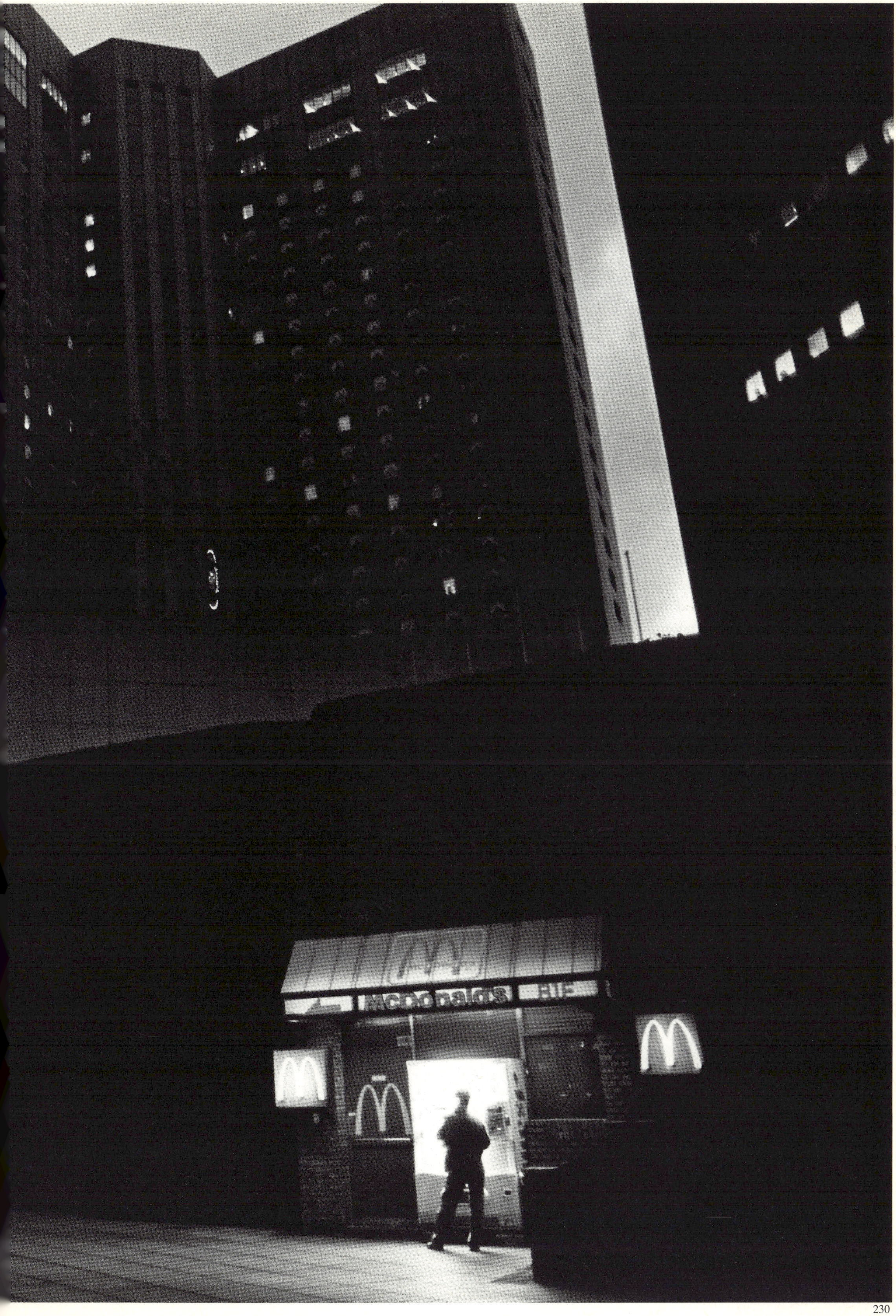
McDonald's
B1F

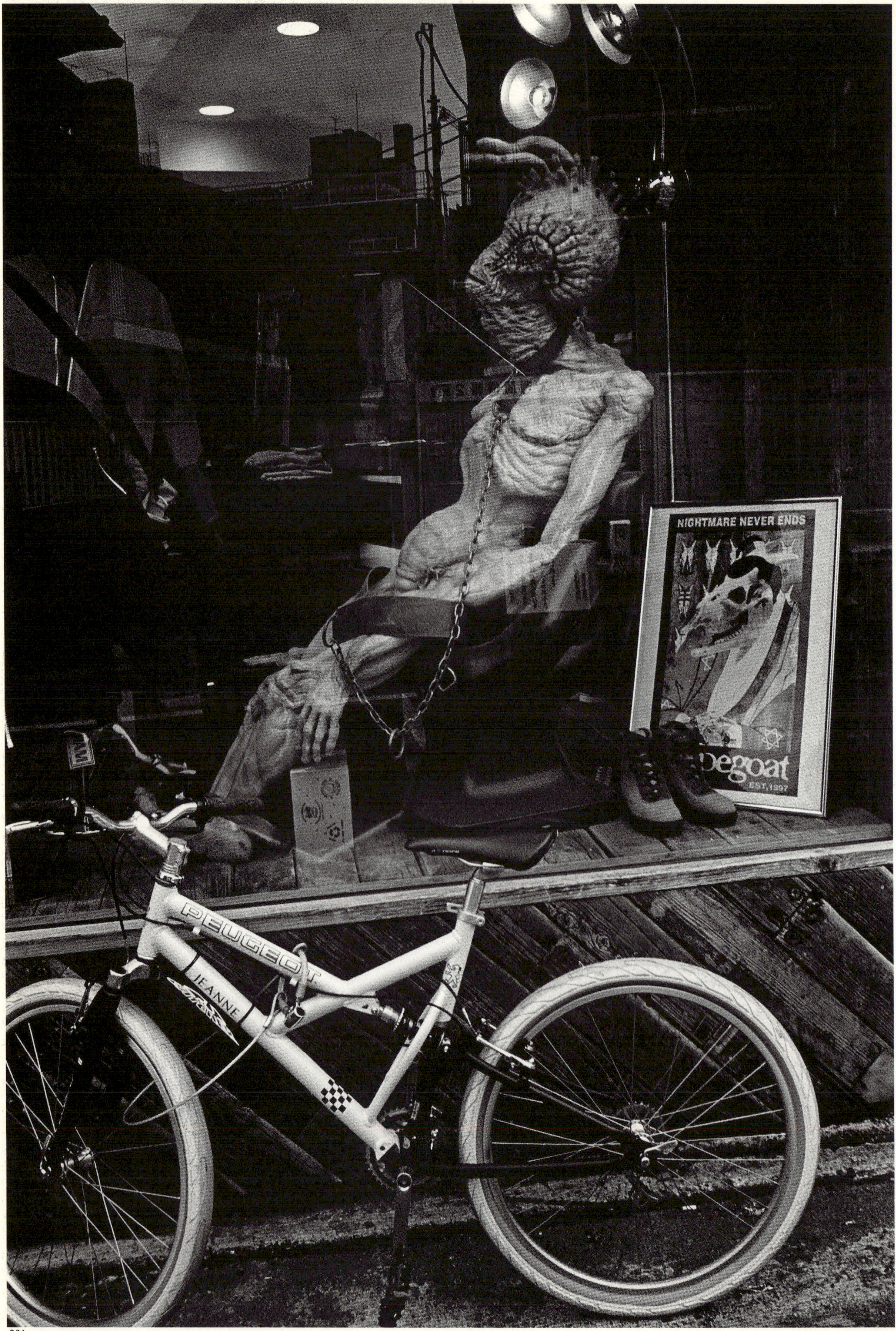
NIGHTMARE NEVER ENDS
pegoat
EST.1997
PEUGEOT
JEANNE

232

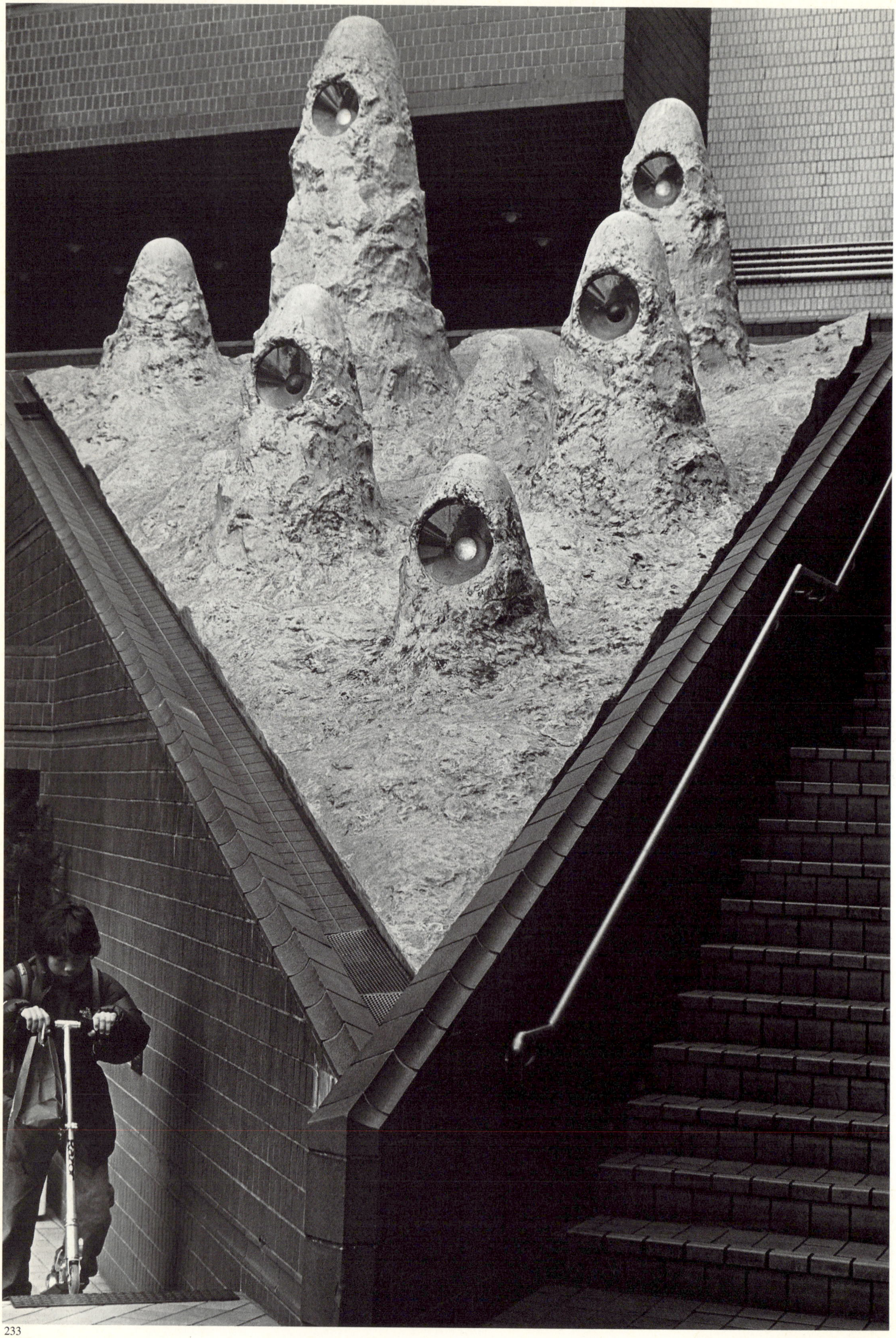

234

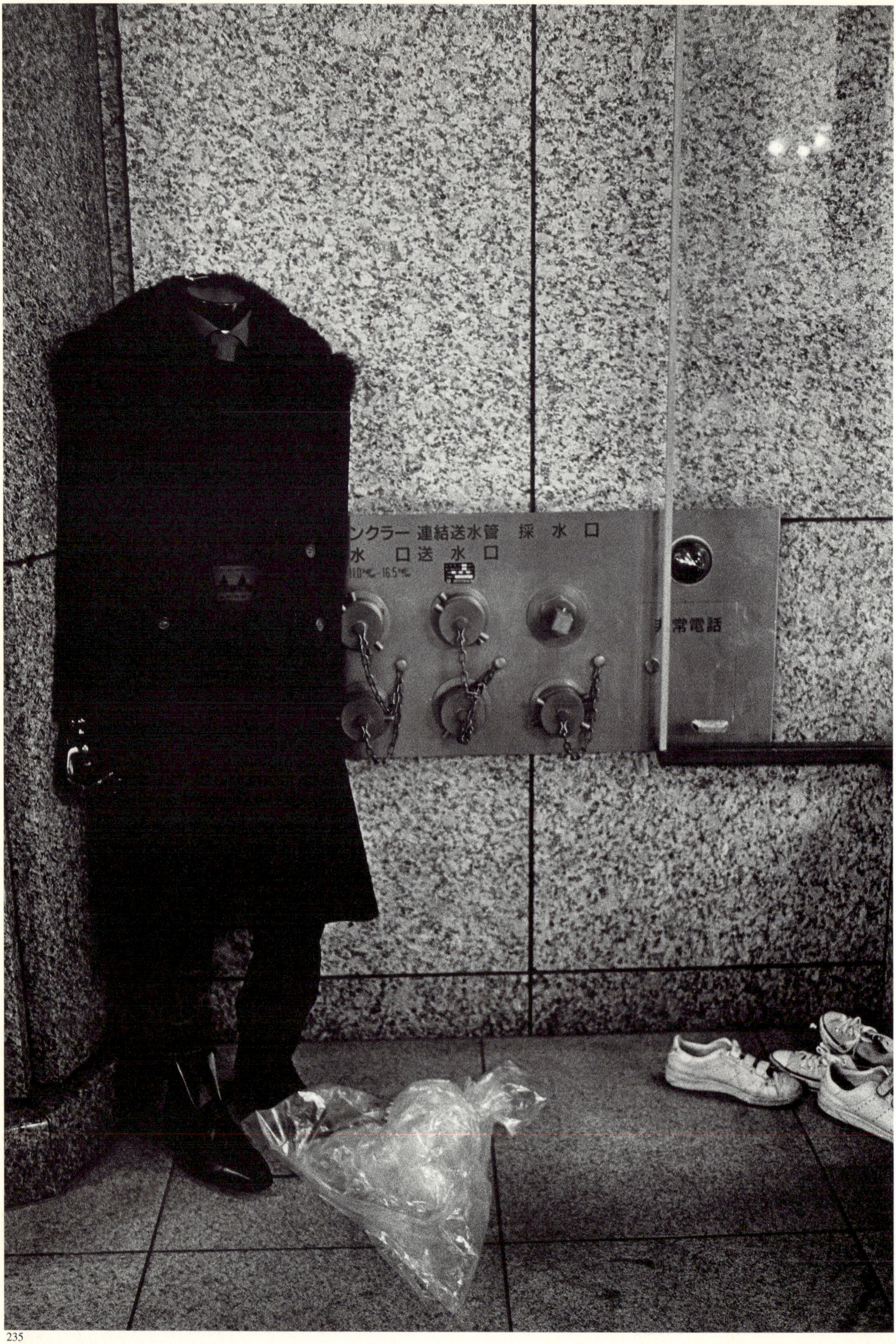
ンクラー 連結送水管 採 水 口
水 口送 水 口
常電話

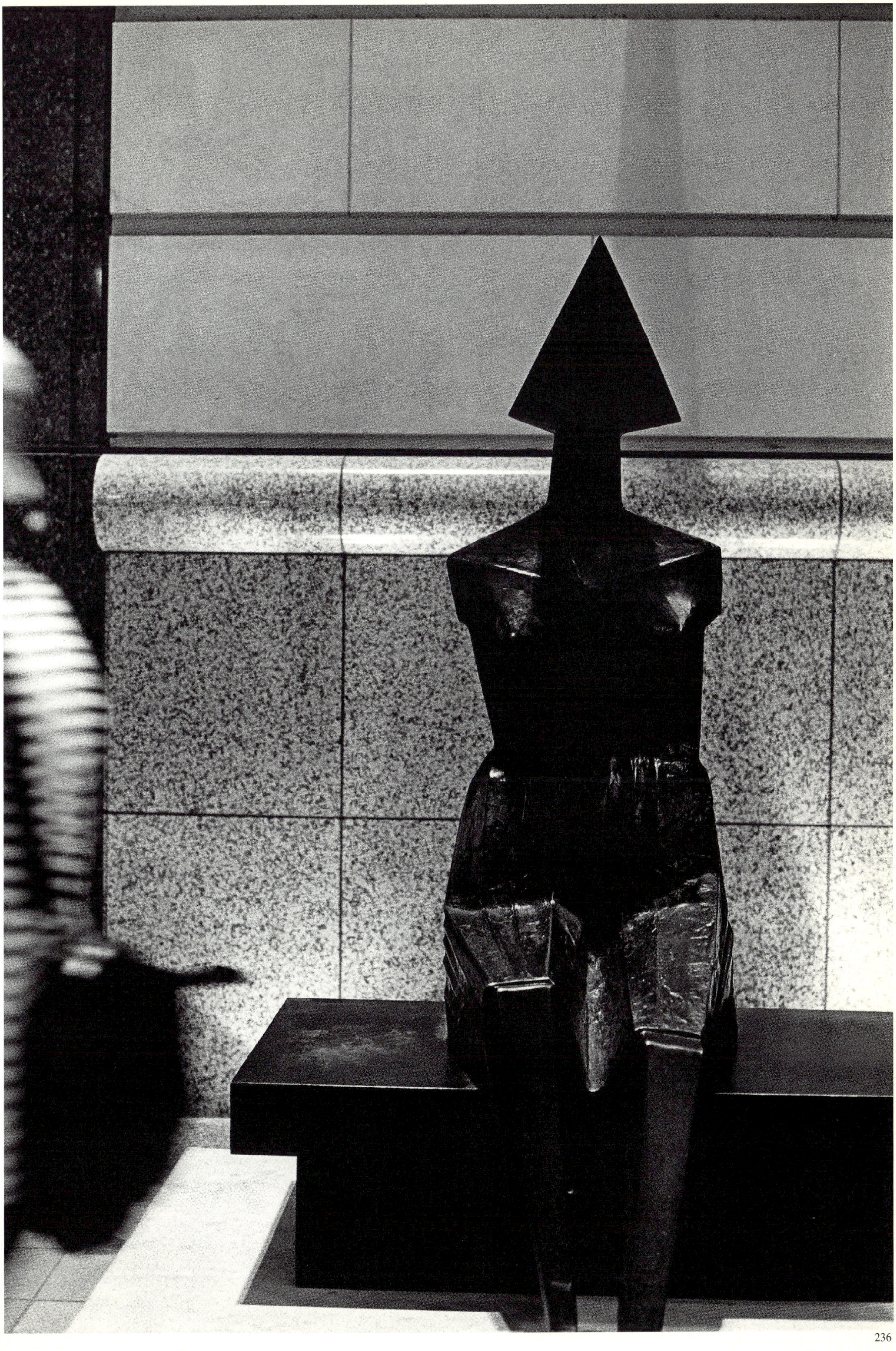

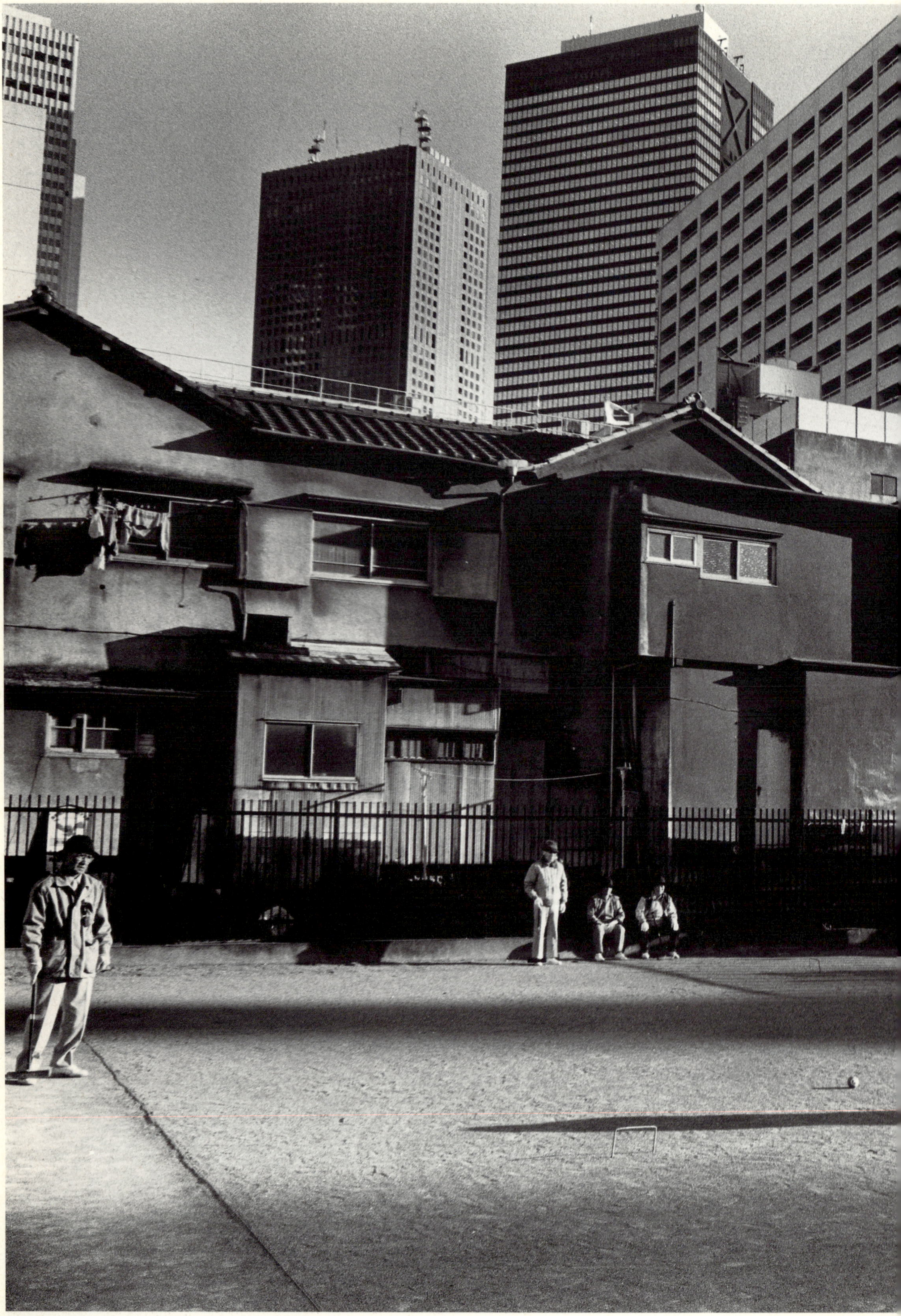

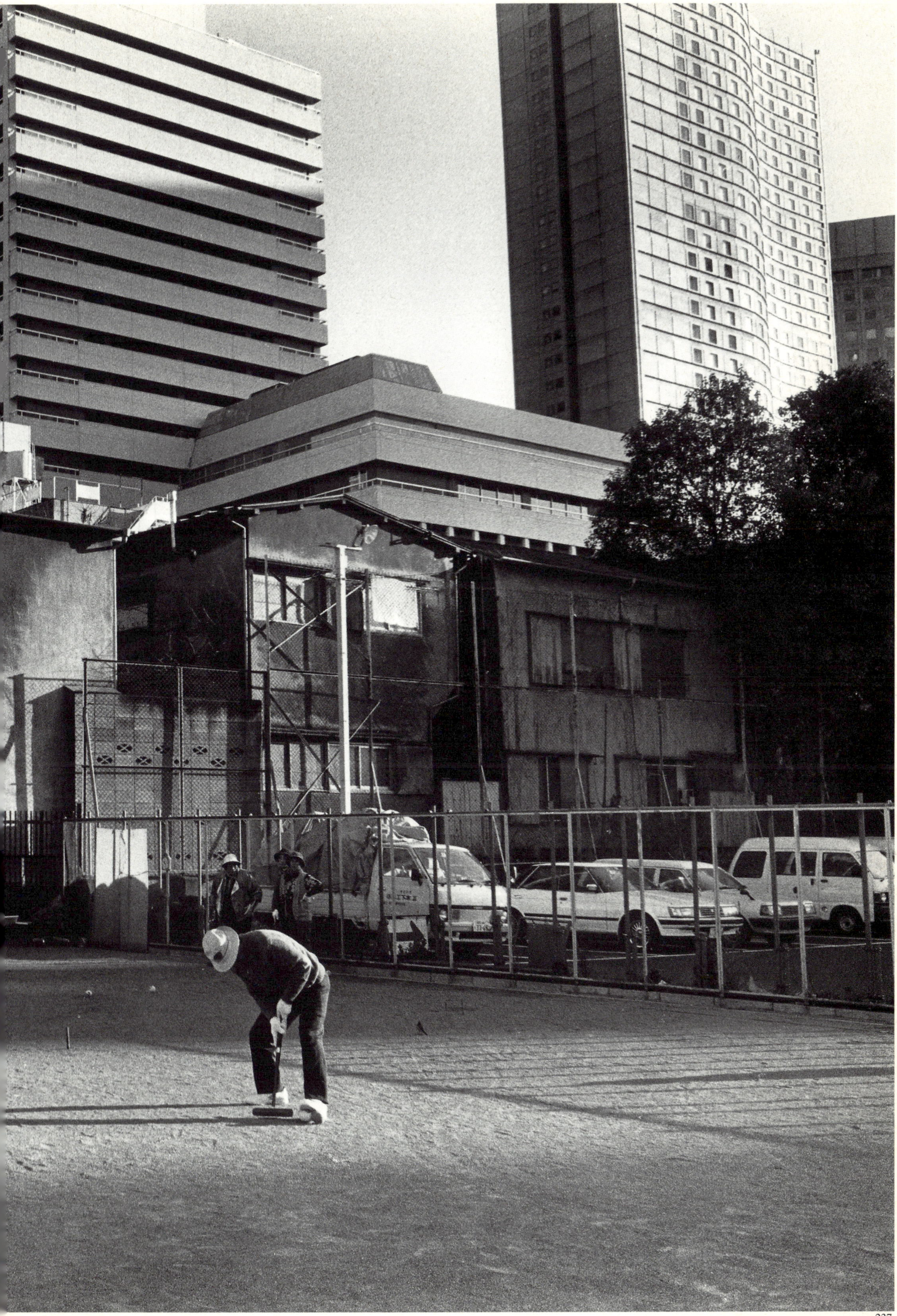

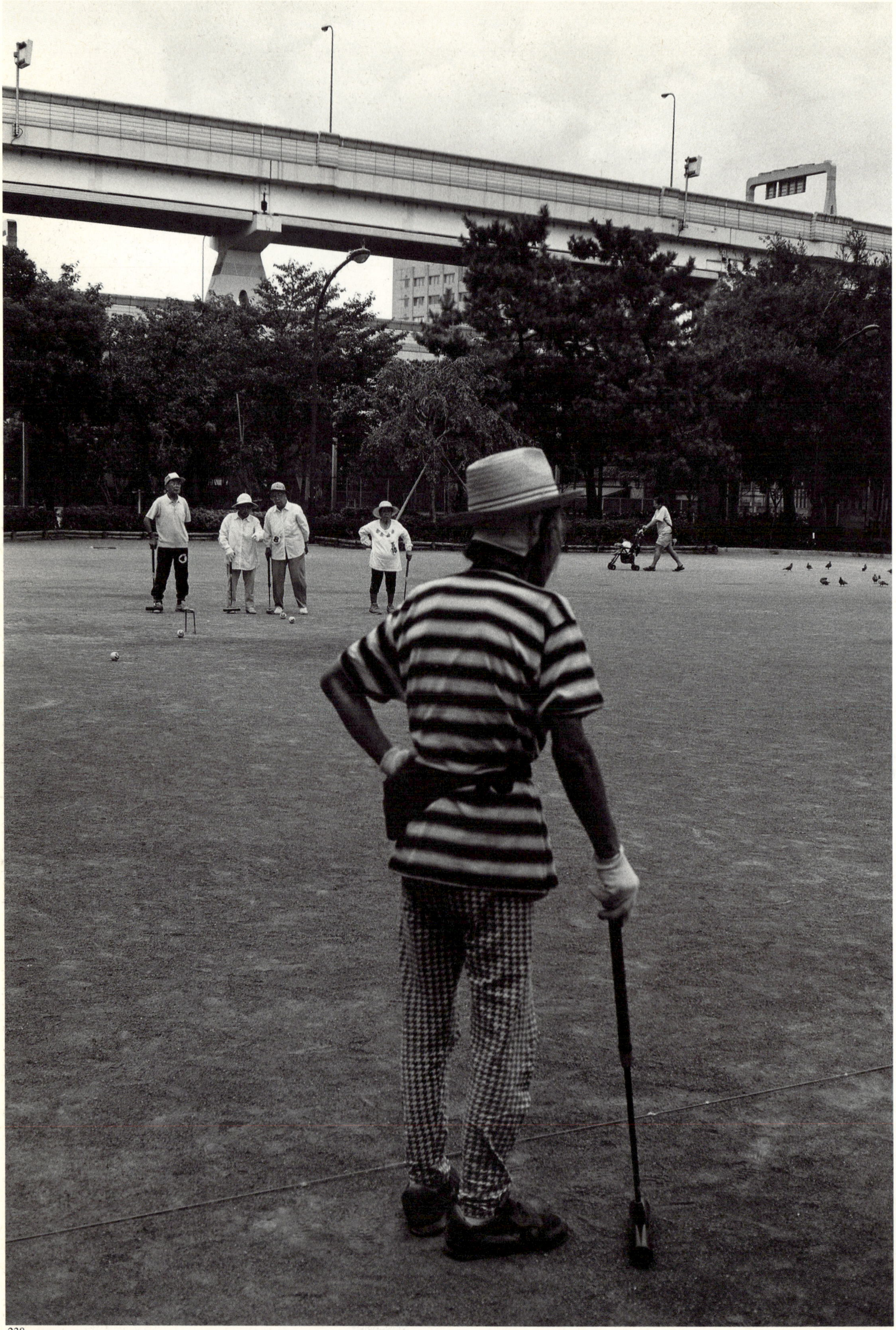

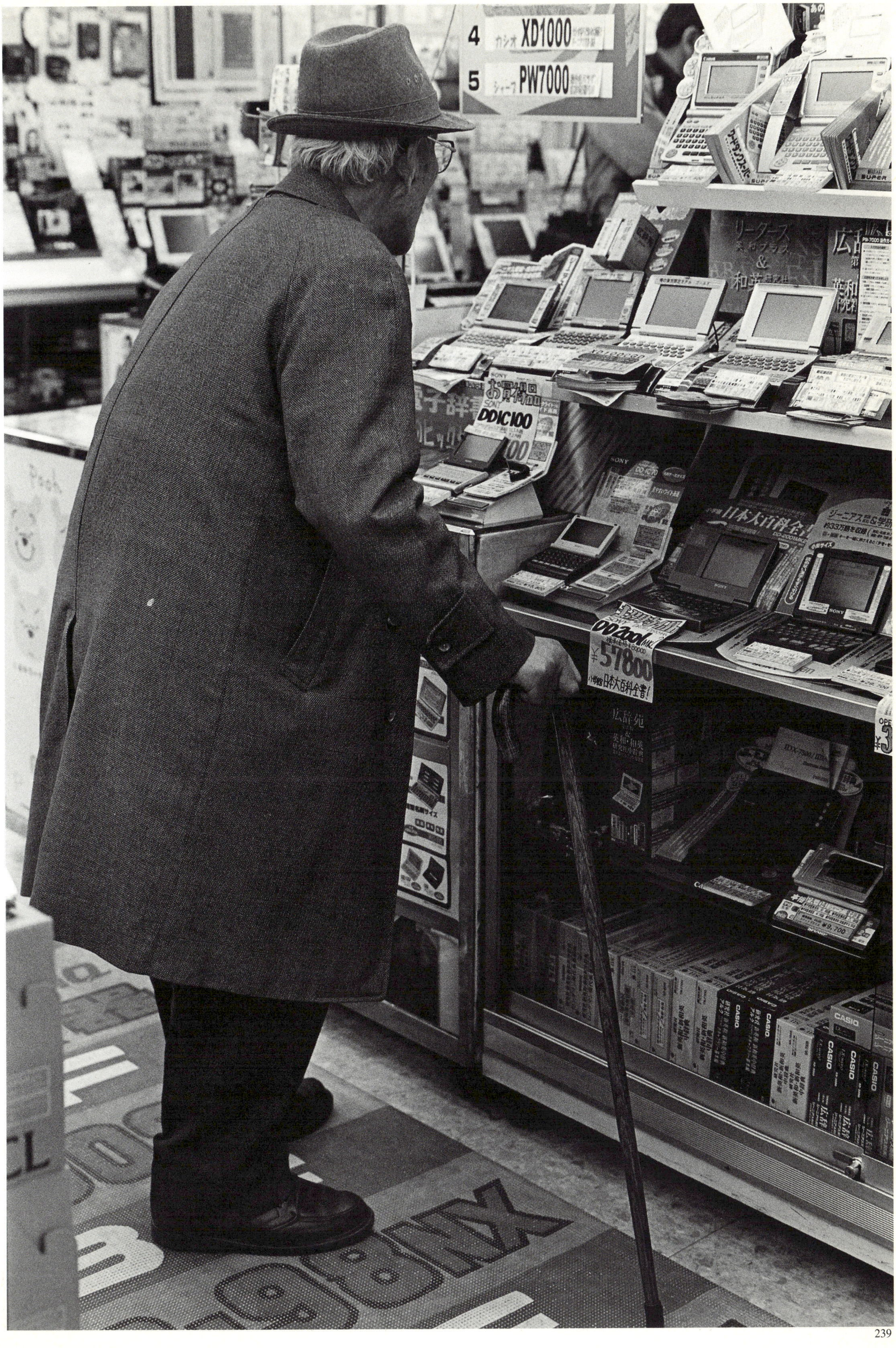
4
XD1000
5
PW7000
DDIC100
¥57800

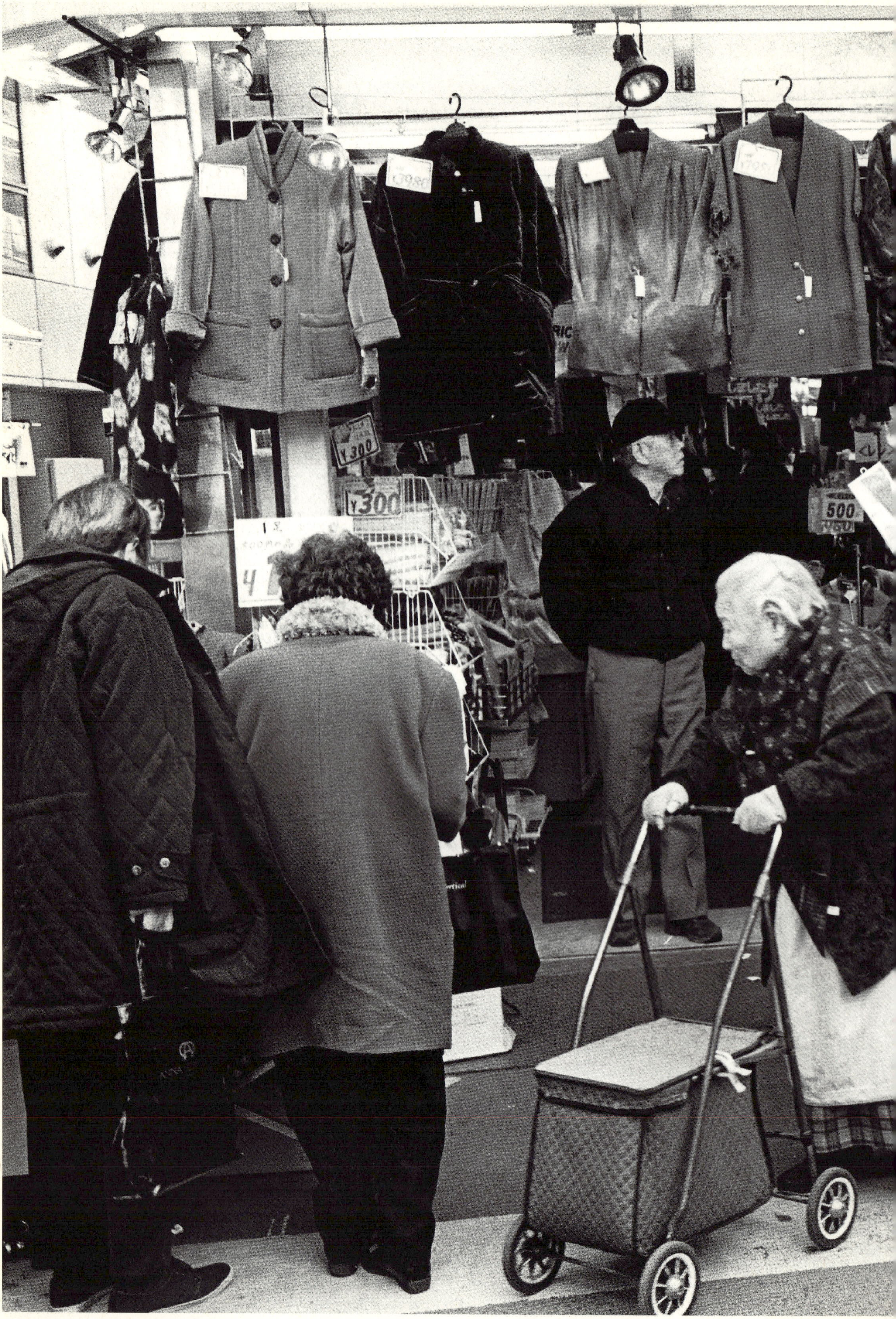
¥300
¥300
500

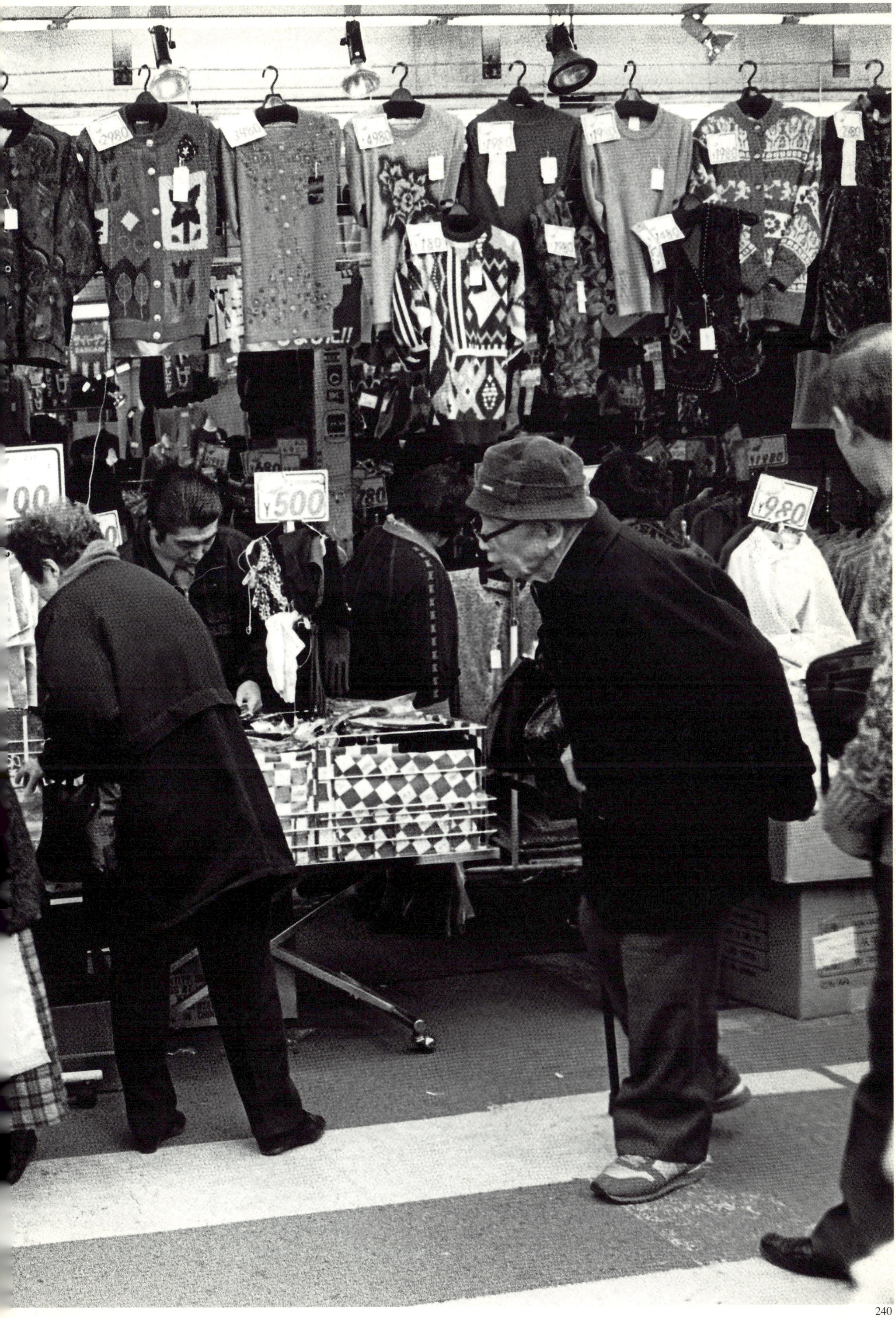
¥500
¥980

241

242

243

244

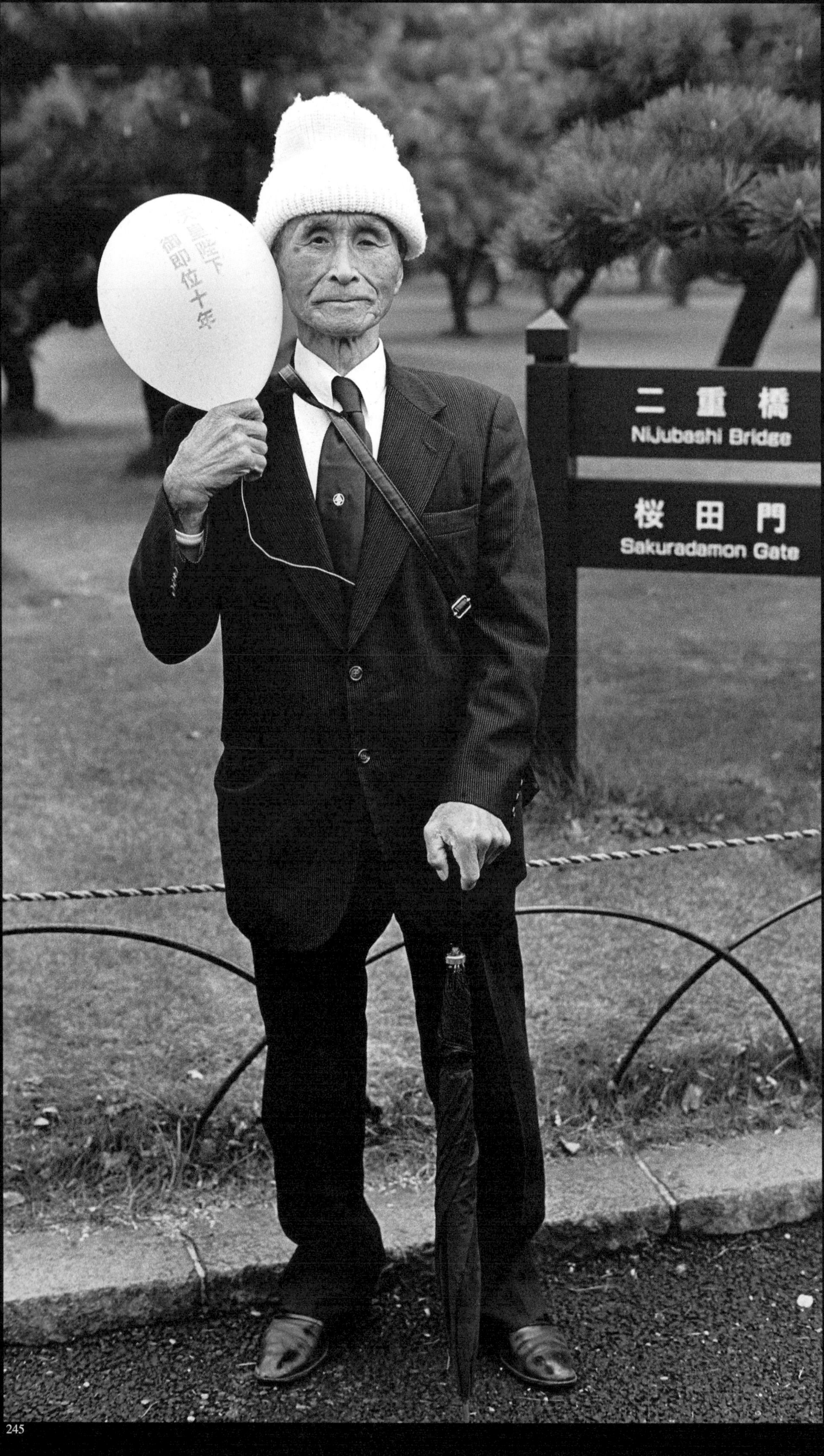
御即位十年
二 重 橋
NiJubashi Bridge
桜 田 門
Sakuradamon Gate

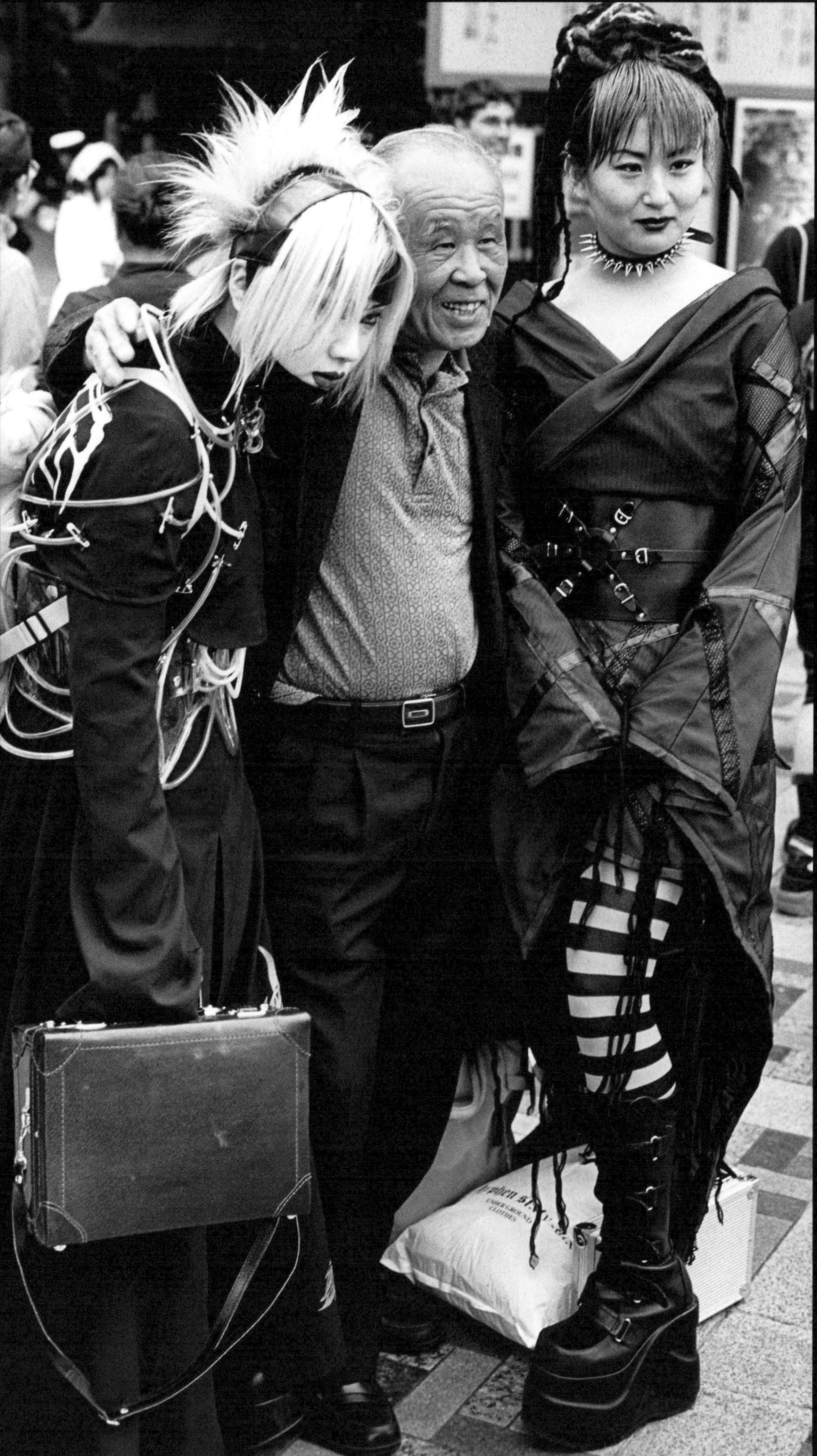

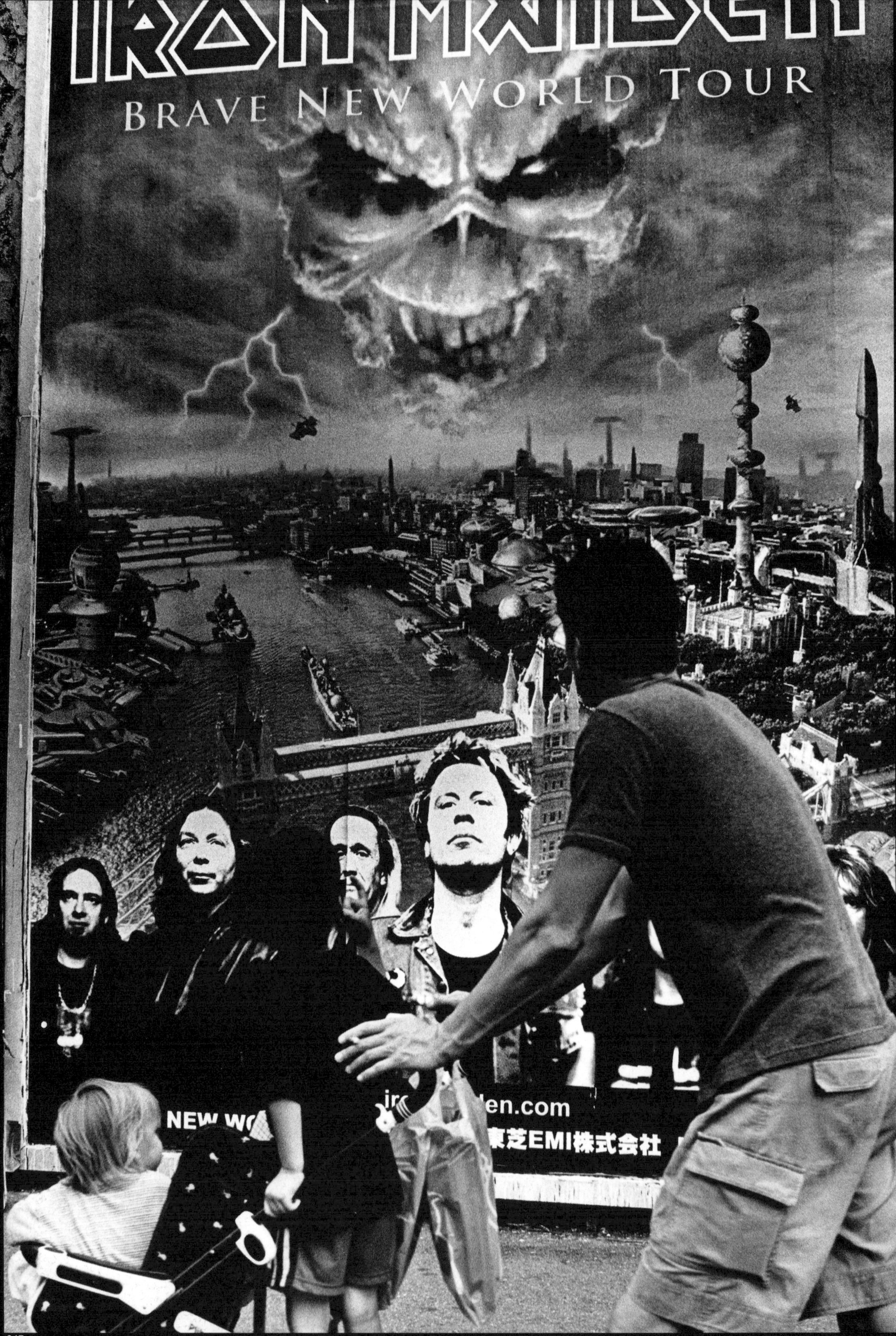
BRAVE NEW WORLD TOUR
東芝EMI株式会社

ALTAVISION
0:00
367日
BAZAR de
ALTA 20th
50%~30%OFF
無期限ロングラン絶賛上演中!!
0120-489-444
劇団四季
ALTA
7F

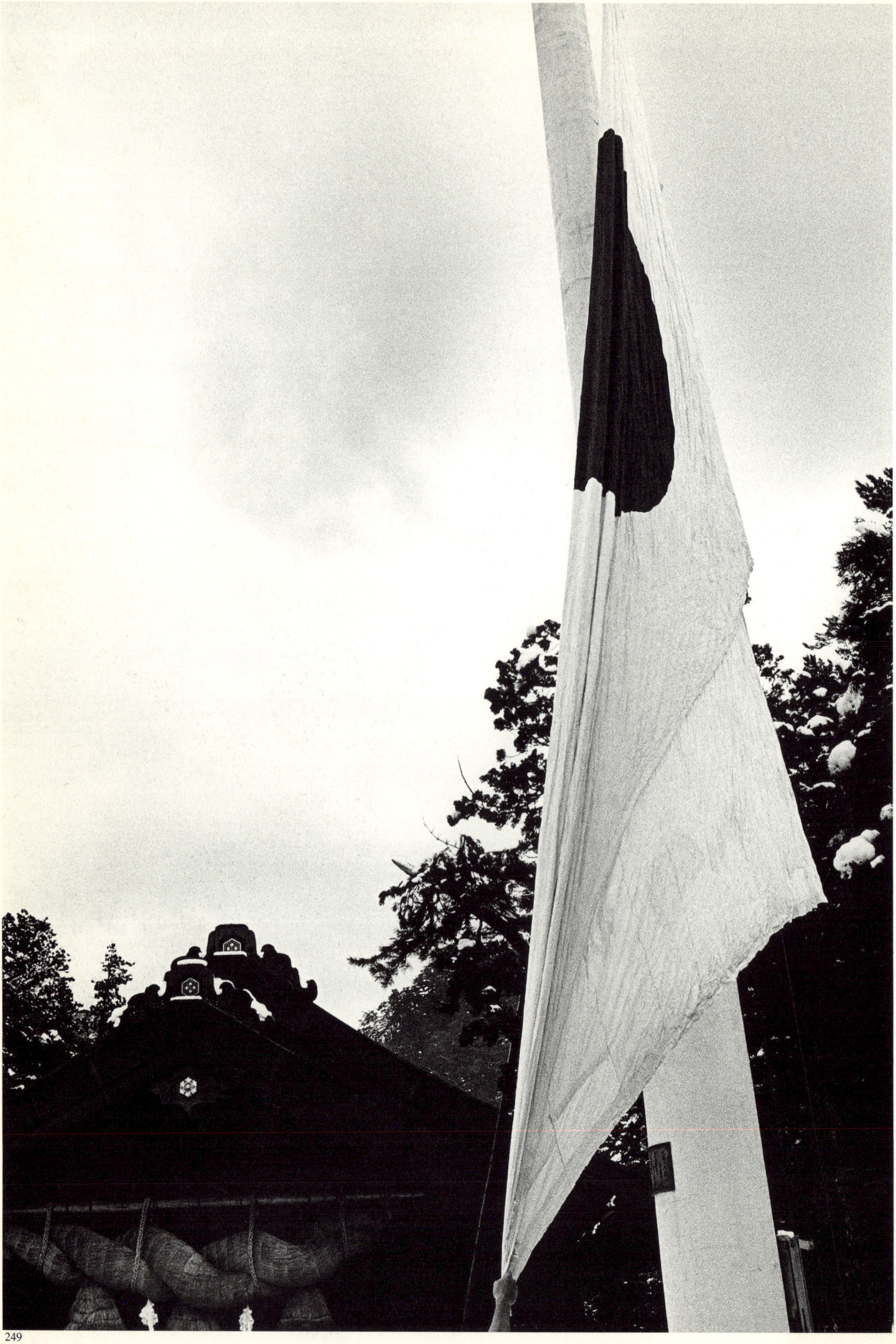

250

251

「なぜ東京Xか」

　1984年の秋だったと思う。

　TVスイッチをもてあそんでいると、NHKが私の興味を引く番組を放送していた。内容は、1948年に発表されたイギリスの作家ジョージ・オーウェルの小説『1984年』を予言書に見立て、1984年の今、世の中がオーウェルが書いた狂信的な圧政主義的世界になっているかどうかを、真面目に検証していたのだ。

　私はオーウェルの『1984年』や『動物農場』も読んでいたから、あれは、絶対の支配者ビッグ・ブラザーが君臨する全体主義的国家体制を風刺嘲笑する、未来思想SF小説ではなかったのかと、奇異な気持ちだった。だがまてよ、そうかも知れん。現在、我々を包む社会状況はオーウェル的世界と、『1984年』以前にオルダス・ハクスリーが書いた、逆ユートピアの『素晴らしい新世界』を混ぜあわせたような、逃げ場のないエレクトロニクス管理社会になりつつあるのも確かだと思った。

　そのような視点で日常の東京を改めて直視すると、異界に迷い込んだかのように街の事物や人々が、いままで気づかなかったメッセージを発信していた。

　私は、そのメッセージの受信者として出来るかぎりを記録したいと思い、カメラを手に街にでた。それは酷く疲れる行為で、体調の悪いときは妄想の映像化などばかげている、喫茶店でうまいコーヒーを飲んだほうがましだと、何度も投げだしたいと思った。だが、かつてない経済的混乱と、すべてがコンピュータに吸収され、バーチャル化する幻のような東京に強い刺激をうけ、気をとりなおして、世紀末における「眼」の語りべとして、この仕事をやり終えることが出来た。

　私は今、この世界にはヒエラルキーの頂点の聖域で、神のような悪魔のような地球を覆い尽くす、人智も宗教も超越した膨大な権力を持った指揮者が存在するのだということを信じて疑わない。タイトルの「TOKYO・X」は文字通り訳がわからない東京であり、怪しげな影が忍びよる東京であり、「？謎」の東京の意なのだが、豚の名前でもある。東京都畜産試験場が7年の年月を費やして、北京黒豚とバークシャー、デュロックの三品種を国際交配し、開発造成に成功した。日本種豚登録協会にも認定されているグルメ向きの輝かしい高級豚の品種名が「トウキョウX」なので、気にいっているのだが、東京以外のカットもあるので『X・JAPAN』とするのが正しいのだろう。

——大倉舜二
00.12.6

WHY "TOKYO X"?

It was 1984—autumn, I believe.

I was flipping through the TV channels when I came across a program on NHK that caught my attention. They were examining the novel *1984*, written in 1948 by the English author George Orwell, and giving it serious consideration as a prophetic work—trying to determine whether or not our world, in 1984, was in fact the world of fanatical oppression and tyranny Orwell had foreseen.

I was taken aback because I'd read both *1984* and *Animal Farm* and remembered the former only as a science fiction novel of the remote future, a biting satire about a totalitarian state ruled by an absolute dictator known as Big Brother. But wait a minute. Maybe the book *had* proved prophetic. It seemed undeniable that we were immersed in the process of becoming a highly regimented, electronically controlled society from which there was no escape, a society that was a cross between the Orwellian vision and Aldous Huxley's pre-*1984* dystopia, *Brave New World*.

Taking a close look at everyday Tokyo in this light, I began to feel as if I'd stumbled into an alien sort of world where everything and everyone was transmitting a certain message—a message I'd never picked up on before.

As the recipient of this message I wanted to do my best to record it; and so, camera in hand, I hit the streets. It was an exhausting endeavor; often, on my more enervated days, the whole idea of trying to capture my delusions on film would strike me as absurd, and I'd wonder if I wouldn't be better off giving up and sipping good coffee in some corner café.

But unprecedented chaos in the economy, and the phantasmal Tokyo I found before me, a Tokyo that had been assimilated whole by computers and transformed into a virtual city—these were strong stimuli, enough to make me repeatedly pull myself together and, seeing myself as an end-of-century visual version of the tribal singer-poet, eventually bring this work to a close.

That at present, in the consecrated space at the very summit of the hierarchy of this world, there exists a godlike, demonlike ruler whose power is so vast that it envelopes the entire planet and transcends all human understanding and religion—this is something I believe to be true beyond the shadow of a doubt.

The title *Tokyo X* means just what it says: unfathomable Tokyo, a Tokyo that crawls with ominous shadows, the [?] or [enigma] that is Tokyo; but it's also the name of a variety of pig. The Tokyo Metropolitan Livestock Experiment Station spent seven years developing this pig through an international crossbreeding program that involved the Beijing black pig, the Berkshire, and the Duroc. The new variety, a stellar source of high-quality, gourmet pork, has been recognized by the Pig Breeders Association of Japan; and the name it goes by—Tokyo X—appeals to me. Since not all the scenes in this book are from Tokyo, however, perhaps *X Japan* would have been a more accurate title.

——Shunji Ohkura
6 December, 2000

Translated by Ralph McCarthy

INDEX

1) 90. 11. 22　東京都港区赤坂（皇太子御成婚パレード）
2) 99. 9. 20　沖縄県嘉手納米軍基地
3) 99. 7. 31　東京都福生市横田米軍基地
4) 98. 7. 8　神奈川県横須賀海岸
5) 00. 1. 21　東京都新宿区西新宿（東京都庁からの展望）
6) 99. 7. 18　東京都中央線の車窓（大久保－東中野）
7) 98. 12. 28　東京都渋谷区渋谷駅前交差点
8) 00. 2. 1　東京都港区新橋駅前（金融のサンドイッチマン）
9) 00. 1. 23　東京都渋谷区駅前（ビルのTV）
10) 00. 2. 27　東京都渋谷区道玄坂（歩行者天国）
11) 00. 6. 4　東京都渋谷区道玄坂（歩行者天国）
12) 99. 9. 6　東京都江東区永代
13) 97. 10. 26　東京都新宿区大ガード
14) 98. 2. 1　東京都荒川区西日暮里
15) 98. 12. 29　東京都練馬区江古田
16) 93. 4. 8　東京都新宿区西新宿
17) 99. 9. 23　東京都中野区中野
18) 97. 9. 15　東京都新宿区北新宿
19) 00. 4. 29　東京都新宿区西新宿
20) 99. 9. 19　沖縄県恩納村
21) 91. 1. 30　奈良県奈良市
22) 92. 5. 5　東京都新宿区西新宿
23) 94. 2. 12　東京都新宿区西新宿
24) 99. 7. 9　東京都新宿区西新宿
25) 99. 3. 5　東京都世田谷区用賀
26) 99. 4. 5　東京都千代田区靖国神社
27) 98. 7. 23　群馬県関越自動車道
28) 98. 5. 27　高速7号小松川線
29) 99. 1. 11　東京湾横断道（海ほたる）
30) 99. 1. 11　東京湾横断道
31) 88. 2. 15　東京都首都高速羽田線
32) 99. 8. 4　東京都中央区晴海
33) 99. 8. 23　東京都千代田区秋葉原
34) 99. 2. 23　東京都台東区アメ横
35) 91. 8. 17　東京都浦安市
36) 94. 5. 7　東京都杉並区大宮和田堀公園
37) 94. 8. 18　東京都渋谷区代々木公園
38) 00. 1. 14　東京都渋谷区センター街（プリクラボックス）
39) 99. 2. 4　東京都新宿区アルタ地下階段
40) 99. 7. 19　東京都渋谷区代々木公園
41) 99. 2. 18　大阪府みなみアメリカ村
42) 98. 12. 8　東京都港区台場（フランスから借りた自由の女神）
43) 98. 9. 1　東京都新宿区アルタ地下階段
44) 99. 3. 14　東京都渋谷区代々木公園
45) 93. 9. 12　東京都渋谷区代々木公園（ロックバンドのファン）
46) 99. 8. 25　東京都渋谷区公会堂前（ロックバンドのファン）
47) 97. 9. 20　東京都新宿区歌舞伎町
48) 99. 10. 21　東京都渋谷区原宿駅竹下通り
49) 00. 6. 2　東京都渋谷区宇田川町
50) 00. 5. 28　東京都新宿区アルタ地下入り口
51) 00. 5. 21　東京都渋谷区原宿駅竹下通り
52) 99. 8. 25　東京都渋谷区公会堂前（ロックバンドのファン）
53) 00. 6. 4　東京都渋谷区渋谷
54) 00. 1. 23　東京都渋谷区ハチ公前
55) 98. 12. 26　東京都渋谷区神宮前
56) 00. 2. 27　東京都渋谷区宇田川町
57) 98. 5. 21　東京都渋谷区原宿駅竹下口
58) 99. 9. 13　東京都渋谷区代々木公園
59) 99. 1. 10　東京都渋谷区神宮橋
60) 93. 9. 5　東京都渋谷区神宮橋
61) 99. 1. 15　東京都渋谷区神宮橋
62) 98. 10. 11　東京都渋谷区原宿
63) 11. 7. 9
64) 98. 10. 11
65) 99. 1. 31　東京都渋谷区原宿神宮橋（日曜ごとに集まる仮装する女の子達）
66) 00. 6. 18
67) 00. 2. 27
68) 00. 6. 18

69) 00. 6. 4
70) 00. 6. 4
71) 00. 5. 21
72) 00. 6. 4
73) 00. 2. 27
74) 00. 4. 9
75) 00. 2. 27　東京都渋谷区原宿神宮橋（日曜ごとに集まる仮装する女の子達）
76) 00. 7. 9
77) 00. 1. 30
78) 99. 12. 26
79) 00. 2. 27
80) 00. 5. 21
81) 00. 6. 4
82) 00. 2. 27　東京都渋谷区道玄坂
83) 99. 10. 30　東京都渋谷区原宿駅竹下通り
84) 00. 5. 21　東京都渋谷区原宿
85) 00. 5. 21　東京都渋谷区原宿
86) 00. 2. 27　東京都渋谷区渋谷駅前
87) 00. 1. 24　東京都渋谷区原宿
88) 00. 1. 10　東京都渋谷区原宿
89) 00. 1. 30　東京都渋谷区原宿
90) 00. 3. 20　東京都新宿区新宿
91) 98. 8. 14　東京都新宿区新宿デパート（ウィンドーディスプレイ）
92) 99. 12. 26　東京都渋谷区神宮橋
93) 98. 7. 18　東京都新宿区西新宿
94) 00. 3. 20　東京都新宿区新宿（高級ブティックディスプレイ）
95) 00. 6. 2　東京都渋谷区原宿駅竹下口
96) 00. 2. 27　東京都渋谷区渋谷駅前
97) 00. . 25　東京都渋谷区渋谷駅前
98) 00. 2. 24　東京都渋谷区原宿駅竹下口
99) 00. 2. 18　東京都新宿区新宿
100) 00. 12. 25　東京都新宿区新宿大ガード
101) 00. 1. 28　東京都渋谷区原宿駅竹下口
102) 99. 12. 13　東京都渋谷区原宿交差点裏
103) 99. 12. 9　東京都新宿区新宿アルタ前
104) 00. 1. 31　東京都渋谷区神宮橋
105) 00. 2. 23　東京都新宿区新宿アルタ前
106) 99. 3. 28　東京都新宿区新宿南口
107) 00. 1. 8　東京都新宿区新宿
108) 00. 1. 23　東京都渋谷区道玄坂
109) 00. 1. 24　東京都渋谷区道玄坂
110) 00. 2. 23　東京都新宿区新宿
111) 00. 2. 16　東京都渋谷区原宿駅竹下口
112) 99. 12. 10　東京都新宿区新宿アルタ前
113) 99. 12. 24　東京都新宿区新宿アルタ前
114) 99. 12. 24　東京都渋谷区原宿駅竹下通り
115) 99. 11. 15　東京都新宿区歌舞伎町西武新宿線駅前
116) 00. 6. 18　東京都渋谷区神南
117) 00. 6. 11　東京都渋谷区原宿駅竹下口
118) 00. 5. 20　東京都新宿区新宿
119) 00. 2. 26　東京都渋谷区原宿駅竹下通り
120) 00. 3. 5　東京都渋谷区原宿駅竹下通り
121) 00. 6. 8　東京都渋谷区表参道
122) 00. 5. 14　東京都新宿区新宿駅南口
123) 99. 1. 9　東京都新宿区新宿駅東口ピラミッド広場
124) 00. 1. 24　東京都渋谷区神南
125) 99. 2. 9　東京都港区赤坂
126) 98. 9. 18　東京都港区芝公園東京タワー
127) 93. 4. 4　東京都港区青山こどもの城
128) 00. 6. 5　東京都新宿区南口デパートのゲームセンター
129) 98. 6. 7　東京都新宿区西新宿東京都庁
130) 00. 6. 1　東京都新宿区新宿
131) 99. 12. 15　東京都営団地下鉄
132) 00. 6. 11　東京都渋谷区原宿駅竹下通り
133) 99. 6. 13　東京都杉並区和田
134) 94. 8. 20　東京都杉並区和田
135) 95. 3. 7　東京都東大和市多摩湖
136) 98. 12. 23　東京都杉並区高円寺南

#	日付	場所
137)	99. 1. 11	東京都新宿区歌舞伎町
138)	99. 1. 17	東京都新宿区歌舞伎町
139)	96. 6. 28	東京都新宿区歌舞伎町
140)	99. 2. 3	東京都新宿区歌舞伎町
141)	00. 6. 7	東京都新宿区新宿
142)	99. 1. 12	千葉県木更津（パチンコ店）
143)	99. 1. 15	東京都中野区中野
144)	99. 11. 21	東京都台東区浅草（場外馬券売場）
145)	98. 11. 29	東京都新宿区新宿アルタ前ピラミッド広場
146)	98. 7. 2	東京都新宿区新宿
147)	99. 5. 21	東京都新宿区新宿（デパートのウィンドーディスプレイ）
148)	00. 7. 7	東京都千代田区神田駅前（電話ボックスの金融チラシ）
149)	98. 5. 27	東京都渋谷区渋谷駅前（金融看板）
150)	00. 3. 3	東京都千代田区東京駅前（株式の電光版）
151)	99. 2. 27	東京都千代田区神田駅前（金融ビルと風俗店の立て看板）
152)	99. 2. 16	東京都港区銀座（倒産した銀行の看板と監視カメラ）
153)	98. 12. 22	東京都新宿区歌舞伎町（金融ネオンとキリスト教の布教）
154)	99. 10. 10	東京都新宿区歌舞伎町（パチンコ店の巨大な1万円札）
155)	98. 12. 9	東京都港区表参道
156)	99. 12. 25	東京都新宿区新宿駅南口
157)	98. 7. 4	東京都新宿区新宿駅東口
158)	00. 2. 23	東京都台東区上野駅前
159)	91. 1. 2	東京都新宿区南口
160)	98. 4. 31	東京都練馬区光が丘
161)	99. 6. 12	東京都文京区目白鬼子母神
162)	98. 10. 6	東京都新宿区西新宿
163)	90. 4. 5	東京都千代田区九段千鳥ケ淵
164)	93. 3. 31	東京都千代田区半蔵門
165)	99. 6. 29	東京都新宿区西新宿
166)	97. 5. 6	東京都台東区蔵前
167)	98. 2. 23	東京都新宿区西新宿（ウィンドーディスプレイ）
168)	98. 5. 15	東京都港区新橋駅前
169)	00. 1. 27	東京都新宿区新宿駅南口
170)	97. 7. 25	東京都新宿区新宿駅東口
171)	00. 1. 19	東京都新宿区歌舞伎町交差点
172)	98. 11. 8	東京都新宿区新宿駅南口
173)	99. 5. 28	東京都新宿区西新宿
174)	98. 6. 21	東京都中野区中野坂上駅
175)	99. 4. 21	東京都新宿区初台（オペラシティ）
176)	99. 4. 23	東京都新宿区西新宿（地下道）
177)	98. 5. 14	東京都千代田区有楽町（国際フォーラム）
178)	97. 11. 6	東京都港区芝公園東京タワー
179)	99. 9. 5	東京都新宿区西新宿
180)	98. 8. 15	東京都新宿区初台（オペラシティ）
181)	99. 9. 3	東京都新宿区戸山
182)	99. 12. 22	東京都千代田区有楽町（国際フォーラム）
183)	98. 5. 28	東京都渋谷区代々木（保険会社ビル）
184)	00. 3. 9	東京都新宿区西新宿
185)	98. 7. 19	東京都新宿区西新宿（十二社からの都庁）
186)	99. 11. 6	東京都港区芝公園東京タワー
187)	99. 5. 26	東京都中野区新井薬師
188)	98-00	1998年から2000年までのTV映像
189)	99. 2. 19	大阪府心斎橋（コーヒーアイスクリーム店）
190)	96. 2. 5	東京都三鷹市
191)	93. 3. 12	東京都新宿区西新宿（ウィンドーディスプレイ）
192)	99. 6. 13	東京都渋谷区原宿（レストラン）
193)	98. 6. 7	東京都新宿区新宿（地下道）
194)	98. 1. 26	東京都港区六本木
195)	96. 6. 28	東京都新宿区新宿伊勢丹前
196)	99. 7. 20	東京都新宿区西新宿
197)	00. 7. 9	東京都新宿区新宿
198)	99. 6. 18	東京都港区芝公園東京タワー
199)	99. 5. 3	東京都台東区浅草
200)	00. 4. 9	東京都渋谷区代々木公園
201)	97. 5. 17	東京都新宿区中央公園
202)	98. 5. 31	東京都新宿区中央公園
203)	00. 5. 28	東京都新宿区内藤町新宿御苑
204)	00. 4. 9	東京都渋谷区代々木公園
205)	00. 5. 14	東京都渋谷区神宮橋
206)	00. 4. 9	東京都渋谷区代々木公園
207)	98. 4. 24	東京都新宿区新宿駅南口
208)	98. 9. 18	東京都新宿区西新宿
209)	99. 8. 5	東京都千代田区麹町（日本テレビ前）
210)	97. 5. 17	東京都新宿区西新宿
211)	98. 5. 31	東京都新宿区新宿東口駅前
212)	93. 8. 18	東京都新宿区西新宿（コンドーム自動販売機とイチジクの葉）
213)	98. 9. 13	東京都新宿区西新宿
214)	99. 2. 21	東京都台東区上野駅前（バベルの塔？オブジェ）
215)	99. 2. 4	東京都港区六本木
216)	00. 3. 10	東京都渋谷区千駄ヶ谷体育館
217)	99. 2. 3	東京都港区台場
218)	98. 12. 30	長野県諏訪市諏訪インター
219)	99. 5. 4	東京都新宿区西新宿都庁地下道（ホームレス人々）
220)	99. 5. 7	東京都台東区隅田川（ダンボールハウス）
221)	99. 5. 3	大阪府淀川（ダンボールハウス）
222)	99. 11. 3	東京都新宿区中央公園
223)	98. 1. 26	東京都新宿区麻布片町
224)	99. 8. 16	東京都新宿区歌舞伎町
225)	99. 7. 19	東京都渋谷区代々木公園（ホームレス作のオブジェ）
226)	98. 12. 25	東京都渋谷区原宿交差点
227)	99. 10. 10	東京都渋谷区代々木公園
228)	00. 2. 13	東京都新宿区中央公園
229)	00. 2. 25	東京都中央区銀座
230)	98. 1. 4	東京都新宿区西新宿
231)	97. 11. 28	東京都渋谷区原宿
232)	99. 2. 18	大阪府心斎橋
233)	00. 3. 19	東京都渋谷区宮下公園
234)	99. 2. 17	大阪府心斎橋付近
235)	97. 8. 17	東京都新宿区新宿（デパートのマネキン）
236)	99. 4. 1	福岡県博多（フランス人作家の彫刻）
237)	90. 1. 3	東京都新宿区西新宿
238)	99. 9. 6	東京都江東区門前仲町
239)	00. 1. 26	東京都千代田区秋葉原
240)	98. 2. 11	東京都豊島区巣鴨とげぬき地蔵
241)	00. 5. 30	東京都渋谷区渋谷駅
242)	99. 11. 27	東京都港区青山三丁目
243)	92. 12. 29	東京都中野区鷺の宮駅前
244)	00. 4. 7	東京都新宿区四谷
245)	99. 11. 12	東京都千代田区皇居前（天皇御在位十年記念祝賀）
246)	00. 10. 22	東京都渋谷区神宮橋
247)	00. 7. 17	東京都港区青山三丁目
248)	00. 1. 1	東京都新宿区東口アルタ前（2000年を祝う人々）
249)	99. 12. 23	島根県出雲大社
250)	99. 9. 20	沖縄県那覇（クラブの入口）
251)	91. 8. 19	長野県美ケ原

INDEX

1) Nov. 22, 1990 — Akasaka, Minato-ku, Tokyo (the parade celebrating Crown Prince's wedding)
2) Sep. 20, 1999 — Kadena, Okinawa Prefecture (Kadena U.S. Air Force Base)
3) Jul. 31, 1999 — Fussa-shi, Tokyo (Yokota U.S. Air Force Base)
4) Jul. 8, 1998 — Yokosuka, Kanagawa Prefecture
5) Jan. 21, 2000 — Nishi-shinjuku, Shinjuku-ku, Tokyo (from Tokyo Metropolitan Government Office)
6) Jul. 18, 1999 — Okubo-Higashi-nakanso, Tokyo (JR Chuo Line)
7) Dec. 28, 1998 — Shibuya-ku, Tokyo (Crossroad in front of Shibuya Station)
8) Feb. 1, 2000 — Shinbashi, Minato-ku, Tokyo (ad men for money lenders)
9) Jan. 23, 2000 — Shibuya-ku, Tokyo (TV screen on the station building)
10) Feb. 27, 2000 — Dogenzaka, Shibuya-ku, Tokyo (car-free mall)
11) June 4, 2000 — Dogenzaka, Shibuya-ku, Tokyo (car-free mall)
12) Sept. 6, 1999 — Eitai, Koto-ku, Tokyo
13) Oct. 26, 1997 — Shinjuku-ku, Tokyo (railroad overpass)
14) Feb. 1, 1998 — Nishi-nippori, Arakawa-ku, Tokyo
15) Dec. 29, 1998 — Egota, Nerima-ku, Tokyo
16) Apr. 8, 1993 — Nishi-shinjuku, Shinjuku-ku, Tokyo
17) Sept. 23, 1999 — Nakano, Nakano-ku, Tokyo
18) Sept. 15, 1997 — Kita-shinjuku, Shinjuku-ku, Tokyo
19) Apr. 29, 2000 — Nishi-shinjuku, Shinjuku-ku, Tokyo
20) Sept. 19, 1999 — Onna-son, Okinawa Prefecture
21) Jan. 30, 1991 — Nara-shi, Nara Prefecture
22) May 5, 1992 — Nishi-shinjuku, Shinjuku-ku, Tokyo
23) Feb. 12, 1994 — Nishi-shinjuku, Shinjuku-ku, Tokyo
24) Jul. 9, 1999 — Nishi-shinjuku, Shinjuku-ku, Tokyo
25) Mar. 5, 1999 — Yoga, Setagaya-ku, Tokyo
26) Apr. 5, 1999 — Chiyoda-ku, Tokyo (Yasukuni Shrine)
27) Jul. 23, 1998 — Gunma Prefecture (Kan-etsu Freeway)
28) May 27, 1998 — Komatsugawa, Sumida-ku, Tokyo (Freeway 7, Komatsugawa Line)
29) Jan. 11, 1999 — Tokyo Bay Undersea Freeway (Sea Firefly)
30) Jan. 11, 1999 — Tokyo Bay Undersea Freeway
31) Feb. 15, 1988 — Tokyo Freeway Haneda Line
32) Aug. 4, 1999 — Harumi, Chuo-ku, Tokyo
33) Aug. 23, 1999 — Akibahara, Chiyoda-ku, Tokyo
34) Feb. 23, 1999 — Taito-ku, Tokyo (Ameya Yokocho)
35) Aug. 17, 1991 — Urayasu-shi, Chiba Prefecture
36) May 7, 1994 — Suginami-ku, Tokyo (Omiya Wadabori Park)
37) Aug. 18, 1994 — Shibuya-ku, Tokyo (Yoyogi Park)
38) Jan. 14, 2000 — Shibuya-ku, Tokyo (Center-gai, *Purikura* window)
39) Feb. 4, 1999 — Shinjuku-ku, Tokyo (Alta Underground Market)
40) Jul. 19, 1999 — Shibuya-ku, Tokyo (Yoyogi Park)
41) Feb. 18, 1999 — Minami, Osaka (America-mura)
42) Dec. 8, 1998 — Daiba, Minato-ku, Tokyo (Statue of Liberty borrowed from France)
43) Sept. 11, 1998 — Shinjuku-ku, Tokyo (Alta Underground Market)
44) Mar. 14, 1999 — Shibuya-ku, Tokyo (Yoyogi Park)
45) Sept. 12., 1993 — Shibuya-ku, Tokyo (Yoyogi Park, rock band fans)
46) Aug. 25, 1999 — Shibuya-ku, Tokyo (Public Hall, rock band fans)
47) Sept. 20, 1997 — Kabuki-cho, Shinjuku-ku, Tokyo
48) Oct. 21, 1999 — Takeshita-dori, Harajuku, Shibuya-ku, Tokyo
49) June 2, 2000 — Udagawa-cho, Shibuya-ku, Tokyo
50) May 28, 2000 — Shinjuku-ku, Tokyo (Alta Underground Market)
51) May 21, 2000 — Takeshita-dori, Harajuku, Shibuya-ku, Tokyo
52) Aug. 25, 1999 — Shibuya-ku, Tokyo (Public Hall, Rock Band fans)
53) June 4, 2000 — Shibuya, Shibuya-ku, Tokyo
54) Jan. 23, 2000 — Shibuya-ku, Tokyo (In front of Hachiko Statue)
55) Dec. 26, 1998 — Jingu-mae, Shibuya-ku, Tokyo
56) Feb. 27, 2000 — Udagawa-cho, Shibuya-ku, Tokyo
57) May 21, 1998 — Shibuya-ku, Tokyo (Harajuku Station, Takeshita entrance)
58) Sept. 13, 1999 — Shibuya-ku, Tokyo (Yoyogi Park)
59) Jan. 10, 1999 — Jingubashi, Shibuya-ku, Tokyo
60) Sept. 5, 1993 — Jingubashi, Shibuya-ku, Yokyo
61) Jan. 15, 1999 — Jingubashi, Shibuya-ku, Tokyo
62) Oct. 11, 1998 — Harajuku, Shibuya-ku, Tokyo
63) Jul. 9, 2000 ⎤
64) Oct. 11, 1998 ⎥
65) Jan. 31, 1999 ⎥
66) June 18, 2000 ⎥
67) Feb. 27, 2000 ⎥
68) June 18, 2000 ⎥
69) June 4, 2000 ⎥
70) June 4, 2000 ⎥
71) May 21, 2000 ⎥
72) June 4, 2000 ⎬ Jingubashi, Shibuya-ku, Tokyo (girls in Sunday getup)
73) Feb. 27, 2000 ⎥
74) Apr. 9, 2000 ⎥
75) Feb. 27, 2000 ⎥
76) Jul. 9, 2000 ⎥
77) Jan. 30, 2000 ⎥
78) Dec. 26, 1999 ⎥
79) Feb. 27, 2000 ⎥
80) May 21, 2000 ⎥
81) June 4, 2000 ⎦
82) Feb. 27, 2000 — Dogenzaka, Shibuya-ku, Tokyo
83) Oct. 30, 1999 — Takeshita-dori, Harajuku, Shibuya-ku, Tokyo
84) May 21, 2000 — Harajuku, Shibuya-ku, Tokyo
85) May 21, 2000 — Harajuku, Shibuya-ku, Tokyo
86) Feb. 27, 2000 — Shibuya-ku, Tokyo (Shibuya Station)
87) Jan. 24, 2000 — Harajuku, Shibuya-ku, Tokyo
88) Jan. 10, 2000 — Harajuku, Shibuya-ku, Tokyo
89) Jan. 30, 2000 — Harajuku, Shibuya-ku, Tokyo
90) Mar. 20, 2000 — Shinjuku, Shinjuku-ku, Tokyo
91) Aug. 14, 1998 — Shinjuku-ku, Tokyo (department store, window display)
92) Dec. 26, 1999 — Jingubashi, Shibuya-ku, Tokyo
93) Jul. 18, 1998 — Nishi-shinjuku, Shinjuku-ku, Tokyo
94) Mar. 20, 2000 — Shinjuku, Shinjuku-ku, Tokyo (high quality boutique)
95) June 2, 2000 — Harajuku, Shibuya-ku, Tokyo (Harajuku Station, Takeshita entrance)
96) Feb. 27, 2000 — Shibuya-ku, Tokyo (Shibuya Station)
97) Feb. 25, 2000 — Shibuya-ku, Tokyo (Shibuya Station)
98) Feb. 24, 2000 — Shibuya-ku, Tokyo (Harajuku Station, Takeshita entrance)
99) Feb. 18, 2000 — Shinjuku, Shinjuku-ku, Tokyo
100) Dec. 25, 2000 — Shinjuku-ku, Tokyo (railroad overpass)
101) Jan. 28, 2000 — Shibuya-ku, Tokyo (Harajuku Station, Takeshita entrance)
102) Dec. 13, 1999 — Harajuku, Shibuya-ku, Tokyo (on sidestreet near Harajuku Crossing)
103) Dec. 9, 1999 — Shinjuku-ku, Tokyo (in front of Alta)
104) Jan. 31, 2000 — Jingubashi, Shibuya-ku, Tokyo
105) Feb. 28, 2000 — Shinjuku-ku, Tokyo (in front of Alta)
106) Mar. 28, 1999 — Shinjuku-ku, Tokyo (Shinjuku Station, South entrance)
107) Jan. 8, 2000 — Shinjuku, Shinjuku-ku, Tokyo
108) Jan. 23, 2000 — Dogenzaka, Shibuya-ku, Tokyo
109) Jan. 24, 2000 — Dogenzaka, Shibuya-ku, Tokyo
110) Feb. 23, 2000 — Shinjuku, Shinjuku-ku, Tokyo
111) Feb. 16, 2000 — Harajuku, Shibuya-ku, Tokyo (Takeshita entrance)
112) Dec. 10, 1999 — Shinjuku, Shinjuku-ku, Tokyo (in front of Alta)
113) Dec. 24, 1999 — Shinjuku, Shinjuku-ku, Tokyo (in front of Alta)
114) Dec. 24, 1999 — Takeshita-dori, Harajuku, Shibuya-ku, Tokyo
115) Nov. 15, 1999 — Kabuki-cho, Shinjuku-ku, Tokyo (Seibu-Shinjuku Station)
116) June 18, 2000 — Jinnann, Shibuya-ku, Tokyo
117) June 11, 2000 — Shibuya-ku, Tokyo (Harajuku Station, Takeshita entrance)
118) May 20, 2000 — Shinjuku, Shinjuku-ku, Tokyo
119) Feb. 26, 2000 — Shibuya-ku, Tokyo (Harajuku Station, Takeshita entrance)
120) Mar. 5, 2000 — Harajuku, Shibuya-ku, Tokyo (Harajuku Station, Takeshita entrance)
121) June 8, 2000 — Omote-sando, Shibuya-ku, Tokyo
122) May 14, 2000 — Shinjuku, Shinjuku-ku, Tokyo (Shinjuku Station, south entrance)

#	Date	Location
123)	Jan. 9, 1999	Shinjuku-ku, Tokyo (Shinjuku Station, Pyramid Square)
124)	Jan. 24, 2000	Jinnan, Shibuya-ku, Tokyo
125)	Feb. 9, 1999	Akasaka, Minato-ku, Tokyo
126)	Sept. 18, 1998	Shiba-koen, Minato-ku, Tokyo (Tokyo Tower)
127)	Apr. 4, 1993	Aoyama, Minato-ku, Tokyo (Castle for Children)
128)	June 5, 2000	Shinjuku-ku, Tokyo (Shinjuku, game center near Shinjuku Station)
129)	June 7, 1998	Shinjuku-ku, Tokyo (Tokyo Metropolitan Government Office)
130)	June 1, 2000	Shinjuku, Shinjuku-ku, Tokyo
131)	Dec. 15, 1999	Underground Railway (Teito Rapid Transit Authority)
132)	June 11, 2000	Shibuya-ku, Tokyo (Harajuku Station, Takeshita entrance)
133)	June 13, 1999	Wada, Suginami-ku, Tokyo
134)	Aug. 20, 1994	Wada, Suginami-ku, Tokyo
135)	Mar. 7, 1995	Tama Lake, Higashi-Yamato-shi, Tokyo
136)	Dec. 23, 1998	Koenji-minami, Suginami-ku, Tokyo
137)	Jan. 11, 1999	Kabuki-cho, Shinjuku-ku, Tokyo
138)	Jan. 17, 1999	Kabuki-cho, Shinjuku-ku, Tokyo
139)	June 28, 1996	Kabuki-cho, Shinjuku-ku, Tokyo
140)	Feb. 3, 1999	Kabuki-cho, Shinjuku-ku, Tokyo
141)	June 7, 2000	Shinjuku, Shinjuku-ku, Tokyo
142)	Jan. 12, 1999	Kisarazu-shi, Chiba Prefecture (pachinko parlor)
143)	Jan. 15, 1999	Nakano, Nakano-ku, Tokyo
144)	Nov. 21, 1999	Asakusa, Taito-ku, Tokyo (off-course betting shop)
145)	Nov. 29, 1998	Shinjuku-ku, Tokyo (Shinjuku Station, Pyramid Square)
146)	Jul. 2, 1998	Shinjuku, Shinjuku-ku, Tokyo
147)	May 21, 1999	Shinjuku, Shinjuku-ku, Tokyo (department store, window display)
148)	Jul. 7, 2000	Kanda, Chiyoda-ku, Tokyo (Kanda Station, money lenders' brochures)
149)	May 27, 1998	Shibuya-ku, Tokyo (Shibuya Station, money lenders' signboard)
150)	Mar. 3, 2000	Chiyoda-ku, Tokyo (Tokyo Station, stock market signboard)
151)	Feb. 27, 1999	Chiyoda-ku, Tokyo (Kanda Station, money lender's building and gay quarter signboard)
152)	Feb. 16, 1999	Ginza, Chuo-ku, Tokyo (Signboard of an insolvent bank and a surveillance camera)
153)	Dec. 22, 1998	Kabuki-cho, Shinjuku-ku, Tokyo (signboard of money lender and Christianity campaign)
154)	Oct. 10, 1999	Kabuki-cho, Shinjuku-ku, Tokyo (signboard of a pachinko parlor)
155)	Dec. 9, 1998	Omote-sando, Shibuya-ku, Tokyo
156)	Dec. 25, 1997	Shinjuku-ku, Tokyo (Shinjuku Station, south entrance)
157)	Jul. 4, 1998	Shinjuku-ku, Tokyo (Shinjuku Station, east entrance)
158)	Feb. 23, 1999	Taito-ku, Tokyo (Ueno Station)
159)	Jan. 2, 1998	Shinjuku-ku, Tokyo (Shinjuku Station, south entrance)
160)	Apr. 30, 2000	Hikarigaoka, Nerima-ku, Tokyo
161)	June 12, 1991	Mejiro, Bunkyo-ku, Tokyo (Kishibojin)
162)	Oct. 6, 1998	Nishi-shinjuku, Shinjuku-ku, Tokyo
163)	Apr. 5, 1999	Chidorigafuchi, Kudan, Chiyoda-ku, Tokyo
164)	Mar. 31, 1998	Hanzomon, Chiyoda-ku, Tokyo
165)	June 29, 1990	Nishi-shinjuku, Shinjuku-ku, Tokyo
166)	May 6, 1993	Kuramae, Taito-ku, Tokyo
167)	Feb. 23, 1999	Nishi-shinjuku, Shinjuku-ku, Tokyo (window display)
168)	May 15, 1998	Shinbashi, Minato-ku, Tokyo (near Shinbashi Station)
169)	Jan. 27, 2000	Shinjuku-ku, Tokyo (Shinjuku Station, south entrance)
170)	Jul. 25, 1997	Shinjuku-ku, Tokyo (Shinjuku Station, east entrance)
171)	Jan. 27, 2000	Shinjuku-ku, Tokyo (Kabukicho crossing)
172)	Nov. 8, 1998	Shinjuku-ku, Tokyo (Shinjuku Station, south entrance)
173)	May 28, 1999	Nishi-shinjuku, Shinjuku-ku, Tokyo
174)	June 21, 1998	Nakano-ku, Tokyo (Nakano-sakaue Station)
175)	Apr. 21, 1999	Hatsudai, Shinjuku-ku, Tokyo (Opera City)
176)	Apr. 23, 1999	Nishi-shinjuku, Shinjuku-ku, Tokyo (underground market)
177)	May 14, 1998	Yurakucho, Chiyoda-ku, Tokyo (International Forum)
178)	Nov. 6, 1997	Shiba-koen, Minato-ku, Tokyo (Tokyo Tower)
179)	Sep. 5, 1999	Nishi-shinjuku, Shinjuku-ku, Tokyo
180)	Aug. 15, 1998	Hatsudai, Shinjuku-ku, Tokyo (Opera City)
181)	Sep. 3, 1999	Toyama, Shinjuku-ku, Tokyo
182)	Dec. 22, 1999	Yurakucho, Chiyoda-ku, Tokyo (International Forum)
183)	May 28, 1998	Yoyogi, Shibuya-ku, Tokyo (Insurance company)
184)	Mar. 9, 2000	Nishi-shinjuku, Shinjuku-ku, Tokyo
185)	Jul. 19, 1998	Nishi-shinjuku, Shinjuku-ku, Tokyo (Metropolitan Government Office)
186)	Nov. 6, 1999	Shiba-koen, Minato-ku, Tokyo (Tokyo Tower)
187)	May 26, 1999	Araiyakushi, Nakano-ku, Tokyo
188)	1998–2000	TV images
189)	Feb. 19, 1999	Shinsaibashi, Osaka, (Coffee and icecream shop)
190)	Feb. 5, 1996	Mitaka-shi, Tokyo
191)	Mar. 12, 1993	Nishi-shinjuku, Shinjuku-ku, Tokyo (window display)
192)	June 13, 1999	Harajuku, Shibuya-ku, Tokyo (restaurant)
193)	June 7, 1998	Shinjuku, Shinjuku-ku, Tokyo (underground passage)
194)	Jan. 26, 1998	Roppongi, Minato-ku, Tokyo
195)	June 28, 1996	Shinjuku-ku, Tokyo (in front of Isetan Department Store)
196)	Jul. 20, 1999	Nishi-shinjuku, Shinjuku-ku, Tokyo
197)	Jul. 9, 2000	Shinjuku, Shinjuku-ku, Tokyo
198)	June 18, 1999	Shiba-koen, Minato-ku, Tokyo (Tokyo Tower)
199)	May 3, 1999	Asakusa, Taito-ku, Tokyo
200)	Apr. 9, 2000	Shibuya-ku, Tokyo (Yoyogi Park)
201)	May 17, 1997	Shinjuku-ku, Tokyo (Central Park)
202)	May 31, 1998	Shinjuku-ku, Tokyo (Central Park)
203)	May 28, 2000	Naitocho, Shinjuku-ku, Tokyo (Shinjuku-gyoen Park)
204)	Apr. 9, 2000	Shibuya-ku, Tokyo (Yoyogi Park)
205)	May 14, 2000	Jingubashi, Shibuya-ku, Tokyo
206)	Apr. 9, 2000	Shibuya-ku, Tokyo (Yoyogi Park)
207)	Apr. 24, 1998	Shinjuku-ku, Tokyo (Shinjuku Station, south entrance)
208)	Sept. 18, 1998	Nishi-shinjuku, Shinjuku-ku, Tokyo
209)	Aug. 5, 1999	Kojimachi, Chiyoda-ku, Tokyo (in front of Nippon TV)
210)	May 17, 1997	Nishi-shinjuku, Shinjuku-ku, Tokyo
211)	May 31, 1998	Shinjuku-ku, Tokyo (Shinjuku Station, east entrance)
212)	Aug. 18, 1993	Nishi-shinjuku, Shinjuku-ku, Tokyo (condom vending machine and a fig leaf)
213)	Sept. 13 1998	Nishi-shinjuku, Shinjuku-ku, Tokyo
214)	Feb. 21, 1999	Taito-ku, Tokyo (Ueno Station, modern Babel)
215)	Feb. 4, 1999	Roppongi, Minato-ku, Tokyo
216)	Mar. 10, 1999	Shibuya-ku, Tokyo (Sendagaya Gymnasium)
217)	Feb. 3, 1999	Daiba, Minato-ku, Tokyo
218)	Dec. 31, 1998	Suwa-shi, Nagano Prefecture (Suwa Intersection)
219)	May 4, 1999	Nishi-shinjuku, Shinjuku-ku, Tokyo (Underground of Metropolitan Government Office, homeless people)
220)	May 7, 1999	Taito-ku, Tokyo (Sumida River, cardboard houses)
221)	May 3, 1999	Yodogawa, Osaka (cardboard houses)
222)	Nov. 3, 1999	Shinjuku-ku, Tokyo (Central Park)
223)	Jan. 26, 1998	Azabu-katamachi, Minato-ku, Tokyo
224)	Aug. 16, 1999	Kabuki-cho, Shinjuku-ku, Tokyo
225)	Jul. 19, 1999	Shibuya-ku, Tokyo (Yoyogi Park, object made by a homeless person)
226)	Dec. 25, 1998	Shibuya-ku, Tokyo (Harajuku crossing)
227)	Oct. 10, 1999	Shibuya-ku, Tokyo (Yoyogi Park)
228)	Feb. 13, 2000	Shinjuku-ku, Tokyo (Central Park)
229)	Feb. 25, 2000	Ginza, Chuo-ku, Tokyo
230)	Jan. 4, 2000	Nishi-shinjuku, Shinjuku-ku, Tokyo
231)	Nov. 28, 1997	Harajuku, Shibuya-ku, Tokyo
232)	Feb. 18, 1999	Shinsaibashi, Osaka
233)	Mar. 19, 2000	Shibuya-ku, Tokyo (Miyanoshita Park)
234)	Feb. 18, 1999	Shinsaibashi, Osaka
235)	Aug. 17, 1997	Shinjuku, Shinjuku-ku, Tokyo (department store, mannequin)
236)	Apr. 1, 1999	Hakata-shi, Fukuoka Prefecture (sculpture by a French artist)
237)	Jan. 3, 1990	Nishi-shinjuku, Shinjuku-ku, Tokyo
238)	Sept. 6, 1999	Monzen-nakacho, Koto-ku, Tokyo
239)	Jan. 26, 2000	Akihabara, Chiyoda-ku, Tokyo
240)	Feb. 1, 1998	Sugamo, Toshima-ku, Tokyo (Togenuki-jizo)
241)	May 30, 2000	Shibuya-ku, Tokyo (Shibuya Station)
242)	Nov. 27, 1999	Aoyama Sanchome, Minato-ku, Tokyo
243)	Dec. 29, 1992	Nakano-ku, Tokyo (Saginomiya Station)
244)	Apr. 7, 2000	Yotsuya, Shinjuku-ku, Tokyo
245)	Nov. 12, 1999	Chiyoda-ku, Tokyo (in front of Imperial Palace, tenth anniversary of the Emperor's reign)
246)	Oct. 22, 2000	Jingubashi, Shibuya-ku, Tokyo
247)	Jul. 17, 2000	Aoyama Sanchome, Minato-ku, Tokyo
248)	Jan. 1, 2000	Shinjuku-ku, Tokyo (in front of Alta, people celebrating the New Year)
249)	Dec. 23, 1999	Shimane Prefecture (Izumo Shrine)
250)	Sept. 20, 1999	Naha-shi, Okinawa Prefecture (Entrance to a social club)
251)	Aug. 8, 1991	Utsukushigahara, Nagano Prefecture

著者略歴
1937年5月2日東京生まれ。
獨協高校卒業。植物写真家、富成忠夫氏に写真の基礎を学ぶ。19歳のとき富成氏と平凡社のペリカン写真文庫「蝶」を共著。社会派「LIFE」写真家、三木淳氏に3日だけ指事。女性写真家、佐藤明氏にファッション写真を学び、22歳で独立、そのまま現在までフリーランス写真家。ファッション写真、料理写真、昆虫写真、生け花写真、舞台写真、ドキュメント、演劇ポスター、コマーシャルと幅広い分野で活躍中。昭和46年度第3回講談社出版文化賞受賞。昭和62年度日本写真協会年度賞受賞。著書に「EMMA」(毎日新聞社)「日本の料理」「画家のおもちゃ箱」(猪熊弦一郎と共著、文化出版局)「松坂慶子写真集」「作家のインデックス」(集英社)「ONNAGATA坂東玉三郎」「七代目菊五郎の芝居」「植田いつ子の世界」(平凡社)「蝶の生態写真集、ゼフィルス24」「松本幸四郎の俳遊俳談」(朝日新聞社)「武蔵野」(シングルカット社)など多数。

Author's Profile
OHKURA Shunji, born in Tokyo on May 2, 1937, studied at Dokkyo High School. He was taught basic techniques of photography by Tominari Tadao, specialist in botanical photography. Co-authored *Butterflies* (Pelican Photo Library, Heibonsha) with Tominari at nineteen years of age. Studied with Miki Jun (documentary photographer for *Life*) just three days. Studied fashion photography with Sato Akira, specialist in female photography, and became freelance photographer at twenty-two. Having been working on fashion, cooking, insects, ikebana, performing arts, documentary, posters for theater, commercial photography, and so on, was given Kodansha Publications Cultural Award in 1971, and Annual Award of the Photographic Society of Japan in 1987.

Among his books are *EMMA* (Mainichi Shimbun), *Japanese Cooking* (Bunka Shuppan), *Toy Box of a Painter* (Co-authored with Inokuma Genichiro, Bunka Shuppan), *Actress Matsuzaka Keiko* (Shueisha), *Authors' Index* (Shueisha), *Onnagata TAMASABURO* (Heibonsha), *Kabuki of Onoe Kikugoro VII* (Heibonsha), *The World of Ueda Itsuko* (Heibonsha), *The Ecology of Butterflies, Zephyrus 24* (Asahi Shimbun), *Matsumoto Koshiro no Haiyu Haidan* (Asahi Shimbun), *Musashino* (Single Cut-sha), and others.

使用カメラとレンズ
Cameras and Lenses Used for This Book

LEICA M2			
Summicron	50mm	F2	
Summaron	35mm	F3.5	
MINOLTA CLE			
M ROKKOR	28mm	F2.8	
MINOLTA α-9			
AF MINOLTA	85mm	F1.4	
AF MINOLTA ZOOM	28–105mm	F3.5–4.5	
MINOLTA XG-S			
MC ROKKOR	28mm	F3.5	
MD MINOLTA	35mm	F2.8	
MC ROKKOR	35mm	F1.7	
MC ROKKOR	55mm	F1.7	
MD ROKKOR	50mm	F1.4	
PENTAX LX			
PENTAX MX			
SMC PENTAX	35mm	F2	
SMC PENTAX	50mm	F1.7	
SMC PENTAX	55mm	F1.8	
Canon NEW F-1			
Canon SSC	35mm	F2	
Canon SSC	50mm	F1.4	
Canon SSC	100mm	F2.8	
Canon SSC	200mm	F4	
SIGMA	24mm	F2.8	
SIGMA	135–400mm	F4–5.6	
Film			
Kodak Tri-X	D76		

TOKYO X

2000年12月21日 第1刷発行

著者 大倉舜二
発行者 野間佐和子
発行所 講談社インターナショナル株式会社
〒112-8652 東京都文京区音羽1-17-14
電話:03-3944-6493(編集部)
電話:03-3944-6492(営業部・業務部)
印刷所 株式会社 フクイン
製本所 株式会社 鈴木製本所

落丁本・乱丁本は、小社業務部宛にお送りください。送料小社負担にてお取替えします。なお、この本についてのお問い合わせは、編集部宛にお願いいたします。本書の無断複写(コピー)、転載は著作権法の例外を除き、禁じられています。

定価はカバーに表示してあります。

© Shunji Ohkura 2000

Printed in Japan

ISBN 4-7700-2738-9